Physical Education and Health in the Elementary School

SECOND EDITION

SECOND EDITION

PHYSICAL EDUCATION AND HEALTH IN THE ELEMENTARY SCHOOL

BY

Charles A. Bucher
Professor of Education and Director of
Physical Education, School of
Education, New York University

AND

Evelyn M. Reade
Professor of Health and Physical
Education and Graduate Coordinator,
New Jersey State College, Glassboro

THE MACMILLAN COMPANY
NEW YORK

COLLIER-MACMILLAN
LIMITED, LONDON

© Copyright, The Macmillan Company, 1971

All rights reserved. No part of this book may be
reproduced or transmitted in any form or by
any means, electronic or mechanical, including
photocopying, recording or by any information
storage and retrieval system, without permission in
writing from the Publisher.

Second Printing, 1971

Earlier edition entitled
Physical Education in the Modern Elementary School
© 1958 by The Macmillan Company.
Earlier edition entitled
Physical Education and Health in the Elementary School
© copyright 1964 by The Macmillan Company.

Library of Congress catalog card number: 71-83066

THE MACMILLAN COMPANY
866 Third Avenue, New York, New York 10022
COLLIER-MACMILLAN CANADA, LTD., TORONTO, ONTARIO

Printed in the United States of America

Dedicated to
teachers responsible for educating
children in physical education and
health education in the early,
middle, and upper elementary
grades.

Preface

The tender years of childhood are most important from the standpoint of social, physical, and mental-emotional development. Personality is being molded, attitudes are being formed, symbols are being learned, and social values are being acquired. The direction of the child's development will depend to a great extent upon his educational experiences and the leadership provided to guide these experiences.

Play, which is often referred to as the child's work, is an educational medium with tremendous potentialities for the optimum development of children. Play offers children opportunities for discovering and expressing themselves, acquiring useful skills, developing strong, healthy bodies, learning how to get along with others, making decisions, and gaining other qualities essential to good citizenship.

Play can be adapted to so many different phases of education in the elementary school that the physical education program is integral to general education. In the physical education program, under the leadership of the classroom teacher and the physical education specialist, educational goals can be brought nearer to accomplishment. Such goals are not achieved, however, merely by having physical education periods in the schools. The results depend on the teacher's ability to plan and administer sound programs.

The school health program also has deep implications for the child's education. Good health is basic to effective learning. Within the elementary school program, there should be health instruction, health services, and a healthful environment. Although health and physical education are separate fields, they are closely related. Particularly in the elementary school with the self-contained classroom, the classroom teacher and the physical education specialist have important responsibilities to know and understand what constitutes both the health program and the physical education program.

In recent years, the classroom teacher has played an important part in directing physical education and health programs in the elementary grades. Although there is a recognized need for the physical education and the health specialist to conduct certain aspects of the program, the classroom teacher's day-to-day role is often the key to success. This development has given the classroom teacher the responsibility of adequate preparation in two phases of education that have become major parts of the curriculum because of their indispensable contribution to the proper growth and development of children. This book has been designed to provide the classroom teacher and the physical education specialist with the background of principle and the specifics of practice needed to provide a rich physical education and health offering to all of the children with whom he or she works from day to day. The text offers an entirely new approach, with a new format, new ideas, and many activities never before published.

This book is divided into five parts and is concerned with both physical education and health education in the elementary school from kindergarten through the eighth grade. The parts are: One, "The Philosophy"; Two, "The Child"; Three, "Recommendations for Program Development"; Four, "Methodology for Planning and Teaching Physical Education and Health Education"; and Five, "Recommended Movement Experiences for Physical Education Programs."

Such topics as philosophy, child growth and development characteristics, and the program of activities are covered. Special attention has been given to the role of physical education in schools and the important factors necessary for fulfilling its objectives. In addition, provisions have been made for such current topics as physical fitness, movement education, creativity, and today's health needs and problems.

The book traces the role of physical education in education and the way in which play can be used as a medium through which educational objectives are achieved. It shows that physical education is not an appendage to the school curriculum but instead an integral part of general education. It stresses new developments in elementary education that offer challenges and opportunities for teachers. It discusses the child as a growing and developing personality and the teacher as the guide who utilizes play as an educational medium to help the child. The classroom teacher and physical education specialist will find principles and information on planning the organization and administration of desirable physical education and health education programs, adapting general instructions to individual classes, providing the program progression needed from grade to grade, correlating physical education and health education with other phases of the curriculum, organizing noon-hour and freeplay programs, and teaching almost 500 activities arranged according to the grade levels, the indoor or outdoor play areas, and the occasions to which they are appropriate. In addition, the book discusses problems—such as evaluation, safety, legal liability, and camping and outdoor education—with which every classroom and physical education teacher should be familiar.

A detailed treatment is given to the total health program in the elementary school. The aim of the authors has been to cover in a factual and condensed manner the practical aspects of what the classroom and physical education teacher must know about school health in order to make it meaningful. The nature and scope of the school health program are discussed in terms of such basic topics as objectives, the factors that influence the child's health, health problems of elementary school children, the school health team responsible for protecting the pupil's health, and the relation of health to physical education. There is a discussion of a well-planned health education program—a discussion that includes the bases for selecting curriculum experiences, health needs and interests of students, psychological principles that promote learning, samples of teaching units, proposals for curriculum development, methods of teaching, sources of free and inexpensive health materials, and principles of evaluation. The components of a healthful school environment, both mental and physical, and the services necessary to maintain and improve the child's health are presented.

The appendix includes sources for records, supplies, and equipment; formations needed for dances, sports, and individual and dual activities; and suggestions for obtaining or making free or inexpensive materials and equipment.

The teachers' manual which accompanies this text contains objectives and true-false, multiple choice, and matching questions for each chapter plus materials from the *AAHPER Youth Fitness Test Manual*.

The authors are confident that the inclusion of physical education and health within the covers of one textbook will contribute to a better understanding and appreciation of both of these specialized fields. It should be especially helpful in those professional institutions where the preparation for teaching physical education and health is encompassed in one course.

The authors wish to express their appreciation to the many individuals whose contributions and consultant efforts have made this book possible. Special thanks are extended to consultants Dr. Pearl Britton, Miss Leah Beverley, Mr. Edgar Knepper, Miss Myra Yoldman, Miss Mary Rice, and Mr. Daniel Stanley.

Particular thanks are due the children and teachers who helped develop and test the many new activities.

Assistance with pictures has been provided by Mr. Jeff Toughill, photographer; Mr. Samuel Pinizzotto, Principal of Campus School, Glassboro State College; Miss Mary Silver, Elementary Supervisor, Woodbury, N.J.; and the children in these schools. Photographs have also been supplied by The Universal Bleacher Company, The Nissen Corporation, Creative Playthings, The Delmer Harris Co., Game-Time Inc., Lind Climber Company, and Miracle Equipment Company. Our sincere thanks go to these persons and companies.

The permission from The President's Council on Physical Fitness, Washington, D.C., to reprint the many developmental activities, and permission from other individuals and companies to reprint quotations, all acknowledged throughout the text, are deeply appreciated.

C. A. B.
E. M. R.

Contents

PART ONE The Philosophy

Chapter 1. Physical Education in the Elementary School 3

The function of the elementary school 4, What is physical education? 7, Physical education as a part of general education 15, Components of the elementary school physical education program 18, Factors affecting the elementary school physical education program 19

Chapter 2. Health in the Elementary School 24

The importance of health in the elementary school 24, Factors that influence the health of the child 25, Objectives of the health program in the elementary school 25, The conceptual approach to school health education 26, The school health program 27, The relation of health education to physical education 37

Chapter 3. Movement Education in the Elementary School 40

History of movement education 40, The key concepts of movement education 41, Developing a movement education program 45, The future of movement education 50

Chapter 4. Physical Fitness in the Elementary School 52

Physical fitness in the new society 52, The role of the school in fitness 54

Chapter 5. Current Trends in Elementary School Physical Education and Health Education 61

General trends in the world of today and their challenge to physical education and health education 61, Current trends in elementary education that directly concern physical education and health education 66, Current trends in physical education in elementary schools 68, Current trends in elementary school health education 72

Chapter 6. Basic Principles of Physical Education and Health Education for Elementary Schools   76

Basic principles of physical education 77, Basic principles of health education 84

PART TWO The Child

Chapter 7. Child Growth and Development Factors   91

Typical patterns of growth and development 92, Basis for development of program 95, Growth and development characteristics and needs of children 99, Play—a means of meeting the developmental needs of children 101, Play—the foundation for balanced adult living 104, Recommended physical education activities 105, Growth through physical activity 105

Chapter 8. Motor Learning and the Elementary School Child   108

The learning process 108

Chapter 9. The Atypical Child   116

Defining the atypical 117, Characteristics and needs of specific types of atypical children in the elementary school 117, Responsibility for the atypical child 122

PART THREE Recommendations for Program Development

Chapter 10. Physical Education Movement Activities for Early Childhood with Examples of Progression and Suggested Outcomes   131

Types of movement activities and suggested time for each 131, The need for progression in physical education 140

Chapter 11. Physical Education Movement Activities for Middle and Upper Childhood with Examples of Progression and Suggested Outcomes   146

Types of movement activity and suggested time for each 146, Some expected outcomes 159

Chapter 12. The Physical Education Program for the Atypical Child   163

The culturally disadvantaged child 163, The physically handicapped child 165, The mentally retarded child 167, The disruptive child 168, The poorly coordinated child 169, The physically gifted and the creative child 170, Suggested activities for the atypical child 172

Chapter 13. The Early Morning, Noon-Hour, and After-School Programs and Tournaments   175

The early morning program 176, The noon-hour program 176, After-school programs 180, Tournament use in programs 181

Chapter 14. Camping and Outdoor Education 189

History of school camping 191, The camp program 192, Outdoor education 195

Chapter 15. The Health Curriculum in the Elementary School 198

Bases for selecting curriculum experiences 198, The conceptual approach in health education 201, Critical health areas 205, Evaluation 212

PART FOUR   Methodology for Planning and Teaching Physical Education and Health Education

Chapter 16. Planning the Physical Education and Health Education Programs 217

Guides for planning physical education and health education programs 218, General planning in physical education 218, General planning in health education 234

Chapter 17. General Suggestions for Teaching Physical Education and Health Education 243

Squad method of class organization 243, Selection of activities to provide full participation for each child 247, Hints for teaching specific game skills 251, Safety and legal liability in teaching physical education 256, Teaching health education 263

Chapter 18. Audio-visual Materials and Other Special Aids 271

Purposes of audio-visual aids 271, Classification of audio-visual materials and other special aids 272, Advantages and disadvantages of selected visual materials 274, Guidelines for the selection of audio-visual and other special aids 276, Guidelines for using audio-visual materials and other special aids 277, Evaluation procedures 278, Organizing audio-visual programs 278

Chapter 19. Evaluation of Physical Education and Health Education Programs 281

Need for evaluation 281, Types of information desired 282, Techniques used in evaluation 282, Specific points to be evaluated 285, Forms for evaluating physical education programs 287.

PART FIVE   Recommended Movement Experiences for Physical Education Programs

Chapter 20. Movement Experiences for Early Childhood (Ages Five and Six) 305

Dances and rhythms 305, Developmental activities with playground equipment 320, Games of low organization 320, Individual and dual activities 325, Self-testing activities and stunts 325, Story plays 327, Classroom games 328

xiv CONTENTS

Chapter 21. Movement Experiences for Early Childhood (Ages Seven and Eight)   330

Dances and rhythms 330, Developmental activities 338, Games of low organization 339, Individual and dual activities 346, Self-testing activities and stunts 350, Story plays 353, Classroom games 353

Chapter 22. Movement Experiences for Middle Childhood (Ages Nine and Ten)   356

Dances and rhythms 356, Developmental activities 359, Games of low organization, including relays and lead-up activities 359, Individual and dual activities 365, Self-testing activities 367, Team games 369, Track and field events 373, Classroom activities 374

Chapter 23. Movement Experiences for Middle Childhood (Ages Eleven and Twelve)   377

Dances and rhythms 377, Developmental activities 379, Games of low organization, including relays and lead-up activities 381, Individual and dual activities 384, Self-testing activities 387, Team games 389, Track and field events 396, Classroom games 396

Chapter 24. Movement Experiences for Upper Grades (Ages Thirteen and Fourteen)   399

Rhythms and dances 399, Developmental activities 402, Track and field events 404, Lead-up activities 405, Individual and dual sports 409, Team games (sports) 413, Classroom games 420

Chapter 25. Activities for Special Occasions and Holiday Fun   424

Assembly programs 424, Demonstrations 425, Playdays 425, Sports days 427, Dance festivals 427, Field days 427, May Day programs 428, Activities for holiday fun 428

Chapter 26. Movement Experiences in Stunts, Tumbling, and Gymnastics   435

Outcomes desired 436, Basic tumbling 436, The basic ten in tumbling including directions, safety factors, and common errors 437, Apparatus activities, including directions, safety factors, and common errors 440

Chapter 27. Movement Experiences in Swimming and Water Safety   448

Needs 448, Values 448, Qualifications of instructors 449, Recommended starting age level 449, Class organization 450, Recommended skills, teaching techniques, and hints 450, Water games 455, Water-safety hints 456

APPENDIXES

A.	Audio-visual Aids and Records	461
B.	Sources of Equipment and Supplies	463
C.	Formations for Games, Dances, and Individual and Dual Activities	464
D.	Suggestions for Making Equipment	471

INDEX   473

PART ONE

The Philosophy

CHAPTER 1

Physical Education in the Elementary School

The need for physical and health education is a much publicized subject in today's world. Emphasis on Olympic development and expanded coverage of sports events on television both help to keep physical education before the public. Many families enjoy recreational activities and increasingly, as a unit, go camping, swim, play tennis, and engage in a wide variety of other lifetime sports. Vast advertising campaigns conducted by health-service agencies and health-product manufacturers also inform parents and their children of the need for, and benefits of, proper health care, rest, and exercise.

The schools are especially active in seeing that children receive sound physical education and health education programs. Educators are as much concerned about physical education as are parents. They are confronted, however, with many different philosophies of what constitutes a good educational program. Some school people advocate great amounts of formal exercise, such as calisthenics and push-ups, as the way to get children into good physical shape. Other persons say that athletic programs are the answer and that leagues and tournaments should be organized in many different sports. A third group says that physical education should be concerned with more than the physical aspects of development. This group advocates that consideration be given also to social and mental development.

The classroom teacher and the specialist in physical education are in the midst of all this wrangling and discussion. The classroom teacher, not being a specialist, wonders at times what is the best approach to follow and what type of program to initiate in his or her classes. Many times he or she finds that the easiest solution is to succumb to the pressures of townspeople and provide the program they advocate without thought of the part physical education plays in total education.

This book is written for the guidance of those classroom teachers and specialists who are responsible for health education and physical education classes in the elementary school. Herein are provided the ingredients for sound programs of health education and physical education. Here is a guide that will enable the teacher to proceed with confidence, knowing that she or he has the answers to what is in the best interests of the child and how to provide him with sound education.

The Function of the Elementary School

More than 360,000 elementary schools throughout the nation have important roles to play in modern education. Through their doors each year walk millions of youngsters. This is the first school experience for most of these children. The attitude they develop toward learning, the degree to which their basic mental equipment is activated, how they look at themselves and the world in which they live, and the degree to which they are interested in their health and physical well-being will be sharply affected by these first few years of formal education. Children can be molded in many different ways. Education should be designed to mold them in the right directions.

Most children who come to school are enthusiastic about the educational process. They have heard mothers, fathers, brothers, and sisters talk about reading, games, spelling, writing, and arithmetic. Their appetites have been whetted and they have a strong desire to partake of the educational fare. Their motivation for learning is probably as great at this point as it ever will be in their lifetimes. The teacher and the school can exploit this enthusiasm, this desire for learning, and make education a very satisfying experience, or they can dampen enthusiasm by poor and uninspired teaching.

Some of the experiences in which the child should have a successful, challenging, and satisfying role and the outcomes that should accrue in the elementary school are as follows:

1. *The child should develop mentally.* There should be training and experience in the basic mental skills. There should be opportunities for study in such areas as language, arithmetic, and spelling. There is need for training in logical thinking and clear self-expression. It is essential for children to learn to read material and comprehend what has been read. It is important for them to be introduced to such fields as literature, music, natural history, and simple physical and natural sciences, and the manner in which these areas of learning affect the world in which they live. To impart knowledge, and the fundamental abilities and skills basic to formal learning, and to foster the development of a wholesome attitude toward learning, are the primary functions of elementary education.

2. *The child should develop socially.* The child must learn to live effectively with other people. The elementary school years can provide an excellent laboratory for the development of many desirable social qualities. For example, elementary school experiences can help the child develop a respect for the rights of others and an understanding of the values inherent in society and the family. There should be a change from the "I" concept with the stress on the individual to the "we" concept with the stress on being a cooperating member of society. There should be emphasis on self-fulfillment, with equal emphasis on expanding home, community, national, and international obligations.

3. *The child should develop physically.* There needs to be stress on health habits and physical well-being in the elementary school. This function is especially necessary during the growing years. It is important that the child be emotionally well balanced. It is necessary that the child have a self-controlled, physically fit body. Interest in physical development and consciousness of proper body care should be inspired in each pupil. Finally, there is need for large amounts of big-muscle activity during this period because various parts of the body are developing. This activity is essential to healthy growth. The elementary years are an important time for educating the pupil for his proper health development because organic foundations are being laid, skills are being learned, and attitudes are being developed which will influence his health all through his life.

4. *The child should develop the foundations for the wise use of leisure time.* The world is faced with increasing amounts of leisure as new kinds of automated aids develop. The hours of work are important, but the nonworking hours are equally important. Whether or not children achieve their full potential in the world in which they live today and will live in the future will depend upon their attitudes, skills, and understanding of the part that leisure plays in their full development.

Education as Preparation for Life. Education has changed over the years to meet a changing society. It has adjusted its curricula to meet the needs and interests of people who are required to live in a changing world. It is designed to help individuals meet their responsibilities in day-to-day living. Education is preparing individuals for fruitful and useful lives. Life is not concerned merely with facts. It is also concerned with such things as ethics, human relations, mental health, citizenship, and emotions. Subject matter and discipline are not enough to fill a total educational curriculum. The total culture to which man is exposed and which influences his actions must be considered. Man has not been born in a vacuum. He has been born into a way of life which he should help to preserve and improve for future generations.

George Counts, writing on principles of education, pointed to the value of having an education that was geared to the needs and interests of the individual. Through an illustration involving a dialogue between teacher and pupil, he accented the need for meeting the day-to-day problems with which children and adults are faced:

> Greeting his pupils, the master asked:
> What would you learn of me?
> And the reply came:
> How shall we care for our bodies?
> How shall we rear our children?
> How shall we work together?
> How shall we live with our fellowmen?
> How shall we play?
> For what ends shall we live?
> And the teacher pondered these words, and sorrow was in his heart, for his own learning touched not these things.[1]

The Meaning and Objectives of General Education. The term *education* has different meanings for various individuals. Some define it as a training process which involves study and instruction; others say it is the sum total of human experiences; and still others say it means growth and adjustment. John Dewey, an educator who did as much as anyone to influence modern educational thinking, defined education as the reconstruction of events which compose the lives of individuals so that new happenings and new events become more purposeful and more meaningful. Furthermore, through education, individuals will be better able to regulate the direction of ensuing experiences. Education as defined by Dewey is a "doing" phenomenon. One learns through doing. Education takes place in the classroom, in the library, on the playground, in the gymnasium, and in the swimming pool.

The job of education is to provide experiences for the student which will be most meaningful in his life. Since education is the preparing of individuals for worthwhile lives, the schools should enable one to live a more purposeful, interesting, and vigorous life. They should help him to live the "good life." The Educational Policies Commission, in discussing policies for education in American democracy, states the following as the purpose of education:

> ... The primary business of education in effecting the promises of American democracy is to guard, cherish, advance, and make available in the life of coming generations the funded and growing wisdom, knowledge, and aspirations of the race. This involves the dissemination of knowledge, the liberation of minds, the development of skills, the promotion of free inquiries, the encouragement of the creative or inventive spirit, and the establishment of wholesome attitudes toward order and change—all useful in the good life for each person, in the practical arts, and in the maintenance and improvement of American society, as our society, in the world of accomplishment. It does in fact, if perfection be expected; but such is the primary business of public education in the United States; theory supports it; practice inadequately illustrates and confirms it.[2]

Education cannot restrict itself to the dispensing of knowledge, according to the Educational Policies Commission. In addition, other factors are essential. As this commission says, "The nature of the knowledge to be disseminated is qualified by the condition, 'useful in the good life and in the maintenance and improvement of American society.' Both ethics and the nature of American civilization are drawn into immediate and inescapable consideration."

The Educational Policies Commission further

---

[1] J. Crosby Chapman and George S. Counts, *Principles of Education*, Boston, Houghton Mifflin Company, 1924, Foreword.

[2] Educational Policies Commission, *Policies for Education in American Democracy*, Washington, D.C., National Education Association and the American Association of School Administrators, 1946, p. 60.

points out that education is as much concerned with the training of the body and spirit as with the transmission of knowledge. The commission states:

> It is not merely with the transmission of knowledge that education is deeply concerned. The functions of the schools are not fully described by a summary of programs, curriculum, and methods. No written or spoken words do, or can, completely convey the meaning of education as the day-to-day living force that it is in fact and may be—in the transactions of pupil and pupil, and in the experiences of the library and athletic field. Here are exchanges, bearings, and influences too subtle for logical expression and exact measurement. Yet we cannot doubt their existence, at least those of us who recall our own educational experiences and see teachers at work. Here, in the classroom, the auditorium, laboratory, and gymnasium, are in constant operation moral and cultural forces just as indispensable to civilization as knowledge or any material elements—indeed primordial in nature and the preconditions for the civilized uses of material things.[3]

The above statements well define and express the role of education as it relates to our educational systems. It is within this pattern that all experiences should be formulated.

Goals of General Education. The goals toward which American education is striving have been enumerated many times in the nation's history. The compilation of objectives which has received the most publicity is the list set forth by the National Education Association in 1918. This list received the label "Cardinal Principles of Education" and included such wellknown aims as health, command of fundamental processes, worthy home membership, vocation, citizenship, worthy use of leisure, and ethical character. Although these principles were stated more than fifty years ago, to a great degree they are still reflected in educational thinking today. Over the years, Americans have held a consistent point of view as to what they felt their schools should accomplish.

Another group of aims reflects the socioeconomic goals for education as presented in ten characteristics which are desired for the individual American. These characteristics were stated in 1937 by a committee that included a philosopher, a lawyer, a sociologist, a superintendent of schools, and two secretaries of state education associations. They include hereditary strength; physical security; skills, techniques, knowledge, values, and standards for effective participation in an evolving culture; an active, flexible personality; suitable occupation; economic security; mental security; equality of opportunity; freedom; and fair play. Also included in the report of this committee, of which John Dewey and Willard E. Givens were members, were statements that "education must be universal in its extent and application, universal in its materials and methods, and universal in its aim and spirit."

In 1946, the Educational Policies Commission, one of the most influential groups affecting the direction of American education, set forth four groups of objectives in discussing the purpose of education. These objectives have become guides for teachers in our schools. On careful analysis, it will be discerned that they reflect the thoughts of previous committees and commissions. The four groups include the objectives of self-realization, objectives of human relationship, objectives of economic efficiency, and objectives of civic responsibility.

The objectives of self-realization deal with such important items as the desire for learning; the ability to speak, read, and write effectively; the acquisition of knowledge and habits concerned with healthful living; and the ability to use leisure time in a wholesome and satisfying manner.

The objectives of human relationship are concerned with such things as an appreciation of the home, friendships, courtesy, the value of human welfare, and the ability to work harmoniously with one's fellow men.

The objectives of economic efficiency pertain to producer and consumer education. On the one hand, they stress such things as the importance of good workmanship, careful selection of one's vocation, and occupational adjustment, appreciation, and efficiency; on the other hand, they stress such factors as consumer judgment, buying, and protection.

The objectives of civic responsibility involve the citizen's responsibility to his fellow men, to

---

[3] *Ibid.*, p. 64.

his country, and to the world; his responsibility for developing a tolerant, scientific, critical, sympathetic, and cooperative attitude within himself; and his responsibility for developing an unswerving loyalty to the democratic way of life.

Under a past administration, a White House Conference on Education was called by the President of the United States. This meeting re-emphasized the many objectives of education that have been listed in this section. The conference clearly pointed out the desire of the

(Courtesy of Creative Playthings, Inc., Princeton, New Jersey, and Los Angeles, California.)

American people that the schools prepare their children mentally, physically, emotionally, and socially for the tasks that lie before them. The White House Committee in its report to the President of the United States stressed that it saw a "genuine public demand" for what historians may look upon as a new concept of education. This concept was stated in the following words:

Schools are now asked to help each child to become as good and as capable in every way as native endowment permits. The schools are asked to help children to acquire any skill or characteristic which a majority of the community deems worth while. The order given by the American people to the schools is grand in its simplicity; in addition to intellectual achievement, the schools must foster morality, happiness, and any useful ability. The talent of each child is to be sought out and developed to the fullest. Each weakness is to be studied and, so far as possible, corrected. This is a very majestic ideal, and an astonishingly new one. Schools of that kind have never been provided for more than a small fraction of mankind.

This concept set forth by the White House Conference places additional importance on the development of the "whole" child, and the "physical" is an important aspect of this "whole" development.

The goals of education as presented by various groups and individuals indicate that a heavy responsibility rests upon the shoulders of teachers who spend a large share of their time with the children and youth of today. If experiences are provided which are satisfying, successful, and directed toward enriching an individual's life, these purposes of education will be accomplished. However, if this responsibility is shunned, if an indifferent attitude is assumed, if attention is not focused on the child, if children are allowed to grow up without having experiences which build for the good life—then education, as provided through organized institutions, is not realizing its potentialities. Each teacher has within his or her power the ability to aid in the fulfillment of the objectives of education. The education that takes place in the total program of the school can accomplish the "majestic ideal"—in the words of the White House Conference—of America.

What Is Physical Education?

The word *physical* refers to the body and to things physical, such as muscle, bones, skin, hair, and blood. The word *education* refers to principles and practices which have to do with learning or the instruction and study which helps to develop the mind and character. Physical education, therefore, refers to the instruction or learning that takes place through the body. One important point to understand clearly is that the term *physical education* implies that learning takes place.

What kind of learning takes place in physical education? It is obvious that much can be learned about the body itself. Children can learn about some of the important parts of the body and how such organs as the heart, lungs, stomach, and liver function. Furthermore, they can understand why it is important to take care of bodily equipment and the relationship of this equipment to optimum physical functioning and to happiness and well-being. Of course, there is other subject-matter information that children can be taught and through which they will have a better understanding of the world about them and their own future role in society.

The elementary school teacher needs to recognize that physical education does not merely mean putting young bones and muscles into action. The activity does not take place in a vacuum. There are other reasons for engaging in physical activities and for activating one's body than the exercise that takes place. The more clearly children realize this, the more they will be motivated throughout life to be physically active and provide for the needs of their bodies.

Another type of learning that takes place in physical education is that of physical skill. An expression that has received considerable use in the advertising world is "that it's easier to start a habit than to stop one." In other words, if a skill is taught correctly it will heighten the learning of more complex activities in which it plays a part. Poor habits and wrong ways of performing skills will not have to be undone. Once a skill has been learned the wrong way it takes considerable time and effort to correct the error. The object, therefore, is to help youngsters during their early years to learn to throw, jump, run, skip, tumble, stand, sit, and dance in a coordinated and skillful manner. The more complex skills used in the highly organized sports and physical activities in which the child will engage at a later age are combinations of such fundamental movements as running, jumping, and leaping. Therefore, during the elementary school years a broad foundation of skillful physical performance should be instilled so that new and more difficult skills will be easily learned and enjoyed later on in life.

A third type of learning that takes place is what happens to the individual child in his or her relationships with other youngsters. The physical education class offers a wonderful opportunity to instill such qualities as courage, initiative, leadership, followership, honesty, and dependability. The give-and-take in the physical education class helps a child to appreciate better the individual abilities of others and the value of playing according to the rules. When games are being played, many situations arise where the youngster must determine what is the right course of action to follow. Under expert and qualified leadership, the right decision will be made.

Physical education, therefore, is not just education of the physical body. It is not merely

(Courtesy of Miracle Equipment Co. Photo by John D. Roche, Inc.)

exercising, sweating, puffing, and building strength and stamina. It goes beyond these and, in addition to developing physical well-being, it uses the body as a vehicle through which knowledge is gained, attitudes are developed, and desirable social qualities are acquired. Physical education is education through and by means of physical activity.

The *physical* part of physical education is a way or means and not an end in itself. If all we hope to have our students achieve is neuromuscular skills, strength, agility, and comparable physical growth, we cannot logically say that we have given them a physical *education*. It would be more correctly called *physical training*, the term used years ago. However, through the physical and by means of many different kinds of physical experiences, we have opportunities to assist our students in reaching other educational objectives.

The major objectives of physical education with which we should be concerned in the elementary school are as follows:

1. To provide for big-muscle activity in order to aid in the growth and development of the body.

2. To develop neuromuscular skills so that the child may participate in various activities such as running, jumping, throwing, catching, dancing, and so on. There is currently a growing emphasis on education for movement in American public school physical education programs. Movement education is especially concerned with these natural movements of childhood, and the free and creative use of these movements by the child.

3. To maintain the child's interest in and love of physical activity by teaching activities based on the needs, interests, and abilities of all children.

4. To teach activities which may be used during the child's leisure time.

5. To teach fair play, sportsmanship, respect for fellow players and officials, and an understanding of the need to abide by the rules of games and sports.

6. To teach safety as it relates to each activity in the program, and to instill a regard for safety at all times in activities in which the child engages.

7. To teach health as it correlates with physical education. (Why is exercise and physical development beneficial to all? Why is it not wise to drink ice-cold water when participating in strenuous activities? How is total fitness developed?)

To get a child to run, jump, or skip is not the only function of physical education. Physical education is designed to get him to think about his bodily makeup, his physical needs, the relation of his body to his total self, and the contribution that physical education makes to his whole development.

The Meaning and Objectives of Physical Education.[4] The term *physical education* takes on a new meaning after a consideration of the word

[4] Charles A. Bucher, *Foundations of Physical Education* (Fifth edition), St. Louis, The C. V. Mosby Company, 1968.

education. The word *physical* refers to the body. It is often used in reference to various characteristics such as physical strength, physical development, physical prowess, physical health, and physical appearance. It refers to the body as distinct from the mind. Therefore, when you add the word *education* to the word *physical* and use the words *physical education*, you are referring to an educational process concerned with activities which develop and maintain the human body. When an individual is playing Run Sheep Run, swimming in the pool, dancing in the gymnasium, skating on the pond, or performing any of the activities which aid in the development and maintenance of his body, education is taking place. This education may be conducive to the enrichment of the individual's life, or it may be detrimental. It may be a satisfying experience, or it may be an unhappy one. It may help to achieve educational objectives, or it may result in antisocial behavior. Whether or not physical education helps or inhibits the attainment of educational objectives depends to a great extent upon the leadership that is responsible for its direction.

Physical education is a very important part of the general educational process. It is not a frill or an appendage to the school program. It is, instead, a vital part of education. It can be defined as follows: *Physical education, an integral part of the total education process, is a field of endeavor which has as its aim the development of physically, mentally, emotionally, and socially fit individuals through the medium of physical activities that have been selected with a view to realizing these outcomes.*

The aim of all education is to enable the individual to live an enriched and abundant life. This is the ultimate goal on which all who are concerned with education have trained their sights. The objectives of physical education are more definite and specific than this aim, and through these objectives, the ultimate goal is brought nearer to realization.

A study of the child reveals four general directions or phases in which growth and development take place: physical development, skill development, mental development, and social development. Each of these phases contributes to the making of a well-rounded individual who will become a worthy member of society. Physical education can play a very important part in contributing to each of these phases of child growth and development. Physical education will prove its vital importance as a part of the educational process if it can accomplish these objectives.

Education Through Play. Play is one of the most significant ways in which the needs and interests of children are met. At the same time it is something that boys and girls enjoy and are anxious to do. Why not take this natural phenomenon, therefore, and direct it into constructive channels? Let's have *education through play*.

To obtain the most value from play experiences, proper attitudes, knowledge, and skills must be provided. By focusing attention on play and utilizing this innate compulsion for educational purposes, a tremendous new avenue for learning is opened. Children can learn and have fun doing it. Thorndike proved that the best education takes place when experiences are satisfying. What is more satisfying than a child's play? As Professor Thomas Briggs used to say to his students at Columbia University, "Let's help people to do better those things they are going to do anyway." Children are going to play whether adults and teachers want them to or not. Nature, a much greater force than man, has dictated this. Therefore, if play can be utilized to help develop young boys and girls into the kind of adults the world needs, it might be said that "two birds are being killed with one stone." Children are satisfying an innate drive and at the same time real education is taking place.

Play is universal. Proof can be found throughout history that people in all ages and in all countries have played. Scientists have found toys and trinkets in their excavations of ancient Egypt and Babylonia. Dancing, contests, singing, arts and crafts are some of the forms of expression used by people in most parts of the world.

As an ingredient which is common to people everywhere, play offers an excellent medium for education—for preparation for living. It can serve as an excellent tool for learning.

Early Objections to Play as an Educational Tool. Play, even today, is not universally accepted as an educational tool. There are those who maintain that they do not send their children to school to play. They want them to spend all their time learning the three R's and to forget such foolishness as running and jumping. Some cannot visualize play as an effective medium for education. Some still feel that play should occupy only the hours after school, at night, and on Saturdays.

History gives us a partial answer to the reason why some individuals today feel play has no educational value. Asceticism, scholasticism, and puritanism offer some insights into this viewpoint. These three doctrines have affected play adversely.

Asceticism, a doctrine that permeated the minds of individuals in the Middle Ages, exalted the spirit and degraded the body. The soul could be saved only through the deprivation and torment of the body. The wants and actual needs of the body were ignored. Therefore, it was felt the body should be disciplined and persecuted in the belief that the spirit would be strengthened. In fact, the body was termed by early leaders as a "lion chained to the spirit mind."

As a result of asceticism, things associated with the body came to be thought of as evil and those associated with the mind and spirit as good. Therefore, play, since it was associated with the body, could not be considered education. The so-called cultural subjects—languages, science, arithmetic, and geography—which were more closely associated with the mind, received the emphasis.

Scholasticism was another dominant Christian philosophy of the Middle Ages. This doctrine is reflected in some educational thinking even today. It exalted the intellect. The physical body and the emotions were ignored. Scholasticism stressed logic, metaphysics, and theology. It emphasized facts—if one knew the facts, he was educated.

Play, on the other hand, emphasized the body as well as the mind. It stressed the "whole" individual. It was not concerned solely with facts but with living as well.

Puritanism was a doctrine that developed during the seventeenth century in England and Europe and which had both religious and political implications. It came to America largely as a religious doctrine and contained many of the concepts of asceticism. The Puritans felt that schools should be characterized by sternness, strict discipline, work, and emphasis on things spiritual. The school was not a place to play. Puritanism stressed a fear of showing emotions and playing. Play in any form was looked upon as sin. Work offered all the physical activity needed for the good of the individual.

A stanza from an early church hymnal characterizes this philosophy:

> Work for the night is coming,
> Work through the morning hours;
> Work while the dew is sparkling,
> Work 'mid springing flowers;
> Work when the day grows brighter,
> Work in the glowing sun;
> Work, for the night is coming,
> When man's work is done.

Everything centered around work. The child was taught that living was a serious business. Things should not be too easy; he should not enjoy himself too much.

Modern Attitudes Toward Play as an Educational Tool. Although such doctrines as asceticism, scholasticism, and puritanism dominated the thinking of the past and even reach into the present, the importance of play is rapidly expanding. Since the late eighteenth century it has been increasingly recognized as an educational tool.

Outstanding educators began to support play as an educational medium. Pestalozzi, the great Swiss educator of the late eighteenth and early nineteenth centuries, stressed play. He believed it to have great value from a recreational point of view and also as a means of achieving the harmonious development of mind, body, and soul.

Froebel, the renowned German educator, developed the kindergarten during this same period in history. He strongly believed that one of the best ways to educate children was through play. He felt that youngsters express themselves more readily in their play than in any other way.

John Locke, the English philosopher of the seventeenth century, stressed activity. His words have lived through history. "A sound mind in a sound body is a short but full description of a happy state in this world. He that has these two has little more to wish for." Locke believed that play could aid in the achievement of this worthwhile goal.

Rousseau in *Émile* stressed the important part that play can render in the rearing of children. Dewey and others who followed also recognized the importance of play as a means of educating the young. Although there has been a lag in the acceptance of play as an educational medium, more and more educators are coming to realize the tremendous potential it has for guiding children in the right direction. Play, a phenomenon which has its own drive, cannot be overlooked as an educational device.

Physical Development Through Directed Play. Play excels as a contributor to the health and physical development of the child. It is essential to optimum physical development—to a healthy heart, lungs, and other organs of the body—and to the development of such characteristics as strength, endurance, agility, speed, and accuracy. All are essential to a healthful, vigorous, and satisfying life.

The physical-development objective is sought through the program of activities which builds physical power in an individual, resulting in the ability to sustain adaptive effort, to recover, and to resist fatigue. The value of this objective rests on the premise that a person will be more active, be able to perform better, and be healthier if the organic systems of the body are adequately developed and functioning properly.

Exercise plays an important part in the development of the organic systems of the body. The term *organic* refers to the digestive, circulatory, excretory, heat regulatory, respiratory, and other systems of the human body. These systems are stimulated through activities which involve such basic movements as hanging, climbing, running, throwing, leaping, carrying, and jumping. The activity should be of a vigorous nature so that the various organic systems are sufficiently stimulated.

Through regular, vigorous exercise several beneficial results are achieved. The heart beats slower and provides better nourishment to the entire body. It pumps more blood per stroke; hence more food is delivered to the cells and there is better removal of waste products. There is a longer rest period between beats. Regular exercise enables the heart to return to normal much more rapidly following intense exercise. As a result, a person who exercises regularly over an extended period is able to perform work for a greater length of time, with less expenditure of energy, and much more efficiency. This trained condition is necessary to a vigorous and abundant life. From the time a person rises in the morning until he goes to bed at night he is continually in need of vitality, strength, endurance, and stamina to perform routine tasks, to be prepared for emergencies, and to lead an active life.

This objective is especially important for the elementary school child because he is in his formative period. Play is the child's work—it helps him to grow and develop, and to build the sound organic base which is so essential to a healthy and vigorous existence. According to recent research, American children are soft compared to European youngsters. Although the evidence is not conclusive, there is danger of young people getting soft. Dependence upon the labor-saving devices and other gadgets that modern technology is giving this country tends to discourage physical activity necessary to develop strong, flexible bodies. Part of the blame for this lies in the increasing trend toward spectatorism. This threat to our youth has attracted the attention of many doctors, educators, and even the executive branch of the government. There is a growing urgency to do everything possible to make the youth of this country strong, and physically fit. Elementary school teachers, in particular, should realize the importance of this objective and strive to organize and administer physical education programs which fulfill this important need.

Skill Development Through Directed Play. The skill-development objective can be defined as performing various physical movements with as little expenditure of energy as possible in a proficient, graceful, and aesthetic manner. This has implications for one's work, play, and anything else that requires physical movement.

Effective skill is dependent upon harmonious working of the muscular and nervous systems. This harmonious relationship allows for peak performance over fairly long periods of time. It is needed in activities involving running, hanging, jumping, dodging, leaping, kicking, bending, twisting, carrying, and throwing. It enables one to perform his daily work much more efficiently and without tiring too quickly.

In physical education activities, the function of efficient body movement—or neuromuscular skill, as it is often called—is to provide the individual with the ability to perform with a desired degree of proficiency. Among other benefits, it will result in greater enjoyment of participation. Most persons enjoy doing those things in which they have acquired a degree of mastery or skill. For example, if a child has mastered the ability to throw a ball consistently to a designated spot and has developed batting and fielding power, he will enjoy playing baseball or softball. If he can swim 25 or 50 yards without tiring and can perform several advanced dives, he will enjoy being in the water. If he can dance the latest steps he will like to get out on the dance floor. A person enjoys doing those things in which he or she excels. On the other hand, people do not enjoy participating in activities in which they have little or no skill. Therefore, it is an objective of physical education to develop in each child as many physical skills as possible so that his interests will be wide and varied. This will not only result in more enjoyment for the participant, but will also allow for better individual adjustment to groups.

Physical skills are not developed in one easy lesson. It takes years to acquire coordinations, and the most important period of their development is during the formative years of a child's growth. The building of coordinations starts in childhood when an individual attempts to synchronize his muscular and nervous systems for such things as creeping, walking, running, and jumping. A study of kinesiology shows that many muscles of the body are used in even the most simple coordinated movements. Therefore, in order to obtain efficient motor movement or skill in many activities, it is necessary to start training early in life and to continue this training into adulthood. Further, a child does not usually object to the continual trial and error process of achieving success in the performance of physical acts. He does not object to being observed as an awkward, uncoordinated beginner during the learning period because most of his classmates are similarly awkward and uncoordinated. Most adults, however, are very self-conscious when going through the period of learning a physical skill. They do not like to perform if they cannot perform in a creditable manner. As a result, the skills they do not acquire in their youth are many times never acquired. Therefore, the classroom teacher and the physical education teacher should do everything possible to ensure that much skill learning takes place when a person is young, willing, and laying the foundation for adult years.

Mental Development Through Directed Play. Children develop mentally when they play. This is sometimes hard for educators and parents to understand. Through play youngsters gain knowledge, learn to reason and make judgments, and develop other intellectual powers. Gesell points out the high degree to which children learn and develop through their play. Many observing parents and teachers have noticed this development while they watched boys and girls in action. Babies learn that a *ball* will *bounce* but a block won't. If you *push* some toys a *bell* will *ring*. When you chew on a spoon it is *hard* and *cold*, but a teddy bear's foot is *soft* and *fuzzy*. Through trial and error in play, children learn many basic facts. Parents often take these things for granted because this knowledge is so fundamental, but these symbols have to be mastered—a child isn't born with an understanding of them. Many other mental concepts are developed through play. Young children learn simple arithmetic in rope jumping: "Mary, after the rope turns *four* times, you run in and take *ten* jumps." When the boys plan a softball diamond they must *compute angles* and handle *measurements*. The baseball team uses *percentages* in figuring batting *averages*. Children dance and march in *circles*, *squares*, *rectangles*, and *parallel lines*. Every activity is a learning situation, if the proper leadership is present to exploit the opportunity it offers.

The individual also acquires knowledge about games. Such things as rules, techniques, and strategies are learned. Basketball can be used as an example. In this sport the participant should know the rules, the strategy in offense and defense, the various types of passes, the difference between screening and blocking, and, finally, the values that are derived from engaging in sport. Techniques that are learned through experience result in knowledge. For example, a ball travels faster and more accurately if one steps with a pass, and time is saved when the pass is made from the same position in which it is received. Furthermore, a knowledge of followership, leadership, courage, self-reliance, assistance to others, safety, and adaptation to group patterns is very important.

Knowledge concerning health should play an important part in the program. All individuals should know about their bodies, the importance of disease prevention, exercise, sanitation, and a well-balanced diet, and the values of good health habits and attitudes. This knowledge will contribute greatly to physical prowess as well as to general health. With it activities will take on a new meaning and health practices will be associated with definite purposes. This will help each individual to live a healthier and more purposeful life.

A store of knowledge will give each individual the proper background for interpreting the new situations which inevitably confront him from day to day. Unless there is knowledge to draw from, he will become helpless when called upon to make important decisions.

Social Development Through Directed Play. The child's social development is greatly advanced through play. Many times he forms his values, ideals, and standards from those endorsed by his teachers and playmates. Directed play should provide suitable social relationships between the child and his playmates and teacher. Constructive behavior patterns of helpfulness, kindness, truthfulness, justice, and sociability should result. Individual qualities such as aggressiveness, ambition, perseverance, and courage should be directed so they will not become objectionable. Children can learn good discipline through play. Good manners, courtesy, truthfulness, consideration for others, and a belief in the Golden Rule are worthy objectives that can be accomplished. Properly guided play does not give the child an opportunity to develop antisocial qualities. As Adler says in his book *Understanding Human Nature*, "The manner in which a child approaches a game, his choice and the importance he places upon it, indicates his attitude and relationship to his environment and how he is related to his fellowmen."

The teacher who engages in physical activities with her children can be a very influential person in shaping their character development. In play she observes them in their most natural state. The personality of the child is displayed in his play reactions. When he misses a ball, is he always looking for an excuse? "Tom threw it too hard." "It wasn't anywhere near me." When he is about to be tagged in a running and fleeing game, does he "accidentally on purpose" fall down? If he is poor at some particular activity or skill, does he project his defense on others. "Sam can't play as well as I can even if I can't hit the ball."

Many individual traits or characteristics may be identified through play. Many can also be corrected by the wise and understanding teacher. The teacher, however, must avoid planning activities for play which are too complex.

14   THE PHILOSOPHY

If the play requires skills beyond the capacity of the child, the challenge may appear too great and he will retreat. The same might be true if attainable results are too elementary and have no challenge—he may retreat from the group and choose something for himself which offers more of a challenge.

All human beings should experience success. This factor can be realized through play. Through successful experience in play activities, a child develops self-confidence and finds happiness in his achievements. Physical education can provide for this successful experience by offering a variety of activities and developing the necessary skills for success in these activities.

If children are happy, they will make the necessary adjustments. An individual who is happy is much more likely to make the right adjustment than the individual who is morbid, sullen, and in an unhappy state of mind. Happiness reflects friendliness, cheerfulness, and a spirit of cooperation, all of which help a person to be content and to conform to the necessary standards which have been established. Therefore, physical education should instill happiness by guiding children into those activities where this quality will be realized.

In a democratic society all individuals should develop a sense of group consciousness and cooperative living. This should be one of the most important objectives of the physical education program. Whether or not a child will grow up to be a good citizen and contribute to the welfare of society will depend to a great extent upon the training he receives during his childhood and youth. In various play activities the following factors should be stressed: aid for the less-skilled players, respect for the rights of others, subordination of one's desires to the will of the group, and realization that cooperative living is essential to the success of society. In other words, the Golden Rule should be practiced. The individual should be made to feel that he belongs to the group and has the responsibility of directing his actions in its behalf. The rules of sportsmanship should be developed and practiced

(Courtesy of Creative Playthings, Inc., Princeton, New Jersey, and Los Angeles, California.)

in all activities that are offered in the program. Such qualities as courtesy, sympathy, truthfulness, fairness, honesty, respect for authority, and abiding by the rules will help a great deal in the promotion of social efficiency. The necessity for good leadership and followership should also be stressed as important to the interests and the ideals of our society.

People's actions can be controlled through proper education. This education can result in effective citizenship, which is the basis of sound, democratic living. Effective citizenship is not something that can be developed by artificial stimuli. It is something that is achieved only through activities in which individuals engage in their normal day-to-day routines. Since play activities have such a great attraction for children and youth, and since it is possible to develop desirable social traits under proper guidance, physical education should realize its responsibility. It should do its part in contributing to good citizenship—the basis of a democratic society.

Physical Education as a Part of General Education

It can be seen that through the fulfillment of its objectives of physical skill, mental and social development, physical education can contribute a great deal to the whole development and growth process. It is important, however, to be able to see more clearly how this phase contributes to each of the objectives set forth for education in general. For purposes of organization, this will be discussed under the four headings which represent the objectives of general education as set forth by the Educational Policies Commission. By realizing how physical education, as an integral part of education, contributes to the fulfillment of each of these objectives, the teacher will have a clearer conception of how physical education fits into a totally integrated educational pattern.

Objectives of Self-realization. Attaining the objectives of self-realization means developing the individual so that he realizes his potentialities and becomes a well-adjusted member of society. Physical education can contribute to these objectives in many ways.

1. *Contributing to an inquiring mind.* New and interesting phases of living are opened up to the child through activity. His motor mechanism enables him to move around so he can see and discover the nature of many phases of his environment. His curiosity is stimulated.

2. *Contributing to knowledge of health and disease.* Physical education contributes to knowledge by giving the child information as to the importance of such things as nutrition, rest, sleep, and exercise; by instructing him in measures that should be taken to guard against disease; by developing an understanding of why the body needs vigorous outdoor activity; by instilling an appreciation of wholesome health attitudes and habits; by giving him knowledge about the correction of physical defects; by stressing safety factors for the prevention of accidents; and by showing him the importance of adequate health services.

3. *Contributing to family and community health.* Physical education can create, within the student, a realization of his responsibility for his own health and for the health of others. He comes to realize that health is a product that increases in importance as it is shared with other individuals. He has a degree of responsibility for the health of others in school, at home, and in the community of which he is a part.

4. *Contributing to skill as a participant and spectator in sports.* Physical education helps the individual to develop skill in many activities. The child, as a result, can enjoy and derive the many advantages that come from actually engaging in a game or other similar experiences. At the same time, some knowledge of other activities is presented so that the value of spectator enjoyment is also enhanced.

5. *Contributing to resources for utilizing leisure hours in mental pursuits.* Education is concerned with developing mental resources for the utilization of leisure hours. Physical education contributes by providing the material for interesting sports stories and biographies of great athletes, such as Wilt Chamberlain, Carl Yastrzemski, and Arnold Palmer. In addition to motivating the child to read, sports can contribute to many interesting hobbies such as designing, building, and caring for equipment, research on

the many statistics involved in sports, and a study of various aspects of nature which would be aroused by an interest in sports.

6. *Contributing to an appreciation of beauty*. The educated person develops an appreciation of the beautiful which can be fostered in early childhood. In addition to beauty of architecture, painting, and music, the child should also appreciate the beauty of trees, animals, the sky, and other aspects of the environment which he meets in his play. He should develop an appreciation for the beauty of his body, and of physical movement, which in sports situations can produce the ultimate in grace, rhythm, and coordination.

7. *Contributing to the direction of one's life toward worthwhile goals*. The educated person conscientiously attempts to guide his life in the proper direction. Physical education can contribute to the child's direction during the early formative years by giving guidance as to what is right and proper, which goals are worth competing for, the difference between intrinsic and extrinsic values, autocratic and democratic procedures, and antisocial and acceptable conduct. The child is a great imitator, and the beliefs, actions, and conduct of the teacher are often reflected in the beliefs, actions, and conduct of the student.

Objectives of Human Relationships. Human relationships may be defined as the manner in which individuals get along with each other. Good human relations imply that people live together, work together, and play together harmoniously. Physical education can make a worthwhile contribution in this area in a variety of ways, of which the following are significant:

1. *Placing human relations first*. Activities are planned with the needs and interests of children in mind; rules and regulations exist for the benefit of the player's welfare; the less skilled are given due attention; and the program is child-centered. If human relations come first, a spirit of good will, fellowship, and cooperation will exist.

2. *Enabling each child to enjoy a rich social experience through play*. Such experience can help to develop a child's personality by teaching him to adapt to the group situation, by developing proper standards of conduct, by creating a feeling of belonging, and by developing a sound code of ethics. There are limitless possibilities for social experiences in "tag" and "it" games. Here the child learns behavior traits which are characteristic of a democratic society. Through these play experiences he will become more willing to abide by the rules, accept responsibility, contribute to the welfare of the group, and respect the rights of others.

3. *Helping children to play cooperatively*. The physical education program should stress cooperation as the basis for achieving the goals an individual or group desires. It should also stress leadership and followership traits. The success of any venture depends on good leadership and good workers or followers. Everyone cannot be captain of the relay team. Everyone does not have leadership ability. Those who are good leaders should also be good followers. A leader in one activity might possibly make a better follower in another activity. The important thing is that both leaders and followers are needed for the accomplishment of any enterprise. All contribute to the undertaking. All deserve commendation for work well done. Cooperation by every member of the group in whatever way each one is best equipped to contribute will insure success for the group endeavor.

4. *Teaching courtesy, fair play, and good sportsmanship*. The amenities of social behavior are a part of the repertory of every educated person. Such characteristics as courtesy, fair play, and good sportsmanship can be developed in the child as he plays with his classmates and others in game situations.

5. *Contributing to family and home living*. The teacher of physical education is often the individual in whom a child puts his trust and confidence and whom he desires to emulate. The nature of physical education work and its appeal to youth are probably the major reasons for this tendency. Consequently, the teacher in charge of the physical education class should utilize his advantageous position to become better acquainted with the youth and his home and family life. Many times a child's home and family problems can be helped through such knowledge. Proper counseling and guidance, helping children to experience success in play activities, talks with parents, and home visits are useful.

Objectives of Economic Efficiency. A third objective of education is sufficient production and consumption of goods and services. Education has the opportunity of informing children in respect to both the vocational aspects of living and the consumer aspects. Both are important and are necessary for a happy and successful life. Physical education can aid in more efficient production of goods and services and also can aid in the establishment of certain standards which will guide the public in the wise consumption of certain goods.

1. *Recognition of the need for good workmanship.* Work is an essential for all individuals. Through work one contributes goods and services to the community of which he is a part. Children should have the opportunity to work. As part of their training, children should be assigned tasks in the home and also in school. In physical education, children could help develop playfields, care for equipment, and assist in the instruction of those with less skill. Through regular duties, they can discover that they are contributing to the welfare of the group and are providing services which will help others to enjoy their activity experiences more fully.

2. *Recognition of the need for successful work.* The success of any job depends to a great degree upon the health and physical fitness of the worker. Experience in physical education activities contributes to physical health, mental health, human relations, and other social assets which help to contribute to better work. As each child develops a strong organic base for future years, he becomes prepared to do a better job.

3. *Recognition of the need for professional growth.* The teacher of physical education should be continually interested in developing new skills, understanding, and appreciation of the contribution that his area of education can make to child growth and development. Physical education is a growing profession. New awareness and knowledge in the fields of biology, psychology, and sociology are continually evolving which have implications for the physical education teacher's job. Only if the teacher is constantly studying new scientific and technological developments can he make the greatest contribution to children.

4. *Recognition of the need for wise consumption of goods and services.* The educated person buys his goods and services with wisdom. He is well informed as to the worth and utility of various goods and services. Physical education helps children to recognize the relative values of goods and services that influence their health and physical fitness. Such things as the need to seek qualified advice in health matters, the dangers of self-medication, and the importance of critical evaluation of advertisements and other material on health cures can be discussed.

Objectives of Civic Responsibility. Civic responsibility falls upon each member of society. Only as each individual assumes his civic responsibility and contributes to group welfare will democratic ties be strengthened.

1. *Recognition of the need for humanitarianism.* Children should be well informed as to the needs of mankind everywhere. A humanitarian view of the conditions of mankind should become a part of every student. Physical education can, within limits, provide democratic play experiences in which children see the importance and value of cooperative living and contribute to the welfare of all. Here is an ideal setting for developing humanitarian values. Children of all creeds, colors, and races and from all walks of life are brought together for a social experience. Interest and a natural drive for activity provide a laboratory for actual practice in developing these values.

2. *Recognition of the need for tolerance.* It is the prerogative of every person to think out solutions to various problems, form his own opinions, and attempt to bring others around to his point of view. The physical education class can be a place where tolerance is developed in regard to other people's opinions in the various activities they conduct. Children may be educated to participate intelligently in the discussion of common problems that develop in a game situation. All can be encouraged to contribute their thinking. Thoughts and ideas are respected by all and final settlement of the problem can be made by the group.

3. *Recognition of the need for the conservation of natural resources.* Physical education should be especially interested in preserving such natural resources of the nation as forests, soil, water, scenic beauty, and wild life. They have implications for active forms of recreation. Children should understand the value of such resources to the health and physical fitness of the country. Through an educational program which points out that natural resources are directly related to the welfare of each resident of this country, much good can be done toward conserving this form of the nation's wealth.

4. *Recognition of the need for conformance with the law.* In a democracy laws are made by the people and for their benefit. Obedience is essential to a well-ordered society. Physical education can contribute to the development of a law-abiding attitude in youth. The rules of the game and the rules of safety that have been established for the playground, gymnasium, and other places where activities are held should be made clear to each student. Furthermore, the purpose behind such rules and the individual's responsibility in each case should be understood.

5. *Recognition of the need for understanding one's civic duties.* It is the responsibility of every citizen to have a clear understanding of his civic duties and to see that they are carried out in an intelligent manner. Physical education can show how games and various aspects of the school program are analogous in many ways to what the child's responsibilities will be in an adult community. The importance of selecting good leaders, living according to high standards of conduct, abiding by the rules, and contributing to the welfare of the group are a few examples.

6. *Recognition of the need for democratic living.* The educated citizen believes in the democratic way of life and his every action is symbolic of his loyalty to its ideals. Physical education can contribute, together with other parts of the school program, by making experiences on the playground or in the gymnasium ones where democratic principles prevail and where such important concepts as respect for the individual, the rights of others, and freedom of action are honored.

Components of the Elementary School Physical Education Program

There are three main components of a well-rounded elementary school physical education program—(1) the required class program, (2) the adapted program, and (3) the intramural program.

The *required class program* is the basic component for all students in the elementary school. It is instructional in nature and should be provided on a daily basis throughout the elementary school years. It should consist of a variety of activities including story plays, rhythms and dances, games of low organization, mimetics, self-testing activities and stunts, classroom games, individual activities, team games, and aquatics. These activities should be presented in a progressive manner, ranging from simple and informal to complex and more highly organized. The activities should be presented to meet the physical, mental, social, and emotional needs of the students.

The *adapted program* constitutes that phase of the physical education program that meets the needs of the atypical individual, who, because of some physical inadequacy, functional defect capable of being improved through exercise, or other deficiency, is temporarily or permanently unable to take part in the regular physical education program. The adapted program can be valuable for pupils with such characteristics as faulty body mechanics, nutritional disturbances (overweight and underweight), heart and lung disturbances, postoperative and convalescent problems, hernias, weak and flat feet, nervous instability, low physical fitness, and crippling conditions. Provisions for restricted and/or remedial physical activity are made for such pupils, in both regular and special classes, utilizing special conditioning exercises, aquatics, and recreational sports. The adapted program is predicated upon harmonious working relationships with school and home medical and nursing personnel.

The *intramural program* is designed to provide competition with the same school in games, sports, and other physical activities for elementary school students. Such a program is most frequently offered in the intermediate grades (fourth, fifth, and sixth). In contrast to the required class program which is instructional in nature, the intramural program is designed to provide an opportunity for students to utilize learned skills in actual competitive situations. Such competition should be friendly and informal, with an absence of pressures usually generated by publicity, gate receipts, and spectators. The competition should be voluntary, should be conducted during out-of-class hours, and should provide for a variety of activities based on the needs and interests of pupils.

The elementary school classroom teacher and physical education specialist also have responsibility for instilling proper health attitudes, knowledge, and practice in the children with whom they come in contact through the physical education program. The desired attitudes and knowledge can be gained in the classroom as well as through the activities of the physical education program, and good health practices can be reinforced.

Health, as well as physical education, is concerned with the individual's physical, mental, emotional, and social development. Good health is but one aspect of the total fitness of the individual, for a person cannot achieve or maintain proper levels of fitness unless he is in good health.

Through a sound physical education program, the teacher can educate the children concerning the value of a regular program of exercise and physical activity in contributing to health. Activities can be selected that are vigorous enough to stimulate the child's organic development, and a sufficiently lengthy physical education period should be provided so that the activities will be effective.

The health of all children in a school can be improved through a regular program of physical activity. The normally healthy and active child as well as the physically, mentally, or emotionally handicapped child will be able to enhance his health status at least somewhat through a well-planned and integrated program of health and physical education.

Physical education is concerned not only with developing, physical, social, or emotional fitness but also with helping the child to accumulate a variety of lifetime skills. In today's world leisure-time use is of vital concern to most people. Many individuals have not experienced a wide variety of activities and cannot successfully utilize their newly found free time for recreational pursuits.

On the elementary school level the teacher must be concerned with including a variety of recreational activities in the physical education program. Older elementary school children can enjoy many modified individual and dual sports; swimming is especially suited to children of any age, along with dancing of all forms.

Recreation is often described as the practical utilization of the skills learned in physical education, and the elementary school is the opportune place to begin instilling recreational skills. Aside from the regular class program, there are many after-school activities on the club and intramural level that are especially suited for, or can be adapted to, the recreational needs of the elementary-school-age child.

Factors Affecting the Elementary School Physical Education Program

Whether or not the physical education program in grades kindergarten through eight is a successful experience for the child and a dynamic part of the educational offering depends upon several factors. Some of the more important of these follow.

Administrative Philosophy. The philosophy of education expressed by the community, the board of education, the superintendent of schools, and the principal plays an important part in determining the place and role of physical education in the total educational program. Upon these people depend the type of facilities that will be provided, the amount of money allocated in the budget, the respect given to the physical education specialist, the time provided in the school day, and the personnel who are hired. Some administrations endorse a philosophy of education that gives lip service to the physical needs of pupils but fail to follow through and provide adequate tangible support for meeting these needs. Such administrations should be questioned as to their sincerity concerning this phase of the educational program. School administrators and communities need to see clearly the important contribution that a meaningful physical education experience can provide boys and girls. They should be willing to back up this philosophy with action in terms of scheduling, facilities, time, personnel, and other essentials.

Time. The amount of time in the school program allocated for physical education will influence the type of experience provided for elementary school pupils. On the primary level, the classroom teacher and physical education specialist should try to provide a minimum of thirty minutes each day for purposes of class instruction. In addition, there should be at least thirty minutes of supervised play in which the youngsters engage in activities in the gymnasium, on the playground, or in the swimming pool. In the intermediate grades and in the middle school the time allocation should be increased to forty or forty-five minutes daily for the instructional phase of the program and twenty to thirty minutes daily for supervised play.

Facilities, Equipment, and Supplies. Not all elementary schools have fine gymnasiums, swimming facilities, or an ample supply of balls, bats, and other equipment. In fact, there are many schools that do not have any facilities or materials with which to work. However, this does not mean teachers should throw up their hands and do nothing about physical education. For the creative teacher, much can be done through improvisation. It may mean using the playground for more months during the year, utilizing the corridors in the school as play areas, adapting activities to the classroom, and collecting broom handles, ropes, and supplies from outside sources for the construction of unique equipment. The ingenious teacher will provide for the physical education of her pupils.

Boards of education and community-minded people are increasingly recognizing the importance of physical education facilities. Teachers of elementary school physical education should be familiar with the following standards and make recommendations accordingly.

1. The playground area should be located near the building and be easily accessible to classrooms.

2. Kindergarten children should have for their exclusive use a section of the playground consisting of a surfaced area, a grass area, and a place for sand and digging. The sand area should be enclosed to prevent the sand from being scattered. It is also wise to have a shaded area for storytelling and similar activities. Essential equipment would include swings, slides, seesaws, climbing structures, tables, and seats.

3. Children above kindergarten (grades one through six) should have play space which includes turf, apparatus, shaded, multiple-use paved, and recreation areas. The turf area provides space for many games and other activities and the apparatus area for such climbing equipment as a jungle gym, horizontal bars, and giant strides. There should be ample space to provide for the safety of the participants. The shaded area may provide space for such activities as marbles, hopscotch, or ring toss, and also storytelling. The multiple-use paved area may serve a variety of purposes and activities on a year-round basis for both school and community. It can house basket-ball, tennis, and handball courts, games of low organization, and other activities. In selecting paving material for this area, resiliency, safety, and durability should be taken into consideration. Rapid and efficient drainage is essential. Lines may be painted on the area for the various types of games. The schools should allow additional space adjacent to this area for possible future expansion.

4. Gymnasiums for elementary schools should have a minimum floor area of at least 50 by 80 feet and include such features as smooth walls, hardwood floors (maple preferred), recessed lights, recessed radiators, adequate and well-screened windows, and storage space for the apparatus and other equipment. It is also generally agreed that it is best to have the gymnasium located in a separate wing of the building to isolate the noise and to provide a convenient location for community groups who may use such facilities.

5. Appropriate equipment and apparatus are suggested in Chapter 6.

Personnel. A controversial issue in elementary school physical education is whether the classroom teacher or the specialist should teach physical education. A discussion of this subject appears later in this book. At this point it will suffice to say that the physical education specialist and the classroom teacher must work closely together in carrying out this important function. In many school systems the classroom teacher is assigned the responsibility but there is a physical education specialist upon whom she or he may call for advice, materials, and help.

Qualifications of the Classroom Teacher. Some of the important qualifications of the classroom teacher are as follows:

1. *A philosophy that appreciates physical education as an important part of education.* The classroom teacher must see physical education

as an important part of the educational program. Frequently, the classroom teacher appreciates reading, arithmetic, and language as important phases of elementary education but does not have the same feeling for physical education. In such cases, this philosophy is reflected in what the teacher does during the physical education period. There are some classroom teachers who use this period as a time to sun themselves while the children play on their own, to chat with other teachers who have their classes on the playground at the same time, or to stay in the classroom and grade papers while the youngsters run and jump outside. A disservice is being done when such conditions exist. It is just as serious as if the teacher failed to carry out the teaching assignments in history or in science.

2. *Interest in children and their play activities.* The classroom teacher who recognizes that boys and girls have a love of play and a desire for action and appreciates and wants to direct these desires into educational channels will do an excellent job in physical education. She or he will recognize that this medium is a natural part of the growth and development of children and will nurture and use it for educational purposes.

3. *Desire and determination to know what physical education is all about.* Unfortunately, most classroom teachers have insufficient training and preparation in physical education. Many have no formal course work whatsoever. Some have had a three-credit-hour course which covered the activities, the philosophy, and other aspects of physical education. A few have had more extensive training. This means that the majority of their training and information must be self-taught, and gained on the job. The classroom teacher can get much of this information and do much toward his or her self-education by (a) contacting the physical education specialist for help and advice and (b) developing a professional library in physical education. There may be a specialist assigned to the elementary school. If not, there are some in the community who will be most eager to offer help and assistance. It might be wise to ask to be notified when physical education staff meetings are held and then attend them. There are also many excellent books on physical education and many fine periodicals that contain helpful articles which will keep the teacher in touch with new trends, provide new methods for teaching classes, and help solve the problems that continually arise.

4. *Diligent effort to provide a good physical education program.* The classroom teacher should make an honest attempt to provide a physical education program for his or her pupils which is in accordance with professional standards. This program should be based upon the needs and interests of pupils and should mesh with the program of the preceding grade and the grade following.

Qualifications of the Elementary School Physical Education Specialist. The qualifications of the elementary school physical education specialist should exceed those of the classroom teacher:

1. *Professional preparation*—graduation from an approved teacher-training institution, accredited by the American Association of Colleges of Teacher Education, with a major in physical education.

2. *General education*—preparation in such general-education subjects as English, science, psychology, foreign languages, and the arts.

3. *Elementary education*—preparation in and an understanding of the elementary school child and the program of studies and activities with which he should be provided, together with an appreciation of how physical education fits into the total pattern.

4. *Health*—freedom from any physical or mental defects which would prevent sucessful teaching in physical education. Because of the important part that a teacher plays in shaping a child's life, it is necessary that specialists have good mental and physical health. Furthermore, in building healthy bodies they should be good examples for their students to follow.

5. *Personality suitable for teaching*—possession of such personality traits as enthusiasm, friendliness, cheerfulness, industry, cooperation, self-control, integrity, social adaptability, and likeableness. Whether or not the right social traits are developed in children will depend largely on the personality of the leader.

6. *Sincere interest in the teaching of physical education*—possession of a deep conviction that he or she is rendering a service to mankind. Physical educators should have an interest in serving children through the teaching of physical activities and in helping them to develop into better adults.

7. *Acceptable standard of motor ability*—possession of skills in the activities he or she teaches. Physical skills are basic to the physical education profession and proficiency in some of them is important to success in this type of work.

8. *Sense of humor*—possession of a lighter side to his or her personality, a requisite for the teacher who works with children. It will make physical education more interesting for students.

The Middle School. There has been a recent trend in American education to attempt to reorganize school systems by introducing the middle-school concept. Traditionally, a majority of school systems have been organized on a 6–3–3 or 8–4 pattern. The 6–3–3 pattern means that youngsters attend an elementary school for grades kindergarten through six, a junior high school for grades seven through nine, and a senior high school for grades ten through twelve. Under the 8–4 pattern, grades K–8 are in the elementary school while grades 9–12 are in the senior high school, and the junior high school is eliminated.

In the middle-school organizational pattern, children in grades 6–8, and in some cases 5–8, are grouped in a school that is more departmentalized than the elementary school but less departmentalized and more informal than the high school. This innovative pattern eliminates the traditional junior high school, which by its nature cannot cater to individual student needs as effectively as the middle school. The middle school is designed to cater especially to the early adolescent who needs to feel secure in bridging the gap between the dependency of the elementary school years and the enforced independency of the secondary school years.

In the middle school the student spends several periods each day in the homeroom but reports to other rooms for such subjects as art, music, science, and physical education. These subjects, among others, are taught by specialists. In his first year in the middle school the child spends most of the day in his homeroom, but as he enters each succeeding grade he becomes increasingly independent and is assigned to special subjects with a variety of student groups other than his homeroom group.

Although the traditional elementary school depends mainly on the classroom teacher to handle the physical education program, the middle schools employ specialists for this assignment. The middle school has many implications for improving the quality of physical education instruction in the upper elementary school grades.

Questions and Practical Problems

1. Do you think John Dewey was in favor of physical education? Why?

2. To what extent did the physical education program in which you participated in elementary school contribute to your physical, social, mental, and emotional welfare?

3. Why is there a great need for understanding the true meaning of physical education? What are your responsibilities for interpreting the work correctly? Explain your answer in as much detail as you can.

4. Define the term "education." What do you consider an acceptable definition of an educated person to be? What are the advantages of being an educated person in light of your definition?

5. What is the classroom teacher's role in physical education in the elementary school? What qualifications should he or she have?

6. How can the elementary classroom teacher prepare herself to do an effective job of teaching physical education? Outline what you consider to be a practical in-service program.

7. Do a research paper, finding as many lists of objectives for education as possible that have been proposed since 1800 by associations, committees, and commissions. Determine the similarities and differences.

8. Make a drawing of the circulatory system of the body, showing the changes that take place during exercise.

9. Discuss the nervous system of the body in relation to the development of skills.

10. Comment on the statement, "All education takes place within the walls of the public schools."

11. List the objectives of self-realization human relationship, economic efficiency, and civic responsibility in four columns on a piece

of paper. Place a check mark after each objective to which physical education contributes. Opposite each list itemize as many as you can of the contributions physical education makes to each objective.

12. Examine a history book and determine how the objectives of present-day physical education compare with the objectives of physical education in Ancient Greece. How might the Greek development of physical education be related to the development of democracy?

13. Make a list of points which show the unique features of physical education that contribute to general education objectives.

14. Show how the organizational patterns of education are changing to meet the needs of today's students.

15. Show how physical education, health education, and recreation may be integrated in the elementary school. Make a chart that shows the ways in which their common objectives are sought in each field.

Selected References

ANDERSON, MARIAN, MARGARET E. ELLIOT, and JEANNE LaBERGE. *Play with a Purpose.* New York: Harper & Row, Publishers, 1971.

Association for Childhood Education International. *Physical Education for Children's Healthful Living.* Washington, D.C.: Association for Childhood Education International, 1968.

BRAMWELD, THEODORE. *Philosophies of Education in Cultural Perspective.* New York. The Dryden Press, 1955.

BROUDY, HARRY S. *Building a Philosophy of Education.* Englewood Cliffs, N.J.: Prentice-Hall, Inc., 1954.

BUCHER, CHARLES A. *Administration of School Health and Physical Education Programs.* (Fifth Edition). St. Louis: The C. V. Mosby Co., 1971.

———. *Foundations of Physical Education* (Fifth Edition). St. Louis: The C. V. Mosby Co., 1968.

———. *Methods and Materials in Physical Education and Recreation.* St. Louis: The C. V. Mosby Co., 1954.

Educational Policies Commission. *Education for All American Children.* Washington, D.C.: National Education Association of the United States and the American Association of School Administrators, 1948.

———. *Education and the Defense of American Democracy.* Washington, D.C.: National Education Association of the United States and the American Association of School Administrators, 1940.

———. *Education of Free Men in American Democracy.* Washington, D.C.: National Education Association of the United States and the American Association of School Administrators, 1941.

———. *Policies for Education in American Democracy*: Washington, D. C.: National Education Association of the United States and the American Association of School Administrators, 1946.

FLEMING, ROBERT S. *Curriculum for Today's Boys and Girls.* Columbus, Ohio: Charles E. Merrill Books, Inc., 1963.

GROUT, RUTH E. *Health Teaching in Schools.* Philadelphia: W. B. Saunders Company, 1968.

McCLOY, CHARLES H. *Philosophical Bases for Physical Education.* New York: Appleton-Century-Crofts, 1940.

NASH, JAY B. *Physical Education: Interpretations and Objectives.* New York: A. S. Barnes and Company, 1948, Chaps. 6–12.

OBERTEUFFER, DELBERT, and MARY K. BEYRER. *School Health Education.* New York: Harper & Row, Publishers, 1966.

PARK, JOE. *Selected Readings in the Philosophy of Education* (Third Edition). New York: The Macmillan Company, 1968.

WHITEHEAD, ALFRED N. *The Aims of Education.* New York: The Free Press, 1929.

WILLIAMS, JESSE FEIRING. *The Principles of Physical Education.* Philadelphia: W. B. Saunders Company, 1964.

CHAPTER 2

Health in the Elementary School

The World Health Organization defines health as "a state of complete physical, mental, and social well-being, not merely the absence of disease or infirmity." The primary purpose of the school health program, therefore, is to promote the total health of the child. To accomplish this goal there must be adequate supervision of the physical, mental, emotional and social experiences the child has during the school day. This, in turn, means that courses of instruction must be developed for the teaching of health topics based on the needs and interests of the pupils; the school plant must be a safe and healthful place in which to live; and proper medical services must be offered to improve and maintain the health of the child.

The Importance of Health in the Elementary School

Well informed teachers know that totally healthy children learn more rapidly, are better adjusted, get along well with their classmates, and make teaching a pleasure. Schools should strive to have every student achieve the best possible state of health.

Many educational organizations have pointed out that the school has a responsibility in regard to the health of students. In 1918, the report of a commission on education of the National Education Association listed health as its first objective. The Educational Policies Commission, an important policy-making group in education, points out that an educated person understands basic facts concerning health and disease, protects his own health and that of his dependents, and strives to improve the health of the community. The American Council on Education, another policy-making group, states that schools should help pupils to improve and maintain their own health. A report of a White House Conference on Education stressed physical and mental health as an educational objective.

Specifically, a concern for the health of the elementary school child is important for the following reasons:

1. *The health of the child determines how he will function.* A child functions physically, mentally, emotionally, and socially. The health of the child will determine not only his physical well-being but also how well he concentrates on mental tasks, how capably he controls his emotions, and how easily he adapts socially to his classmates and other people. Without good health a child is ineffective and unproductive. The healthy child is an integrated organism in

which all aspects of his growth and development have a bearing upon the learning process.

2. *The healthy child has a better chance to be a success in school.* To be a success in school requires a sound physical base upon which intellectual fitness can operate. The healthy child is more alert, thinks more clearly, and enjoys school more than does the unhealthy child.

3. *The mental aspects of a child's growth cannot be separated from other aspects of his total development.* The physical affects the mental—a child with a stomach-ache finds it difficult to do his school work. The mental affects the physical—when a child spends *all* his time studying, he finds that lack of physical activity, proper rest, and failure to meet physical needs results in harm to his health. The mental, physical, emotional, and social are all closely interwoven into the human being's makeup. One cannot be slighted without harming the other.

4. *Education has a legal responsibility with respect to the child's health.* The child is required by law to go to school. Accordingly, the school has the responsibility to provide for the child's health and safety while in school, similar to the way a parent provides for them while the child is at home. Therefore, in addition to being a moral and educational responsibility, health is also a legal one.

Factors That Influence the Health of the Child

There factors that affect each child's health are his heredity, the physical, biological, social, and economic environment in which he lives, and the way he lives.

Heredity determines the height of a person, the color of his eyes, the size of his body, the shape of his head, his blood type, the kind of nervous system he has, and many other characteristics. There is nothing that he can do about most of these traits. They are a part of him throughout life. Heredity makes him an individual and education helps him to accept what heredity has given him and encourages him to make the most of it.

Environment influences a child's health. Although heredity sets the limits of achievement, environment will determine whether or not the full potential is achieved. Environmental factors play a part in health and disease. Factors in the physical environment, such as climate and air pollution, affect the child's health. Plants and animals, a part of the biological environment, play a part in the nutritive value of foods eaten and also are instrumental in the transmission of some diseases. Family, community, church, and other phases of the social environment affect mental, emotional, and social aspects of health. Finally, the economics of the society in which a child lives affects many factors that influence health. Such socio-economic factors include housing, food, and medical services.

The way a child lives plays a major role in his health. The daily routine of the child, including the clothes he wears, the sleep he gets, the play he experiences, and the food he eats, will affect his well-being as much as any other factor. It is important, therefore, to note that ways of living can be conditioned by education. A child can be taught to live in certain ways that will be conducive to good health. He can be taught to practice cleanliness of person, to be considerate of others, and to look before he crosses the street. Unfortunately, many older people have poor health habits because they never were taught the harmful effects of certain practices such as smoking and overeating. As a result, their health has suffered. Society has an obligation to educate young people so they understand why good health habits are important and are motivated to develop them.

Objectives of the Health Program in the Elementary School

Specific objectives are frequently listed for the school health program, including the correction of health defects and the reduction of communicable disease. There are four general and major objectives with which the elementary school teacher should be concerned. These are health knowledge, wholesome health attitudes, desirable health practices, and health skills.

Health Knowledge. The teacher in the elementary school has the responsibility of transmitting to the child scientific health information that is readily understood and meaningful at his stage of growth and development. School children should know about such things as how their bodies function, the importance of sanitation, why it is important to eat the right kind of food, and the need for brushing their teeth regularly. This information can be presented in a meaningful and positive manner, together with experiences which show the children in the class the importance of living healthfully.

Health Attitudes. Health attitudes are linked to health interests of children and to the motives which impel children to act as they do. The health knowledge that is imparted will be applied only if a wholesome attitude exists on the part of the child. This is a challenge to the teacher because in some subjects it is important to get across only facts, but in health the facts are of little value without interest, drive, or motivating force. The teacher must help the youngster to develop wholesome attitudes toward health. These attitudes should be developed early in life.

Health Practices. Health practices, such as washing hands before eating, drinking milk, wearing proper clothing, and getting adequate sleep and rest, represent the end product of the educational process. If the teaching has effectively imparted the knowledge and has developed the right attitudes toward health, the right health practices will be developed. To have an effective school health program, it is important to recognize the close relationship that exists among health knowledge, health attitudes, and health practices. One contributes to the other.

Health Skills. Another objective of the school health program is the development of skills. In the elementary school such skills might be home nursing and first aid. The teacher has the opportunity to develop some of these skills during the intermediate grades and in the middle school.

The Conceptual Approach to School Health Education

School health education has never been a static area of the curriculum. The leaders in the field have consistently attempted to keep abreast of the latest health findings and the newest teaching methodologies. The conceptualized approach to the teaching of health in the elementary school is gaining successful entry into today's schools.

The mind does not concern itself exclusively with percepts, i.e., isolated bits of knowledge which are gained through conscious experience. For example, the sensation of light, shape, and form suddenly takes the name "mother," or "bottle," or "bed." The mind instead looks for the "big picture"—for what one percept has in common with others. A group of percepts may share common experiences which form a generalized idea which is called a concept. The process by which you transform a group of percepts into a concept is called conceptualization. For example, a health concept might be, "A person can learn to control his emotions." Therefore, the teaching of this concept would be aimed at providing experiences for the child which would reinforce this concept in his thinking and actions.

The conceptualized approach to teaching and learning has been applied to a variety of subject-matter areas, but it is in the field of health teaching that the most dynamic changes have come about. The conceptualized approach places much of the burden for learning on the child himself. This approach does away with rote learning and encourages the child to seek his own solutions to health problems and questions and thus form concepts for himself. This helps the child to relate health knowledge, attitudes, and practices directly to himself. This personal application is much more meaningful to the child than is any series of sterile memorized health facts.

The School Health Program

The school health program is that phase of the educational process which is concerned with developing an understanding of health and providing those experiences and services which play an active part in maintaining and improving the health of both pupils and school personnel. It includes teaching for health, living healthfully at school, and supplying services for both health maintenance and health improvement.

Teaching for health or health instruction refers to those experiences provided for the purpose of imparting knowledge and influencing attitudes and practices relating to both personal and group health.

Living healthfully at school includes providing a healthful physical environment as well as such aspects of the nonphysical environment as teacher-pupil rapport, organization of the school day, and school activities which affect the social and emotional health of pupils.

Services for health improvement refer to the six procedures which are vital to a desirable school health program:

1. Appraisal of the physical, mental, emotional, and social health status of children and school personnel.
2. Procedures used by teachers, physicians, nurses, and others to counsel pupils and parents in regard to health appraisal findings.
3. Follow-through procedures for correcting remediable health defects.
4. Provision for the exceptional child.
5. Procedures for prevention and control of communicable diseases.
6. Emergency care in cases of sickness and injury.

School Health Council. School health councils are organized in some schools to meet the health needs of pupils and school personnel. Councils are made up of people who devote their efforts to studying health problems and planning a course of action for their solution. Members of the team include such persons as the school nurse, a dental hygienist, the classroom teacher, the school principal, a physician, the custodian, and others who are interested and can contribute to developing a sound school health program.

The Teacher and Health Education. Throughout the course of modern educational history health has been a primary objective. As much as the child needs to become physically educated, he also needs to be health educated. Such education quite properly begins in the elementary school and should be continued throughout all of the school years.

Any school health program must be especially concerned with the needs, interests, and existing health knowledge of the children in the class or school. Frequently, elementary-level school health programs have not been geared to the real needs of the children involved in the program but have instead been designed around the teacher's conception of needed information. Often, health education is centered around a negative approach, that is, children are taught the names of the disease-causing germs and viruses, the symptoms of various diseases, and methods of treatment. A more recent trend has been to introduce a positive approach to health education, that is, the child learns how proper diet, rest, sleep, and exercise, plus all the other facets of daily living, contribute to the attainment and maintenance of a state of good health and general physical well-being.

Health education on the elementary school level has as a major purpose the improvement of the child's health behavior. Health behavior can only be changed in a desirable direction if the child's attitudes toward health develop in a worthwhile direction. The imparting of sound health knowledge, the development of desirable health attitudes, and resultant health behavioral changes depend in large measure on the teacher's training and background in health and on the teacher's imagination and creativity.

In order to be able to conduct a meaningful program of health education the teacher must have a command of basic health knowledge and must be willing to take extra courses and do additional reading in order to keep informed of the many new advances in the field of health and school health education. The teacher must not only be knowledgeable about the subject matter of the field but must also be enthusiastic about teaching health, be creative and innovative in the use of health-teaching aids, and be fully supported

Table 2–1. The School Health Program[a]

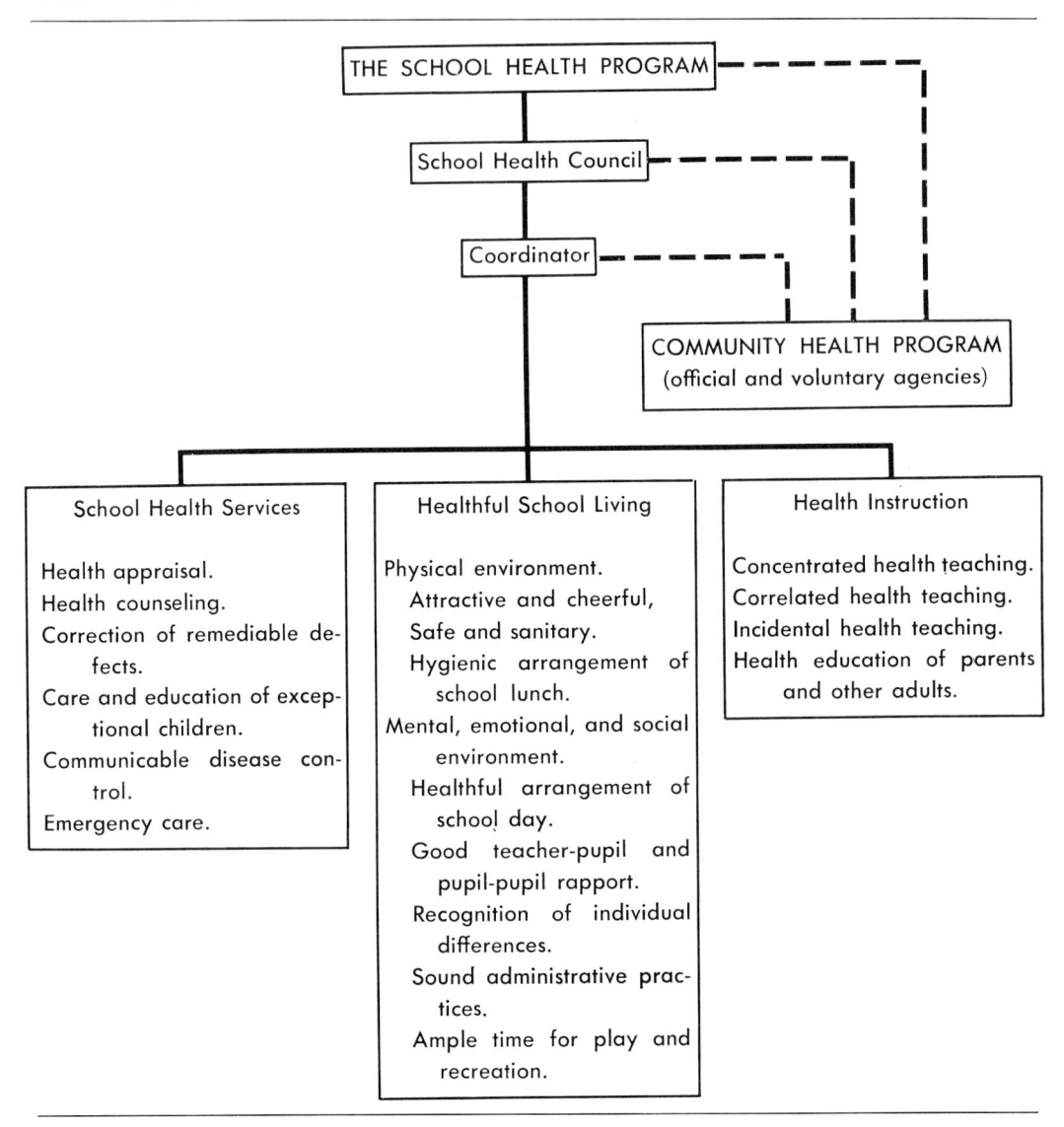

School Health Services	Healthful School Living	Health Instruction

Health appraisal.
Health counseling.
Correction of remediable defects.
Care and education of exceptional children.
Communicable disease control.
Emergency care.
	Physical environment.
	  Attractive and cheerful,
	  Safe and sanitary.
	  Hygienic arrangement of school lunch.
	Mental, emotional, and social environment.
	  Healthful arrangement of school day.
	  Good teacher-pupil and pupil-pupil rapport.
	  Recognition of individual differences.
	  Sound administrative practices.
	  Ample time for play and recreation.
		Concentrated health teaching.
		Correlated health teaching.
		Incidental health teaching.
		Health education of parents and other adults.

The School Health Program → School Health Council → Coordinator, linked to Community Health Program (official and voluntary agencies).

[a] Charles A. Bucher, *Administration of School Health and Physical Education Programs* (Fifth Edition), St. Louis, The C. V. Mosby Co., 1971.

by the school administration in the conduct of the program.

Health education has one of the brightest futures of all of the curricular areas in the elementary school. The emphasis on the conceptual approach has already brought about many changes. New health-centered courses in professional preparation programs for the elementary teacher, the increased training of elementary level health specialists, expanded and more comprehensive school health services, and the increased use of educational television and other such teaching aids will help to bring health education into the spotlight in the elementary school curricula of the future.

The School Health Team. The objectives of the school health program cannot be achieved unless the various members that make up the health team function smoothly and effectively. Some of the important members of this team are the elementary school teacher, the school administrator, the school physician, the family physician, the school nurse, the physical educator, a dentist, a dental hygienist, the custodian, the nutritionist, and the health coordinator.

The Elementary School Teacher. The classroom teacher is the key school person involved in the health of the elementary school child. The organization of the school with its self-contained classroom enables the teacher to observe the pupils continually and to note deviations from normal. Continuous contact with the same children over a long period of time also makes it possible to know a lot about their physical, social, emotional, and mental health. The classroom teacher can help the pupils develop the right knowledge, attitudes, and practices. Some of the responsibilities which fall to the classroom teacher in regard to the health of his or her pupils are as follows:

1. Understand what constitutes a well-rounded school health program and the teacher's part in it.

2. Meeting with the school physician, nurse, and others in order to determine how he or she can best contribute to the total health program.

3. Becoming acquainted with the parents and homes of students; establishing parent-school cooperation.

4. Discovering the health needs and interests of pupils.

5. Organizing health teaching units which are meaningful and are related to the health needs and interests of the students.

6. Seeing that children needing special care are referred to the proper place for help.

7. Knowing first-aid procedures.

8. Participating in the work of the school health council. If none exists, interpreting the need for one to the school administrator.

9. Providing an environment for children while at school which is conducive to healthful living.

10. Being continually on the alert for children with deviations from normal behavior and with signs of communicable disease.

11. Providing experiences for living healthfully at school.

12. Helping pupils assume an increasing responsibility for their own health as well as for the health of others.

13. Setting an example for the child of what constitutes healthful living.

14. Motivating the child to be well and happy.

15. If possible, being present at pupils' health examinations and contributing in any way which is helpful to the physician in charge.

16. Follow-through in cooperation with the nurse to see that remediable health defects are corrected.

17. Interpreting the school health program to the community and enlisting its support in solving health problems.

18. Providing a well-rounded physical education program for the class.

19. Helping to supervise various activities which directly affect health, such as school lunch, rest periods, and so on.

20. Being familiar with teaching aids and school and community resources for enhancing the health program.

21. Being aware of the individual differences of the pupils.

The School Administrator. The school administrator plays a key role in the school health program. To a large degree he will determine how much money is allocated for health purposes, what personnel will be appointed to the faculty to teach health courses, what facilities are available for healthful school living, health instruction, and services, and the degree to which there is public understanding of the health program in the schools. Some ways in which the teacher may help the school administrator to understand the need for and support a better school health program follow:

1. Preparing and submitting to him periodic reports on the health needs and interests of the pupils.

2. Utilizing some time in faculty meetings to acquaint the administration and colleagues with the job that needs to be done.

3. Requisitioning supplies and materials to enhance the program.

4. Inviting the principal and/or superintendent to speak to the class on some aspect of health.

5. Stimulating the formation of a school health council at which the school administrator would be asked to preside.

6. Stimulating in the school program interest among citizens' study groups and parent-teacher associations.

7. Cooperating with community health agencies in interpreting the role of health in the school and community.

8. Working with the school physician, nurse, and school administrator in coordinating school health efforts.

The School Physician. Most school physicians serve under one of two types of appointment: as a full-time school physician employed by the state or local community, or as practitioner who supervises the health of the children on a part-time basis.

The school physician has responsibilities which frequently include administering medical examinations to children, giving advice to parents, having medical control of the teaching staff, maintaining liaison with public health authorities in connection with communicable disease in schools, supervising the health of kitchen personnel, having medical supervision of handicapped pupils, providing medical assistance during the athletic programs, maintaining health records, and preparing reports.

The classroom teacher can work effectively with the school physician through such means as:

1. Attending medical examinations of pupils (with permission of the physician).

2. Discussing results of medical examinations with the physician.

3. Passing on observations of pupils, especially in respect to any atypical conditions that have been noted.

4. Discussing with the physician how she or he can most effectively contribute to the school health program.

5. Orienting the physician about other phases of the educational program.

6. Assisting the physician in following through to see that remediable defects are corrected.

The Family Physician. In many school systems, the family physician, who knows the child's background, home conditions, and health habits, is in an excellent position to perform some meaningful health counseling. He can also discuss the child's health problems with parents.

The classroom teacher can work effectively with the family physician in much the same manner as she or he works with the school physician.

The School Nurse. The nurse works closely with medical personnel on one hand and with students, teachers, and parents on the other. Some of the duties she performs include the administration of health tests and other forms of measurement, assisting in medical examinations, screening for hearing and vision, holding parent conferences, keeping full health records, teaching health, coordinating school and community health efforts, and helping to control communicable disease.

The classroom teacher can work effectively with school nurses through such means as:

1. Working on the administration of tests of health status.

2. Working cooperatively on health observation techniques.

3. Discussing medical follow-up and health records.

4. Discussing ways to contribute to a more healthful school environment.

5. Cooperating in the health education of parents.

6. Determining what community health resources have value for the children.

7. Exploring ways of meeting the needs of pupils who have health problems.

The Physical Educator. The physical educator can contribute much to the school health program. Training in areas such as first aid and foundational sciences makes such services an important contribution to the team effort. In many school systems physical educators test hearing and vision, weigh and measure the children, teach health, give first aid, and conduct adapted physical education classes for handicapped children.

The classroom teacher can work effectively with the physical educator through such means as:

1. Seeking advice on the best procedures for carrying out the physical education class.

2. Consulting with the physical educator on health problems of children upon which physical education has a bearing and with which physical educators are qualified to deal.

3. Working with the physical educator on posture and pupils' problems with body mechanics.

4. Developing an adapted physical education program for the handicapped.

The Dentist. The dentist employed to work with school children frequently performs such duties as conducting dental examinations of pupils, giving or supervising oral prophylaxis, and advising on curriculum material in dental hygiene.

The classroom teacher can work effectively with the school dentist through such means as:

1. Asking advice on the selection of curriculum material for classroom teaching.
2. Discussing dental problems of students.
3. Inviting the dentist to participate in classroom experiences of pupils.

The Dental Hygienist. Dental hygienists usually assist dentists and do oral prophylaxis. The classroom teacher can work effectively with this specialist in much the same way as she or he works with the dentist.

The Custodian. Since the custodian is largely responsible for the cleanliness of the building and a healthful school physical environment in general, he is a member of the health team. He can contribute by regulating lighting, ventilation, and heating and by removing any hazards that exist on playgrounds, stairs, and other school areas.

The classroom teacher can work effectively with the custodian through such means as:

1. Calling the custodian's attention to improper heating, ventilation, and other health conditions.
2. Assisting him in maintaining a clean school by having pupils keep their desks, classroom, and other facilities in good condition.

3. Inviting him to help plan pertinent aspects of the health curriculum.

The Nutritionist. The nutritionist's duties include planning school menus and advising with respect to the nutritional problems of students.

The classroom teacher can work effectively with the nutritionist through such means as:

1. Asking advice on subject matter concerning nutrition for the health education program.
2. Inviting the nutritionist into class to speak to students about food and nutrition.
3. Discussing nutritional problems of students and working to see if they can be corrected.

The Health Coordinator. Some schools are fortunate to have a health coordinator whose job is to see that all aspects of the school health program are functioning. This individual assists teachers, works closely with medical and dental personnel, suggests materials for teaching, conducts in-service health education for staff members, coordinates school-community-home relationships, organizes a health council and is an active member of it, maintains health records, and formulates the policies and the procedures for the total school health program.

The classroom teacher can work effectively with the health coordinator through such means as:

1. Attending meetings which he calls and to which he or she is invited.

2. Having frequent conferences on the health program for the class.

3. Asking for advice on teaching aids, methods, and techniques.

4. Discussing health interests and problems of students.

5. Reporting pertinent observations with respect to the health of pupils.

6. Assisting in the follow-through program.

7. Assisting in the evaluation of the school health program.

Health Education. Some general guides for the elementary school teacher to keep in mind in teaching health to pupils are as follows:

1. *Health education must be planned.* Much thought must be given to the planning process if health education is to be effective. The planning will help in determining such things as the subject matter to be taught, the learning experiences to be provided, the methods to be used, the community and school resources to be tapped, and the health problems to be covered.

2. *Planning for health education should be a total endeavor.* Although the classroom teacher will spearhead the planning for his or her own pupils, there must be continuity and progression throughout the various grades and schools in an educational system. To accomplish this, there should be committees of teachers, specialists, and consultants who plan the over-all school program. Units on health problems and topics can be outlined, correlation with other subject-matter areas can be thought through, and curriculum experiences can be explored.

3. *Objectives are important in determining health education experiences.* The general objectives of the school health program, including knowledge, attitudes, practice, and skills, have previously been discussed. These need to be reviewed and a further delineation of the knowledge, attitudes, practice, and skills, grade by grade, should be listed. Then, on the basis of the outcomes desired, the program can be planned intelligently and meaningfully.

4. *The community can contribute to health education.* The health department and other official agencies, the mental health society and other voluntary associations, doctors and dentists and other health specialists, and parents can contribute much to a health education program that recognizes the school as a part of a broader community in which its students live and into which many graduates return.

5. *The classroom teacher is the person responsible for health teaching.* Although there may be specialists in health education at the elementary level, the classroom teacher in most schools at the present time has the major responsibility for health education and is in a strategic position to plan an effective role in the health program. The teacher has special preparation in elementary school teaching. The teacher has the opportunity to see students throughout the school day, observing them at play as well as in study. The teacher knows the health problems of her pupils. The teacher works closely with the parents, school nurse, and other persons concerned with health in the elementary school. The teacher is in a position to make a greater contribution to the total health of the child than a specialist who may see the children only one period a day. This, however, does not mean that the specialist cannot play an important role. In meetings and consultation with the teacher, materials can be furnished, aids and techniques explored, and discussions held about ways in which health teaching can be made effective.

6. *Health education can be included in any of the variety of curriculum patterns that are followed in elementary schools.*

a. Health and safety can be taught as a *separate subject-matter course* like science, art, physical education, or geography. There is a body of subject matter that fits well into the elementary school curriculum. Such a curriculum pattern would give health its rightful place in school education programs.

b. Health can be *correlated* with other subject-matter courses. For example, the English class could write essays concerned with health, the art class could make posters showing safety precautions at street intersections, the foreign language classes could translate health material into French and Spanish, and the science class could explore the biological foundations of health. The correlated plan, however, is regarded as a method of presenting supplementary health material rather than one by which all the essential material can be satisfactorily covered.

c. Health can be taught in a *core-curriculum pattern*, where there is a center, or core, around which many educational experiences are planned.

Included in these experiences could be health and safety activities.

There are other ways in which subject matter may be organized, including the *integrated,* and *areas-for-living,* and the *broad fields* approaches. Regardless of the curriculum pattern followed, health education can be planned to be compatible with the rest of the program.

7. *Incidental health education should be utilized.* Incidental health education refers to that education which can take place when attention is suddenly focused on some news development or event that is of interest to pupils. Such occasions may arise as a result of a question asked by a student; when a personal health problem confronts a member of the class, a family, or the community; or when a sudden illness, accident, or similar event takes place. Incidental health education represents an opportunity for the teacher, physician, dentist, or nurse to provide information that is educational in nature. It can be planned for in advance. Situations and incidents should be anticipated and utilized to their fullest in the interests of good health teaching.

8. *The time allotment for health education should be in line with that of other subjects in the curriculum.* Health is as important for the child as other experiences, including arithmetic, social studies, and music. As such, it should be provided for in the school's schedule. At the same time, it should be understood that health instruction in the kindergarten and primary grades is given in an informal manner, while in the intermediate grades it is more systematic and should be allotted additional time. Anderson suggests the following principles for scheduling health education.

1. A weekly schedule provides for extended time periods and allows for necessary flexibility.

2. A daily health period is not required for health instruction.

3. Two fairly extended periods per week may be sufficient scheduling for health instruction in the primary grades and three periods a week will serve the intermediate grades.

4. A flexible schedule allows for continuation of an activity which is particularly challenging.

5. Opportunities should be provided for the varieties of activities that health instruction entails.

6. When special health needs or interests require it, the schedule should be rearranged. Extra time invested in health instruction during one week can be followed by incidental instruction in the following week or weeks.

7. Opportunities for incidental and integrated health instruction should not be sacrificed to maintain a rigid schedule.

8. Correlation of health with other areas, to be effective, must be given a definite place in the organization of health instruction.[1]

9. *The kindergarten and primary grades represent a setting where stress should be placed on the development of wholesome attitudes and habits.* The early school years are an ideal time to impress upon children the importance of healthful routines, proper attitudes, and habits. Through attention to clothing, cleanliness, ventilation, rest, eating, safety, and other health goals, the foundations of good health for a lifetime can be laid down.

10. *The health education offered through the school should be closely integrated with home conditions.* If what is taught in the school is not practiced at home and in out-of-school situations, the education has not been meaningful. Furthermore, to have the knowledge gained at school applied at home means working closely with parents and knowing something about the home conditions in which the child lives.

Living Healthfully at School. The school should be conducive to healthful living. First of all, this means that the physical environment is attractive, sanitary, and functional. The buildings have been constructed with health and safety standards in mind. Secondly, the mental and emotional environment is conducive to good health. This is as important as the physical environment. These two phases of living healthfully at school are discussed in this section.

The Physical Environment. The elementary classroom teacher should be familiar with the aspects of the physical environment that affect teaching and learning.

[1] C. L. Anderson, *School Health Practices,* St. Louis, The C. V. Mosby Co., 1960, p. 274.

1. *School site.* In urban communities the school should be situated near transportation facilities, but at the same time away from industrial plants, railroads, noise, heavy traffic, fumes, and smoke. It should be attractive and well landscaped. In rural communities the school should be located in an attractive setting where the physical environment is conducive to healthful school living.

2. *Play and recreation area.* Standards recommend at least five acres of land for elementary schools. The play area should consist of a minimum of 100 square feet for each child.

3. *Buildings.* There is a trend toward one-story construction, where possible, with stress on functional planning rather than ornamental structure. In addition to an adequate number of classrooms, school buildings should contain such facilities as a health suite; special rooms for activities like music, dancing, arts and crafts; a gymnasium; a cafeteria; and, if possible, a swimming pool.

4. *Lighting.* It is important to conserve vision, prevent fatigue, and maintain and improve morale in the classroom. Light intensity in most classrooms varies from fifteen to fifty foot-candles. Most authorities recommend between twenty and forty foot-candles for reading and close work.

5. *Heating and ventilation.* Heating standards vary according to the activities and the clothing worn by the participants. The following specifications are generally accepted. Classrooms, office, and cafeterias: 68°–72° F (thirty inches above the floor); kitchens, closed corridors, shops, and laboratories: 65°–68° F (sixty inches above the floor); gymnasiums and activity rooms: 55°–65° F (sixty inches above the floor). Ventilation should provide from eight to twenty-one cubic feet of fresh air per minute per occupant. The recommended humidity ranges from thirty-five to sixty percent. The type and amount of ventilation will vary with the specific needs of the particular area to be served.

6. *Furniture.* Seats and desks which are adjustable and movable are recommended by most educators. Desks should be of proper height and adjusted to fit the pupil comfortably and properly. This helps to avoid fatigue and faulty posture habits.

7. *School plant sanitation.*

a. Water supply should be safe and adequate. One authority suggests that at least 25 gallons per pupil per day is needed to serve all purposes.

b. Drinking fountains at various heights should be recessed in corridor walls. Approximately one drinking fountain should be provided for every seventy-five pupils. The stream of water should flow from the fountain in a manner that does not require the drinker to get his mouth too near the opening.

c. Water closets, urinals, lavatories, and washroom equipment such as soap dispensers, toilet paper holders, waste containers, mirrors, bookshelves, and hand-drying facilities should be provided as necessary.

d. Waste disposal should be adequate.

8. *Other essentials for a healthful environment.*

a. A well-planned school lunch program should include good, wholesome food, adequate time for eating, and a pleasant, quiet, attractive atmosphere.

b. Necessary custodial help and cleaning supplies should be secured for maintaining sanitary conditions in all classrooms, lavatories, gymnasiums, cafeterias, and so on.

c. Safe, uncrowded transportation to and from school and on all trips sponsored by the school should be provided.

d. Special arrangements should be made for handicapped children, such as seats near the front of the room for auditory handicapped individuals.

Mental and Emotional Environment. The mental and emotional environment is equally important if pupils are to live healthfully at school. Some of the factors that the elementary school teacher should recognize as contributing to good mental and emotional health are as follows:

1. The teacher, school officials, and pupils work harmoniously and happily together.

2. The teacher exemplifies good physical, mental, emotional, and social health.

3. The educational curriculum is adapted to the needs and interests of the child.

4. An atmosphere of friendliness and consideration of the rights of others exists in all personal school relationships.

5. The teacher gives each child a feeling of belonging and security.

6. The teacher does not use sarcasm or ridicule children.

7. Frequent opportunities are provided for relaxation and play.

8. Pupils are encouraged to improve themselves rather than to excel over their classmates.

9. A permissive climate prevails.

10. Pupils help in making decisions.

11. A variety of teaching methods is used.

12. Individual differences are recognized.

13. The length of the school day is in conformance with the age of the child.

14. Classes are scheduled in a way that does not result in excessive fatigue.

15. Excessive emphasis is not placed on marks.

16. School attendance is not overemphasized to the point that the health of the individual is disregarded.

17. As much freedom as possible is given to the pupils.

18. The teacher takes a personal interest in and loves each child.

19. The teacher has a pleasing personality.

20. There is good rapport between the teacher and the parents of each child.

Services for Health Improvement. Health services represent a very important part of the total school health program. In this section, each of the six areas of the health service program will be discussed in light of the elementary school teacher's responsibilities.

Health Appraisal. Health appraisal is that phase of the school health service program which is concerned with evaluating the health of the whole child, through examinations, observation, and records.

The aims of health appraisal have been well stated by the American Association of School Administrators in their *Twentieth Yearbook:*

1. To identify pupils in need of medical or dental treatment.

2. To identify pupils who have problems relating to nutrition.

3. To identify pupils who are poorly adjusted and in need of special attention at school or of treatment by a psychiatrist or a child guidance clinic.

4. To measure the growth of pupils and to assist them in attaining optimum growth.

5. To identify pupils with nonremediable defects who may require modified programs of education—for example, the crippled, partially sighted, hard-of-hearing, mentally retarded, and those with speech defects.

6. To identify pupils who need a more thorough examination than is usually provided at school—for example, X-ray examination, examination by a specialist, or a laboratory examination of one kind or another.

7. To identify pupils who may be cared for best apart from the regular school situation—for example, the blind, deaf, and tuberculous.[2]

The classroom teacher's responsibilities in regard to health appraisal include the following:

1. To weigh and measure children periodically when it is requested or desired.

2. To give vision and hearing screening tests where required or desired.

3. To orient children as to the nature and purpose of medical examinations.

4. To be present at medical examinations to give the physician further health information on pupils and also to provide various health records for the physician's information.

5. To help make the medical examination and other forms of appraisal worthwhile educational experiences for the child.

6. To be familiar with the health history of the student.

7. To refer pupils needing special medical or psychological help to the proper clinic.

8. To help in dental examinations.

9. To know the various physical and behavioral conditions that have implications for children's health for which the teacher should be alert.

10. To be observant in noting digression from normal health appearance or behavior in children.

11. To keep health appraisal findings in strict confidence.

Health Counseling. In light of the findings gathered through appraisal techniques, health matters should be discussed with pupils and parents. Such matters as the need for medical and dental treatment, better health practices, diagnostic examinations, special services, and analyzing behavior problems require conferences. Through

[2] American Association of School Administrators. *Twentieth Yearbook. Health in Schools.* Washington, D.C., 1951, pp. 261–262.

counseling procedures a better understanding of the health of children can be achieved. Some of the teacher's responsibilities in respect to health counseling follow:

1. To work closely with the nurse and other school officials on counseling problems.

2. If he or she is requested to do counseling, to get to know the pupil and parents well enough to do it effectively.

3. To have face-to-face conferences rather than writing letters or using the telephone.

4. To understand desirable health counseling procedures.

5. To have all necessary records at hand.

6. To have a knowledge of health defects and the proper action to be taken, plus an understanding of the problems surrounding the particular pupil in question.

7. To be sympathetic and understanding of both the pupil's and the parents' points of view (a friendly atmosphere is necessary for good results).

8. To be a good listener.

9. To refrain from talking down to pupils or parents.

10. Not to divulge, except to proper persons, results of counseling conferences.

11. To understand that the success of the counseling conference will depend on the counselor's skill and the degree to which he or she has planned for the conference.

12. When the conference is concluded, to arrive at a common understanding with pupil and parent concerning the next step to be taken in the elimination of health problems.

Correction of Remediable Defects. After health appraisal and health counseling have been carried out, there must be a follow-through to see that remediable defects are corrected. The teacher can help by the following means:

1. Continually being informed and keeping accurate records as to the status of her pupils' remediable defects, both those that have been corrected and those still needing correction.

2. Constantly encouraging pupils and parents to correct remediable defects.

3. If lack of money or some other insufficiency is responsible for failure to correct defects, trying to remedy the problem (in most communities there are charitable organizations, civic groups, or others who are ready to help such cases).

4. Visiting the home if this is essential for better results.

5. Tapping community resources (public clinics, welfare agencies, and voluntary organizations should be utilized; a list of hospitals, specialists, and clinics for various types of treatment should be provided when parents want additional information).

Care and Education of Exceptional Children. The term *exceptional* refers to those children who are handicapped mentally, physically, socially, or emotionally, and also to those who are gifted intellectually or in other ways.

The elementary teacher can help these children in the following ways:

1. Developing a planned procedure for determining those pupils who are exceptional.

2. Knowing the exceptional children and their needs.

3. Adapting the educational program wherever possible to help meet the needs and interests of the exceptional child.

4. Referring for special services those exceptional children who need such care.

5. Observing children closely—through continuous observation, deviations from normal behavior may be identified.

6. Treating exceptional pupils as individuals and giving individual consideration in every case, rather than viewing children as groups with similar characteristics. (Whether or not the exceptional child should be a part of the regular group in the school situation, a part of a separate group, or in a separate school will depend upon the individual. The decision should be in favor of the situation which will allow the greatest possibility for improvement of the child's condition and for his total growth and development.)

7. Providing an adequate supervisory program in connection with special classes for exceptional children. (Good supervision will insure periodic examinations to determine the status of the individual in respect to his handicap or atypical condition, making sure that the program is as much like a regular school program as possible and seeing that the child is returned to the regular class as soon as possible.)

8. Being aware of the many ways that the school can make special provisions for handicapped children, such as scheduling all classes for handicapped on the same floor, providing rest periods for children with cardiac and other

impairments, transporting them to and from school, and providing specially constructed chairs and desks.

9. Possessing emotional stability and cultivating the personality attributes that are suitable for working with exceptional children.

Communicable Disease Control. Wherever children congregate there is the possibility of spreading disease. The school, as a place for children and youth to assemble, is unique in that the law requires attendance. Therefore, if school attendance is compulsory, precautions should be taken to insure that everything is to guard the health of the child. This includes the necessary procedures for controlling communicable disease. The teacher can play a very important part as follows:

1. Knowing the symptoms for various communicable diseases.

2. Being continually vigilant so that such symptoms will be noted, isolating affected individuals immediately, and referring these cases to the school or family physician.

3. Consulting regularly with the nurse and school physician as to what other contributions she can make.

4. Providing a healthful classroom environment which will help prevent the spread of communicable diseases. (This should include proper ventilation and heating, safe running water, cleanliness, use of pasteurized milk as a safeguard against milk-borne diseases, control over readmission of students who have had communicable diseases, and avoidance of overemphasis on perfect attendance for both pupils and teacher.)

5. Stressing the importance of immunization against preventable diseases.

6. Having good rapport with the childrens' parents so that unnecessary risks will not be taken.

Emergency Care. The school is responsible for providing each child with the necessary protection and care while the child is at school. The school acts in place of the parent, and it is assumed that the child will receive the same care and protection during the hours of school that he normally would receive at home. Children often become sick or injured during school hours. Therefore, the school must provide the necessary attention until the responsibility can be taken over by the parents. The classroom teacher has such responsibilities as the following:

1. Every teacher should have a definite plan to follow in event of emergency. Such a plan should be in writing. There should be an over-all school plan; however, if such a plan does not exist, the teacher should have one of her own. This plan should cover such essentials as first-aid instructions, staff responsibilities, procedures for obtaining medical help, transportation, notifying parents, and having supplies, equipment, and facilities available for needed emergency care.

2. All teachers should know where the first-aid supplies are and how to use them.

3. Every teacher should be trained in first-aid procedures.

4. Each teacher should have complete personal information on each of her pupils: parent's name, address, and phone number; parent's business address and phone number; family physician's address and phone number; family dentist's address and phone number; parent's instructions in case of emergency; choice of hospital; and anything else that is pertinent.

5. A complete record should be kept of every accident, including first aid given and emergency care administered in the event of illness.

6. The legal aspects of health problems in regard to emergency care should be understood.

7. Various insurance plans should be discussed at parent-teacher and other school meetings.

8. All teachers should possess foresight—disaster or accidents can happen at any time. Be prepared.

The Relation of Health Education to Physical Education

The layman is sometimes confused about the relationship of health education and physical education in the school program. Unfortunately, some educators feel they are one and the same. Although both are closely allied and concerned with the health of the students, they are separate and distinct subject-matter fields. Each area has its own specialized subject-matter content, its specialists, and media through which it is striving to accomplish its goals. Physical education at the elementary school level is concerned with the many physical activities that are discussed in this book and through which the teacher strives to achieve the physical, mental, and social goals. On the other hand, health education is concerned with imparting knowledge about all phases of health, such as nutrition and communicable-disease control, and developing the right attitudes and practices for physical, mental, social, and emotional health.

The elementary school teacher should recognize that she is not meeting all the health needs of the child simply by conducting regular periods of physical activity. This section on school health should have helped to clarify in the teacher's mind how she can meet the requirements for a broader health program.

Questions and Practical Problems

1. Study various lists of objectives that have been set forth for education during the past one hundred years. Determine how many refer to health as an objective.

2. Describe a physical education program and a health program, showing their similarities and differences.

3. Make a chart, outlining the three aspects of a school health program. List the components of each phase of the program.

4. Set up a school health council within your class. Have a mock meeting at which the most important health problems in the school are discussed.

5. Visit the local health department and report on the services available to the elementary school child.

6. Visit several elementary schools and prepare a report on the school health programs that exist. Evaluate each one.

7. Describe the term *health*.

8. What are some responsibilities of the classroom teacher for the health of her children?

9. Write an essay on the subject of "School Health Services." In this essay, list essential services for the elementary school child, and some of the factors involved in the accomplishment of each.

10. What are some of the factors that should be taken into consideration in providing a healthful school environment for children?

11. What are some of the factors that the elementary school teacher should recognize as contributing to good mental and emotional health?

12. Describe what you consider to be an ideal classroom from a physical point of view. In your description include standards for play and recreation area, lighting, heating, ventilation, furniture, and color scheme.

13. Prepare a mock counseling session for your class which will show an elementary school teacher having a conference with a parent on her child's health.

14. What are five ways in which an elementary school teacher can help to prevent the spread of communicable disease?

15. Tell how the conceptual approach to health education has helped to modernize the field.

16. Draw a series of implications for the role of health education in the schools projected ten years *into* the future. Your answer should include information on time allocation, topics covered, and teacher's graphics.

Selected References

American Assocation for Health, Physical Education, and Recreation. *Health Concepts: Guides for Health Instruction.* Washington, D.C.: American Association for Health, Physical Education, and Recreation, 1967.

BUCHER, CHARLES A. *Administration of School Health and Physical Education Programs* (Fifth Edition). St. Louis: The C. V. Mosby Co., 1971.

GROUT, RUTH E. *Health Teaching in Schools.* Philadelphia: W. B. Saunders Company, 1968.

IRWIN, LESLIE W., et al. *Health in Elementary Schools.* St. Louis: The C. V. Mosby Co., 1962.

Joint Committee on Health Problems in Education of the National Education Association and the American Medical Association. *Health Education.* Washington, D.C.: National Education Association, 1961.

KILANDER, H. FREDERICK. *School Health Education* (Second Edition). New York: The Macmillan Company, 1968.

LASALLE, DOROTHY, and GLADYS GEER. *Health Instruction for Today's Schools.* Englewood Cliffs, N.J.: Prentice-Hall, Inc., 1963.

OBERTEUFFER, DELBERT, and MARY K. BEYRER. *School Health Education.* New York: Harper & Row, Publishers, 1966.

SMOLENSKY, JACK, and L. RICHARD BONVECHIO. *Principles of School Health.* Boston: D. C. Heath and Company, 1966.

TURNER, C. E., et al. *School Health and Health Education.* St Louis: The C. V. Mosby Co., 1957.

VANNIER, MARYHELEN. *Teaching Health in Elementary Schools.* New York: Harper & Row, Publishers, 1963.

WILLGOOSE, CARL E. *Health Education in the Elementary School.* Philadelphia: W. B. Saunders Company, 1969.

CHAPTER 3

Movement Education in the Elementary School

Movement education seeks to utilize the natural play activities and drives of children to help them to become better physically educated individuals. Through movement education many of the activity drives of children may be successfully and satisfactorily directed and channeled. Movement education is very intimately associated with play—the child's work. Movement education attempts to make the conduct of this work more efficient and pleasurable for the child.

Movement education is the newest look in today's elementary school physical education programs in the United States. Movement education is not separate from physical education, but rather is viewed as the basis upon which specific physical education skills can and should be developed.

Movement educators view the human body as the tool through which physical movement takes place. Some physical educators have traditionally conceived of the human body as a force to be overcome before effective and efficient movement can take place. This stand is in direct opposition to the theory and principles of movement education. In today's world where the major emphasis is on the individual, movement education is that phase of physical education that is directly and purposefully directed to the individual child.

History of Movement Education

Movement education is a fairly recent innovation in elementary school physical education programs in the United States. The initial impetus came from Rudolf Laban, a dancer and student of human movement. Laban settled in England during World War II and proceeded to train teachers of movement education. Eventually Laban's theories were seen to have merit and movement education became an integral part of physical education programs in the English schools. The principles, theories, and methodologies developed by Laban and introduced in the English schools form the foundation of the movement education programs in the United States today and have influenced elementary school physical education programs.

The Key Concepts of Movement Education

Movement education is activity-centered rather than word-centered and depends upon a problem-solving approach to physical-skill development. Thus movement education is closely allied with dance in principle, but it is not synonymous with dance. Moreover, movement education does not supplant physical education but is a phase of the total field known as physical education. To be able to form a picture of movement education, it is necessary that the teacher of physical education understand some of its key concepts.

1. *Movement education is intimately concerned with the natural movements of childhood.* Children enjoy running, jumping, climbing, leaping, and other physical movements, and they tend to perform these movements of their own volition. Movement educators seek to capitalize on these natural movements of childhood as they guide the child through an individual exploration of their many varieties.

2. *The childhood ability to move freely and easily should be sustained.* Formalized physical education programs tend to stress conformity to stylized patterns of movement. Through movement education, it is felt, the child's individualized patterns of movement can be reinforced and retained.

3. *Freedom to create, and opportunities for self-expression through bodily movement are essentials.* Movement education classes provide an unlimited opportunity for children to explore the uses of their bodies for movement in ways that are creative and self-expressive.

4. *Guidance is a facet of the process of movement exploration.* The elementary-school-age child tends to be highly active physically. While this child does explore many varieties of physical movement spontaneously he still requires teacher guidance so that many more varieties and broader ranges of movement will be attempted.

5. *The body needs to be educated so that it can be used as a tool for enhanced motor-skill development.* The natural movements of childhood form the basis for future motor-skill development. These movements will tend to develop haphazardly, and future skill performances will be inefficient, unless the body is effectively educated in movement.

6. *Movement education stresses the learning of skill patterns through movement exploration.* Children are challenged in movement education programs to discover their own unique methods and techniques for solving problems in movement or in a skill performance. No one method is assumed to be the only acceptable answer to a problem; thus the children are free to use their own bodies in an individually suitable manner.

7. *Movement education is based on a conceptual approach to human movement.* The child learns to perceive intellectually the position of each segment of his body prior to attempting any physical-skill performance. Through the utilization of the problem-solving approach, the child begins to think about what his body can do, and how he can best utilize his body. The understanding that results helps to give the child insight into individual differences in skill performance. They also help him to develop confidence in the capabilities and capacities of his own body for movement.

8. *Time, space, force, and flow of a movement are key words for the movement educator.* The child learns to consider intellectually each of these factors before attempting to solve a problem in movement. These factors are the core of the movements executed by the child and are exploited each time movement takes place.

9. *Movement education is concerned with each child as an individual.* Each child is able to set his own standards for the successful solution to a problem in movement. He need not strive to meet the standards of performance set by any other child or individual. Movement education adapts itself to the needs of each individual child.

10. *Movement education is highly organized and structured.* Movement education programs have definite objectives that must be met. Thus each class in movement education follows a logical sequence and progression leading to the realization of the program objectives and goals.

The Theories Basic to Movement Education. Movement education is not a panacea that will make highly skilled performers out of children who have only average or low levels of motor-skill ability. Instead, movement educators have as a primary goal the education of the child in

(Courtesy of Nissen Corporation)

movement so that he will be able to make the best possible use of his motor-skill abilities.

1. *The problem-solving approach underlies all classes in movement education.* In traditional physical education classes, much of the learning takes place through mimicry of the teacher's demonstration or verbal explanation of the skills to be performed. In movement education classes there is no teacher demonstration. Instead the child experiments with different solutions to a skill-performance problem until he discovers one that best suits his own abilities. For example, a teacher would not dictate nor demonstrate to a class of children a single prescribed method for scaling a jungle gym. Each child would instead be challenged to discover his own unique method for reaching the top of this piece of equipment.

2. *Each child is helped to develop confidence in the capabilities of his own body for movement.* Because no single acceptable standard of skill-performance is expected of each child in a movement education class, each child is free to work at his own peak capacity. Each child competes with himself to improve in successive performances of a skill, and builds up his confidence as his efficiency and effectiveness increase.

3. *The natural developmental activities of childhood are the core of future skill learning.* Comprehensive exploration of the natural movements of childhood—including such activities as running, leaping, climbing, twisting, and hopping —form the foundation for learning more sophisticated skills. When these activities have been explored thoroughly at different speeds, on different levels, and in different planes and patterns under the guidance of a movement educator, the child is more ready to exploit them as parts of physical education skills.

4. *Specific physical education skills are best taught by traditional methods.* Movement education is primarily concerned with exploiting the natural activities of childhood. It is not concerned with teaching the child, for example, how to play soccer or basketball. While ball and implement-

handling skills are an important part of movement education, the use of these skills in competitive games is left to the province of traditional physical education classes and methodology.

5. *Movement education is a phase of physical education and thus shares the same developmental objectives.* A curriculum in movement education is devised so that it fulfills the objectives of physical, mental, emotional, and social development.

6. *Movement education attempts to help the child to become mentally as well as physically aware of each movement he performs.* Everything an individual does involves bodily movement of some sort. The better able the child is to understand a movement pattern mentally, the easier it will be for him to develop the concomitant physical skills.

7. *The ability of the child to perceive of his body as an entity helps to promote physical-skill development.* Children who are retarded in physical-skill development often do not have the insight to consider their bodies as wholes. They tend to be concerned first with the individual segments, and thus they attempt to correct performance errors by altering the position or action of a single arm or leg and fail to measurably improve their performance. Movement educators feel that the child must learn to consider the interaction of all of the parts of his body before skill performances can be significantly improved.

8. *The child's movement education must begin in his earliest school years.* Movement educators feel that adult problems in physical-skill performance are the result of poor habits developed in early childhood. Children generally do not, on their own, explore a variety of movement patterns and the patterns they do use tend to become stereotyped unless movement exploration is encouraged and guided. The early school years are thus the most opportune time in which to begin the child's education for movement.

9. *Each child possesses inherent natural movements.* Through the imposition of rigid and formalized exercises, the child tends to lose his ability to move freely and easily. Experiences in spontaneous and exploratory movement help the child reach his potential for efficient and effective movement through the development of increased kinesthetic awareness.

10. *Education in movement is the first step in becoming physically educated.* Movement education teaches proper use of the body as a tool for movement. Through movement education the child discovers the speed, balance, force, timing, leverage, and other physical principles that must be applied to each performance of a physical skill.

The Methodology of Movement Education. Where physical education on the elementary school level has traditionally emphasized the learning of certain low-organizational games, dances, and beginning activity skills, movement education on this same level stresses the learning of skill patterns through movement exploration. Education for movement is especially important for the elementary-school-age child for it is at this age that the child is most active physically and requires the most direction in his exploration of movements of all kinds.

Movement educators contend that traditional physical education programs as conducted on the elementary school level serve to stereotype certain movements. These programs effectively prevent the child from freely exploring the many varieties of movement patterns by setting common performance criteria for the mass of children. Because movement education is focused on the individual child, the child sets his own standards for the successful solution to a problem and works within the limits of his own abilities and capacities.

1. *Movement education employs a problem-solving approach.* Each new movement or variation of a movement that is to be explored presents the child with a unique challenge. Learning takes place when the child accepts, attempts to solve, and overcomes increasingly more difficult challenges.

2. *The teacher of movement education serves as a guide through the learning process.* A movement educator devises problems and challenges for the children, he guides the children through a thinking process, observes their attempts at problem solving, and stimulates and encourages them as they move toward solutions to the problems assigned. The movement educator, in the role of guide, does not explain or demonstrate skills, conduct formal drill and practice, nor dictate corrections for performance errors.

3. *Traditional patterns of class organization are not properly a part of movement education.* Classes in movement education do not employ the more formalized circles, lines, and rows of traditional class organization for the teaching and

practice of a skill. Because movement education helps the child to discover how much space he needs to perform a certain skill, the child is free to utilize any part of the play area he desires so long as he does not interfere with the movements of other children.

4. *Movement education asks the child to compete only with himself.* Movement education is concerned with the individual child, and no class time is allocated for activities of a competitive nature either between individual children or between groups of children who have been organized into teams. Games that incorporate class-learned skills are used, however, and frequently include games of the tag type, follow-the-leader, or teacher-devised play situations.

5. *Movement education classes are not informal to the extreme nor lacking in discipline, organization, or structure.* Much of the discipline in movement education classes comes from the activity and from the inner direction of the children themselves. These classes tend to be very highly organized and structured.

6. *Movement education classes involve a more highly structured approach than do traditionally conducted physical education classes.* Movement education classes demand much of the teacher with respect to concrete philosophy, sound objectives, logical progressions, the understanding of proper techniques and methodology, and liberal amounts of imagination and creativity.

7. *Equipment is an important part of movement education programs.* Many of the pieces of apparatus and equipment found in a regular physical education classroom can be used in movement education classes. At times, the teacher will have to devise various unique pieces of equipment to fit the needs of a particular lesson. When apparatus or equipment is used, the child is expected to observe the rules of safety, space, and appropriateness of use of the equipment.

8. *Equipment and apparatus used must conform to the age and size of the child.* Balls that are easy to grasp and paddles that fit the hand of the child are examples of some equipment essentials that must be carefully considered. Likewise, heavy apparatus such as vaulting boxes and climbing ladders must be scaled to the most appropriate size for the children by whom they will be used.

9. *Problems set for a group of children must not cause too great a strain for the children.* Challenges presented to a group of children must reflect the readiness of the children to cope with them. If a problem is too advanced, motor development will be hindered.

10. *The program must be constantly evaluated.* The need for program modifications and adaptations is frequent in movement education. The need for revision will be noted only if the program is objectively evaluated following each class session.

Developing a Movement Education Program

The elementary-school-age child requires a wide variety of experiences in basic movement and movement patterns. Many movements and movement patterns have common elements and provide the movement educator with a multiplicity of skills with which to work. Furthermore, these common movement elements help the movement educator to devise a program that advances toward its objectives in a logical progression.

1. *In the early elementary school grades, K–3, the major emphasis should be on the natural movements of childhood.* The locomotor movements, including running, walking, jumping, skipping, hopping, and sliding, and the nonlocomotor movements, including pulling, pushing, lifting, twisting, and stretching, should be emphasized.

2. *Beginning with grade four, the techniques of handling implements should be a major part of the program.* In grades 4–8 locomotor and nonlocomotor movements should still be emphasized, but in a more sophisticated form. During these years, however, the child should be introduced to the handling of such implements as softball bats and field hockey sticks, and to such skills as soccer-type kicks and traps that can be used in lead-up games.

3. *The movement educator must have a thorough understanding of each skill before presenting it to the children in a problem-solving situation.* The teacher must understand the mechanics involved in a skill such as twisting before a child's performance of this skill can be evaluated. Furthermore, the teacher must know the end result desired from the performance of this or another skill or combination of skills.

4. *Problems must be properly devised and set by the teacher so that the desired end result can be achieved.* If, for example, the teacher has planned a lesson in walking for a first-grade class, certain specifications must be made so that the children will achieve the desired response. Proper use of space, force, timing, and flow of the movement must all be considered and presented to the children as parts of the problem before they can begin any physical movements.

5. *Variety must be present in each movement education class.* On any given day a movement education class should include a review of problems that have been solved previously, and new challenges should be presented in progressive order. After new problems have been explored the class should conclude with a noncompetitive game that incorporates many of the skills the children have already learned or are currently practicing.

6. *Skills must be progressively taught from grade to grade.* Although in a unit on running a class of first-grade children will concentrate their efforts upon correct performance of the skill and on body control, a second-grade class should progress to running with a partner or running through obstacle courses that require starting, stopping, and changes of direction, and should concentrate their efforts on general and various specific uses of this skill.

7. *Standards of skill performance must relate to the individual child.* Each child in a movement education class must be evaluated on the basis of individual performance. The exploratory nature of movement education demands that individual rather than group criteria be set. A single common standard of performance cannot be demanded or expected.

8. *The program must help the child to gain confidence in his own performance.* Satisfaction in meeting basic and simple challenges will help the child to gain confidence. More difficult problems, such as cooperating with a partner in tumbling skills like Eskimo rolls and in pyramid building, should be introduced only after the children have

gained control of their own bodies and confidence in the use of their bodily skills.

9. *A sound formation of basic movement skills should precede the introduction of games of low organization.* Many games of low organization can be adapted to use on any age and grade level. For example, games of the tag type can be introduced as soon as the children have learned the skills essential for that activity. Low-organization games that contain elements unfamiliar to the children in a particular class should not be incorporated into the program for that class until the children are thoroughly ready for them.

10. *A sound foundation of basic movement skills should precede the introduction of specific sport skills.* In traditional physical education programs in the elementary school, such games as kickball and softball are often mainstays of the program. Frequently, children play these games without having had adequate instruction and practice in the highly specific skills involved. Introduction of these activities as a concomitant of a sound movement education experience helps place them in their proper perspective in the elementary school physical education program.

The Movement Education Program. Because movement education is new and still in the experimental stage in the elementary schools of the United States, no set procedures or standardized methodologies have as yet been developed. The unique nature of movement education may indeed preclude its standardization. A movement education curriculum must meet the needs of the children concerned, and the teaching approach and methodology must also be directly concerned with the children to be served.

The following guidelines for specific grade groupings are intended as a general outline only, and are not inclusive of all of the activities that may be offered in a program. Specific activities can be appropriately chosen by the teacher only after the specific needs, interests, and abilities of the children in a particular program have been determined.

Programs for Grade K–3. Basic locomotor and nonlocomotor skills should receive the major emphasis in these grades. Locomotor skills to be practiced should include:

Walking	Falling
Running	Leaping
Skipping	Hopping
Sliding	Jumping

Nonlocomotor skills to be practiced should include:

Lifting	Twisting
Pulling	Stretching
Pushing	Bending
Swinging (of the parts of the body)	Turning

In performing a locomotor or nonlocomotor skill, balance should be emphasized, as well as the use of the different parts of the body. In walking, for example, the use of the arms for momentum and the position of the trunk and head are as essential as the action of the legs.

After skills have been practiced as entities at different speeds, with various forces (a hard or soft step, for example), with free or restricted movement, and in limited or unrestricted spaces, two or more skills may be combined. For example children may be asked to combine various patterns of leaps and hops, or runs and skips, or twists and stretches, or they may be asked to perform these movements with a partner.

Many locomotor-movement problems may incorporate obstacles. For example, children may be asked to run along an inclined plane, hop over a low rail, and finally jump on and off a low platform. Nonlocomotor skills may be combined into similarly imaginative patterns devised by the children under the guidance of the teacher. Locomotor and nonlocomotor skills may be combined in infinite variations and patterns.

Rhythmic skills may also be introduced during these early years. Many movement education classes can and should be conducted to a musical accompaniment. Children enjoy music and relate and react well to it.

Games of low organization incorporating the locomotor and nonlocomotor skills learned and practiced by the children are especially adaptable to movement education. A few of the many games suitable for grades K–3 include:

Brownies and Fairies	Three Deep
Red Light	Odd Couple Out
Squirrel in the Tree	Streets and Alleys
Cat and Mouse	Steal the Bacon
Crows and Cranes	Numbers Change
Thief O Thief	Simple Tag and variations

Simple tumbling stunts, such as forward and backward rolls, animal walks, basic ball throwing and catching skills, and physical fitness skills should also be parts of the program.

Program for Grades 4–8. In these grades work on the basic locomotor and nonlocomotor skills should be continued. However, more advanced challenges, such as running more sophisticated obstacle courses requiring the child to perform varied movements and combinations of movements are important. Also, the children should gain additional experience in working with a partner or with several other children.

During these years the use of the vaulting box, parallel bars, vaulting horses, and bucks can be introduced, and by the end of the elementary school movement education experience the children should be able to perform simple routines on this equipment.

Sport skills, such as dribbling a basketball or soccer ball, can be developed as concomitants of the movement education program. The use of striking implements such as softball bats and hockey sticks can properly be introduced.

As adeptness and confidence in the use of the body as a tool for movement increase, tumbling and gymnastics of intermediate and advanced level should be included in the curriculum.

Teaching Movement Education. The methodology of movement education is specific to the group of children being educated in movement, and to the teacher of that class. The following examples suggest approaches that may be used.

Walking Lesson—Grade One. The teacher begins the lesson by simply asking the children to walk around the play area in any way they wish. The only restrictions are that the children are not to collide with each other or with any objects in the room or with the walls of the room.

After the children have utilized the space for a short period of time, the teacher will call the group together, praise their efforts, and present a series of new problems involving the walking skill. In general, these problems will be stated as questions:

1. How can you use your arms to help you walk more freely? Think about it for a minute and then try it.
2. How can you use your legs to help you cover more space? Think about it, then move out on the floor and see what you can do.

3. Are there any other ways you can use your body to change the way you walk? Think about it, then try out a few ways.

Each problem represents a slightly more difficult challenge, but does not exceed the intellectual or physical abilities of the children. After each of these problems has been explored, the teacher will have called the group together and asked individual children to demonstrate their discoveries. Thus, after working on problem 2, the children will see that Mary, who takes short steps, cannot cover as much ground as Johnny who takes longer strides with his longer legs. All of the children will then test out their own methods again and be able to come to their own conclusions about the use of their legs for covering space in walking. This learning comes from the children themselves. In traditional physical education classes the teacher would simply direct: "Stretch your legs to cover more space," or "Mary, try to take longer steps." The children would comply and perform the task, but they would not have gained the valuable insights that come from self-discovery.

This same lesson might include work with bean bags or utility balls, depending on the readiness of the children. The teacher may ask the children to see if they can toss the bean bag (or the ball) to themselves and catch it; then put the questions:
1. How high can you toss the bean bag?
2. How can you use more of your body to make the bean bag go higher?
3. How can you use your body to make the bean bag travel faster?

This lesson might conclude with a game of Giant Steps or a modified game of Spud.

Soccer Dribble and Trap—Grade Five. The teacher would begin the lesson with a review of basic movement skills that are essential to running and controlling the soccer ball, all of which will have been covered in previous lessons. These skills would include such things as start-and-stop running, running in straight lines, running with swift directional changes, and some nonlocomotor activities such as twisting, leg swings, and body bends. Then the members of the class would be given soccer balls and presented with a series of problems to solve:
1. How can you move this ball along the ground? For this first problem, the teacher would not prohibit the use of the hands.
2. How can you move this ball along the ground without using your hands?
3. Are there any ways you can think of to move the ball along the ground in a fairly straight line? At this point some children will have begun to use both feet and will have good control of the ball in an approximation of a dribble. Other children will gain insights from demonstrations by their classmates.
4. How can you use your arms and body more for better balance?

After a series of brief practice sessions on these lead-up skills necessary to the development of a controlled soccer dribble, the teacher may then ask:
1. How many ways can you think of to stop a rolling ball? At this juncture, the teacher would caution the children about the dangers of stepping on the ball, but would not prohibit the use of the hands.
2. Can you stop the ball by using only your legs?
3. Can you stop the ball by using only one leg?
4. Can you discover a way to stop the ball by using only one foot?
5. How can you use the rest of your body to help you keep your balance and stop the ball better?

At this grade level, the children should be able to work effectively in pairs with one partner rolling the ball while the other attempts to stop it.

This class might conclude with a circle-dribbling game, an obstacle dribble, or a game that combines many previously learned skills, as well as the dribble and elementary form of trap that the children have practiced.

These examples can be used with almost any class in movement education, subject to modifications and adaptations preferred by the teacher. At the conclusion of his movement education experience each child will have learned his skills not through mimicry but through an individualized process of discovery and conceptualization.

Table 3-1 lists the essential locomotor and nonlocomotor skills that should be thoroughly covered in grades K-8. Additionally, it shows the major physical principles of each movement and the common performance errors.

Table 3-1. Essential Locomotor and Nonlocomotor Skills for Grades K–8

Movement	Major Physical Principles	Common Errors
Locomotor		
Walk	1. The child should push off with the toes into the direction of movement.	1. Excessive upward push-off.
	2. Maintenance of correct center of gravity for stability and balance.	2. Walking with feet too close together or too far apart. Toeing in or out excessively.
	3. The weight should be transferred from the heel to the outside border of the foot and finally to the toes.	3. Walking flat-footed, on the toes, or maintaining weight on inside border of foot.
	4. The entire body should move straight ahead in an erect and fluid manner.	4. Legs swinging in an abnormally wide arc, excessive arm swing, forward head and trunk.
Run	1. The ankles, knees and hips should relax as the ball of the foot makes contact.	1. A stiff-legged landing on the heel.
	2. The elbows and knees should bend to enable proper leg push-off.	2. Straight arms and legs, lack of forward-upward movement.
Skip	1. One-foot push-off in a forward-upward direction.	1. Transfer of weight at wrong phase of movement.
	2. Extra momentum is added by an arm swing.	2. Failure to use the arms at all.
Slide	1. A one-footed push-off combined with a lateral step and weight transfer from leading to trailing leg.	1. Incorrect lead and incorrect shift of weight.
Leap	Same as the run, except that the force of the push-off is increased while there is an increased extension of the knee and ankle of each leg.	
Hop	1. One-foot push-off in an upward direction. The nonactive leg remains bent at the knee so that the foot makes no contact with the ground.	1. Two-footed take-off and landing.
	2. The weight of the landing proceeds from the toes to the ball of the foot to the heel.	2. Flat-footed or heel landing or off-balance landing forcing the nonactive leg downward.
	3. The arms are swung upward for increased vertical lift.	3. Loss of vertical lift results in a loss of balance.
Jump	1. The child bends at the hips, knees, and ankles to provide for increased forward movement.	1. Failure to bend decreases forward movement because correct amounts of force cannot be gained.
	2. The arms should swing in the direction of the motion.	2. Lack of swing leads to loss of momentum.
	3. The child should lean forward for *distance*, stand more erect for *height*.	3. A forward lean in a jump for height increases the resistance and reduces the height of the jump. The reverse is true for jumps for distance.

(continued)

Table 3–1 (continued)

Movement	Major Physical Principles	Common Errors
Falling	1. The relaxed weight of the body should be absorbed by the fleshier body parts—buttocks, hips, thighs, etc.	1. Falls on vulnerable body parts, such as limbs. Failure to relax and roll and tuck the chin and head.
Nonlocomotor		
Lift	1. The knees bend to help absorb the weight of, and help lift, a heavy object.	1. Back muscles will have to absorb an excess of weight unless the powerful leg muscles assist with the lifting of heavy objects.
Pull	1. The stance is widened to increase stability while the body leans slightly toward the object to be pulled.	1. Loss of balance due to small base of support; incorrect body position.
	2. With heavy objects, the knees are bent so that the leg muscles can assist.	2. Back strain can result from pulling heavy objects unless the leg muscles are used.
Push	1. The reverse of the pull. A heavy object can be moved most easily if it is contacted below its center of gravity.	
Swing	1. The arms, legs, head, feet, hands, etc. may be swung as independent units.	1. Too much or too little force applied to the swing. Twisting the part rather than swinging.
Twist	1. The spine, hip, wrist, shoulder, and neck are the only parts of the body that can twist.	1. Turning or swinging rather than twisting.
Stretch	1. Stretching is an extension of the body joints.	1. Vertical or lateral reaching or shifting of weight without accompanying joint extension.
Bend	1. Bending is a flexion of the various body joints.	1. Failure to curl or tuck in accordance with the range of flexibility of the body.
Turn	1. Turning involves a rotatory movement of a body part or of the whole body.	1. Loss of balance, improper take-off when whole body turns. Lack of preliminary twist when speed is desired.

The Future of Movement Education

There are many changes being made in today's world and in today's schools. Many of these changes are directly related to technological advances, but still others have evolved because educational curriculums have been static for too long a time. Movement education is the first breath of fresh air for physical education, and it is directly in step with the times because it places full emphasis on the individual. Movement education does not diminish the teacher's role but rather makes the teacher a guide through the process of physical education. Movement education may be taught by the classroom teacher as well as by the specialist in physical education.

Movement education does not supplant physical education. It does add a new dimension to a field that is becoming increasingly important in the elementary school curriculum.

Questions and Practical Problems

1. Why should elementary schools emphasize movement education? Develop a position paper giving your own point of view.

2. Discuss the similarities and differences between movement education and traditional physical education.

3. Prepare a curriculum in movement education from grades K–8 and tell how this curriculum helps to meet the developmental objectives of physical education.

4. Trace the history of movement education and show the status of movement education in the schools of the United States at present.

5. Compare the role of the teacher and the role of the child in traditional physical education classes and in movement education classes.

6. How does the problem-solving method of teaching help movement education to succeed?

Selected References

BOYER, MADELINE HAAS. *The Teaching of Elementary School Physical Education.* New York: J. Lowell Pratt and Company, Publishers, 1965.

BROER, MARION R. *Efficiency of Human Movement.* Philadelphia: W. B. Saunders Company, 1966.

CRATTY, BRYANT. *Movement Behavior and Motor Learning.* Philadelphia: Lea & Febiger, 1964.

Department of Public Instruction, State of Wisconsin. *A Guide to Curriculum Building in Physical Education—Elementary Schools.* Madison, Wis.: Department of Public Instruction, 1964.

SINGER, ROBERT N. *Motor Learning and Human Performance.* New York: The Macmillan Company, 1968.

SMITH, HOPE M., ed. *Introduction to Human Movement.* Reading, Mass.: Addison-Wesley Publishing Company, Inc., 1968.

TRICKER, R. A. R., and B. J. K. TRICKER. *The Science of Movement.* New York: American Elsevier Publishing Company, Inc., 1967.

CHAPTER 4

Physical Fitness in the Elementary School

The subject of fitness is a topic of much interest to people in America. Ever since test results indicated there was a tendency toward softness among American children as compared with European children, the question in professional circles as well as among many civic and business groups has been "How can we improve the fitness of our children?" The active enthusiasm of the Presidents of the United States toward solving this problem has acted as a catalyst, pushing it to the front lines of American thought. The national government has been especially concerned since a pilot program conducted by schools in several states for what was formerly the President's Council on Physical Fitness showed that almost half the 200,000 school children in grades four through twelve who were tested failed minimum physical achievement tests. In addition, the Council pointed out that only about 28 per cent of the nation's schools had adequate physical education and health education and that more than 50 per cent of our children had no daily physical education period. Statistics such as these have justly aroused alarm.

Physical Fitness in the New Society

The development of physical fitness must be a concern of the classroom teacher as well as the physical education specialist. Each has an important responsibility to the elementary school boy or girl in relation to providing opportunities for the development of total fitness.

Societal changes are bringing about rapid alterations in our way of life. The pace of life is increasing and only the fit individual can realistically attempt to cope with modern tensions and frustrations. The elementary school child also falls victim to today's hurried and restless way of life. He needs proper guidance so that he will not have to drop by the wayside and let life pass him by. Advances in technology have been a boon, but they have also engendered many problems. Expanded use of communications media such as television have helped to make the world smaller, but at the same time television producers have begun scheduling wider and more frequent coverage of sports events. One hallmark of modern life is that this is the age of the spectator. Many people prefer to watch sports and games on television or at a nearby stadium rather than to get into the out-of-doors and participate in some form of physical activity of their own choosing. The attitude of the adult population affects the attitude of the child toward physical activity and its worth to his present and future life,

Some authorities have pointed out that, while lack of physical activity seems to affect the health of the individual adversely, the reverse seems to be true when the individual gets adequate amounts of physical activity.

The elementary school child needs to begin developing a love of physical activity early in life so that he will, as an adult, continue to be physically active rather than seek out the passive role of the spectator.

What Does Fitness Mean? Although the word fitness means different things to different people, the professions of health, physical education, and recreation subscribe to the concept of total fitness—physical, mental, emotional, social, and spiritual well-being. The former Director of Selective Service for the Federal Government has given this definition: "Fitness is that quality, inherent and acquired, which renders a person qualified to serve to the limit of his or her physical strength; to render the maximum of his or her mental capabilities and capacities, and on a high moral plane, and which recognizes, fully, his or her obligations to the family, the neighbor, the community, the state, and the nation."

Fitness is the ability of the individual to live a full and balanced life. The totally fit person has a healthy and happy outlook on life. He satisfies basic needs, such as physical well-being, love, affection, security, and self-respect. He likes people and lives happily with them. As he grows older, he develops a maturity that is characterized by submersion of self and an interest in serving humanity. He makes peace with his God and believes in and exemplifies high ethical standards. He lives what is known as the "good life."

The American Association for Health, Physical Education, and Recreation stresses that fitness is the ability of the individual to function, which means that he possesses organic health, coordination, strength, vitality, emotional stability, social consciousness, knowledge, desirable attitudes, and spiritual and moral qualities.

What Does Physical Fitness Mean? Although it is recognized that the various aspects of fitness are closely interrelated, physical fitness is discussed separately because of its close relationship to our professional fields of endeavor.

Physical fitness is one aspect of total fitness. The term has been defined in different ways. Gallagher and Brouha[1] provide an excellent description when they point out that physical fitness is composed of (1) static or medical fitness which refers to soundness of the organs of the body such as the heart and lungs; (2) dynamic or functional fitness, or the degree to which the body functions efficiently under strenuous work; and (3) motor skills fitness which refers to coordination and strength in the performance of activities.

Physical fitness is related to the tasks the person must perform, his potential for physical effort, and the integration of his total self. The same degree of physical fitness is not necessary for everyone. It should be sufficient to meet the requirements of the job plus a little extra as a reserve for emergencies. The student who plays football needs a different type of physical fitness from the student who plays in the school orchestra. The question "Fitness for what?" must always be asked. Furthermore, the physical fitness of a person must be appraised in relationship to that person's own human resources and not those of others. It depends on his potentialities in light of his own physical make-up. Finally, physical fitness cannot be considered by itself, but, instead, as it is affected by mental, emotional, and social factors. Human beings function as a whole and not as segmented parts.

Physical fitness is not achieved solely through exercise. It is a complex quality which depends upon many factors. Although heredity plays a part in physical fitness, the environment in which an individual lives and the personal daily regimen which he follows play more significant roles.

Physical fitness is acquired to a large degree. Most persons can contribute immeasurably to their own well-being. The food they eat, the rest they get, the exercise in which they engage, and similar factors will determine the degree to which they will achieve and maintain physical fitness. The American Medical Association has listed seven paths to physical fitness: proper medical care, good nutrition, dental services, exercise, satisfying work, healthy play and recreation, and adequate amounts of rest and relaxation.

To understand the meaning of physical fitness and how it is achieved and maintained is an

[1] J. R. Gallagher and L. Brouha, "Physical Fitness," *Journal of the American Medical Association*, 125:834–838, July 23, 1944.

important responsibility for any teacher in the schools as well as any youth leader in the community. Unless the many facets of fitness are known, educational programs may become distorted and physical fitness may never be developed in the children.

The President's Council on Youth Fitness, now called the President's Council on Physical Fitness and Sports, was initiated by executive order under President Dwight D. Eisenhower on July 16, 1956. It has been continued under the succeeding administrations.

The President's Council, with the cooperation of nineteen leading national educational and medical organizations, has developed a basic physical fitness program for schools. This recommended program is called the Blue Book[2] and can be obtained from the Superintendent of Documents, Washington, D.C. The basic recommendations of this program are as follows:

1. A health appraisal for each child to discover remedial defects and determine his capacity for exercise.

2. A screening process to identify underdeveloped children.

3. At least 15 minutes of vigorous activity as part of a daily physical education program.

4. Periodic achievement tests to measure progress and provide incentive.

The President's Council strongly urges every school to adopt the basic philosophy expressed in these four points.

The President's Council has put forth a noteworthy effort to enhance the physical fitness of the nation's children and youth. In general, the publicity that has been given by the Council has had a salutary impact on the schools. Parent-teacher associations have held meetings, schools that have not had programs have instituted them, and provisions have been made for facilities and equipment to implement the Council's recommendations.

The Role of the School in Fitness

The school program that best contributes to physical fitness must take into consideration not only exercise but also the various health habits that a child is forming. The school can help in great measure by determining pupil needs through such means as health appraisal by medical personnel, identification of pupils with special health problems, screening of children to ascertain those who are physically underdeveloped, identification of posture problems, use of health surveys, and evaluation in physical education to determine status in regard to physical fitness, skills, knowledge, and attitudes. After this job has been accomplished, the school can provide a very well-rounded physical education and health education program that meets the needs of its students, grade by grade.

The best way to meet the recommendations of the President's Council on Physical Fitness and Sports is to provide a well-rounded physical education and health program. Through such a program the physical fitness of the children will be enhanced. But, equally and perhaps more important from an educational point of view, many other positive physical, mental, and social results will be achieved.

Education in its broadest sense means preparation for life. It should help each individual to become all he is capable of being. Therefore, it is inexorably tied in not only with physical fitness but with total fitness. Education and physical education must be concerned with developing in each individual organic health, vitality, emotional stability, social consciousness, knowledge, wholesome attitudes, and spiritual and moral qualities.

Schools have the responsibility for providing many opportunities for understanding and developing fitness. The school programs should provide experiences and services that contribute to fitness. This means that health knowledge, attitudes, and practices are stressed; protective health services are provided; physical activities are available to and engaged in by all, not just the few who are skilled; necessary facilities are provided; the environment is conducive to proper growth and development; and experiences in every area stress proper social and ethical behavior.

[2] President's Council on Youth Fitness, *Youth Physical Fitness—Suggested Elements of a School-Centered Program*, Washington, D.C., President's Council on Youth Fitness, 1961.

School leadership should exemplify fitness and all disciplines in the school should be concerned with this quality. It should permeate the entire program and all persons associated with it. It is not the responsibility of only one curricular area and just a few teaching personnel.

Schools should provide community leadership in this area. They should work closely with, and play a leading role in, the utilization of the entire resources of each community to do the job.

The American Association of Health, Physical Education, and Recreation has listed the following goals as "What the Public Schools Hope to Achieve for your Child Through Fitness Programs":

1. Excellent health, through knowledge of the human body and its needs.
2. Self-protection, through knowledge about safety, alcohol, narcotics, wise purchase of products.
3. Sufficient strength, vitality, and coordination to meet emergencies as well as the requirements of daily living.
4. Emotional stability to meet the stresses and strains of modern life.
5. Skill in meeting the requirements of group living.
6. Attitudes, values, and skills which help achieve and maintain fitness.
7. Spiritual and moral qualities that make for personal maturity.[3]

The elementary school in particular has an important function in the development of fit children. Attitudes toward physical activity and education essentials are being formed, knowledge is being imparted, and habits which will contribute to or detract from good health are being developed. An educational program is needed which takes into consideration the fact that physical fitness is the foundation of intellectual fitness and is an area in which the child recognizes the importance of all phases of his growth.

Physical Fitness Testing. Physical fitness testing has become the vogue in many of the nation's schools. Children are tested periodically and reports are posted and in many cases sent home to parents. On the basis of these tests many youngsters are declared to be strong and healthy or weak and unhealthy Sometimes the tests used are good, sometimes poor; sometimes the analysis of the results of physical fitness tests are used in the right way, sometimes they are misused. Because of the confusion that exists in regard to physical fitness tests, a short discussion of them is included here.

Physical fitness tests include such activities as running, pull-ups, sit-ups, throwing, and jumping. On the basis of individual performance in these items, conclusions are reached as to whether or not a person is physically fit. In a strict sense, however, such tests are merely indexes of physical performance in these particular activities. Many other measurements are needed—medical examinations, for example—to get an accurate picture of the child's total physical fitness.

Physical fitness tests vary in respect to the number and type of items that are included. Some of the components of physical fitness commonly assessed are muscular strength, tested when the child has his hand grip checked; cardiorespiratory endurance, tested when the child is asked to run for a certain period of time; muscular power, tested when the child is required to broad jump; and muscular endurance, tested when the child is required to do push-ups.

A good test is one that meets certain criteria. Some of the more important criteria are validity, reliability, administrative economy, and norms. The *validity* criterion means that a test must measure what it is supposed to measure—for example, if a test is to measure strength, then it should measure strength and not endurance. *Reliability* means that a test must give the same results to different teachers or administrators. *Administrative economy* means that the time, equipment, and other technical essentials of the test must be reasonable and practicable for the situation in which they are used. *Norms* means that performance standards must be established for the test so that a measure of comparison exists among students. The test set up by the American Association for Health, Physical Education, and Recreation, for example, has national norms for boys and girls, so that students in a New York school may be compared with those in a California school.

Several physical fitness tests are widely available today. In addition, some teachers make

---

[3] American Association of Health, Physical Education and Recreation, "Your Child Can't Sit and Keep Fit," Washington, D.C., Division of Press and Radio Relations in cooperation with the American Association of Health, Physical Education, and Recreation, National Education Association.

up their own tests. Many of these tests do not have objective evidence of validity. Furthermore, not all physical fitness tests measure the same kind of physical fitness. Therefore, when selecting a fitness test it is necessary to select one that has validity and measures the kind of fitness the program is aiming to achieve.

In spite of the many limitations of physical fitness tests, they can be utilized to advantage in the elementary school physical education program. They can also be used for purposes of motivation. When a student sees his score and compares it with those of his classmates and with others in other parts of the country, it motivates him to try to make a commendable showing and spurs him on to develop the strength and other qualities essential to such an accomplishment. Physical fitness test scores show the progress a student or class is making in regard to such qualities as muscular strength, endurance, and power. Test results offer information which can be used as a guide to group a class for special work in areas of physical performance that need improvement. Test results can be utilized as one consideration when giving grades in physical education. Tests can help identify strengths and weaknesses of pupils and aid in curriculum planning. Tests also can give direction and supply information for guidance purposes.

One important point should be brought out, however. The test results must never be used as the final and absolute analysis of a child's physical fitness. The results are only a guide to be utilized in conjunction with other evidence and information.

The American Association for Health, Physical Education, and Recreation has developed its own physical fitness test[4] for national use. It consists of seven basic items plus a swimming test.

1. Pull-ups (modified for girls): to test arm and shoulder-girdle strength.
2. Shuttle run: to test speed and change of direction.
3. 50-yard dash: to test speed.
4. Sit-ups: to test strength of abdominal muscles and hip flexors.
5. Standing broad jump: to test explosive power of leg extensors.
6. Softball throw for distance: to test skill and coordination.
7. 600-yard walk or run: to test cardiovascular system.
8. Swimming test (jumping into water, resting, and swimming 15 yards): to test protective powers in the water.

The first seven tests are included in Teachers' Manual, along with tables of percentile rankings for ages ten through seventeen for boys and for girls.

Physical Fitness Guides for the Elementary School Teacher. Some guides for the teacher in developing physical fitness in elementary school children are as follows:

1. *Periodically appraise the health and physical fitness of each child through a medical examination.* A complete medical examination should be given to each child by either the family physician or the school doctor at least once a year. The family physician is best suited for this because he knows the child and his health history.

2. *Provide for a variety of vigorous physical activities in the program.* The regular program of physical education activities will provide a core of experiences which will develop the necessary strength, speed, agility, balance, coordination, flexibility, muscular endurance, good posture, and organic efficiency essential to the development of optimum physical fitness. Special groups of games and sports are not needed.

[4] American Association of Health, Physical Education, and Recreation, *AAHPER Youth Fitness Test Manual*, Washington, D.C., American Association for Health, Physical Education, and Recreation.

3. *Adapt activities to the individual pupil.* A blanket program cannot be prescribed for all students. Instead, each child should have a program adapted to his needs, interests, and capacities. It is especially important to identify pupils who have a low level of muscular strength and other components of physical fitness and plan a developmental program in light of their needs.

4. *Be alert to teachable moments.* There are many teachable moments in the life of a child. It may be when he is curious about his physical makeup, when he is trying to compare his physical performance with that of another pupil, or when someone in the class is sick. These are the times when the teacher can get across important information which will have much meaning for the child.

5. *Motivate pupils to be physically fit.* Through discussion with pupils in class and individually, test results, audio-visual aids, performance charts, and other techniques, boys and girls can be motivated to become physically fit.

6. *Provide for a sound testing program.* Each teacher should determine what he or she wants to measure in the area of physical fitness, and what test will provide the most valid results. After the test has been selected and administered, the results should be utilized in a meaningful manner.

7. *Establish a guidance program.* The teaching program should provide an opportunity for individual guidance of students in the area of physical fitness. Individual conferences could be held, for example, after a physical fitness test has been given. Personal problems and weaknesses could be discussed in light of test results. When a teacher is able to offer this personal attention to each student and can suggest methods of improvement, the boy or girl will benefit considerably.

8. *Provide instruction in health and safety education.* Concentrated instruction relative to specific health concepts and problems should be provided at each grade level. Such topics as cleanliness, nutrition, sleep, rest, and exercise, if taught effectively, will contribute to the physical fitness of boys and girls.

The American Association for Health, Physical Education, and Recreation lists some suggestions for further promoting physical fitness.[5] A few are presented here in adapted form.

1. Establish a system for parental reporting and counseling on the health and physical fitness of the school's children.

2. Install and maintain a bulletin board devoted to health and physical fitness. Keep it attractive and current with stimulating ideas, announcements, posters and flyers.

3. Make prominent use of such slogans as "Think Fit—Look Fit—Be Fit," "You Can't Sit and Be Fit," and, "Shape Up or Ship Out."

4. Plan demonstrations and exhibitions of fitness and involve as many children as possible in a program for the public.

---

[5] American Association for Health, Physical Education, and Recreation, *Operation Fitness—U.S.A., 1963*, "The Year of Cooperation, Coordination, and Concerted Action in the Nation," Washington, D.C., American Association for Health, Physical Education, and Recreation, 1963.

(Courtesy of Game-Time Inc.)

5. Plan a school assembly program with a physical-fitness theme.

6. Develop a homework program for physical fitness. Require some activities to be engaged in during out-of-school hours.

7. Plan and conduct occasional weekend hikes and bicycle treks to points of interest, with packed lunches.

8. Plan a special school fitness club and establish standards for membership. Provide membership cards and public recognition.

Working with Parents for the Physical Fitness of School Children.[6] At a recent parent-teachers association an impetuous mother jumped to her feet and wanted to know why the school permitted her child to remain a physical weakling. "Roger can't run without puffing, push-up without grunting, and he looks like a girl every time he throws a ball." She continued in a dejected tone of voice, "My boy is frail, pale, and lacks vitality. Our school has a physical education program, yet Roger is soft." As the confused woman sat down her last words were "I can't understand it."

If the physical education department had been represented at the meeting, the staff could have pointed out that Roger is a physically underdeveloped youngster, but that a program with only two 45-minute periods a week, 75 youngsters in the class, and 15 minutes out of each period devoted to dressing and showering makes such a bodybuilding task difficult to accomplish.

It is also important to realize that physical fitness is the responsibility of the home as well as of the school. Parents should conceive of themselves as half the team. After all, the child is in school only 180 or so days a year, 5 days a week, from 8:30 A.M. until 4:00 P.M. He is at home much more than this—or should be. The control that is exercised by an understanding mother and father is also important.

[6] Adapted from an article by Charles A. Bucher entitled, "What Can Parents Do? (About Their Child's Health and Fitness)," *National Education Association Journal*, February, 1962.

Physical educators need public support for a daily class program that has no more than thirty-five to forty pupils in a class, support that is readily given to English, science, and mathematics teachers. Parents must develop values concerning physical fitness in their children so that when their youngsters are in class they will want to work hard to be physically fit. The author once heard a father remark that he would rather have a soggy body than a soggy mind. His children look at it the same way and try to skip physical education class every time they can. But it isn't an either/or proposition. The late John F. Kennedy's words "... the foundation of intellectual fitness is physical fitness" have deep meaning for all parents.

Studies have shown that a child is more likely to smoke if his parents smoke and that he is more likely to use alcohol if his mother and father do. The same thing is probably true where physical fitness is concerned. If parents take pride in their bodies and keep them in good physical shape, the child is likely to follow suit. Whenever you see an obese girl or boy, take a look at the parent—the old block may give off fat chips.

Too many parents think of physical fitness in terms of stereotypes such as a Mr. World or Miss Universe strolling up and down Muscle Beach. Or their minds turn to Joe Namath, Jerry Lucas, or the high school football or basketball star. Because a boy or girl doesn't know which end of a tennis racket to hold, mothers and fathers may assume that fitness is a quality far removed from their youngsters. Such erroneous and misleading beliefs make it imperative that each parent know what physical fitness is, how important it is, and how it is acquired and maintained.

It is important for grownups, by example and precept, to create in the minds of youngsters the feeling that to be a good American one must be physically fit. This is a responsibility that each of us has if our democratic way of life is to be preserved and our national purposes accomplished.

Democracy is not a spectator sport; it is a game in which all are participants. In this life-and-death struggle we must have total effort on the part of all. This means total fitness—emotional, mental, and physical.

A newspaper article once stated that Russia, instead of having the American coffee break twice a day, allotted time for required calisthenics for all employees. In a democracy this regimentation is out of place; yet in America, where physical fitness is a voluntary thing, we must motivate our young to recognize that their own physical development is important to them as individuals and also to the nation. Each person has the responsibility to be in good physical condition and not to detract from our national power and strength.

More specifically, here are some practical suggestions that parents can follow to promote their children's physical fitness.

1. See that their children get proper rest, medical care, nutrition, and the other essentials to physical fitness.

2. Buy toys that give children a good physical workout as well as fun. Instead of an electric train buy a horizontal bar that fits in the doorway. Each child should chin on it before passing through.

3. Construct a gymnasium in the basement or backyard complete with climbing ropes, trapeze, badminton court, swings, and other equipment.

4. Provide a meaningful work schedule around the house which includes mowing the lawn, shoveling snow, and other jobs which provide healthful physical activity.

5. Arrange for more total family participation in physical activities, where mother and father and all the children go camping, bowling, square dancing, ice skating, or engage in other appropriate physical activity.

6. Insist that the older children walk or ride their bicycles to school and other places if the distance is not more than one or two miles.

Questions and Practical Problems

1. Write an essay on the relation of physical fitness to the fitness and health of the elementary school child.

2. Your school principal has asked you to make recommendations for a broad and comprehensive physical education program that will

achieve the recommendations of the President's Council on Physical Fitness and Sports. Outline such a program for the elementary school.

3. Prepare a list of five outstanding physical fitness tests found by research and prepare a table showing the validity, reliability, availability of norms, and administrative feasibility of each.

4. Develop a newsletter that you could send to parents to acquaint them with the responsibilities they have and the role they can play in the physical fitness of their children.

5. What is the relation of the physical fitness objective to all the objectives of physical education?

6. Prepare a file of materials on physical fitness which would be of value to the classroom teacher.

Selected References

Many of the materials needed on physical fitness can be obtained in pamphlet form in individual or economy lots through the American Association for Health, Physical Education, and Recreation, 1201 Sixteenth Street, N.W., Washington, D.C. These materials include:

AAHPER Youth Fitness Test Manual. Directions for administration of the AAHPER Youth Fitness Test, with test descriptions, percentile scores, and norms for fifth grade through college.

Children and Fitness. Report of the National Conference on Fitness of Children of Elementary school age.

Excercise and Fitness. Joint statement by the American Medical Association and American Association for Health, Physical Education, and Recreation.

Selected Fitness Articles. Packet of 25 articles on fitness.

Your Child's Health and Fitness. A series of articles reprinted from the *National Education Association Journal*, February, 1962.

Youth Physical Fitness—Suggested Elements of a School-Centered Program, President's Council on Youth Fitness, 1961. This pamphlet is available from the United States Government Printing Office, Washington, D.C.

CHAPTER 5

Current Trends in Elementary School Physical Education and Health Education

Trends may be defined as movements or changes in educational thinking or practice that take a particular direction reflecting a change in the traditional pattern.

Trends in education do not just happen. They are the result of historical developments. Trends may be difficult to trace, however, because they usually result from many different influences. The advancements in science and research techniques and the rise or decline of a culture are among the factors which produce changes and directly or indirectly cause various trends.

After World War I there were definable trends in citizenship education, health education, curriculum studies, and toward more liberal education in elementary schools.

Educational trends today continue to reflect such factors as the national income, a greater understanding of child behavior, recent findings in child growth and development, a saner understanding of mental health, and an increased emphasis on school planning and development.

Trends which will be discussed in this chapter have direct bearing on and offer specific challenges to programs of physical education and health education. They show needs in the over-all structure in content, planning, and organization.

General Trends in the World of Today and Their Challenge to Physical Education and Health Education

A major trend of our era is automation. Automation is greeted with joy by some people, yet others regard it with consternation and fear. Some feel it represents a new utopia where electronic tapes, push buttons, and giant brains will do all the work while humans live an ideal life. To others it represents the vehicle which will carry the world into the worst depression in history, characterized by unemployment and degradation of the human spirit. The result of automation probably will not be as drastic as either of these two extremes. However, it will, according to most experts, result in a new way of life for millions of Americans with many new problems to challenge their thinking.

The automation era, with its ability to perform with less time and energy work which formerly took hundreds and thousands of man hours, is giving mankind more and more free time. The worker in the United States today produces as much in a 40-hour week as three men did in 1870 in a 70-hour week. In 1850, approximately 66 per cent of all power was produced by man or animal muscle, while 100 years later it had dropped to only 2 per cent. If the trend continues for another 100 years, one 7-hour work-day will produce as much as a 40-hour work week does today. In 1800, the average work week in industrial establishments consisted of 84 hours; in 1900, it averaged 60 hours; and today, 40 hours. Experts predict that with the application of atomic energy to industry the time of the 30-hour work week is not far off. This means there will be twice as many hours for leisuretime activities as their are hours devoted to work.

It has long been the task of education to prepare for those hours spent in work. For years the schools have trained the mind and body for earning a living and accomplishing the many daily tasks. This was its main challenge when everyone was faced with long hours of hard work and no opportunity for relaxation and recreation. But now, education must adjust its goals if it is to fit in with modern living. Surely it should be of utmost importance to prepare for those hours which will soon take up twice as much time as work. There should be thinking and planning for those many leisure hours so that they may be used to greatest advantage—to help develop the human body and mind, to enhance one's total fitness. A noted educator has said, "Education also consists in knowing what to do when you have nothing to do." If education is truly preparation for life, then surely this important responsibility cannot be ignored.

Use of Leisure and Its Relation to Health. If education accepts the challenge of the automation era, then teachers and other leaders should be interested in developing in the pupil a proper attitude toward leisure. A child should not grow up thinking that free time is something to waste, to get rid of recklessly or foolishly. He should not feel that the purpose of leisure is to kill time, but rather to use time wisely, every golden minute of it. It should be viewed as an opportunity for self-development, for achieving many of those worthwhile things which cannot be accomplished during hours of work—a time for travel, for engaging in refreshing physical activity to meet bodily needs, and as a main spoke in the wheel of balanced living to which work, play, rest, and recreation must all contribute.

Each young person should have as his or her objective the development of an integrated personality in which the mental, physical, social, and emotional are in harmony and all supplement and complement each other. If such an attitude can be instilled in each young mind, the misuse of leisure will not exist. According to Henry Thoreau, students should develop the attitude that the new age of leisure affords new avenues for plucking the "finer fruits of life."

Mental and emotional health problems will diminish if people know what to do in their leisure and gain satisfaction from their activities.

Perhaps the greatest challenge in the 1970's will be what to do with spare time. The groundwork must begin in schools with the curriculum aimed at readying today's children who are tomorrow's adults for play and wholesome recreation as well as for work.

Emotional health problems now on the increase may be helped considerably by preparing people for wise use of leisure time.

Another important responsibility of teachers in preparing students for worthy use of leisure is to see that a wide variety of skills which can be utilized in leisure hours is developed by each boy and girl. These skills can be a source of health and happiness during youth and also in the adult years. Possession of these skills will greatly determine the pleasures that attract youngsters, the types of amusements they want during their free time, and the luxuries they consume. The late Dr. Jay B. Nash, a leader in the fields of physical education and recreation, has said that the early years of life are the crucial ones for the child in regard to skill learning. He conducted a study which showed that skills and hobbies learned by children under twelve years of age constituted 78 per cent of their hobby interest when they became adults, and those skills and hobbies learned under ten years of age made up 62 per cent of the leisuretime pursuits during their middle and later years.

Physical education must be concerned with developing a wide range of skills which will serve as a motivating force for insuring the worthy use of leisure time. These should include skills involved in such activities as cycling, camping, skating, skiing, boating, swimming, fishing, hiking and such individual and group sports as archery, tennis, bowling, badminton, golf, and so on.

Another important implication of the automation era for elementary school teachers and other educators is the growing concern regarding the fitness of youth. Today's children and youth are threatened with physical and moral bankruptcy as a result of modern push-button technology and materialism.

Today's children ride to school instead of walking. Even in situations where they are close enough to walk, many times they are transported.

Home chores once necessary and which led to excellent muscular development are diminishing. Instead of lawn mowers being pushed, they are ridden, power snow plows are replacing the man-powered shovel; walking is replaced by the auto and, in most other cases, by the bicycle. Climbing trees is a lost art because of urbanization. Few trees exist in the densely populated areas or in the new developments in semi-rural sections. The opportunities to run across fields, jump brooks, and chase butterflies are being slowly but surely lost.

Homes are being built today on small lots with no special space set aside for play areas. Yet real estate statistics tell us we may expect two and one-half children per house. Why do we not require all building areas to set aside two acres of playground for every 250 children? Children are not allowed to play in one neighbor's yard because of damage to the flowers, in another because a window has been broken by a fly ball. In still another the swimming pool is interesting, yet dangerous unless supervised, so they must leave there. Where will they play? How will they use up their abundance of energy and how will they become physically strong if denied the place and opportunity for play and big-muscle activity? Is it any wonder then that they sit hour after hour in front of television sets, munching potato chips and drinking soda.

Because of these factors it is an increasing challenge to educators to educate children and parents to the need of activity, so that they will find places for it and plan programs which will be usable in smaller areas than were formerly available.

Education can help by providing experiences for children which will give them an understanding of the human body—its needs and limitations—the ability to discriminate fad from scientific fact, the interest and desire to be physically fit, the resources for spending leisure hours in a manner that contributes to fitness, and skill in activities which provide release from strains and tensions associated with modern-day living. They should also be provided with experiences that contribute to wholesome personal and group adjustments and opportunities for creative expression. These are only a few of the contributions that the schools can make. If total fitness is to be within the reach of a larger number of children and youth in this nation, schools and teachers must be aware of and take active steps to fulfill the many contributions they can make.

The Need for Extracurricular Programs. The school's job does not end when the three o'clock bell rings. Its influence extends into the child's life throughout the school day and is also reflected in those activities in which he engages after regular school hours. How the child spends his free time after school, on Saturdays, Sundays, and holidays will influence his health and also his success in life.

The out-of-school part of the child's daily life is entirely his own, from which he should get the most fun and satisfaction. This period of the day is especially important to mental health and well-being. During this time he can find outlets for aggressive drives, he can create, and he can learn. Activities engaged in during this period can meet his physical needs and also play a part in meeting his social needs. Through play with other children he has an opportunity to satisfy the need for recognition. This time can also offer opportunities for developing hobbies. The interests developed will carry over into adult life and will supply many happy and profitable hours.

The elementary school teacher and the physical education specialist can help guide youngsters in the selection of their activities during out-of-school hours. By taking an interest which extends beyond the school day, she will be helping to pave the way to a satisfying future for each of her students. Here are some suggestions of things the teacher can do.

1. Develop an intramural program for out-of-school hours in various sports, games, and other physical activities.

2. Through the regular class program, draw attention to activities which will be an extension of the curricular program.

3. Have those youngsters who have special talent or skill in selected activities put on a demonstration for the rest of the class.

4. Arrange clinics for certain activities where experts are brought in to work with children.

5. Form clubs which have as their primary purpose the exchange of ideas and the development of skills and interests in special activities.

6. Encourage parents to devote some time to family recreation where such interest can be explored more thoroughly.

7. Utilize parent-teacher associations as a medium for promoting recreational interests.

8. Set aside special days for sports days and play days where all children can demonstrate their choice of activities.

9. Help parents obtain and/or evaluate outside instruction for children in recreational activities—dancing, singing, swimming, and so on.

Table 5-1. Possible Leisure-Time Activities

Camping	Ice skating	Swimming
Bicycling	Sailing	Bowling
Fishing	Mountain	Golf
Dancing	climbing	Archery
Horseback riding	Tennis	Hiking
Badminton	Table tennis	Softball

A few of the activities related to physical education that teachers should encourage pupils to explore as possible leisure-time pursuits are shown in Table 5-1.

In selecting recreational activities it is important to use some guide. Here are some points the teacher should have each child consider:

1. Is he interested in the activity? One of the main considerations for selection is an interest in the activity. The choice is his. Do not select an activity for him; he should not participate in one unless he has an inner desire to do so.

2. Are facilities available for pursuing the activity? He shouldn't select swimming as an activity if there are no pools, beaches, or other accommodations.

3. Is the activity within his financial means? Some activities, such as photography, require expensive equipment. He must ask himself (and his parents) if he can afford such an expense.

4. Will the activity be useful later in life? All other things being equal, activities should be selected in which he can participate throughout life.

5. Will the activity enhance his social relationships? If possible, leisure-time pursuits should enable him to develop his social self. Therefore, it may be wise for him to choose group activities in preference to those done alone.

6. Does the activity interfere with such important phases of his life as his work, religion, and home life? Activities selected should allow opportunity to improve these essential pursuits rather than detract from them.

7. Does the activity compensate for some of the shortages of schoolwork? Activities should help meet emotional and physical needs that sometimes fail to be achieved in regular required activities.

8. Does he have time for the activity? The time needed for participation should be considered in light of his required daily responsibilities.

The teacher can make an important contribution to the education of her youngsters by taking an interest in what they do out of school. Although the daily class work is very important, the after-school activities of children should not be left to chance. By having an understanding of the place of recreation in balanced living and a desire to have her children recreationally educated, she can do much to guide their energies and interests into channels that will be constructive and will further their self-development.

Need for Safety and Survival Techniques. The ease of travel today, the numbers of national and state lakes, and the rise in the amount of leisure time have brought an increase in boating, canoeing, water skiing, skating, fishing, and home pools.

Today, boating is enjoyed by more than 40 million people. These boaters either pull skiers, haul fishermen, or try for the best speed from their powerful motors. From these boats many swimmers dive into unknown waters, some never to return. Many of the people riding in boats and canoes do not know how to swim. Over seven thousand drownings occur each year. While many may say this is a small number compared with the number engaged in these water sports, most of them could have been saved if they had been taught swimming in their physical education programs or in Red Cross classes conducted at YMCA's, YWCA's, YMHA's, or Boy Scout or Girl Scout organizations, because 50 per cent of these seven thousand drownings involve nonswimmers.

Companies constructing permanent pools in the yards of home owners estimate that over 150,000 were completed in 1969. Conservative estimates for the purchase of portable or temporary plastic pools ranging in size from the very small to those of 40-foot diameter and 5-foot depth indicate that over one million are bought annually.

Drownings rank third among causes of death of people between the ages of fifteen and twenty-four and second in cause among children between the ages of five and fourteen. There is a great need for increased instruction in swimming and in water safety. More schools should be able to include swimming as part of their program of physical education. When pools are not available in schools it is possible many times to use community facilities for this excellent program.

Winter sports on ice—including skating, ice hockey, ice fishing, skiing, kite skating, ice sailing, and curling—are increasing annually. Interest in the use of the snowmobile has increased 500 per cent since 1965. T. W. Koskella of the U.S. Forest Service predicts a million snowmobiles will be in use within the next five years and believes this will create the same interest in winter recreation that boating enjoys in the summer. While no accurate record of drownings is available they will undoubtedly increase in winter recreation unless all safety, survival, and rescue methods are taught.

Current Trends in Elementary Education that Directly Concern Physical Education and Health Education

The Total-Child Development Concept. Teachers must be prepared to educate the child in his infinite variations of behavior and reactions to his environment. This means that the teacher is responsible for the development of the emotional, social, intellectual, and physical learning and well-being of each child.

Story, an administrator in elementary education, believes the responsibility of the school is to

> ... administer a program of activities for children developed in relation to the achievement purposes of the school, activities that reflect teacher understanding of a student's needs, abilities and interests, activities which in their scope and sequence indicate a knowledge and sensitiveness to the total development of the "whole child."[1]

It is impossible to separate the various parts of the child and teach each part separately. All parts are interrelated and the child learns as a whole individual. This whole is important and the individual elements alone are unimportant except as parts of the whole.

The elementary schools must serve the child, the community, and the nation. They will serve the community and nation to the greatest degree by serving the individual child to the best of his ability.

The dualist notion of a separate mind in a separate body is not acceptable today. The whole child goes to school and there he gains skills, techniques, knowledge, and appreciation. This necessarily challenges the school to assist him in his physical, mental, social, and emotional growth and development.

It is agreed among educators that physical education is an integral part of the program and will assist in the development of the whole child.

Our machine age has made great changes in the lives of children, and the school must accept the responsibility to substitute activities once believed unnecessary for the physical activity no longer necessary for mere survival. Man is by nature active. Physical activity today is becoming less and less necessary for maintaining a livelihood and consequently the needs must be met in other ways.

Physical Education as an Aid in Total Development. Because of our changing world the need for physical education as an integral phase in the development of the whole child becomes apparent. Each individual needs activity for biological growth and development. Physical education exists as a good constructive social force to guarantee all youth the fulfillment of these needs.

Thus it appears that to educate the whole child, the school must assume many jobs and these are in a great part the responsibility of the elementary classroom teacher. Each classroom teacher must understand the ways in which physical education contributes to the development of the whole child and must be prepared to plan and administer an adequate program. Much learning may be gained through a program of physical education and motor activities because these cannot be isolated from the mental, social, and emotional learning of the child,

The Challenge of Increased Consolidation of School Districts. Some of the reasons for this trend are as follows.

1. The shift of population from farms to cities is reducing enrollments in rural areas and making it increasingly difficult for the population in these areas to finance good schools.

2. Consolidation of districts makes it easier to provide better schools and more services.

3. With the cost of education rising, consolidation is essential to make the best possible use of financial resources.

4. Recruitment of good teachers is easier in consolidated districts than in small, poorly managed ones.

A recent commission on school district organization of the American Association of School Administrators pointed out that in general any district that contains fewer than 1,200 pupils or 40 teachers is too small to operate efficiently. This commission pointed out some of the limitations of small districts. They provide meager high school programs; they are unable to construct needed school plants; the cost per pupil is un-

---

[1] Bascum H. Story, "The Good Life in the Elementary School," *Thirty-first Yearbook*, Association of Department of Elementary School Principals, National Education Association, p. 22.

reasonably high; and their low pupil-teacher ratio results in loss of manpower.

This trend toward consolidation of school districts offers a direct challenge to physical education to plan and administer adequate recreation programs during the noon hour because there are many children transported by bus to these schools who must remain there all day. The need for planned activity is great.

In addition to the noon-hour programs, early morning programs are also advisable. Because the same buses are often used to transport two or three different groups of children, causing many to arrive at school long before the actual beginning of the school day, some planned worthy activities should be available then, also. Opportunities for these children to secure equipment and supplies in order to participate in a safe and organized program of activities during this time is a responsibility of educators. A similar plan to that of the noon hour has been used with great success in many schools.

Additional time for similar programs is again prevalent at the close of school when the same buses must make two or three trips to transport all the children home. The opportunity for worthy use of leisure is again the responsibility of leaders in these elementary schools.

Chapter 13 devotes more space to the consideration of ways and means by which teachers may organize and administer worthy programs of recreational activities before school, during the noon hour, and after school to meet a great desire and need for children to be busy in educationally sound activities.

Importance of Camping and Outdoor Education. Various educational agencies and associations recommended in May 1948 that camping be a part of every child's education. These associations included the American Association for Health, Physical Education, and Recreation, the U.S. Office of Education, the National Secondary Principals' Association, the American Association of School Administrators, and the American Council on Education.

Many educators believe that camping and outdoor education should be an integral part of the child's total education. Federal funds have made it possible to increase camping and outdoor education in the United States. The new programs in operation now, however, are but a mere trifle compared with those to come. Already we find some schools organized for twelve-month education, requiring at least one of the months to be spent in camping and outdoor education.

Use of national parks from 1960 to 1968 shows a 72.3 per cent increase, according to statistics compiled by the U.S. Department of the Interior, National Park Service, Washington, D.C. These figures are very small compared with those for the use of our state parks for family outings and camping activities. There are in addition, of course, thousands of individuals who, during their vacations, camp on land that is privately owned.

Camping education offers an opportunity to further the democratic living relations between teachers and children. These relationships have great carry-over value into adult life. All phases of education benefit from camping education. No subject or part of the curriculum is unaffected by it. It is a fine chance for integration of the total education of the whole child.

The trend toward camping and outdoor education is well established and will show great strides within the next decade. This movement may well be directed and coordinated by physical education departments.[2]

New Modes of School and Program Organization. The integration and correlation of subjects today make team teaching possible, posing a challenge to teachers in all areas to assist. The physical education specialist teams with the music and art specialists who in turn work directly with the classroom teacher to make the unit in social studies much more meaningful to the students. Dances of the countries studied, their games, songs, types of music and musical instruments, costumes, colors, and drawings change words in a text into living experiences that bring home to children the reality of life in strange and far-off lands around the world.

Teacher assistants who help with clerical work, lunches, special programs, and so on, are working well today in many areas of the elementary school.

Educators are becoming more aware that individuals learn in different ways and at different rates. They are attempting to make schools more nearly like life situations. Different forms of organization within schools and districts,

---

[2] Chapter 20 is devoted entirely to camping and outdoor education.

such as the nongraded school, the multigraded school, and the middle school, are examples of changes in the structure of the school which help place the child where he will gain the most from his education. These changes challenge both health education and physical education to plan their programs and instructional methods accordingly.

The conceptual and problem-solving approach has been tried and proved successful. Making the school closely related to life problems helps the child to understand educational values. Children are being offered opportunities to help in planning and are being given more learning experiences through participation in the conceptual or problem-solving approach.

Team teaching, teaching machines, programed learning, and a greater use of community facilities and consultants are all contributing to increase the educational experiences of the child.

Current Trends in Physical Education in Elementary Schools

There are specific trends in physical education which directly affect the educational offerings of our schools. These trends make necessary demands on programs both internally and externally and may not be disregarded if physical education is to be an integral part of the education of each child. Understanding and awareness of them assist in program planning, administering, and evaluating. Those considered the most important are discussed.

Importance of the Classroom Teacher. The elementary classroom teacher is one of the most important educators in our society. He or she is the person who has contact with and guidance of more children than almost any other one person in the field of education. He or she has the child during his impressionable growing years. The child can be considered a work of art to be fashioned by the teacher into something wonderful. Furthermore, many children, because of drop-outs, receive their *only* formal educational guidance from the classroom teacher.

The classroom teacher needs to be prepared to teach physical education to the children. The aid of specialists and consultants is desirable, but this help is often lacking. The self-contained classroom with consultants on call is popular. Each year districts are hiring more physical education specialists to assist in the elementary education programs.

Stress on Individual Differences. Good results in schoolwork are accomplished only when the teacher has a thorough knowledge of the children being taught. The outstanding work being achieved in the kindergarten and primary fields of education is attributed to this knowledge and understanding.

In education today, leaders stress the understanding of growth, development, and behavior characteristics of children as basic requirements for the professional preparation of teachers.

The growth processes of children are uneven in physical, organic, and psychological aspects as well as in mental, social, and emotional development. Therefore, programs of physical education should be based on these findings and be attuned to meet the needs of the individual child. Children possess different physical abilities in the same chronological age group and these must be considered in planning and administering programs.[3]

Development of Leisure and Lifetime Activities. Today's work week of 35 to 40 hours will gradually be reduced. But even when people work an eight-hour day and a five-day work week, much time is available for leisure. Today there are more people, more goods, more money, more workers, more paid vacations, more cars, more places to go—all of which add up to the need for more leisure-time activities and facilities.

Physical education must broaden its offerings for leisure-time activities to meet some of these needs by teaching an appreciation of sports and by adding more recreational activities that are valuable for leisure-time use now and in later life. Worthy use of leisure time may tend to lessen juvenile delinquency and promote good mental and emotional health. This challenge to physical education is very important. Programs must also be changed to offer instruction in activities suitable to be carried on in smaller areas because of urbanization.

[3] Chapter 7 is devoted to a discussion of the program of physical education attuned to meet needs found in research in growth and development.

Current Trends in Physical Education and Health Education

Physical Education as an Aid to Democratic Living. Democracy derives its strength from the worth of each individual. In turn, each individual must learn to live in a democracy and value himself, his status, and his fellow man. He must learn to live in harmony with others, despite the conflicts in and about him which he cannot change. He must learn respect for all people.

Physical education has an opportunity to aid in democratic living because it is primarily concerned with the qualitative aspects of human

(Courtesy of Game-Time Inc.)

behavior. It does not have as its only aim mere strength, endurance, and motor skills. These are not ends in themselves. They are only means toward an end and are aimed at assisting the child in his total development by giving him the ability to cooperate and succeed in a complex society.

Youth may be taught to reach mutual understanding through a program of physical education. They may be taught to play with others, to win and lose, to give and take, and, whatever the outcome may be, not to give up.

The gymnasium, playground, and athletic field are laboratories wherein attitudes and ideals are developed into worthy patterns of socially acceptable conduct and behavior for our democracy. Fair play, respect for the rights of others, willingness to abide by rules and regulations and accept an official's decision, the development of leadership and followership, the place and value of self-sacrifice for the sake of the team, loyalty and respect for oneself and one's teammates may all be taught in the program of physical education. From the situation on the playfield, true tolerance and the democratic way of life may be won or lost.

One of the most important contributions of physical education is the insight it provides into human nature. Games are intensive social experiences. Participation in them aids children in forming ideals, habits of judgment, and the basic social organization needed now and in adulthood in a democracy.

In the physical education program, teams and squads give vent to the gang instinct. There must, however, be a differentiation between childhood gang and gangsterism. Team play correctly planned and guided will fill the needs children gain from belonging to gangs. *Gang* need not be a word with bad connotations. Gangs can be good as well as evil.

Physical education develops socializing experiences, builds character, and provides opportunities for developing leadership and followership so urgently needed in a democracy. Physical education may be a laboratory for aiding the development of harmonious teamwork, a democratic spirit, and the ability of the child to accept his place in sharing with and belonging to the group.

Evaluation of Physical Education Programs. Much is claimed for physical education, but how can teachers know what they are accomplishing unless they evaluate their programs? Effectiveness and efficiency should be developed and maintained in planning and administering programs of physical education.

Evaluation is a process. It is not accomplished by one test or one measuring device. Most parts of the curriculum may be evaluated. The physical education program should be also. This is a responsibility of the teacher.[4]

[4] Chapter 19 discusses evaluation needs and techniques.

Special Developmental Activities. Today, the trend to use gymnastic equipment in all schools, including the elementary school, is gaining ground. Whether or not the poor results of the Kraus-Weber tests created this interest is hard to determine. Elementary playgrounds throughout the nation are being equipped with more climbing apparatus such as jungle gyms, horizontal ladders, and horizontal bars. In a report made by the U.S. Department of Health, Education, and Welfare concerning physical education in 12,217 urban elementary schools, we find that one third of the schools have a climbing apparatus, 20 per cent have horizontal ladders, and 21 per cent have horizontal bars. Indoor facilities for elementary schools are also being equipped with climbing ropes, balance beams, and combination pieces of apparatus which include the horizontal ladder, vertical ladder, ropes, and rings.

Several companies are now manufacturing pieces of apparatus in smaller sizes especially for use in elementary schools.

This trend toward developmental activities in the elementary schools is very popular among children where they are being taught because they meet the children's needs for climbing, hanging, and testing themselves, needs which used to be satisfied in their own yards and the out-of-doors, by ropes attached to tree limbs, by climbing trees, and skinning the cat over tree limbs.

Such a development is indeed worthy of a place in our programs.

Intramural Sports and Play Days. Interest among children in participating in activities during the noon hour and after school has increased the number of intramural sports, play days, and sports days in our elementary schools. In a recent survey of over 12,000 urban elementary schools, 57 per cent were busily engaged in intramural programs as part of their activities. Play days were popular in 58 per cent of these same schools.

Because many children remain at school during the noon hour, this is an opportune time to carry out intramural programs in grades five through eight, using activities taught in the regular physical education program. Many who must wait for late buses or who walk to school may engage in such programs after school and gain much value from participation.

Intramurals, play days, and sports days must be well planned and correctly administered to be of value. If children of different grades are to play together they must be mixed. Do not challenge the fifth graders against the sixth graders or the seventh graders against the eighth graders.

Play days usually include many children participating simultaneously in many different activities. For example, while one group participates in dodge ball, another is playing kickball, another softball, and as many other activities are going on as interest warrants and space will permit.

Movement Education. Movement education is centered around the concepts of body use, space, and the quality of movement. These concepts fit well with the problem-solving approach and afford satisfaction to the participant in that he moves within his own capacities. Skills are developed as an outgrowth of carefully structured problem-solving experiences *without* specific directions as to how to perform them. When these skills are gained they are later used in various situations.

Movement education has aroused great interest among those working with elementary school programs. Its application is ever important in dancing and gymnastics which are included as an important part of elementary programs today.

The concepts of movement education are now being included in some professional education programs in colleges to develop personal skill. Chapter 3 discusses movement education.

Perceptual Development as an Aid to Motor Activity. Acceptance of the significance of the level of perceptual/motor development in the academic achievement of children is increasing. Hence, the challenge to teachers in different areas to work together becomes ever more important.

We think of perception as the intermediate stage between sensation and response. The response action or pattern is caused by impulses sent out by the brain. This response is determined by the effect the stimulus had on the individual. Sensory perception—auditory, visual, and other sensory modes—may be said to interpret the stimulus. The brain organizes the data and, if a motor response is required, sends out signals to the various muscle groups. Perception of external stimuli may be faulty—thus we can expect poor or faulty responses.

Movement education in early life seems to be very necessary for the development of perceptual ability. Since it is thought perception arises from sensory experience, then children must have the opportunity for many experiences. If motor activity is one important factor in perceptual development, then no child should want for activity.

If children do not perceive correctly, activity performance may be poor. It may be that poor motor ability stems from perceptual problems and are not motor problems per se. We must direct careful attention to the stimuli presented to our children in physical education and accept individual differences in perception as well as in response. Our one main goal is to find ways in which we may be able to assist those with motor problems. Some activities which aid us in the study of perceptual/motor development include those which will show body control, balance, and hand-eye, foot-eye, and throwing-and-striking coordination.

Building Trends and Programs. Elementary schools are now being planned and built with fully equipped gymnasiums rather than the multipurpose rooms which were so popular at one time. Parents have been educated to the value of indoor facilities and are passing bond issues to include this facility.

In a few areas indoor pools are added. However, in many areas Port-a-Pools are in use on the playground. These are relatively inexpensive and are well liked by persons using them. (See Appendix B for manufacturer of Port-a-Pool.)

School facilities are being used by the community more frequently and community resources are being used by schools. This tends to create a better understanding of needs and program values. It will perhaps help even more in future building programs than at present.

In summary, trends give challenge and direction to physical education programs. If there is not to be an educational lag, these challenges in all of our educational processes must be met. Physical education is no exception if it is to be justified as an integral part of the program of education for elementary children. All programs should be planned to meet the needs shown through the trends of the times. To be successful, education must meet the challenges of the day and because trends do not remain static, we must expect, accept, and plan for changes.

Current Trends in Elementary School Health Education

Because of the increase of knowledge concerning health, it has become difficult for the public as a whole to keep abreast of developments. Keeping the child alive and in reasonably good health until he reaches school age is the responsibility of the parents. They use the medical assistance they know is available. Some children receive instruction concerning safe and desirable health practices in the home and others receive none. It becomes the responsibility of the school to give proper instruction in health education to all children so they may be informed of how each can maintain and improve his own health and that of others.

The increased abuse of drugs and narcotics and the new discoveries concerning the harm of smoking, coupled with changing social mores, have focused the country's attention on the need for more health education. The incidence of venereal disease, and the increased dangers from pesticides, radiation, and air and water pollution make it evident that health education must have a revised curriculum.

Societal pressures and needs have focused attention on health instruction and have resulted in certain trends.

Emphasis on Preventive Medicine. Changes in preventive medicine have become possible because of advances in science and technology. Advancement in the methods of teaching the public by mass communication media in order to cause greater acceptance and utilization of these changes is a must in preventive medicine. Research without the successful application of its results is useless.

Through the educational media, extensive application of the research on polio was brought about, virtually resulting in the elimination of that disease. For example, in 1950 polio caused 2.6 per 1,000 deaths among five and six-year-old children in the United States. In 1965 the rate was zero, according to data provided by the

National Center for Health Statistics, Washington, D.C.

In addition to polio we find that diphtheria, tetanus, smallpox, malaria, and typhoid fever have also been nearly eliminated. Others are on their way out. Measles and mumps may be next. Notice in the doctors' offices signs reading "Wipe out Mumps" and "Wipe out Measles."

Scientists tell us that an average of ten years could be added to man's life expectancy if all available medical knowledge were applied. In order to accomplish this, the combined effort of every available educational medium is necessary. The application of knowledge and research will depend on positive health attitudes and practices which are challenges to education. School education faces the greatest challenge ever.

It can well accept this challenge because today it has more resources than ever, including printed materials, audio-visual aids, wholehearted interest and cooperation of consultants such as doctors, dentists, and psychiatrists; all these may be used in bringing knowledge to children and in helping to create wholesome attitudes needed for the application of such knowledge.

The improvement of man's total environment will be a cooperative venture. Developing ways and means through research, imparting knowledge of them through education, and bringing about their application by inducing a change in the public's attitude is the recipe.

Health education is one of the most important fields in our educational system. Well-prepared teachers, interested in a continuous education, must be called on to assist in teaching preventive medicine. Policies, laws, and rules and regulations also are necessary. However, these must in turn be imparted to the public through education.

New Subject Matter in Health Education. Today scientific advancements have provided us with many wonderful products. To use these effectively, we must be aware not only of their advantages but of their dangers. Abuses and harmful effects are causing the public to be much concerned, and demand for instruction is the result.

The misuse of drugs, narcotics, and alcohol, and the prevalence of glue sniffing are frightening. Education must accept the challenge to inform students of the dangers by teaching the pertinent facts. We hope that on the basis of these known facts, behavior patterns will be developed that will not lead to abuse.

The danger of pesticides, and the problems of water and air pollution require study. Whatever is presently known and the results of research advancement must be imparted to students.

Accidents on the rise among teen-age students make instruction in safety education mandatory. Safety education is agreed by many educational leaders to be a vital part of health education. Much needs to be done about this most important area.

Problem Solving and the Development of Concepts Related to Daily Living. Because of the increase in factual materials available to health education, it is not possible or desirable to have children memorize facts. When children are engaged in activity which has meaning for them, learning becomes easier and more lasting. Activities are being planned for the development of concepts which can be applied throughout life. The trend is for curricula to be child-centered. Health education is being based on the needs of the child in order to help him function at his highest potential level.

Children ask many questions. These can often be used as a basis for exploration and concept formation. The question "Where do mosquitoes come from?" can lead to the discovery that illness can be transmitted by insects and that water pollution can give rise to illness. The entire community today is being utilized as a laboratory for the solution of problems. Visits to the water-purification plant and the sewage-disposal plant help children understand the Board of Health's work in protecting health. This brings out better cooperation and understanding between school and community. When parents are involved in such explorations, they become better informed regarding what the school is attempting to do and will better understand how they can help to reinforce learning in the home.

Concepts Related to Community and World Health as Part of the Health Curriculum. Schools have begun to provide time and encouragement for teachers to work together in building a curriculum which will be sequential through the grades and which will meet needs of children at each age level and grade level. In some cases this is done through released time from teaching; in others, extra remuneration is provided for work of this nature to be done outside of school time. Regardless of the method used, time must be released and set aside if this task is to be done well. Curricula are being planned on a cooperative basis with the school providing the leadership. Community agencies, doctors, nurses, psychiatrists, dentists, and children are being involved today in planning.

There was a time when we could consider only our own health and that of a few neighbors and friends. Today, with our rapid means of communication, increased world travel, and frequent moves made by many families from one area to another, neighbors may be people who have just returned from the opposite side of the world. Disease which started in one small area of the world may spread to other parts with great speed. Poor health in one area may place a financial burden on other areas for the improvement of health conditions. Unless the health of all peoples is improved to at least a minimal standard, the health and economy of the remainder of the world's population is affected.

It is necessary for children to be taught that which will help them to understand their responsibilities for global health. Tracing the spread of a specific disease, learning methods of prevention, and exploring ways in which these preventive methods could be made available to others is a practical example of the type of problem-solving activity that can be used.

Sex Education and Instruction with Respect to Drugs, Narcotics, and Alcohol. Because of (1) recent findings concerning the connection between smoking and lung cancer and heart disease, (2) the illegal use of narcotics, drugs and harmful chemicals, and alcohol by youth, and (3) the changing mores concerning sex, people are beginning to seek ways of reaching young people with correct information respecting all these topics. Because the majority of children can be reached in public schools, there is increased demand to include these areas in health instruction. Laws alone do not alleviate the problems. Parents are often unsure of the best sources of information and the best ways in which to present such information to their children. In order to assure that all children receive factual information, the schools are being urged to do this teaching. This means that schools are being given a great responsibility to assure that the most recent information is presented in the way best suited to the age level. There is no doubt that all of the areas in which health abuse occurs must be touched upon early in the child's schooling, but the material presented must be suited to the age and needs of the group. To present facts about many drugs to children in early elementary school will have little value, but to make them aware of the danger of colorful pills in attractive bottles, found in medicine cabinets and elsewhere, may prevent accidental poisonings. From the use of barbiturates, their derivatives, and from children swallowing "pretty pills," eleven people per million die annually. This means over 2,000 lives will be lost each year and shows a 16 per cent increase in 1968 over 1960. The need to teach facts concerning the use of drugs, narcotics, and alcohol, and concerning family living, which includes sex education, is underscored daily by events reported in newspapers, magazines, radio, and television.

The Teaching of Health Education by Classroom Teachers. In a health education study directed by Dr. Eleana M. Sliepcevich[5] under a grant from the Samuel Bronfman Foundation of New York City, an extensive survey of instructional practices in 38 states representing 1,101 elementary schools, it was found that most health instruction in elementary schools was taught by the classroom teacher, without supervisory assistance, and was included in the curriculum with other subjects.

Separate health classes were taught in grades seven and eight in 59 per cent of the schools. This pattern ranged from 61.2 per cent in large schools to 48 per cent of schools in small districts. Health education was a required subject in grades seven and eight in approximately 55 per cent of the schools.

Hence, the classroom teacher must be well prepared and must study continuously in order to be up to date with respect to factual materials. She surely needs the assistance of health education specialists, community consultants, and administrators in the school health services as well as healthful school living areas if she is to be successful.

Federal Support for Health Education. Federal funds and industrial and private grants have aided and will continue to aid health education.

[5] Sliepcevich, Eleana M, *School Health Education Study: A Summary Report*, Washington, D.C., 1964.

These grants make it possible to study present curricular patterns and the needs of children, communities, and countries, and to assist in the development of curricular materials.

During the first year of Title I of the Elementary and Secondary Education Act, about nine million children were reached. These children attended school in 17,481 different districts located in every state. About $22 million was expended for health resources, primarily for additional professional personnel including nearly five thousand nurses, one thousand physicians, and eight hundred dentists. Over two million children were affected by these services. It is interesting to note that more than one third of the projects submitted for consideration under Title I had a health component as an integral part of the programed project.

Up to November 1967, there were one hundred Title II elementary and secondary school projects involving health education services and mental health and safety education at a total cost of over $11 million.

Results from these grants have already shown many improvements and experiences in various areas. Private grants have made it possible to do research on a national level and to use the findings to advantage.

Much more aid to health education will be forthcoming from funded programs.

Need for In-Service Classes for Elementary Teachers and for Elementary Health Specialists. Because the preparation of elementary teachers may have included too little or no instruction in the area of health and because of constant development of new materials and research, there is demand for in-service classes. Sometimes these classes are held on a college campus and other times individual schools or school districts make it possible for their teachers to receive such opportunities locally. Frequent requests reach colleges for assistance in planning and administering health education courses and workshops during the school year, as well as in summer sessions. These in-service workshops and courses will always be in demand because of ever changing and increasing health education materials and because of the needs of children in a changing world.

A number of colleges across the United States have organized departments specifically for the preparation of health specialists. Others are planning to add this special program. At the present time, the actual teaching of health education in grades one through six is the responsibility of the classroom teacher. There seems to be greater emphasis on having teachers specifically trained to teach health education starting in grade seven. However, much of this teaching is done by physical education specialists who may or may not be adequately prepared. While health education and physical education are both aimed at improving the health of the child, they are separate subject areas, each having its own body of knowledge. Elementary teachers should have specialists in health education available to whom they may turn for assistance. Health coordinators or supervisors are becoming increasingly needed. In schools where team teaching is prevalent, it certainly is desirable to hire at least one teacher who is adequately prepared in health education. All of this points to the need for more teachers prepared with a major in this important area.

Questions and Practical Problems

1. Trace the history of physical education and health education in the schools of the United States.

2. Predict trends and their influences on our educational program in the next decade. Be specific in explaining how these trends will challenge the programs of physical education and health education.

3. Read several educational articles. Summarize them and show either how present trends influenced the philosophy of the author or how the author is proposing to meet educational needs caused by new trends.

4. How do physical education and health education contribute to the development of the "whole child?"

5. Discuss five trends in physical education and five in health education in elementary schools.

6. Develop a bibliography of outstanding references which discuss trends in physical education and health education.

7. For a grade level of your choice, write a

concept to cover a block of work to be taught daily for two weeks. Show how the community could be used as a laboratory. Indicate the practices you would like to have the children develop and how you would evaluate these.

8. List five colleges in your state preparing elementary teachers and the health courses required in their preparation.

9. How and by whom is health taught in an elementary school which you attended? When was the most recent change made in health teaching in this school? Does the school have a sequential program for health running from the lowest through the highest grade?

10. Talk with five parents and find out what health information they would like to have their children receive while in elementary school. Ascertain what these parents know about the health instruction their children are presently receiving.

Selected References

American Association for Health, Physical Education, and Recreation. *Education In and For the Outdoors.* Washington, D.C., 1963.

BROWNELL, C. L. "Role of Health, Physical Education, and Recreation in the Space Age." *National Association of Secondary School Principals Bulletin,* 44:3–9, May 1960.

BUCHER, CHARLES A. "A Ten-Point Program for the Future of Physical Education." *Journal of Health, Physical Education, and Recreation,* Vol. 38, No. 1, Jan. 1967, pp. 26–29.

BURDON, GWEN. "You Can Drown in Winter." *Today's Health,* Vol. 46, No. 11, p. 48.

CARLSON, REYNOLD E., THEODORE R. DEPPE, and JANET R. MACLEAN. *Recreation in American Life.* Belmont, Calif.: Wadsworth Publishing Co., 1963.

Commission Study Report 26, "Prospective Demand for Outdoor Recreation." *Outdoor Recreation Resources Review,* Washington, D.C.: Superintendent of Documents, U.S. Government Printing Office, 1962.

DAVIS, ELWOOD C., and GENE LOGAN. *Biophysical Values of Muscular Activity.* Dubuque, Iowa: William C. Brown Company, 1961.

FAIRBANKS, BERTHAIDA. "Teaching How to Swim Is Not Enough." *Journal of Health, Physical Education, and Recreation,* Vol. 38, No. 3, March 1967, pp. 38–40.

GRAY, JAMES E. "Balance Work and Play." *Journal of Health, Physical Education, and Recreation,* Vol. 38, No. 1, Jan. 1967, pp. 22–23.

GROUT, RUTH. *Health Teaching in Schools,* 5th ed. Philadelphia: W. B. Saunders Company, 1968.

HUNSICKER, PAUL. *Physical Fitness.* Washington, D.C.: Department of Classroom Teachers, National Education Association, 1963.

KINSER, JAY. "Leisure Time—A Challenge for Physical Education." *The Physical Educator,* Vol. 25, No. 2, May 1968, pp. 57–58.

KRAUS, RICHARD. "Riots and Recreation." *Journal of Health, Physical Education, and Recreation,* Vol. 38, No. 3, Mar. 1967, pp. 42–45.

LEHMAN, EDNA S., CORINNE SCHUMACHER, and MILDRED VITEK. "The Conceptual Approach to Health Education." *Journal of Health, Physical Education, and Recreation,* Vol. 38, No. 2, Feb. 1967, pp. 32–35.

MARSHALL, R. M. "Toughening Our Soft Generation." W. Gill, ed. *Saturday Evening Post,* 235:13–17, June 23, 1962.

MOHR, DOROTHY R. "Team Approach to Staff Functioning." *The Physical Educator,* Vol. 25, No. 2, May 1968, pp. 54–56.

NASH, JAY B. *Recreation: Pertinent Readings, Guide Posts to the Future.* Dubuque, Iowa: William C. Brown Company, 1965.

National Society for the Study of Education. Sixth Yearbook, *The Changing American School.* Chicago: University of Chicago Press, 1966.

RAGAN, WILLIAM. *Modern Elementary Curriculum.* New York: Holt, Rinehart & Winston, Inc., 1966.

SANTORO, JOEL T. "Advantages of Team Training for Physical Education." *The Physical Educator,* Vol. 24, No. 2, May 1967, pp. 73–74.

SCHNEIDER, ROBERT. *Methods and Materials of Health Education.* Philadelphia: W. B. Saunders Company, 1964.

CHAPTER 6

Basic Principles of Physical Education and Health Education for Elementary Schools

Webster's defines the word *principle* as a fundamental truth; that which is an essential or characteristic constituent; and that which gives a substance its essential properties. For general understanding, principles may be considered as beliefs, based on facts, which are used as guides or criteria. They are needed to form judgments and to determine actions. Discussion of some basic principles as they apply to physical education and health education in the elementary school and which may act as guideposts in developing programs is the purpose of this chapter. Complete textbooks have been written on principles of physical education and health education. The authors have in no way endeavored to include all of them in this chapter. They will discuss only those which they believe to be absolutely necessary in planning and administering worthy programs in elementary schools.

Through the years, educational leaders have deemed physical education and health education important enough to pass laws making them a mandatory part of the public school curriculum. This shows that their importance is realized by educators and legislators and challenges the planning and administration of worthy programs. Such programs must be based on sound principles.

Educators believe that programs of physical education should be based on physiological, psychological, and sociological principles. Each principle, in turn, should be related to the needs, interests, and abilities of the individual child in the program of each school.

Physiological principles stress opportunities for a wide range of physical movement and activity as essential to organic development. *Psychological principles* stress the learning situation in the teaching of skills and activities based on natural play activities. *Sociological principles* urge the selection of activities that are adaptable to leisure-time pursuits and which contribute to education for citizenship and to accepted character development.

Education for the immediate present and the future may be either good or bad, depending on the teacher or leader, the environment, and all interactions. Although children are primarily concerned with the present, some thought must be given to preparation for adulthood. Hence, the principles on which programs of health and physical education are based must endeavor to meet the immediate needs of childhood as well as help prepare him to meet the future needs of adulthood. Bearing these criteria in mind, the authors believe that the following basic principles are essential and must be carefully considered in planning and administering worthy programs.

Basic Principles of Physical Education

Physical Education Must Consider the Needs, Interests, and Abilities of the Child. Today the needs of children have been well defined according to various age groups through studies of child growth and development. Some of the needs of children which may be met through a program of physical education have previously been discussed. The following specific needs and supporting reasons challenge programs of physical education:

1. Programs of physical education should include activity to satisfy biological needs for growth because (a) physical activity is essential to good health and a satisfying and vigorous life; (b) today many children are deprived of outdoor farmwork, fishing, hunting, and similar activities; (c) out-of-school time is curtailed because of wide and varied interests and opportunities for instruction in music, art, and dramatics; (d) the failure to provide appropriate play facilities in many areas, both urban and suburban, is a problem; (e) the television fad encourages inactivity.

2. Programs of physical education should include activities to aid organic health and emotional stability because (a) modern competition and stress sometimes prove disastrous to those who are unfit; (b) labor-saving inventions result in less need for large-muscle activity; (c) the incidence of strain, illness, and fatigue decreases with physical fitness; (d) a strong body, well cared for, may lessen emotional instability.

3. Physical education programs should increase skills, responses, and coordinations essential for a productive, active life. There should be a direct correlation between accident prevention and the possession of these skills. Hazardous conditions are ever present and accident prevention may be aided through good mind and muscle coordination, good reflexes, and quick mental reactions.

Children learn best when they have a purpose and interest. If activities in physical education are selected according to their interests and needs, and taught according to sound principles, they will be of educational value to the child.

Anything for which children see an immediate purpose is easier to teach than that which is planned to help them only later in life. Play is a fundamental part of the life of each child. Most children are more interested in play than in anything else. Because of this interest, they throw themselves wholeheartedly into it. With programs based on these interests, it is possible to direct the children into proper growth channels through this phase of education.

If interest is lacking, children learn less rapidly and may acquire a dislike for the activity and for the leader who is forcing them to participate. Because of these factors they may develop bad habits.

It has been said by educators that motivation plays the leading role in education. The interest drive in play is the motivation from which we direct it into useful channels through properly planned programs of physical education. Play interests change with age, and for this reason programs must also change.

Children's abilities also change as they grow. Boys and girls differ in ability as they mature. The best programs of physical education should be flexible enough to be adapted to a wide range of activities at different levels of ability, often within the same grade as well as in different age groups. This principle also implies that activities will be planned for the atypical child, who will be discussed in Chapter 9.

Chapters 10 and 11 will discuss the types of activity, time elements, and other program factors based on the needs, interests, and abilities of the child to further assist the teacher in the application of this principle.

Programs of Physical Education Must Plan for Large-Muscle, Social, and Emotional Development. Unless a program of physical education activities is planned, it will be slipshod and relatively unimportant. Good planning avoids mistakes, confusion, needless and boring repetition, and meets the needs, interests, and abilities of the children.[1]

Once a program is planned it is easier to administer. The therapeutic value received by the child from the play situation in physical education often depends on the provisions made for the activity, i.e., planning and the way it is planned and administered. All teaching principles used

---

[1] Refer to Chapter 16 for further discussion of planning.

Table 6–1. Recommended Supplies: Apparatus and Playground Equipment for Primary Grades

Supplies	Recommended Number	Apparatus and Playground Equipment	Recommended Number
Balls (rubber) 12"	20	All Purpose Climber	1
Balls (rubber) 10"	20	Balance Beams (Low 6")	2
Balls (rubber) $8\frac{1}{2}$"	20	Giant Blocks	4
Balls (rubber) 5"	20	Horizontal Bars (Multiple sizes)	2
Bats (small)	8	Horizontal Ladder	1
Bean Bags	30	Jungle Gym	1
Dance Drum	1	Merry-go-round	1
Footballs (Jr. size)	6	Record cabinet	1
Hoops	30	Rope Ladder	1
Piano	1	Sand Boxes	2
Plastic Fun Balls	10	Scramble Net	1
Pogo Sticks	10	Slides—6'	2
Record Player (Portable)	1	Swings (Safety seats)	6
Records (Creative Rhythms, Folk Dance, Fitness)	Many	Walking Boards $1\frac{1}{2}$" thick (Various lengths and widths)	6
Ropes (Various lengths)	30	Various pieces of creative apparatus for climbing and crawling over and through	
Ropes (8' to 10' long)	10		
Rubber Cone Markers	12		
Stilts	10		
Supersoft Softballs 12"	15		
Tambourine	2		
Yarn Balls	20		

in education apply to the physical education program.

Activities necessary for large-muscle development are based on the needs of the individuals within the program. Types of equipment and facilities are factors which have some bearing on the physical education program. Various play apparatus such as jungle gyms, horizontal ladders, merry-go-rounds, and ropes for climbing are excellent for developing the muscles in the arms, legs, and chest. Self-testing activities, stunts and gymnastics as well as games will also aid in big-muscle development.

Participation in games should create an atmosphere conducive to acceptable and desirable social development. Activities taught in the program which have carry-over value for leisure time aid in the social development of the child. Social qualities of play may provide suitable relationships between the child and his playmates and develop constructive behavior patterns of helpfulness, kindness, truthfulness, justice, and sociability. If these experiences through play are adequate and properly guided, they should assist the child at the time and also aid him to take his place as a better-adjusted adult.

A child learns self-discipline through his play in physical education. The experiences he gains through the program must be honest, give him satisfaction, present cooperative social experiences, and emphasize the group ideal. Children who play fair learn to get along with others, become good sports, and learn to give and take, to win and lose, to accept decisions made by the majority and those made by the elected captain or official. All of these assist in teaching him the democratic way of life. He knows no distinction of color or creed. His teammates and he are striving for the same goals of success and fun. Barriers do not exist.

Providing Necessary Equipment, Facilities, and Leadership Is the Responsibility of Every School. How well a teacher teaches depends on her education, love for the work and the children, teaching conditions, facilities, equipment, administration, and a happy, cooperative, democratic environment. Each of these factors is important no matter what field or branch of specialization one prefers. To plan, administer, and execute a program of physical education that will meet the needs of individuals requires varied personal as well as physical equipment. Supplies, equipment, facilities, and leadership are all essential.

Recommended equipment and supplies for elementary schools are listed in Tables 6–1 and 6–2. The amount recommended is for classes of 25–30 pupils and presupposes all equipment, supplies, and apparatus will be available to each class.

Quiet games such as Checkers, Flinch, Lotto, Scrabble, Chinese Checkers, Monopoly, and the like are recommended for classroom use.

The proper care and distribution of equipment are essential. If kept in a central equipment room, a systematic way of checking items out and in must be planned so that each person using them will be responsible for them. If it is possible to keep some equipment in each classroom, it will undoubtedly be used more and there will be less conflict. Naturally the amount of equipment needed varies according to the number of students. One ball for each four to six students is suggested. Rubber balls which may be inflated the same as leather ones are recommended. They are less costly as it is possible to buy two or three for the cost of one leather ball. Also, they last longer when used on wet playgrounds. When leather gets wet, unless it is carefully cared for, which is time-consuming, it becomes very hard and rough, the stitches break, and the balls are then short-lived.

Safety equipment should include eye guards for those who must wear glasses, safe markers for sectioning play areas, safe bases for games and protective equipment such as body protectors, masks, and gloves for catchers in softball games.

Apparatus or permanent playground equipment is essential for large-muscle activity and social pleasure. The most popular and useful

Table 6–2. Recommended Equipment, Supplies, and Apparatus for Intermediate and Upper Grades

Equipment and Supplies for Games and Sports	Recommended Number	Apparatus and Equipment (*Indoor and Outdoor*)	Recommended Number
Miscellaneous		All Purpose Portable Standards	4 sets
Balls—Rubber 5″, 8½″	30	(Badminton, Aerial Tennis,	
Bases (Indoor and Outdoor)	4 sets	Deck Tennis, Volleyball, and	
Bowling Sets	3	all net games)	
Color Bands or Pinnies for		Archery Stands (Portable)	4
marking teams (4 colors)	48	Batting Tee	2
Indian Clubs	24	Basketball Goals (Portable)	2 sets
Pogo Sticks	12	Crossbars	4
Ropes (Various lengths for		Field Marker	1
individuals)	30	Football Goals	1 set
Rubber Cone Markers	24	Gymnastics Apparatus	
Aerial Tennis		Balance Beam (Regular)	1
Birdies	36	Balance Beam (Low)	2
Paddles	24	Horizontal Bars	
Archery		(Multiple sizes)	2
Targets 48″ Butts	4	Horse	1
Target Faces 48″	24	Mats (5′ × 7′)	30
Bows (Various lengths and		Mini Tramp	1
pulls)	24	Parallel Bars (Regular)	1
Arrows (Various lengths)	72	Parallel Bars (Uneven)	1
Badminton		Rings	1 pr.
Rackets	25	Ropes (Climbing)	4
Shuttlecocks	10 doz.	Reuter Board	1
Basketball		Scramble Nets	2
Balls (Official)	12	Vaulting Box	1
		Hockey Goals (Portable)	1 set

80 THE PHILOSOPHY

Table 6–2. (continued)

Equipment and Supplies for Games and Sports	Recommended Number
Deck Tennis	
Rings	12
Football	
Balls (Junior)	3
Balls (Official)	10
Belts for Flag Football	24
Hockey	
Sticks (Various lengths and weights)	36
Balls	24 sets
Goalie Pads	2
Paddle Tennis	
Balls	30
Paddles	24
Quoits	
Sets	4
Rhythms	
Record Player (Variable speed)	2
Records (Folk, Square, Social, Modern, Fitness)	Many
Dance Drum	2
Tambourine	4
Piano	1
Shuffleboard	
Complete Sets	6
Soccer	
Balls (Official)	12
Softball	
Balls (Official)	24
Super-soft 12"	10
Bats 28"–31"	12
Catcher's Mitt	2
Catcher's Mask	2
Chest Protector	2
Table Tennis	
Paddles	24
Balls	6 doz.
Tennis	
Rackets (Official)	20
Rackets (Shortie)	10
Balls	6 doz.
Tetherball	
Balls	12
Volleyball	
Balls	12

Apparatus and Equipment (Indoor and Outdoor)	Recommended Number
Hurdles (Rocker Type)	16
Jump Standards	2
Nets (Badminton, Deck Tennis, Paddle Tennis)	8
Nets (Tennis)	2
Record Cabinet	1
Soccer Goals (Portable)	1 set
Scramble Nets	2
Table on Wheels for Record Player	2
Permanent goals, courts, and markings should be established for outdoor shuffleboard, tetherball, badminton, volleyball, deck tennis, tennis, and basketball	

pieces include jungle gyms, horizontal ladders and bars, swings, seesaws, slides, merry-go-rounds, and sand boxes. Care and inspection of this apparatus and equipment are essential for safety. Proper instruction in the use of all apparatus is necessary. Planned and organized periods need to be worked out so that each group will have an opportunity to use it with a minimum of conflict or hard feelings. Properly supervised play apparatus provides excellent opportunities for big-muscle activity and teaches safety and respect for individual rights.

The recommended space for play areas is a minimum of 10 acres for each 500 students. This is, of course, not possible in many schools already functioning. However, when purchasing land for new buildings, administrators are keeping this recommendation in mind and are preparing large playground areas. The minimum recommended area for outdoor play is 100 square feet per child. In a recent issue of *Educational Summary*, it is stated that new sites for elementary schools average 10 to 15 acres. Facilities in the community may also be used by the school to good advantage and the community should be encouraged to share and make use of the school's recreational facilities. Community facilities are always great assets. This is especially true for the school that is already functioning with a small playground area and little opportunity for expansion.

Minimum indoor facilities recommended include a playroom or gymnasium 50 by 80 feet with a 20-foot ceiling. More is desirable if possible. It is natural to suppose that the play area both indoors and outdoors will be one factor which determines the types of activity in which children may engage.

Adequate locker and shower rooms should be available for children in the intermediate grades. Children from eight years of age and up are ready for showering. It seems only educationally sound when we endeavor to teach children good grooming and healthful living that we continue this teaching during our physical education programs. We should make it possible for students to have facilities where they may leave their street clothes and dress appropriately for their physical activity program. After 30 to 50 minutes of vigorous activity, showers should be available and be used. Surely, each teacher who has used these facilities knows children feel more like continuing their classroom work after showering and dressing than they do when they return to their classroom without that privilege.

Lockers should be provided for all children who will be changing clothes. Storage lockers for gym clothes should equal the number of children changing clothing. Street clothes lockers should equal the greatest number using the area at any one time.

Showers should be mostly group type. A few individual showers may be desirable in the girl's area. One shower head for each four users during the peak load period is recommended. Shower heads should be placed at varying heights so that they may be used without getting the hair wet.

A report of the National Conference on Physical Education for Children of Elementary School Age suggests the following necessary qualifications for leaders:

1. A genuine liking for children.
2. Good health, physical vitality, sound mental attitude, emotional balance, and social adjustment.
3. Physical skills, efficient posture and body mechanics, and ability in a variety of recreational activities.
4. Ability to get along with pupils.
5. Understandings and interests that stem from a broad cultural background.
6. Knowledge of how children grow and learn and skill in using that knowledge in practical situations.
7. Competence in teaching and guiding elementary school children.[2]

There Should Be Progression in All Programs. Maintaining interest in any area of education is essential if learning is to be successful, adequate, and challenging. It is also necessary to remember the individual differences of children, the differences between boys' and girls' interests in the intermediate level, and differences in interest span, abilities, and needs in general.

A well-planned program will include specific materials for the grade level so that each

[2] National Conference on Physical Education for School Children of Elementary Age, *Physical Education for Children*, Washington, D.C., National Conference on Physical Education for School Children of Elementary Age, 1951, p. 29.

teacher will know when she receives a new class what they have had in their physical education program, in addition to how they score in reading and other parts of the curriculum. Forms for keeping these records may be found in Chapter 19. Too much repetition in the same activity is often boring. Children tire of the same activity year after year in the elementary grades. They like new activities and new challenges. Each new experience is a learning situation for them. The lack of planning for progression may lead to a program of activities either too hard or too easy for the group. Either is dangerous.

Little children need plenty of big-muscle activity such as running, climbing, throwing, and chasing. This may be gained through play that is not too highly organized. Creative rhythms and dances give free expression and are fun. As children grow older, they need more difficult types of activity. They are less interested in games of low organization, such as circle and running and tagging games. Advancement should include team games which give them more challenge and require more skills and techniques to provide the needed physical activity as well as the social and psychological development suitable to their needs and abilities.

The teacher who does not know the correct materials for her children and who does not plan a progressive program will find that interest lags, the children may grow to dislike the physical education period, and there are many problems to settle.[3]

Programs Must Develop Free-Time and Recreational Skills. The physical education program should meet the play desires of children and teach them activities which they may use in their leisure time when they are not at school. These needs challenge the program to include activities which may be used in homes, back yards, basements, or sand lots. Children are often in groups of two, three, or four when out of school. Activities must be taught which may be enjoyed by a few as well as by larger groups.

A good program should include activities usable for parties or picnics and on trips with the family. Games suitable for small areas, the beaches, and picnics are necessary if the recreational needs of children are to be met. Participation in wisely selected activities under proper guidance is needed and should aid the development of character and citizenship for the following reasons:

1. There is an increased amount of leisure time.
2. There is a rise in reported juvenile crimes and delinquency.
3. Older pupils are interested in the social or gang stage and physical activities can be a constructive outlet.
4. Home conditions are changing in many instances and are creating greater needs and responsibilities for outside organizations, including the schools.
5. Facilities and adequate provisions for wholesome leisure time activities are many times not provided by society.

Activities for leisure are needed to develop skills and techniques and a love of wholesome recreation because:

1. The shorter work day and week results in more free time.
2. There is need for recreation to assist in a well-balanced life to preserve good mental and emotional health.
3. Youth has much freedom and the number of questionable modern commercial attractions is great.
4. Outdoor recreation is good for the many sedentary workers in our society.
5. Modern conveniences have given housewives more time for leisure.

The late Dr. Jay B. Nash stressed the fact that the early years are crucial and that 78 per cent of all hobby interests are developed before the age of twelve years. This would surely challenge the elementary school to include activities of a recreational type.

Undesirable commercial recreation may well replace that of the desirable wholesome type if programs are inadequate.

Interscholastic Sports Are Not Recommended in Grades One Through Six. Interscholastic competition means competition of team games or individual and dual activities between two or more schools or outside groups. Highly organized, high-pressured competitive athletics have no place in the elementary schools.

Interscholastic competition places too much stress on winning and permits too few children to participate. Facilities, equipment, and leader-

---

[3] Further discussion of progression may be found in Chapters 10 and 11.

ship are often used for the approximate 10 per cent who have already developed the greatest skills and techniques and who show the greatest potential. The remaining 90 per cent are supposed to be satisfied as passive observers rather than active participants. Such competition lacks group focus by isolating many from participation and impedes the desired outcomes for children.

Children are not developed emotionally, physically, or psychologically to stand the stress and strain of interscholastic competition. Programs should be planned on a wide basis to include the participation of all children.

Many important educational organizations, such as the American Association for Health, Physical Education, and Recreation, the Department of Elementary School Principals of the National Education Association, the National Council of State Consultants in Elementary Education, the National Recreation Association, the National Federation of High School Athletic Associations, and the American Association of School Administrators emphasize no interscholastic competition in elementary schools because it may be physically, emotionally, sociologically, and educationally harmful.

For a better understanding of competition for elementary school children, the Joint Committee on Athletic Competitions for Children of Elementary School and Junior School Age has published a report entitled *Desirable Athletic Competition for Children*. Every educator should read this report. The reader's attention is also called to "The Report of the Committee on School Health of the American Academy of Pediatrics."

Intramural and extramural sports, including sports days and play days, satisfy the competitive desire of children in the sixth, seventh, and eighth grades. However, some elementary schools are now sponsoring interschool competition. The reaction of principals and educators appears to be mixed; a much greater percentage being against than for.

Awards Are Not Recommended Incentives. Each child should engage in a program of physical education for the enjoyment and benefit he gains from it, not for the awards he may be given.

Motivation in the teaching process has often emphasized the external or incentive aspect of the program at the neglect of internal factors of readiness based on growth, needs, and interests. Studies prove that educators cannot expect as much positive behavior from children who are competing for individual awards, prizes, and similar incentives as when they are working and playing together. Competition usually creates out-group hostility and antisocial behavior patterns. At best, awards are artificial incentives. They should be ruled out in favor of the real goals of participation. These should be sufficient reward.

Educators frown on awards which are impossible to be achieved by all, as they tend to point out individual differences. An example of this is the abolishment of the awards for perfect attendance which were so popular at one time. These have been found to be educationally unsound because children who were physically unfit at times came to school merely for that award. Many children in the physical education program might overindulge to gain an award and thus, instead of benefiting from participation, would be harmed by it. Prizes and awards are artificial and questionable ways to stimulate participation and learning and may create a false standard of value.

Physical Education Programs Must Meet Community and Family Needs. Emphasis is being placed on getting parents and members of the community into the schools and teachers out into the community. The needs of each community should aid in determining the organization, procedures, and methods of education. For the best programs, the maximum support of all concerned persons is needed.

Interests in a given community are guides for programs of physical education. Facilities present in the area should be used. Surely, if the community boasts of swimming, fishing, and boating areas, they should be a part of the program of physical education, and planned and administered in joint cooperation with the school, the home, and the community.

It is generally agreed that the greatest success in the educational process emerges when the school and the parents who make up the community share common goals. In this way, parents may learn the true value of play for their children.

Play days, May days, and sports days serve to acquaint the public with the physical education program. Through this medium it is often possible to interest the parents in coming to school to see programs in action. These special programs should be an honest outgrowth of the physical education program and not be planned only for publicity and public entertainment.

Physical education may serve the school and community by providing recreational and leisure activities for children, families, and adults. Civic groups and organizations, both for adults and for children, such as 4-H Clubs, Boy Scouts, Girl Scouts, Rotarians, Kiwanians, Lions, women's clubs, and the like may play an important part in the cooperative planning of physical education programs in community and school.

There appears to be greater family unity when good recreation habits are practiced. It would appear wise for the school to act as the leader, and gain the cooperation of the homes in all programs of physical education and recreation. Parents are willing to aid and cooperate under wise guidance and leadership, especially when they understand the purposes and needs.

Five more principles, discussed in other chapters throughout the text, are only listed here. Reference to their discussion may be found listed below and also in the chapters in which they are discussed.

Provision for the Exceptional Child Must Be a Part of Each Program. See Chapters 9 and 12.

Physical Education Should Be Coordinated with the Whole Curriculum. See Chapter 16.

Facilities, Equipment, and Leadership Should Be Available Before School, at Noon, and After School. See Chapter 13.

Evaluating Physical Education in Terms of Pupil Growth Is Essential. See Chapter 19.

All Audio-Visual Teaching Aids and Resource Materials Should Be Used. See Chapter 18.

Basic Principles of Health Education

What has been said concerning principles of physical education is equally applicable in a discussion of principles of health education. Unless there is understanding of these principles and their application, planning and administering the curriculum for health instruction may become haphazard. As in other areas of education, many changes have taken place in health education. So much progress has been made in health knowledge that teachers are challenged more than ever before to fulfill their obligation for the development of desirable health habits in their children. A consideration of some basic principles will help give direction to program planning and development.

Well-Planned and Sequential Health Instructional Programs Are Necessary. Unless health instruction is planned so that it takes into account the needs and interests of children and is sequential, unnecessary repetition can occur. Repetition has some value in impressing children with the importance of certain materials, but too much can lead to boredom and inattention and create an atmosphere where little learning takes place. There must be sequence and progression so that concepts in each grade or age level can be based on that which has previously been learned.

Planning must be a cooperative project if it is to be the best available. The school should give direct guidance and leadership; however, consultants and children should also be included.

Sequential planning and instruction in health education is no more a mystery than that in other areas of education, yet it has in many cases taken a "back seat." To meet the needs of children today and to use the knowledge given us in research, we can no longer afford haphazard planning.

A Healthful School Environment and Adequate Health Service Are the Responsibility of Each School. A healthful school environment is necessary if the health of children is to be protected. Not only must the building itself be kept clean and free from hazards, but every possible opportunity must be provided for children to practice desirable health habits during the school day. Unless there are adequate facilities and time provided for showers following vigorous exercise and for hand washing before lunch as well as adequate clean toilet facilities, clean water-fountain facilities, pleasant well-lighted classrooms, pleasant and clean lunchroom facilities, children are justified in feeling that instruction is of little value. They must be given opportunity to practice in school those things they have learned.

Adequate health services should be available

at all times. Because laws make attendance mandatory in our elementary schools, provision must be made for individual care in the event of accident or illness. Such services should also make it possible for the child to secure individual attention from a nurse or physician in such matters as medical examinations, eye testing, audiometer testing, and so on. This period of attention often provides an opportunity for individual health guidance for both the child and his parents. Because records of these services are maintained, the nurse and physician involved are able to alert the classroom teacher to special needs of an individual as well as to those common to numbers of children.

The services of dentists, psychologists, and psychiatrists are becoming increasingly important in elementary schools.

Safety inside and outside on the playgrounds demands attention. Periodic examination of all equipment used by children may prevent accidents.

The Conceptual Approach Is the Best Known Way to Help Students Understand the Complexities of Healthful Living. There has been rapid development in the area of health knowledge. It is neither possible nor desirable to expect a child to absorb a multitude of facts and then assume he will be able to apply new knowledge. Facts must be taught in order to arrive at concepts, but these facts must be scientifically and medically sound and general enough to cover large segments of healthful behavior.

The conceptual approach has been used for a long time by effective teachers who have taught not only isolated facts, but the reasons for them. An understanding of both cause and effect is essential to learning, regardless of the terms used. Concepts must be developed in the mind of the child and they result from such factors as motivation, good teaching, favorable environment, and the opportunity to practice.

The influence of many unfavorable environmental factors may defeat the positive health instruction necessary for a child to develop desirable concepts because concepts grow out of a combination of learning and living. Hence, the school, the home, and the community must all be engaged in assisting to develop favorable environmental factors.

Health Education, Evaluation, and Revision, Must Be a Continual Process. New discoveries in teaching techniques and behavioral science and new findings from scientific research and other new knowledge make it necessary to evaluate and revise materials and curriculum constantly. Unless there is some evaluation of what has been done, there is no real basis for change. Good evaluation techniques, when properly used, can show strengths and weaknesses in the health knowledge and habits of children. New approaches and curriculum revision may remedy the latter. Too often new curricula are developed and nothing further is done to discover weaknesses nor to update materials included. This may result in outdated courses of study being presented by the latest, best-known methods. Teaching techniques and curricular content must both be evaluated and changed to reach the desired outcomes.

School, Home, and Community Must Cooperate in Order to Meet Needs of Children in the Societal Setting. Health councils made up of representatives from all concerned segments of society can help to improve health and facilities for healthful living. Unless the society does cooperate to improve conditions and provide healthful settings, the child becomes frustrated in an attempt to practice what he has learned.

It is necessary that adequate provision be made in the home for the practice of desirable health habits. Parents must be aware of what has been taught in school so they can encourage application of this knowledge in daily living because children practice what they see their parents do.

If parents want children to obey the law, they must obey the law themselves. To drive sixty miles an hour in a clearly marked forty-mile speed zone does not indicate to the child that adults show obedience to law. To leave the house daily without eating breakfast is not setting a good health example for a child.

Unless healthful and safe settings are provided in the school and in the community, the child is unable to see the application of those things he has been taught and will not make the necessary change in behavior patterns.

Safety and Accident Prevention Should Be a Part of Health Education. Many educators today believe safety education must be a part of health education. Surely we cannot teach it adequately only when incidents arise. If safety education is planned and made an important part of instruction, we may expect positive results.

The need for safety orientation becomes

more crucial daily. More cars, people, drugs, toys, bicycles, boats, playground and gymnasium equipment, and home appliances represent but a few of today's potential causes of accidents. Accidents rate as the number one killer of children in the age group of one to fourteen years. While statistics show some decline in certain types of accident, we find an increase in others.

Community leaders such as firemen, police, and Red Cross workers, can be valuable aides in the safety program. Audio-visual devices, newspapers, and free and inexpensive materials obtainable from many industries can be invaluable instructional media.

Audio-visual Aids and Materials, Consultants, and Other Educational Media Are Essential to Modern Day Education. No longer are we interested in teaching health education merely from a textbook. While value is found in a text, it should be only one small segment of the means used in health instruction.

Experiences become more meaningful when audio-visual aids are used. Many companies and libraries furnish them. Chapter 18 suggests sources and available materials.

Consultants from the immediate community, the staffs of nearby hospitals and clinics, the school physician, nurse, and dentist, and physical education teachers and coaches all help make health education meaningful and interesting. Visits to health agencies and clinics may also be helpful.

Articles in current magazines and newspapers, and special programs on television and the radio make the subject current to children.

Many schools may be in areas where professional athletes, Olympic participants, or special health clubs are located. These persons and organizations are more than willing to assist in motivating healthful living.

It is estimated that there are nearly 25,000 voluntary health agencies in our nation. These are on the national, state, and local levels and they comprise hundreds of thousands of health professionals and lay workers as well as extensive facilities. Assistance from these agencies is invaluable, as they can help in providing materials, audio-visual aids, speakers, and consultants. It is also important to introduce them and their objectives to students who may need assistance from them later in their lives.

Health Education Is a Specific Part of the Curriculum. Incidental health teaching, offered only when special opportunities arise, cannot meet the major objectives of health education. These objectives are to improve health practices and attitudes and to help solve individual and community problems through the application of scientific knowledge. These objectives must be foremost in all planning and teaching.

How experiences that will embody the application of knowledge are planned and administered will vary. Naturally, incidental teaching is important. So also is correlation with science, language arts, fine arts, and social studies. However, health education has an important body of knowledge of its own which, to be most effective, must be taught as an integral part of the curriculum in addition to being correlated with other subject areas when and where possible.

Questions and Practical Problems

1. Organize a planning committee for the development of the physical education program in grades one through four, or five through eight. Organize committees and assign each a task to plan the program, its administration, and evaluation based on the principles discussed in this chapter.

2. Write an address to be given before the citizens of your town relating to the ways the school and community may cooperate for the betterment of the physical education, health education, and recreational programs within the area. Discussion following your presentation will indicate whether you have aroused sufficient interest by showing the needs and values necessary to accomplish you objectives.

3. Assume that you do not have sufficient equipment for the physical education program in your school. Discuss ways in which you could approach the administrator of your school to convince him of the need for your requisitioned equipment. Be specific in what you need and why you need it.

4. Choose the grade you wish to teach, or are teaching, and plan ways in which you can

correlate physical education with units of work in various parts of the curriculum appropriate for the grade.

5. Prepare an additional list of principles for health and physical education programs.

6. Your principal has asked you to speak before the Board of Education on the need for well-planned health instruction. Prepare an outline for such a speech.

7. How might you keep parents informed of what children are being taught concerning health?

8. List ways in which the teacher might evaluate the application of desirable health knowledge.

9. List concepts in health which you would feel most important to develop during a year of instruction for a grade of your choice.

Selected References

BUCHER, CHARLES A. *Administration of School Health and Physical Education Programs* (Fifth Edition). St. Louis: The C. V. Mosby Co., 1971.

CLARK, EVELYN A. "Needed Improvements in Elementary School Health Education Programs," *Journal of Health, Physical Education, and Recreation* Vol. 38, No. 2, Feb. 1967, pp. 28–29.

EBERLY, VIRGINIA D. "What the New Look in Education Implies for Physical Education," *Journal of Health, Physical Education, and Recreation*, Vol. 37, No. 7, Sept. 1966, p. 28.

FODOR, JOHN, and GUS DALIS. *Health Instruction—Theory and Application*. Philadelphia: Lea & Febiger, 1966.

Joint Conference of the Division for Girls' and Women's Sports and Division for Men's Athletics. *Values in Sports*. Washington, D.C.: American Association for Health, Physical Education, and Recreation, 1963.

KILANDER, FREDERICK H. "An International Recommendation on Health Education in Primary Schools," *Journal of Health, Physical Education, and Recreation*, Vol. 39, No. 2, Feb. 1968, p. 37.

LOCKE, LAWRENCE F. "The Movement Movement," *Journal of Health, Physical Education, and Recreation*, Vol. 37, No. 1, Jan. 1966, p. 26.

MAYSHARK, CYRUS, DONALD SHAW, and WALLACE BEST. *Administration of School Health Programs—Its Theory and Practice*. St. Louis: The C. V. Mosby Co., 1967.

NEMIR, ALMA. *The School Health Program*. Philadelphia: W. B. Saunders Co., 1965.

School Health Education Study, *Health Education—A Conceptual Approach to Curriculum Design*. St. Paul: 3-M Company Educational Press, 1967.

VANNIER, MARYHELEN. *Teaching Health in Elementary Schools*. New York: Harper & Row, Publishers, Inc., 1963.

VANNIER, MARYHELEN. "Toward Better Physical Education," *The Instructor*, Vol. 72, No. 5, Feb. 1963.

WILLIAMS, JESSIE F. *Principles of Physical Education*, 8th ed. Philadelphia: W. B. Saunders Co., 1964.

PART TWO

The Child

CHAPTER 7

Child Growth and Development Factors

It has been an established practice for many years for teachers to accept individual differences in children. The organization of two or three reading groups within the same grade is not uncommon. This is a good educational procedure because it accepts individual differences. We know that all children do not learn at the same rate.

To select meaningful activities in elementary physical education programs, all known facts relating to child growth and development must also be applied. Differences in ability within a given age group must be accepted. All children do not develop alike at the same rate nor do they all grow alike in size and stature. Children do not all have the same start in life. Some are ill at birth and in early childhood, the home atmosphere makes a difference, and actual mental abilities differ. How can these facts in child growth and development be used to aid a physical education program?

In addition to applying general facts gained from her knowledge of child growth and development, each teacher should secure data from all sources relating to each individual child. These data may come from medical records, tests and examinations, conferences with former teachers, parent conferences, and individual discussions with the child. The teacher should spend some time trying out recommended activities for her class and note through careful observation the range of abilities and interests among the students.

Specific patterns of maturation will perhaps fit the majority of children at a given age level, but provisions should be made in the program to provide experiences in physical education which will meet individual differences and which will aid each child. If this is accomplished a teacher will be presenting meaningful activities because she has selected those which are within the child's range of ability and meet his needs and his interests.

A study of the physical, social, and emotional development of the child may aid the teacher in understanding why John is afraid of a ball, why Mary fears the swings, and why Jack seems to gain the most pleasure from not sharing anything with anyone. What causes these fears and the lack of cooperation and sharing? Is it something related to home and play experiences? These are questions which must be answered before the teacher can succeed in helping the individual child. Was John hit by a ball and injured? Did Mary fall from a swing or have an unpleasant experience with swings? Is Jack an only child or is he not permitted to share his toys with neighbors at home? Children are sensitive to their peers. Why isn't Jane accepted? Why won't the children hold Jimmy's hand in a circle game? The teacher must recognize the motivating forces behind these actions and correct them accordingly. She must respect all individual differences and needs. She must have a thorough understanding of the children for whom she is planning the program.

Typical Patterns of Growth and Development

Each human being passes through certain stages of development. During the early years these stages are infancy, childhood, the preteens, and the teens. As members of a single species, all human beings follow the same pattern and grow and develop in a similar, predictable sequence, controlled by enzymes. However, there is a wide range of individual growth patterns. Body parts, organs, and systems develop in each individual in a unique way. Each of us inherits a different genetic makeup, a different potential, and so each stage of development comes to us at a time generally determined by heredity. The process of growth and development is called maturation and is largely controlled by the endocrine system. At each stage the course of maturation is influenced by physical and social factors in the environment. Of course there is much overlapping from one stage of the life cycle to the next.

Stages of Growth

The First Five Years. The moment of birth is the organism's first experience of independent functioning. The death of newborn children is a cause for great concern. Prenatal maternal care, modern medical techniques for delivery, and hospital care of the newborn give many children a better start in life. From the moment of birth, the body's systems—respiration, circulation, digestion, excretion, nervous activity, and endocrine-gland activity—begin the functions that will continue throughout life.

The newborn baby—one of the most helpless of beings—must struggle to survive. One of man's most basic biological characteristics is the long period of his infancy and immaturity. But the slowed-down growth rate is of great importance to the human being. At birth the human being is a bundle of potentialities waiting to be actualized. More than for any other living creature, self-development in the human being will determine whether or not his unique potential is fulfilled.

The first year of life is one of remarkable growth. By the end of the first year, the birth weight is tripled. The brain, one fourth of its adult weight at birth, is now half its adult size. The skeleton, soft and pliable at birth, has begun to harden.

At birth, most bones are quite soft and resemble cartilage, a connective tissue. Bone tissue begins to form and harden. The process of hardening, called ossification, includes the gradual fusion of the 270 bones of the newborn infant to the lower number (206) in the adult. This includes the fusion of the bones of the cranium which protect the brain.

Teeth may erupt during the sixth or seventh month, so that on the first birthday a child may have as many as six temporary teeth. The heart has doubled its size by the end of the first year.

The Childhood Years. The year-old child is ready to explore his environment, and in the years that follow, he will learn to walk, climb, jump, talk, and sing. He will also learn to feed and dress himself and to attend to other physical needs. The use of tools, paint, clay, hammer, and nails mark another area of development.

By the end of the period of infancy, a child is deemed ready for school—for the discipline of classroom life and for such learning activities as reading, arithmetic, and physical education.

Preadolescence. The growth and development of boys and girls during preadolescence (6 to 12 years) can be identified with a variety of physical and social-emotional changes.

By obviously slow but steady physical growth, followed by a marked "resting period," nature appears to be preparing the child for a sudden growth spurt. This often occurs as early as eleven years of age.

Social-emotional changes occur gradually, sometimes hesitatingly, through situations that provide the preadolescent child with opportunities to extend or to modify his feelings of self-dependency, cooperation, antagonism between boy and girl groups, sportsmanship, and loyalty. Just prior to the onset of adolescence, he may become overcritical, rebellious, changeable, and uncooperative.

The Teen Years. The most striking changes of the teen years begin when the pituitary gland brings about changes in the reproductive system. This is the beginning of a wonderful and often bewildering period of growth and development. There is no absolute time when these changes begin. They may start anywhere between the tenth and fifteenth years. With the onset of sexual maturation, the individual arrives at puberty. We speak of this stage as adolescence, or the teen years.

(Courtesy of The Delmer F. Harris Co. Photo by J. Louis Browne.)

Early adolescence is a period of rapid growth. This accounts for the lack of coordination which is sometimes referred to as "the awkward age." All people mature at different rates. Girls, on an average, tend to develop earlier than boys. During early adolescence, girls are often taller and heavier than boys of the same age. Bones, still in the process of hardening, are susceptible to injury. For this reason contact sports with the risk of broken bones can be dangerous in the early teens. Most of the permanent teeth (usually about twenty-eight) have appeared by fourteen years of age.

The heart muscle, however, is relatively small. It may not be able to supply the body with adequate supplies of blood during strenuous exercise. For this reason, youngsters should heed signs of fatigue and avoid excessive activity when they are tired or tense.

Many teen-agers begin to feel the "moods"—sometimes of enthusiasm and exhilaration, sometimes of indecision and unhappiness—which can be explained by the changes in body chemistry taking place at this time.

Motor Development and Its Implications for Physical Education. Classroom teachers and physical educators should be familiar with the characteristics of motor development in children from infancy to adolescence. A thorough knowledge of these factors will enable the classroom teacher and physical educator to plan a program of activity that will meet the needs and interests of each individual with whom they work.

Individuals are classified in various ways according to age. The most common are estimations of chronological, anatomical, physiological, and mental age. These may all be helpful to the teacher and the physical educator.

Chronological age represents the age of an individual in calendar years and months. *Anatomical* age is usually related to the ossification of bones. Quite frequently the small bones in the wrist are used as a measure of this development. An x-ray examination is needed to determine anatomical age. Sometimes the stage of dentition is also used to determine on this scale. *Physiological* age is related to puberty. It may be determined by the quality and texture of the pubic hair in boys and menstruation in girls. X-ray of bones is also used for such purposes. The last classification is *mental* age, which is arrived at by determining, through tests, the degree to which an individual has adjusted to his environment and is able to solve certain problems.

Although the teacher and physical educator will be interested in all the age classifications of children, he should have special interest in anatomical and physiological ages. These, it seems, are very important to motor learning and in selecting activities related to the needs and interests of the student.

The characteristics of physical and motor growth in the child during infancy, the preschool years, early school years, and middle school years are very important for the classroom teacher and physical educator to know. A study of these characteristics reveals the child as a dynamic individual, craving activity.

Infancy. We have seen that during prenatal life the fetus grows very rapidly. At birth and for about eighteen months thereafter development occurs from the head downward or in the *cephalocaudal* direction. The fact that the arms develop faster than the legs is an indication of this. During prenatal life the arm buds develop before the leg buds. Development also is from the axes of the body to the extremities or in the *proximodistal* direction. For example, the ability to use the hand develops in the palm of the hand before the fingers. This may be seen by watching a baby manipulate a block. He pushes it around with the palm of his hand for some time before he is able to pick it up with his fingers.

In discussing the cephalocaudal and proximodistal directions of development, it should be brought out that questions are frequently raised as to whether educational programs for young children should be concerned mainly with big-muscle activity or with the fine-muscle activity that is associated with the use of the fingers, eyes, and the like. Some educators feel that the child's main concern during the growing years should be big-muscle activity. This is based on the premise that fine-muscle coordinations develop after the large-muscle coordinations in the child. On the other hand, some educators point out that although there is some basis for this argument, it is not entirely true. They note that a child can pick up objects with his thumb and forefinger and perform many manual manipulations, thus utilizing the fine muscles, before he is able to walk and run, activities that utilize the large muscles. According to some psychologists the choice of activities should not be based only on whether they involve large-muscle or small-muscle actions, but should provide for both types of activity. In regard to the physical education program, big-muscle activity plays an important part in normal growth and development and during the growing years the child should have ample opportunity for such activity in order to become a well-developed, healthy human being.

Preschool years. During the preschool years the child develops many physical skills. He develops skills in running, climbing, and skipping. These not only aid in his physical development but also provide a basis for social relationships. He associates with other children and finds out how they react to their environment. During this period the child gains great pleasure from his physical activity. This affects his emotional life. As he gains ability in certain physical acts, he gains self-confidence. He has better use of his arms and legs and utilizes more and more skills. This motor development makes possible more avenues of learning as he begins to explore his environment.

Certain maturation levels should be recognized in children. If allowed to develop independently, a child will do things, to a certain point, as a part of the natural growth process. Experiments have been carried out in which two-year-old children have been prompted to button their own clothes. However, at the end of several weeks of practice they did not do any better than another group of children of the same age who had not practiced. Other experiments have shown that this also applies in the learning of such skills as skipping and tricycling. The motor skills that are provided for children should be related to their readiness to utilize and perform them. There is an urgent need for more research as to what skills children should develop at certain ages. More should be known about skills that are of value in themselves, as distinguished from skills that develop a child socially and intellectually, and skills useful for a limited period of time, as contrasted with skills that are developed for future use.

Motor learning has been recognized as an essential for all children and important to the social and emotional life of a child. It helps him to become independent. It plays a part in his intellectual development. Through motor skills

(Courtesy of Lind Climber Company.)

the child acquires concepts as to size and weight and finds out about such things as gravity and balance. Emotionally they help him to solve problems that would otherwise enrage and stump him. Newell Kephart, while head of the Achievement Center at Purdue University, conducted much research that supports the relation of motor skills to the mental as well as physical development of the child.

Early School Years. During early school years the child acquires fundamental skills that affect his current existence and that he will also use throughout life. One study of men twenty years old and older found that many of their hobbies and adult leisure-time interests were based on their childhood experiences. The physical educator should recognize the implications of this for his work. If adults are to have physical skill in various activities, their foundation should be laid during the early years of life.

During the early school years the child develops socially. He makes contacts through motor activities. He is accepted by the group if he can participate with some degree of skill. He gains independence by learning to do things by himself. He increases his knowledge in respect to his environment. In all this development, motor skills play an important part. Through them he develops his whole organism.

The classroom teacher and physical educator need to know what skills children possess at certain age levels—those skills possessed by most children, and those possessed by just a few—the importance of skills in the lives of children, and the environmental factors contributing to or thwarting skill development. These are essential facts if physical education is to contribute further in the development of the child.

Middle School Years. During the years that approach adolescence as well as during adolescence, the body's musculature and capacity to learn motor skills is markedly increased.

During the elementary years boys are superior to girls in many activities, such as running, jumping, and throwing. This is even more pronounced in the middle school years. This can be explained by the fact that boys usually have more opportunities than girls to participate in these activities, and also because of certain anatomical differences. A girl has a wider pelvis, and the angle of attachment of the femur to the thigh is different in girls than in boys. Boys are also stronger than girls. After the age of thirteen, fourteen, or fifteen years, boys and girls probably should not participate together in the more strenuous types of physical activities.

Developmental Facts About Children That Have Implications for the Physical Education Program. The State Department of Education for the State of Wisconsin has developed as a result of much research and study *A Guide to Curriculum Building in Physical Education— Elementary Schools.* This bulletin is designed to give direction in respect to program development and also teaching procedures. Part of this bulletin is reproduced here by permission, under the subheads (1) Physical Growth and Development, (2) Motor Skill Development, (3) Knowledge and Understanding Development, and, (4) Social and Emotional Development; all these have implications for the classroom teacher and the physical educator.

Basis for Development of Program

Decision making in the development of a physical education program for boys and girls must be based on a thorough knowledge of growth and development needs of children.

Any program must be constantly reviewed, evaluated, and revised periodically, in the light of research findings and experience, if it is to keep pace with the needs of children in our time. In the development of this guide the following important points have been selected for consideration in the development of sound bases for decision making in the process of development of program in physical education. . . .

Physical Growth and Development. Physical growth progresses in a sequential, predictable manner. This process is called maturation.

Growth proceeds from simple to complex and from general to specific.

Growth and development are characterized by periods in which the dominant activity is that of acquiring new experiences followed by periods of integrating the newness into the child's life.

In development, one aspect of growth may be slowed down while another dominates, i.e., during concentration in acquisition of language skill, motor development may be slowed.

Hereditary factors are important in shaping the design, but growth and development can be markedly influenced by environmental forces.

Growth is continuous but varies in rate; the body does not grow as a whole nor in all directions at once.

Each human being has his own peculiar way of developing even within a uniform growth pattern sequence, therefore both normative data which indicates age level expectancies and sequential individual records are important in proper assessment of growth progress of individual children.

Children who are tall or short at birth, tend to maintain the same relative position at six and at nineteen although during adolescence the trend may be temporarily changed.

Tall children tend to become pubescent early and have an early growth spurt.

Growth of the respiratory and vascular organs tend to keep pace with growth in bone and muscle tissue thereby reducing the possibility of physiological imbalance in meeting the needs of expanding body frame.

Throughout childhood and especially during adolescence, the heart grows more rapidly than the arterial system; as a result, relative cardiac competency increases, heart rate decreases, and blood pressure increases.

Girls are consistently more mature than boys in their skeletal development with this sex difference tending to increase with age.

Fat-bone ratio decreases with age in boys and increases with age in girls.

The legs grow faster than the arms; the arms grow faster than the trunk; and the trunk faster than the head.

Rapidly growing arms and legs demand use; children have an insistent need for activity.

A child broadens out in the first year of life, then slims down to the age of seven or eight, broadening again as the child faces adolescence (shoulders for boys and hips for girls).

Motor Skill Development. Motor learning is only one type of learning important in the development of the young child, but a high percentage of the child's time and energy is devoted to it; motor learning is frequently closely associated with other learnings in the young child's development.

Skill development is dependent upon structural (skeletal and muscular) development and neurophysiological maturity.

Motor skill development proceeds in generally the same sequence, but not at the same rate for all children.

Most children have developed skill in basic motor activities in a rudimentary form by the age of six or seven, but these basic motor skills are refined and developed into more complex skills only through repeated use in a variety of situations as the child grows.

While all children love physical activity, not all children automatically become skilled in movement. Most children require instruction in basic motor skills as well as opportunity for practice if these skills are to progress to a mature useful level.

Environmental opportunity is essential in skill development. Children may be maturationally ready long before the environment stimulates them to action.

Adequate opportunity to explore and move freely as well as wise encouragement and assistance by parents in preschool movement experiences are essential to rapid progress in development and refinement of motor skill in the early school years.

Much of the deceleration in the rate of motor development that sets in about the age of three is attributable to the lack of challenging environmental stimulation and to stereotyped playground equipment.

During the elementary school years the child learns many new motor skills and improves on those previously acquired.

Changes usually observed in the refinement of motor skills are in the direction of increased strength, speed, versatility, precision, and smoothness of execution.

Performance scores in basic motor activities increase as a function of age but little is known concerning the patterning of movements as these skills are refined.

Increase in speed of eye-hand coordination accompanies increase in age during the elementary school years.

Motor reaction time shows a marked decrease during the elementary school years.

Two sidedness in motor functioning is gradually replaced by one sidedness during early childhood but stability is not often established until the age of six. Intra-individual discrepancies with respect to different body parts and even with respect to different activities performed by a single part (writing, throwing, batting) are not uncommon after the age of six.[1]

The extent to which a child develops his inherent potentialities for motor skills depends somewhat on temperamental and personality factors, such as venturesomeness, aggressiveness, persistence and curiosity.

Energy level affects the development of motor skill.

Children from over-protecting homes

---

[1] Considerable research is now in progress concerning the importance of established unilaterality in the acquisition of such skills as reading and writing.

tend to be physically apprehensive and relatively retarded in gross motor development.

High levels of personality anxiety have been found to inhibit trial-and-error learning in children.

Development of skill in basic motor activities can be a "game" or "stunt" to a child in his early development. Once learned, the child needs a challenge to use it in a variety of ways if it is to be improved, or even maintained at a high performance level.

Participation in a game or organized activity will not guarantee improvement of motor performance; only when a child has the minimum level of skill to meet successfully the demands of the game is there likely to be maximum motivation and opportunity for motor learning in the situation.

Understanding of and appreciation for quality of performance are important to the child in the development of improving motor performance.

Goals set for the child in the light of previous achievement and not merely in terms of class norms on general class goals are essential to the child's understanding and satisfaction in his own individual progress.

Sex differences in ability and interest are apparent as early as kindergarten in some activities and are quite marked by second grade in such activities as throwing, catching, jumping, striking and most locomotor activities.

It is probable that the difference between boys' and girls' performances can be in a large measure attributed to cultural expectations which tend to limit the boy's or girl's experience to certain movement or activity areas; it is also probable that differences in performances by boys and girls, at least in efficiency of movement patterns, can be reduced through physical education programs.

Achievement in skills must be evaluated in terms of quality of pattern of movement as well as in terms of the end product of movement if progress in motor skill development is to be accurately assessed.

Knowledge and Understanding Development. Knowledge and understanding of the body in movement are important to the child if he is to:

Develop a full appreciation of what is possible in movement.

Recognize the common elements in a variety of movement situations.

Recognize and apply principles of movement in many different movement situations.

Movement experiences are important in the development of concepts of time, space, motion, acceleration, deceleration, force, balance.

Movement experiences can make use of and can contribute to many other areas of interest in the child's living such as science, reading, art, music, mathematics, and health.

Through movement education, the child can gain a personal understanding and appreciation of the physiological effects and benefits of activity.

Through movement experience, the child can learn to recognize psychological effects of stress or excitement.

The child can learn to recognize muscular tension and to understand the value of skill in conscious relaxation in helping him meet the stresses of modern daily living.

Social and Emotional Development. Physical education can provide opportunity for the child to gain understanding and skills necessary to balance satisfying activity with control and release of excessive tension.

The child can learn to relax consciously and can make use of this skill in his daily living.

Social and emotional growth through group games and activities requires readiness to meet the demands of such activities; children not ready to meet the physical demands of the games being played by their peers either because of lack of previous opportunity for practice or because of immaturity, may tend to withdraw, or to become aggressive or distracting in a class in a "cover-up" attempt.

Social and emotional readiness to meet the demands of games and activities requires planning the program at a child's level and not in terms of those things on which an adult pattern is imposed.

Good habits of sportsmanship, development of sensitivity to the needs and to feelings of others, positive leadership characteristics are not automatic results of group participation in physical education; activities must be examined for emotional and social growth potential, followed by careful planning, teaching, and guidance if the potential is to be realized for individual children.

The total child is involved in any learning situation, therefore while the contribution of physical education to the physical growth and development of motor skill in children should be the center of emphasis, sensitivity to the possibilities for self-realization through movement experience is essential in a good program.

The child's view of the goals or motivation in a movement experience may not coincide with the teacher's view; it is essential that the teacher be sensitive to the way in which the child views his movement experiences if they are to be made meaningful to him in his everyday living outside of the gymnasium and classroom.

Dull, unimaginative, narrow, repetitive programs may be the cause of discipline problems in class and underachievement in physical education.

The shy, or the unskilled child is frequently lost in the demands of "low, unorganized games"; programs of physical education must provide for the development of the slow learner in motor skills, as well as for the challenge of the highly skilled performer.

Well-planned and guided experiences in physical education can affect the child's development of confidence in self and can influence him to become more outgoing, venturesome, and persistent in trying activities which require some courage and initiative.

Socially ascendant behavior may be increased by improving a child's motor skills.

Motor activity is an important outlet for emotional expression and a source of basic satisfactions and self-expression. Increased motor competence can help reduce frustrations encountered in the child's environment.

Emotional release possible through satisfying physical activity may be dependent to a large extent on skill in movement; this can be important to the mental health of the child and the adult.

Proficiency in motor skills determines to a large extent a boy's prestige and leadership status in his peer group at elementary school age. Programs of physical education should provide opportunity for boys to experience success in areas of interest suited to them rather than force conformity and limit opportunity to a narrow range of "major" sports.

Development of basic motor skill is not as important for social success for girls in elementary school, but will affect the ability of girls to develop desired skills in such culturally important activities as bowling, golf, tennis, badminton, skating, skiing, and swimming in young adult and adult life. High school and college age is too late for maximum satisfaction in the development of skill in these areas of specialization, if careful movement background has not been developed.[2]

Growth and Development Characteristics and Needs of Children

The following list[3] of needs of children in age groups from five to thirteen should assist the teacher in understanding the needs of children in various age groups and present a challenge to the program of physical education.

Needs of Age Group Five, Six, Seven

1. Expression through movement is necessary for growth.

2. It is part of the child's development to play in mud, wade in puddles, fall in snow, walk in fallen leaves and roll down hills. He may approximate rock and tree climbing activities on playground climbing apparatus. Playing animals (walking on all fours) will develop muscles of the back and

[2] Curriculum Bulletin No. 28, *A Guide to Curriculum Building in Physical Education.* State of Wisconsin, Department of Public Instruction, Madison, Wisconsin, Aug. 1963.

[3] From "Growth and Development Characteristics and Needs" (Chart), *Organizing the Elementary School for Living and Learning*, Association for Supervision and Curriculum Development, Washington, D.C., The National Education Association, 1947.

abdomen. Use of the walking board (balance beam) will help correct pronation (flat feet). Scooters and coaster wagons develop the leg muscles and fulfill a need for speed.

3. There must be opportunity to organize simple group play, to skip and dance in small groups. Half a dozen children are capable of playing together for a fifteen minute period or longer. All demand attention from one another and demand their own "turns."

4. Dramatic activities and rhythmic activities are essential.

5. The withdrawn child must be encouraged gradually to find his place in the group.

6. Since the attention span is short the periods should be short.

7. The child should sleep about eleven hours.

8. Although the child from time to time may reject certain foods because of texture and strong taste, variety in the menu will provide the necessary nutritional requirement.

9. The child needs training both at home and in school in habits of personal hygiene; covering coughs and sneezes, using the handkerchief, keeping fingers away from the mouth and nose, etc. He needs training in the choice of clothing appropriate to weather.

Needs of Age Group Eight, Nine, Ten

1. The child needs an assured position in a social group. Membership in a gang or secret club fills this need. At this period children need a certain amount of freedom in setting up their own standards and rules, yet strongly desire understanding and sympathy from adults. Participation in family affairs is important.

2. There must be full opportunity to develop body control, strength, and endurance. The child of 8, 9, or 10 years needs activities involving use of the whole body; stunts, throwing and catching, running "it" games, with their accompanying noise, etc. Seasonal play is important; kites, marbles, and the like.

3. The child needs organized team play. He is willing to practice in order to become adequate in skills for games; he may gain self-confidence by excelling in some one thing.

4. It is as important for children to learn good followership as it is to learn good leadership.

5. Encouragement to exercise creatively in rhythms should be given.

6. Activities such as playing in caves and brooks, gathering nuts, and making campfires are needed. Bicycles and skates are enjoyed.

7. The child should sleep about ten hours. He usually does not get enough rest. A quiet period in the afternoon, not necessarily bed, may prevent overfatigue.

8. The child's increased interests in foods provide a basis for better understanding of the seven basic foods in maintaining good health.

9. The teacher must see that pupils having visual or aural defects are always seated in strategic positions in the classroom.

10. Close supervision is required to assure properly adjusted furniture and to prevent slumping over desks. Creation of an awareness that good posture is a comfortable posture is important.

Needs of Age Group Eleven, Twelve, Thirteen

1. There must be careful supervision in order that children of these ages may choose games proportionate to their strength and appropriate for their development needs.

2. Skill is essential for successful group participation. The child is willing to practice skills in order to gain proficiency, but needs informed guidance.

3. Games of increased organization such as softball, kickball, modified soccer, and so on, are needed. The sedentary or self-protective child may need encouragement to play out of doors. Differentiation of activities for boys and girls may begin at these ages.

4. Special provision must be made for the child who is reaching his literate capacity and may be able to gain his chief satisfactions from muscular activities.

5. It is as important for children to develop good spectatorship as it is for them to develop good sportsmanship.

6. More mature interests must be met by more mature programs. There must be opportunities for many types of social contact. Club programs, church groups, Boy and Girl

Scouts, YMCA, Campfire Girls, camping and the like fill the need for guidance.

7. Provision must be made for a growing interest in social dancing.

8. The rest needs are about eight or nine hours or longer.

9. The child's increasing desire to improve his personal appearance provides excellent opportunity to remedy habitual postural defects and to establish a balanced diet.

These needs challenge the physical education programs to provide activities which are significant and meaningful to children; which meet and satisfy the needs, ages, development, and abilities of children; and which are adaptable to the areas and places available for children to engage in play. Participation in activities which give opportunity for vigorous physical activity to aid in organic growth and development and which develop specific skills and techniques is a must. Challenging experiences and activities which assist in developing attitudes of pride in success and accomplishments and those which have definite carry-over values for future use help spell out the criteria to be used in the selection of activities to meet the needs of children.

Play—A Means of Meeting the Developmental Needs of Children

The fifth-grade children of the Salamanca Elementary School were restless and impatient. Fidgeting in their seats they watched the hands of the clock slowly work toward eleven o'clock. Then, as the bell rang marking the end of the period, their faces lit up with smiles, and there were uncontrollable whoops of joy. Little arms and legs moved at double time to the school exit and on toward the playground. As they left the confinement of school corridors behind, the fast walk turned into a gallop. There were cheers and yells. Jack Worth, ten-year-old, shouted, "Come on, Rich, let's get the balls." Doris Brown and six other girls legged it as fast as they could to try and beat them out.

These children were anxious and in a hurry to get where they were going. The eager looks on their faces, tenseness of their muscles, and explosive, limitless energy demonstrated that play is the child's work. It carries its own drive. It is something children want to do. As Arnold Gesell, the well-known child psychologist, said, "[Play] rises spontaneously out of instinctive promptings which represent developmental needs. It prepares for maturity. It is a natural enjoyable exercise of growing powers." He continued, "Play never ceases to be a major business throughout childhood. Nature plants strong play propensities in every normal child to make sure that certain basic needs of development will be satisfied."

Nature has not left children's play to chance. It has literally kicked them into activity. It has pushed them into action so that their hearts, lungs, muscles, and the rest of their bodies will develop properly.

Observe elementary school children over a period of hours. They are a mass of activity. It is hard for them to sit still. They must have action. It is not deviltry created in the mind of the child in order to annoy the teacher. It is activity that cannot be suppressed—it must be expressed. This desire for activity is being satisfied when children burst out of the schoolroom doors onto the playground. It is being met as they climb through the maze of the jungle gym. It expresses itself in creative dance movements. Growth and development are proceeding in harmony as the girls jump rope or the boys play tag.

Some years ago an Eastern university conducted an experiment. The investigators asked Mel Ott, then a professional baseball player, to come to the playground at nine o'clock one morning. They also requested six-year-old Johnny Beckett to be there. Mel was asked to do everything Johnny did for as long a time as he could. It was a "follow the leader" game and in this case Johnny was the leader. Mel started out enthusiastically—eager to go. Every time Johnny took a somersault, Mel followed suit. When Johnny ran, Mel ran. After Johnny, Mel came swishing down the slide. As Johnny wriggled through the bars on one side of the jungle gym, Mel twisted and turned up and down on the other side.

Those who are familiar with children know the result of such an experiment. Although Mel was in excellent physical condition, he became very tired by eleven o'clock, exhausted at twelve, and had to give up a short time later. Johnny's thirst for activity, his boundless energy, and his continual craving for something more to do proved too much for an adult.

W. R. Smith, a psychologist, says, "Play is the most direct motivation possible and is the vocation of youth and avocation of the mature." Webster's defines it as an exercise or series of actions intended for amusement or diversion. Many years ago in his book *Play in Education*, Joseph Lee termed play an instinctive activity, looking toward an ideal. John Dewey, the well-known educator, believed play consisted of activities not consciously performed for the sake of any results beyond themselves. *The Dictionary of Education* defines it as any pleasurable activity carried on for its own sake, without reference to ulterior purpose or future satisfactions. *The Encyclopedia of Modern Education* states: "Play is defined not by the type of activity engaged in but by the distinctive attitude which the players take toward activity. In play, it is the activity itself, rather than the result, that counts."

These are a few definitions of play. To a great degree they all say the same thing: play is a natural activity which carries its own drive and is characterized by joy, pleasure, and happiness.

Directed Play. Play is a medium for the education of children but *it must be properly directed* if it is to achieve desirable outcomes. There must be qualified leadership lest it become misdirected and diverted into destructive channels. This fact was well illustrated recently at a school where there were no planned activities or leadership during a long noon hour. A factory, two short blocks down the railroad tracks from the school, had recently closed and moved its business out of town. At the end of the noon hour the first day after the industrial site had been vacated, 300 panes of glass were broken by the boys from this school. Was this "play?" The answer is "Yes." Was it directed? The answer, of course, is "No." The fellow who won this noon-hour game was the one who broke the most panes of glass. Pleasure was gained by the boys and they gratified their desire to play. This play was destructive in nature. It was misdirected because of lack of planning and qualified leadership. No planned activities of a constructive type were offered by the school. The school had failed to provide equipment, facilities, and leadership for wholesome play.

The question can be asked, is it necessary to teach a child to play? In a sense the answer is "No." It is not necessary to teach him, but it is necessary to direct his play to worthwhile activities. One professor has stated that education should help an individual to do better those things he is going to do anyway. The child is going to play. But the school has not fulfilled its responsibility unless this play is properly and meaningfully directed and guided.

The play of children is spontaneous. Educators should work *with* this motivation and not *against* it. Through play they can help to develop the most sound standards for living.

Achieving Children's Goals Through Directed Play. Every child has certain goals which represent basic human needs. Each of these may be satisfied in many ways. Play is one important way. A few of these goals are discussed.

1. *The child's desire for new experiences and adventure.* The child desires new experiences and adventure. He constantly wants new challenges to meet, new mysteries to unravel, and new adventures to stir his blood. In play he is constantly meeting these new experiences. Each game affords a different adventure depending on its nature, where it is played, and with whom it is played. New learnings are outcomes of these new experiences. Those which are satisfying he will seek again. Those which are annoying will be avoided. As he grows older and his backlog of experiences becomes greater, his store of knowledge, attitudes, skills, and understanding will be richer. An individual is the sum of his experiences. Therefore, it is important that as many rich and satisfying experiences as possible be provided. Play is one avenue for achieving this goal.

2. *The child's desire for security.* The child needs security. It is one of the most important essentials for a happy life. It may or may not come from his father and mother. It can come to the child from his own group in school. How secure is he with them? Do his buddies include him in their play when they go on a hike or to a birthday party? Is he standing on the sideline at the playfield hoping Jim will want him on his team? Through play and proper leadership each child can be provided with the opportunity for the success and security that he needs.

3. *The child's desire for recognition.* The development of self requires recognition. Each individual wants others to know he exists and has something to contribute to the group. It is human nature to want to receive some form of recognition. Through play the teacher can provide varying situations where each child has the opportunity to be acknowledged.

4. *The child's desire for participation.* All children want to participate, either with a group or with another individual. Each wants to be able to contribute something to this individual or group. Basically, no child wishes to stand on the sideline and be a wallflower. No child wishes to be left out of the plans for the Christmas party or ball game. Play offers innumerable situations where all can participate regardless of skill and ability.

5. *The child's desire for pleasant emotions.* Every child wants to feel happy. His physical and mental well-being are dependent on it. Each desires the satisfaction of those things which bring pleasant emotions. The natural urge to play and the joy that it brings help to satisfy this basic need.

It can be seen that play offers many avenues for satisfying the desires and wishes of children. As such, it can be utilized in an educationally constructive way. It offers an excellent medium for guiding the child toward adulthood.

Adapting Play to the Child. In order to achieve the greatest possible benefits, play *must be adapted to the needs of the individual child.* Individuals differ. They vary in respect to intelligence, emotions, physique, social background, race, economic standards, educability, and in many other ways. In respect to play, individual differences are significant.

Physical Differences. The body comes in many sizes, shapes, and models. Sheldon, in his *Varieties of Human Physique,* found that there are 76 different body types. There are the fat, the lean, the short, the tall, and the many combinations of these. In respect to physical aspects, there are also those who are strong, weak, sickly, healthy, well-skilled, poorly skilled, and who possess other physical traits. Each physical characteristic has its influence on the total response of the child. One must consider these factors in play. The child who is overweight will not have the same endurance, skill, or perhaps even the same interest in a fast running game as one who is an alert live wire of normal size and weight. A wise teacher notes all these factors and works accordingly with each individual child—not insisting that what is good for one is good for all.

Intellectual Differences. The fact that intellect varies with each individual has implications for the benefits each individual will derive from play situations. All of the children participating in activities will not learn the same things or be able to learn them at the same rate. This will mean more individual guidance and help for some, clearer explanations, more time to grasp the rules and understand the strategies involved, and helpful demonstrations. The learning curve of each boy and girl will differ. The progress of each must be analyzed and noted separately. A wise teacher knows this is true when the child is attempting to solve a mathematical problem. It is also true in a play situation.

Neuromuscular Differences. The ability to perform such fundamental activities as hopping, skipping, jumping, throwing, running, leaping, and combinations of these movements varies with each individual. One has only to watch a group of children to observe the differences. Mary can skip on her right foot but not on her left. John can throw a ball pretty well but cannot catch one skillfully. Each child differs as to the skills he possesses and the rate at which he is capable of learning new ones. Each individual should be guided to develop to the best of his or her ability. Neuromuscular differences, as well as physical differences, intelligence, and other factors, determine what each child will achieve.

Emotional and Social Differences. Temperament affects play. What is the emotional range of the child? Is he optimistic or pessimistic? Is he a good competitor? Does he have self-assurance or is he timid? Such factors may determine the success of a child in his relations with fellow students and group participation in play. The very factor of timidity, for example, may slow him considerably in developing skills. Through careful guidance the teacher may give the timid child needed assurance in developing a skill and may help cheer the pessimist through his accomplishments. This is also true of other emotional traits. Some children lack the desire to excel. Others have too much for their own good. Some are too easily satisfied with just the bare necessities of life and never accept a challenge to go further or do more than merely meet these. Others go too far in the opposite direction. The child with the drive to be always on top, the child with the revenge drive, and the child who refuses to accept reality and habitually rationalizes—each of these may possess too strong a desire to excel. These drives may be good or bad, depending on the direction in which they are guided. The play situation is an opportune place for these traits to develop and to be properly directed.

Types of Play. Play may take several forms, all of which may be beneficial and contribute to the educational program. There should be proper balance among the various types. Three types are discussed: active, passive, and intellectual.

Active Play. Active play includes physical movement and participation in various forms of activity such as tumbling, swimming, and tag. The children are active participants and the exercise and activity are beneficial to each child. This is the most desirable form of play for growing children. Only by being a participant can the child realize many physical, mental, social, and emotional dividends.

Passive Play. In the passive type of play, the spectator approach is used. One does not take part as an active member of the group or team but gains enjoyment by watching others participate in play or athletic contests. Passive play takes place at a big-league baseball game, a tennis match, or a play, sports, or field day in the local school. Fun, relaxation, and other values can be gained from such activity. However, it should be recognized that the majority of values from play can only be gained by active participation.

Intellectual Play. The last type of play is the intellectual kind. This does not mean that the intellect is not used in the other forms of play. However, as in chess or checkers, intellectual play requires deep thinking and concentration. It should be reiterated that children need active physical play for optimum results. Young bodies need vigorous movement and exercise in order to grow and develop and build a sound, strong physical organism for the many years to follow. But it is also important that a physical education program include intellectual play.

Play—The Foundation for Balanced Adult Living

Dr. William Menninger, the famous psychiatrist and physician, once stated that too few adults know how to play. He also stressed that play is essential to balanced living. In one study he compared a group of psychiatric patients with a group of well-adjusted individuals. One characteristic of the well-adjusted group that was lacking in the psychiatric patients was that they had many hobbies, knew how to play, and took their play seriously. Dr. Menninger concluded from years of studying maladjusted individuals that play is very important to enriched living.

The proper attitudes toward play, the skills for play, and many other foundations are developed during the elementary school years. However, teachers who do not understand its importance are sometimes responsible for destroying this drive and making play unpalatable. Consequently, as some individuals mature they tend to shy away from play and seek other pursuits. Some of these persons are in mental hospitals today. They had no healthy form of release from the tensions of modern-day living. They had no wholesome outlet for their aggressive drives. They could not find relaxation from their competitive living. They did not know the formula for good mental health. It is estimated that one out of every twelve children in our schools today will someday find his way into a mental hospital. Every teacher should recognize the importance of giving each child the foundational equipment so they know how to use play for balanced living. This is true education. This is living. This is teaching children how to live rich and happy lives. This is meeting a basic need of society. This is the responsibility of every teacher who comes into contact with a child in any type of play situation.

Recommended Physical Education Activities

Early Childhood Activities. Recommended types of activity for the physical education program of children in early childhood are as follows:
1. Dance and rhythmic activities.
2. Developmental activities using equipment and other specific types with no equipment.
3. Games of low organization.
4. Individual and dual activities.
5. Self-testing activities and stunts.
6. Story plays.

Additional activities for consideration:

7. Classroom games (to be used when other indoor facilities are not available).
8. Aquatics (to be used if facilities and qualified teachers are available).

Middle and Upper Childhood Activities. Those types of physical education activity recommended for the middle and upper childhood grades (four through eight) may be listed as follows:
1. Dance and rhythmic activities.
2. Developmental activities (specific).
3. Games of low organization.
4. Individual and dual activities.
5. Preliminary and lead-up games and activities.
6. Self-testing activities, stunts, and gymnastics.
7. Team games.
8. Track and field events.

Additional activities for consideration:

9. Classroom games (to be used if other indoor facilities are not available).
10. Aquatics (to be used if facilities and qualified teachers are available).

Growth Through Physical Activity

If the physical education program is planned, based on the knowledge of child growth and development, it will be guided by the needs, interests, and abilities of each child. If it is then correctly administered, one may readily expect that it will aid the child in organic development, neuromuscular skill development, and grace in movement. It should also continue to guide natural play instincts so a child may gain pleasure through participation in games and develop a carry-over interest in activities to be used in leisure time.

A child learns through play, and learning is synonymous with living. Joseph Lee says, "Play to a child is growth—the gaining of life; to the adult, recreation."[4]

To gain the most from physical education each child should be assisted in his natural growth

[4] Joseph Lee, *Play in Education*, New York, The Macmillan Company, 1915, p. 174.

patterns without force. Each one may need this assistance by different processes, but every process should supply an acceptable social pattern and achievement. How physical education may help meet a child's needs is ably summarized in *Physical Education for Children*.

> Every child needs sufficient muscular strength to maintain good posture at rest and in motion and to do with ease the tasks of each day. He attains this strength through vigorous physical activities. Strength coupled with a flexible body gives him ability to move quickly and effectively. He needs the stamina and endurance that depend on well-developed heart and lungs to persist in work and play without undue fatigue. Strength, agility, and endurance come from play that is long and intense enough to tax the body beyond the ordinary.
>
> A child's ability to use his body skillfully in work and play requires coordination of brain and muscles that comes only from purposeful practice. Skills learned in a variety of rhythmic activities, dances, games, and stunts, will remain through life. . . .[5]

Physical education must involve guidance to be educational. Children learn certain activities such as creeping, standing, walking, and the like which are not greatly affected by teaching. However, the game situation, learning to play with others, and developing certain needed skills and techniques are all acquired faster and improve through good teaching. These game situations aid a child in meeting his organic and social needs, are interesting, and should influence his life. Anderson believes a child is aided through play in the following ways:

> A game or contest has rigid rules which are well-defined and well-administered . . . probably more so than are rules of conduct in any other area of human affairs, even including government. As a result, the child acquires not only the skills needed for a game or sport, but also knowledge of the activity and its rules. Although the process is gradual and largely informal, its completeness causes some wonder as to what would happen if similar methods could be used for regular school work.[6]

Each person should bear in mind the fact that no program of physical education activities may be justified unless all the facts available in child growth and development have been applied in its planning and administration.

Questions and Practical Problems

1. Using books on child growth and development and psychology, list the social, physical, mental, and emotional characteristics of children in the early and middle childhood grades. Show how each must be considered in planning a program of physical education.

2. Show specifically how each recommended type of activity will help meet the specific and general needs of the children in each of the six grades.

3. Give examples of types of children who may challenge the teacher to meet their needs through a program of activities which differs from the one you plan for the group in general. How will you be guided in planning such a program? What will be your difficulties in administering it?

4. What challenge do you meet in evaluating your program in relation to child growth and development? Be specific and concrete.

5. Discuss factors which influence children's behavior. Apply the various behavior patterns to a program of physical education and show how you will attempt to assist the child.

6. How may many of the physical, social, and emotional tensions of children be removed? How may physical education aid? May it cause more tensions and strains if not planned and administered according to principles and knowledge of child growth and development?

---

[5] National Conference in Physical Education for School Children of Elementary Age, *Physical Education for Children*, Washington, D.C., National Conference in Physical Education for School Children of Elementary Age, 1951, pp. 9–10.

[6] John Anderson, *The Psychology of Development and Personal Adjustment*, New York, Henry Holt and Company, 1949, p. 375.

7. What are the basic changes in skeletal, muscular, and organic development in children in the six-, seven-, and eight-year age levels compared with those in the nine-, ten-, eleven-year-old child? What significance do these changes have to the program of physical education?

Selected References

Association for Supervision and Curriculum Development. *Growing Up in an Anxious Age*. Washington, D.C.: Association for Supervision and Curriculum Development, 1952.

BALLER, WARREN R. *Readings in the Psychology of Human Behavior and Development*. New York: Holt, Rinehart and Winston, Inc., 1962.

BRECKENRIDGE, MARIAN, and VINCENT LEE. *Child Development: Physical and Psychological Growth Through Adolescence* (Fifth Edition). Philadelphia: W. B. Saunders Company, 1966.

BRISBANE, HOLLY, and AUDREY RIKER. *The Developing Child*. Peoria, Ill.: Charles A. Bennett Company, Inc., 1965.

CROW, LESTER D., and ALICE CROW. *Child Development and Adjustment*, New York: The Macmillan Company, 1962.

ENGLISH, HORACE G. *Dynamics of Child Development*. New York: Holt, Rinehart and Winston, Inc., 1961.

ESPENSCHADE, ANNA. *Physical Education in the Elementary Schools. What Research Says to the Teacher, #27*. Washington, D.C.: Department of Classroom Teachers, National Education Association, 1963.

JENKINS, GLADYS. *Helping Children Reach Their Potential*. Chicago: Scott, Foresman and Company, 1961.

RADLER, D. H., with NEWELL C. KEPHART. *Success Through Play*. New York: Harper & Row, Publishers, 1960.

RARICK, G. LAWRENCE. *Motor Development During Infancy and Childhood*. Madison, Wis.: College Printing and Typing Company, 1961.

CHAPTER 8

Motor Learning and the Elementary School Child

The techniques of effective teaching are important to each educator. Teachers attempt to create a learning environment that is conducive to learning. They build lesson plans based on realistic objectives and goals in order to have an efficient plan for teaching. Additionally, teachers attempt to make themselves as knowledgeable about the teaching-learning process as possible so they can carry out their professional commitments to the children they teach.

Effective teaching is dependent upon the educator's understanding of the learning process and the interrelationship of the teaching-learning process. The elementary school classroom teacher who is responsible for teaching physical education, as well as the physical education specialist, needs to have a comprehensive knowledge of the learning process. These individuals must also understand how motor learning takes place within the over-all process of learning. Motor learning is not separate from the learning process, but rather is one phase of the entire process.

The Learning Process

While learning has been given many definitions, the one most commonly used is that learning is a procedure through which alterations or changes are made in the behavior of the individual. A child who learns to skip has undergone a change in behavior as has the child who learns to ride a bicycle or whose swimming skills are improved through practice. Learning-induced behavioral changes may be negative as well as positive, however. It is the responsibility of the teacher to see that behavioral changes in the child take place in the desired direction.

The experts are in agreement that there is more than one type of learning, but they do not agree on exactly how many different types of learning there are. Nor do they agree on how these types of learning should be classified or titled. Some authorities have said that learning takes place in three broad general areas that may be called the cognitive domain, the affective domain, and the motor domain. Other authorities include classical conditioning, trial-and-error learning, discriminatory learning, verbal learning, and motor learning in their lists of various types of learning experiences. It is important to note that each list of learning domains or types that has been compiled includes motor learning.

There are three essential ingredients necessary before learning, and specifically motor learning, can take place. These ingredients are the learner himself, the motor-learning process, and the conditions in and under which motor learning will take place. In the physical education classroom, motor learning is the primary desired behavioral outcome of the physical development program. Motor learning is involved in developing increased coordination of the various muscular responses that lead to physical movement. This chapter will be devoted to a discussion of motor learning as a part of the entire learning process.

The Elementary School-age Child and Motor Learning. The child's ability to learn, the rate at which he learns, and the child's ultimate attainment of knowledge depend on a variety of factors both within and outside of the child's control. The teacher and the school combine to provide the proper atmosphere and the supplies and equipment that help learning to take place. The teacher provides the learner with a series of challenges and attempts to motivate the child to accept each challenge, overcome it, and to be willing to accept increasingly more difficult challenges.

The Laws of Learning. Educators have consistently based some of their insights into the learning process on what are known as Thorndike's Laws of Learning. These three laws—the law of readiness, the law of exercise, and the law of effect—describe the interrelationship of the learner with the learning process. Each of these laws has implications for physical education and especially for the process of motor learning.

The Law of Readiness

1. *In the process of education a child is systematically exposed to many different learning experiences as his growth, development, and maturity dictate.* For example, a child is assumed to be mentally mature enough to learn algebra at about the age of thirteen or fourteen. He has the maturity and experiences only for far simpler kinds of arithmetic at earlier ages. Were he exposed to algebra at the age of six or seven he would not be able to give the desired responses.

2. *In physical education the child must be physiologically ready in order to effectively undertake specific motor-learning tasks.* The skills necessary for basketball are inappropriate to the physiological maturation level of the first-grade child. This child is, however, developmentally ready for rhythmics and for movement education and for other activities that are not overly stressful, either physically or mentally.

3. *Physiological readiness as applied to motor learning is a complex phenomenon that is generally described as having three components.* These three components are briefly discussed in paragraphs 4, 5, and 6.

4. *Physiological maturation depends on the child's neurological condition and resultant neuromuscular functioning.* An infant's increasing ability to roll over, grasp objects, and sit up are responses that are controlled by the extent of his physiological maturation. Physiological maturation is apparently controlled by hereditary factors rather than by environmental ones. There is some disagreement as to whether this development is completed by the time the individual has reached his twenties, or whether it continues beyond that age.

5. *The second component of physiological readiness is called motor development.* Certain components of bodily movement—such as agility, strength, and endurance—develop only as a result of practice. If this practice is lacking, the individual will not be able to reach an adequate level of motor development. Children who have not participated in the natural physical activities of childhood to any great extent will be impeded in reaching a satisfactory state of motor development.

6. *Foundational learnings are the third component of physiological readiness.* Foundational learnings refer to those basic skills which must be learned before the child can attempt more complex motor tasks. They are the premise upon which teaching progressions for physical education activities are based. Physical education teachers learn, through such courses as child growth and development, that it is the gross-muscle skills that must be developed first and that this development enhances the later learning of the finer-muscle skills and coordinations.

The Law of Exercise. *The learner must continually practice a skill in order to reinforce the initial learning that has taken place.* The more often the desired response is repeated, the less likely the learner will be to forget the skill. If a class of third-grade youngsters, for example, has learned to dance the polka step, they should review the step from time to time so that the initial learning is reinforced.

The Law of Effect. *When the child receives satisfaction from giving an appropriate response, he will tend to repeat this response in order to* *continue receiving satisfaction.* The child is much more likely to repeat a satisfying response than he is to repeat a response that is not satisfying. This is the essence of the law of effect. As applied specifically to motor learning, the child will tend to repeat satisfying skill performances. That is, if a fourth-grade child has learned to bend his knees and use his arms for balance when landing after a jump from a low platform, he will be more likely to continue using this landing for future similar landings. He will be less likely to continue to use a stiff-legged, awkward landing that jars his body, throws him off-balance, and gives no satisfaction.

Motivation and the Child. Most children enjoy being physically active. During their preschool years they engage, of their own volition, in a wide variety of activities that are movement-oriented. Much of this activity is unsupervised and undirected. Children engage in these activities because they find pleasure in the physical activity. When children enter elementary school, their participation in physical activity takes on a new light. Their play is generally structured, directed, and highly supervised. They begin to learn, through their physical education classes, how to refine their natural movements into certain physical skills.

1. *A child must be motivated to want to refine his basic skills as a prerequisite to continued motor-skill development.* Some of this motivation will come from the teacher of physical education, but the major portion of the motivation must be inner directed by the child himself. The child must personally have an interest in learning a particular skill, such as rope climbing, before he will be motivated enough to attempt the skill.

2. *The child must have a need to learn a skill before he will attempt that skill.* Within a group of children who are learning to swim, those who are motivated through need and interest will learn the strokes by faithful practice and by making repeated attempts at skill improvement. Those children who are not interested in learning to swim, or who see no personal need for learning the skills of swimming, will not be intense in

their efforts and will take long periods of time before making any observable improvement in skill performance.

3. *Unless the learner is motivated, he will not learn skills effectively.* Children will tend to learn skills much more slowly if all, or the majority, of the motivation is externally imposed by the teacher.

4. *There must be a challenge to, and stimulation in, the performance of a skill.* Unless challenge and stimulation are present, the performance of a skill will not be as effective as it otherwise might be.

5. *There must be some excitement or tension created within the individual before skill learning will result.* It has been variously pointed out that while tension and excitement can facilitate the learning of the simpler motor movements and gross-muscle coordinations, the learning of complex skills involving the finer-muscle coordinations is sometimes impeded by high levels of tension and excitement within the learner. The teacher of physical education must know how to exploit these levels of tension and excitement in order to promote effective skill learning. However, motivation on the part of the learner himself is the most important prerequisite to the learning of motor skills.

Individual Differences Among Learners. No two children will be identically motivated in regard to the learning of skills. No two children will attain exactly the same levels of motor ability. No two children will develop the same facility of performance of a single motor skill or set of skills.

1. *Each child has a learning rate that is individual to him.* Some children learn a specific skill more quickly than others do, and the same child is often able to learn some physical skills easier and faster than he can learn other skills. There are many individual differences in the rate of skill learning both among children and within the same child. These individual differences must be accounted for by the teacher each time a series of skills to be learned is presented to a group of children.

2. *A child's level of aspiration also helps to govern his ultimate level of motor ability.* Each time a skill-performance challenge is set for a group of children, each individual child within that group will set his own personal standards for attainment in relation to the challenge. Some children will aspire to exceed themselves in the performance of the skill, others will aspire to meet the challenge at a minimal level, while still others will set a goal so low that they will be totally unable to meet the challenge.

3. *Research seems to indicate that to succeed at optimum levels the child must be able to go beyond his aspiration level each time he performs a skill.* But if the level of aspiration is set so low that it is too easily exceeded, the child will not receive the benefits of finding his optimum level of success in physical-skill performance.

4. *Levels of aspiration vary between individuals and within the same individual.* The level of aspiration for each individual depends upon the specific nature of the challenge to be faced, and the relationship of the challenge to each child as an individual.

Teaching Motor Skills. The elementary-school-age child is a beginner as far as the learning of motor skills is concerned. Because he is a beginner, his initial skill performances are generally characterized by inefficient movement.

1. *The child's efficiency improves as he continues to learn more and more motor skills.* For the elementary-school-age child, motor skills are acquired best through practice. Therefore, elementary school boys and girls learn skills more effectively and efficiently when their physical education program is heavily activity-centered. Programs that overemphasize verbal explanations have been found to be generally ineffective with this age group.

2. *The beginner needs to achieve and to realize the satisfaction of achievement on his own level of ability.* This is best accomplished through an activity-centered program. The shorter interest span of the younger child dictates that the teacher keep verbal instructions to a minimum. However, a variety of audio-visual aids such as short movies or loop films do hold the interest of the elementary-school-age child, provided they are appropriate to the level of understanding and are illustrative of the skills to be learned.

3. *The older elementary-school-age child in grades 5 to 8 cannot be considered a beginner in regard to skills, provided he has had a background of skill learning in a sound physical education program in his earlier years.* The boy or girl in grades 5 to 8 is more receptive to verbalized teaching techniques, provided these are not employed to excess. All elementary school children,

however, must have full knowledge of what is expected of them in regard to skill learning and skill improvement. Thus, the teacher must be able to balance the verbal explanations necessary against the optimum amount of time that should be spent in actual participation in physical activity.

4. *How well any child will learn motor skills is directly related to how much experience he has had in utilizing the basic movements of childhood.* This has vast implications for programs of movement education beginning with the kindergarten year. Movement education helps the child to learn how to exploit his body as a tool for movement by working through the natural movements of childhood as a foundation. Programs of movement education are designed to make motor skill learning easier for the child by providing him with a sound foundation of experiences in physical activity.

The Conditions for Motor Learning in the Elementary School. Environmental conditions that help to promote learning, such as adequate heat and light and proper ventilation, are essential for creating the proper atmosphere in the classroom or gymnasium. These factors and others, such as the cleanliness of the locker room, are not often problem areas with which the teacher of physical education needs to be unduly concerned. There are, however, other conditions outside of the environmental ones that are the direct concern and responsibility of the teacher, and that are applicable to every class in physical education.

Learning is a phenomenon that is specific to the individual child. No one learning style is common to all children, and no one teaching methodology will be equally effective with each elementary school boy and girl in a single class. Some general concepts have been developed, however, that will help to guide the teacher who is responsible for physically educating elementary-school-age boys and girls.

1. *Motor educability is specific to the individual child.* No two children will learn physical education skills with the same facility. The child

who learns new skills with great ease is said to be highly motor educable.

2. *Motor skill learning is specific to the individual child.* The rate at which a child learns motor skills depends upon his genetic inheritance, motivation, prior experiences in physical activity, amount of physical-skill practice, and his ability to transfer learning in regard to movement principles from one skill to another.

3. *Skill performances are specific to the individual child.* The child's motor abilities, body build (which must be suitable for the activity), age, and personality, and the nature of the activity are determinants of skill performance for each child.

4. *The child's initial skill attempts are generally inefficient.* Success in performing a skill is more important to the child than is its form. Proper form and efficiency of movement develop as the child gains experience in performing the skill.

5. *Mental imagery is essential to motor-skill learning.* A child who is simply told to perform a forward roll will have no concept of how to attempt the task, The child must have a mental image and concept of the skill he is to perform before any physical attempt at performing the skill is made.

6. *Skills and abilities are specific to the activity for which they will be used.* Different kinds of balance are needed in different activities. For example, the balance skills a child learns in walking a balance beam reflect a different kind of balance than that required for doing a headstand. Speed, leverage, agility, flexibility, and strength are among the attributes that are specific in their use, depending on the activity. None of these abilities, nor related ones, can be taught or developed only once and then generalized by the child for a variety of dissimilar activities.

7. *A child who is initially highly skilled will tend to maintain his abilities.* Motor skill has an enduring quality. While children will hit plateau periods in their learning of motor skills, those who are highly skilled will tend to remain so. Motor skill is also a general quality, and a child who

shows high levels of motor ability in one area of the physical education program will also tend to have above-average motor abilities in other areas of the program.

8. *The practice of a skill should be closely related to the actual performance requisites of that skill.* If a group of children is to be taught the skills of kickball so they can play a game, then their kicking technique should be practiced on a rolled ball as is done in the actual game. If these same children were to concentrate their practice only on a stationary ball, then they would encounter difficulty when faced with a rolled ball in a game situation.

9. *Distributed practice is more effective than massed practice.* Elementary-school-age children do not have the attention span or the physical endurance necessary for intensive practice periods on a skill. They learn new skills more efficiently, and achieve greater success in skill performance, when their practice periods on a single skill are fairly short in duration. Further, these practice periods should occur frequently and be alternated with practice on other skills or with participation in other activities.

10. *Physical fitness is an important aspect of the program.* The elementary-school-age child cannot be expected to perform skills well unless he is physically fit enough to meet the demands of the skill.

The Motor Learning Process. Even though the child is fully ready and motivated to learn motor skills, and even though the teacher has full knowledge of the conditions needed for learning, the learning process itself must still be initiated and carried through.

The methodology for teaching skills and the teaching techniques used are a part, but by no means all, of the motor-learning process. The application of the process is individual to each child and must be adapted and modified to meet each child's needs and interests.

1. *The proper performance of a skill should become a habit.* The teacher's praise for a correctly performed skill does not necessarily insure that the child will perform the skill correctly again and again. The child's correct performance of a skill must be reinforced through his personal sense of kinesthesis. In other words, the child must understand the movements he has made in his initial proper performance in order to be able to repeat this performance.

2. *Kinesthetic awareness can be transferred from skill to skill.* A child is often taught the skills of the balance beam but preparatory training frequently is done not on the beam itself but on the gymnasium floor. The child perfects his movements on the floor, develops the kinesthesis required, and applies these to the balance beam. General kinesthetic awareness may also be transferred in swimming, where dry-land practice is often the rule, and in many other skill areas.

3. *Skills are retained when they are practiced from time to time.* A child will lose his efficiency in a skill unless he is given an opportunity to reinforce his learning through periodic practice.

4. *Learning cues are essential to the beginner.* A child is generally unable to isolate the essential parts of a skill. The teacher of physical education must point out the essential parts so the child will know which parts of the skill he must concentrate on in order to improve his performance.

5. *Overlearning is essential in motor-skill learning.* A single correct performance of a skill does not guarantee retention of the skill. A child needs to repeat correct performance over and over until the pattern of action becomes overlearned through practice.

6. *Performance levels are not constant.* A child who performs a skill perfectly for a week may suddenly show a decline in his performance of that skill. When this occurs, the child must be remotivated to improve his performance.

7. *The criteria for performance must be suited to the child.* If the standards for a performance are set too high, the child will fail. Criteria must be set that are reachable through challenges appropriate to the child.

8. *The child needs to know how he is doing.* A child will tend to perform better if he is given knowledge of the results of his efforts, whether this is positive or negative information. This phenomenon is known as "feedback," and has been found to be an essential ingredient in all learning.

The preceeding sections have been designed to give the reader some general knowledge about the area of motor learning. This complex area is continually being reviewed and is subject to much scholarly research. It is suggested that each classroom teacher or physical education specialist working on the elementary school level become as knowledgeable as possible about motor learning so that the greatest contribution can be made to the boys and girls in their elementary school years.

Questions and Practical Problems

1. List and describe as many different types of learning as you can.
2. Explain the differences between each of the three essential ingredients for learning.
3. Show how Thorndike's law of readiness applies to the elementary school child specifically.
4. Interview a kinesiologist to determine the latest thinking in regard to physiological readiness. Prepare an oral report to present in class.
5. Describe the process of motivation in physical education in the elementary school. Tell how you would motivate a seventh-grade boy to want to learn how to square dance if he was resistant to this activity.
6. List all the individual differences you can think of among learners. Show how each relates to motor learning specifically.
7. How does word-centered teaching differ from activity-centered teaching? Prepare a lesson plan using each method.
8. Define practice, reinforcement, feedback, overlearning, and motivation and show how they affect motor-skill learning.

Selected References

CRATTY, BRYANT J. *Movement Behavior and Motor Learning*. Philadelphia: Lea & Febiger, 1967.

JOHNSON, WARREN R. Ed. *Science and Medicine of Exercise and Sports*. New York: Harper & Row, Publishers, 1960.

OXENDINE, JOSEPH B. *Psychology of Motor Learning*. New York: Appleton-Century-Crofts, 1968.

SINGER, ROBERT N. *Motor Learning and Human Performance*. New York: The Macmillan Company, 1968.

SKINNER, B. F. *The Technology of Teaching*. New York: Appleton-Century-Crofts, 1968.

CHAPTER 9

The Atypical Child

For years educators have taken the individual needs and differences of children into consideration in many parts of the school curriculum. They have established within a given grade or class several different reading groups and have given work according to the abilities of children. There has, however, been too little planning for the atypical child in physical education. The whole range of atypical individuals, from the highly skilled to the mentally, orthopedically, and socially handicapped, needs attention. The atypical should not be completely bypassed and left in the classroom during each period of physical education. Harvey was an example of this until grade four, when he came to the attention of a wise teacher.

Harvey was a polio victim. Large, heavy steel braces on both legs from his hips down were fastened around his waist to his knees and extended down his legs to specially built shoes. His face was pale, his eyes were haunting. He needed fresh air, sunshine, friends, and a feeling of being needed. Instead, as each play period rolled around, Harvey was left in the classroom to do as he wished in the belief that it was too strenuous for him to travel out-of-doors or to the gymnasium. That was the teacher's opinion only. Harvey had not been asked. No excuse had come from the doctor requesting that he remain indoors. In fact, when the case was discussed with the school physician and the boy's own doctor, they both wanted him to be given incentives and encouragement to walk. They felt it would tend to aid and strengthen his legs.

One day the physical education teacher purposely permitted the class to go to the playground without the equipment she needed for the planned program. She started getting it ready to carry outside and found she needed some help. Harvey sat in the room watching her get the equipment from the closet. After finding she could not carry all of it she said, "Harvey, I surely need your help. Would you please carry this ball out to the playground for me?" His eyes lit up. He got up from his desk and slowly came to the closet. There was a slight smile on his face and he said, "Do you think I can get there fast enough?" Assured that he could, he started out after the teacher. It was a beautiful, sunny fall day. The class was busily engaged in the activities they had chosen before they left the classroom, and were playing happily under the guidance of their squad leaders and classroom teacher. Haste was not necessary so the teacher walked and talked with Harvey in an attempt to break some of the three-year formation of ice. This was the start of Harvey's part in the physical education program.

Daily he went to the playground. He was asked to assist in scoring the squads' accomplishments for the day. This interested him greatly and at home one evening he made a score pad. It was fastened together with colored yarn his mother gave him, and he was as pleased as one could be when he showed it to his teacher and classmates. His daily trips to the playground gave him some needed physical activity. He got sunshine and fresh air. He learned the rules of games rapidly. He was then asked to umpire and act as a judge in relays. He felt he was needed and wanted. The class accepted him wholeheartedly through the fine work of the teacher. He was equipment manager, score keeper, umpire, judge, or referee as the activity demanded. Then another happy occasion occurred in his life. The class wanted to learn to play the game of batball. In the process, they decided Harvey had arms as good as theirs. "Why can't he have his turn up at bat and we'll take turns running for him?" The look on Harvey's face was worth a million dollars. His classmates had found another place for him in the physical education program. He could play with them. He hesitated because he said he had never hit a ball with his hand. They offered to help him, and so it was that he entered into every activity which required no running on his part and many where his peers took turns running for him.

The doctors were very pleased with the progress of his physical condition. He was happy and lost the haunted look, his paleness disappeared, and his legs seemed to grow stronger. His mother said his appetite was much improved and he was happier at home. He was now *a part of* his group and not *apart from* it during the play period and the physical education program. He went outside during the noon hour, also, and was the most popular official in the school. All of this participation gave him physical activity, social and psychological growth, satisfaction, and an interest in games and activities. This illustration is an example of how a child with a physical handicap was aided by working with his regular class in the physical education program. This child was classified as an atypical child due to a locomotion handicap. Other handicaps are discussed below.

Defining the Atypical

The atypical child is so classified because of a variety of factors. These may be physical, emotional, mental, or social in nature.

Included under the classification of physical deviations are those of a postural nature, heart malfunction, nutritional difficulties, locomotive problems, speech impediments, vision and hearing defects. Also, there is the problem of the physically gifted and the creative child.

Emotional deviations include the many emotional maladjustments such as aggressiveness, antisocial behavior, withdrawal, or depression. These maladjustments will not be helped by programs which are not adapted to the physical and mental abilities of the child and which fail to insure his satisfactory emotional and social development.

The mentally atypical child may be either gifted, possibly to the point of genius, or retarded. Socially atypical children include those who have specific deviations in their human relations, are culturally disadvantaged or exhibit disruptive behavior for any reason.

Characteristics and Needs of Specific Types of Atypical Children in the Elementary School

A single classroom in any subject area may contain children who fall into several different atypical categories. Each classroom teacher and each teacher of physical education must know how to best serve the educational needs of these youngsters.

The Culturally Disadvantaged Child. Culturally disadvantaged children, meaning those children who are deprived educationally and economically, or in some other way, and frequently live in the slums of large cities or in rural poverty pockets, come from various sections of the United States, but most of them come from families that have migrated to the large cities.

The Ford Foundation has estimated that in 1960 one in three city children was culturally disadvantaged. Today this number has increased to one out of two.

The culturally disadvantaged child usually does not perform well in school because his home atmosphere and neighborhood environment have not equipped him to meet the challenges of daily school life. The culturally disadvantaged child suffers greatly from a lack of ability to communicate. Reading, conversation, the use of logic, concept formation, and abstract thinking are totally new and strange to this child.

Because the culturally disadvantaged child meets with constant failure in the classroom, he is generally unmotivated and has a low level of aspiration. He also tends to have a short attention span and to be emotionally unstable, excitable, and restless.

Despite his seeming inability to cope in the classroom, the culturally disadvantaged child generally enjoys and excels in physical education activities. Within the physical education classroom, this youngster can gain a release of tension in an acceptable manner, participate in a supervised and structured program, and compete on his own level.

The elementary school physical education program for the culturally disadvantaged must be designed so as to meet these needs. It can do this by providing an opportunity for the child to be creative and self-expressive. The program should include work designed to help the child improve his physical fitness and motor skills. There should be an opportunity for competition that is related to the needs, interests, abilities, and competition-readiness of the children. Lifetime sports and activities should be important parts of the curriculum. The children in any class must be treated as individuals first. Good health habits, attitudes, and knowledge should be concomitants of the physical education program for these children. Discipline should be handled on an individual basis and be firm and consistent. The physical education class should provide for learning, understanding, and insights that can be carried over into the regular classroom. Finally, the entire physical education program should be specifically geared to the needs of this culturally disadvantaged child. A more complete discussion of a physical education program for the culturally disadvantaged is discussed in Chapter 12.

The Physically Handicapped Child. There are more than two million children of elementary school age who are physically handicapped to some extent. While not all of these children attend public elementary schools, those who do must be of special concern to their teachers.

Physical handicaps may be permanent or temporary in nature and may range from minor to major in severity. Some physically handicapped children will also have developed negative behavioral and social traits while others will be well-adjusted individuals.

In the elementary school classroom, the physically handicapped child is often at a severe disadvantage because his classmates may not understand his disability and may ostracize him from the group. Furthermore, in spite of any motor abilities approaching normal that this child may have, he is frequently not invited to participate in the regular physical education activities of the class because his presence is viewed as a detriment.

Many physically handicapped children are fully capable of participating in a regular program of physical activity. Some handicapped students can participate if minor adaptations and modifications are made while others will need to be placed in a specially designed program of adapted physical activity. In cooperation and consultation with each physically handicapped child's physician, the teacher or physical educator should assess the capacities and abilities as well as the needs of each handicapped child. Only in this way can handicapped children be provided with individually tailored programs.

Physical education programs that contribute to the well-being of physically handicapped children in the elementary school make special provisions for this condition. The child's own personal physician is consulted wherever possible for advice as to the type of activity program that will be best for the child. The child's abilities in motor skills and physical fitness are tested. Careful records are maintained that show such information as the child's test scores, activities he participates in and that interest him most, progress he is making, and the nature and extent of his disability. When a child is so severely handicapped that he must be placed in an adapted rather than a regular class, the program is so structured that it is as similar to the regular physical education program as possible. Physically handicapped children are provided with the stimulation and challenge of a program that has definite goals and an orderly skill progression. A program is available after regular school hours for those physically handicapped students who wish to receive extra help of a remedial nature. The fitness level, recreational needs, sex, and age of each child, as well as his interests and any medical recommendations and limitations available, are reviewed by the teacher to determine the activities the children will benefit from and enjoy most when all physically handicapped children in that school are grouped in the same class regardless of age, grade level, or physical disability. The program of activities is individually adapted to each physically handicapped child. Extra safety precautions are taken to insure the welfare of each child. Suitable after-school activities are provided where possible. Early elementary-school-age children have a club program in physical education making it possible for them to participate with their more normal peers in a common activity of interest. A more complete discussion of a physical education program for the physically handicapped is discussed in Chapter 12.

The Mentally Retarded Child. Today there

are more than seven million mentally retarded children and adults in the United States. Current estimates cite six million mentally retarded children and adults, and each year this number is swollen by the birth of over 126,000 mentally retarded babies.

Mentally retarded children may fall anywhere within a broad range of mental and physical abilities. In general these children are more advanced in physical maturity than they are in mental maturity.

The mentally retarded child is generally placed in an academic class where his special needs can be met by specially trained teachers. However, there may not be any special provisions made for the physical education of this child within the regular framework of the school. In the academic classroom, these children usually have an extremely short attention span and are frequently restless and impulsive. Other characteristics may include a low threshhold of irritability, a tendency to emotionally over-react, and destructiveness. These characteristics are individual to each mentally retarded child.

Many mentally retarded children can participate in the regular physical education program while others will need to be placed in an adapted class. Many mentally retarded children have not had a physically active life and thus must be taught how to play and how to use their bodies as tools for movement.

Guidelines that will be helpful in constructing a physical education program for mentally retarded elementary-school-age children include such factors as the following. Activities that develop physical fitness should be stressed. Movement education experiences should be provided to help the mentally retarded child develop his gross motor abilities. Mentally retarded children should be encouraged to compete against themselves and to engage in a variety of self-testing activities. Since mentally retarded children and normal children have identical activity needs, the former should be provided as carefully structured a physical education program as are normal children. Opportunities should be available for the development of desirable social skills. New activities should be introduced at the beginning of a class period to offset the effects of fatigue and loss of interest that are so often apparent at the later stages of a class period. The children should share in the program planning, as this helps them to feel important and stimulates their interest. Lifetime recreational skills, such as swimming and dancing, should be provided. Good health and hygienic habits should be stressed and practiced. In schools where facilities are available, the children should dress appropriately for the activity and follow appropriate health procedures before, during, and after the activity. Accurate and complete records should be kept regarding each mentally retarded child and his progress within the physical education program. The program itself should constantly be evaluated to see if it is meeting the needs of these children. A more complete discussion of a physical education program for the mentally retarded is discussed in Chapter 12.

The Disruptive Child. The disruptive child is in need of guidance and counseling. These emotionally unstable children are often restless and unable to pay attention in a class. In a physical education class, they may poke and prod a child near them, call out nonsensical remarks during the teacher's presentation, or use other nonconforming means of gaining the attention of other children and the teacher. Some of these disruptive children have mental or physical handicaps that contribute to their bizarre behavior. Whatever the cause of the problem, these children are in need of understanding and competent help from the teacher and other trained professionals who serve the schools.

Some guidelines that provide suggestions to the teacher for preventing and dealing with behavioral problems that may adversely affect an entire physical education class, include the following. The teacher should understand and be able to recognize and appraise individual behavioral patterns because of his knowledge of child growth and development. Children should know and understand the expected behavior in the physical education class and that misbehavior is not expected. Discipline should be firm and consistent. Children who misbehave should have private conferences with the teacher and a child should never be ridiculed in front of his peers. A child who is a continual problem should be given extra opportunities to find success since continued failure helps to perpetuate disruptive behavior. All children should receive praise for their accomplishments rather than hearing only about their failures since recognition of a skill well done often helps a child to discipline himself. Children should be provided with opportunities to assume responsibilities. Interested school personnel should be informed of the progress of especially disruptive children. A more complete discussion of a physical education program for the disruptive child is included in Chapter 12.

The Poorly Coordinated Child. The poorly coordinated child is found in almost every classroom. This child requires remedial help so he can increase his motor ability scores, improve his skill performances, and attain higher levels of physical fitness.

The poorly coordinated child lacks general physical ability. This handicap may result in certain psychological problems. Poorly coordinated children on the elementary school level take physical education along with their age peers. Too often they receive special attention in the class only when the teacher wants the child to show his classmates the wrong way to perform a skill.

The poorly coordinated child will be resistive to learning new activities because the challenge they present offers little chance for success or for an end to ridicule. The challenge of a new activity or skill may create such tension in the child that he becomes physically ill, or the tension may result in negative behavior.

The following suggestions may assist the teacher in working with and helping a poorly coordinated child. The activities the child engages in must present an attainable goal and therefore offer an almost certain chance for success. The program should be progressive, varied, and interesting. Physical fitness and self-testing activities should not monopolize the program. Low-organization team games such as Brownies and Fairies, and games such as Squirrel-in-the-tree do not demand a high level of skill or coordination but do provide an opportunity for competition. Children should be involved in some of the planning for the program. The program should be progressive so the children will have a feeling of accomplishment and achievement. Lifetime sports should be provided that can be applied to future adult needs and interests. A more complete discussion of a physical education program for the poorly coordinated child is included in Chapter 12.

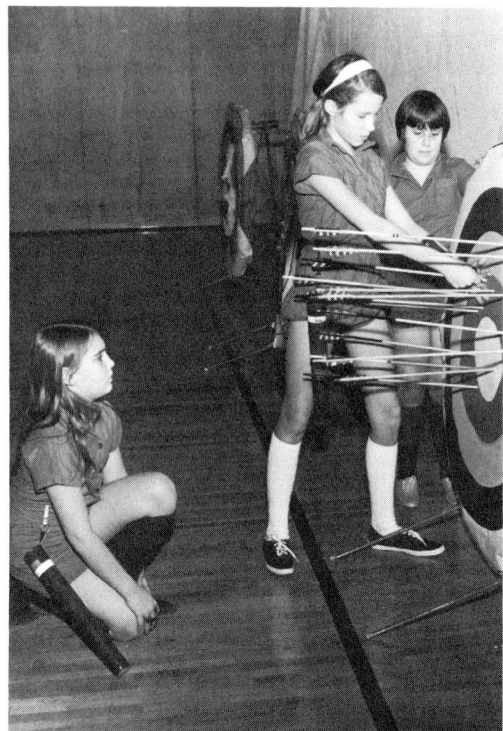

The Physically Gifted and the Creative Child. Physically gifted boys and girls have superior motor abilities which they demonstrate in a variety of activities or skills. These children learn quickly, are enthusiastic about physical activity, and pursue many recreational activities during after-school hours and on weekends. These children usually have a very well-developed kinesthetic sense.

These suggestions may help the teacher to assist the physically gifted and the creative child more effectively. Each child should be enabled to develop new insights into performance skills. The skill work for the child should represent a challenge. Elementary-school-age children can assist each other in practicing skills. The exceptional child may be stimulated and challenged by a special club that is geared specifically to his level of ability. A more complete discussion of a physical education program for the physically gifted and the creative child is included in Chapter 12.

Responsibility for the Atypical Child

Emphasis on the democratic ideal means a realization of the full responsibility due to atypical children to help them grow and develop to their fullest potentialities. The Recommendations on Children and Youth from one White House Conference states that a program for children and youth with handicaps must be expanded to provide for their physical, mental, emotional, and occupational needs.

Most atypical children gain many educational experiences through association with other children. Unless these children are so atypical that they require the services of teachers especially educated to care for them, they should be permitted to remain with the regular class.

In every thousand children, the estimated number with physical handicaps which require special school adjustment is between fifty and sixty. In the same group there will probably be about forty who deviate from the average in mental ability. Other atypical conditions are also very much in evidence, including those in the emotional and social realms.

The deviations from normal create serious problems for children. Such problems are at times made more serious by adults who do not understand them and who leave children out of learning situations because of overprotection, fear, or indifference. These children challenge the teachers and parents to help them with all the skills they can master and to substitute for those they cannot.

Play releases frustration and pent-up energies. The atypical child needs to learn to use swings, slides, jungle gyms, and the like and to be a part of the regular group so he may learn from contact and experiences with other children.

The atypical child has all the desires and ambitions of a physically, emotionally, and, many times, socially normal child. These are intensified and thwarted by the abnormal condition. Such children also need an outlet for their desires. A well-planned program of physical education, having the approval of the school physician and the family physician, is a good way to help them in the physical, emotional, and social phases of their lives.

It is the duty of educators to stress in great measure the similarities of children—not their differences. The atypical child must be helped to accept himself and to find ways in which he may substitute activities and gain satisfaction from these substitutions. To permit him to take part in a physical education program gives him a chance to be accepted socially and an opportunity to be part of the group.

The National Committee on School Health Policies recommends that all pupils should participate in the physical education program. Where necessary, the program should be adapted to meet the needs of each child.

A corrective program for the atypical child is not a complete program. While it is true that some children require much special help, it is just as true that many will gain from social contacts with children in the regular program. In any case, where the program of games and other activities will meet some of the desired objectives, the child should be permitted to participate rather than assigned to a class to take only special exercises. Harvey was an example of this. It is true that he needed special exercises for his legs, apart from his regular class, but if he had had only remedial work, he would have missed the other essential part of his living. Many times special activities are needed to supplement what the child can do in the regular physical education program with his classmates, but it is the belief of the authors that atypical children should in every possible case be permitted to remain a part of their group and take part in whatever ways they can in addition to engaging in special activity recommended by the doctor.

Ways the Program Should Serve. The philosophy accepted by educators is that if a child is well enough to be in school, he is well enough to participate in a program of physical education, even though it must be adapted to meet his individual needs. This is the responsibility of the school.

The physical education program should make an honest attempt to improve the health status of each child. This can be accomplished only if individual needs and abilities are taken into consideration. Programs of physical education have too long been designed solely for the physically gifted child and have neglected those who are under par. The physical education program should include a gamut of activities such as correctives, body mechanics, active sports, quiet games, and vigorous exercises to increase strength and endurance—all designed to fit the needs of every child.

In a report of a National Conference on Physical Education for Children of Elementary School Age, it was found that every child received more benefit from physical education when the programs were planned for individual needs. A majority of children can take part in all activities, some need a modified program and can take part in only certain phases, while still others can participate only in quiet games and activities.

A National Committee on Adapted Physical Education stressed that their specialty had much to offer each individual who faces the combined problems of seeking an education and overcoming a handicap. This adapted program should serve the individual in each of the following four ways if the program is to be successful:

1. Aiding and discovering deviations from normal and making proper referrals where such conditions are noted.

2. Guiding students in the avoidance of situations which would aggravate new conditions or subject them to undue risk or injury.

3. Improving general strength and endurance of individuals who are poorly developed and those returning to school after illness or injury.

4. Providing opportunities for needed social and psychological adjustment.

No teacher or administrator should feel that his or her job is well done unless physical education is planned to meet the needs of each child in the school with an adapted program. As one educator expresses it, "We must be as interested in the handicapped child as in the potential all-American halfback,"

Guidance in Meeting the Needs. The teacher must naturally be guided in the programs of physical education for the atypical child by such persons as the school doctor, school psychologist, and the family physician. Many times the first referral comes from them in the form of a blanket excuse stating that a certain child must not take any physical education. To take the path of least resistance this excuse could be accepted and no program would then be attempted for the child.

On the other hand, in order to be fair to the child, a prepared form giving all of the types of activity in the physical education program should be sent to the doctor asking him to check the activities in which the child may participate and to recommend the amount of time advisable for each.

Many times physicians do not know that the school is willing to offer activities other than the usual program, mapped to fit the needs, interests, and abilities of the greatest number of children within the given group and often too strenuous for the handicapped child. Hence these physicians send the school the blanket excuse.

A letter to a physician in reply to a blanket excuse might read:

Dear Doctor ———,

We have just received your excuse stating that ——— should not participate in any physical education activities.

May we, through this letter, acquaint you with the types of activity we are capable of rendering in our program and ask you if there are some which would be beneficial to ———?

If you note any in which it would be possible for him (her) to participate, would you be kind enough to check them? It would be helpful to us if you would also suggest the length of time you believe would be best for participation.

We have the interest of each individual in mind and endeavor to plan our programs to fit the needs, interests, and abilities of each child in our school.

Sincerely yours,

———

Enclosed with this letter should be a form giving all the types of activities offered in the program. Such a form may be planned as below. It should be checked and signed by the family and school physicians and returned to the teacher in charge of the child.

Dear M———,

I have checked the activities you are offering in your program of physical education and the time I believe it would be beneficial for ——— to participate in them. The diagnosis of my patient's condition requires a special program as follows:

Type of Activity	*Recommended Time for Participation*
1. Special conditioning activities	
2. Special developmental exercises for:	
a. Arms	
b. Legs	
c. Feet	
d. Back	
3. Quiet table games	
4. Swimming	
5. Boating	
6. Hiking	

7. Biking
8. Individual and dual activities:
    a. Shuffleboard
    b. Marbles
    c. Croquet
    d. Archery
    e. Hopscotch
9. Rhythmic work
10. Less strenuous circle games and relays

[Signed] _____, M.D.

In following this procedure, the teacher is working with the exceptional child directly under the guidance of a medical person and is not taking any chances. Without the help of a physician, what she believes may benefit the child may actually be harmful to him.

Regardless of whether the teacher working with the child is a specially trained physical education major or an elementary classroom teacher, it must be stressed that neither is qualified to plan and/or administer most phases of a program for the atypical child without the direction and guidance of a medical authority. Even a physical therapist works under a physician's recommendation and supervision. This point cannot be too strongly emphasized.

Teachers have been known to conduct programs, especially those of a corrective nature, which could definitely injure the child rather than help him. At the same time, there is the possibility of a legal liability suit if harm results to the child.

An example of the need for caution is shown in postural defects. These defects may be symptoms of fatigue caused by poor nutrition or skeletal disease such as bone tuberculosis and osteomyelitis. They may be caused by nervous and muscular disorders such as polio or cerebral palsy. Unless one knows the cause of a postural defect, great injustice may result in overstressing mechanical correction through exercises. Proper attention must be given to each individual child through the health services department to determine the underlying cause before the teacher may safely endeavor to aid the child through a special program of corrective work.

The close cooperation of the home is also needed in aiding the atypical child. This may be partially accomplished by inviting the parents to be present at the annual medical examination of their child and through the home visits of the nurse, the classroom teacher, the school psychologist, and/or the special teacher of physical education. The parent-teacher conferences, which are so popular today, may serve as the necessary link for close cooperation of the parent and the school in their endeavors to assist the atypical child.

Evaluation of the Program. The progress and accomplishment of the atypical child in the program of physical education is especially important. Some means of evaluation are necessary; some will be subjective and others objective in their nature.

Conferences with the child; observation of his social behavior as exhibited in various informal play situations; the results of certain skill achievement and knowledge tests planned specifically to show the progress he has made—all will aid in evaluating the program of activities in which he is engaged.

These children should be carefully examined by the school physician or other specialist every two or three months to ascertain whether the planned program is meeting the physical needs of the child and to recommend changes for his benefit. Teachers usually can help the child by assisting him to prepare an evaluation sheet for himself on which he records what he desires to accomplish and how he is succeeding. As in all cases of evaluation, if it is to be meaningful to him, the child must know his goals and his growth.

Suggestions for the Teacher

1. Each child may benefit from some phase of the physical education program if it is carried out with his needs, interests, and abilities in mind and planned under the close guidance of the medical profession.

2. The corrective program is *not* the complete answer. Many children will not be able to have their handicap removed, and it is the teacher's responsibility to help them to adjust and enjoy themselves in spite of it.

3. The atypical child gains needed social adjustment, fun, fresh air, sunshine, and emotional help through participating and being with his peers.

4. Physical education can help the child in many ways other than physical development.

5. All children need not participate in the same activity during the physical education period any more than all will participate in the same

activities in the other parts of the school curriculum. Several activities may be enjoyed at one time during the period with one class or group.

6. Do not attempt to do the impossible.

7. Accept the situation and do your best for the child.

8. At times you will meet children who are unable to participate in the regular program. These students should be referred to the school physician for guidance. This may be necessary when a new child enters a school and is assigned to a class prior to the annual school medical examinations. It is the classroom teacher's responsibility to bring each case to the attention of the health services department so that the examination and recommendations may be made during the first days of school.

9. The teacher should familiarize herself with the complete physical records of all new children admitted to her room each September and at other times during the year.

10. Refer to the health service department a child who has returned from a prolonged illness or accident and develop his program based on its recommendations. These children will need, in most cases, only a temporary adapted program.

11. Keep an individual record of each child's daily activities and the length of time he spends in each.

Questions and Practical Problems

1. Plan a meeting with the school nurse and doctor regarding some atypical child. Be specific. Know what you wish to discuss and what help you need.

2. Use hypothetical cases, if you know of no real ones, of children with specific handicaps. Plan activities which are generally accepted for handicapped children.

3. Set up an evaluation chart for the teacher to use in her work with the atypical child.

4. Organize an evaluation chart for each atypical child to use in his physical education program. Devise a rating rule or guide easy enough for him to understand and use.

5. As part of your health and physical education program, plan a unit on posture for the grade of your choice.

6. Can you justify giving a child a mark on posture?

7. What is your stand on the planning and administration of a corrective program for children by a physical education specialist? By a classroom teacher? Your class may be interested in debating the negative and positive sides of this question.

8. Ask the personnel of the health services department in your school to speak to your class about the atypical child and the physical education program.

Selected References

AAHPER Project on Recreation and Fitness for the Mentally Retarded. "Activity Programs for the Mentally Retarded." *Journal of Health, Physical Education, and Recreation*, April, 1966, Special Journal Feature.

Association for Supervision and Curriculum Development. *Learning More About Learning*. Washington, D.C.: Association for Supervision and Curriculum Development, 1959.

BUCHER, CHARLES A. *Administration of School Health and Physical Education Programs* (Fifth Edition). St. Louis: The C. V. Mosby Co., 1971.

Council for Exceptional Children and AAHPER. *Recreation and Physical Activity for the Mentally Retarded*. Washington, D.C.: American Association for Health, Physical Education, and Recreation, 1966.

CRATTY, BRYANT J. *Social Dimensions of Physical Activity*. Englewood Cliffs, N.J.: Prentice-Hall, Inc., 1967.

DANIELS, ARTHUR. *Adapted Physical Education*. New York: Harper & Brothers, 1965.

———, "What Provision for the Handicapped?" In *Children in Focus*, 1954 Yearbook of the American Association for Health, Physical Education, and Recreation, 1955, p. 134.

Fantini, Mario D., and Gerald Weinstein. *The Disadvantaged: Challenge to Education.* New York: Harper & Row, Publishers, 1968.

Franklin, C. C., and William H. Freeburg. *Diversified Games and Activities of Low Organization for Mentally Retarded Children.* Carbondale, Ill.: Southern Illinois University, no date.

Hayden, Frank J. *Physical Fitness for the Mentally Retarded.* Toronto, Canada: Rotary Clubs, 1964.

Information Center—Recreation for the Handicapped. *Recreation for the Handicapped: A Bibliography.* Carbondale, Ill.: Information Center—Recreation for the Handicapped, 1965.

Martmer, E. E. *The Child with a Handicap.* Springfield, Ill.: Charles C. Thomas, Publisher, 1959.

National Conference in Physical Education for School Children of Elementary Age. *Physical Education for Children.* Washington, D.C.: National Conference in Physical Education for School Children of Elementary Age, 1951, p. 11.

Ratchick, Irving, and Frances G. Koenig. *Guidance and the Physically Handicapped.* Chicago: Science Research Associates, Inc., 1963.

Riessman, Frank. *The Culturally Deprived Child.* New York: Harper & Row, Publishers, 1962.

Snyder, Raymond A. "The Gifted Student and Physical Education." *Journal of Health, Physical Education, and Recreation,* 33:18, Jan. 1962.

Stafford, George T., and E. D. Kelly. *Preventive and Corrective Physical Education* (Third Edition). New York: The Ronald Press Company, 1958.

Woodward, Everett W. "Camping Motivation in Communication Skills for Speech-Impaired Children." *Journal of Health, Physical Education, and Recreation,* 32:26, May–June 1961.

PART THREE

Recommendations for Program Development

CHAPTER **10**

Physical Education Movement Activities for Early Childhood with Examples of Progression and Suggested Outcomes

Children differ in their needs, interests, and abilities in physical education just as they do in all areas of education. Certain types of activity have been found to be desirable to meet these needs in early childhood. During this period of growth and development children need big-muscle activity. They may receive it through play which is not too highly organized but which is planned to meet their interests and abilities.

Recommended types of activity for this group—with definitions, objectives, and examples of each—will be discussed in this chapter. New materials and more of each type may be found in Chapters 20 and 21.

Types of Movement Activity and Suggested Time for Each

The types of activity recommended for children in grades one, two, and three are shown in Table 10-1.

The suggested time for each type of activity in the over-all physical education program is given only as a rough guide. All children differ, and the teacher must use her judgment in the use of the activities. The percentages of time recommended here are in agreement with those proposed by leaders in the field of physical education. The program should not consist of only one type of activity. For example, a program of games alone is not justified. Aquatics should be included when availability of facilities and qualified leaders permits.

Classroom games are listed because many times in the elementary schools there are no special indoor facilities for physical education in inclement weather. Hence, if a program is offered it must be carried on in the classroom. There are various types of activity suitable for use in classrooms which should be used when the weather will not permit children to go out-of-doors and when there are no gymnasiums, playrooms, or other such indoor facilities.

Dances and Rhythms. Rhythms are activities in which a child responds to music, percussion instruments, or singing. His response includes physical, mental, and social reactions. Rhythmic activities may include:

1. *Fundamental rhythms.* All fundamental rhythms are basic experiences utilizing such movement skills of locomotion and nonlocomotion as running, hopping, leaping, jumping, and walking. Combinations and variations of these in patterned, regular rhythmic sequence will result in skips, slides, and gallops.

2. *Dramatized rhythms.* Dramatized rhythms

Table 10-1. Activities and Times Recommended for Grades One Through Three

Types of Activity	Suggested Time for Each (*Per Cent*)
1. Dances and rhythms	25–30
2. Developmental activities using equipment	10
3. Games of low organization	25–30
4. Individual and dual activities	10
5. Self-testing activities and stunts	10
6. Story plays	10
7. Classroom games (to be used during inclement weather if other indoor facilities are not available)	
8. Aquatics (to be used if facilities and qualified leaders are available)	10

include the rhythmic dramatization of nursery rhymes, poems, or stories, such as "Hickory Dickory Dock," "Humpty Dumpty," and "Jack-Be-Nimble."

3. *Folk dances and singing games and dances.* Selected folk-dance steps are combinations of the fundamental locomotor movements. They may be characterized by variations in the accented beat or may be combined with selected nonlocomotor movements. All dance steps should be performed accurately. Folk singing games and dances are those traditional dances which characterize different groups or races. They involve definite group relationships. Examples of these would include "Shoemaker's Dance," "Chimes of Dunkirk," "Looby Loo," and "The Farmer in the Dell."

Folk dances are those traditional dances which originated to satisfy the needs and interests of particular folk groups. The combinations and variations of step patterns are more complicated than the simple folk singing dances. They usually have instrumental accompaniment.

4. *Creative dancing and mimetics.* Movement exploration aids self expression by allowing the child to express himself creatively and satisfies a great need within him. It helps him to understand himself. If properly developed it becomes a form of communication—a "show-and-tell" method of speaking through motion rather than verbally. The child may develop his own movement patterns of design with musical accompaniment or with just a narration. The child poses himself in his imaginary world and interprets suggested subjects, such as bicycles, dolls, tops, animals, or clocks.

Objectives. The objectives of dances and rhythms are as follows:

1. To develop a sense of rhythmic coordination.
2. To develop a sense of grace.
3. To teach an interest in and love of rhythmic and dancing activities.
4. To develop desirable social attitudes and courtesies through group activity.
5. To develop a strong, well-coordinated body.
6. To develop a means of expressing oneself through rhythmic movement.

Teaching Hints. Introductions are important means of motivation. Tell something about the dance and the country from which it comes, show pictures of people and dance, bring in personal group experiences, or correlate the activity with other subjects in the school. These are only a few methods.

1. Be sure the children know the beat of the music. Have them listen to the music and then clap out the beat.
2. Demonstrate the step to be used (i.e., skip, slide, polka).
3. Let each child try the step alone in an informal organization, not in the set formation called for in the dance.
4. Give individual help.
5. Organize the children in the formation called for in the dance.

6. Teach a small part without music and let the children practice it.

7. Next try it with music.

8. Teach the next part; practice this.

9. Combine parts one and two; continue with each part until the dance is complete.

10. If there are words which may be sung, teach only a part of them at a time. Do not try to teach the entire dance at once. Words may be taught in music class.

11. For more enjoyment, leave enough time so the entire rhythm or dance may be gone through once or twice after it has been completely learned.

12. Do not expect all children to do it equally well.

13. Commend for work well done and also for improvement.

14. Never humiliate one child before the class. An example of this was seen after a teacher had spent parts of several periods on the fundamental rhythm of skipping. All children had mastered it but John. He skipped on his right foot and walked on the left. Finally the teacher asked all the class to sit down while she worked with John. Naturally, he was worse, much embarrassment was created, and all learning ceased as did everyone's fun.

15. Stop the rhythm or dance while the children still like it. Do not bore them with it.

16. If a rhythm gives certain children in the circle a chance to be more active than others, make certain that each child has a good opportunity for activity before stopping it. This is readily accomplished by placing more than one child in the center to start an activity. In this way, the rhythm or dance will be completed faster and the children will not be bored by repeating it too many times nor will they be discouraged and disappointed because each one did not get a chance. An example of this is shown in the singing game, "Here Comes a Bluebird through My Window." Standard directions for this game and a suggestion for getting more activity will be discussed.

HERE COMES A BLUEBIRD THROUGH MY WINDOW

Formation

Children form a circle, which represents a large imaginary house. The directions call for one child to be chosen as a bluebird and to take his place in the center of the circle or house. Change this. Choose more than one. If there are 24 or 32 in your class, choose three or four bluebirds. Select one for the leader of the birds, and have the others follow him to avoid confusion.

First Verse (Tune, "London Bridge")

Here come some bluebirds through our windows,
Through our windows, through our windows.
Here come some bluebirds through our windows,
My fair lady.

Teaching Directions

1. Teach the words and have the class sing it and clap to the rhythm. (Words could be taught in a music class before going out for physical education.)

2. Children hold hands and raise arms upward opening imaginary windows.

3. Bluebirds skip, with arms extended for wings, through the windows in time to the words sung by the class. All birds follow the leader.

4. When the music stops, each bluebird should stand directly behind the person nearest him in the circle.

Second Verse

Take a little partner and tap her on the shoulder,
Tap her on the shoulder, tap her on the shoulder.
Take a little partner and tap her on the shoulder,
My fair lady.

Teaching Directions

1. Teach the words and have the class sing them.

2. Each bluebird taps the shoulders of the partner behind whom he is standing. He taps in rhythm with the music. (Make certain that the children understand the meaning of *tap*.)

3. Children in the circle clap their hands in rhythm as they sing.

Third verse

Take a little partner for a hip-skip-scholar,
A hip-skip-scholar, a hip-skip-scholar.
Take a little partner for a hip-skip-scholar,
My fair lady.

Teaching Directions

1. Teach the words and have the class sing them.

2. Each bluebird takes the hand of the person he tapped and skips around the outside of the circle in rhythm to the singing of the group.

3. All children remaining in the circle hold hands and swing their arms forward and backward, keeping in rhythm with the music. The circle is now much smaller. Repeat the entire rhythm with all partners as bluebirds. If the activity started with only one bluebird, after the completion of the song there would be only two skipping and it would take a long time before each child had a chance to do the skipping and be either a bluebird or a partner. Children could tire of the activity, and problems might result. But, if it is started with three bluebirds, six are busily engaged as partners at the completion of the song. The second time it is played, there would be twelve bluebirds going in and out windows and tapping partners. By playing and singing it three times, a circle starting with thirty-six children would be completely engaged. Replay if children desire, with new bluebirds selected. In this way each child has a chance to participate in some part of the activity and is happy.

Developmental Activities Using Equipment. The special category, "developmental activities using equipment," refers to activities offering more use of big muscles than the other categories. Included here are activities on playground and indoor equipment such as climbing bars and jungle gyms, horizontal ladders, horizontal bars, ropes and climbing poles, large tiles for crawling in and out, swings, seesaws, slides, merry-go-rounds, and various new kinds of equipment made by creative leaders. Creative Playthings, Inc., is one company with excellent creative playground equipment. (See Appendix B for a list of suppliers and addresses.)

It must be understood that all classifications of activities by their very nature offer big-muscle activity. However, the category here under consideration creates the opportunity for muscles to be used in ways and combinations different from those of many other categories.

The pieces of equipment mentioned above provide opportunity for exploratory experiences. Learning the safe and best way to walk on balance beams, to climb jungle gyms, to use swings, and to ride merry-go-rounds gives children confidence and courage. It helps them to continue to have fun without injury while they develop strong muscles.

Jumping rope is an excellent developmental activity. It aids in developing rhythmic coordinations, strengthening leg muscles, and developing endurance.

Children in early childhood learn first to jump a rope that is turned by two people. After they can coordinate the timing and are successful, they are ready to add the skill of turning their own ropes. As the child develops skill, jumping to music adds much fun.

Children of this level develop so they are able to jump on both feet and on alternate feet, to run

(Courtesy of The Delmer F. Harris Co. Photo by Switzer Studio.)

in the front door and back door while the rope is turning, and to jump to several rhymes. They should also be able to jump at different speeds, from slow to fast.

Objectives. The objectives of developmental activities are as follows:

1. To give opportunity for vigorous activity developing strength, agility, and dexterity.

2. To teach children the safe way to use the various pieces of equipment.

3. To teach courtesy and respect for others.

4. To provide the fun and delight that accompany free movement and development of control.

5. To help children discern many different ways of moving.

6. To develop independence.

7. To help children become skillful in movement.

Teaching Hints

1. Teach respect for each piece of equipment.

2. Teach respect for each individual child.

3. Teach safe ways to use the equipment—for example, to hold on with at least one hand where possible.

4. Teach certain children first and permit them to demonstrate to others.

5. Organize groups so that after the proper instruction much activity is possible for all without too long an interval between turns. A class of 25 may be split in four groups (after instruction) and may be assigned to play on four different pieces of equipment. Rotation may be used so each will have the opportunity to use each piece.

6. Check each piece of equipment daily to ascertain its safety (for example, check for worn chains or ropes on swings).

7. Do not use these pieces of playground equipment on rainy or snowy days or when they are wet or icy because of the dangers involved.

Games of Low Organization. Games of low organization are activities which have few rules and involve relatively simple skills and techniques so that children may learn them fast and progress quickly from the learning stage to that of enjoyment. This is necessary because of the relatively short interest span of the children in grades one, two, and three. These games can be adapted to varying conditions such as facilities and sizes of the group. Games of various types are included in this category. They are classified in Table 10–2 and examples of each are given.

Table 10–2. **Games of Low Organization**

Classification	Examples
1. Games with equipment	Teacher Ball
	Call Ball
2. Circle games without equipment	Three Deep
	Run for Your Supper
3. Fleeing and tagging games	Red Rover
	Bear in the Pit
4. Relays (not below third grade)	Running and Jumping Relay
	Ball-Passing Relay

Objectives. The objectives of low-organization games are as follows:

1. To provide vigorous physical activity.

2. To teach children to play together.

3. To teach activities which have a carry-over value for leisure-time use.

4. To develop mind and muscle coordination.

5. To teach specific skills and techniques.

6. To provide good fun and lessen emotional stress.

Teaching Hints

1. Analyze the game before you teach it and know the skills and techniques needed.

2. Be sure all necessary equipment and facilities are available, including marked areas.

3. Introduce the game in an interesting way.

4. Use as little time as possible to explain and demonstrate the game.

5. Get children into the activity fast.

6. Give children a chance to ask questions.

7. Permit children to act upon their own suggestions.

8. Teach as the game progresses by giving hints and help to the children.

9. Encourage each child to try.

10. If possible, participate in the games with your children.

11. Stress sportsmanship and fair play at all times.

12. If tagging is a part of the game, teach the proper way to tag so that a child is not too rough and does not tear clothing or push another child down.

13. If a game is started and the children appear to lose interest, stop it. Analyze it later. It may have been too hard or too easy, or it may

have been presented in a way the children did not understand.

14. Have an adequate ending for the game. Review the name, objective, winners, if any, and why they won. Do not overemphasize winning.

15. Evaluate the activity: (a) What did the class learn? (b) How did they respond? Why? (c) What needs to be taught and practiced to make the game better? (d) How will you practice the skills and techniques needed? (e) Were all children playing? (f) Was there bickering and poor sportsmanship? If yes, why? (g) What can you do to help them avoid this?

16. Provide chances for repetition of the activity to improve skills and techniques.

17. Many games of low organization, after being taught to the class as a whole, should then be played simultaneously by several groups to increase student participation.

Individual and Dual Activities. Individual and dual activities are activities which may be enjoyed by one, two, or four individuals. They are perhaps best known for their recreational value.

Children of this age group need to work often in twos or fours to help develop needed skills such as tossing and catching a ball at different distances. Tossing bean bags through special boards such as the clown's mouth develops accuracy in throwing. Various rope-jumping games, marbles, hopscotch, and jacks are additional examples of this type of activity.

Objectives. The objectives of individual and dual activities are as follows:

1. To give opportunity for children to improve certain skills.

2. To teach activities that have great carry-over value for use at home in leisure time.

3. To teach activities that may be used in small areas.

4. To give opportunity for each child to be aware of his own growth and feel a satisfactory sense of accomplishment.

5. To provide social experiences that develop desirable behavior patterns.

Teaching Hints

1. Teach activities to the entire group and then give them the opportunity to participate with different individuals and couples.

2. Plan necessary areas for participation.

3. Be sure sufficient equipment is available.

4. Give individual help to those in special need.

5. Encourage those who are better skilled to assist others.

6. Do not plan for competition!

Self-testing Activities and Stunts. Self-testing activities and stunts entail big-muscle activity. They may involve imagination as in imitating certain actions of animals or fowls, such as the bear walk, kangaroo hop, or duck walk. They provide opportunities for children to frolic in such activities as barrel rolls and forward or backward rolls. They may include activities in which one may work individually or with a partner. Examples of each type include:

1. *Individual activities:* Seal Slap, Kangaroo Hop, Inch Worm, Duck Walk, Seal Crawl, Bunny Hop.

2. *Couple activities:* Sit-ups, Wheelbarrow, Churn the Butter, Wring the Dish Rag.

Objectives. The objectives of self-testing activities are as follows:

1. To afford an opportunity for big-muscle activity.

2. To develop fine-muscle coordination, flexibility, balance, and timing.

3. To develop individual skills.

4. To give children a chance to use their imagination and to mimic actions.

5. To give children an opportunity to work individually and to see success in accomplishment.

6. To develop strength, body control, and agility.

7. To provide opportunities for genuine fun and the release of emotional tension.

Teaching Hints

1. Create an interest in the activity through the proper introduction.

2. Teach one or two children the activity before presenting it to the class so they may demonstrate it, or demonstrate it yourself.

3. Permit each child to work at his own rate.

4. Give individual help and encouragement by analyzing what the child is doing wrong and how he may correct it.

5. Never use these activities for races or in relays. For example, teachers have used the duck walk as a race for children. Naturally, when done correctly it is a slow pace. The children who win are always the ones who do not stoop correctly and who do not walk like a duck. These activities are not for speed, but should be taught for skill and fun.

6. Watch for safety. Racing will tend to cause danger.

7. Do not pit one child against another. Some can never do certain stunts.

8. Use a wide variety of activities so that each child may accomplish some. Do not expect all children to be able to do each stunt.

9. Use each activity for a short time in any given period of physical education. Do not expect the children to practice it for long periods at one time.

Story Plays. Story plays give the child a chance to use his vivid imagination and play in the land of make-believe. Often little girls dress up in their mothers' clothes, including shoes, hats, handbag, and gloves, really being the "lady of the hour." Boys pretend they are cowboys, Indians, robbers, and policemen. All have seen boys and girls playing fathers and mothers with dolls as their children, or playing school, with one child acting as the teacher and the others acting as the pupils.

Story plays are dramatizations of activities which are interesting to children. They may be taken from stories children read or they may be planned to show the roles of citizens in communities, such as policemen and firemen. They may also be made up and may very interestingly portray various leaders in history, or holidays and seasons of the year.

Objectives. The objectives of story plays are as follows:

1. To give big-muscle activity.
2. To give the child a chance to use his imagination.
3. To teach him to play with others.
4. To help him relax and have fun.
5. To provide opportunities for children to act and play in informal situations.
6. To teach cooperation.
7. To teach leadership and followership to each child.

AN EXAMPLE OF A STORY PLAY

An example of a story play entitled "The Firemen" is used to illustrate the steps in planning and progression, because the teacher will find very little help available where story plays are concerned.

The selection of this title may arise from a true incident following a fire in the area the night prior to the presentation. Perhaps most of the children heard the siren and knew about the fire. Some of their parents may have gone to the fire. Thus it provides a true situation from which children may gain the desired objectives. It also affords an excellent opportunity for teaching about community and civic helpers and may develop great respect for a fireman. Safety hints for the prevention of fires may be outgrowths of this story play. One way to proceed and use such an incident as a story play in the physical education class is as follows.

Introduction—Setting the Stage

Certain lead questions may be used to start the children's discussion and to motivate their interest. Some might be as follows:

"How many of you heard the fire siren last night?"

"Do you know where the fire was?"

"Was anyone hurt?"

"Who put the fire out?"

The teacher may now wish to make a definite suggestion in a very enthusiastic manner and say, "Today let's play we are firemen and we are called to a fire." To gain suggestions from the children, certain lead questions may again be asked. In this story play the teacher may ask the children, "What will we need to play firemen?" Their answers may start with trucks, a fire chief, drivers, sirens, and so on. After the necessary pieces of equipment and personnel have been suggested, the teacher will permit the children to decide in a democratic manner who will act each part and drive each piece of equipment. From this point the activities begin.

Logical Activities Sequence

1. Let's pretend we are firemen and asleep at the fire house when the siren blows. (Ascertain whether children know the difference between *paid* and *volunteer* firemen. Later, have children check in their home town to learn which they have.)

2. Put your hands up and your face on them and pretend you are asleep.

3. Blow an imaginary siren.

4. Hop out of bed. Stretch way up high.

5. Get dressed. Reach high for clothes; bend low for shoes. (Use various types of physical activity.)

6. Pretend to slide down poles or go down stairs.

7. Get in your trucks.

8. Fire chief goes first.

9. Start motors. (Children make sounds of running motors.)

10. Follow the fire chief. Clang bells, blow sirens to warn all traffic. Drive carefully.

11. Stop at the area designated for the fire.

12. All choose a job to aid in putting the fire out and rescue work: (a) Put up ladders. (b) Attach hoses to hydrants. (c) Go in house, if possible, to rescue people. (d) Climb ladders, rescue people. (e) Direct hoses on the fire, make hissing noise of water on fire.

13. (Finally, declare the fire out.)

14. All work to get ready to return to the fire house: (a) Take ladders down and put them on trucks. (b) Roll up hoses on trucks. (c) Climb back in trucks. (d) Start trucks.

15. Follow the fire chief back to the fire house.

16. Jump out of trucks—off with boots, raincoats, and fire clothes. Hang them up to dry.

17. Aren't you hungry? I am. All right, let's pretend it's time for breakfast. What makes a good breakfast? (Health correlation. While eating, talk over how the fire might have happened and how we may prevent fires.)

18. Breakfast is over. Now it's time for the new firemen to come to work and we may go home.

19. (Stress safety while going home—lights green before crossing street, and so on.)

20. Good-by. I'll see you at the next shift of duty.

Note: Physical activities included bending and reaching while dressing, bending to slide down imaginary pole, climbing in and out of trucks and up and down ladders, running while driving trucks, and so on.

Teaching Hints

1. Make story plays interesting to children by getting them ready with a good introduction.

2. Guide the suggestions for the activities so they move quickly.

3. Get the children into the activity quickly.

4. The entire activity should not last longer than ten minutes.

5. Do not tell the whole story first and then have them act it out. They will remember the first and last parts only.

6. Never repeat a story play because it did not go well. Check why it was not successful. It is usually the fault of the teacher.

7. Use every available chance to teach; for example, in the firemen story play teach respect for the fireman, show the responsibility of his job, how he risks his life to help others, and so on.

8. Make the story complete. If you do not, the children will tell you about it. Have a logical beginning and ending.

9. Get suggestions from your children for the activities to be included.

10. Take part yourself or at least go with them so you may talk to them at the areas designated for specific actions. Do not stand still and shout to them.

11. Evaluate when you are through. Did the children have fun? Why? Did the action include big-muscle activities? Were all the children active? If not, why? Ask the children what they learned? Did all children cooperate with each other; for example, were they willing to select a chief, drivers, and so on, in a democratic way or were some sulky and did they refuse to play because they could not be the driver? How can you help them?

12. Use every opportunity for carry-over in the classroom. In the fireman story play, for example, children could draw pictures of any part of the equipment used, write about the firemen, draw pictures of clothes worn by firemen, learn new words and terms, write and discuss safety rules for preventing fires, learn how to report a fire on their phones, and learn how to use fire alarms. Emphasize respect for alarms, so no false alarms are spread. Visit the fire house and have a fireman come and talk to the children at school. Each of these offers excellent teaching situations.

Suggested Topics. Make use of the seasons of the year, all holidays, and special occasions in addition to stories the class enjoys reading.

Classroom Games. Classroom games are informal activities which usually permit little vigorous activity but offer fun, relaxation, and group cooperation in an educational situation in the classroom. They are usually appropriate for various recreational situations.

Some examples of classroom games are Lost Child; Seven-Up; Huckle Buckle Beanstalk; Coffee, Tea, and Milk; Bean Bag Toss; and Cat and Mice.

Objectives. The objectives of classroom games are as follows:

1. To help children relax after the constant mental work of the school day when the weather does not permit physical education to be held out-of-doors and there are no other indoor facilities.

2. To help children have fun.

3. To provide some physical activity.

4. To teach the social qualities of play and cooperation.

5. To teach indoor activities which will have carry-over value at home, parties, or other social gatherings.

6. To develop sportsmanship and respect for the rights of others through the proper respect for playmates and through gaining cooperation in quiet play so individuals in other rooms are not disturbed.

7. To aid in the all-round development of social and emotional qualities.

Teaching Hints

1. Be sure the children understand why they must be quiet when playing these games in the classroom (respect for the other teachers and pupils).

2. Do not use much running (safety). Have children walk with giant steps or skip if games call for running.

3. Ventilate your room as well as possible during this play period.

4. Use rhythms and mimetics to advantage while in the classroom.

5. Where games call for balls, use bean bags, yarn balls, or clean blackboard erasers instead.

6. Many classroom games are of an elimination type. Change the rules of these so that all children may play and need not sit and watch others.

7. Do not permit children to use walls for goals. Make all goals a safe distance away from them.

8. Choose activities which will permit all children to play in the given space. Do not expect some to be happy while watching others.

9. Have fun with your children.

10. Teach them to be good sports and to have fun in spite of the weather, little space, and other handicaps.

Aquatics. If facilities and qualified instructors are available, swimming should be taught as a part of the physical education program. As is true with many other activities, younger children may be taught to respect and enjoy the water. Floating, doggie paddle, and basic strokes are teachable to a child of this age group (see Chapter 27 for a complete discussion of aquatics).

The Need for Progression in Physical Education

Children tire of the same activities day in and day out, and they also tire of the same ones in each grade. The same principle of progression used in other parts of the curriculum needs definite application to physical education.

New things are challenging to all. They also provide new learning experiences. No child likes to know that he must participate in a certain activity each day in physical education. He grows bored, endeavors to find excuses to stay away from the class, or creates a problem.

There should be progression in the programs of physical education from very easy to more difficult activities within each grade. Provision should also be made to assure progression in activities from grade to grade.

At first a child learns certain fundamentals like running, tossing a ball, and catching. As skill in these fundamentals is acquired, they are put in simple game formation using only one fundamental skill at first. Later activities include more than one skill and become more difficult.

Example. An example of progression in games of low organization would be to teach first the game named Teacher Ball, then advance to Call Ball, and then to Ball Stand.

TEACHER BALL

In the game of Teacher Ball, one child acts as the teacher and stands a few feet in front of his squad of from four to seven other children.

The distance from the teacher to the squad members depends on the capabilities of the children. Each teacher must judge this according to the children. The teacher tosses the ball to child number one, who tries to catch it, and then to toss it back to the teacher. Next the teacher tosses the ball to child *two*, and so on, until each child has received the ball from the teacher and returned it to the teacher. The teacher may then go to the end of the line if the children are interested in playing it again. Child *two* would become the new teacher. This game may progress until each child has had a chance to be the teacher if interest warrants. The interest of the children will determine how long it should be played.

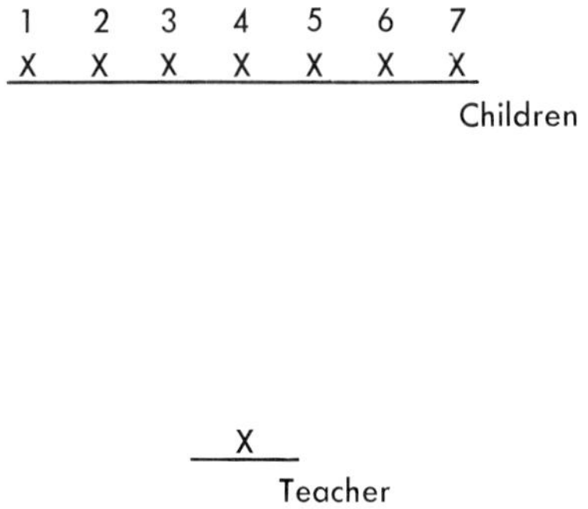

The skills involved are tossing and catching. Attitudes involve sharing equipment and playing together. From Teacher Ball we may progress to Call Ball.

CALL BALL

Call Ball starts with the children in a circle position. One child is chosen to be the "thrower" and stands in the center of the circle. He tosses

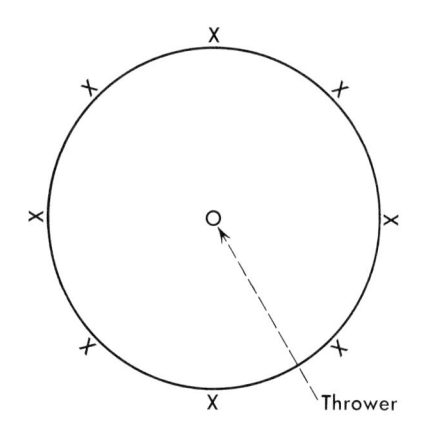

```
    1   2   3   4   5   6   7
    X   X   X   X   X   X   X
                                Children



                    X
                  Teacher
```
Figure 10–1. Teacher Ball

Figure 10–2. Call Ball

the ball straight up in the air and as he does calls the name of one child out loud. The child whose name is called runs to the center of the circle and endeavors to catch the ball before it hits the ground. If this is impossible, he recovers it on the first bounce. Although the rules of this game call for the first thrower to remain in the circle until a player called successfully catches the ball, the game is better if that rule is deleted. This will afford more opportunities for each child to practice tossing the ball straight in the air as well as endeavoring to run and

Table 10-3. Suggested One Month's Progression in Physical Education for Grade One, 30 Minute Period

	Monday	Tuesday	Wednesday	Thursday	Friday
	First week: New story play—10 min. New game—15–20 min., running and tagging type.	Review game learned Monday—10–15 min. New rhythm—15–20 min.	Review rhythm learned Tuesday—10–15 min. Teach two self-testing activities (new).	Choice of activities by squads. Each squad will choose one activity, get equipment, and be designated a play area. Rotate once.	Review testing activities taught on Wednesday—10 min. Teach new Jump Rope verse and jump.
	Second week: New rhythmic dramatization—10–15 min. Teach new game of Hopscotch—15 min.	Choice by class of two activities. Use each one for one-half period.	New story play on and give instructions on safe and courteous use of playground equipment—15–20 min.	Review self-testing activities learned last week. Teach one new—10–15 min.	New game using equipment—15–20 min. Choice of action by class—10 min.
	Third week: Review game learned Friday of last week—15 min. Review rhythm—10–15 min.	Use entire period for individual and dual activities such as Hopscotch, Jump Rope, activity on playground equipment.	Review any game using equipment—15–20 min. One or two new self-testing activities.	New circle game—10–15 min. Review any rhythm.	Choice of activities by squads, four different activities going on at one time. Rotate activities once.
	Fourth week: Review two games using equipment. Teacher selects, based on skills needed.	Review one rhythm based on teacher's judgment of steps needed—15–20 min.	New game with equipment—15 min. Choice by class—10–15 min.	Review game taught Wednesday—15–20 min. Review individual and dual activities including playground equipment.	Permit choice of activities by the four different squads. Rotate once (each engages in two activities).

The number of new activities taught will depend on various factors, such as: (a) What repertoire of activities does class already know? (b) What is their learning speed? Some classes will naturally demand more in new activities because of their quickness to comprehend and their eagerness for new experiences. (c) The time of year. (d) Weather governs choice as to the necessity of very active types of games or dances for colder days and the quiet type for very warm days.

catch it. Some children who wish to remain "It" for a longer period may purposely toss the ball so it cannot be caught.

Notice the added progression in relation to skills involved. *Throwing straight up* and *running* to catch the ball are necessary instead of *standing* to catch it as in Teacher Ball. This calls for greater skill than when a child is standing and the ball is tossed directly to him. After this game has been taught to the entire class, it should be played by squads so that there is more chance for each child to play in the *same* amount of time. The next game used in the progression is called Ball Stand.

BALL STAND

Ball Stand, like Call Ball, starts with the group in a circle. A thrower is chosen. He throws or tosses the ball straight up in the air and at the same time calls the name of a player out loud. The player whose name is called runs forward and tries to catch the ball before it hits the ground. If he misses it, he hurries to get his hands on the ball as soon as possible. All other players in the circle including the thrower run away from the ball. When the player called to catch the ball has his hands on it, he calls "Stand." Players who are running must stop and stand where they are. The player with the ball may advance three steps in any direction. He then endeavors to hit a player, below the waist, with the ball. If he succeeds, the player whom he hits is "It" and tosses the ball up the next time. If the thrower misses, he remains "It" and all children return to the original circle formation after each throw.

The progression of these three games shows more skills involved in each. The skills in Ball Stand are as follows:

1. Tossing or throwing a ball straight up in the air.
2. Running to catch a ball.
3. Running away from a ball.
4. Throwing at a target.
5. Dodging a thrown ball.

Thus progression provides more skills and techniques, more rules in the game, and a greater challenge to think. This same idea of progression is valid in all other types of activity, both within a given grade and from grade to grade.

Recording Activities. To assist teachers during the year and the teachers in the succeeding grade who receive the children, a complete record of all activities taught should be kept and filed with other records of the class.

A suggested form which can be easily mimeographed is shown in Table 10–4. Teachers may wish to change the form completely. The important point is to develop a form, use it, and pass it along.

With such a record and evaluation, though brief, the teacher throughout the year may examine the progress in her class, may note that she has had a good variety of activities, and may determine the response of her class. The next teacher who receives the children will know exactly what they have had in their physical education experience and may plan her program accordingly. Her plans should include review work, progression for maintaining interest and challenge, and opportunities to enlarge the repertory of activities children may engage in during school and leisure time.

Some Expected Outcomes. A program of physical education activities, well chosen as to variety in content and properly taught, gives us some ideas of what development and growth in skills and attitudes we may expect.

The following chart suggests some outcomes which should be attainable.

Social learning we may expect to develop can be broken down as follows. This is not meant to represent the child's total and full development. However, it gives some idea of the growth outcomes, based on planned physical education experiences, which may be hoped for.

Some Expected Social Learning. Children should learn to:

1. Share equipment with peers.
2. Take turns using playground apparatus.
3. Help each other.
4. Play together without arguing or tattling.
5. Admit when tagged; play fairly.
6. Enjoy themselves without boisterousness and screaming.
7. Make new friends.
8. Abide by rules, follow directions, respond to signals.
9. Play and work safely according to boundaries, space, rules, and equipment.
10. Play games well enough to enjoy them and use them outside of school.
11. Be able to act as squad leader.
12. Be able to follow a leader.
13. Demonstrate some self-direction, responsibility, and initiative.
14. Play successfully as a member of a group.

Table 10–4. **Physical Education Record of Activities**

Year:_____

Grade:_____   Teacher:_____

Activities Taught	Response of Children	Rating of Group
I. Games: 　Teacher Ball	Excellent.	Excellent—good skills in catching and tossing. Good group relations.
II. Self-testing activities: 　Seal Slap	Fair—not too thoroughly enjoyed. Response only warm.	Fair—many could not accomplish this. Appeared too difficult.
III. Rhythms and dances: 　Looby Loo	Fair.	Fair—children do not have a good sense of rhythmic coordination.
IV. Classroom games: 　Huckle Buckle 　Beanstalk	Excellent.	Very good—children cooperate well in respecting rights of other classes by being quiet. They were generous in sharing turns and thoroughly enjoyed the game.
V. Story plays: 　Fireman 　Santa's Helpers 　A Trip to the Zoo	Excellent.	Excellent—vivid imagination, very interested, asked to repeat activity.

Table 10–5. **Some Expected Learning Outcomes (Kindergarten through Third Grade)**

Activity	Some Expected Outcomes
1. *Movement Fundamentals*	
Walk	Efficiently, easily; with good posture; change of step—light, heavy, short, long; walk with 2 or more people.
Run	Fast, without falling; stop suddenly and change direction without falling, as needed in dodging a chaser; tag a runner correctly (not push); run 20 to 40 yds.
Jump and leap	In place vertically, forward, backward, sideward—without falling; run and leap over objects 12″ or more in height; run and jump forward, covering distance.
Hop	On right foot or left for a distance of 20′–30′; on alternate feet changing distance covered on each hop.
Gallop, skip, slide	Changing lead foot; different directions; with a partner. In second or third grade, combine in series of movements (4 skips forward, 4 back steps, 4 slides to right, 4 to left, etc.)
Leap and jump 　(third grade)	In series (e.g., leap, run, run, run, leap); gain height and form.
2. *Rhythmic Movement*	
Walk, run, hop, skip, gallop, slide, jump, leap	Different steps in time to accompaniment and in tempos of fast, slow, very slow; move in different directions; create patterns of movement using these locomotor skills.

Table 10-5 (continued)

Activity	Some Expected Outcomes
Perform nonlocomotor skills—sway, bend, swing, stretch, pull, push, rise, fall, etc.	Expressively with music; combine with locomotor movements such as walk and pull; walk and bend and sway.
Use movement for creativity	Imitation—toys, horses, tops, elephants, rag dolls, skating, elevators, airplanes.
Use movement in singing games and folk dances—toe-heel, step-hop	"Jolly Is the Miller," "Looby Loo," "Dance of Greeting," "Jump Jim Joe"; In third grade—Bleking, Indian Dances, etc.
3. *Stunts and Tumbling*	
Agility, balance, flexibility, strength	Perform several stunts requiring each; be able to perform successfully 5–10 stunts in each grade level including rolls, crab walk, seal crawl, duck walk, etc.
Climb	Climb up and down jungle gyms or appropriate apparatus; climb a pole or rope 3'–6'.
Hang and travel	Hang for several seconds from bar (drop lightly); hang and raise knees (try for chest height); travel by hands across bar or horizontal ladder.
Balance	Walk a balance beam or facsimile 4" wide, 5"–6" off floor; be able to move forward, backward, and turn around on it.
4. *Skills with Equipment*	
Balls	Roll a ball; catch a rolled ball or underhand toss from a partner; bounce a ball to self and to a partner; throw to a partner; throw in air to self and catch; throw at a large target and hit it at 8'–15' distance; kick a ball 20'–30' distance.
Rope jumping	Jump on both feet and on alternate feet; run in and out while rope is turning; jump to rhymes; jump with another child (second and third grades); change rhythm (slow-pepper).
Hoops	Rotate on arms, legs, and waist; jump in and out in different ways when placed on floor; roll hoops; throw rope quoits, beanbags, balls through hoops at different levels and distances.
5. *Combined Skills*	
Play skillfully 15–20 games using locomotor movement	Ability to run to goals—tagging, dodging, jumping, leaping as required to meet objectives in organized games.
Play 10–20 games using equipment	Success in throwing, catching, control, speed, and accuracy, as called for in organized activity.
6. *Swimming*	Respect water but have no fear of it; feel at home in shallow water; know how to float and doggie paddle; know how to use life preservers.

Questions and Practical Problems

1. Make up two complete story plays. Plan exactly how you would teach them, including the introduction. Plan and illustrate ways you may correlate them with other parts of the curriculum. Be certain the story plays include good physical activities.

2. Plan a program of physical education for a ten-week period for the grade of your choice.

3. Show two weeks' progression in daily plans for this same class, using the activities you have chosen.

4. Choose several self-testing activities you wish to teach your class. Plan how you will teach them. Show progression from very easy activities to more difficult ones.

5. Use your originality and make up two classroom games suitable for the early childhood grades.

6. Your second grade insists on playing softball, perhaps because your community is very baseball minded. Will you permit this? If so, justify it. If you will discourage it, be specific and show how you would do it and what activities you might substitute.

7. Mary will not enter any activities on the playground with her classmates. She does not show this attitude in the classroom. What will you do? Will you ignore it? If so, why? If not, how will you endeavor to gain her confidence and interest?

8. You have a jungle gym, a merry-go-round, slides, swings, and seesaws on your playground. How may they be used by your class?

Selected References

See end of Chapter 11.

CHAPTER 11

Physical Education Movement Activities for Middle and Upper Childhood with Examples of Progression and Suggested Outcomes

Children in the middle and upper childhood grades need considerable physical activity and are capable of gaining it through activities which are more difficult to accomplish than those listed in the previous chapter. Activities with more difficult skills and techniques and more complicated rules meet their challenge. These children have a longer interest span and will practice to be successful in activities they like and are motivated to accomplish. They are very interested in team games and group activities. The social and gang stages are present. Team games will aid in meeting some of these needs, in addition to providing vigorous activity.

The types of activity recommended for this age group—with definitions, objectives, examples, and specific teaching hints for each—will be discussed in this chapter. New materials, including some of each recommended type may be found in Chapters 22, 23, and 24.

Types of Movement Activity and Suggested Time for Each

The types of activity found suitable and recommended to meet the needs, interests, and abilities of the children of this age and grade level are listed in Table 11-1. It is hoped that interests developed through the years in school and experience in activities of various types will be of value to the child as he grows older and needs a more recreational type of program.

The suggested time element is for guidance purposes only. The total of 100 per cent of time is suggested without classroom games.

If other indoor facilities are not available for use during inclement weather, the classroom activities might necessarily be 10 per cent. Rhythms, certain self-testing activities, and some developmental activities may be used to advantage in the classroom. The main point for teachers to remember is that it requires each of the types listed to present a well-balanced and interesting program in order to meet the needs and interests of all children. The allotment of time for aquatics is included in arriving at 100 per cent of the time. The teacher will use her judgment in the amount of time for each activity to meet the factors of facilities, space, and equipment. If aquatics cannot be included, the suggested amount of time may be used at the discretion of the teacher.

Dances and Rhythms. The actual definition of rhythms is, of course, the same for any grade level. In the middle-childhood grades, dances are

Table 11-1. **Activities and Times Recommended for Middle and Upper Grades**

Types of Activity	Suggested Time for Each (Per Cent) Middle	Upper
1. Dance and rhythms	25–30	20–25
2. Developmental activities (specific)	5–10	10–15[a]
3. Games of low organization	5–10	5–10
4. Individual and dual activities	10–15	10–15
5. Lead-up games	5–10	10–15
6. Self-testing activities and stunts	10–15	5–10
7. Team games	25–30	25–30
8. Track and field events	5–10	10
9. Classroom activities (for use during inclement weather when playground or gymnasium is not available)	Some	Some
10. Aquatics (if facilities and qualified personnel are available)	10	10

[a] Including gymnastics if facilities and qualified instruction are available.

more highly organized and require more difficult and complicated steps and patterns to challenge the participants.

The recommended types differ. They include more folk dancing, including the American square dance. More creative and interpretive dancing may be offered, particulary to the girls. Boys enjoy strenuous athletic dances. The social dance for coeducational groups is often recommended for the fifth or sixth grades. It is highly recommended for seventh and eighth grades. The success of it will depend largely on whether the children are interested in it and the social needs of the children in the area.

Objectives. Children in the middle and upper grades should have a good start in accomplishing the basic objectives of rhythms and dances through participation in them while in grades one, two, and three. It is hoped they will be further developed in the middle and upper grades. Objectives, in addition to those listed in Chapter 10, include:

1. To develop skills which will not only provide present enjoyment, but also meet possible future needs and interests.

2. To develop a wholesome social relationship between boys and girls.

3. To develop an understanding of socially acceptable standards and courtesies of individuals and groups in dancing situations.

4. To aid in learning and appreciating the characteristics and activities of people in other countries.

5. To develop the desire and ability to create rhythmic and dance patterns and movements.

6. To develop skill, grace, balance, and agility in body movements.

7. To overcome awkwardness.

8. To establish fun and happy recreational experiences that decrease nervous tension.

9. To increase poise.

Teaching Hints

1. Create an interest in the dance through a proper introduction. In addition to the name and derivation, the correct atmosphere may be developed by the use of pictures and costumes of the people of its origin and by making it a part of a unit of work.

2. Permit the group to hear the music before endeavoring to teach the dance. This usually creates interest.

3. Assist them in getting the beat of the rhythm.

4. Describe and demonstrate the first step and permit them to do it in an informal grouping.

5. After they have practiced, try it with the music. If it is a couple dance, have them try it next with a partner.

6. Teach the dance in parts. Add a new part

to those already practiced, and continue to the completion.

7. Do not force children to be partners. It is much wiser to permit them to select. Many times boys of this age wish to work out the steps with boys, and girls with girl partners. Usually, when they are at the enjoyment stage of the dance, they will volunteer to mix partners.

8. Give them encouragement and individual assistance without embarrassing them before their group.

9. In the social dance situation, boys may wish to have some classes apart from the girls until they gain some confidence.

10. Create social situations where folk, square, or social dancing may be enjoyed to achieve their value.

Developmental Movement Activities. This category of activities is very vigorous and includes specific movements in a planned sequence to increase the efficiency of body use, strength, and agility. They are planned appropriately for each grade and age level with care being noted for individual differences in relation to body structure and build. In these activities it is usually best to have each child challenge himself to increase his record as he increases his strength, movement coordination, and ability. The activities include sit-ups, pushups, squat thrusts, jumping, climbing, flexing and bending, and so on. Rope jumping and circuit training are also excellent developmental activities.

Continuation of rope jumping for development is excellent for children in the middle and upper grades. Athletic coaches find that jumping rope is very helpful in the hand-foot coordination in balance and foot dexterity needed in many sports. It is of value in training and conditioning. Because of its use today in many sports, boys should no longer think of it as a "girls' activity." Many routines and combinations of movements make it challenging and interesting. Special routines may be created by children in rhythmic patterns and performed to music.

Circuit training is very popular today as a developmental and conditioning activity. While it has perhaps been used for a longer period of time in colleges and secondary schools, it is an equally valuable activity in elementary schools. Circuit training is built around desired goals and well defined objectives. The use of equipment for climbing, hanging, and jumping is excellent and very popular for use in developmental activities and circuit training.

Circuit training is an exercise method that aims to develop certain components of physical fitness. It is designed to increase muscular strength, muscular endurance, cardiovascular endurance, and flexibility. A circuit refers to a group of selected exercises or activities that are arranged in a definite order around a gymnasium or play yard. Each exercise is referred to as a station and is given a number. The performers move in order from station to station performing the exercises. A description of the exercise as well as the number of repetitions to be performed is posted at each station. It is suggested that about ten minutes of a physical education period be devoted to the circuit. Students are divided into small groups and each is assigned a definite station as a starting point. They then proceed at their own rate to complete as many circuits or parts of a circuit as they can in the allotted time. Class-

(Courtesy of Game-Time Inc.)

record cards are kept and the student reports his score each day. In a ten-station circuit, a student who started at station 1 and arrived back at station 1 in the allotted 10 minutes has a score of 1 for that day. If in that time he had passed his starting station and had completed station 2 of his second trip, his score would be 1.2 and so on. A target of two complete circuits could be set. When individuals reach that target the number of repetitions at each station could be increased for them, thereby setting a new target. This applies the principle of progressive loading. One of the greatest advantages of circuit training as a method of developing physical fitness is that it is adaptable to individual needs and achievement. A student goes around the circuit at his own rate and when he reaches a set target a new one is set for him. A circuit aims to keep everyone busy all of the time and presents exercises in an interesting manner. It also permits a large number of performers to train at the same time.

In selecting activities for a circuit it is important to keep the objectives clearly in mind and to select exercises that contribute directly to them. It is also important to set the number of repetitions at each station at a level that is realistic. Everyone should experience success at each station. Sometimes a modification of an exercise is suggested as an alternate in individual cases. For instance, a rope climb may be a prescribed exercise but may be impossible for some students. Those unable to climb could be given the exercise of lowering their backs to the floor and pulling themselves upright. It is also important that stations be arranged in an order that will permit students to move freely from one station to another without waiting for their turn. This can be accomplished by having enough equipment available and by having the slower stations placed strategically. A slower station should be followed by one which accommodates many students. In case performance is delayed at one station, the student could skip that one momentarily and move on. He could then move back to pick it up when the station is not overcrowded.

Two sample circuits are outlined in Table

11-2, one for a gymnasium and one for a playground. Both are designed to increase muscular strength, muscular endurance, cardiovascular endurance, and flexibility. With slight changes they may be applicable for various age levels.

Objectives. The objectives of developmental activities are as follows:

1. To increase the strength of all muscles of the body.
2. To increase endurance.
3. To improve total physical fitness.
4. To show the relationship of special activities to strength and a better feeling of physical well-being.

Teaching Hints

1. Use progressive exercises to meet the needs in various age and grade levels.
2. Start with short periods of time and gradually increase time in order to build endurance.
3. Identify all activities carefully to the students and teach the benefit of them in relationship to general health and physical well-being.
4. Accept individual differences as to body build and endurance. Challenge each to better himself and not necessarily compete with his classmates.
5. Encourage a wholesome attitude toward desirable health attitudes and the promotion of physical strength and endurance.

Games of Low Organization. The definition and objectives for these games are the same in middle-childhood grades as in the early-childhood grades. Skills and techniques required are naturally more difficult and challenging.

These games are valuable and very enjoyable to use when there is a short time for activity; when a teacher is not working on a special team game; for activities with carry-over value for children to use when they are not at school; for social relationships within the group; and for uniting a class.

Examples of games of low organization include Three Deep, Beater Goes 'Round, Freedom, and Jump the Shot.

Teaching Hints

1. Help your children to understand the game by explaining how it was named. For example, Three Deep received its name because three people are not permitted to stand in a triple circle.

2. Before attempting to teach the game, analyze it to ascertain its exact objectives and determine whether it will meet the needs and interests of your children.

3. Check very carefully the skills and techniques involved to ascertain whether they meet the abilities of your children. They may be either too easy and give no challenge or too difficult for them to enjoy.

4. Teach the game to your entire class. Then, if more active participation is desired, play two or more games at the same time by combining two squads for a game or permitting each individual squad to play a game.

5. Assist the children with the skills and techniques both as a group and as individuals.

6. Give recognition for good group relationships shown through respect for each other, such as taking turns so a few are not being given all the opportunity to be "it" at the expense of the other children.

7. Analyze the activity while your children

Table 11–2. Out-of-Doors

Station	Exercise	Repetitions	Objective
1	Step-up	10	Cardiovascular endurance
2	Shooting baskets	5 shots	Strength, flexibility
3	Agility run (zig-zag run)	3 laps	Flexibility, cardiovascular endurance
4	Horizontal traveling on ladder (15 feet)	1	Strength, muscular endurance
5	Long run (30 to 75 yds., depending on age level)	1	Cardiovascular endurance
6	Flexed-arm hang	10 sec.	Strength, muscular endurance
7	Rope jumping	15 times	Cardiovascular endurance
8	Skin the cat (over bar)	3 times	Flexibility
9	Jump and reach	10 times	Strength
10	Jungle gym climb	2	Flexibility
11	Sliding board	3	Strength
12	Over and under (A pole on two chairs a short distance apart. Student goes over 1st and under 2nd)	3	Flexibility

In-Doors

Station	Exercise	Repetitions	Objective
1	Shuttle run	1	Flexibility
2	Wall bounce	15	Muscular strength
3	Rope climb (10 ft.)	1	Strength and muscular endurance
4	Log roll	1 mat	Flexibility
5	Wrist curls	1	Muscular strength
6	Squat thrust	5	Cardiovascular endurance
7	Over and under	3	Flexibility
8	Step-ups	10	Cardiovascular endurance
9	Sideward bends (weights)	3 each	Muscular strength and endurance
10	Rope jump	15	Cardiovascular endurance
11	Basket shooting	5	Strength, flexibility
12	Bent-arm hang	15 sec.	Muscular strength and endurance

are participating in it to ascertain if it is meeting your objectives. If not, change certain rules to meet them or change to another activity.

8. Remember, games of low organization may be for either small or large group play. This means that a small number of children may play them with enjoyment or the entire class may participate in the game together and receive the needed physical activity, social development, fun, and challenge.

Individual and Dual Activities. Individual and dual activities are defined as activities which require from one to four players for participation. They are of value not only for immediate use but for recreational pursuits in later life as well. Shuffleboard, archery, deck tennis, advanced forms of hopscotch and rope jumping, croquet, quoits, marbles, and table tennis are examples.

Objectives. The objectives of individual and dual activities are as follows:

1. To teach activities which may be engaged in during leisure time—now and later in life.

2. To give a child an opportunity to choose and become proficient in an activity he desires.

3. To develop an interest in and love of physical activity.

4. To give an opportunity for each child to recognize his own individual growth and development and to feel a sense of accomplishment.

5. To provide activities for times when only a few children are present.

6. To provide corecreational activities for boys and girls above the fifth-grade level.

7. To provide social experiences which develop desirable social behavior patterns.

Teaching Hints

1. These activities may be taught to the group as a whole so that all children understand rules, play area, and the necessary skills.

2. After the group is oriented, individuals should be encouraged to work in small groups for practice and play.

3. Visual aids are available and helpful.

4. Blackboard diagrams which show playing areas are essential.

5. Equipment must be shared so that each person has an opportunity to use it.

6. The children should agree on a schedule for the use of available equipment and facilities.

7. Individuals should be encouraged to work at their own rate of speed and to choose partners. Many times they know with whom they can best work and play to gain the most from the experiences.

8. Aid each child individually with constructive teaching suggestions and hints.

9. Help those who wish, after they have the necessary skills and techniques, to plan tournaments. This desire should come from the class and not be forced on them at the wish of the teacher.

Lead-Up Activities for Team Games. Certain skills and techniques are necessary for successful participation and enjoyment of team games. Teachers should analyze the team game or games they desire to teach their children and note the specific skills and techniques required. Many times these may be presented to the class in the form of a preliminary or lead-up game, thus providing an opportunity for practice.

Lead-up activities include relays, certain modified games which include one or more skills and/or techniques, and specific drill and practice. Students in the fifth and sixth grades are often sufficiently interested in improving their skills in team games to practice in actual formal drill. Others will dislike drill practice and will need to develop the necessary skills and techniques in a game situation.

Examples. Three lead-up games will be discussed showing the skills and techniques they involve which are needed in the team game of Bat Ball. They are Catching and Throwing Relay, Hot Potato, and Dodge Ball.

CATCHING AND THROWING RELAY

Use an even number of squads for this game. Arrange squads in four equal lines as shown in Figure 11–1.

Number *one* on each team is given a volleyball

Table 11–3. Lead-Up Games

Lead-Up Games	Skills and Techniques of Each Game	Requirements for the Team Game of Bat Ball
1. Catching and Throwing Relay	Catching Throwing Running	All the skills used in the lead-up games are needed.
2. Hot Potato (circle passing game)	Speed in throwing Speed in accurate throwing Skill in catching	In addition, one needs to be able to bat the ball from his hand and there is much teamwork required.
3. Simple Dodge Ball	Catching Throwing at a moving target Dodging a ball Running Jumping	

or an inflated ball of similar size and weight. At the signal, "Go," he throws the ball to number *two* in his line. Number *two* catches it and quickly passes it back to number *one* and then runs to the end of his line behind the last player.

This brings number *three* to the front of the line. Number *one* passes the ball to him and number *three* returns it to number *one* and runs to the end of the line. Number *one* remains at his starting position until he has passed the ball to everyone in his line. When number *two* returns to the front of the line, he runs up and takes the place of number one. Number *one* then runs to the end of the line and participates in play the same as all others. Number *two* now passes the ball to each one in the line until number *three* is in front of the line. Number *three* replaces number *two*, and so the game continues until each person has had a turn to be up front and pass the ball to everyone in his line. The team finishing first wins. The distance the thrower stands from his teammates is determined by the ability of the students. The first time the distance should be short but it may be lengthened as the game proceeds and the throwing skills increase.

It takes a short time to play this game and each person receives much practice in catching and throwing the ball. As the players increase their skills, the speed will also increase. Skills of catching, throwing, and running are practiced and should show improvement.

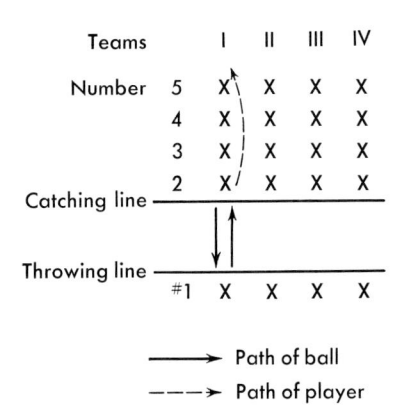

Figure 11-1. Catching and Throwing Relay.

HOT POTATO—CIRCLE GAME

Hot Potato is played in a circle formation. It is wise to start with one ball. The object is to pass the ball from one person to another as fast as possible. At intervals the leader claps his hands or blows a whistle. At this signal, the ball passing stops and the person holding the ball is caught with the "hot potato." The object, of course, is not to have the ball when the whistle blows.

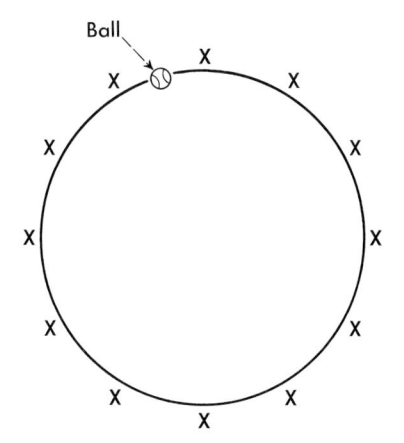

Figure 11-2. Hot Potato.

If the class remains together in one circle for this game, several balls should be used to add interest and challenge. When more than one are used, they must be passed around the circle in the same direction, skipping no one. Balls should be given to each third or fourth student in the circle to start the game. A change of direction may be made at a given signal from the leader. Winners are those who were never holding the ball at the stop signal. Skills of speed and accuracy in catching and throwing are increased. After the game has been taught to the entire group, several games may be played with each group, using one or more balls as their skill permits. The same signal to stop could apply to all groups, so one leader will suffice.

DODGE BALL

The rules of this game, discussed in Chapter 17, are familiar to most people. Children gain practice in the skills of catching, throwing at a moving target, dodging, and running. Each of these skills is needed in the team game of Bat Ball which is used here to illustrate how lead-up games aid in preparation for a team game.

BAT BALL—TEAM GAME

Two teams of from eight to twelve players each are recommended, with a rectangular playing area marked off as illustrated in Figure 11-3. A volleyball or inflated ball of similar size and weight is used. One team is at bat and the other in the field as diagrammed. There are no specific places for fielders to stand, except that no one may be closer than 6 feet to the base.

The game is played by innings. Three outs constitute one-half an inning and the fielding team then has its turn at bat. When each team has batted and made three outs, one full inning is completed. Seven or nine innings may be set for a game. The score of the last complete inning may be used to designate the winning team.

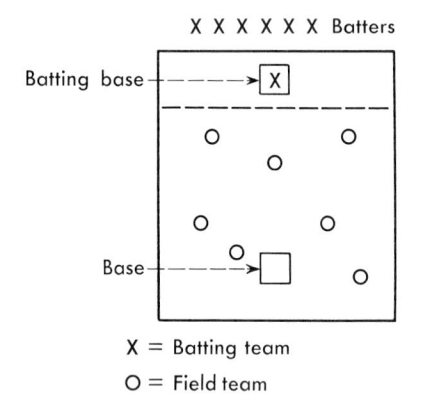

```
                    X X X X X X  Batters
Batting base ┼─────▶[X]
             │────────────────
             │      O      O
             │         O
             │
             │      O      O
             │         O
    Base  ───┼────▶[ ]
             │              O

X = Batting team
O = Field team
```

Figure 11-3. Bat Ball.

The first person at bat holds the ball in one hand and endeavors to bat it over the dotted line so the fielders may not catch it. A fly ball caught by a fielder is an out. If the ball fails to cross the dotted line, the batter is out. The distance of this line from the batter's base varies from 3 feet to 5 feet, depending on the ability of the children and the size of the playing area. The court may vary in size according to the amount of space available. The size will again vary with abilities of children.

Once a batter bats the ball over the line, he becomes a runner and endeavors to run to the one base and return home without being hit with the ball. He may either circle the base or touch it. He is never safe on the base.

The fielders endeavor to hit the runner below the waist before he returns home and crosses the dotted line. Fielders must pass the ball from one to another. They may not walk or run with it nor hold it longer than three seconds. The batter, then, either makes a run or an out before another player is up to bat. Note the speed element needed which was practiced in the Catching and Passing Relay and in Hot Potato.

By the use of the Catching and Passing Relay, Hot Potato, and Dodge Ball, one may readily understand the value of preliminary games as aids for teaching skills and techniques needed in the team game of Bat Ball. This plan of progression, using lead-up games and activities to assist with skills needed in team games, is recommended very strongly.

Teaching Hints

1. Analyze the team game you and your children have agreed to play. Then plan lead-up games to include the skills and techniques necessary for it.

2. Interest your children in the games by giving them the reason for practicing the skill or technique.

3. Demonstrate with another child or have children with whom you worked prior to class time demonstrate the game.

4. Provide an opportunity for questions.

5. Use as little playing time as possible before starting the activity.

6. Encourage all children to participate.

7. Expect and encourage good sportsmanship and social relationships.

8. Discourage comparison of one student with another. All will not perform equally in physical education activities any more than all will be at the same level in other parts of the curriculum.

9. If relays are used, plan the scoring so each team or squad may score each time it is played. For example, if four squads participate, the winner may score ten points; second place, eight; third place, five; and last place, two. Play relays more than once. They do not take long and give good opportunity for needed practice.

10. Never have more than 8 players in a squad or team for a relay. Some teachers with 32 children divide them into two groups of 16 each. When this practice occurs, children lose interest because they must spend too much time waiting for a turn. Remember, four groups will give each child twice the fun and activity in the same amount of time, and in addition will prevent waning interest and problems.

Self-testing Activities and Stunts. Stunts and self-testing activities are those activities which afford the participant an opportunity to test his skill with others, to manipulate his body in many unusual positions both stationary and locomotive, and which are concerned with large-muscle development, flexibility, strength, and agility.

Table 11–4. Types of Self-testing Activities and Stunts

Individual Activities	Couple Activities
Pushups	Indian Wrestle
Jump-the-Stick	Acrobatic Handshake
Forward Roll	Cock Fight
	Tandem

Group Activities	Pyramids
Skin the Snake	Rick Rack
Merry-Go-Round	Ten Pins
Wooden Man	Picket Fence
Thousand-Legged Animal	Heart

Objectives. The objectives of self-testing activities and stunts are as follows:

1. To develop agility, flexibility, balance, and strength.
2. To offer an opportunity for big-muscle development.
3. To provide opportunities for a student to develop satisfaction through his own accomplishments.
4. To provide fun and social relationships.
5. To provide an activity which develops a rhythmic sense.
6. To develop initiative and courage.

Teaching Hints

1. Demonstrate each activity or teach it to student leaders in advance so they may demonstrate.
2. Make necessary arrangements so that proper clothing will be worn during the program.
3. Do not hurry children in these activities.
4. Do not expect each child to do all of them.
5. Teach safety measures necessary for each activity.
6. Progress from relatively easy to more difficult activities.
7. Provide mats, mattresses, or other safe protection.
8. Avoid strain.
9. In couple stunts, choose partners wisely and carefully.
10. Do not force any child to participate who is afraid.

Gymnastics. Gymnastics is becoming an important part of the elementary school physical education program today when qualified teachers and the necessary equipment and apparatus are available. Because of the specific needs and presentation of this program, Chapter 26 presents it in detail.

Team Games. Team games are activities which require more organization and are played between two or more groups, units, or squads. They are concerned with the development of specific skills and techniques, group understanding and participation, specific attitudes in relation to sports, and the understanding of teamwork with emphasis on the "we" and cooperative spirit.

Objectives. The objectives of team games are as follows:

1. To teach social responses through cooperation and competition.
2. To teach the child to work for the good of the team, which at times requires repression of his own individual desires.
3. To teach the child, through group cooperation, self-discipline and self-control.
4. To develop respect for officials and to show the need for definite rules and requirements.
5. To develop specific skills and techniques as required in the game situation.
6. To develop the ability to officiate through an understanding of the rules, sportsmanship, alertness, and impartiality.

Examples. Some examples of team games suitable for middle childhood are Line Soccer, Newcomb, Bat Ball, Kick ball, Kick Baseball, Kick Pin Baseball, Captain Ball, and Long Ball.

Teachers should choose and teach team games to their children which meet their needs, interests, and abilities. The fourth grade requires team games with fewer rules and less highly developed skills and techniques than the sixth grade.

An example of progression using three team games mentioned above will be discussed so teachers may thoroughly understand how they may work for progression from team game to team game within a given grade or from grade to grade.

The three games to be used for illustrative purposes are Kickball, Kick Baseball, and Kick

Pin Baseball. Each game is played on a diamond like a softball diamond. The size of the diamond will differ depending on the ability and ages of the children and the available play area.

KICKBALL

Kickball may begin in the fourth grade. It is played by two teams of from eight to twelve children. One team is at bat and the other is in the field as shown in Figure 11–4. X's indicate the batting team and O's indicate the fielding team. The game is played by innings like Softball and Bat Ball. Seven or nine innings may be agreed on for a complete game. These may not all be completed in one period of physical education and the game may be continued during the next period.

A soccer ball, volleyball, or inflated rubber ball of approximately the same size is used.

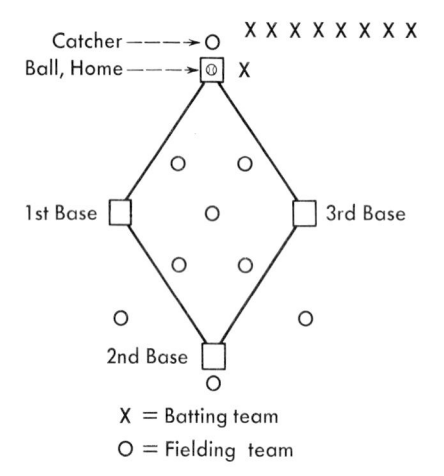

```
Catcher ----> O   X X X X X X X X
Ball, Home ----> ⊙  X
              /         \
            O   O
    1st Base □              □ 3rd Base
            O   O
          O           O
              2nd Base □
                  O

X = Batting team
O = Fielding team
```

Figure 11–4. Kickball.

The fielding team has only one specific player, a catcher, who stands behind home plate. Other players cover the field as they desire so they may field the balls kicked by the team at bat.

Number *one* of the batting team kicks the ball which lies stationary on home plate. If he kicks a fly ball and it is caught by a fielder, he is automatically out. The next batter is then up. If he kicks a fair ball which is not caught by a fielder, he becomes a runner. He runs as many bases as he can before the fielders recover the ball and throw it home to their catcher. When the runner sees the ball nearing home, he stays on base until the ball is kicked by another player.

Fielders have but one rule to remember when they field a ball. They must always throw it home to the catcher—never to any other base. As soon as the catcher receives the ball, he immediately places it on home plate. The object is to catch the runner off any base. Only one player may be on any one base at a time. Base runners may not advance on caught fly balls. If they do run on a caught fly, they must return to base before the ball is thrown home and placed on home plate or they are out.

Notice the few rules necessary to play the game. For the runners they are as follows:

1. Keep running as long as the ball is away from home plate.

2. Do not run on a caught fly ball. If you advance, quickly return to the base you have just left, before the ball is placed on home plate.

For the fielders the rules are as follows:

1. Field the ball immediately and throw it home to the catcher.

2. Keep all areas of the field covered and endeavor to catch fly balls.

The skills and techniques needed for the game include:

1. Running.
2. Kicking a *stationary* ball.
3. Throwing a ball to one specified base.
4. Catching a ball.

Kick Baseball, another team game played on the same diamond with two teams of equal numbers of children, will be discussed next.

KICK BASEBALL

The rules for Kick Baseball game are harder. More actual thinking is necessary. More skill is required because the kicker must kick a ball which is rolled or bowled in from a pitcher. The fielding positions include a catcher, bowler (pitcher), and a player on each base. The runner is played at each base as in a regular softball or baseball game. He may stop at any base and advance on the next kick. Hence the fielders have to think and know, when each new person comes up to kick, where they will throw the ball when they field it. The game is played by innings the same as Kickball.

Progression to this game involves more rules, more skills, and more techniques.

1. Each player must be able to kick a moving ball rolling toward him from the bowler or pitcher.

2. Skill is required to bowl the ball.

3. Fielders must catch and throw the ball as in Kickball, but must know which base to make their throw to for an out.

4. Many more people must be skilled in catching because each baseman, first, second, and third, as well as the catcher, will receive many thrown balls as well as kicked balls.

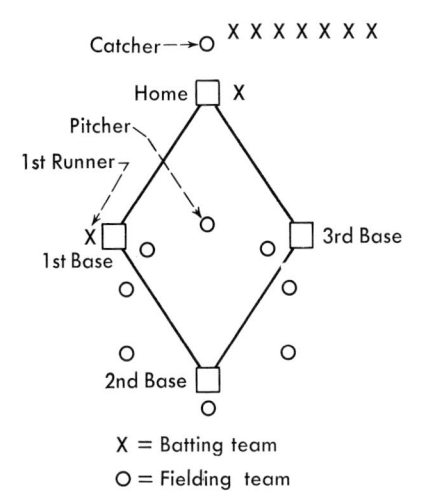

```
        Catcher→O  X X X X X X
              Home □ X
       Pitcher
      1st Runner
           X □           □ 3rd Base
       1st Base  O     O
                O     O
                O     O
              2nd Base □
                  O
        X = Batting team
        O = Fielding team
```

Figure 11–5. Kick Baseball.

KICK PIN BASEBALL

Advancing to Kick Pin Baseball requires more speed and skill. This game is also played on a diamond by two teams. On each base, including the home base, stands an Indian club, an old bowling pin, a milk carton, or a similar object.

The bowler (pitcher) bowls the ball to the kicker. If the bowler knocks over the pin at home plate, the kicker is out. Notice the accuracy needed by the bowler. If the kicker knocks his own pin over, he automatically puts himself out. He should stand by the side of the pin so that he will not kick it with the backward swing of his leg, and so that the bowler has an opportunity to aim at the pin.

If the kicker kicks a fly ball which is caught, he is out. When he kicks a fair ball he becomes a *runner* and if he makes a complete circuit of bases he scores a run. He must run behind each club, so he does not knock them over, and return to home plate. He is never safe on any base. He either scores a run or makes an out before a new kicker is up.

The fielders field the ball and pass it to first base, to second base, to third base, and home, endeavoring to get it to a base ahead of the runner.

The ball must make the same complete circuit of bases as the runner. If the ball reaches any base ahead of the runner, the baseman kicks the pin down. This makes the runner out, if the runner beats the ball home, he makes a run for his team.

Notice the skill and speed needed in fielding the ball and the accurate throwing to each base which is required to put a runner out. Notice also the additional speed needed in running the bases. Remember, a runner is never safe at any base. He is safe only after he crosses home base ahead of the ball.

Skills and techniques involve all of those mentioned in the other two games plus additional ones:

1. Skill in bowling a ball to hit a pin.
2. Timing the kick correctly to obtain placement and distance.
3. Good judgment in order to protect the pin at home plate from being bowled over.
4. Accurate and fast passing of the ball to every baseman.
5. Skill in catching and getting the throw away rapidly.

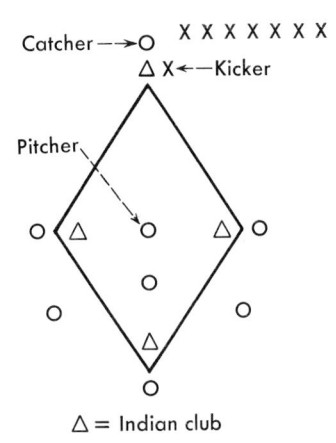

```
        Catcher→O  X X X X X X
                  △ X ← Kicker
       Pitcher
         O △      O    △ O
                O
         O              O
                △
                O
        △ = Indian club
```

Figure 11–6. Kick Pin Baseball.

From the discussion of these three team games it is hoped the teacher will understand their use for progression in different groups or grades. For example, Kickball might be used in the fourth grade, Kick Baseball in fifth grade, and Kick Pin Baseball in sixth grade.

When planning programs of activity, teachers will be able to find games which develop in skills, rules, and techniques from relatively easy to hard. They will also find their children happy and interested in progression and continued advancement to more challenging play experiences.

Teaching Hints

1. Use the blackboard and all possible visual aids to teach children the over-all view of the field, playing area, and positions of players.

2. Prepare children for skills and techniques needed through the use of lead-up games or games of low organization before the actual team game is started. It is very difficult to teach new skills and techniques as well as new rules at one time.

3. After the team game has been started, analyze the children's needs and plan the first five or ten minutes of the period with games or situations in which they may practice the skill.

4. Prepare various children to act as umpires, judges, or referees. In this way a class of 32 children may have two team games going on at once with twice as much fun, activity, and learning experience.

5. Use every possible teaching opportunity to encourage teamwork. For example, a ball will travel faster if thrown to a teammate than it will if a player runs with it to a given base; when one fielder goes after a ball, other players should wait to relay it to the needed base instead of all running after it.

6. Encourage students with good skills to help those who have lesser abilities, the same way they help each other with work in a classroom.

7. Encourage sportsmanship at all times.

8. Stress cooperation, not competition.

9. Teach children to be good winners as well as good losers and to know that the important

thing is not the score but the way they play and cooperate.

10. Plan tournaments if the class is interested in them.

Track and Field Events. Track and field events are activities which are competitive and self-testing and which are excellent for the development of agility, strength, speed, and endurance. A child enjoys them because they are able to be measured and he may see his own improvement as well as compete with others.

Track events include dashes at varying distances depending on age level, shuttle relays and, if desired, novelty relays such as sack, obstacle, and three-legged races.

Field events include the high jump, running and standing broad jumps, hop step and jump, throws for distance using balls such as basketball and softball, shot put (8–10 lb.), punting footballs and kicking soccer balls for accuracy and distance.

Objectives. The objectives of track and field events are as follows:

1. To develop strength, speed, and endurance.
2. To assist in developing the locomotor skills of running, jumping, and throwing.
3. To increase interest in self-improvement through individual participation and measurement.
4. To meet the desires of children to challenge and be challenged.

Teaching Hints

1. Teach the need for safety in each activity.
2. Select activities and distances on basis of age.
3. Have a diversified program.
4. Work with each individual and do not eliminate anyone.
5. Do not have boys and girls competing with each other.
6. Use modified meets as a culminating activity with children classified according to age and weight groups.

Classroom Games. Classroom games for children in the middle-childhood grades do not differ in definition or objectives from those used in early childhood (see Chapter 10). They may place additional emphasis on social and recreational and worthy leisure-time pursuits. Relatively little physical activity may be developed in the classroom program.

Examples are Black Magic; Bird, Beast, and Fish; Telegrams; Coffee, Tea, and Milk; Going to Jerusalem; Upset the Fruit Basket; and various relays, pencil and paper games, and blackboard games. Games such as darts, indoor quoits, and ring toss are suitable for these purposes.

Teaching Hints

1. Teach games which will be suitable for recreational pursuits.
2. Teach the need for close cooperation and respect for other people. Children can have fun without disturbing those in other rooms.
3. Permit children to choose activities by democratic procedures.
4. Change rules of games if they are not safe in your classroom situation.
5. Substitute yarn balls, bean bags, or clean erasers for balls.

Aquatics. For many schools it is not possible to use aquatics as a part of the physical education program. However, if facilities in the community or school and qualified instructors are available, swimming, boating, and canoeing should be a part of the program. Only a qualified instructor should attempt to teach aquatics. Assistance may be received from qualified persons in the community. The Red Cross will assist in planning and administering the program when facilities are available. Chapter 27 discusses the aquatics program in detail.

Some Expected Outcomes

The following chart shows some outcomes we might expect to see from the use of recommended activities in physical education programs. We expect those suggested in Chapter 10 to have been reached by most children.

Some Expected Social Learning. Some social skills we might expect children to develop from their continued experiences in physical education programs are:

1. Accept self as an important member of a group.
2. Accept teammates as being equally important as self.
3. Accept differences in abilities of peers.

RECOMMENDATIONS FOR PROGRAM DEVELOPMENT

Some Expected Learning Outcomes

Activity	Expected Outcomes

1. *Movement Fundamentals*

Walk — Correct posture. Varying movements such as cross step, goose-step, drum major step.

Run — *Fast*—without collisions, with quick starts and stops, and with quick directional movement. Fifty or seventy-five yards for 7th- and 8th-grade girls and a hundred for 7th- and 8th-grade boys.

Hop — Both feet or each foot *fast* in place or moving forward, backward, sideward either side—25 times or more.

Jump — Standing broad, running broad, vertical jump 10" or higher, jump down from a 2'–4' height lightly with bent knees and without falling. Combine a hop step and jump; combine runs and leaps; hurdle over low obstacles; high jump over bar.

Hurdle — Run and hurdle, height from 18" for 4th grade up to 36" for 8th-grade boys, girls up to 24" in 7th and 8th grades.

2. *Rhythmic Movement*

Combine locomotor and nonlocomotor movements — Perform in even and uneven patterns any called-for combinations, such as walk-run-leap. Advance to specific dance steps called for in folk and square dances and execute them alone or with partners. These include the toe-heel step, step-hop, schottische, polka, mazurka steps, waltz, etc.

Creativity — Be able to express feelings and actions in dance, such as fear or happiness. Create new patterns of movement and combine patterns for a dance routine.

Body control — Show grace and poise in all rhythmic movement—good control of body, graceful moves, light steps, high leaps with soft landing, etc.

3. *Developmental Activities; Stunts, Tumbling, and Gymnastics*

Vault — Over bench, box or buck, using basic, straddle, squat, or flank vault.

Climb — Climb and descend a rope or pole 10' or more, using both arms and legs correctly. Learn to do different things on ropes.

Chinning — Boys—at least five times; girls—use modified pull up on low bar 10–15 minimum.

Strength, agility, flexibility, balance — Be able to perform individual forward and backward rolls; rolls with partners (i.e. Eskimo). Accomplish handstand against wall, head stand, hand stand, cartwheel, etc. Be able to work on the various pieces of apparatus available.

Hanging — Hang by hands from rope higher than the head of the performer, do bicycle with leg movement. Using two ropes side by side, do an inverted hang.

4. *Rope Jumping* — Be able to do a variety of jumps for increasing periods of time, for endurance and agility.

5. *Games Skills*

Throw and catch — Using various size balls, be able to throw and catch to self at different heights in air and against a wall; throw over a net and run and catch it on the other side; throw to a partner with accuracy at different distances; hit a stationary target and a running target (player running); throw for distances, endeavoring to beat own record; catch rubber rings used in deck tennis and throw one accurately.

Some Expected Learning Outcomes (*continued*)

Activity	Expected Outcomes
Bounce and dribble	Accurately to self while moving and covering ground; without losing control of ball, bounce and toss to a standing or moving partner; dribble a ball with the feet (alternating feet); continuous bounce in place at various speeds according to rhythmic beat used.
Kick	For accuracy—through goals; for distance, to break own record; kick a moving ball rolled toward kicker with consistency and for distance; punt a football (boys).
Strike	Strike a volleyball against a wall 10 times or more in succession; serve a volleyball within the court boundaries; bat a pitched softball 4 or 5 times out of 10; successfully hit a ball in games such as tetherball; serve a volleyball over 6′ net; successfully use racquets and paddles in tennis, badminton, and table tennis.
Shoot a ball	Make three or four baskets shooting from the foul line; dribble and shoot lay-up shots; shoot from various distances after dribble and when standing.
Volley	Successfully volley a ball to a partner over a net 6–10 times. Direct ball to different areas of the court.
Combine skills and movements	Be able to play 10 or 15 new games annually, including those of low organization, individual and dual activities, lead-up, and team games. Know rules so games may be played away from school when no adult leader is present.
6. *Swimming*	Be able to float and to use at least one stroke well enough to have confidence in deep water.

4. Recognize and adjust to own abilities and limitations.
5. Accept teaching suggestions cheerfully and apply them.
6. Accept decisions of any official, whether a teammate, a teacher, or a professional official.
7. Be able to serve as a leader.
8. Be able to act as an official of games played with his own peer group.
9. Play honestly and fairly without constant bickering and arguing.
10. Accept wins and defeats without boasting or making excuses.
11. Be able to carry on some activities without an adult leader.
12. Apply sportsmanship in assisting peers needing help rather than fault finding.

Questions and Practical Problems

1. Some activities in the middle and upper grades are recommended to be used with boys and girls in separate groups. Discuss all of the pros and cons of this principle from the viewpoint of the physical, social, psychological, and biological bases.

2. Select one team game you wish to teach. Analyze this game thoroughly and then choose the preliminary or lead-up activities you wish to use before starting the team game. What class organization will you use for your lead-up activities? Why?

3. The children in your fifth grade are not interested in rhythms or the dance. You have been told you must include them as a part of your physical education program. Plan ways of motivating your class and show how you will work this problem through to a successful end.

4. Plan a well-balanced, 10-week program of physical education for the grade of your choice.

5. Show the progression for this program based on suggested daily activities for the 10-week period.

6. Your school has no gymnasium or playroom. All of your physical education program during inclement weather must therefore be held in your classroom. Plan pieces of equipment your children may make to use for classroom games. What activities will you use other than games? Specify types and names of each activity. Plan the most satisfactory class arrangement for the average size classroom to insure maximum benefit for all children.

7. Make up two original classroom activities for the grade of your choice.

8. You are in an area where there is a nice lake near the school. How would you make use of it? Plan specifically for its use, including going to and returning from the lake.

9. Your boys and girls do not wish to participate together in their physical education program. You are teaching the sixth grade. How will you meet this problem? Be specific.

Selected References

AARON, D., and B. WINAWER. *Child's Play*. New York: Harper & Row, Publishers, 1965.

American Association for Health, Physical Education, and Recreation. *This Is Physical Education*. Washington, D.C.: American Association for Health, Physical Education, and Recreation, 1966.

BARROW, CRISP, LONG. *Physical Education Syllabus*. Minneapolis, Minn.: Burgess Publishing Co., 1967.

HALSEY, ELIZABETH, and LORENA PORTER. *Physical Education for Children: A Developmental Program*, rev. ed. New York: Holt, Rinehart & Winston, Inc., 1963.

HIXSON, CHALMER G., JR. "Bowling in the Elementary School?" *Journal of Health, Physical Education, and Recreation*, 33:30, Jan. 1962.

IRWIN, LESLIE W. *The Curriculum in Health and Physical Education*. Dubuque, Iowa: William C. Brown Co., Inc., 1960.

"Playgrounds—Design for Children." *Architectural Forum*, 117:84–105, Nov. 1962.

PRUDDEN, BONNIE. "Let Dancing Help Them." *Dance Magazine*, 34:26, Nov. 1960.

SCHURR, EVELYN L. "A Suggested Volleyball Unit for the Fourth Grade." *Volleyball Guide*, 1965–1967. Washington, D.C.: American Association for Health, Physical Education, and Recreation, Division of Girls' and Women's Athletics, p. 48.

SMITH, HOPE M., et al. *Introduction to Human Movement*. Reading, Mass.: Addison-Wesley Publishing Co., 1968.

WHITLOW, GARY. "Elementary Circuit Training." *Journal of Health, Physical Education, and Recreation*. Vol. 39, No. 5, May 1968.

WILBUR, HELEN. "Plus Values for Rope Jumping." *Journal of Health, Physical Education, and Recreation*, Vol. 37, No. 2, Feb. 1966, pp. 32–33.

CHAPTER 12

The Physical Education Program for the Atypical Child

The beginning teacher soon discovers that the children in a single class cannot accurately be said to form a homogeneous group. While most of the boys and girls in a single class may fall within a certain narrow age range, not all of these children will possess the same physical, mental, social, and emotional traits. A large majority of the children will fall into the "normal" or "average" classification for their age and grade. Others will deviate to a smaller or larger degree from their peers on a physical, mental, emotional, or social measure or on a combination of measures. This latter group, the atypical children, need special physical education experiences.

It is important that the classroom teacher or physical education specialist know the characteristics of these atypical children because upon this base of understanding a contributory physical education program will be built. This chapter will give the classroom teacher or physical education specialist some guidelines to follow for each of the atypical conditions described in Chapter 9 and will offer some activity suggestions for the teacher.

The Culturally Disadvantaged Child

Educational and physical education curriculums for the disadvantaged child cannot be conventional middle-class curriculums with traditional middle-class objectives and goals. The teacher cannot use middle-class teaching techniques or methods or expect to be able to impose a middle-class disciplinary standard. The traditional and conventional approaches to education and physical education do not help the culturally disadvantaged child to succeed in his school work; they only succeed in driving him away from the school and its educational offerings.

Many authorities have criticized the unrealistic educational atmosphere to which the culturally disadvantaged child is systematically exposed. On the elementary school level especially, they point out, textbooks describe and laud a way of life that is totally alien and unreachable to the culturally disadvantaged child. Educators are constantly seeking to adjust curriculums or to introduce innovative curriculums that will best serve the culturally disadvantaged child. As yet definitive answers as to how education can realistically serve the needs of the culturally disadvantaged child have not been found.

The classroom teacher or physical education specialist must have the ability to develop rapport with the culturally disadvantaged so the teacher can respect, understand, and help these children. The teacher must be able to provide the experiences and learning in physical education that are most needed by the culturally disadvantaged child. The teacher must be able to provide an enriched program that will help to motivate the culturally disadvantaged child to make the best use of his physical, intellectual, and creative skills.

Some guidelines that the classroom teacher and physical education specialist can follow in planning a meaningful program for the culturally disadvantaged child follow.

1. *The physical education program for the culturally disadvantaged should be focused on the individual child.* The culturally disadvantaged are especially aware of their individuality and the program therefore needs to exploit this quality and permit each child to express himself and to be creative in his play. Individual accomplishments in the physical education program, even though they may appear to be of a minor nature, if properly recognized and praised by the teacher will be of utmost importance and achieve desirable results.

2. *The physical education program for the culturally disadvantaged should recognize that two important goals are the development of physical fitness and the improvement of motor skill abilities.* The physical education program should include activities that will help these children to raise their physical fitness levels. Lack of structured programs in the ghettos and poverty pockets of our cities and communities and outside the school often prevents the culturally disadvantaged child from participating regularly in a program of physical activity and consequently prevents the child from maintaining even a minimal fitness level. Motor skill abilities are frequently not developed for the same reason. A sound and regular program of physical education and physical activity under outstanding leadership has been denied them.

3. *The physical education program for the culturally disadvantaged should be designed to meet the child's needs and interests.* Culturally disadvantaged children are not physically deprived in respect to physical goals. They enjoy vigorous activities as well as creative and self-testing activities. The program should offer a wide choice of activities so that these children can select not only those experiences they find pleasurable, but also those in which they can find success.

4. *The physical education program for the culturally disadvantaged should provide for "carry-over" recreational activities.* Recreational interests and habits of participation in regular physical activity of one's own choosing are important to culturally disadvantaged children. The elementary school physical education program should provide opportunities for these children to begin developing interest in and a background of skills for present and future recreational pursuits.

5. *The physical education program for the culturally disadvantaged should provide for a wholesome type of competition.* The culturally disadvantaged need and enjoy wholesome competition that is suitable to their age and grade level in school. However, the stress on competition should not be excessive. Competitive games and activities are important, particularly if the child is able to compete with himself to raise a physical-fitness-test score, to score higher on a motor-ability test, or to engage in a low organization game or sports contest. For younger elementary school-age children, there are many club programs that could be initiated, and older elementary-school-age children will enjoy the give and take of an intramural program. Highly competitive sports should not be included in such a program.

6. *The physical education program for the culturally disadvantaged should provide teaching aids, supplies, and equipment that have been purchased or constructed with care to suit the special needs of the program.* Rhythmical and creative activities are enjoyed. Therefore, the teacher should try to have phonographs, records, and a variety of instruments that have been purchased or made especially to carry out the program. Many warm-up activities, as well as games of low organization and other activities may be performed with musical accompaniment.

7. *The physical education program for the culturally disadvantaged should see that disciplinary measures are firm and consistent.* The culturally disadvantaged need and want firm, consistent, and appropriate disciplinary measures. It will help if each child knows what is expected of him and is encouraged to conform to these standards. The disciplinary measures that are imposed should relate directly to these children and they should understand the need for having such measures.

8. *The physical education program for the culturally disadvantaged should stress the need to achieve desirable health goals.* The program offers many opportunities to influence the health of deprived children. Showers, for example, should be available to the children whenever the school facilities permit. Each child should have a pair of sneakers and some kind of special clothing for physical education that will permit freedom of movement. Girls should have shorts, tights, or slacks to wear while participating, and all of the children should be provided with space to store their physical education clothing. Cleanliness and proper care of this clothing should be stressed by the teacher and followed up during the year through periodic inspections.

9. *The physical education program for the culturally disadvantaged should have implications for behavior patterns in the rest of the educational program.* From the give and take of physical activities and games the child can be helped to learn how to get along with others and how to cooperate as part of a larger group. Under outstanding leadership he will gradually become more aware of the needs, abilities, and talents of his peers and see how he differs. If these experiences are provided in the physical education class, some of the basic lessons, it is to be hoped, will be transferred and applied to other educational and life situations.

10. *The physical education program for the culturally disadvantaged should be correlated with the rest of the school academic program.* Through physical education activities that are imaginatively taught, many general education knowledges, skills, and abilities will be enhanced for the child. Through folk dances, for example, it is possible to acquaint the child with the customs of various cultures. These insights will help the child to better understand other countries and people and perhaps take more pride in the customs of his own culture. Knowing the origins of various folk dances may help the child to develop an interest in history, while the need to keep score in various games or figure baseball batting averages may stimulate the child's interest in arithmetic.

The Physically Handicapped Child

Some handicapped children will be able to participate in a regular program of physical education providing certain minor modifications are made to accommodate them. A separate adapted program must be provided for those children who cannot participate in the regular class program. The physically handicapped child cannot be allowed to sit on the sidelines and live a life devoid of any physical activity. The handicapped child needs to have the opportunity to develop and maintain appropriate levels of physical fitness and motor-skill ability. If no provision is made for special classes, the teacher should provide time in the regular class period for activities that are suited to these children. Placing all handicapped children in the regular physical education class has the advantage of giving them a feeling of belonging to the total life of the school. This advantage is not always possible when separate adapted classes are provided. The teacher or physical educator must know the capacities and abilities of each handicapped child so he can provide these children with an individualized program.

The following are some general guidelines for physical education programs for the physically handicapped in the elementary school.

1. *The physical education program for the physically handicapped should be directly related to the child's disability as well as to his total welfare.* The child's disability and medical recommendations concerning that disability determine the activities he can engage in. Therefore any modifications or adaptations that are made must be made in the activity that is selected. There should be consideration for the physical, social, emotional, and other aspects of the child's welfare.

2. *The physical education program for the physically handicapped should provide for a close working relationship with the medical profession.* The child's own physician will be in the best position to provide recommendations for a physical activity program for the child. If the child comes from a family that does not have a personal physician, then the school should take the responsibility for seeing that community or school health services cooperate to provide the

counseling that is needed for planning a program for the handicapped child.

3. *The physical education program for the physically handicapped should appraise skill and physical fitness levels.* The child's abilities in different motor skills and his physical fitness rating should be known if intelligent planning is to take place. Tests should be given to each child insofar as medical approval has been given. Such appraisal will not only help to ensure a proper physical education program for each child, but will also help to assure that the needs of the child are being met.

4. *The physical education program for the physically handicapped should receive continuous evaluation.* Careful records are very valuable when they indicate such information as medical findings, health habits, test scores, activity recommendations, physical disabilities, and activities engaged in. Records might also be kept on the child's interests and whether or not they are being met. Various sound means of evaluation should be utilized by the teacher to determine the effectiveness of the program. In this way the teacher will know whether the program is reaching its goals for each child, the child's parents can be appraised of progress, and the child's physician will be aided in recommending future activities for the child as he matures and progresses through the program.

5. *The physical education program for the physically handicapped should be similar in substance to the regular physical education program for normal children.* If the school makes provision for separate adapted classes and the program is totally different from the regular class program for children of the same age and grade, the physically handicapped child may feel even more isolated from his peers than he would be otherwise. When the adapted and regular class programs are made as similar as possible, the handicapped child can be helped to feel that he is, in his own way, accomplishing the same things as his classmates. He will be helped to gain self-confidence and self-respect, and will feel that he really is a part of the larger group. Similarity of programs will also serve as a motivator and stimulus to the handicapped child to achieve as much as possible in light of his limited abilities.

6. *The physical education program for the physically handicapped should be challenging to the child.* Physically handicapped children need the stimulation and challenge of a program that has definite goals and a definite skill progression. The physically handicapped like to test their abilities and need to experience the fun of a challenge and the success of meeting it on their own level of performance.

7. *The physical education program for the physically handicapped should provide time for additional help from the teacher.* The handicapped should be given an opportunity to have remedial help during after-school hours or club periods. Such a service on the part of the teacher can result in more individualized instruction than is usually permitted in a class period. Such out-of-class opportunities are especially needed if the handicapped are placed in the regular physical education class.

8. *The physical education program for the physically handicapped should attempt to select activities suitable for each individual.* On the elementary school level, all handicapped children in the school may meet in a common adapted physical education class. Although some of these children may be able to participate in several common activities, their differing ages may not stimulate a common interest in these activities. The fitness levels of each child, recreational needs, and sex and age as well as interest and medical limitations will help the teacher to determine the activities the children will enjoy and want to participate in.

9. *The physical education program for the physically handicapped should emphasize safety.* Safe facilities and safe equipment, for example, are essential to any sound physical education program. Special vigilance on the part of the teacher and school officials should be taken when a physical education class includes handicapped children. This is particularly true at the elementary school level where the school acts *in loco parentis.*

10. *The physical education program for the physically handicapped should provide suitable out-of-class activities.* Early elementary school children can profit from a club program in physical education where they can participate with their normal peers in an activity of common interest. When club and intramural programs are provided, they must be of such a nature that the physically handicapped child can enjoy them in a safe and controlled atmosphere. Child growth and development experts feel that the older elementary school child is placed in an unduly hazardous situation when he engages in highly competitive activities.

The Mentally Retarded Child

The mentally retarded child needs a physical education teacher with special training, special skills, and a special brand of patience. The mentally retarded child often lacks confidence and pride and needs a teacher who will help him build up his self-image. The physical educator must be able to provide a program designed to give each child a chance for success. The goals of the program cannot be so high that they are unreachable for the child.

Physical education can make a very positive contribution to the mentally retarded. Not only must the program be a suitable one, but the teacher must also be adequately prepared and professionally dedicated to teaching these children.

The following are some general guidelines for physical education programs for the mentally retarded.

1. *The physical education program for the mentally retarded should provide a well-organized and progressive program from grade to grade.* Mentally retarded children have the same activity needs as normal children. A progressive program will help to stimulate and motivate these children to be physically active as well as to develop useful skills in a sequential manner.

2. *The physical education program for the mentally retarded should utilize the beginning of the class period for introducing new activities.* The mentally retarded tire easily and have a short attention span. Therefore, new activities will be learned best before fatigue sets in and while the interest of the child is still high.

3. *The physical education program for the mentally retarded should provide for movement education experiences.* Movement education experiences as described in this text are especially suited to the mentally retarded. These children have not as a general rule experienced the natural play activities of childhood and therefore need to develop their gross motor skill abilities.

4. *The physical education program for the mentally retarded should take into consideration the physical-fitness level of children.* The mentally retarded do not usually seek out physical activity on their own initiative. Consequently, lack of a regular program of exercise means that the mentally retarded child may be lacking in physical fitness. Such a condition means the provision for a sound physical education program that includes physical-fitness activities.

5. *The physical education program for the mentally retarded should include a wide variety of self-testing activities.* Providing the mentally retarded child an opportunity to compete against himself will help even the youngest to gain

confidence and pride in accomplishment. Experiencing such success will provide many rewards and be very worthwhile. This feeling of accomplishment can also carry over into other school activities.

6. *The physical education program for the mentally retarded should provide opportunities for the development of desirable social skills.* The mentally retarded can participate in games of low organization and other activities where there is group interaction. The experiences gained in these activities will help the child to develop needed social skills provided the leadership creates such opportunities.

7. *The physical education program for the mentally retarded should provide for a choice of activities.* Even the kindergarten-age child will feel that he is more a part of the program and is more important in the eyes of the teacher if he can be given some share of the responsibility for helping to plan the program. This worthy goal can be accomplished in such a way as giving children the opportunity to select a game to play from some they are familiar with. Such opportunities will help to stimulate their interest in the class.

8. *The physical education program for the mentally retarded should provide for the future activity needs of the students.* The mentally retarded especially need to start early in building a background of recreational and lifetime skills. Swimming is one recreational activity that is suited to the child of any age level, as is dance in its various forms. There are many other activities that fall into this classification.

9. *The physical education program for the mentally retarded should provide for a sound system of record keeping.* Carefully kept records will help in assessing the child's abilities and limitations in regard to physical activity. The children's parents will also be interested in their progress and keeping them informed will help with public relations. Accurate and complete records will be of invaluable aid to the school guidance counselors, the school doctor, school psychologist, and nurse, and the child's personal physician. Records of this sort also help the teacher to make an objective evaluation of the program and make planning for future programs easier.

10. *The physical education program for the mentally retarded should stress health goals.* Such requirements as showers and special dress for physical activity aside from school clothing will point up the need for good habits of health. Safety, of course, must be continuously stressed in all activities and related to the other phases of the school program.

The Disruptive Child

The teacher cannot impose discipline on the disruptive child before the causes for his behavior have been determined. When the teacher of physical education is faced with a disruptive child, the teacher should first confer with the child to try to find a common solution to the problem. If the problem is a continual one, school personnel who are especially trained for the task should be consulted and their aid enlisted in uncovering the cause or causes of the negative behavior.

The following are some general guidelines for physical education programs for the disruptive child.

1. *The physical education program for the disruptive child should communicate clearly to these children the behavior that is expected of them.* While physical education classes are usually conducted in a less formal manner than are classroom subjects, this does not mean that lower standards of behavior should be acceptable or desirable. Children should know what the standards for the physical education class are and should be expected to measure up to these standards. If the disruptive child feels that poor behavior is the expected behavior, he will probably react in just this way in order to attract attention. However, if he knows good behavior is expected from him the chances are better for his behaving in acceptable ways.

2. *The physical education program for the disruptive child should encourage a form of discipline that is firm and consistent.* When rules are rigid one day and relaxed the next, the children will not know how to react. Discipline should be enforced in a firm and consistent manner during all physical education class periods.

3. *The physical education program for the disruptive child should involve teachers and admini-*

strators who understand children. Recognizing a particular child's needs early will help in anticipating future behavior problems. If the administrators understand child growth and development they will give the teacher greater support and be more sympathetic to the various procedures and techniques she utilizes.

4. *The physical education program for the disruptive child should provide for a dialogue on behavioral problems between the physical educator and the individual child.* Respect for the individual child is a necessity no matter how young the child is. Children do not like to be criticized or placed in an embarrassing position in front of classmates. When a child is singled out from a group and used as a disciplinary example, the behavior of the entire class will be adversely affected. Children who misbehave should have a private conference with the teacher rather than having their problems discussed in front of the larger group.

5. *The physical education program for the disruptive child should provide for frequent praise.* If the disruptive child has a special skill or talent, for example, he might be asked to demonstrate for the class. This will give him some of the recognition and attention he craves, and will channel his energies into the right direction. Give praise for even the most minor accomplishments in physical activities. There are many daily occurrences that provide opportunities for praise and commendation.

6. *The physical education program for the disruptive child should try to ensure that the child experiences success.* Constant failure abets disruptive behavior. If the child is known to be hostile and disruptive, an attempt should be made to avoid placing him in situations where he feels inadequate which will only result in adverse behavior. Opportunities should be provided to enable him to experience success. Having a backlog of successes is the best way to meet failure.

7. *The physical education program for the disruptive child should allow the child to assume some form of responsibility.* Make the position of helping the teacher with the equipment, for example, a desirable position to be earned. See that each deserving child, including disruptive ones, get this and similar honors and responsibility when they have merited them. The alert teacher will see that such opportunities are provided.

8. *The physical education program for the disruptive child should welcome the child to after-school activities and special events.* If a child voluntarily participates in an after-school program he must really want to. These experiences, therefore, offer an opportunity to establish behavioral standards for such activities. The desire to participate may help the disruptive child to gain a measure of self-respect, peer recognition, and teacher approval and result in a more desirable behavior.

9. *The physical education program for the disruptive child should provide for keeping interested school personnel informed of the progress of disruptive children.* Too often the school administration and the child's parents are informed only of the negative actions of the child. They should also know about the progress the child is making.

The Poorly Coordinated Child

The physical education program frequently motivates children with specific problems to perform better in the classroom by offering an opportunity for success in physical activity. There is some evidence that shows this to be true with the mentally retarded, for example. This process may work in reverse with the poorly coordinated or awkward child. If a child dreads his physical education class, this will have a detrimental effect on his ability to perform satisfactorily in the classroom. Both his behavior and academic achievement may be adversely affected. The teacher of physical education must understand child growth and development and use the principles derived from a scientific study of children in formulating a physical education curriculum. Additionally, the physical education teacher must be able to select activities and devise progressions that are appropriate to the age and grade level of poorly coordinated children.

In working with poorly coordinated or awkward children the teacher must exercise the utmost patience. He must find out why the child is poorly coordinated and provide an individual program to help the child. He should further be certain that the child understands why he needs special help, and he must attempt to motivate the child to succeed. Immediate successes will not be forthcoming, and the teacher should be careful not to push the child beyond his limits. When a skill is performed with even a modicum of improvement, the effort should be praised and the achievement reinforced. Any goal set for the poorly coordinated child should be a reachable goal.

The teacher has a very definite responsibility to the poorly coordinated child. Poor attitudes developed in the elementary school concerning physical activity may too easily be carried over into adult life. If negative attitudes toward physical education can be stemmed early in the child's elementary school experience, the child may find that he can develop a lifelong love of physical activity.

The following are some general guidelines for physical education programs for the poorly coordinated child.

1. *The physical education program for the poorly coordinated child should represent a sound, well-organized, and carefully structured experience.* Many different types of experience should constitute the program. Physical fitness improvement work and self-testing activities should form only a part of the program for the poorly coordinated child. Games of appropriate level, rhythmics and dancing, and activities such as swimming will also help to stimulate the child, let him sample success, and maintain his interest and motivation.

2. *The physical education program for the poorly coordinated child should provide for an offering of suitable activities.* Activities should be selected to fit the needs of each child. If a child has poor eye-hand or poor eye-foot coordination, for example, he will not be able to succeed in such activities as Batball or Kickball. Activities must be chosen that suit the abilities of the children and at the same time help them develop the needed coordinations.

3. *The physical education program for the poorly coordinated child should involve the children in program planning.* Children should be surveyed to determine their activity interests. Then a selection of activities should be offered that will appeal to the children, and their selections should be guided in relation to their abilities.

4. *The physical education program for the poorly coordinated child should provide for lifetime sport skills.* Swimming and dancing of all kinds are ideal for future recreational use. Rather than attempting to develop championship-level skills, poorly coordinated children need to develop enough skill to be able to appreciate and enjoy voluntary participation in physical activity.

5. *The physical education program for the poorly coordinated child should be progressive in nature.* The children's performance should be periodically checked to see how they are progressing. When a sufficiently high level of success has been reached, a slightly more difficult task should be added, but this task should be within the child's reach.

6. *The physical education program for the poorly coordinated child should provide for competition of a wholesome nature.* The intensity of the competition should be low. Low-organization team games such as dodge ball, squirrel in the tree, and other competitive activities that do not demand a high level of skill or coordination can be used to give the poorly coordinated child confidence in his abilities to perform both as an individual and as a member of a team. He should, however, experience success in such "low key" competition.

The Physically Gifted and the Creative Child

The physically gifted child or the creative child may not have attempted a wide range of physical activities, but may have experienced only those that are offered in the school physical education program. Or on the contrary, he may have private lessons in some sport after school hours and on weekends. Both the physically gifted or creative child and the average performer will be stimulated and challenged by the introduction of new activities.

The classroom teacher or physical education specialist has a contribution to make to each child in the physical education program. The challenge presented by children of exceptional ability will help to keep the teacher alert, stimulated, and enthusiastic about teaching.

The teacher can maintain the interest of exceptional students by using her ingenuity and such methods as the following.

1. *The physical education program for the physically gifted and creative child should make use of audio-visual aids.* Posters, illustrations, or demonstrations by skilled performers will interest even the youngest elementary school child. Older elementary school children will benefit from watching slides, movies, or loopfilms. On his own level, each child will be able to develop insights into performance skills and can be introduced to new activities.

2. *The physical education program for the physically gifted and creative child should provide the students with challenging experiences.* If the skill work for the child is too easy he will lose interest and become bored. New challenges should continually be provided. Special skill challenges on a more advanced level can easily be worked into the program for the exceptional child without isolating him from the other children in the class.

3. *The physical education program for the physically gifted and creative child should encourage the exceptional child to help his classmates achieve a higher degree of skill.* Elementary-school-age children are quite capable of assisting each other with skills. When assigned as partner for a less-well-coordinated child, the better performer can help his partner on a level of understanding that it is at times impossible for the teacher to reach. The leaders' group that physical education teachers frequently utilize in the secondary school might have possibilities for elementary school physical education and for utilizing the skills of exceptional children and increasing their interest in the program.

4. *The physical education program for the physically gifted and creative child should provide a special club program.* The exceptional child will be stimulated and challenged by a special club that is geared specifically to his level of ability. Within this framework the exceptional child can receive much individual instruction and attention and can work on developing new

skills. For the middle school students, an intramural program will help to provide challenging experiences.

5. *The physical education program for the physically gifted and creative child should encourage additional reading on various skills and also the cultural implications of such activities.* Today there are many books on various physical education games and other activities. These books provide additional information on how skills should be performed, strategies that should be utilized, and how to be a better performer. In addition, many books provide information on the history of such activities, where they originated, what people play them at the present time, the skill level of various people around the world, and other information that provides background information for the activities. Exceptional students should be encouraged to read such material in order to become more knowledgeable about the various activities and the role they play in the cultures of the world.

Suggested Activities for the Atypical Child

Activities suitable for the atypical child may advance from those of very little physical activity to those with vigorous exercise, especially for some parts of the body or limbs.

Quiet games may be needed such as card and table games. Darts, horseshoes, quoits, and such activities are often suitable. Croquet, marbles, and archery answer many needs. Bowling, shuffleboard, ring toss and quiet circle games, bicycling, hiking, simple rhythms, simple stunts, and quiet relays requiring no running but which include catching and passing balls, beanbags, and rings will aid many. Camping, fishing, swimming, and boating are both interesting and helpful if it is possible to include them in the regular program.

It should always be remembered that the atypical child has the same basic needs as the normal child and must be helped to meet these needs. The challenge is always present to include something in an adapted program of physical education which will aid him in making the necessary adjustment and make him a better integrated and emotionally and socially happier individual. The physical education program may help the exceptional child in many ways, though it is not the claim that it will be able to aid all handicapped children to the same degree.

It is the belief of the authors that the physical education program which stresses only corrective work is not meeting the needs of the child since it neglects the other phases and objectives of providing opportunities for needed social and emotional adjustment.

The following activities have been selected on the basis of the guidelines given for each of the atypical conditions described earlier in this chapter. These lists are not meant to be all-inclusive of the activities that are appropriate to each child described, but rather are meant to serve as suggestions that the teacher can follow in planning a physical activity program.

The Culturally Disadvantaged Child. In grades kindergarten through four, the culturally disadvantaged child will be especially in need of movement education. Other activities that should be included for this child in these lower elementary school grades are relays, dancing and rhythmical activities, swimming, Kickball, running activities, and physical-fitness work. In grades 5–8 the basic program should be continued while track and field, tumbling, and more sophisticated games and activities should also be included. Bowling, body mechanics, volleyball, softball, and basketball skills are especially appropriate.

The Physically Handicapped Child. There are many categories of physically handicapped children, and each handicapped child has individual abilities and limitations according to his handicap. However, many physically handicapped children can engage in such activities as movement education, physical-fitness work, calisthenics swimming, and dancing activities in grades K–4. In the middle-school grades, running, tumbling, bowling, horseshoes, track and field, volleyball, and dancing may be added to the program for many of the children.

The Mentally Retarded Child. In grades K–4, swimming, story plays, animal walks, Kickball, tug-of-war, body mechanics, running and running games, relays, obstacle courses, and movement education are appropriate. In the middle-school grades, games and relays, recreational activities, and certain individual sports such as archery can be added to the program.

The Disruptive Child. No special program needs to be planned for the disruptive child outside of the regular class program. This child needs to be handled slightly differently than the well-disciplined child, but does not need to be given any extraordinary program allowances.

The Poorly Coordinated Child. In grades K–4, the program for this child should concentrate on movement education and on building physical fitness while increasing the motor-skill abilities of the child. Specially adapted games, such as crab soccer, are essential to the development of the child. In grades 5–8, swimming, archery, dancing, bowling, soccer, and other developmental activities may be added to the program.

The Physically Gifted and the Creative Child. These children do not need a special program, but do need to be given special challenges within the regular program. The gifted child can develop tumbling or gymnastic routines while the creative child can work out special dances or acrobatic stunts of his own choosing and design.

Questions and Practical Problems

1. Describe the culturally disadvantaged child and tell how a sound physical education experience in the elementary school can help him to become better adjusted to the educational process as a whole.

2. Make a chart of the varieties of physical handicaps and show the physical education activities that are suitable to each handicap in grades K–4 and 5–8.

3. Interview a teacher who specializes in the mentally retarded. Find out what special physical experiences are offered to this child, and attempt to evaluate the program in light of your own knowledge of these children.

4. Tell how you would deal with a child who refused to participate in the activities of the physical education class. Give the step-by-step procedures.

5. Make a series of record forms that you would recommend be kept in the physical education area for each of the atypical conditions described in this chapter.

6. Observe a class of elementary school children while they are participating in physical education. Make a descriptive list of all the atypical conditions you see and write a commentary on the value of the program for each of these children.

7. Assume you have a physically gifted child in a third grade physical education class. Write a lesson plan that provides for special challenges for this child.

8. Develop your own set of program objectives and goals for an atypical condition of your choice.

9. Show how physical education needs to be especially adapted to serve the needs of the culturally disadvantaged child.

10. Write a position paper telling how physical education can better serve the needs of the atypical child in the elementary school.

Selected References

AAHPER Project on Recreation and Fitness for the Mentally Retarded. "Activity Programs for the Mentally Retarded." *Journal of Health, Physical Education, and Recreation*, April, 1966, Special Journal Feature.

BUCHER, CHARLES A. *Administration of School Health and Physical Education Programs*. (Fifth Edition). St. Louis: The C. V. Mosby Co., 1971.

Council for Exceptional Children and AAHPER. *Recreation and Physical Activity for the Mentally Retarded*. Washington, D.C.: American Association for Health, Physical Education, and Recreation, 1966.

CRATTY, BRYANT J. *Social Dimensions of Physical Activity*. Englewood Cliffs, N.J.: Prentice-Hall, Inc., 1967.

FANTINI, MARIE D., and GERALD WEINSTEIN. *The Disadvantaged: Challenge to Education*. New York: Harper & Row, Publishers, 1968.

FRANKLIN, C. C., and WILLIAM H. FREEBURG.

Diversified Games and Activities of Low Organization for Mentally Retarded Children. Carbondale, Ill.: Southern Illinois University.

HAYDEN, FRANK J. *Physical Fitness for the Mentally Retarded.* Toronto, Canada: Rotary Clubs, 1964.

Information Center—Recreation for the Handicapped. *Recreation for the Handicapped: A Bibliography.* Carbondale, Ill.: Information Center—Recreation for the Handicapped, 1965.

RATHCHICK, IRVING, and FRANCES G. KOENIG. *Guidance and the Physically Handicapped.* Chicago: Science Research Associates, Inc., 1963.

REISSMAN, FRANK. *The Culturally Deprived Child.* New York: Harper & Row, Publishers, 1962.

CHAPTER 13

The Early Morning, Noon-Hour, and After-School Programs and Tournaments

The consolidation of schools often means that students are transported to school in the morning and back home in the late afternoon. They remain in the school all day.

Many times the same buses are used two or three times to transport children to school in the morning and again to return them to their homes in the late afternoon. Because of this, children arriving on the first or second morning bus usually have from one-half to one hour free before school opens. This is a wonderful time for them to engage in physical activities that are carry-overs from the physical education program. Today, many teachers and principals are successfully and happily removing a one-time disciplinary headache with happy, worthy, leisure-time activities for their "early morning children." Free time may be filled in the same way for those children who are waiting after school to be transported home by the second or third bus; again, physical activities may occupy the time creatively.

It does not take more teachers to supervise these programs before and after school than it does to keep the children orderly when they are not occupied and to solve problems created because of this inactivity. The same planning applied to the noon-hour program will work successfully, including the sectioning of the playground.

Today, it is also true that many children remain in school during the entire day because both parents are working and no one is at home during the noon hour. Other children, though not transported, may remain in school all day because of physical reasons. Some children, also, desire to remain during the noon hour for fun and comradeship and there are others whose parents find it psychologically sound for them to stay at school because they will eat a better lunch and more of the correct foods when they see their friends eating them.

Thus, the schools, because of several factors, have many children all day and, if they are doing a good educational job, they are challenged to plan, administer, and supervise programs of activities during the early morning, the noon hour, and late afternoon that meets the needs, interests, and abilities of the children. Children like activity. Educators, doctors, and psychologists appear to agree that the child in elementary school needs from two to five hours of physical activity per day. Some of it may well be gained during morning, noon-hour, and after-school programs that meet the objective of worthy use of leisure time. The teacher should keep in mind that these times represent an opportunity to achieve educational goals outside regular physical education periods.

The Early Morning Program

When the first buses unload their passengers, students should be permitted to take their personal belongings to a safe place for storage. Leaders should be permitted to obtain the equipment needed for their fun and participation, and, within a period of five to ten minutes, all should be engaged in activities of their choice on the playground.

The areas of the playground may be designated for use as indicated in the discussion of the noon-hour program. Many times, however, larger areas may be used if there are not as many children as at noon.

Some teachers or administrators are present when the first buses arrive. They should arrange for equipment to be used and supervise the playground. Squad leaders, bus captains, and safety leaders should assist and readily assume responsibility when organized and correctly informed of their duties. Through careful organization, only certain students will necessarily be charged with the responsibility of getting equipment. These leaders may remain active for several months, making the organization simple and changes relatively few.

The Noon-Hour Program

In relation to the total health of the child, one may reasonably ask if it is physically sound and beneficial for children to eat and then immediately start vigorous physcial activity? According to good health standards, it is certainly not advisable for a child to use five or ten minutes to hurriedly gulp his lunch and immediately rush to the playground and engage in vigorous activity.

During the noon hour there should be sufficient time to eat followed by some relaxation and fun such as quiet table games, group singing, listening to music, or the like, before the children plunge wholeheartedly into a program of strenuous activities. If children know the noon-hour plan, they will find it unnecessary to eat in haste and this period may and should be pleasant, socially acceptable, relaxing, healthful, and a worthy social and educational experience.

Planning for the noon hour must be done both for clear weather when the playground and all outdoor facilities may be used and for rainy days when only indoor facilities are available. Children, representing leaders from each class, should definitely assist in all planning and organization for the noon hour. They have good ideas, can see problems and help solve them, work well as leaders for small- and large-group activities, make fine officials for games, and help make the noon-hour assignment a happy occasion for the teacher in charge rather than a police duty without the privilege of the night stick. This group of teachers and children could well be named "The Planning Committee."

If the physical education program is adequate, there can be much carry-over from it to the noon-hour activities. A sufficient number of activities should be planned to interest all children.

Each teacher should assume the responsibility for assisting children in her class to plan and organize the activities they wish to engage in during the noon hour. Responsibility should be given to the student leaders in each grade. They are capable and accept it well. The authors know this is possible through experience in elementary schools from kindergarten through eighth grade.

Activities for Clear Weather. For the noon hour program during clear weather, individual activities for children should include the use of all play apparatus such as merry-go-rounds, slides, jungle gyms, and swings. Also among the individual and dual activities should be such games as Marbles, Ring Toss, Hopscotch, and Jump Rope. If these activities are planned, they may well be self-directed by the participants. If more children desire to use the stationary apparatus than the amount of equipment allows, a time schedule may very conveniently be planned. For example, the first grade could use it from 12:30 P.M. to 12:45 P.M., the second grade from 12:45 P.M. to 1:00 P.M., and so on. A schedule may also be planned for grades to use the apparatus on alternate days. Some children will be interested in games which use equipment such as Dodge Ball, Stealing Sticks, and Stand Ball. These games may be directed by responsible student leaders.

Girls, in particular, may desire circle games, singing games, and folk dances while the older group of boys and girls may be interested in tournaments in Bat Ball, Kickball, and other team games which can be played within the given area. When possible, it is also desirable to offer, during the noon hour, activities which may not be a regular part of the physical education program. These might include such games as Shuffleboard, Croquet, Table Tennis, Tether Ball, Deck Tennis, Parchesi, or Dominoes.

Activities for Inclement Weather. Rainy weather plans call for use of table games, classroom games, and gymnasium and playroom activities. Auditorium programs which include singing, skits, motion pictures, good radio programs, or television are also popular. Each teacher should plan to have games such as Lotto, Checkers, Dominoes, Scrabble, and Hearts in her room ready for use during a rainy noon-hour program.

Programs in the playroom or gymnasium may include darts, novelty relays, social, folk, and square dancing. Classroom activities could include ring-toss games, blackboard games, rhythms, hunting games, and magic games. Many pencil-and-paper games are also fun and usable in the classroom.

Planning a program of activities for the noon hour must be done well in advance so that one is ready for any type of weather.

Efficient Use of the Play Area. Sectioning

the playground into areas for various groups to use in their play is most important. With more children on the playground during this period than at any other time, good organization and planning and sectioning of areas are imperative if accidents are to be avoided and if chaos is not to be the order of the hour.

Space limitations automatically make certain activities impossible and impractical. Children who help with the planning can understand this very well and can help their group accept it. This will prevent an antagonistic attitude and belligerence on the part of those who cannot play the games they wish and will keep them from doing such things as interfering with other groups. The spirit of cooperation and sharing, giving and taking, thought and respect for others may all be taught in this plan of action.

Points to bear in mind in the sectioning of play areas for various groups depend on such factors as nearness to street or road; fenced or unfenced playground; stationary apparatus such as swings, slides, jungle gyms, and sand boxes; the number of children to use the area at one time; and the actual space available.

The area near the stationary apparatus should be used only for quiet nonrunning games and activities such as marbles, hopscotch, ring toss, and rope jumping. This will, for example, keep a child who is fleeing "It" in a running-tagging game from running directly into the path of a swing. The same danger would exist with a child chasing a ball if such games were played near this area.

Games using balls should be played in fenced-in areas or in areas as far away from the road or street as possible to avoid having the balls fly into the street. This automatically lessens the danger of children dashing into the street to recover equipment. All safety rules must be well established and understood and *one* person in each group should be designated to recover equipment which goes into the street, road, bushes, or dangerous places An example of playground sectioning is shown in Figure 13–1.

The areas may be marked with red markers fastened on rubber standards so children cannot get hurt if they fall on them, or by using white slaked lime, which will not harm the eyes. If lime is used dry and put on very thick it will remain a long time. White field-marking paint is available at nominal cost and may easily be applied by an inexpensive mechanical field liner. Areas 6 through 11 may be subdivided to meet the needs and interests of the group. These suggestions do not mean that boys and girls must remain sep-

S T R E E T	Area 1 Jungle gyms; swings, slides, teeter-totters, etc.	Area 5 Circle games, rhythms	Area 8 Active games 5th and 6th grade boys	Area 10 Active games 7th and 8th grade boys
	Area 2 Quiet games (no running), marbles, jump rope, jacks, etc.	Area 6 Active games 3rd and 4th grade girls		
	Area 3 Sand box and quiet area for story tellng, etc.		Area 9 Active games 5th and 6th grade girls	Area 11 Active games 7th and 8th grade girls
	Area 4 Active games (no equipment)	Area 7 Active games 3rd and 4th grade boys		

Figure 13–1. Sectional play area for eight grades.

arated in their activities nor does it prevent various age groups from playing together if desired by the children. Any exchange is possible to meet needs and interests but the basic plan must be understood by all children.

The Use of Equipment. The problem of equipment must be discussed and well understood by all children. What may be used? Who is responsible for taking it out and returning it? Some schools make the mistake of permitting no equipment to be used during the noon hour. These schools usually do not plan activities or designate specific areas for various age groups to play in, thus causing the teacher in charge of the noon hour to detest the assignment. Children will assume responsibility if the desire to do so is created. They will use equipment carefully and will not abuse it because they realize their noon-hour play will be more fun if they have equipment to use.

Student leaders may be organized and assigned the responsibility of checking out and receiving equipment if the school stores all of it in a central storage room. If each room has some equipment, the student who takes it may merely write his name on the board, indicating what piece or pieces he has taken. When he returns it, his name is erased.

Students should be permitted to use all available equipment needed to carry on the activities which have been approved by the planning committee for the noon-hour program. Substitutions for some popular games may have to be made. For example, if space does not permit softball for the fifth- and sixth-grade boys, they may have as much fun using all the rules of softball but pitching a volleyball or rubber ball of the appropriate size and using the fist to punch it in place of a bat. This will be a safe game for all children playing nearby, will require a smaller space for the diamond, but will meet the interests and needs of the boys for team play and vigorous activity.

Assistance for Teachers. The authors are fully aware of the tremendous task and great responsibility of today's classroom teacher. It is hoped that a general understanding of planning the early morning program, the noon-hour program, and the afternoon program will ease a problem for her. The physical education teacher, if available, can be of great assistance.

The health of the teacher is important. Administrators should *insist* that each teacher have some time for herself during the day—away from her children. All teachers should not have to be in the cafeteria and/or on the playground during the noon hour. Through proper planning and scheduling, cooperation of all teachers and supervisors, and the inclusion of students in planning and executing the programs, good programs will be provided and teachers will need to spend less time on duty during the noon hour. The time they do spend will be rewarding as they observe a group of young people truly enjoying themselves under student leadership and gaining valuable educational experiences plus worthy use of leisure time.

The safety club members, Girl Scout and Boy Scout leaders, and leaders chosen by students from each class will answer many problems and needs.

It should be arranged so the teacher assigned noon-hour supervision has an opportunity to eat her lunch and relax either before the period or after coming from noon supervision. This may be handled in many ways. One method would be for a teacher who has a free lunch hour to take the students of the teacher assigned noon-hour supervision either the period before lunch or the period after it. She might use this time with the two classes combined for an art lesson, music, singing, or story-telling program. Thus the teacher assigned to noon-hour supervision would have an opportunity to eat and relax. Perhaps the best solution is a floating teacher and assistance from the supervisors and administrators. No one answer is the solution. If the teachers are permitted to assist in planning the noon-hour program and supervision, it is believed they can reach a workable plan. No teacher should be assigned more than one noon period per week. She needs the other four noon periods to relax in order to be refreshed before meeting her afternoon responsibilities.

The noon-hour program may be beneficial to the teacher if she approaches it with the right attitude. During the noon hour she has a chance to see children in informal situations and get to know them better. She learns more about them, their habits, their sportsmanship, and how they react in various situations. She may use these observations as teaching aids within her own group. She also has an opportunity herself to be out in the fresh air and sunshine.

The noon-hour program is a good time to develop student leadership and followership. The greatest amount of teacher time should be devoted to planning and organization meetings with individual groups and with combined groups when tournaments are desired by the children. This time utilized in organization is well spent and can easily make the noon hour a pleasant experience. Teachers ought to feel the noon-hour program is an integral part of the day.

After-School Programs

Because their buses make several trips, some children must wait for their bus after school. In addition, many children whose parents work and those who walk to school can benefit greatly by a program of activities after the last class. These programs again should be planned by teachers and students.

Those children who return to empty houses, whose parents do not get home from work until 4:30 or 5:00 P.M., would surely be better off playing on the school playground than running and playing unsupervised in dangerous streets. Those who must wait for their buses should also be given the opportunity to have fun.

The Question of Supervision. An after-school program brings up the question of who shall supervise it. Classroom teachers usually have a right to leave at 3:30 P.M. or whenever their class is dismissed. However, the after-school program is important from the standpoint of the child's welfare. A staggered plan of teacher supervision for an after-school program will work and will not be an overly heavy burden on any one teacher. With proper planning and organization, the

(Courtesy of Game-Time Inc.)

children will have a joyful and beneficial experience. When physical education teachers are available, this is a natural part of their program.

Schools which have worthy programs in operation for early morning, the noon hour, and after school have reported finer attitudes and a better spirit of cooperation among the children throughout the entire school day. These schools are helping to meet the needs of the child for physical activity under correct conditions, and the child is enjoying worthy use of leisure time. A mother worries less when her son or daughter has a place to play in the proper environment and in a safe area under the proper leadership.

Playgrounds, apparatus, and equipment should be used after 3:30 P.M. Mothers and fathers, retired teachers, as well as other interested citizens in the community, are often happy to help with the supervision if the school assumes the leadership in community and school planning. This affords the school a good chance for community cooperation. Parent-teacher association groups and mothers' clubs often reveal much interest, willingness, and cooperation in a supervisory capacity.

The programs for after school can be an outgrowth of the physical education program and need not require further teaching.

Tournaments

Children, especially in the middle and upper grades (5 to 8), enjoy tournaments. These should be planned and administered with regard for the interests and desires of the children. The after-school program gives good opportunity for the use of tournaments as the time is usually longer than the noon-hour period for activity, However, if time permits, they are of value at noon also.

It is believed that intramural competition, in selected activities which have been well planned and are well controlled, aids in building social status in a group. The child learns to cooperate and not to depend solely on himself. He learns to accept success and defeat. He learns his abilities and limitations.

These worthy experiences may be gained through participation in games which give incentive for better skills and performance because of individual desire rather than through stress from an outsider to win. Such games and programs give every child a chance to play rather than just approximately 10 per cent of the "top notchers" who benefit from highly organized competitive sports programs.

Children are being prepared for good adult living when they can accept competition and cooperation because this is the basis of our democracy. Hence, the right kind of competition, well planned and organized, carefully supervised, and open to all regardless of ability has proved helpful for elementary children. Accepted kinds of intramural competition would include activities that are outgrowths of the regular physical education program such as Kickball, Bat Ball, and Newcomb. They would also include various types of recreational, individual, and dual activities, such as marbles, hopscotch, shuffleboard, croquet, quoit pitching, and the like. Sports days and play days are recommended within a given school, or for an occasional invitation to a nearby school. For these purposes a knowledge and understanding of the types of tournaments and how they may be organized is essential.

Types of Tournaments. The most popular and successfully used tournaments include the round-robin, the ladder, the pyramid, the elimination, and the double elimination. These will be discussed separately. Examples will be used to show how they may be utilized either alone or in combination to promote desired interest, learning, and satisfaction.

The Round-Robin Tournament. The round-robin tournament is set up so each team, squad, unit, or individual has an opportunity to play with all others in the tournament play. If there are six groups or six individuals who wish to participate, a round-robin tournament would be organized by using the steps shown in Table 13–1.

To make the organization of the tournament relatively easy, and to insure that each team or individual is scheduled to play with all five, begin by matching all participants against number *one*.

The number of steps necessary is determined by the number of groups competing—for example ten groups would require nine steps. There is always one less step than the number of participants.

When all participants have been matched through the step process, it is then possible to plan the tournament schedule. It must be decided whether each participant will play each day, two times a week, or once each week. Time, space, facilities, and equipment will be the determining factors.

To avoid error, as the schedule is being planned each combination listed in the five steps should be crossed out or checked as soon as it is scheduled.

An example of a round-robin tournament with six contestants, groups, or individuals scheduled to play each day is shown in Figure 13–2.

The same organization may be used for schedules other than daily ones. It could be used for play two or three times a week or on a weekly basis.

A round-robin tournament with six groups or individuals affords an opportunity for each to play five games. In order to declare a winner, the tournament may award each contestant two points for winning, one for tie games, and nothing for a loss.

The round-robin tournament is most popular. It is the fairest, as it permits all participants an equal chance to play. It maintains interest because all who start participate to the end. The only objection to it is the time element. If one has a short time for tournament play, it may not be possible to use it.

If there should be ten teams or individuals who wish to participate in a tournament, it is advantageous to divide the group. For example, teams numbering one through five could play together and numbers six through ten would play in another tournament. A winner could be declared in each group. If a single winner is desired, the winners from the two groups would be matched to play each other. A three-game match is preferable to a single game, and the winner of

Day	Date	Place	Time	Winner	Points
Monday 1 vs. 4 2 vs. 5 3 vs. 6	May 6	Play area #1 Play area #2 Play area #3	3:00 P.M.	#4 #2 #3	
Tuesday 5 vs. 6 3 vs. 4 1 vs. 2	May 7	Play area #1 Play area #2 Play area #3	3:30 P.M.	#6 #4 #2	
Wednesday 2 vs. 4 3 vs. 5 1 vs. 6	May 8	Play area #1 Play area #2 Play area #3	3:00 P.M.	#4 #3 #6	
Thursday 4 vs. 5 2 vs. 6 1 vs. 3	May 9	Play area #1 Play area #2 Play area #3	3:00 P.M.	#5 #2 #3	
Friday 2 vs. 3 4 vs. 6 1 vs. 5	May 10	Play area #1 Play area #2 Play area #3	3:30 P.M.	#3 #5 #1	

Contestants scoring
Number 1 = 2 points
Number 2 = 6 points
Number 3 = 8 points = Winner
Number 4 = 6 points
Number 5 = 4 points
Number 6 = 4 points

Figure 13–2. Round-robin tournament with six contestants.

Table 13–1. **The Round-Robin Tournament**

Step	Matching	Explanation
I	1 vs. 2 1 vs. 3 1 vs. 4 1 vs. 5 1 vs. 6	The completion of this step assures the organizer that number one is scheduled to play all others. In a tournament with six contestants or teams, it means each one will play five games.
II	2 vs. 3 2 vs. 4 2 vs. 5 2 vs. 6	Notice that this step starts with number two since two is already scheduled to play one in the first step. Number two is now assured that he is scheduled for five games.
III	3 vs. 4 3 vs. 5 3 vs. 6	Step three starts with number *three* and, when completed, number *three* is scheduled in five games.
IV	4 vs. 5 4 vs. 6	Step four starts with number *four* and *four* is scheduled to play his five games.
V	5 vs. 6	As the illustration has shown, the step number and the number of the team corresponds each time.

two out of three games would be declared the one winner. For example, if number five won in the first group and eight in the second, numbers five and eight would play each other to determine a grand winner.

A round-robin tournament with an uneven number of teams or individuals makes it impossible for each participant to play every day of tournament play, This fact will not mean that the children will lose interest. Round-robin tournaments afford good opportunity for teamwork and aid in developing skills and techniques. They provide much fun and cooperative competition.

The Ladder Tournament. The ladder tournament is planned as follows. Contestants names are placed on rungs of a ladder made of oaktag. The exchange of names is made very easy if the contestants' names are written on a piece of oaktag longer than the width of the ladder itself. At the end of each rung on the ladder, a slit is made and the name tags are slipped into the slits and remain in place. The children are then ready to compete with each other. If eight players wish to participate, the ladder would contain eight rungs. Eight is a recommended number for each ladder. If there are more participants, more ladders should be planned.

Contestants receive their places on the rungs of the ladder by having their names drawn from a box. The first name drawn should be placed on rung number one, the second on rung number two, and so on until each contestant receives a place on the ladder.

The rules of the tournament should be agreed on by the contestants and be well understood before play begins. This type of tournament is usually given a time limit. It may operate for one month—the month of April, for example. The object, of course, is to be on the top rung on May 1.

Players may advance to rung one by challenging the person directly above them or two rungs above. A contestant may never skip more than one rung. A winner automatically exchanges his name with the loser.

Each person must accept challenges. No one may challenge the same player twice in succession.

Rung		
	1	Dunn
	2	Regan
	3	Gross
	4	Scarpa
	5	Mazzoni
	6	Thomas
	7	Scott
	8	Saric

Figure 13–3. **Ladder tournament, eight players.**

For example, if number *three* challenged number *two* and won, he would automatically move up to the second rung and *two* would go down to the third rung. *Two* may not immediately rechallenge *three*. He must challenge number *one*. If he loses to number *one*, he may then be rechallenged by *three*. The players themselves make this tournament work. The opportunity of being able to challenge either directly above or two rungs above avoids lack of interest for persons who do not win. It is surprising to see how many times places are exchanged in a given length of time in this type of tournament. Rules may be changed to permit contestants to challenge three rungs above them if desired by the group and more than eight may be on a ladder. The important thing is to establish rules before tournament play begins and for each contestant to understand them thoroughly. The ladder tournament may be used either for individual or dual activities or for team games. It is, however, most popular for the former, as fewer persons are involved and two or four contestants can easily agree on a time to play, while 16 or 20 team members must have their dates and times scheduled in advance so they may plan their time accordingly. Space and facilities also make this necessary.

Regarding the use of equipment, space, and facilities for the participants of the ladder tournament, it is recommended that when the first two contestants are ready to set a time and date for a match they enter this on a tournament schedule sheet posted by the ladder. Other challengers will be guided accordingly.

If there are many contestants, several ladders may be used. The same rules apply. If there are 24 contestants for example, there could be three ladders composed of eight contestants each. At the close of the scheduled playing time, the players on the top rung of the three ladders would each have won in their respective groups. If a grand winner is desired, the three may play in a round-robin tournament.

The Pyramid Tournament. A pyramid tournament is similar to a ladder tournament. All

```
Row 1      X
    2     X X
    3    X X X
    4   X X X X
```

Figure 13–4. Pyramid tournament.

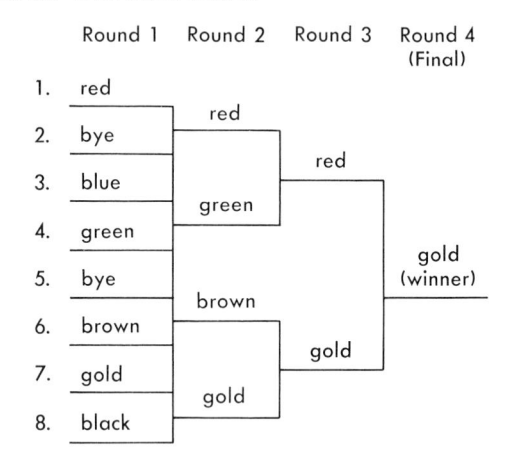

```
            Round 1   Round 2   Round 3   Round 4
                                          (Final)
1. red
              red
2. bye
                         red
3. blue
              green
4. green
                                   red
5. bye
              brown                     gold
                                        (winner)
6. brown
                        gold
7. gold
              gold
8. black
```

Figure 13–5. Elimination tournament

names of contestants, either individual or team, are drawn from a box and placed in pyramid formation. The first names drawn form the base of the pyramid. Figure 13–4 shows a pyramid based on ten players, which places four at the base.

Row three is filled next with the names as they are drawn, then row two, and the last person is at the top of the pyramid.

Contestants challenge in the row directly above them and endeavor to be at the top when the time for the closing of the tournament arrives. Names may be moved back and forth as they are in the ladder tournament.

The Elimination Tournament. The elimination tournament is well named. As individuals, couples, or teams compete and lose they are eliminated. Figure 13–5 is an illustration of a tournament draft for six teams.

The procedure for structuring an elimination tournament is as follows: Select the multiple of the number 2 which is larger than but closest to the number of teams entered in the tournament. This will determine the number of positions to be drafted for the first round. This is necessary in order to place all byes in the first round. A bye means that a person, couple, or team does not play in that round. Figure 13–5 shows a 6-team entry; therefore, the number of positions needed in the first round is 8 ($2 \times 2 = 4 \times 2 = 8$). The difference between the number of positions and the number of entries indicates the number of byes in the tournament. With reference to Figure 13–5, this would be 2 byes ($8 - 6 = 2$). The word "bye" is then substituted for a team name in the necessary number of spaces in the first-round draft (positions

#2 and #4 in Figure 13–5). The numbers of the remaining positions are placed in a hat and a representative of each team draws from it to determine placement of the team in the first round. Byes must be at least one position apart and generally they are equally distributed throughout upper and lower half of the tournament bracket.

The elimination tournament is not highly recommended to be used alone. As one can readily see, a team or person has but one chance, and half who start never get a second chance. Interest lags; it is not popular. There are misunderstandings and excuses. The outcome does not necessarily mean that the winning individual, couple, or team is the best. Too much stress is placed on winning and too little on fun and friendly, cooperative play. The one advantage is that little time is required.

This type of tournament is often used to declare a winner when there are three or more winners at the completion of a ladder tournament or a round-robin, as mentioned in the previous discussion. For this purpose it can be justified.

The Double Elimination Tournament. A double elimination tournament is preferable to the previous type because all starters play more games. A tournament for eight is diagramed in Figure 13–6.

Note that the first round is shown in the center and the winners' side is on the right and the losers' on the left. Eight contestants play in the first round, eight in the second, and four in the third. Ten games complete the tournament. In the straight elimination tournament for eight contestants, only seven games are played.

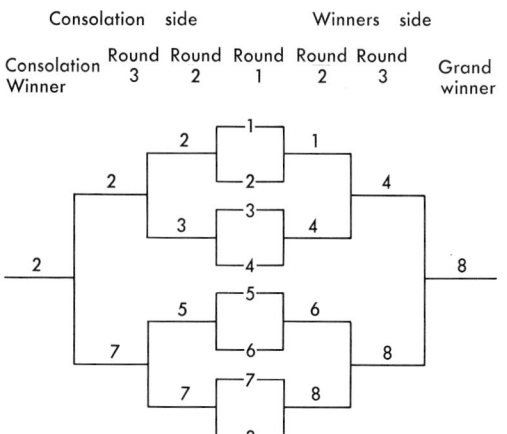

Figure 13–6. Double elimination tournament.

Grouping Individuals for Tournaments. Regardless of the activities used in the intramural program in a school, it is advisable to group individuals and teams on as even a basis as possible. Factors used in determining the groupings should include size, age, skill, sex, and, in many cases, grade. For example, it would be rare—all things being equal—for a sixth-grade boy to be a fair match for a fourth-grade boy. An exception might be found in an activity such as a marble tournament. Even in that activity it would be advisable to schedule the tournament on a ladder basis for each grade and plan one tournament for girls and another for boys. By doing this, it is easy to declare a winner of each sex by grade. Interest would determine whether a grand winner should be chosen for each grade or for two or more grades.

In the case of team games, tournaments should be planned for those children of the same grade and not for children from different grades. For example, if there are three sixth grades in a school, these three might plan a tournament among their grades. One could not expect the sixth-grade boys to be in fair competition against the eighth-grade boys in a game of Bat Ball or softball.

If there is only one section of each grade in a school and a tournament is desired, a good way to organize the groups would be to have fifth-grade boys who desire to participate sign one sheet. Sixth-grade boys would sign another sheet. The same should be done for the girls. The total number of players would indicate the number of teams possible and should be decided by the students and the teacher together. If the sport or game calls for nine players, the group may decide to place two extra players on a team in case illness, absence, or some other reason eliminates a player or two. The total number who have signed for the tournament should then be divided by the number agreed on for each team. For example, if sixty-six had signed and the teacher-pupil group decided that eleven are needed on each team, there would be six teams. All players' names would then be numbered consecutively from one to six and repeated until each player received a number. This would be done for both grades. If the fifth-grade boys' list stopped with number *three*, the first name on the sixth-grade list would start with number *four*. Teams would then be organized by placing all number *ones* on a team, number *twos* on another, number *threes* on a third, and so on to make six teams of eleven players each. The girls may be organized in teams by the same method and would play in a separate tournament. This same plan works well with seventh- and eighth-grade boys and girls.

It is always interesting to note how evenly matched teams become when they are organized in this manner. It is impossible for children to know where to sign in order to stay in a clique and be on the same team, because the number of players agreed necessary for each team decides the final number of teams. It is also good to mix players in this or a similar way so the students from one classroom are not playing against another room. It is a well-known fact that some classroom teachers are more interested in physical education activities than others. Many times children dislike a teacher who in their opinion does not assist them enough or who does not give them as much time as they desire in their physical education program. Competition between two rooms should never be developed. Children should play *with* members of other groups rather than *against* them. The proposed plan is also usable to mix two or more groups of the same grade for tournaments.

Tournament Hints for Teachers

1. Be sure the children help with all plans.
2. Permit them to choose the activities they desire to use for tournament play.
3. Be sure the grouping is as impersonal as possible.
4. Organize all rules and have them well understood before a tournament starts—for example, rescheduling of outdoor activities in case of rain; the least number of players a team must have in order to play; and what happens if a team forfeits.
5. Do not overstress winning. Participation and activity under proper conditions should be the aim. Children should learn to accept defeat graciously.
6. Do not permit winners to become braggarts. Teach them to win graciously.
7. Be sure officials know the rules and are fair, and that players respect the officials and their decisions.
8. Stress playing *with* rather than *against*.
9. Stress teamwork and cooperation.
10. Do not give prizes to winners.
11. Use activities for a tournament which have been taught as a regular part of the physical education program.
12. Plan a variety of individual, dual, or couple activities as well as team participation. Too much emphasis should not be placed on team activities. Marbles, hopscotch, shuffleboard, archery, and the like are very necessary and popular.
13. Plan all ground rules, places for play, and time for schedules before starting any tournament. Be sure all members know these rules and agree to abide by them.
14. Arrange for members of groups to choose their own captains or co-captains. If it is impossible to work with all children in planning tournaments, these captains should represent their groups,
15. Make sure the necessary equipment is available and used.
16. Set up all necessary safety precautions regarding the use of equipment, place to play, need for wearing protective equipment such as body protector, mask, and glove when catching in softball, and glasses guards for protection of those wearing glasses while playing with balls.
17. Stimulate the group to have good clean fun and to be good sports at all times.
18. Never accept poor sportsmanship. This should be well understood before a tournament begins and captains should be responsible for their players' conduct. This will aid in developing leadership and followership.
19. Use tournaments only as fun to climax or close an activity at a given time in the program.
20. Make it possible to complete tournaments in a short time. Too long a period finds interest waning and cannot be justified.
21. Remember that tournaments are only interesting learning experiences—not matters of life or death. Teach and use them accordingly. They will prove happy, valuable educational experiences if properly planned, administered, and executed by educators.

Evaluation of Tournaments. Some means of evaluation is necessary for determining the value of tournaments. The following points would be helpful in making such an evaluation.

1. Are the children thoroughly enjoying the activities?
2. Is there too much competition?
3. Is there too little cooperation?
4. Are children good winners? Good losers?

5. Do the activities meet the needs of the children? Should others be planned?

6. Is there good cooperation and spirit among team members?

7. Are children emotionally stable or is this tournament play overstimulating to them?

8. Is each game a learning experience?

9. Is interest maintained throughout the tournament or does it wane?

10. Are schedules completed or are there many forfeited games or matches?

11. Do children *discuss* their tournament play among themselves or do they argue it?

12. What is the reaction of the parents toward the program? Favorable? Unfavorable? Why?

13. Do the children ask for other tournaments?

14. Are all children who wish to play, regardless of their ability, included in the program?

15. Do the children appear to be growing and developing good social qualities and group consciousness through the program?

Hints for Morning, Noon, and After-School Programs

1. Organize a planning committee and plan the early morning, noon-hour, and after-school programs with the help of students and fellow teachers.

2. Time spent in organization is well worth the effort and pays high dividends in program enjoyment.

3. Be sure that the equipment and apparatus used are in safe condition.

4. Plan play areas with the understanding and cooperation of all the children and fellow workers. Nothing is worse than bickering about play space.

5. Accept these three activity periods as real educational experiences for the children. Make them worthwhile experiences.

6. Use the extra programs to learn more about the individual students.

7. Be proud of your part in the programs. Do not grudgingly give of your time.

8. Use activities taught in physical education for the early morning, noon-hour, and after-school programs.

9. Be sure all children understand the three W's. *What* are the objectives of the program? *Why* are certain rules and regulations necessary? *When* may they use certain apparatus and equipment?

10. Understanding usually leads to cooperation.

11. Build character and sportsmanship during the early morning, noon-hour, and after-school programs.

12. Develop leadership and followership.

13. Plan well in advance. Both short-term and long-term planning are desirable and necessary.

14. Enjoy the period and your children.

15. Be prepared for rain as well as clear weather.

16. Plan tournaments if children are interested and desire them.

Evaluation of Programs. To ascertain whether the early morning, noon-hour, and after-school programs are meeting sound educational objectives, these standards may be used for evaluation. To what degree does each of the ten ideal conditions apply to your school?

1. Activities are diversified to meet the needs, interests, and abilities of all.

2. Children are entering wholeheartedly into the activities with no coercion from leaders or teachers.

3. There is a genuinely happy spirit at all times.

4. There is a good social and group relationship.

5. There is much physical activity for all who are capable and desire it.

6. Cooperation and sportsmanship prevail.

7. Problems which arise are used as means of educating the children in democratic ways of solving them.

8. Children are accepting the role of leadership.

9. As the program progresses, more children desire to participate.

10. You hear happy discussion and comments among the children.

Questions and Practical Problems

1. You are the teacher in charge of the early morning program in a school. Develop plans and steps you would use in the organization of a planning committee composed of teachers and students.

2. Set up a noon-hour program of activities for grades one through six (one class in each grade), suitable for play on a playground of approximately one acre of land. Each class consists of 35 children. There is no playground apparatus available. Show by diagram where the various groups of children would play and what activities might be used in each area. Students in the class should work on different size play areas and with different numbers of children.

3. Plan specifically the responsibility you would wish each student leader to assume for the noon hour. How would you work with these leaders? How would you seek to gain the full cooperation of the other children with the leaders?

4. How would you organize a program of after-school activities? Would you recommend that citizens in the community assist? If so, organize a specific plan of action. If you believe the teacher should assume the entire responsibility, defend your stand.

5. What is the responsibility of the physical education specialist in the morning, noon, and after-school program?

6. You are asked to speak at the Parent-Teacher Association meeting on Little League Play. Prepare your talk and substantiate your stand.

7. The boys in the fifth through eighth grades are steaming with enthusiasm to organize an interschool schedule with other schools in the town and nearby areas. How would you go about working out this problem? Be thorough and exact in your planning and be sure you can substantiate your stand.

8. One of the local civic service clubs wishes to donate awards for winners in each tournament you play. What will your stand be? How can you put it in effect without ill feelings?

9. What will be guiding criteria for tournaments in various grade levels? Explain them fully.

10. What are some of the recommendations of the joint committee on athletics for children of elementary school age?

Selected References

American Association for Health, Physical Education, and Recreation. *After-School Games and Sports, Grades 4–5–6.* Washington, D.C.: American Association for Health, Physical Education, and Recreation, 1964.

―――. *Classroom Activities.* Washington, D.C.: American Association for Health, Physical Education, and Recreation, 1960.

―――. *Desirable Athletic Competition for Children of Elementary School Age.* Washington, D.C.: American Association for Health, Physical Education, and Recreation, 1969.

―――. *Recreational Games and Sports.* Washington, D.C.: American Association for Health, Physical Education, and Recreation, 1963.

Athletic Institute. *Desirable Athletic Competition for Children.* Chicago: Athletic Institute, 1967.

―――. *Intramurals for Elementary School Children.* Chicago: Athletic Institute, 1964.

EVANS, RUTH. "The Noon Hour in Elementary Education." *Children in Focus*, 1954 Yearbook of the American Association for Health, Physical Education, and Recreation, Washington, D.C.: American Association for Health, Physical Education, and Recreation, 1955, *Recreation*, p. 213.

McCOOE, DAVID, and CLIFFORD HUTCHINSON. "An Experiment in Noon-Time Recreation." *Journal of Health, Physical Education, and Recreation* 22:26, October 1951.

SAUBORN, MARION, and BETTY HARTMAN, *Issues in Physical Education.* Philadelphia: Lea & Febiger, 1964.

CHAPTER **14**

Camping and Outdoor Education

Jim was a boy who lived in a middle-sized Michigan city. His home was a two-room apartment in the poor section of the town. As in most cities, this undesirable section had little grass, poorly constructed homes, narrow streets, and congested quarters. Jim was faced with the usual problems of the culturally disadvantaged. In addition, he was a Negro.

He soon realized he was different from the boys who lived in the more advantaged areas of the city. It was especially noticeable in school. His public school was a common meeting ground for the poor and the rich—all classes and religions since laws forbade segregation. However, though Jim was tolerated he wasn't included when the gang had a picnic, and he was never nominated when a school election came up. He was not treated as an equal. He was not given the same opportunities. During his last year in elementary school, however, a new development in the educational program of the city did a great deal to break down this prejudice against Jim.

Jim and all of his classmates were taken to camp as part of their regular school program. They lived together as a family group. They ate together, worked, played, and slept in the same room. The youngsters realized for the first time that Jim wasn't different after all. Except for the color of his skin, he felt and acted just like they acted in a camp. He pitched in and did his share of the work, he was happy and fun to be with, he was the best tenor when they sang songs around the campfire, and he was named honorary second chef when he turned out to be an excellent outdoor cook. As the youngsters talked over their week at camp they realized that Jim had actually contributed a lot more to the success of their outdoor experience than some others had. This admiration carried over even after they returned to the classroom. School camping accomplished more in wiping out prejudices than any other school or community activity had been able to do. It helped Jim and it may have helped the other youngsters even more.

Experiences in camping and outdoor education are especially suited to the culturally disadvantaged child. Such an experience can give this child invaluable practice in social skills that he might otherwise fail to gain during the normal course of his school years. Further, a school camping experience can help the city child who is culturally disadvantaged to leave his ghetto existence for a brief time and sample the adventure of the out-of-doors. Many of the healthy learnings that this child needs can also be gained from a period of school camping, and the culturally disadvantaged child can be introduced to new and needed nature interests and recreational skills.

Children in many other Michigan communities experience school camping and learn to respect and admire people for their abilities as individuals. California, Minnesota, New York, Florida, Illinois, and many other states are also realizing such values from their school camping programs. Children learn to live democratically in these settings. Besides living, sleeping, eating, playing, and learning with all types of youngsters, they aid in planning programs and assume responsibility for upkeep of the camp.

The development of good human relations is only one of the many values derived from school camping. The child also learns many things that could never be acquired in a formal classroom. Such things as soil, forests, water, animal, and bird life take on new meanings. The child learns the value of the nation's natural resources and how they can be conserved. He learns by doing rather than through the medium of textbooks. Instead of looking at the picture of a bird in a book, he actually sees the bird chirping on the branch of a tree. A Michigan school camp uses letter writing to the family back home to develop the language arts, the camp store to practice budgeting one's allowance, and the camp bank to make arithmetic a real learning experience. The child has experiences which are not available at home or within the four walls of a school building. Several years ago, New York City conducted a camping experiment for fifth- and seventh-grade children at Life Camps, Mashipacong, New Jersey. The Board of Education's Research Division, in evaluating the experience, found that children attending camp learned more than those who stayed within the school buildings, especially in such things as nature study, vocabulary, arithmetic, and interest inventory. It was also shown that there was no loss in the other academic subjects.

The health needs of the child are better met through camping. Camps are located away from the turmoil, confusion, noise, and rush of urban life. Children have their meals at regular times, obtain sufficient sleep, and participate in wholesome activities in the out-of-doors. There is also the fun and relaxation that come from participating in recreational activities. The parents of an underweight boy in Dearborn, who had tried unsuccessfully for years to have the boy put on weight, found their son had gained five pounds in two weeks at camp.

The mentally retarded child has been found to receive immense benefits from programs in school camping and outdoor education. The Joseph P. Kennedy, Jr. Foundation has funded research into camping for the mentally retarded, has initiated and supported camps for the mentally retarded, and has sponsored a variety of training programs for physical educators and other individuals who have been chosen to work with the mentally retarded in a camp or recreational setting.

The Kennedy Foundation has found that the mentally retarded function very well in a camping atmosphere. Within a camping program, the mentally retarded can gain skills in a far shorter period of time than they usually do in the closed and formal environment of the schoolroom.

The values of camping do not accrue only to the children. Teachers who have been part of a school camping experience have pointed out that they learn more about their pupils in two weeks of camp than they do all the rest of the year in the classroom. Parents feel better when they see their children maturing socially, assuming responsibility, and becoming emotionally independent.

Ernest O. Melby, former Dean of Education at New York University, summed up what a camp experience means when he said, "[The general education outcomes of a good camping program are] a keener sensing of the responsibilities of citizenship, concern for the welfare of others, reverence in the presence of nature and of other human beings, and capacity for living and working with others in an artistic and wholesome fashion."

History of School Camping

When historians look back at the twentieth century there is a good possibility they will acclaim the school camping movement as one of the greatest educational innovations of the era and nature's classroom as one important means of preparing the child more effectively for successful living in today's world.

The state of Michigan has pioneered in the school camping field for some time. In the early 1930's Tappan Junior High School in Ann Arbor utilized a camp setting for its junior high school students, and the Cadillac Board of Education developed a summer camp for its elementary school children. A little later, schools in Battle Creek, Decatur, and Otsego utilized camps in their educational programs. In 1945, the state government passed legislation making it possible for school districts to acquire and operate camps as part of their education programs. A year later the departments of Public Instruction and Conservation, together with the W. K. Kellogg Foundation, joined forces to develop the program further. The late Lee M. Thurston, State Superintendent of Public Instruction, and P. J. Hoffmaster, State Director of Conservation, set as the goal for the state of Michigan, "a week of school camping for every boy and girl in the state."

The educationally significant way in which the program is operated is largely responsible for the rapid development of camping in Michigan. The groups going to camp usually include fifth or sixth graders on the elementary level or home rooms and special subject-matter areas on the secondary level. The camps are run by the teachers and students. Preplanning takes place in the classroom where such essentials as necessary clothing, projects that are to be developed, and jobs are assigned. The usual procedure is to have two teachers for the average classroom-size group plus extra help for food preparation and camp maintenance. The family assumes the cost of food, with special provisions for those children whose families are unable to pay the expenses.

Any child who wants to go to camp is given the opportunity. Schools assume the instructional cost. The school district or government agency bears the cost of the camp and its facilities.

Over 100 educational systems in Michigan include camping in their school programs at the present time. More than one-half of the school districts provide camping experiences for elementary school children. This state is pioneering in an educational movement which has many potentialities for furthering the social, mental, physical, and emotional growth of children. More than twenty other states have started school camping programs in their elementary schools. Many communities across the nation are taking Michigan's example and programs are starting to flourish in their schools. However, this movement is still embryonic. The fact that fewer than 10 per cent of the children of camp age in America ever get any type of camp experience presents a challenge for other states to follow this trend.

In the coming years people will have more and more leisure time available for their use. At present the elementary school child has more than 2,000 free hours per year to use at his will. These represent far more than the number of hours he spends in school each year. An experience in school camping will give the child many recreational skills that he can put to future use. Outdoor education will help open many new vistas for the child and introduce him to a variety of new interests that he can carry over into the future.

American society is becoming highly mobile. Families, as a unit, are traveling great distances in very short times over new superhighway systems. This has effectively helped to make the nation smaller, and has led to the opening of many new family camping and public recreational lands. Under the aegis of the Federal Government, many lands have been turned to recreational use that might otherwise have been lost for all time to commercial purposes. Since 1965, the Bureau of Outdoor Recreation of the Department of the Interior has administered the Land and Water Conservation Fund Act of 1964. This twenty-five year plan provides for the special funding of federal money for recreation development programs, recreational projects, and land acquisition.

Since 1960 many of the individual states have approved bond issues for recreational planning and the purchase of recreational lands. The open spaces provided by federal, state, and local action have helped to create many opportunities for family camping. This is a burgeoning phenomenon in today's society.

The elementary schools, through sound programs of school camping and outdoor education, can help to prepare children for the worthwhile use of their leisure time and for the family camping skills that may help them to meet some of their future recreational needs.

The Camp Program

The program in most camps consists of such sports activities as swimming, boating, fishing, horseback riding, tennis, badminton, hiking, horseshoes, basketball, and softball; such social activities as campfires, frankfurter and marshmallow roasts, dancing mixers, and cookouts; opportunities to develop skills and appreciation in arts and crafts, photography, Indian lore, drama, music, and nature study.

Julian W. Smith, one of the nation's leaders in the fields of camping and outdoor education, has listed a sample elementary school camp program as shown in Table 14–1. Table 14–2 shows a more detailed program.

A camping and outdoor education program in California that has won much recognition throughout the country is the Camp Hi-Hill program. Table 14–2 shows how the experience in this camp helps to meet the objectives of general education.

Getting a Camping Program Started. The classroom teacher can be instrumental in establishing a camping program for the school. Any teacher interested in providing such an experience for the pupils might pursue the following steps:

1. Obtain as much information about school camping as possible. Explore fully what is being done by other school systems across the country in this field. The names of these schools can be obtained from such places as (1) American Association for Health, Physical Education, and Recreation, 1201 Sixteenth Street, N.W., Washington,

Table 14–1. **A Sample Elementary School Camp Program**
(60 Campers = Three Program Groups)[a]

Day	Teamsters	Cruisers	Lumberjacks
Monday	Planning Hike around lake Cookout Paul Bunyan stories	Planning Hike to abandoned farm Crafts	Planning Camp cruise Tapping trees Square dance
Tuesday	Blacksmith's shop Scavenger hunt Sock hop	Logging Making ice cream Cookout	Treasure hunt Planting trees Fishing
Wednesday	Boiling sap Crafts Square dance	Hike around lake Fishing Square dance	Fire building Compass hike Crafts
Thursday	Breakfast cookout Compass hike Council fire	Compass hike Plan for council fire Council fire	Cookout Boating Council fire
Friday	Evaluation Clean-up and packing Going home	Evaluation Clean-up and packing Going home	Evaluation Clean-up and packing Going home

[a] Julian W. Smith, *Outdoor Education*, Washington, D.C., American Association for Health, Physical Education, and Recreation, 1956, p. 26.

Table 14–2. **School Camping as an Extension of the Classroom**[a]

Basic Scientific Understandings and Appreciations

How soil is formed. How plants grow. The rain-water cycle. How forest animals live. Dependence of man upon plants and animals. Causes of soil erosion and prevention.	Operation of a weather station. Use of man and compass. Significance of fire damage. Study of stars. Meaning of contour, grade, and slope.

Study of Seasonal Changes

Bird, animal, and insect life. Uses of flood control dams. How snow is used for protection and water supply for vegetation. Migration, fire hazards.	Barometric pressure. Weather observations. How animals use the food they have stored. Watersheds.

Worthy Skills in Recreation

Hiking to discover, study, explore, and collect native craft materials. Outdoor cooking techniques. Outdoor survival skills. Nature workshop. Square dancing.	Outdoor sports such as skiing, boating, canoeing fly-casting, bait-casting, swimming, skating, and mountain climbing. Crafts. Building outdoor shelters. Appreciating wholesome outdoor recreation.

Table 14–2 (continued)

Spiritual Values	
Experiencing the beauty of nature. Appreciation of living things developed from personal contact. Better appreciation of the personal worth of others from living together.	Development of finer group unity. Appreciation of the beauty and worth of the out-of-doors.

Wholesome Work Experiences	
Conservation projects. Planting and terracing to arrest erosion. Repairing trails. Building small check dams. Planting and maintaining a forest nursery.	Setting tables. Washing dishes. Cleaning cabins. Caring for animals and pets. Learning safe use and care of simple hand tools.

Democratic Social Living	
Cooperative planning by groups. Evaluation by students. Discussing camp safety standards. Living in cabin groups. Participating in campfire activities. Improving relationships of pupils and teacher.	Solving problems arising from living together. Understanding duties of the forest ranger. Acting as host, hostess, and hopper at dining table. Enriching and fostering democratic living.

Healthful Living	
Maintaining personal health, cleanliness. Maintaining regular hours of sleeping. Keeping cabin neat and clean. Participating in wholesome exercise.	Developing better table manners and eating habits. Planning menus. Practicing first aid.

[a] Adapted from the Division of Instruction, Long Beach, California, Public Schools, *Guide for the Camp Hi-Hill Program*, Long Beach.

D.C.; (2) Commissioner of Education, United States Office of Education, Department of Health, Education, and Welfare, Washington, D.C.

2. Discuss the camping program with the colleges and universities in the states which are active in promoting camping programs.

3. Invite a school camping specialist to discuss this program with you in more detail. Such a person might be a representative of a school system where a successful camping program is being conducted or a professor from a nearby college or university where such projects are sponsored and studied.

4. Investigate to determine if enabling legislation exists which permits school districts to operate camps as part of the educational program. Also, determine if there are any legal barriers to camping programs in the state.

5. Organize a plan of action which, if followed step by step, will ultimately make it possible for school children to have the benefits of a school camping experience as part of their regular educational program.

6. Develop a camping program on paper showing the organization, program, grades that will attend, teachers interested, financial outlay, relationships with regular education program. Distribute to school officials and other interested parties.

7. Meet with the principal and superintendent of schools to discuss the matter in detail.
8. Investigate possible camp sites where the school could carry on such an experience. Camps could be leased, rented, or some other provisions made.
9. Have the parent-teacher association discuss its possibilities.

Outdoor Education

In simple terms outdoor education means using the out-of-doors as a place to learn about things which are peculiar to nature's classroom. It can take place in a camp, but there are many other settings where such experiences take place. It isn't a separate subject in itself; instead, it cuts across departmental and subject-matter lines. It is applicable to science and art in both elementary and secondary education.

An outdoor education program, where children actually learn by direct experience, has many proved benefits. It provides direct experiences for learning about such things as plant and animal life, conservation, rock formation, and other wonders of the universe. It enables youngsters who are removed from rural life actually to see things which before were known only through books and experienced vicariously. It allows for the tapping of community resources to a great degree. It also provides additional avenues to knowledge, understanding, and skills for children, broadening their educational horizons, and furthering their total development.

Outdoor Education Experiences for the Elementary School Teacher. There are many ways the elementary teacher can use the out-of-doors for educational experiences. Some of them follow:

1. Taking a hike to a nearby woods to study the flowers, trees, and other plant life in connection with a nature lesson.
2. Planting trees or shrubs to enhance the beauty of a nearby landscape and to prevent soil erosion.
3. Walking around the school grounds to acquaint students with some of nature's works of art.
4. Going on an overnight camping trip to an historic site.
5. Making a direct study of how animals live.
6. Taking an early morning walk to identify the many different birds that inhabit the community environs.
7. Visiting a nearby farm to see at first hand some of the jobs performed and services rendered in agriculture.
8. Having a garden in a section of the school grounds set aside for the class where pupils can do their own planting and gardening.
9. Drawing pictures of some works of nature such as trees, leaves, landscape, lake, woods, or mountains.
10. Going on a fishing trip to study the habits of various types of fish and how to catch them.
11. Caring for animals and pets.
12. Building small dams.
13. Repairing or laying new trails through the woods.
14. Engaging in new forms of outdoor recreation.
15. Mastering the art of outdoor cooking techniques.
16. Collecting craft materials peculiar to the section of the country in which the school is located.
17. Learning how to use a map and compass.
18. Having pupils meet at night to study the stars and the moon.
19. Learning the meaning of such terms as slope, erosion, conservation, contour, terracing, and geology.
20. Going to the zoo to see the animal and bird life.
21. Visiting a quarry as a means of introducing a new unit on earth science.
22. Developing and arranging a picture exhibit of plant and animal life in the area.
23. Visiting a museum, planetarium, botanical garden, or bird or animal sanctuary.
24. Visiting the local weather station to learn about weather forecasting.

Camping and Outdoor Education—An All-School Affair. Camping and outdoor education are not limited to one grade in a school or to one subject. They have important contributions to make to the total school offering. Paul E. Harrison has pointed out the contributions various departments in many schools are making to camping and outdoor education programs. These suggestions point out the role of the total school offering in such an educational experience.

Speech. Activities in speech and dramatics can take many forms:

1. Short plays, comedy, drama, and so on.
2. Pageants.
3. Folk festivals.
4. Readings, recitations.
5. Marionette and puppet shows.

Music. Campers can spend many happy hours with music:

1. Informal campfire sings.
2. Pageants.
3. Camp orchestra.

Mathematics. Arithmetic is a must in many camp activities.

1. Food costs.
2. Surveying and mapping.
3. Camp stores and banks.
4. Figuring land areas, elevation, tree heights, lumber footage, tree age.

Industrial Arts. Using appropriate tools and nteresting natural materials where they are found:

1. Camp maintenance and repair.
2. Building new camp equipment.
3. Reading blueprints.
4. Camp activities, dramatics, staging, and so on.
5. Craft programs.

Homemaking. Good food and appropriate clothing make for a happy camp:

1. Planning and preparing foods for cookouts, campouts, and regular menus.
2. Care of clothing and camp equipment.
3. Social graces.
4. Helping with camp food service.

English. The camp can provide an opportunity for the practice of effective communication and appreciation of literature.

1. Proper language usage.
2. Writing letters, plays, poems.
3. Storytelling.
4. Reading.

Social Science. The history of the area—its land, its people, and its customs—is always an interesting problem for study:

1. A study of the area's industries.
2. Indian lore and the lumber camps.
3. Use of public property.
4. Camp government.

Science, Physical and Biological. A study of the land, water, and living things is always interesting and useful.

1. A study of forest and forest life.
2. Experiences in botany.
3. Activities in Geology.
4. Study of the skies, stars, constellations, weather stations, and so on.
5. Soil.
6. Sanitation.
7. Rivers and lakes.
8. Fish and fishing.
9. Fire protection.
10. Photography—aerial, and so on.
11. Map development.
12. Reforestation.

Physical Education. Exercise is basic to camp happiness.

1. Hiking.
2. Cookouts and campouts.
3. Swimming and boating.
4. Snowshoeing.
5. Archery.
6. Bait casting and fishing.
7. Hunting and tracking.
8. Wood crafts.
9. Games and athletic events.

Art. The camper has a chance to study nature as it develops.

1. Creative drawing and sketching.
2. Painting (dramatic-music pageants).[1]

[1] Paul E. Harrison, "Education Goes Outdoors!" *Journal of the American Association for Health, Physical Education, and Recreation,* 24:10–20, Dec. 1953.

Questions and Practical Problems

1. Visit a school camp. Describe its physical aspects as well as the program that is followed.
2. Prepare a camp program for a period of one week as an extension of some classroom activity.
3. Prepare a list of camp projects which are

normally taught in the classroom but which could be done more effectively in a camp setting.

4. Make a list of the basic needs of children that can be met in a camp setting.

5. Read extensively on school camping throughout the United States and report on some outstanding programs that are written up in the professional literature.

6. Develop an outdoor education project for a class of elementary school children of one particular grade.

7. Plan a trip to the zoo. Include the details that would need attention and list the values that could be derived from such an experience.

8. Describe in detail how various subject-matter areas can be utilized in outdoor education projects.

9. List ten outdoor education experiences that every child should have.

10. Write a short report on the contributions physical education can make to camping and outdoor education programs.

Selected References

BRIGHTBILL, CHARLES K. *Man and Leisure: A Philosophy of Recreation.* Englewood Cliffs, N.J.: Prentice-Hall, Inc., 1961.

BUCHER, CHARLES A. *Administration of School Health and Physical Education Programs* (Fifth Edition). St. Louis: The C. V. Mosby Co., 1971.

———. *Foundations of Physical Education* (Fifth Edition). St. Louis: The C. V. Mosby Co., 1968.

DE GRAZIA, SEBASTIAN. *Of Time, Work, and Leisure.* New York: The Twentieth Century Fund, 1962.

HUTCHINSON, JOHN L., ed. *Leisure and the Schools.* Washington, D.C.: American Association for Health, Physical Education, and Recreation, 1961.

KAPLAN, MAX. *Leisure in America: A Social Inquiry.* New York: John Wiley & Sons, Inc., 1960.

KRAUS, RICHARD G. *Recreation and the Schools.* New York: The Macmillan Company, 1964.

NASH, JAY B. *Philosophy of Recreation and Leisure.* St. Louis: The C. V. Mosby Co., 1953.

Participation in National Recreation Workshop. *Recreation for Community Living: Guiding Principles.* Chicago: The Athletic Institute, 1952.

SHIVERS, JAY S. *Leadership in Recreational Service.* New York: The Macmillan Comapany, 1963.

———. *Principles and Practices of Recreational Service.* New York: The Macmillan Company, 1967.

SMITH, JULIAN W., et al. *Outdoor Education.* Englewood Cliffs, N.J.: Prentice-Hall, Inc., 1963.

CHAPTER 15

The Health Education Curriculum in the Elementary School

Health education is an important part of the elementary school program because this is where scientific knowledge is imparted to youngsters about their health. Health education is no longer a "sometime" experience, but is, instead, a planned and regular part of the educational program. It should be given equal status with such other subject-matter areas as arithmetic, science, and art.

Bases for Selecting Curriculum Experiences

The Joint Committee on Health Problems of the National Education Association and the American Medical Association stresses that the bases for selecting curriculum experiences should be the *biological needs* of boys and girls such as rest, sleep, and food; the *characteristics of children* at different age levels and their growth and developmental needs; *health problems* as revealed through a study of mortality records by age groups; *health status* by age groups as revealed by health records, accident and illness records, special studies, and surveys; *analysis by age groups* of activities related to health in which the majority of boys and girls engage; *analysis of environmental health hazards* in school, home, and community; *analysis of citizenship responsibilities* relating to health; *analysis of major social trends* relating to health; and *analysis of vocational opportunities* in health education.

Health Needs and Interests of Students. Health education in the elementary school should be based to a large degree upon the health needs and interests of the children it serves. There is no single procedure that can be followed or set formula that can be applied to determine the health needs and interests of children. The procedure will vary with the particular school and community involved. Some of the procedures for determining children's interests and needs are as follows:

1. *Pupil observation.* Observing the pupil and watching his habits will reveal his knowledge, attitudes, and health practices.

2. *Records.* Pupils' general health history, attendance, communicable-disease history, and other health records give information concerning certain diseases, health defects, behavior, and abnormalities.

3. *Tests.* Diagnostic health knowledge, atti-

tude and habit tests, and health-interest inventories may be of value for older elementary pupils.

4. *Class discussions.* Many of the interests and needs of children are revealed during classroom discussions.

5. *Surveys.* Utilizing such instruments as check sheets and questionnaires for school and community use will give wanted information. For example, a survey of food habits may suggest nutritional needs.

6. *Consultations.* School physicians, family physicians, nurses, parents, public health workers, and others can provide important health information.

7. *Visits.* Observing practices in other schools may indicate needs not previously revealed.

8. *Health conferences.* Discussions of school health problems in general frequently focus attention on needs and interests that have been overlooked.

9. *Professional literature.* Examining material concerned with needs and interests of children can be of value.

10. *Parent-teacher association meetings.* Meetings of teachers with parent groups can sometimes provide valuable health data.

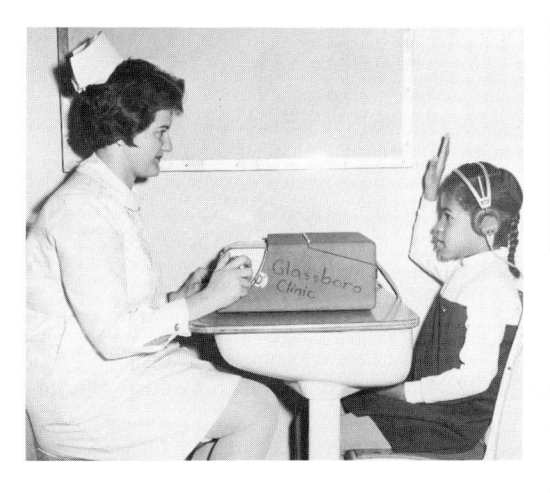

Health Problems of Elementary School Children. Respiratory conditions such as sore throats, colds, influenza, and tonsilitis, infections and parasitic conditions such as measles, mumps, and chickenpox, and injuries and digestive disturbances are the health conditions that most frequently keep children home from school.

A significant number of children between the ages of five and seventeen have eye conditions needing special care, orthopedic defects, cerebral palsy, epilepsy, and impaired hearing.

The nation's children just beginning school have on the average three or more decayed primary teeth.

Accidents are the leading cause of death among school-age children. In a single recorded year, more than seven thousand children aged five to fourteen years were killed by accidents.

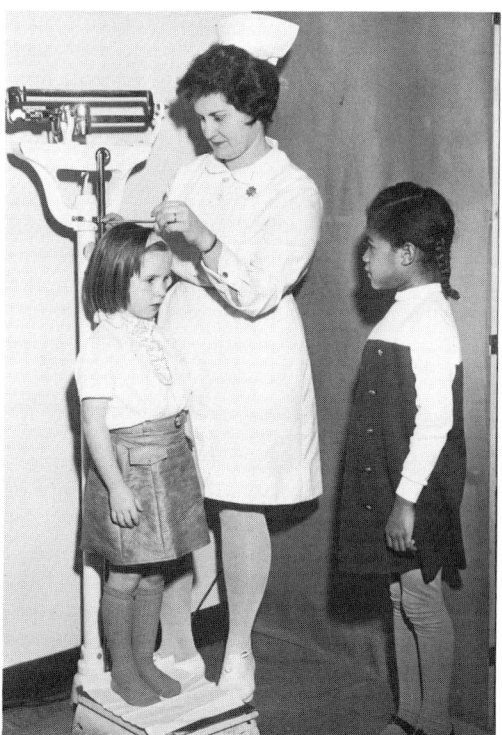

A large proportion of the nation's children have been declared physically soft.

Leading causes for death among children five to fourteen years for one year were accidents, cancer and leukemia, influenza and pneumonia, congenital malformations, heart disease and rheumatic fever, meningitis and meningococcal infection, vascular lesions of the central nervous system, and acute kidney disease.

Health surveys have shown that nutritional inadequacies are common among elementary school pupils.

The Health Education Curriculum. Health education at the elementary level is aimed primarily at helping the child to develop good health habits and health attitudes and to live happily, healthfully, and safely. These objectives can be achieved by imparting scientifically based knowledge adapted to the child and by incorporating good health practices to the regular routine of school and home living. The classroom teacher is the guiding influence and his or her understanding of good health will determine to a great degree the effectiveness of such a program. The American Association of School Administrators in its *Twentieth Yearbook* stated that the health problems which confront and interest children in the primary grades included such topics as: (1) growth and health, (2) nutrition, (3) elimination, (4) exercise, relaxation, rest and sleep, (5) personal hygiene, (6) prevention and control of disease, (7) care of eyes and ears, (8) medical and dental attention, (9) emotional and social adjustment, and (10) safety. These various subjects must, of course, be adapted to the individual child. At the intermediate level health problems may cover many of the same topics with more information and experiences being adapted to the child's level of understanding. Specifically, topics that are appropriate for the intermediate grades include: (1) growth and health, (2) nutrition, (3) exercise, relaxation, rest, and sleep, (4) personal hygiene, (5) care of eyes and ears, and (6) prevention and control of disease.

The Norfolk, Virginia, public schools have listed fourteen basic areas of health instruction for the elementary school: (1) play and physical education, (2) social hygiene, (3) mental and emotional health, (4) personal hygiene, including diet, rest, sleep, exercise, clothing, elimination, handwashing, and exposure, (5) experiences in healthful living, (6) communicable diseases, including diseases listed under health service, (7) nutrition, (8) dental hygiene, (9) eye hygiene, (10) posture education, (11) safety education, (12) first aid, (13) experiences in health service, and (14) foot hygiene.

The authors' college classes have suggested the following as some of the important health topics and experiences for consideration in the elementary school:

Kindergarten
1. Getting acquainted with school nurse, doctor, and dietician.
2. Location and proper use of school facilities (bathrooms, drinking fountains, and lunchroom).
3. Safe practices in classroom and playground.
4. Safety procedures in travelling to and from school.
5. Learning skills of handwriting, toothbrushing, and use of handkerchief.
6. Wearing appropriate clothing for different weather conditions.

Primary Grades, One to Three
1. Social and mental adjustment to school life (sharing with others, and so on).
2. Need for cleanliness and good grooming (eyes, ears, hair, teeth, clothes, and so on).
3. Nutrition (eating habits, kinds of foods, manners, and so on).
4. School safety and accident prevention (fire drills, crossing streets, and so on).
5. Growth (height and weight).
6. Communicable diseases and infections (colds, wounds, immunization, and so on).

Intermediate and Middle School Grades, Four to Eight
1. Learning body structures and systems.
2. Posture and body control.
3. Relation of rest, exercise, and relaxation to health.
4. Essential food elements for a balanced diet.
5. Relation with peers.
6. Safety and accident prevention.
7. Personal appearance and cleanliness, caring for the eyes, ears, teeth, and so on.
8. Common health disorders (stomachache, headache, and so on).
9. How to cope with and resolve fears and frustrations.
10. Importance of medical and dental examinations.
11. Basic first aid procedures.
12. How the community provides for healthful living.
13. Family living, alcohol, tobacco, and drugs.

The type of health program offered should be adapted to the child's level and planned in accordance with his or her interests and needs. It should also be remembered that health education is a continuous process and cannot be completely compartmentalized within a definite subject area or within a specific class period. It should embrace all the activities and subjects that are a part of the child's life.

The Conceptual Approach in Health Education

Health instruction must proceed in a systematic way if optimum results are to be achieved. This means planning subject-matter areas which are based on the needs and interests of the pupils concerned. Following a textbook, chapter by chapter, will not provide the best type of learning experience for the student. Instead, it is recommended that the classroom teacher identify concepts, and then plan units of instruction based on the concepts that are appropriate for a particular age group or class.

Various authorities, for example, have recommended that health teaching in the elementary school be concerned with safety and first aid teachings as well as with what is usually considered to be a normal part of the health curriculum in the elementary school. These authorities also recommend that the health program for the child in kindergarten through grade three or four concentrate on the development of good health practices and that the development of health attitudes and knowledge be allowed to accrue as a concomitant of these practices developed earlier. In the later elementary and middle school grades, they feel, attitudes and knowledge can be emphasized and better related to the existing foundation of good health practices.

Health teaching in the elementary school begins when the child enters kindergarten, and it is here that certain health practices are learned and reinforced. For example, most kindergarten teachers provide a nap or rest period for their pupils, require that they wash their hands after using the toilet or before eating lunch or a snack, and make certain that there are several periods during each day when the children can participate in vigorous physical activity. Further, such activities as group games and class parties enhance the social-development objectives of both health and physical education. Trips to dairies to see milk processed and tours to fire stations and other community facilities such as food-processing plants or sewerage-treatment plants are all health-related and help to stimulate the child's thinking about matters concerned with health.

Older elementary school children also enjoy trips to places of interest that are related to the classroom health program, and where they can gain the knowledge they need from personal experience. The children in the upper elementary grades are capable of sharing in the planning of their school health program. When the teacher and the children combine to plan the program, it will be more closely related to the needs and interests of the children. These older children might, for example, wish to plan, prepare, and serve a simple breakfast or lunch based on their study of nutrition, or they might decide to visit a home for handicapped children or to work as volunteers in a hospital or other agency to gain experience in this area of health. The kinds of experience that are directly related to health education motivate the child to form his own personal concepts concerning health practices. These concepts can then be related to the child's developing attitudes toward health and can be based upon the child's increasing store of health knowledge.

There are specific health teachings that can and should be accomplished during the elementary school years. The following concepts are general ones and are not intended to be all-inclusive of the health teachings that should result during the elementary school years. Each of these general concepts can be broken down and further refined. These particular broad concepts have been selected for illustration because they are representative concepts. It would be impossible, within the confines of this chapter, to list the several hundred health concepts appropriate to grades kindergarten through eight.

Six General Concepts for the Health Program for the Early Childhood Years—Grades Kindergarten through Four

1. *Proper care of the body is essential to good health.* The development of this concept would include a foundation of learning in the areas of posture, care of the eyes, teeth, personal cleanliness, and the importance of fresh air and proper sleep and rest. The teacher might wish the school dental hygienist to visit the classroom to demonstrate proper techniques for brushing the teeth, or where facilities permit, might arrange time for the children to shower after each of their physical education classes.

2. *If proper health precautions are taken, many diseases can be prevented.* The need for regular dental and physical examinations, the wisdom of staying away from people who have communicable diseases, the necessity of having one's own personal hygiene items such as toothbrushes and wash cloths, and the contribution of a healthful environment would be among the developmental facts leading to the formation of the general concept. A visit to a laundry to see the proper washing of clothes, or to a pharmacy to learn about drugs and their proper use would help to stimulate the childrens' learning in this area.

3. *Proper diet enhances good health.* Children are interested in learning how proper food, properly prepared and eaten in the right amounts, contributes to their growth and development. A visit to the school nutritionist to see how the meals are planned for the week, observation of the practices in the school kitchen, and a survey of the children's own practices in regard to diet add interest to the development of this concept.

4. *The home and community atmosphere influences health.* Community health services and their effect on the child and his family are important considerations. The place in the community and relationship to the family of the physician and dentist should be emphasized. Field trips to community sanitation facilities and surveys of community needs in regard to sanitation will help the children to become more aware of the factors that influence their health status.

5. *Personal adjustment is a part of health.* The place of the emotions in daily life, the ability to cooperate with others, and ways of making and keeping friends are all aspects of health. Story plays about different ways of behaving in certain social situations, the planning of a class celebration, and attempting to make new friends during recess periods or in the lunchroom are practical ways to help children develop an understanding of this concept.

6. *Obeying safety rules is an aspect of healthful living.* Obeying the school-crossing guard, swimming in a safe place and with supervision, and knowing the rules for school fire drills are some of the aspects of safety that help to protect the health of the individual. Practicing proper fire-drill procedures and discussing the need for these and other safety measures, and accounts of personal experiences in the area of safety are methods of enhancing this concept's formation.

Six General Concepts for the Health Program for the Middle and Later Childhood Years—Grades Five through Eight

1. *The maintenance of good physical health is a personal matter.* The children in grades five through eight are about to enter, or have entered, the adolescent period. For many, their bodies are going through a series of strange and startling changes. The teacher can aid the children immeasurably during this period by attempting to help them to understand their newly developing selves. These children need to understand how their bodies function, and how they can help their bodies to function better. Grooming, posture, and personal appearance are particularly important during this time. The relationship of physical growth and development to the use of alcohol, drugs, and tobacco are also essential learnings. Where the school system permits, well-planned units in sex education are extremely important. An entire class, in order to enhance the development of the general concept, might have a panel discussion or debate on the relationship of smoking to sports performance. Girls would find a grooming demonstration by an expert helpful, while boys might be interested in devising their own personal physical health and fitness improvement program.

2. *Society is founded on the independent family unit.* Preadolescent and adolescent youngsters sometimes have difficulty in their home and family relationships. As they begin to approach

maturity youngsters at times tend to withdraw from the family unit as they seek increasing independence. Through the school health program these children can come to a greater understanding of the role of the family in society, cultural and economic differences among families, their own roles in their families in the present, and their future roles as heads of families of their own. The school psychologist or school social worker will be an excellent resource person in the work on this concept.

3. *A knowledge of safety and familiarity with first aid techniques is essential to healthful living.* Children in grades five through eight are often prone to accident and injury. They are more independent in their recreational endeavors and frequently are not aware of proper safety procedures when their play is unsupervised. Many teachings in this area can take place in the physical education class. A course in first aid and trips to a pool for swimming lessons and water-safety procedures are some of the measures that can be successfully employed.

4. *Mental health is an essential element in the total health of the individual.* The older elementary school child is interested in the mental as well as the physical aspects of health and in the phenomenon of mental and emotional disturbances. Through the health education program these youngsters can be helped to understand the ways in which mental and physical health are interrelated. The need of each individual for self-respect, a feeling of success, and respect for and from others, and the effect of the home, community, and school upon each of these mental-health aspects are important. The development of this concept also includes understanding of drug use and abuse, personal standards of integrity, and the relationship of crime and juvenile delinquency to mental health and physical and mental well-being.

5. *Satisfying social relationships are an important aspect of health.* Children in grades five through eight are just beginning to come to an understanding of their relationships with their friends, with their parents, and with other adults. The on-going health education program should help these youngsters to understand the necessity of choosing their close companions wisely. The importance of the individual within the group, respect for individual differences, boy-girl relationships, popularity, and home and school relationships with adults also need to be considered. Coeducational activities, especially formed youth groups and clubs, and child-parent forums and discussions are several methods that can be used to point out the ways in which good social relationships are formed.

6. *Good health depends on a sound body.* Proper diet, rest, exercise, and sleep all enhance health. Methods of disease prevention and home, school, and community environments and their relationship to health are features of this concept. National and local health agencies and services, and the types of medical care available to individuals should also be stressed. New techniques of preventing and controlling diseases and innovations in medical and scientific technology are also important areas of concern. A discussion led by a representative of a health-service agency or a narcotics-bureau agent would help children to better understand the part these agencies and services play in their lives and in the maintenance of their personal physical health.

Outline for Teaching the Health Concept. *Dental health is assured with proper personal and professional care of the teeth.* The following is an outline for developing a concept for dental health for a fifth-grade class.

Rationale to Support the Need for Concept. Observation of fifth-grade children showed that their permanent teeth were still erupting and their deciduous teeth were disappearing. Children were curious about their teeth, asking where they came from, what their purpose was, why first teeth come out and new ones come in, and why some are crooked and others straight. A survey of the fifth-grade class showed an average of three carious teeth to each child. An interview with the dental hygienist at the school showed that many of the children didn't brush their teeth regularly and parents seemed indifferent to the dental needs of their children. The doctor, nurse, and dentist all felt that the children could benefit greatly from health instruction in the care of their teeth.

Objectives for Instilling Concept in Minds and Thinking of Students

1. Provide pupils with an understanding of the structure and function of their teeth.

2. Develop an appreciation for proper care of teeth.

3. Acquaint students with the services rendered by the dentist and dental hygienist.

204 RECOMMENDATIONS FOR PROGRAM DEVELOPMENT

4. Develop skill in how to brush teeth correctly.

5. Familiarize pupils with the relationship of nutrition to healthy teeth.

Procedures for Initiating Thinking About Concept

1. Show a film such as "Behind That Smile."
2. Follow showing of film by a discussion of the importance of teeth to appearance and to health in general.
3. Elicit participation of students in planning for unit—what they would like to learn about teeth and what educational experiences they would enjoy having as part of this unit.

Questions or Problems to be Answered and Solved Regarding Concept

1. Why is good dental health important?
2. How many teeth do we have? What is the purpose of each type of tooth?
3. What are the various parts of a tooth?
4. What are the causes of tooth decay?
5. How do we protect our teeth from decay?
6. Why is it important to see the dentist regularly?
7. What is the best diet for good dental health?

Activities and Learning Situations to Help Develop Concept. Several different methods should be utilized for teaching the concept such as charts, visits to the dentist's office, experiments, films, discussions, and resource people.

A committee of students meeting with the teacher and dental hygienist might select such activities as the following to help students answer questions and solve problems:

1. Examining teeth by use of mirrors.
2. Obtaining a large chart showing the structure of a tooth; studying the chart.
3. Using a large model, demonstrating and discussing the proper method for brushing teeth; individual toothbrushes to be brought from home by students to use for personal practice.
4. Reading about the reasons for dental decay.
5. Preparing posters illustrating good dental hygiene.
6. Researching the effectiveness of fluoridation of water supplies for dental health.
7. Doing a case study of a boy and a girl on what they have done for a period of three years to provide for their dental health.

8. Making a graph to show incidence of dental caries among pupils at each grade level, using information provided by dental hygienist.

Other Steps to Reinforce Concept

1. Working with dental association.
2. Gathering materials from various commercial concerns, such as toothpaste concerns, and evaluating materials.
3. Evaluating toothpaste ads in magazines.
4. Discussing television programs which relate to dental health or advertising.
5. Preparing and presenting student-committee reports on such topics as "Should primary teeth be retained as long as possible in order to have good dental health?"

Some Teaching Aids That Can Be Utilized in Developing Concept

1. Reading materials in textbook.
2. Materials obtained from the American Dental Association, 222 East Superior Street, Chicago, Illinois.
3. Materials and information obtained from the State Health Department.
4. Discussion of dental problems with a dentist.
5. Dental hygienist to speak to class.
6. Films, filmstrips, recordings, and other audio-visual aids.

Evaluation of Extent to Which Concept Was Developed in Students. The accomplishment with respect to the development of this concept within students in terms of the original purpose might be determined by:

1. Giving an examination to pupils about material covered in the unit to see if the children have knowledge of structure of tooth, dental caries, and health practices that promote good dental health.
2. Conducting daily health-regimen checks to see if children demonstrate a continued interest in brushing teeth and providing for their dental health.
3. Carrying out a dental survey of parents to see how many children visit the dentist regularly to have teeth examined and treated.
4. Determining the children's skill in brushing teeth through actual practice in the classroom.
5. Having the children write their own evaluation reports on what worth this concept has for them.

Critical Health Areas

Certain health areas are receiving increasing attention from educators because of the acute problems associated with them in today's world. For this reason they have been called "critical health problems." Four of the most pressing of these problems are concerned with sex practices, tobacco smoking, and the use of drugs and alcohol. Although youngsters in the elementary school may not be experimenting with these materials and engaging in harmful sex practices, a foundation should be laid during these years that will insure proper understanding and appreciation of these health areas when young people are faced with decisions concerning them. Teachers in the elementary and middle schools have a responsibility for developing key concepts in each of these health areas.

Family Life Education. Family life education, which includes sex education, should play a prominent role in elementary and middle schools. Through adequate planning, effective community interaction, outstanding teaching, and appropriate subject matter, much good can be done. The emphasis throughout the program should be on human sexuality, or how boys and girls and men and women fulfill their roles in life. Each child should be helped to identify his own masculine or feminine role in school, at play, at home, and at work. The core of one's identity is one's sexual role.

Family life education should be designed to help boys and girls grow and develop in a way that will be meaningful and lead to the achievement of maturity, emotional independence, and a responsible relationship with the opposite sex. In order to achieve these goals boys and girls need a knowledge of their physical, mental, social, and emotional selves, an understanding of their role in the family, and the means of achieving good human relationships.

During the elementary school years an opportunity is provided to impart information and understanding about such things as the child's responsibilities, satisfying his curiosity about various questions concerning his body and sex, providing him with an understanding of the reproductive process, helping him to develop good habits concerned with his toilet, and the importance of getting along with members of the other sex. Such a program can be effectively implemented through such means as observation of nature and pets, good teaching, and the many visual aids that are available on this subject.

Schools should help their teachers in meeting the need for family life education so that the subject is an integral part of the school program, not an adjunct. Teachers should know their subject matter, be comfortable in using the language of sex, and be aware of the great social changes in progress in our society. Audio-visual aids, books, and other materials that are used should be up-to-date and appropriate for students. Resource people, such as nurses, clergymen, doctors, psychologists, and social workers can make a valuable contribution to the program.

In general, in the elementary schools, boys and girls can be grouped together for most discussions and activities. In the middle school, there would be need for separating the sexes in such matters as discussion of menstruation and similar topics where students might be fearful or flippant.

In general, a family-life-education program should concern itself in early childhood with such matters as an understanding of sex differences, developing a wholesome attitude toward sex, helping boys and girls to relate emotionally to others, helping them to be good family members, and understanding such physiological facts as that a baby grows in the body of a mother. In middle childhood an attempt should be made to help boys and girls develop wholesome attitudes toward themselves, respecting their right to have opinions, helping them to experience success and develop confidence. There is a need to help boys and girls to understand the growth process and the role of inheritance in this process, to develop respect for social customs, and to respect life itself. Later childhood should find the student recognizing his appropriate sex role, mastering the social graces in boy-girl relations, and developing a sound standard of values in human relations. Early adolescence should find boys and girls accepting masculine or feminine roles through appropriate behavior in boy-girl relations and developing an understanding of the physical changes they experience as adolescents.

Examples of concepts to be developed, learning activities to be utilized, and resources to be used for a family-life-education program at the elementary school and middle school levels follow.

Examples of Concepts To Be Developed at the Elementary School Level (Grades K–4)

1. The family is the basic unit of society and as such plays a major role in influencing the development of each of its members.
2. Family cooperation is imperative for family health.
3. A successful family is characterized by love and the sharing of effort.
4. Love for another person can be shown in many different ways.
5. A father and mother are essential to the birth of a baby.
6. Each person receives his inherited characteristics from his mother and his father.
7. The human body is composed of many parts which have specific terminology.
8. Boys and girls have different physical characteristics.
9. The animal kingdom produces babies.
10. Most animals, including human beings, start their lives as eggs.
11. Living things reproduce.
12. All living things have basic needs which must be satisfied if there is to be optimum growth.
13. Each person should respect the rights of others.

Examples of Learning Activities To Be Utilized in Grades K–4

1. Discussing the many ways that happy families work and play together.
2. Preparing reports after talking with their parents, regarding the arrangements that were made prior to their being born.
3. Role-playing with children assisting in the care of the baby.
4. Viewing the film "Animals Growing Up."
5. Caring for pets in the family or at school.
6. Observing how animals protect and feed their babies.
7. Taking a trip to the zoo to see newborn baby animals.

8. Having the nurse visit the class to discuss cleanliness and grooming.
9. Planning a class party to simulate a family get-together and relate to family sharing.

Examples of Resources To Be Used in Grades K–4

1. *Films*, such as "Mother Hen's Family (The Wonders of Birth)," Coronet Instructional films, Chicago.
2. *Records*, such as "Sex Education for Children" (For Parents), by Francis Filas, Faith Through Education Corporation, Skokie, Illinois.
3. *Books and pamphlets*, such as: Francis L. Filas, "Sex Education in the Family," Prentice-Hall, Inc.
4. *Sound Filmstrips*, such as "The Zoo Trip (Show and Tell)," Eye Gate House, Inc., Jamaica, New York.

Examples of Concepts To Be Developed at the Middle School Level (Grades 5–8)

1. Although the growth and development patterns follows the same sequence for all persons, each individual follows the sequence at his own individual rate.
2. The human body experiences several changes during the preadolescent period.
3. Puberty initiates the physical changes leading to manhood and womanhood.
4. The endocrine system influences body functions and behavior of individuals.
5. The sex drive is a natural phenomenon that assures the continuation of the species.
6. As boys and girls grow older they assume more responsibility for their own welfare and also that of others.
7. Emotions need to be expressed but there are constructive and destructive ways of expressing emotions.
8. Appropriate behavior is essential in social activities between boys and girls.
9. Developing a healthy sexuality is a developmental task for teen-agers.

Examples of Learning Activities To Be Utilized in Grades 5–8

1. Discussion of growth patterns and rates of development of human beings; members of the class compare themselves with others in class in regard to body build, size, weight, height, and other physical factors.
2. Panel discussion on ways to control emotions, such as avoidance of emotional outbursts.
3. Question box in which members of the class can deposit questions; teacher screens questions.
4. Discussion of the question: What makes for popularity? Include desirable and undesirable qualities for developing friendships.
5. Viewing the film "Human Reproduction."
6. Preparing charts of the endocrine glands and identifying function of each.
7. Utilization of transparencies of male and female bodies showing location of the endocrine glands.
8. Development by class of a Code of Behavior to guide the students in their social relationships.
9. Inviting the school physician to class to discuss the implications of puberty for boys and girls.

Examples of Resources To Be Used in Grades 5–8

1. *Films*, such as "Growing Up (Preadolescence)," McGraw-Hill Book Co., Inc., "Human Heredity," E. C. Brown Trust, Portland, Oregon.
2. *Sound filmstrips*, such as "Especially for Boys," Sy Wexler Film Productions, Los Angeles (Pubescent Growth and Development of Boys and Girls).
3. *Books and Pamphlets*, such as Charles Wilson, and Elizabeth Wilson, "Growing Up," Bobbs-Merrill Company, Inc., Indianapolis.

Tobacco Smoking. The smoking of tobacco is a very ancient practice. Early Anglo-Saxon, Chinese, and Roman history indicates that people long before the first century were using a potent mixture and implements for drawing smoke through the nose and mouth for the purpose of deriving pleasure. Today the American public carries on this practice by smoking billions of cigarettes, cigars, and pipefuls of tobacco each year.

It is obvious to anyone who is willing to observe that poisons present in tobacco smoke taken into the body can cause damage to the person doing the smoking. The physiological effects of smoking are not compatible with a healthy, efficient body. Cigarette smoking is damaging to the cilia of the lungs, affects heart and respiration rate, and affects blood pressure. It is linked with cancer of the lung, chronic bronchitis, and heart disease. Cigarette smokers have a higher death rate from certain diseases than nonsmokers. Smoking sometimes interferes with physical activities. Smoking is the greatest single cause of fires.

Perhaps the most significant change in smoking in recent years is the increase in the number of smokers at an early age. One frequently sees students in the elementary and middle schools puffing on cigarettes. Partly as a result of intensive advertising that glamorizes the habit and partly because parental influences have relaxed, young people now smoke in public and sometimes at home with little adult disapproval. Slightly less than one out of every three American teen-agers smokes, and an estimated two million new smokers between the ages of twelve and seventeen are added each year, many of them acquiring the habit early in life. According to the United States Public Health Service, if present lung-cancer rates continue an estimated 1,000,000 of today's school children will develop lung cancer during their lifetime. Nearly 10 per cent of habitual smoking starts at seventh grade level with youngsters experimenting at earlier ages. It is very important, therefore, to start adequate instruction in the intermediate grades concerning the use of tobacco.

The middle school period is an excellent time to provide the beginning of instruction on tobacco and smoking. This educational level provides an opportunity to acquaint boys and girls with an understanding of such things as what tobacco is, the health hazards associated with smoking, and the economics of smoking. Through meaningful instruction, proper understanding and attitudes can be developed which can result in intelligent decisions on the part of youngsters as to whether or not they will use tobacco.

Examples of concepts to be developed, learning activities to be utilized, and resources to be used for the middle school level follow:

Examples of Concepts To Be Developed
1. Smoke from tobacco is composed of gases and particles that have damaging physiological effects on the body.
2. Tobacco production plays a major role in our national economy.
3. Cigarette advertising is sometimes misleading and inaccurate.
4. Cigarette smoking is a very expensive habit.
5. Smoking is the greatest single cause of fires.
6. The decision to smoke or not to smoke is a personal one that should be based on sound evidence.
7. The decision as to whether a person will smoke will greatly influence his health throughout life.
8. Smoking may interfere with physical performance.
9. The evidence associating cigarette smoking with various diseases is very substantial.
10. The Surgeon General's Report on Smoking and its conclusion have been accepted by the medical profession.
11. Persons interested in optimum growth, development, and performance avoid the use of tobacco.
12. There are many psychological reasons why young people smoke.
13. Many adults now using tobacco were not aware of the consequences of smoking when they started at an early age.

Examples of Learning Activities To Be Utilized
1. Collection of advertisements on tobacco and analysis of them from a scientific point of view.
2. Discussion of the relationship of tobacco use to lung cancer.
3. Exhibit containing a variety of charts, graphs, and other materials from the American Cancer Society on the extent and effect of smoking tobacco upon the human body.
4. Experiment whereby some nicotine is placed in a fish bowl containing a tadpole and observation of the results.
5. Invitation to medical doctor to visit class to discuss and answer questions about smoking and its impact on one's health.
6. Analysis of the Surgeon General's report on smoking; formulation of conclusions for students in the middle school.
7. Survey of several adults who smoke, asking the question, "Would you start

smoking if you had the opportunity to roll back the clock to when you were young and started to smoke?"
8. Report on the cost of smoking one pack of cigarettes a day for the lifetime of the average individual.
9. Request to Roswell Park Memorial Institute, Buffalo, New York, for posters and materials relating to smoking and health, and use of these materials for a classroom display.

Examples of Resources To Be Used
1. *Pamphlets* from the American Cancer Society, such as "Shall I Smoke?" and "Your Health and Cigarettes." Many pamphlets can also be obtained from the State Departments of Health, U.S. Department of Health, Education, and Welfare, and Public Affairs Committee.
2. *Books*, such as C. M. Fletcher and others, "Common Sense About Smoking," Penguin Books, 1963.
3. *Periodicals*, such as M. B. Neuberger, "Hazards of Teen-age Smoking," Parents Magazine, 39:51, January, 1964.
4. *State Department Guides*, such as "The High Cost of Smoking," New York State Department of Health, 1966.
5. *Filmstrips*, such as "I'll Choose the High Road," American Cancer Society.
6. *Films*, such as "Is Smoking Worth It?" American Cancer Society.

Drugs and Drug Addiction. Americans spend more than five billion dollars each year on medical drugs. Drugs as they are used to treat disease have proved to be a very worthwhile contribution to humanity. New discoveries by scientists are constantly producing new drugs that assist in fighting disease, alleviating pain, and providing treatment for various human ailments.

In order that drugs may be used properly and constructively by human beings, there is need for an educational program to help adults and especially youth understand their use, the contributions they make, and the dangers involved when they are misused.

There is increasing concern among many health authorities and interested citizens regarding not only the indiscriminate use of drugs by adults but, even more important, drug experimentation among our youth. Narcotic, or habit-forming, drugs detach a person from reality. They make him unaware of danger. Some drugs induce a sense of well-being by postponing feelings of fatigue. Some drugs have been used by participants in sports where a high level of energy is required but such practice is denounced by physical educators, coaches, and sports medicine associations.

Marijuana is a drug that young people sometimes experiment with, thinking it will not be harmful; however its use can result in intoxication and reckless, and even violent behavior. The immediate effect of smoking marijuana is a temporary mental disturbance. The user of marijuana loses touch with reality and is likely to act on suggestions which in a more normal state of mind he would not consider. The use of marijuana is dangerous not only for these reasons but because it may pave the way to addiction to more powerful and dangerous drugs. The user learns to depend upon a drug for pleasure. Later, in an effort to get pleasure, he will turn to stronger drugs such as morphine, heroin, and Lysergic Acid Diethylamide (LSD). These stronger drugs are usually peddled by the same law-breaking individual who first introduced the victim to marijuana. This constant search by the "pusher" for new victims and, therefore, new markets for his illegal wares, has caused much crime and the practice of preying upon young and innocent youth. The typical drug addict needs from $10 to $40 per day to maintain his habit. Thus, as the illegal sellers push their drugs on the market, the drug user must turn to petty thefts, shoplifting, burglary, and other crimes to secure the price of a fix.

Plastic cement, model airplane glue, gasoline, and other chemical substances have been used in recent years by unsuspecting youth who sniff these materials to acquire sensations that resemble acute alcoholic intoxication. The results of such sniffing can be very harmful. Continuous inhaling can produce double vision, hallucinations, stupor, amnesia, and unconsciousness. The fumes can seriously damage the liver, the kidneys, the brain, and other parts of the body. Moreover, the use of such chemicals can also lead to using stronger drugs and ultimately to addiction with its dreaded withdrawal sickness.

The time to help youth with respect to drugs and drug addiction is before they are tempted to experiment with dangerous drugs.

This, of course, means an educational program regarding drugs and drug addiction starting in the middle school years. If youngsters are well informed regarding drugs—their nature, use, and abuse—when they encounter this problem and are tempted they will have a resource of information that will enable them to make an intelligent choice as to whether they want to experiment—with all the harmful impact upon their health, success, and future that it implies. Without such information they may readily fall prey to addicts and other uninformed youth who are seeking some form of a "kick" of which they do not know the consequences.

Examples of Concepts To Be Developed at the Middle School Level

1. Drugs have been used by man since ancient times for relieving pain and other purposes.
2. Man has been concerned with the use and misuse of drugs since earliest times.
3. Modern drugs help in the control of disease, in surgery, childbirth and dentistry, and in other humanitarian ways.
4. There are several types of drugs, including those that can be purchased legally only with a doctor's prescription, and nonprescription drugs.
5. In general, narcotics and dangerous drugs may be divided into two main categories: depressants and stimulants.
6. Drugs can prove harmful if not used properly.
7. The government and the medical profession have taken steps to control the manufacture and sale of drugs.
8. The effects of drugs upon the organic systems of the human body can be very harmful.
9. Drug addiction, a state of periodic or chronic intoxication produced by continual use of drugs, can produce a life of pain and suffering that affects not only the user but society as well.
10. Environment and personality deficiencies separately or together play significant roles in acquiring the drug habit.
11. Drugs should never be accepted from strangers.
12. The social consequences of drugs are addiction and crime.

Examples of Learning Activities To Be Utilized

1. A magazine-and-newspaper-article display on drugs and drug addiction is prepared.
2. A member of the local police department or state narcotics office is invited to class to discuss narcotic drugs.
3. The psychological reasons why people become addicted to certain kinds of drugs are discussed.
4. The history of drugs is traced back to ancient times.
5. A panel discussion is conducted on the use of drugs in the local community.
6. The street names for various drugs, and the nature and use of such drugs as "bennies," "coke," "hemp," "horse," and "weed," are discussed.
7. Production of various drugs is discussed.
8. Patent medications that are used for headaches, upset stomach, colds, and other ailments are listed and evaluated as to their worth.
9. Lists of the contents of medicine chests in students' homes are prepared and evaluated.

Examples of Resources To Be Used

1. *Books*, such as "The Real Voice," by Richard Harris, the Macmillan Company, 1964.
2. *Pamphlets*, such as those provided by the United States Department of Health, Education, and Welfare (Food and Drug Administration): "Drugs and Driving," FDA Publication #15, January, 1965, or "First Facts About Drugs," FDA Publication #21, November, 1965.
3. *Periodicals*, such as "Today's Health," published by the American Medical Association, and articles like "Magical Cures for An Ancient Disease," by Lenz, August, 1963.

Alcohol. Seven out of ten Americans use alcoholic beverages at the cost of more than twelve billion dollars a year. Drinking enjoys a place in the social scheme that is accorded few other practices. Millions of dollars are spent on advertising by alcohol producers to promote the sale of alcoholic beverages. Tax revenues from the sale of alcoholic beverages help fill local, state, and federal treasuries in the amount of approximately four billion dollars annually.

Despite the large role that alcohol and drinking play in our economy, their use presents serious personal and social consequences that cannot be ignored. Drinking may well lead to absenteeism from work, crime, automobile accidents; an increased workload and cost placed upon hospitals, jails, and welfare agencies; to say nothing about the problems that acrue to the alcoholics' children and families.

Although some persons drink to relax and to socialize, others use alcohol as a means to escape from their problems or for other deep-seated psychological reasons. Young people sometimes start drinking as a result of giving in to social pressures or of a desire to go along with the group. What these people want is the approval of their friends and they fear that if they do not drink, they will not be accepted. Some young people drink because they think it is adult to do so. Others say they drink to have fun or excitement.

Persons vary in the way they behave under the influence of alcohol. The only general statement that can be made is that they will not display their normal personality, but instead, one which has been altered by the depression of the mental processes by intoxication, or the accumulation of the toxic effects of alcohol. Some persons will be happy or silly whereas others become belligerent, noisy, vulgar, or morose.

One of the truly serious problems concerned with alcohol is alcoholism. One of every fifteen drinkers will fall victim to that sickness. Unfortunately, there is no way to predict who that one will be.

In making the choice whether or not to drink, the important thing for young people is to make a decision based on the facts. Most young people know the arguments in favor of social drinking in moderation. But it is also important for them to know about drinking in our society as it involves law-breaking, automobile deaths, wrecked lives, and broken homes. Young people if they choose to drink should look at the health risks they run and, most important, at the responsibility the drinker must bear for his actions. If young people choose not to drink they will have decided that the liabilities of alcohol far outweigh its benefits and that good health habits suggest they abstain. Whatever their choice, it should be their own, made freely, based upon the facts as to what is best for them.

The middle school years are not too early to develop concepts that will help children better to understand the role of alcohol in our culture and whether or not they should drink when they are older.

Examples of concepts to be developed, learning activities to be utilized, and resources to be used for an alcohol-education program at the middle school level follow.

Examples of Concepts To Be Developed
1. There are various types of alcohol, manufactured differently, some of which are used in industry and others in medicine.
2. There are many commercial uses of alcohol.
3. Ethyl alcohol as a beverage has been used by people since ancient times.
4. Alcoholic beverages represent a large economic outlay in some family budgets.
5. The production of alcoholic beverages represents "big business" in our society.
6. The consumption of alcohol affects the various organic systems of the body in various ways.
7. Alcohol has very little nutrient value.
8. Alcohol can be used for medicinal reasons.
9. Alcohol is responsible for many social problems.
10. Alcoholism is an illness.

Examples of Learning Activities To Be Utilized
1. Class is divided into buzz groups to discuss the question, "Should I drink alcoholic beverages when I get older?"
2. The physiological, psychological, and sociological effects of alcohol on the human body are outlined.
3. The nutritional elements found in a quart of milk with those of a quart of whiskey are compared.
4. A chart is prepared showing the outlay of money for alcohol compared with that spent on schools and education.
5. A member of Alcoholics Anonymous is invited to class to discuss this organization.
6. A survey is conducted among pupils to find out whether or not they expect to drink alcohol as they get older, with a list of reasons "pro" and "con" being prepared for the class as a whole.
7. A study is made of the causes of automobile accidents as they relate to drinking.

8. The topic "America, A Drinking Culture," is discussed.
9. The chemistry teacher is invited to class to discuss the uses of alcohol.

Examples of Resources To Be Utilized

1. *Books*, such as "Drinking Among Teenagers," by G. L. Maddox and B. C. McCall, Rutgers Center for Alcohol Studies, New Brunswick, New Jersey, 1964.
2. *Films*, such as "What About Drinking?" Young America Films, Department of Mental Hygiene, State Health Department, Albany, New York.
3. *Filmstrips*, such as "Drinking, Drugs, and Driving," McGraw-Hill, Inc.
4. *Pamphlets*, such as "A Guide to Twelve Steps of A.A.," Alcoholics Anonymous, 337 East 33rd Street, New York, N.Y. 10016.

Evaluation

There should be periodic evaluation of the school health program. Such evaluations assist the teacher in determining knowledge achieved by the students, whether the students' needs are being met, if objectives are being realized, marks for grading purposes, if certain methods are effective, the need for curriculum revision, if the teaching is effective, strengths and weaknesses of the program, and the value and importance of health in the educational program. They also motivate the students to greater effort.

The Joint Committee on Health Problems of the National Education Association and the American Medical Association has listed some methods that can be used in the evaluation process.[1] These may be summarized as follows:

1. Observation of students in respect to their behavior and skills.
2. Surveys of health conditions.
3. Questionnaires and checklists which are submitted to students and parents to determine their knowledge about health matters.
4. Interviews with pupils, parents, teachers, and various school personnel.
5. Diaries and other records kept by pupils.
6. Health and growth records of students.
7. Records of other health conditions or improvements such as vital statistics from the local health department, or improvement in school's health conditions.
8. Samples of pupils' work, such as charts, models, exhibits, and reports.
9. Case studies of individual pupils.
10. Health-knowledge tests, both oral and written.

It is important to recognize that many factors need to be evaluated to appraise the entire school health program. In addition to health knowledge, there are health attitudes and health practices. Furthermore, it is important also to evaluate the school environment and school health services.

Questions and Practical Problems

1. What are ten bases for the selection of curriculum experiences for the elementary school health education program? Discuss how each may be used.
2. Prepare a health unit for the teaching of nutrition to a third-grade class.
3. What are some psychological principles that could be applied in the teaching of health in the elementary school?
4. Write to ten national health organizations and collect materials for the elementary school health program from each. Prepare a file of materials according to a topical index.
5. Survey ten state departments of education and obtain their courses of study for teaching health in the elementary school. Analyze the ten reports and prepare a statement of findings.

---

[1] Joint Committee on Health Problems in Education of the National Education Association and the American Medical Association, *Health Education*, Washington, D.C., National Education Association, 1961, pp. 342–343.

6. Survey an elementary school class and find out what pupil interests are in the field of health.

7. Interview a dentist, a doctor, and a psychiatrist to formulate a list of health problems that should be covered in the elementary school health education program.

8. Select a health-knowledge test and evaluate the health knowledge of a fifth grade class.

9. Prepare a lesson plan for teaching about bicycle safety for a sixth-grade class using a problem-solving approach.

10. What are ten sources of health materials for the elementary school?

Selected References

American Association for Health, Physical Education, and Recreation. *Health Concepts: Guides for Health Instruction.* Washington, D.C.: American Association for Health, Physical Education, and Recreation, 1967.

BUCHER, CHARLES A. *Administration of School Health and Physical Education Programs* (Fifth edition). St. Louis: The C. V. Mosby Co., 1971.

GROUT, RUTH E. *Health Teaching in Schools.* Philadelphia: W. B. Saunders Company, 1963.

IRWIN, LESLIE W., et al. *Health in Elementary Schools.* St. Louis: The C. V. Mosby Co., 1962.

Joint Committee on Health Problems in Education of the National Education Association and the American Medical Association. *Health Education.* Washington, D.C.: National Education Association, 1961.

KILANDER, H. FREDERICK. *School Health Education* (Second Edition). New York: The Macmillan Company, 1968.

LASALLE, DOROTHY, and GLADYS GEER, *Health Instruction for Today's Schools.* Englewood Cliffs, N.J.: Prentice-Hall, Inc., 1963.

Nassau Tuberculosis and Health Association. *Curriculum Guide for Health and Safety—Kindergarten through Grade Twelve.* Roslyn, N.Y.: Nassau Tuberculosis and Health Association, 1966.

OBERTEUFFER, DELBERT, and MARY K. BEYRER. *School Health Education.* New York: Harper & Row, Publishers, 1966.

SMOLENSKY, JACK, and L. RICHARD BONVECHIO. *Principles of School Health.* Boston: D. C. Heath and Company, 1966.

VANNIER, MARYHELEN. *Teaching Health in Elementary Schools.* New York: Harper & Row, Publishers, 1963.

WILLGOOSE, CARL E. *Health Education in the Elementary School.* Philadelphia: W. B. Saunders Company, 1964.

PART FOUR

Methodology for Planning and Teaching Physical Education and Health Education

CHAPTER **16**

Planning the Physical Education and Health Education Programs

It is the purpose of this chapter to give the elementary classroom teacher and the health or physical education specialist suggestions in planning programs of physical education and health. Suggested types of activities for physical education for various age levels and the placement of health education materials by age or grade will be found in later chapters.

No architect attempts to build a house, a school, or a hospital without blueprints. No engineer builds a bridge, a clover-leaf intersection, or a tunnel without plans. Similarly, no teacher should attempt to teach physical education or health to elementary school children without plans.

Mistakes made by the carpenter using the architect's plans may be rectified. True, this will cost some money, but a carpenter works with materials that are replaceable. The same applies to the construction foreman working from an engineer's plan. The teacher's mistakes, however, prove much more costly, because she is working with a human being—a child—who may never be replaced. Others will come and go but Johnny will always be Johnny and mistakes may scar him for his entire life. Hence, the teacher is charged with great responsibility and has the pleasure of working with the most precious and the most important thing in the world—an individual, a human being, the child.

Planning will never guarantee that errors will not be made, but the builder with good plans, the engineer with good plans, and the teacher with good plans will certainly err less than those with none. Most satisfactory accomplishments result from clear and challenging anticipation followed by careful planning.

Teachers who have the privilege of teaching elementary children are presented with one of the greatest challenges in education. They teach, guide, and direct a greater percentage of children than teachers in any other field or area of education. Laws require children to attend school. Since many leave school early, they may never have the guidance of any teacher other than their elementary teachers. The elementary school teachers must, in many cases, assume the complete responsibility for the child's formal education and do everything within their power to aid him in developing his potentialities to the fullest possible extent. Properly planned and administered programs of physical education and health education will assist the teacher to help the pupil reach the goals necessary for his happiness, growth and development, and healthful living, and to develop proper attitudes and behavior patterns.

Guides for Planning Physical Education and Health Education Programs

General guides will aid in planning programs of physical education and health education. The minimal ones which must be taken in consideration are:

1. Physical education and health education must be planned as an integral part of the total curriculum and be developed by the cooperative planning of school personnel, the pupils, and community leaders. The leadership must be provided by the administration, specialists, and the best qualified personnel.
2. Progression must be planned for various age levels to meet the needs, interests, and ability of the children.
3. Correlation and integration must play an important part in order to show the interrelationship of these two areas with other parts of the curriculum.
4. Each teacher must use the coordinated, planned program in such a manner as to best meet the needs of a particular group.
5. Planning must be a continuous process.
6. Changes must be made when evaluation or experience shows the need.

General Planning in Physical Education

In planning physical education, the teacher must keep in mind individual differences. She must know the needs, interests, and capabilities of the children in her group. She should plan to meet them at their own levels of ability and to assist them in reaching an educationally desirable goal.

She must also consider the outdoor play area, indoor facilities, equipment, type of class organization, and time allotment in relation to the state laws and local regulations.

In general, planning gives purpose and meaning to the program. It will prove helpful in coordinating physical education with other parts of the school curriculum. It aids in efficiency and is time saving. It assists in maintaining pupil interest both by meeting needs and avoiding repetition.

Bearing these specific points in mind, the teacher may plan her program of physical education on a yearly, seasonal, monthly, and daily basis.

Yearly Planning. What does the teacher expect or want her children to gain in skills and techniques, social growth, leadership qualities, carry-over values for leisure-time activity, and the like? Which recommended activities for children in the age and grade level of her class will best help them reach these desired goals? How much of each shall she include in her program?[1]

The teacher must know the needs of her children and then plan to meet them. She will make her yearly plan accordingly, with her overall objectives based also on the interests and abilities of her children. She may then break this yearly plan into seasonal plans.

Seasonal Planning. The wise teacher uses seasons to assist with the child's interest and also in the correlation of her physical education program with other parts of the curriculum.

Spring and the glory and splendor of its beauty and color are great aids to her. Spring means interest in softball and/or baseball for the middle childhood grades. For various reasons her group may be unable to participate in either. Perhaps the playing space is too small. The wise teacher will plan activities which are similar to these and may be played in the space provided. Flowers and Wind, a fleeing game, will be taught in the spring and be correlated with nature. Bird Catcher, another running and tagging game for early childhood, belongs in the spring program and again gives good opportunity

---

[1] Patterns are fully discussed, with recommended types of activity and time allotment, in Chapters 10 and 11.

for correlation with nature study, art, and reading.

The fall season brings interest in soccer and touch football to children in the middle childhood group. In many instances the elementary classroom teacher may have few facilities for these activities and in most cases finds them too advanced for her group. She will, therefore, choose activities resembling these highly organized team games. To the early childhood group, fall means possible dramatizations in the form of story plays, rhythms, or dances using such symbols as falling leaves, raking leaves, and gathering nuts.

Winter is the season to teach dances, using the "Skaters' Waltz" as an example. Dramatizations of building snowmen and skating and skiing to music bring interest to rhythmic and dance activities during the cold days. Games resembling basketball and volleyball will be seasonal interests for middle childhood groups.

Indoor programs suited to the available facilities must also be considered in this seasonal plan. A good teacher plans a flexible program for each season. To meet hot days there is less-active play and for brisk days there is active movement for the health of all concerned.

The alert teacher will think of a wealth of possibilities. Seasonal planning may then be broken up into monthly planning and used to advantage.

Monthly Planning. Every school month gives the teacher many ideas for choosing interesting activities for her physical education program. All special days and events are clues. October brings Halloween, November means Thanksgiving, December denotes Christmas, March or April brings Easter. These are but a few examples of holidays falling in certain months which may be used advantageously in physical education.

Early childhood classes may use each of these holidays in story plays, rhythmic and dance dramatizations, games of low organization for outdoor play, and classroom games for indoor activity. A goblin dance, the game of Old Mother

Table 16–1. Block Plan—Track and Field Unit

	Monday	Tuesday	Wednesday	Thursday	Friday
First week	*Introduce unit:* Description Purpose Types of events History and origin of Olympic and Pan-American competitions *Explain:* Kneeling start *Practice:* Starts *Conditioning:* Game of Overtake	*Review:* Kneeling start *Practice:* Starts Review Conditioning Act of Game of Overtake *Introduce:* Walk, jog, run	*Explain:* Standing start *Practice:* Standing starts Shuttle Relay *Review:* Walk, jog, run	*Explain:* High jump Scissors kick *Practice:* Over the rope or bar *Conditioning:* Walk, jog, run	*Review:* High jump Kneeling start *Practice:* Jump—over the rope or bar Starts—Overtake
Second week	*Explain:* Standing broad jump *Practice:* Broad jump Number of jumps High jump *Conditioning:* Walk, jog, run	*Explain:* Running broad jump *Practice:* Running broad jump High jump Broad jump Singles jump Number of jumps	*Explain:* Sprints *Practice:* Sprinting *Conditioning:* Walk, jog, run *Explain—practice:* Softball throw	*Review:* Sprinting *Practice:* Sprinting Softball throw High jump	*Explain:* Baton relay *Practice:* Baton race Walk, jog, run Broad jump

Third week	*Explain:*
	  Low hurdles
	Practice:
	  Approach and jump
	    over hurdles
	Conditioning:
	  Walk, jog, run
		Review:
		  Low hurdles
		Explain:
		  Western roll
		Practice optional:
		  Hurdles
		  High jump
		  Scissors or Western
		    roll
		  Softball throw
			Practice:
			  Sprints
			    50 or 100 yds.
			    (Permit students to
			    make choice.)
			  High jump
			  Scissors or Western
			    roll
			  Standing broad jump
				Practice:
				  Baton relay (240 yds.)
				  Running broad jump
				  Low hurdles
					Introduce:
					  220 yd. run for boys;
					  150 yd. run for girls
					Practice:
					  High jump
					  Scissors or Western
					    roll
					  Standing broad jump

Fourth week	*Conditioning:*
	  Walk, jog, run
	Set up stations for each event. Divide class into groups.
	Rotate groups from one station to the next every 8 minutes.
	On Wednesday permit the student to concentrate on events of his preference.
			Conditioning:
			  Walk, jog, run
				Class Track Meet	Class Track Meet

Witch, and a story play of Santa's helpers are examples of activities based on special days.

Middle childhood may use gay Christmas music in December for rhythms and creative dancing. Self-testing activities and stunts may be based on toys of interest to the children. Running and tagging games such as Catch the Caboose, which uses the nationwide Christmas interest in electric trains, will be thoroughly enjoyed.

In planning, the teacher usually works with two types of plans—the unit plan and the separate or individual class plan. Illustrations of each are given and points are discussed for the use of each type.

Unit Plans. Much interest is maintained through unit planning in each specific subject field and through correlation with the other subjects in the curriculum. Physical education is no exception to the subject fields which derive value from unit planning.

For example, a teacher in the sixth grade may wish to use softball as a team game in the spring program. Such a unit plan could include:

1. Introduction to the activity.
2. General objectives to be attained: (a) worthy use of leisure time, (b) team-work, (c) social qualities, (d) sportsmanship, (e) safety.
3. Specific skills: (a) preliminary games used to develop these skills, (b) organization of class to best advantage.
4. Teaching rules: visual aids, (a) films, (b) blackboard.
5. Motivating interest.
6. Correlation with other subjects.
7. Evaluation techniques.

From such a unit of work, planned both by the *teacher* and the *pupils*, the weekly and the daily progression necessary to reach the established goals would be determined. Thus a weekly and/or daily plan is developed.

Table 16-1 illustrates the way a resource unit in track and field may be developed in a block unit. It gives a picture of the time and sequential development possible for the presentation and teaching of each part of the unit culminating in a class meet (Upper-Grade level).

This unit of work should be correlated with the program in social studies. A study of the Olympic and Pan-American Games, their origin, history, and purpose, should prove a highly motivating factor for participation in the unit activities. Continued investigation concerning the preservation of the Olympic Games, their organization and administration, and the people participating in them will further the students' understanding of international relationship, excellence of performance, and the qualities necessary to become a champion.

Weekly and/or Daily Plans. Each specific plan should be the result of combined efforts of the teacher and the pupils. Teacher-pupil planning stimulates more interest and results in worthy experiences in group dynamics. These plans will consider space, equipment, weather, size of class, and differences in individual skills and techniques. General and specific objectives from the yearly plan that are to be accomplished each week and day must be decided.

All planning must be directed toward the specific objectives of physical education which in turn are based on the general purposes of education. Children need to understand these goals and the teacher must help make them attainable. These goals may be accomplished much better and faster if the child has a clear concept of what he is trying to attain.

An example of a simple daily form for a plan in physical education is as follows:

1. Aim of lesson.
2. Specific objectives.
3. Activities: (a) type (b) time for each (c) equipment needed.
4. Method of procedure: (a) introduction (b) class organization necessary (c) demonstration (d) teaching hints (e) ending.
5. Anticipated difficulties (i.e., small playing space, roughness).
6. Outcomes desired: (a) skills (b) knowledge (c) attitudes.
7. Integration with other subject area, (i.e., new words for spelling and vocabulary, the use of playing areas and circumference of balls for mathematics).

After each lesson, details should be discussed by the teacher and the students. The teacher wants to know the answers to the following questions.

Did the children learn? How could I have improved my teaching? Was the activity too hard or too easy with little challenge? Was there genuine fun displayed? Did it meet their needs and abilities? Did they work and play well together? Did I give opportunity for any creativity or ideas by the children? Are there safety measures which need to be stressed next time? How may I help children evaluate their learning? Is there any carry-over for their leisure time? Was there correlation with another part of the curriculum?

When teachers and children together discuss their lesson, much may be accomplished.

An example of a daily lesson plan for grade two follows in Table 16–2.

Creativity in Physical Education. Time and opportunities for children to create new patterns of movement and new activities must be permitted. Creativity is not new in body movement and/or activities for physical education. However, we have perhaps been giving too little opportunity for its use in our programs and therefore depriving children of this means of self-expression. Basically there are no new physical actions. Cavemen walked, ran, jumped, swam, hung, and threw. All motions were necessary for their livelihood.

Today few physical activities of any consequence, required in a strenuous combination, are necessary for us to use to maintain our homes or earn our living. Hence, since man by nature desires activity and since physical activity is necessary for physical well-being, the fundamental activities have been put in other forms for the enjoyment of children and adults. These forms consist basically of games, gymnastics, dances, team sports, and track and field events.

Each game and activity we know, participate in, and teach has been created by some imaginative person to meet the physical needs of certain age groups. Through the use of such activities, the physical activity necessary for the growth and development of the body is provided.

Instead of running from dangerous animals we run to catch a ball, to tag a player in a game, to get on base in a team game, and, perhaps, in later life, to catch a bus. We throw not to kill an animal with a stone or a spear, but to engage in many games and sports. We jump not to move from ledge to ledge or to cross a brook, but to clear a jump rope or a crossbar, to better our previous broadjump from the toe board toward the far end of the jumping pit.

Someone, sometime, had to use imagination and create new patterns of the needed physical activities for use by humans. Hence, imaginative uses of the basic physical activities in the form of games and activities that give pleasurable experiences to those participating in them is old. Most of these activities, however, have been planned to be used in exact ways. They are organized with exact and specific rules that leave some room for creating new ways to do things but not as much as we perhaps desire.

To create is to produce, to bring into being, or to cause to exist. To be creative means to have the power to create or to bring something new into being. Imagination must be used and connotes creative power. In physical education the use of imagination results in a creation of the mind that can be shown or demonstrated through the movement and expression of the body. This is what is meant by creativity in physical education.

Children learn when they create. They interpret what they see or feel when confronted with specific music or certain situations in which the teacher has directly or indirectly guided them. Creativity is a way of expression and of putting into action the imagination of a child or an adult. Each will be able to use his imagination and create something based on his *experiences*, the *motivation* used to start or help him gain a desire to create, what he *sees*, and what he *thinks*. He will then *express* through his body movements the way he *feels*. There are many opportunities and challenges for children to be creative in physical education as well as in art, music, and other parts of the curriculum.

Creativity in physical education brings into existence a child's conception produced by body movements. The individual thinks and produces ideas, ideals, and movements. Through the challenge of the creative process he explores and investigates all known experiences, actions, and ideas and emerges with a reorganization or rearrangement of these in a unique and individual pattern. These are new patterns, previously unknown even to the producer, the child. These movements may be created in dance, in a new way to move about in a story play, or by depicting a different character in a dramatization.

How can we assist, challenge, and encourage the creativity of children in physical education? First, we must think of certain basic principles. These may include elaborations of and additions to the following six over-all guides:

1. Our desire and understanding of creativity and its worth to the child.

Table 16–2. Lesson Plan for Second Grade (Time 30 minutes)

Objectives: To develop strength, body control, flexibility, and balance.
To experience success in achieving movement task.
To experience the fun of movement response to music.
To further develop the pupil's sense of rhythmic coordination through performance of specific dance patterns.

Activities	Time	Equipment	Procedure	Anticipated Difficulties	Outcome—Knowledge, Skills, Attitudes
Self-testing Activities					
1. Human Rocker	10 min.	Whistle	1. Human Rocker a. Ask pupils what a rocking chair looks like. How does it move? What is the part that moves called? b. Ask pupils to make their bodies into rockers and move as the chair does.	1. Human Rocker a. Some pupils may not be able to grasp ankles. Suggest they grasp feet. b. Pupils may not understand how to achieve an arch in the back. Help individuals to "lift head and chest." c. Pupil may not be able to start rocking motion. Help him by starting motion for him and explain that it is done by first leaning head and trunk toward floor, then pushing away.	1. Learning of body parts and how they can be used in new movements. 2. Large muscle coordination. 3. Increased strength in arms and legs. 4. Flexibility. 5. Enjoyment. 6. Experiencing success in working with partner.
2. Indian Get-up			2. Indian Get-up a. Ask pupils to seek partners about their own size. Stand back to back with partner and hook arms with partner. b. Ask pupils to lower their bodies to a sitting position without breaking arm hold. c. Ask them to return to standing position.	2. Indian Get-up a. Pupils may need help pairing off. Suggest a partner, check arm positions. They should be "hooked" above the elbow. b. Pupils may be unable to perform stunt. Explain how legs are used, timing, and position. Change partners if necessary.	
3. Wheelbarrow			3. Wheelbarrow a. Ask the pupils what a wheelbarrow is. How does it work? Who pushes it? b. Ask partners to make themselves into a wheelbarrow being pushed by a gardener. Change positions and repeat.	3. Wheelbarrow a. Weak arm and shoulder muscles causing "wheelbarrow" to fall. Encourage slow movement and several attempts to cover distance.	

Rhythmic Activity	20 min.	Record Player R.C.A. record #2-432	1. Introduction (pupils seated in a circle).
			   a. Children's dance from Germany.
			   b. Kinder—German word for *child*; Polka—a dance.
			2. Play music through once and have children listen.
			3. Ask pupils to clap the beat as they listen to music.
			4. Assemble group in a single circle with partners facing each other by:
			   a. Asking boys to stand in a circle.
			   b. Having the girls stand between the boys.
			   c. Boys face girls on right; girls face boys on left. (If number is odd, teacher becomes a partner).
			5. Walk through directions for part 1 without music; repeat. Dance part 1 to music.
			6. Follow the same procedure in teaching parts 2 and 3 of the dance, adding the new part to previous part when children dance to music.
			7. Perform complete dance to music.
			8. Give assistance to pupils who need it.
			9. Voice encouraging comments as pattern is learned.
				1. None.
				2. Encourage all to listen.
				3. Some pupils might not recognize beat. Give help.
				4. Circle could be crowded. Ask girls to move back so boys can assemble. When boys or girls outnumber each other, have the extra boys or girls dance together.
				5. Steps may be too large. Ask for smaller steps. Movement may be stiff. Suggest pupils put balls of feet down first, and bend knees as step is taken.
				6. Pupils may have difficulty keeping rhythm. Call movement in rhythm with music.
				7. Slow the music when necessary. Note: This is usually a MUST when learning a dance.
					1. Performance of a dance pattern in response to music; grace; poise.
					2. Enjoyment and relaxation.
					3. New words for vocabulary.
					4. Learning about children in the country.

1. Kinderpolka

2. The creation of an atmosphere conducive to challenge the imagination and hence produce a creative response. This requires freedom for action and not a stereotyped program.

3. Arrangement of situations which are necessarily challenging for exploration.

4. Supplying materials which call for exploration.

5. Planning experiences which give various skills and knowledge to the child so he may have background from which to create.

6. Encouraging all children to be creative by accepting this as an important and vital part of their education and encouraging each one to remain an individual in his or her creativity.

Examples of Creativity. Based on the specific types of activity recommended in the well-rounded program of physical education, the following examples illustrate how each activity area may be used by the alert teacher to challenge creativity. In greater detail, specific experiences in physical education and some ways in which these experiences, which start on the playground or in the gymnasium, may be made meaningful in the over-all curriculum, will then follow in Tables 16–1 through 16–5.

Playground Equipment. Children think of playground equipment in many ways and with different uses and movements. Some look at a jungle gym as a high house with no outside walls, a big tree, a monkey cage in a zoo, a tower for looking out far over the land, or, to some, a space station near the moon. On it, they will explore and create movement. Some will climb high, others will use only the lower bars. Some will sit astride a bar and make believe they are riding a horse or pedaling a bicycle. Some will skin a cat or hang by their knees. Encouragement given by an understanding teacher gives confidence to the fearful child to also start experimenting in various forms of movement on such equipment.

Story Plays

1. Dramatize basic activities common to children's experiences in the readers, during the holiday seasons, in everyday life (deep snow walk, for example).

2. Portray community helpers at work—the fireman, the ambulance driver, the policeman.

3. Create results of nature activities—wind blowing, leaves falling, leaves swirling, snowflakes falling and being blown by the wind.

Dance

1. Integrate movements based on certain types of music showing free axial movements: up-down, sideways, forward, backwards, and rotating.

2. Create dance patterns based on fundamental locomotor movements of walking, running, skipping, hopping, leaping, sliding, and galloping.

3. Add patterns using nonlocomotor movements of pushing, pulling, lifting, swinging, and striking.

4. Plan creative dances of countries studied in social studies, e.g., Indian dances, Mexican dances, and so on.

5. Interpret music as to big steps, high steps, heavy running, and light running.

6. Create accompaniment on percussion instruments.

7. Make percussion instruments.

8. Create additional movement patterns based on characters from outer space, songs and poems, television, and different sports.

9. Create movements in specific floor patterns and designs such as squares, circles, and figure eights and then develop the sequence of movements to be used.

Games

1. Create new games of several different types.

2. Create new challenges by changing rules or adding rules and skills to games already known.

3. Formulate games and rules to fit unique situations—small areas, little equipment, many participants, few participants.

4. Plan and make new pieces of equipment, e.g., yarn balls, different kinds and shapes of bean bags.

Two Games Created by Children. Two examples of children's creativity in games are given. The first game was created by a fifth-grade child to help his smaller brother to learn colors, counting, various shapes, and accurate tossing of a bean bag, rubber mason jar rings, or rubber heels from old shoes. Needless to say, the game was also used and enjoyed by the fifth-grade children.

CREATIVE TOSS-BOARD

Each section of the board is painted a different color and is numbered, as shown, from one to five.

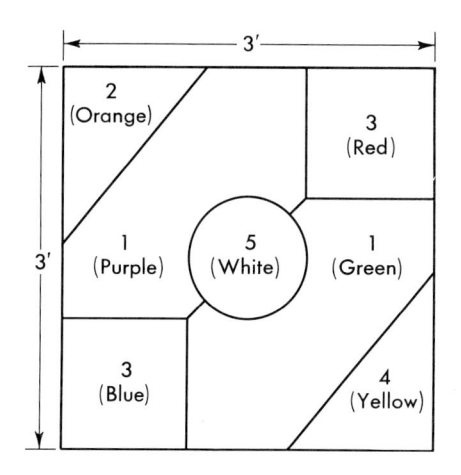

Planning the Physical Education and Health Education Programs 227

Figure 16–1. Creative Toss-Board.

The board contains squares, triangles, one circle, and two uneven and unnamed geometrical figures.

The board is placed on the floor at different distances from the players according to age and ability.

Each child has a chance to toss three bean bags, jar rings, or rubber heels at the board. He then tells the colors he has hit and adds his score, which is taken from the numbers in the areas hit. Next, as he picks up the rings or bean bags, he names the geometric figure each was in.

The second game, shown in Figure 16–2, involves creating scrambled words in specific forms. This arrangement was made by a sixth-grade student. Other children were challenged and designed forms. These included a witch on a broom, used at Halloween; a turkey and a pumpkin, used at Thanksgiving; rabbits, ducks, and a tulip plant for Easter; and a snowman, used during a snowy season.

Self-Testing Activities and Stunts. The following self-testing activities and stunts involve creative action.

1. Action showing animals walking or running, showing fear or happiness.
2. Airplanes starting, taking off, flying, and landing.
3. Various combinations of body movement in new patterns, e.g., run—jump—roll; hop—skip—jump.
4. New combinations, e.g., hanging—swinging—jumping.

Individual and Dual Activities. Creativity is called for in the following individual and dual activities.

1. New ways to jump rope, including new rhymes to use.
2. New hopscotch court diagrams and ways to play on the new areas.
3. New activities for restricted areas.
4. New activities with new equipment.
5. Activities using certain groups of muscles for those children with physical handicaps, such as arm or hand paralysis or heart conditions.

Swimming. Where swimming supervision is available, swimming activities can also be creative.

1. Create different swimming patterns, such as line, circle, and star formations.
2. Plan a theme and work out appropriate water activities.
3. Swim in time to music, using different strokes.

Camping and Outdoor Education. Many creative outdoor-education activities can be added to the following:

1. New ways to mark trails.
2. New types of shelters.

Correlation of Physical Education with Whole Curriculum. It is advisable to consider the correlation of physical education with the entire curriculum rather than merely to teach

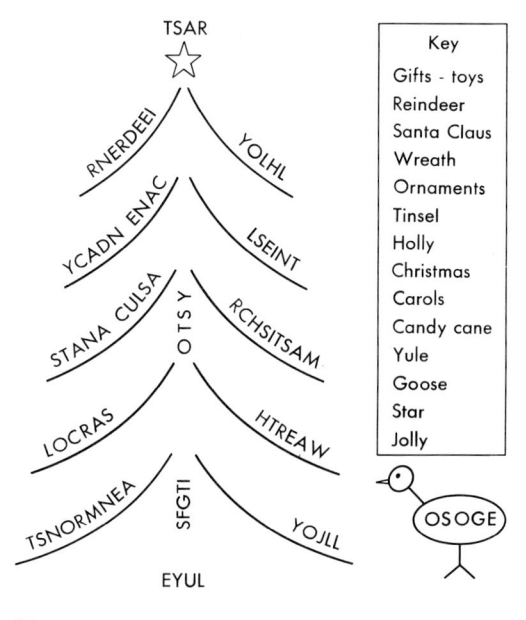

Figure 16–2. Creative Scrambled Words.

it—for thirty minutes a day or whatever time is required by state or local regulations—as a subject apart from overall educational goals. Correlation is an attempt to bring out relationships among the subjects of the curriculum.

In schools where teachers have correlated physical education with other programs much interest is found among the children. It also makes possible a greater understanding of the total physical education program for parents and educators.

A unit of work in social studies being planned or studied in the sixth grade might be the United Nations. Physical education could easily become a real part of this unit through studying and participating in games and dances of the various member countries of the United Nations. Many schools today are fortunate to have children from various countries. A wise teacher will ask these children to assist in the presentation of games, dances, and other physical activities of their native countries.

The two examples of units of work show in a small way how physical education may be correlated with other parts of the curriculum. The examples are by no means complete. However, through them, the teacher may understand some ways she may make her physical education a part of the total unit. If she does, it will provide more unity and will elicit more meaningful physical education activities. The names of games and activities may be changed to meet particular situations.

Specific Subject Correlations. Physical education may be correlated with various subject fields in the following ways:

Language Arts. Some projects in this area related to physical education are (1) learning names of games and equipment; (2) learning new words—vocabulary and spelling; (3) reading the directions for new games; (4) recording physical education activities on daily individual records; (5) giving oral directions for games and discussing the day's activities; and (6) performing pageants, plays, and dramatizations.

Social Studies. Some projects in this area relating to physical education are (1) studying various manners of play and recreation in different countries; (2) noting environmental conditions in relation to their activities—for example, certain activities are possible and desirable because of weather and the general climate; (3) learning democracy through group work and team cooperation; and (4) noting historical changes in activities.

Safety. Some projects in this area relating to physical education are (1) learning and observing all safety rules and regulations pertaining to sports and play; (2) knowing safe use of equipment and apparatus; (3) checking playgrounds and apparatus; and (4) learning the need for using safety equipment in games and activities.

Table 16–3. **Correlation of the Dance (All Rhythmic Work) with Other Subjects**

The Fine Arts	The Sciences	Social Studies	Language Arts
1. Costumes of peoples where dance originates: (a) make sketches of costumes, (b) collect pictures of costumes and make bulletin-board display, (c) bring in dolls in native costume, (d) make simple costumes.	1. Transportation in the country where the dance originates: (a) types of transportation in that country, (b) scientific principles involved.	1. Geography and history of the country where dance originates.	1. Read folk tales and stories of peoples where dance originated.
2. Make scenery for dance presentation.	2. Agriculture in that country: (a) types of soil, (b) types of food, (c) animals raised there, (d) types of farm machinery used, (e) financial value of crops.	2. Customs of the people there: (a) weddings, (b) holidays.	2. Tell stories to classmates or another grade.
3. Make program covers for presentations.	3. Health: (a) basic health needs of people in the specific country, (b) contributions to science and medicine.	3. Products of that country used by us (food, clothing, etc.).	3. Write an original play about peoples of the country for assembly program.
4. Make simple instruments (drums, gourds, musical glasses).		4. Government of that country; (a) type, (b) ambassadors to U.S.? (c) member of United Nations?	4. Write invitations to parents to attend play.
5. Draw the flag of the country.			5. Write letters to travel bureaus or foreign information centers to collect pamphlets, posters, and pictures.
			6. Make a vocabulary list of new words learned while studying this country.
			7. Make use of these words for spelling.

Health. Some projects in this area relating to physical education are (1) knowing all health rules pertaining to play and sports; (2) learning training rules for athletes; (3) safeguarding health by proper clothing for play, showers after activity, not drinking while warm, and so on; (4) knowing the effect of exercise on the body; and (5) knowing the need for food as fuel.

Mathematics. Some mathematics projects relating to physical education are (1) determining areas and perimeters of play spaces; (2) figuring averages in tournaments and various games, such as the batting average in softball; (3) marking courts, angle computation, and measurements; and (4) determining diameter, circumference, and radius of balls and circles used for games.

Science. Possible projects in science are (1) camping and outing activities; (2) hiking; (3) planning playgrounds; and (4) planting

Table 16-4. Correlation of Class Organization (Squads, Leaders) with Other Subjects

The Fine Arts	The Sciences	Social Studies	Language Arts
1. Make attractive charts for each squad: (a) list name of squad, (b) list names of players.	1. Divide class into equal groups.	1. Democratic organization: (a) selection of leaders, (b) division into squads.	1. Read true stories about some of our great sports leaders. List characteristics of great leaders.
2. Make attractive charts listing: (a) characteristics of good leaders, (b) characteristics of good followers.	2. Set time limit for incumbency of squads and leaders.	2. Teach cooperation, responsibility, and respect.	2. Have oral discussions: (a) characteristics of good leaders, (b) characteristics of good followers.
	3. Keep scores accurately.	3. Teach safety rules for all games: (a) use protective equipment, (b) set up safe play areas, (c) have an active safety patrol.	
	4. Make graphs of progress of squad.	4. Teach need for cooperation in a democracy. Substitute "we" for "I" in group responsibilities.	
	5. Learn how to use a stopwatch.		

Table 16–5. **Correlation of Games and Sports with Other Subjects**

The Fine Arts	The Sciences	Social Studies	Language Arts
1. Make charts showing positions of players for game.	1. Make scale drawings, showing perimeter and area of playing courts.	History of the game or sport (Basketball-Naismith, Soccer-Rugby, etc.).	1. Make vocabulary list: (a) names of equipment—balls, jacks, ropes, (b) names of apparatus—jungle gym, slides, swings, (c) learn to spell the words.
2. Draw pictures of characters in games (squirrels in trees or fox and chickens, etc.).	2. Find diameters and radii of circles used for games.	2. The Olympics: (a) history of countries participating, (b) types of sports involved, (c) outstanding Americans participating.	2. Read stories of outstanding athletes.
3. Draw sketches of equipment and apparatus.	3. Find angles of rectangular playing fields.	3. Teamwork needed in democracy; teamwork needed in sports.	3. Make up original game; write rules; explain to class.
4. Collect pictures of athletes in action; make bulletin-board display.	4. Find percentage of games won or lost.	4. Respect for authorities in life—sports present this respect for officials.	4. Make a collection of rope jumping rhymes.
5. Show film of Olympic games.	5. Learn training rules for athletes.		5. Read sports articles in newspaper.
	6. Learn personal health habits: (a) outdoor play, (b) fresh air—day and night, (c) showers, (d) individual towels, (e) sufficient rest.		6. Write sports articles for school paper.
	7. Effect of alcohol and tobacco on athletes.		7. Make oral report as sports announcer of a class game.
	8. Types of activities suitable for the exceptional child (rheumatic fever or polio victim)		
	9. Safety rules and regulations.		

types of hedges and shrubbery in place of fences.

Music. Projects directly related to physical education are (1) learning the words for rhythms and singing games; (2) making tom-toms, gourds, rhythm sticks, and sandblocks; (3) improving rhythmic response through movement to various forms of accompaniment; and (4) understanding and appreciation of phrasing, accent, and quality of music through use of a wide variety of accompaniment.

Art. Projects related to physical education are (1) drawing children participating in various kinds of activities; (2) diagraming the formations of a dance created by the children; (3) comparing roundness in line of a drawing to the roundness in

Table 16–6. Correlation of Self-testing Activities and Stunts with Other Subjects

The Fine Arts	The Sciences	Social Studies	Language Arts
1. Draw sketches of animals or things children mimic; (a) Duck Walk, (b) Wheelbarrow.	1. Learn life story and uses of animals mimicked (seal, duck).	1. Take field trip to farm or zoo to see animals mimicked.	1. Write letters to plan field trips.
2. Do stunts in time to music.	2. Learn how these animals protect themselves—their safety versus ours.	2. Talk about countries where stunts originated.	2. Have oral discussion of field trips.
3. Sketch people participating in stunts (circus personnel).	3. Physiology of exercise and value to man.	3. Watch TV stunts and activity programs.	3. Early childhood group can make experience chart and learn to read it.
		4. Visit circus.	4. Make vocabulary list of activities and stunts.

movement to a 3/4 or 6/8 rhythm; and (4) dancing to the quality of a finger painting—curving or straight lines.

Play Ideas Motivate Learning. The discussion thus far has been centered on ways in which physical education activities may be made meaningful in units of work and in specific parts of the curriculum and how specific physical education experiences may be made meaningful in the classroom in other parts of the broad curriculum areas. Attention is now focused on the idea of fun and play as a means of motivating children to learn and to create fun in learning.

Each idea discussed here has been contributed by an elementary classroom teacher and has been used in typical classroom situations.

Social Studies Example. In social studies, one teacher hung the map of the area or country being studied on the wall. Several suction darts were provided. The class was arranged in committees. One member from a committee threw a dart at the map. That committee then told facts about the country or area which was hit by their dart. Each committee had its turn.

Mathematics Example. Multiplication Bingo was successful in gaining interest in skill and speed. Cards were made with various number combinations appearing on them. These were flashed by one person. The first child, or group, to get five correct called "Multiplication Bingo" and flashed the cards for the next game. The same idea may be used for addition, subtraction, and

Table 16–7. Correlation of Story Plays with Other Subjects

The Fine Arts	The Sciences	Social Studies	Language Arts
1. Make simple costumes.	1. Learn safety rules (fire drill, traffic, playing rules).	1. Develop respect for, and appreciation of, characters in story plays (policeman, fireman, milkman, and so on).	1. Read stories that could be used as bases for story plays.
2. Draw pictures of characters, equipment, and apparatus.	2. Learn about fire prevention.	2. Lead up to study of community occupations.	2. Tell about favorite stories and characters.
3. Sing songs related to story plays.	3. Learn about seasons and weather changes.	3. Learn about holidays used to develop story-play text.	3. Keep a list of story plays enjoyed.

division. This may be worked with groups, as well as with individuals.

Committees, squads, or groups also engaged in arithmetic fact games organized on a wheel-and-spoke idea. This may be changed to meet the needs of the class and may be used for multiplication, addition, or subtraction. Groups are given turns in answering.

Spelling Example. Spelling Bingo added to the enjoyment of learning new words and reviewing words. Each student folded his paper so it made 25 squares. As the spelling words were dictated, the children wrote them in any square they chose. The word was then dropped in a box. When all words had been dictated, each was drawn from the box, one at a time, pronounced, and spelled.

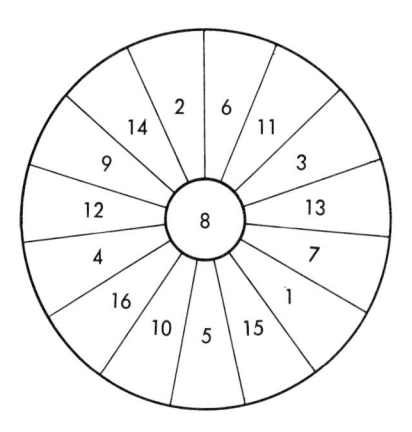

Figure 16–3. Wheel and Spoke—Arithmetic can be fun.

The first child to have five in a row spelled correctly called "Bingo." Teachers who used this game reported children learned words which before had seemed impossible for them.

Science Example. Children gained much interest in their study of rocks when they played a game based on Upset the Fruit Basket. Each player was given the name of a rock in one of the rock classifications. When sedimentary was called, for example, each child in that group rose and gave the name of his rock and told where it was found. Then they all exchanged seats while the "Pebble" (caller) tried to get a seat. When metamorphic was called, all children had to change seats. This same idea could be used in health, for example, with the basic food groups.

General Examples. Variations on the game of Bird, Beast, and Fish are fun in all subject fields. A review of the names of countries, cities, rivers, history dates, and health rules may also be great fun with this game idea. Number facts may be used, too. Individual differences may be taken into account by counting at different rates and giving the child a longer time to think before he must answer. He may also be given easier facts to answer.

A softball game idea works well with various questions in any subject. The class may be divided into two groups. The teacher may take individual differences into account by preparing very hard questions, moderately hard ones, fairly easy ones, and easy ones. Correct answers to these questions represent a home run, a three-base hit, a two-base hit, and a single, respectively. One team, committee, or group is at bat. The first child selects the hit he desires to try for. If he answers correctly, he is on base or makes a run, accordingly. If he misses, he is out. When he misses, another child, either from his group or another, immediately answers the question, so the learning process is continual. To change the questioning often from one group to another, the teacher may wish only one out before switching questions to the next team. Runs made count for the group. One child may place the runners on the correct base on the blackboard ball diamond and keep advancing them correctly or they may move around the room on an imaginary diamond.

Respect for Individual Differences. There are many ways in which teachers may use the play incentive to challenge children to think and learn. Each teacher will be able to plan and use many more than have been discussed. It is true that those discussed here, as well as any other one particular plan, may be abused and overdone. Good judgment must be exercised in taking individual differences into account so that no child is embarrassed and made to feel inferior to his classmates. These activities may be used in different groups within a given grade in much the same way that one works with different reading groups. The entire class need not participate at one time. Each teacher knows her children. If she believes they will enjoy trying the game idea at certain times, she should use it. Otherwise, she should forget it. Remember, the game idea may be used for fun and learning *only* and should *not* be used solely on a *competitive* basis.

Summary of Planning Hints in Physical Education
1. Plan the program of work yearly, seasonally, monthly, weekly, and daily.
2. Plan activities which are appropriate for your group and which meet their needs, abilities, and interests.
3. Plan to help each child learn or accomplish something each day. Bear in mind individual differences in rates of learning.
4. Give children a chance to be creative.
5. Plan for correlation of physical education with other parts of the curriculum.
6. Plan activities for the atypical child through the help and advice of his physician (refer to Chapter 9).
7. Plan to play outside every day the weather will permit.
8. Plan for inclement weather and for indoor programs either in the all-purpose room or the classroom in case a gymnasium is not available.
9. Plan your program and teach the time allotment required by your state or local regulations. Remember, their recommendations or requirements are minimums.

General Planning in Health Education

Some discussion of planning health education can be found in Chapters 2 and 15. Additional emphases are included here.

In planning effective health education in our schools, many things must be taken into consideration. Planning in health education should be life-oriented for the student. Health education should aim for the promotion and protection of the individual. In order to accomplish this, it must instill in him the desire to be a healthy individual and help him to gain the knowledge needed for a healthy, happy life.

In general, planning must consider (1) the goals desirable for the child at his age level, (2) his present status, (3) the corresponding needs of the group for whom the planning is intended, and (4) what is the best help for the individual and/or group to reach the goals found to be needed. Reaching these planned goals means knowledge and understanding transferred into positive action and behavior-pattern changes in individuals.

Needs. The needs of children in each school or area are most important. These needs may well be established through medical and dental examinations, community studies concerning availability of clinics and hospitals, and social and economic status which may suggest specific needs for poverty areas. Geographic locations may also show specific needs and present environmental problems for study such as air pollution and water pollution. Major social trends relating to health, such as preventive medicine, points to needed direction and planning. Accidents and other hazards peculiar to the area also define needs.

Cooperative Planning. Teachers, pupils, administrators, doctors, nurses, dental hygienists, psychologists, and community leaders should be involved in the total planning for health education.

These groups can logically help in organizing and planning, in the collection of materials, in establishing objectives, and in selecting and organizing the content of health instruction. They may also assist in determining the correct learning experiences and in evaluating the end results. They are most helpful in securing resource personnel and materials needed for successful health teaching.

Conceptual Approach. Broad curriculum planning with critical problems identified and then concepts established for various age levels has proved successful. From this approach a framework is established which provides direction in the selection of objectives, specific content, and materials needed. In this approach the child sees each part as it relates to a large concept (picture) and in turn understands better the knowledge and actions necessary to make this concept (picture) complete.

An example of one health concept printed in "*Guides for Health Instruction*"[2] is the following:

"Family members experience physiological,

[2] *Health Concepts; Guides for Health Instruction*, Washington, D.C., American Association for Health, Physical Education, and Recreation, 1967, p. 38.

psychological, and sociological problems and make adjustments as they progress through part or all of a family cycle." (See Chapter 15 for other examples.)

Since families differ in size and in economic status, these two factors may show needs for health teaching. For example, if a teacher knows her class is from a low socioeconomic income group, she may apply this knowledge in deciding to work with students on a unit in nutrition, emerging with well-balanced menus easily within their income range. Cooperation among members of families is always essential. Good mental and emotional health may be aided if each child recognizes his worth to the family and his responsibility to aid in home chores.

Progression. In order for children to learn and remain interested and challenged, the health program must be planned to avoid repetition.

It appears necessary for schools to accept and define concepts they wish to use and then decide in which grade or at what age level each will be taught in depth and where it will be introduced only incidentally. The fourth-grade teacher surely needs to know the health education concepts her children have learned in the first, second, and third grades. If a curriculum is planned for the total school, progression will be considered and developed more readily than if each teacher plans independently.

Progressive programs will also provide for appropriate learning experiences and planned programs will give meaning to health content which in turn will be more likely to contribute to desired behavior changes.

Planned programs are built upon the values, attitudes, and interests of children. They present accurate and factual material. They challenge the student to think as well as offer him knowledge. When the interaction of knowledge plus thinking occurs, we have more chance of change in behavior patterns than when facts are memorized and not fully understood. Applications will then lead to more desirable health action which in essence is the major concern of health education. The use made of materials learned and the effect they have upon a child's life is the crux of all education.

Integration and Correlation. Health education should be integrated with other subjects and be an integral part of a curriculum. Integration demands natural relationship between the content being taught and the area to which it relates. Any artificial injection of health instruction at random would not be used in the best interests of the students nor would it accomplish the desired goals. Integration does not tend to lessen the importance of health education. It helps to make it more meaningful to children.

The basic areas which offer excellent opportunities to teach health correlating it with the subject-matter concerned, include the sciences, social studies, home economics, and mathematics.

With respect to the broad areas of education —science, language arts, fine arts, and social studies—the following chart shows some possible correlation. The illustrations start with specific topics in health education and show their correlation with the other studies, the examples having been chosen from the representative areas of health habits, the physiological and anatomical structure of the body, and problems of community health.

Incidental Planning and Teaching. Often situations arise which offer an opportunity for successful teaching through the incidental approach. An observation of the social non-acceptance of new students who have recently been transferred to a particular class, carelessness in not using tissues or handkerchiefs when coughing and sneezing, and prevalence of colds in a near epidemic stage are but a few examples that show the need for a teacher to move from her ready-made program to introduce important teachings.

One illustration of the value of incidental teaching occurred when Bob, a fourth-grader, became very ill after taking medicine prescribed for his grandfather.

Regardless of planned work, these are problems which can be best taught when the immediate need is apparent. Opportunities for incidental health instruction should not be missed in order to follow a rigid schedule. When special health needs and interests appear, the schedule should be rearranged to make the best use of it for learning.

Daily newspapers, radio, and television often present topics which are of great interest to students. Opportunities for incidental teaching are plentiful and may well aid the planned program. For example, the following concepts and experiences with reference to the correct use or

Table 16–8. Correlation of Health Instruction with Other Subjects

Health Education	Science	Language Arts	Fine Arts	Social Studies
Area I **Good Health Habits**				
Diet	Chemical changes necessary for the body to use food. Preparation of foods. Graphs; calories; types; sources; measurement (liquid); weight (fractions).	Writing of well balanced menus. Invitations to outside speakers to come to school. Planning field trips and writing for all information and films to be used. Oral discussion of trips: New words for vocabulary. Read articles in news media.	Draw posters, caloric charts, and study cards. Draw pictures of foods illustrating well balanced breakfast, lunch, and dinner.	Where do "specific" foods grow? Why there? Transportation to consumer.
Exercise	Changes which occur in the body during exercise and during rest. Count normal pulse and then check for increased rate after exercise; leverage in movement and lifting effect on body. Muscle strengthening; speed of running; height of jumping; measurement (area of playing fields).	Written and oral discussion of exercise. Read magazine articles. Study of leisure-time needs.	Pictures of equipment and apparatus used for exercise. Stick figures showing various types of movement. Illustrate different joints in motion and in rest positions.	Source of materials (i.e., wood in bats, gut in rackets). Difference in activities based on culture, age, temperature of countries, etc. Clothing worn, why; material; source of raw materials.
Area II **Knowledge of the body**				
Growth	Individual differences of growth. Measurement, height, weight, averages, fractions. Cell growth, division, multiples, etc.	Names of different body types and builds. Names of cells. Reading new words for vocabulary, spelling.	Posters, growth charts, graphs showing growth from infancy to various ages. Weight charts.	Comparative sizes of people of various countries at various ages. Life span. Why do they differ?

Teeth	Study: Numbers of teeth (baby and permanent) Composition of teeth. Foods necessary for good teeth. Food and necessary dental costs.	Names of teeth (i.e., bicuspid, molar, etc. New words for vocabulary. Plan field trips to dental supply houses and dentists' offices.	Drawings or diagrams to show structure of teeth (internal to external); full sets—upper and lower—baby and permanent.	Where do foods come from? How grown? How transported to consumer?
Circulation	Study: Heart as a pump and blood pressure. Exercise and its effect on heart and circulation. Types of blood; Rh factors; composition of blood.	Build vocabulary. Learn needs and uses of blood. Write an invitation to a physician to speak to class, and then thank-you letters. Request permission of Civic Associations to assist in collecting blood for bank.	Diagrams of organs involved in circulation. Diagram of complete circulation cycle.	Learn about agencies assisting in blood collection for hospitals; clinics and their valuable work. Red Cross organization and work.
Body Temperature	Fractions and decimals (98.6°); causes of temperature variance; cost of thermometers; reading thermometers; centigrade and Fahrenheit, differences.	Write articles, read news media concerning different effects on the body during work, play, and rest depending on temperature. Use new words in oral and written assignments.	Graphs; differences of temperature—normal compared with fever, animals compared with humans, children compared with adults.	Where are thermometers made? Of what materials? By whom invented? How packed and shipped?
Ears	Pressure; proper care; machine used for testing; cost of machines; new methods of operations to assist hearing problems; hearing aids.	Build vocabulary. Learn parts of ear; ear specialists and their work; know machines used for testing purposes. Reading assignments; oral discussion and field trips to clinics.	Posters; clay models of ear; draw inner and outer ear; use bulletin boards for display of work.	Learn of doctors and other persons responsible for audiometer; materials needed for manufacturing; where manufactured.
Eyes	Study light rays; testing procedure; instruments used; measurement in foot candles; fractions of 20/20, 20/40 vision; use of dark glasses; compare camera and eyes. Costs of care of eyes.	New vocabulary: retina, cornea, optic nerve, ophthalmologist, etc. Learn how to protect eyes at work and play. Occupations which require intensive eye use; night blindness, cause and effect.	Draw posters illustrating correct care of eyes; correct reading position and glasses of different kinds. Make safety posters. Make color charts for testing eyes. Draw models of the eye showing cross section.	Research to find important contributors concerning glasses, eye testing, machines used and glass eyes. Where are machines made? Of what materials? Manufacturers? Means of shipping machines?

Table 16–8 (continued)

Health Education	Science	Language Arts	Fine Arts	Social Studies
Area III Community Health				
Water	Purification; sources; chemicals; measurement (meters); gravity; pressure.	Preparation of articles for bulletin-boards. Discussion of findings in other classes. Visit to filtration plant. New words for vocabulary.	Charts showing sources of water and lines to reservoir. Diagrams of filtration systems.	Laws governing water rights, disposal of debris, etc. Men who perfected various systems, etc.
Clinics	Immunization. Sterilization techniques. Costs of building; staffing; and general operational budgets. Special needs of caring for the younger and older citizens.	Vocabulary building. Write letters seeking permission to visit clinics. Write thank-you letters. Reports on clinics in the area and their functions. Future needs as population increases.	Draw plans for building a clinic (scaled to size). Show special rooms designed according to medical needs (i.e., x-ray, therapy, etc.).	Laws concerning immunization; countries from which scientists have come. Study of their lives. Effects age span has on special needs.
Smog	Causes; prevention; effect on individuals. Future problems.	Write requests for materials. Invitations to guest speakers. Study articles in news media. Write town or city Council seeking special help needed in own community.	Bulletin-board.	Study of laws concerning new antismog devices. Why invented? What is patented? Future prospects and needs.

abuse of drugs were gained by a class of children who, because of their interest, asked for information on glue sniffing and other drugs they had heard about.

Additional Experiences Gained

1. A field trip was taken to a local drug-manufacturing firm and also to a local pharmacy.
2. The school doctor and nurse visited the class and helped them to find materials and solve problems.
3. The children asked parents to keep all medications out of the reach of children and to discard old prescriptions.
4. They wrote letters to obtain information from the Food and Drug Administration, their local Health Bureau, the County and State Medical Societies, and the Pharmaceutical Association.
5. They learned how to reach Emergency Service from each of their homes when needed if drugs or poisons were taken by accident. They learned that these centers are manned twenty-four hours a day.

Patterns of Curriculum Planning. Generally we think of four patterns of curricular development in today's schools. They are the core curriculum, the experience curriculum, the subject matter curriculum, and the area curriculum.

1. The *core curriculum* emphasizes present needs and is centered about life today. Such a curriculum in health education would consist of many problems and might extend several weeks. Examples of units which might be found in the core curriculum are: the value of leisure-time activities, the preventive medical approach, and conserving and improving good mental health.

2. The *experience curriculum* is planned mainly around the needs and interests of the students. This type of curriculum offers pupils assistance in their planning.

3. The *subject-matter curriculum* is the oldest. It isolates each subject and presents it independently. Thus, some information may not be meaningful to students because they cannot see the relationship of what they are learning to the total school program. Many times subject matter becomes more important than children.

Table 16–9. **Grade 4. Drugs, Their Use and Abuse**

Concepts	Content
Man has always sought a cure for illness and a means of relieving pain.	Find stories about early use of drugs by Aesculapius, Hippocrates, Greeks, Romans, American Indians. Discuss ways in which cures were found and the history of some of the medicines we have in our homes.
Medication prescribed by the physician should be used as directed and only by the person for whom it was prescribed.	Secure labels from over-the-counter and prescription drugs and have the students observe what the labels contain, why, and the value of this information. Be sure children understand what should be done with prescription drugs when the patient has recovered. Discuss with the children the use, effects, and dangers of stimulants and depressants and the possible harm which may result if they accept medicine or something which anyone other than parents or a physician tells them will make them feel better or different.
There are medicines which will prevent illness.	Have the school nurse discuss with the children the various forms of immunization and the frequency of renewal. She should urge those who have let any immunity lapse to have it renewed.
Minor, short-term illness can be cared for through self-medication but serious illness should have the attention of a physician.	Invite the school physician to talk with the students about those conditions which can be cared for through home remedy and contrast symptoms which need the attention of a physician.

The following lesson outline was used for the concept; Medication prescribed by physicians should be used only as directed and only by the person for whom it was prescribed.

Table 16-9 (continued)

Specific Concept	Procedure	Content
Over-the-counter drugs must be correctly labeled.	Have labels from over-the-counter drugs such as aspirin, cough medicine, etc. The pupils should be encouraged to bring some. Have children read these to observe the label requirements.	1. Name and address of manufacturer or distributor. 2. Name of product. 3. Name and quantity of ingredients. 4. Strength of dosage unit. 5. Frequency of dosage. 6. Preparation (shaking, diluting, measuring, etc.). 7. Warnings such as age of user, maximum dosage per day.
	Ask children the reason for such labels and who makes regulations and why.	1. Protection of public. 2. Federal Food, Drug and Cosmetic Act. 3. Drugs must be safe for people.
	There are some general warnings on containers. Why?	1. Example: "If condition continues see physician." 2. There might be some other illness.
Prescription medicine also has a label containing certain information.	Now show the pupils labels which they or the teacher have brought in and notice what is on the label.	1. Name and address of druggist. 2. Name of physician. 3. Prescription number. 4. Date. 5. Dose or any special instructions. 6. Name of patient. 7. Refill instructions.
Prescription drugs must be taken as directed by the person to whom the prescription was given.	Have children discuss the importance of following directions and not using the medicine prescribed for another person.	1. Physicians know what you need. 2. Medicine should be taken until the doctor tells you to stop. 3. If the patient has not improved in a given period of time, see the physician again. 4. A prescribed medicine has been prepared for you and your needs.
	Why should you tell the physician if you have been taking any other medicine?	1. So he will know if the two can be taken at the same time or will react on each other. 2. So he can tell you if you should continue both medicines.
	What should be done with left over prescription drugs and why?	1. Destroy them so no one else can get them. 2. Such drugs might make another person ill. 3. Very young children may even die from taking adult medicine.

4. The *area curriculum* integrates, correlates, and fuses related subject areas and assists children in seeing the total relationship among them. It may include the four broad areas of language arts, the sciences, the fine arts, and social studies, or it may be divided into seven less broad areas consisting of social studies, health, physical education and safety, language arts, general mathematics, general science, and art.

Health education fits well in any of the curricular patterns which the elementary school chooses to use.

Unit Planning. A unit is a convenient subdivision of subject matter which integrates and unifies selected experiences. Unit planning provides many opportunities for various activities, creates learning situations, and will be most successful when it uses the conceptual and problem-solving approach.

In general we think of three types of unit. The subject-matter unit, the experience unit, and the resource unit.

A complete unit plan includes concept, general objective, specific content to be learned (including practices and the development of correct attitudes), the outline guide of the material, activities which may be used (such as group discussion, dramatizations, field trips, and the like), evaluation (including knowledge and improvement indices), and resources for use by the teacher and the students.

Summary of Planning Hints in Health Education

1. Representatives from all areas of the school, the community, and students should help plan.
2. Organize a broad plan at the beginning of the year and make it an integral part of the total curriculum.
3. Base the plan on needs, interests, and abilities of the children and needs of the community in which they live.
4. Establish priority needs for progressive planning.
5. Keep the plan flexible in order to include needs not heretofore seen. Incidental teaching is important.
6. Know the outcomes which should be the result of each unit of work and each lesson.
7. Plan to use the conceptual approach.
8. Plan to integrate health and physical education with other parts of the curriculum.
9. Plan means of motivation which will create a desire for new learning.
10. Plan to give opportunities for new experiences.
11. Make use of health consultants in all areas possible (i.e., dentists, doctors, nurses).
12. Plan for the use of audio-visual aids, field experiences, and all meaningful educational media.
13. Plan to assess and evaluate results in as many ways as possible.
14. Keep in mind the significant home and community factors in all planning.
15. The time element is important. What is the relationship of physical education and health instruction to the total program? Plan your program in accordance with this allotted time.
16. Keep your program current with new scientific developments.

Questions and Practical Problems

1. Plan two lessons in physical education using the suggested outline for the plan. Choose one early childhood grade and one middle or upper grade.

2. Select a unit of work you wish to teach in grade six, seven, or eight. Develop a complete unit.

3. Select suitable activities for various seasons of the year for each of the eight grades.

4. Make up one new game to be used at certain times of the year for each of the first eight grades.

5. Visit a grade of your choice. From discussion with the classroom teacher, ascertain the units of work being taught. Plan a health education unit, correlating it with other parts of the curriculum. Be sure you learn the needs and abilities of the children before planning.

6. Write a daily health education plan drawn from your unit. Prepare also a weekly plan.

7. Be prepared to defend each type of unit planning.

Selected References

American Association for Health, Physical Education, and Recreation. *This Is Physical Education*. Washington, D.C.: American Association of Health, Physical Education, and Recreation, 1965.

BEYRER, M. K., A. E. NOLTE, and M. K. SOLLEDER. *A Directory of Selected References and Resources for Health Instruction*. Minneapolis: Burgess Publishing Company, 1966.

FAIT, HILLIS F. *Physical Education for the Elementary School Child*. Philadelphia: W. B. Saunders Company, 1964.

FLEMING, R. S. *Curriculum for Today's Boys and Girls*. Columbus, Ohio: Charles E. Merrill Books, Inc., 1963.

GROUT, RUTH. *Health Teaching in Schools*, 5th ed. Philadelphia: W. B. Saunders Company, 1968.

HARRISON, CLARKE H., and FRANKLIN B. HAAS. *Health and Physical Education for the Classroom Teacher*. Englewood Cliffs, N. J.: Prentice-Hall, Inc., 1964.

HUMPHREY, JAMES, et al. *Readings in Health Education*. Dubuque, Iowa: William C. Brown Company, Inc., 1964.

Joint Committee on Health Problems in Education of the National Education Association and the American Medical Association. *Health Education*. Washington, D.C.: National Education Association, 1961.

LITTLE, BILLY JEAN. "Creativity in Physical Education." *The Physical Educator*, Vol. 24, No. 2, May 1967, p. 754.

NEILSON, NELS, NELO P. VAN HAGEN, and WINIFRED LOMER. *Physical Education for Elementary Schools*. New York: The Ronald Press Company, 1966.

PREGNIA, ANTHONY. "Helping Youngsters Read Through Physical Education Experiences." *The Physical Educator*, Vol. 25, No. 2, May 1968.

School Health Education Study. Washington, D.C.: School Health Education Study, 1507 M Street, N.W., Room 800, 1964.

VANNIER, MARYHELEN, and MILDRED FOSTER. *Teaching Physical Education in Elementary Schools*. Philadelphia: W. B. Saunders Company, 1963.

CHAPTER 17

General Suggestions for Teaching Physical Education and Health Education

The first part of this chapter gives the teacher general and specific suggestions which will be helpful in teaching physical education. Included are suggestions for the squad method of class organization, the selection of activities which will give all children a chance for an equal amount of participation, discussion of safety and legal liability needed for successful accident-free classes, general teaching hints, and specific teaching hints for game skills.

The second part discusses some health-teaching suggestions. These include motivation, methods and materials, and general teaching hints for health education.

Squad Method of Class Organization

The physical education program offers the teacher a challenge for good class organization which will not only be of great assistance to her teaching but will offer worthy experiences to each child. The learning accomplished through good class organization is invaluable to all children if it is properly planned and administered. The children should always assist in the planning. It is not the prerogative of the teacher alone.

Terms frequently used in class organization for the physical education program are *squads*, *units*, or *teams*. Of the three, squads or units are preferable terms. The word *team* almost always connotes competition, and class organization should not be used to foster a sense of competition. It is a recommended means of teaching cooperation, group consciousness, leadership, followership, and similar desirable traits.

Number of Squads. Four or more squads are usually recommended, depending on the total number of children. For a class with 32 pupils, four squads of eight each is a satisfactory number. Each teacher should plan the number which will best suit the group. Some prefer eight squads of four each.

Organizational Methods. Squads may be organized in many ways. Two of the most widely used methods will be discussed.

Homogeneous Grouping. Children may be grouped according to their abilities. The results of skill tests, strength tests, physical-fitness indices, and/or general all-round ability, as well as size and age may be bases for grouping.

The teacher who has no means of measuring the specific abilities of the children but who knows their over-all abilities may wish to organize the children on this basis. To accomplish this he or she would select four children of similar abilities and place each one on a different squad. This method may be continued until each child has a place. Groups will then be very evenly matched. While the squad plan is not used mainly for competition, it does help to have children of near-equal ability on each side when they are playing relays, team games, or running and tagging games.

Random Placement. Squads may be organized by random methods in several ways. They may count off by fours if the number of desired squads is four. Then all "ones" are together, all "twos" are together, and so on.

Leaders may be selected first and they may choose the members of their squads. This is the least recommended method of all. Squad leaders know the differences of ability among their classmates. The few children who have poor muscle coordination, skills, and techniques are always last to be selected. They know that no squad wants them and they are there because they must be. It points out individual differences to the entire group and is not desirable for certain children.

The drawing method may be used. An equal number of four different-colored pieces of paper are placed in a box. Each child draws a piece. All greens form a group, all reds another. Each color indicates one squad.

Grouping by months of birthdays, house numbers and the number of letters in either the child's first or last name are other methods of random placement. Children will contribute many ideas for different means of organization, and the teacher may think of other methods. It is interesting to note that squads chosen through the random placement method are usually evenly matched in skills.

Length of Service. Squad membership should be changed often. If children are permitted to work and play together for too long a period of time, cliques result and the children lose the desired social experiences. One example of this was illustrated in a school where teams, the term they used, were organized in September and stayed together until June. Undesirable rivalry built up between the teams both in school and outside.

It is desirable to change squads every three or four weeks to avoid undesirable antisocial experiences. This will give more children a chance to act as squad leaders and to develop desirable qualities of leadership as well as followership. Children need to be able to work and play with each person in their class, either individually or in small or large groups.

Selection of Squad Leaders. Squad leaders may be selected in various ways. Whatever way is used should be thoroughly understood by the children and also should meet with their approval.

In some instances teachers arbitrarily select the squad leaders, either before the children are organized in squads or from the squads. This is not recommended because the children gain no learning experiences and many times resent the leader because of the honor bestowed on him by the teacher. Where this plan is practiced it appears to be an assumed arbitrary right of the teacher.

If desired, leaders may be nominated and elected by the children before squads are organized. The qualifications necessary for leadership should be discussed, posted, and well understood by all children. When children are given the opportunity to nominate and elect, they are learning the method by which leaders are elected in a democracy. Voting may be by a show of hands or by written ballot.

Squads may be organized first, after which each squad may elect its own leader. This is another method worthy of a try.

The teacher who works carefully with the class and teaches the desirable qualifications for leaders need not worry that the children will merely choose the most popular student. Given an opportunity, under careful guidance, they do a fine job of selection.

Children need to know desirable leadership and followership characteristics to enable them to be valuable members of a group. Teachers should encourage their children to help establish these qualifications. If the age level permits, they may make one chart listing the qualifications for good leaders and one for good followers. In grades where children are unable to make the charts, it is a valuable teaching aid for the teacher to make them. Children may learn new words for their vocabulary and spelling from the charts, as well as learn to read them.

While leadership and followership abilities differ among children, it is hoped that through clear understanding of the qualifications each child will work toward reaching them and may some time during the school year have an opportunity to act as a leader. If squads are reorganized each month, a classroom operating on a four-squad plan would need forty leaders for a ten-month session. This would make it possible for each child to act as a leader once, and some twice, during the year. It is strongly recommended that teachers plan the process of reorganization period with their classes.

Leadership Qualifications. The specific qualifications needed for leaders should be thoroughly understood by the children. They may add other qualities not listed below. In general, it is believed that a good leader must:

1. Be able to take care of himself before he can aid in the organization of others.
2. Be well prepared to organize his group.
3. Be honest and a good sport.
4. Be dependable.
5. Have and keep the respect of his group.
6. Be courteous and thoughtful.
7. Be able to give and receive suggestions.
8. Be enthusiastic.
9. Give encouragement to all participants by giving constructive help.
10. Have the interest of his entire group in mind.
11. Be fair in making decisions and be able to act as judge or referee in game situations.
12. Have the ability to keep everything running smoothly in his squad during each activity.

Followership Qualifications. It is as important for a child to possess the qualities of a good follower as of a leader. This should be taught and stressed. Each child may add additional qualifications for followership to those listed. Specifically, it is believed essential that a good follower must:

1. Be respectful to the leader.
2. Be willing to cooperate and participate to the best of his ability.
3. Be able to accept constructive help.
4. Be a good sport at all times.
5. Listen to the leader's opinions as well as those of his teammates and be guided by good judgment.
6. Follow directions well.
7. Be conscious of his part in the social group and abide by group standards.
8. Be unselfish.
9. Have a desire to gain a knowledge of the rules and directions for all activities.
10. Be able to follow and not try to take over the leader's responsibilities while he is in charge of the group.
11. Be able to discipline himself and have self-control at all times.
12. Work as a part of the group for group consciousness and harmony and forget himself as an individual.

Value of Squads to Teachers. Squad organization is a great aid to teachers. Squad leaders may help by:

1. Assisting with the planning of the program of activities.
2. Acting as equipment managers.
3. Helping assign the positions of various players in games.
4. Making decisions concerning their players.
5. Ascertaining that each child has his rightful turn in play.
6. Checking the play area and equipment for safety factors.
7. Assisting with their groups in securing wraps and in going to and from the play areas, the basements, and the lunchroom.
8. Acting as leaders in the classroom as well as on the playground.
9. Acting as leaders for small-group play, individual activities, skill tests, and so on.
10. Acting as referees, umpires, and score keepers.
11. Aiding in sectioning the playground into playing areas and in marking courts or specific areas needed for play.
12. Aiding, through their understanding of problems pertaining to facilities and equipment, in the mutual understanding and cooperation of their groups.
13. Acting as demonstrators of skills and activities in their groups if the teacher works with them first in a leader's corps.
14. Assisting in evaluating activities and the entire program.
15. Assisting in setting a good example of sportsmanship for others.
16. Helping to make the teacher less necessary, which helps meet the objective set by John Amos Comenius, "To find a method of instruction by which teachers may teach less and learners learn more."

Squads aid the teacher by:

1. Saving valuable time for each class period because children are already in groups and ready for various activities and formations.
2. Making it easy for the teacher to work on skill tests.

3. Assisting the teacher in being ready for relays and games requiring several groups.

4. Facilitating small-group work and offering good opportunities for her to notice children who need specific help. (This is easier to spot in a group of eight than one of 32.)

5. Being combined in one large group or in two groups for team activities.

6. Aiding in teaching group consciousness by departing from the "I" stage to the "We" stage.

7. Offering a fine opportunity to teach democratic relationships.

Value of Squads to Children. Squad organization offers many varied experiences which may aid children by:

1. Developing leadership.
2. Developing followership.
3. Providing helpful socializing opportunities.
4. Providing a laboratory for aiding teamwork.
5. Eliminating individual emphasis through group consciousness.
6. Developing responsibility.
7. Teaching democratic procedures and actions.
8. Presenting social experiences of a group nature which give vent to the gang instinct.
9. Developing sportsmanship.
10. Giving individual satisfaction through belonging to a group and being needed.
11. Teaching cooperation.
12. Teaching the child to accept his place in a group.

Hints for Teachers

1. Squads may be organized in all grades including the first.
2. Be sure children understand the values and objectives of organization.
3. Give them an opportunity to aid in the organization.
4. Help them develop by aiding them in assuming leadership and followership positions.
5. Do not use squads merely for competitive purposes. This will add to problems rather than assist in solving them.
6. Change squads often.
7. Provide opportunities for each child to

act as a leader at some time during the year, if at all possible.

8. Give the leaders responsibility both on the playground and in the building.

9. Use the squads for other purposes than in the physical education program.

10. Use each reorganization period as a valuable teaching opportunity.

11. Evaluate the group organization constantly.

12. Make it a cooperative experience at all times.

Evaluation of Pupil Growth. Teachers may use the squad organization for evaluation purposes to assist the group in seeing its growth and accomplishments. She may help each individual squad to prepare a chart. This may be done during an art class. Children usually like to name their squads. A chart may be made for each squad containing the name, an appropriate drawing characterizing its name, and all members' names. Adequate space should be permitted for leaders to write in the daily accomplishments of their squads. These accomplishments may include the names of the games played, rating of sportsmanship and various other characteristics, skills and techniques learned, specific positive comments by the teacher, and the like.

Each child may also wish to keep his own monthly record, listing the name of his squad, his specific accomplishments while working with the group, and his comments on and reactions to each particular squad.

Children may write about their reactions or speak before their group. They should gain much from the organization experiences and should be given an opportunity each week to think together and evaluate their experiences.

In conclusion, it appears that organization gives an opportunity for the correct adjustment of relationships between children and/or adults in an effort to accomplish certain specific goals.

A good program of physical education, correctly organized, offers a great opportunity to teach democracy because it aids in developing social consciousness, which assists a child in taking his place in a group.

Good class organization in physical education is an invaluable teaching aid to the teacher and to the child.

Selection of Activities to Provide Full Participation for Each Child

When reference is made to games and activities used in the program of physical education that give opportunity for full participation, the intent is that 100 per cent of the group, each and every child, regardless of his or her skills and techniques, will remain in the game until the time allotment for it in a given period is completed. Full participation, 100 per cent participation, does not mean that each child must expend himself or herself to the fullest every minute of the time. This would be most dangerous for the health of the child.

In contrast, the elimination type of activity refers to activities containing rules which make it necessary for a child to stop playing a game when he is caught by "It," hit by the ball, or put out by some other means. The objection to this type of activity is that too many of the games prevent extensive participation on the part of *all* children.

Each period of activity should give *every* child the fun he desires; allow him to participate as long as the game continues and he is physically fit to play; keep him a part of the group and not send him away from it; aid him to develop desirable skills and techniques; teach him to get along with his peers, to be a good sport, to know himself as he is, and to give him a chance to improve. These objectives are possible only if the child *continues to participate* with his peers. The law of learning, "We learn by doing," is as necessary in physical education as in any part of the curriculum.

If a child is eliminated from a game because he is a slow runner and is caught by "It," has not mastered good mind-and-muscle coordination in dodging and darting away from a ball, cannot catch a ball well, or lacks other skills and techniques—when will he learn these? Will he continue to like to play with his group or will he find rationalizations and excuses to stay away from the play period? "I have a headache; may I stay inside today?" "Mother said I should not run and play today because I was sick last night."

It is well to analyze the results of activities of the elimination type.

Elimination from Games an Undesirable Factor. It must be remembered first of all that children are by nature active and crave physical activity. They should be permitted to play and not be eliminated because of certain rules of games.

How will the eliminated child react? What will he do? How will he learn? How will he be looked upon by his group? Will he be wanted or rejected? What will his attitude be regarding the activity and, perhaps, play in general? Will this create any problems for the teacher?

All people, especially children, want to be liked, accepted, and wanted by their peers. All children and individuals differ. They differ in stature, looks, color, likes and dislikes, mentality, physical coordination, and in many other characteristics. Factors of individual difference are accepted in the general over-all education of children, and provisions are made to meet them. The same practices should be part of our physical education programs.

A child cannot be taught or helped if he is eliminated from an activity. If he cannot read his part when in the reading circle, he is not sent away from the group. Why then must he stop playing because he has skills and techniques which are not as well developed as others in his group? If he is stopped, the teacher can give him no help nor can he help himself. Learning ceases and different undesirable reactions occur.

Effects on Attitudes. The reactions of children who are eliminated from games and play will differ just as surely as the children differ. It may make one seek attention in an undesirable way. He may create a behavior problem for the teacher to try to solve. He will strive to gain attention as his way to have fun and perhaps take the teacher's time and attention away from the group from which he was eliminated.

Another child may withdraw completely. She feels bad. She knew she couldn't run as fast as many. Now it has been proved to her and she knows she'll never be like her classmates.

Still a third child may be able to cover up his disappointment and remain interested in the activity and vow he'll do better once he gets back in— if he does.

Sam blames his elimination on someone else who got in his way. John says, "They do not play fair and I do not want to play with them, anyway." Nancy admits she never did like to play ball.

There may be as many different reactions as there are children. Some will dislike the activity and find excuses for not participating when it is used as a part of the program again. When the opportunity to choose an activity for the group arises, these games will not be mentioned by those who have less ability than their peers.

Effects on Learning. All persons learn by doing. Surely no one will argue that this law of learning is incorrect. All persons will not learn the same amount or at the same speed, but if activities for a given group are correctly chosen to meet its needs, interests, and abilities, there will be learning situations in each one. If the child starts to participate and is not permitted to continue, will he learn by doing?

Learning may be aided through repetition. If a child is out, and therefore not permitted to participate, will he learn? Where will the repetition come in? He is not going to stand off by himself and practice catching a ball off a fence while his playmates are playing together. He will not run up and down the sidelines to increase his speed. Mary cannot practice keeping her eye on the ball and then dodging, jumping, or running away from it when there is no game in which she may play.

Some may ask, "Why are these activities not good ways to teach the child we are not all alike? They will have to find it out when they go out into the world." The answer perhaps is that there is a correct time and place for this to be learned. During childhood, when there is much to be derived and desired in the education of children through play, their differences should not be publicized by eliminating them from an activity.

The child who needs the activity and comradeship of his peers, to gain confidence in himself and to develop certain skills, may be the first eliminated from the activity. It paves the way for classmates to note extreme differences in certain children. When the time comes to choose or elect squads or teams, the child with the lesser ability may be rejected. The majority of children do not want him or her in their squad. Thus the child's differences are exaggerated and he is unhappy and emotionally upset.

Some of these activities of the elimination type need not be deleted from the program. Instead, rules may be changed and they may remain

General Suggestions for Teaching 249

an accepted part of the physical education program.

Examples of Modifying the Elimination Factor. For discussion and illustration purposes three types of games will be presented which contain rules for eliminating players. In each activity, changes will be suggested showing how these games may continue to be used by deleting the elimination element. When the teacher understands them it will be easy to spot games of an elimination nature and to make the necessary changes before teaching them in order to insure full participation of the children. There is no objection to changing the rules in any activity excepting standard rules for highly organized team games such as Soccer, Volleyball, Basketball, Baseball, and the like. If situations arise when the rules of these must be modified in any way, children should be definitely informed of these changes and why they are necessary.

DOG CATCHER—A GAME OF LOW ORGANIZATION

The rules of Dog Catcher, a running and tagging game, direct each child in the class to choose the name of a dog. One person is "It" and receives the name of dog catcher. There are two safety goals or kennels to which the dogs may run. All dogs stand at one end of the rectangular play area in one kennel. The dog catcher takes his place midway between the two kennels.

The dog catcher calls the name of one breed of dog. Players who have selected this name run and try to reach the other kennel at the opposite end of the play area without being tagged. All dogs tagged by the dog catcher are placed in the imaginary dog pound. The pound is a small square marked outside of the regular playing area. The dog catcher then calls another breed of dog from the first kennel, tags all he can, and places them in the pound. This continues until all the dogs from the first kennel are either in the pound or have successfully reached the second kennel. Dogs are then called back to the first kennel—one breed at a time—and as each dog is tagged he goes to the pound. The last remaining dog who is not tagged is the winner. He becomes the new dog catcher if another game is to be played; the rest of the children may choose new breeds.

It is quite possible that some children will only have one chance to run the length of the play area during the game. Some will undoubtedly be tagged the first time they attempt to run to a new kennel and will be placed in the dog pound where they remain until the game is completed. Their activity and participation will have consisted of one minute or less. What do they learn? Do they have fun? How can the rules of this game be changed to permit all children to remain in it?

A Suggested Change to Avoid Elimination

The following is one suggested change. Others are possible. Eliminate the dog pound. Permit the children to decide how many times or chances the dog catcher may have. They may agree on three turns. He may call collies and tag two. These two do *not* go in the dog pound since there is none. They merely give the dog catcher two points and remain with the group in the game. The second time the dog catcher may call beagle hounds and catch two more. His score is now four. The two caught remain in play. For his third and last turn he may call "all the dogs in the kennel." If he does, all dogs must run. The dog catcher may feel he has a chance to tag more if he calls them all at one time. If he tags three this third time, these three are added to his original score of four and his total score would be seven. Then another dog catcher would be chosen in a way designated by the class and the game played again. By the use of this one suggested change, all the children in the group participate from the beginning to the end of the play time. A winner may be declared from among the dog catchers by the number each tagged. The one who tagged the most would be declared the winner. Other winners may consist of all those who were never tagged.

Thus, with this change, the game ceases to be of the elimination type. Children use their

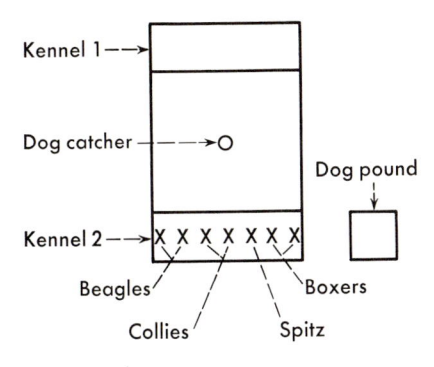

Figure 17–1. Dog Catcher.

250 METHODOLOGY FOR PLANNING AND TEACHING

imagination, gain skill in running and tagging, learn sportsmanship—how to tag and to admit when tagged—and have a lot of fun with total participation of the group.

COFFEE AND TEA—A CLASSROOM GAME

Coffee and Tea is a classroom game whose written rules make it a game of the elimination type. Directions for playing it are as follows. On the floor in the classroom two or four areas, each about 3 feet wide, are marked off with chalk. An even number of areas are marked "tea" and "coffee." To start the game all children move around the room by either walking, hopping, skipping, or any way they choose or are directed. The teacher or leader claps hands at intervals and this is the signal for all children to *stop moving*. Each child who is standing in an area marked coffee or tea is eliminated and must take his seat. The game continues until there is only one child left. This last child is declared the winner.

Undoubtedly the first clap will eliminate at least one child and maybe four, depending on the number of marked areas. That constitutes their fun and activity for a period of probably 10 to 15 minutes or until the game ends. These children who are no longer playing may become restless in their seats, cause excess noise, and create a problem for the teacher.

A Suggested Change to Avoid Elimination

One way to change the game and use it for maximum fun and activity for the entire group is to allow all the children to remain in the game regardless of whether they are standing in a coffee or tea "pot" when the leader claps hands. They will, however, keep their score. A score of one point is made each time a child is standing in a pot when the leader claps hands. The object of the game is to get the lowest score. The persons with no score would be the winners of the game. If the game is played this way, the length of time desired to play it may be established. Even if it is to be used for only five minutes before changing to another activity, it is justifiable because all children have had participation and fun for the entire time.

DODGE BALL—A TEAM GAME

Dodge Ball is a popular game and may be played many ways. Intermediate and upper grades

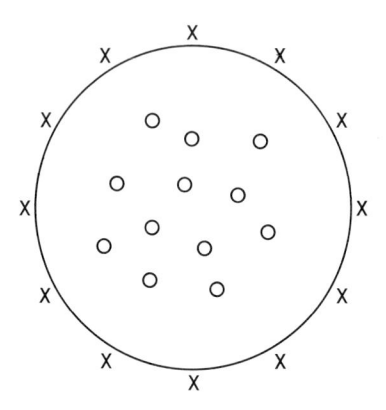

X Denotes throwing team
O Denotes dodging team

Figure 17–2. Dodge Ball.

often like to have competition among squads. Many times it is used in this way and eliminates children as they are hit. Organization of the game places one group in a circle surrounded by the other groups. The team which forms the circle has a volleyball or an inflated ball of similar size and weight. At the signal "Go," the captain throws the ball at a person in the center. The object is to hit the players in the circle with the ball. When a player is hit by the ball he is eliminated from the circle and from the game until all of his teammates have been hit. When only one player remains in the circle, he makes his team's score. A point is counted for each throw it takes to hit him. If 12 throws are made before he is hit, the score of the team which started in the center is 12. The throwing team then goes in the circle made by those who were eliminated. They make their score in the same manner. If it takes 15 throws to hit their last player, their score is 15 and they win the game.

Probably the first throw will eliminate some child. What fun will he have? What will he learn? Will he learn to keep his eye on a moving ball and to jump or dodge it any better? It is true he will have an opportunity to throw the ball at the other team, but there are ways the game may be changed to provide each child with an equal amount of time to practice dodging and running away from a moving ball as well as time to practice throwing it.

A Suggested Change to Avoid Elimination

Start the game in the usual manner, but agree on a specific length of time for each team or group to remain in the circle. Perhaps a three-minute period will be chosen. Instead of eliminating players as they are hit, all players will remain in the circle for the entire three minutes. The captain of the throwing team or squad is responsible for keeping count of the number of hits his team makes. He calls each hit a point and keeps his score *aloud*. Every child knows at all times what the score is. All children are playing all of the time. Since time is an element, there is little ball hogging—which wastes time. There is team cooperation. If a ball leaves the circle, one child recovers it and throws it to a teammate. This saves time and gives them more chances to hit players. The score of the throwing team is the number of hits made during the three minutes of play. Teams then exchange places, and play for another three-minute period. Score is kept the same way. At the end of the last three-minute period the winning team is the one which earned the highest score by hitting the most players.

Notice in the suggested rule changes that all children play all of the time. No one is eliminated. Playing for time gives more incentive for good teamwork. The score is not dependent on one person who is already tired and may overdo in running, jumping, and dodging in order to make a high score for his team. Thus the activity continues to be a team game and is worthy of a place in the program. Skills and techniques involve throwing at a moving target, catching, running, jumping, and dodging. Each is repeated many times. No one player is the star. The entire team cooperates. It is fun and the total group participates all the time.

From the discussion of these three different games, with rules which make them the elimination type, and the suggested changes made to maintain participation for all children during the entire game, teachers will be able to spot games of the elimination type at once when planning their programs. It is recommended that they make the necessary changes to insure full participation of their group and avoid eliminating children from an activity. The first child eliminated may need the activity and fun the most. By avoiding the use of games of the elimination type, the tendency to show individual differences in children's abilities to the entire group is lessened. The children with poorer skills will have less tendency to dislike the play period and physical education. Each child will have a chance to play and practice and to become better in skills and techniques. Full participation will aid in giving the social and psychological incentives and understanding needed to develop as normal individuals. A happy, healthy learning situation should exist at all times.

Hints for Teaching Specific Game Skills

The following principles need to be observed by teachers when engaged in teaching throwing, catching, and striking skills to children.

1. *Opposition.* When throwing, the motion of the hand and arm is opposite that of the foot and leg (i.e., right handed thrower—left foot forward; left handed thrower—right foot forward).

2. *Follow-through.* Good performance depends on follow-through. For example, any striking or throwing requires a complete follow-through of the body. One should not stop the movement when the hand, foot, racket, or other equipment used makes contact with the object. Continuing the body movement assists one to gain good skills to throw further, hit harder, and be more successful. For example, kicking requires body movement and follow-through after the foot makes contact with the ball.

3. *Focus.* Eyes should be kept on the object. When striking or catching, the eye watches the ball. When throwing, eyes should be focused on the target. When children understand the principles of opposition, follow-through, and focus, they will usually develop more skill and grace in total movement. This in turn makes it easier for the child to perform the skill. Energy conservation is inherent in good performance, thus the performer does not tire as quickly and is capable of greater participation.

Personal Hints

1. Dress comfortably. Many teachers keep a pair of loafers, saddle oxfords, or sneakers in their closet to wear for physical education. This saves damage to expensive footwear, makes the teacher more comfortable, and gives him or her a greater incentive to enter into the activity.

Table 17–1. Teaching Hints for Catching, Throwing, and Striking Skills

Skill	Basic Principles	Common Faults
1. *Catching* Palms face direction from which object approaches. To catch an object below waist, fingers point downward (little fingers together). To catch an object above waist, fingers point upward (thumbs together). Fingers are spread and slightly curved.	1. The force of the oncoming object is closer to the center of gravity when the body is in line with the object. 2. Greater body stability is achieved with a stride position in the direction of the oncoming object (forward stride). 3. "Giving" with the object (i.e., pulling it toward the body) reduces the speed by increasing the time and distance over which force can be reduced.	1. Reaching to side for catch. 2. Failure to "give" with object. 3. Fingers straight and rigid, causing ball to rebound off fingers. 4. Heels of hands together, causing ball to bounce out of hands. 5. Failure to keep eyes on object.
2. *Throwing* Three basic patterns: Overhand, underhand, sidearm.	1. The speed of object thrown is controlled by momentum given it by the body. This momentum is developed by the total action of the throw—backswing, proper stance, body rotation, forward shift of body weight, and follow-through. 2. Distance is dependent upon how fast the object is moving when released and the angle at which it is released. 3. Direction in which the object travels is dependent upon the direction the hand is moving when object is released.	1. Little or no body rotation. 2. Failure to focus on target. 3. Failure to shift weight. 4. Failure to follow through.
2–a. *Overhand Throw* Stance: Stride position, nonthrowing side of body toward target, arm shoulder level. Backswing: Throwing arm brought back, elbow bent, arm away from body and at right angle to it, ball approximately ear height, wrist cocked. Rotate trunk in direction of throwing arm, shift weight to foot on throwing side of body. Forward swing: Bring ball forward, elbow leading, wrist and hand "snap" forward, ball is released. Body rotates toward target during this motion and weight is shifted to forward (nonthrowing) foot.	1. A wide base stance, with foot opposite ball (object) hand toward the target, allows for weight transfer to rear foot and insures maximum rotation of body. This means a longer backswing, permitting more time to build momentum which is transferred to the object. 2. A short lever is easier to move; therefore, the elbow is bent at all times in backswing. 3. Follow-through (continued movement in the direction of the throw) is essential as it enables the object to be released at the center of the throwing arc when the hand is moving fastest. *Note;* Stopping the hand with release of the ball would reduce momentum and result in loss of speed. Thrown objects move in a tangent to the arc the hand travels	1. Starting throw with body facing (square) target. 2. Failure to rotate trunk. 3. Holding ball in palm of hand. 4. Failure to keep elbow bent and to lead throw with elbow (particularly girls). 5. Using pushing motion—result of elbow being held close to body. 6. Forgetting to transfer weight forward. 7. Dropping wrist before ball is released. 8. Failure to follow through.

General Suggestions for Teaching 253

Skill	Basic Principles	Common Faults
Release and follow-through: Ball is released at shoulder height, the throwing arm and hand continue movement (follow through) toward target.	at point of release; therefore, the flatter the arc the greater the accuracy of the throw. 4. Trunk rotation and transfer of body weight forward are essential to move the shoulder forward.	
2-b. *Underhand Throw*		
Stance: Feet together, facing target. Backswing: Throwing arm brought straight down and back as body rotates to throwing side and weight shifts to foot on that side. Forward swing: Throwing arm is brought forward (swing) quickly as a step forward is taken onto the foot on the nonthrowing side of the body. Release and follow-through: Ball is released when arm is at right angle to target and hand and arm continue motion toward target. Nonthrowing arm swings backwards to maintain balance. *Note:* First attempts at throwing are usually a two-hand toss or underhand throw. As the hands get larger and throwing object smaller, the one-hand throw develops.	1. Straight arm results in greater arc through which object travels, building momentum. 2. Follow-through enables hand to be moving fastest at moment object is released. Object moves in tangent to arc in which hand travels at time of release. Point of release is when arc of hand is tangent to target.	1. Little or no trunk rotation. 2. Backswing short. 3. Failure to shift weight backward. 4. Ball released too high (late). 5. Failure to step forward on foot opposite side of body from which object is thrown. 6. Failure to follow through.
2-c. *Sidearm Throw*		
Stance: Forward stride position. Large object held against lower arms with palm of hand. Small ball or object held with fingers. Backswing: Throwing arm swings back in horizontal arc as body rotates in direction of throwing arm; weight is transferred to foot on throwing side. Forward swing: Small object—same as overhand except for horizontal arc. Large object—arm moves as one lever rather than in a series of joint actions.	1. Long backswing, rotation of body, forward transfer of weight and follow-through result in force and speed being transferred to object as it leaves the hand.	1. Failure to rotate body. 2. Failure to shift weight to throwing side (back), then nonthrowing side (forward). 3. Early release—object travels wide of target in direction of throwing side of body. 4. Late release—object travels wide of target in direction of nonthrowing side of body.

Table 17-1 (*continued*)

Skill	Basic Principles	Common Faults
Release and follow-through: Object is released when arc is tangent to target; arm and hand continue in direction of target.		
3. Striking Definition: Hitting an object with some part of the body or an implement which is controlled by the hand. Object may be stationary or moving. Pattern: Much the same as that of throwing. Types: 2-hand underhand; 2-hand overhand; 1-hand underhand; 1-hand overhand; sidearm; batting—striking with implement controlled by hand (i.e., bat, paddle, racket).	1. The applied force must be great enough to overcome the weight and speed of the object to be hit. 2. A stable base provides more efficient application of force. (Forward stride; opposition of motion). 3. Complete extension of the body parts involved should occur at the moment of impact. 4. The eyes must focus on the object to be struck. 5. Maximum force is generated when the object is hit through its center of gravity. 6. The striking implement must be held firmly to utilize the rebounding properties of object struck. 7. Direction can be imparted by turning the surface of the implement or by moving the implement in the direction of the desired hit.	1. Incorrect judgment of force and speed of object. 2. Reduction of the base of support. Result is loss of force. 3. Stepping forward on the same foot as side applying force (should be opposite). 4. Gripping implement with too much tension prior to contact. Relaxing at point of contact or impact. 5. Taking eyes off object. 6. Failure to use sufficient backswing. 7. Insufficient body rotation. 8. Elbows too close to body. 9. Failure to follow through. 10. Contacting object above the center of gravity. Result is "topping" or top spin. 11. Contacting object below the center of gravity. Result is back spin.
3-a. Kicking Definition: Striking an object with the foot. (Use top of instep for contacting object.) Types: Stationary object; rolling object; bouncing object; drop kick; dribbling.	In addition to the principles that apply to striking, the following also apply to the kick: 1. With balance centered over one foot, aid body balance by extending arms sideward. 2. Apply force below center of object with free foot. 3. Continue movement of free foot in direction of desired kick.	1. Free foot misses object completely or rides over the top losing force. 2. Failure to focus on object. 3. Poor direction—result of improper extension of free foot. 4. Increased tension, resulting in too much force.

2. Keep your voice natural and conversational. This may be accomplished by having your class know the meaning of a whistle, a piano chord, or a hand clap and abiding by it. Do not talk when your class is noisy. Teach the rules of etiquette and social manners and use the physical education class to develop these social qualities acceptable to all. Use your signal sparingly but whenever necessary.

3. Accept your responsibility to teach physical education the same as you do your responsibility to teach reading. Remember that the whole

child comes to school and you teach this child in his entirety. Physical education can be fun for the teacher as well as for the pupil. The wise teacher will learn much about each individual during physical education which will be beneficial in her total guidance of him.

Organizational Hints

1. Organize your class in the most efficient way possible. This will avoid much trouble and loss of time and may be used to match students evenly in competitive activities.

2. Use student leaders for squads, teams, and/or units. Develop responsibility in all students by making them responsible for equipment.

3. Use students for demonstration. Work with these children before actual class time.

4. Use color bands, pinnies, or other distinguishing emblems to mark squad players when they are mixed during activities.

5. Have your organizational plan for going to and returning from physical education well understood. Plan this with your class so they understand the standards expected of them. Student leaders should be given responsibility for carrying out the accepted procedure.

Safety Hints

1. Keep playgrounds free of dangerous obstacles.

2. Do not use stones or sticks for bases in games or to mark running areas.

3. Have rules about the recovery of balls or other equipment going into a busy road or street thoroughly understood.

4. Do not permit children to run to walls or fences as goals. Make goal lines a safe distance from such barriers.

5. Inspect equipment regularly.

6. Inspect facilities regularly.

7. Provide proper safety protection for children in all game situations (e.g., mask, body protector, and glove for catcher in softball).

8. Teach children the proper way to tag so they do not injure each other or tear clothing.

9. Teach respect for each other and for all equipment and facilities.

10. Good organization will aid safety.

11. Be sure students awaiting their turn in certain games, such as softball, stay away from the batter to avoid injury.

12. Have your own playing area. Do not permit children participating in a running and tagging game to run across a soccer field, a ball diamond, or any area of play being used by other students.

13. Have children remove glasses or wear eyeglass guards.

Health Hints

1. Do not permit any child to over-strain.

2. Be sure children know that if they become too tired they may drop out of an activity and rest without gaining permission from the teacher.

3. Know the health records of your children. Remember you will have physical education classes before the doctor examines your children in the fall. Use the last health records available. Discuss this with your class in your health teaching. Be cognizant of the child who has just returned from an illness. What is best for him?

4. Ventilate and light your indoor facilities in the best way possible.

5. Be sure children wear proper clothing for the place and type of activity.

6. Do not permit your children to sit on the damp ground while awaiting turns in games or other activities.

Teaching Hints

1. Know your work thoroughly before attempting to teach.

2. Have the necessary equipment ready.

3. Make your playroom, gymnasium, or playground as attractive as possible.

4. Use a positive approach rather than a negative one. "Let's do it this way," rather than "Don't do it that way."

5. Make explanations simple and concise, using as little of the play time as possible.

6. Demonstrate or have demonstrated each step, skill, or technique necessary. Remember, lengthy explanations cause interest to wane. Use visual aids whenever possible. Blackboards are very helpful.

7. Remember that children want action. Have 100 per cent participation.

8. Once rules are established for a given condition, teach your children to accept them.

9. When officiating, make quick and accurate decisions.

10. Teach sportsmanship and character education at all times. Teach children to accept and respect decisions given by officials.

11. Revise rules, if necessary, to increase activity and make it purposeful.

12. Do not permit certain children to monopolize the activity, equipment, or facilities at the expense of all.

13. Aim for knowledge, habits, attitudes, and appreciation which lead to social efficiency and acceptance.

14. Use incentives to reach desired outcomes and goals. Remember that praise is good. Comment whenever possible even though improvement is small.

15. Vary your procedures.

16. Watch closely for waning interest. Kill an activity rather than have it die.

17. End your lesson appropriately.

18. Analyze the lesson each day. Did it go well? If so, why? If not, why? Was it a wrong activity? Was the presentation faulty? Was it not challenging enough for your group? Was it too hard for your group?

19. Enjoy yourself and your class.

20. Be enthusiastic! It's contagious and good contagion.

21. Given opportunity for questions and suggestions by pupils.

Safety and Legal Liability Considerations in Teaching Physical Education

It is tragic that so many of the accidents which occur in the United States today involve young boys and girls with lives of hopes and desires still to fulfill. Accidents are the leading cause of death and an important cause of disability for boys and girls of school age.

Although the school has proved to be a safer place than the home, there is still much room for improvement. Accidents occur going to and from school and in classrooms, auditoriums, gymnasiums, playgrounds, laboratories, shops, corridors, and stairways. About one out of three accidents occurs in gymnasiums. Classrooms run second with one injury in five. These accidents take place during organized activities such as sports as well as during unorganized ones involving running and falls. The accidents which occurred to pupils in kindergarten through the sixth grade during a recent year were classified into four main categories depending on the location and the activities engaged in at the time of the accident. These categories were (1) *in the school plant*—auditoriums, classrooms, playground apparatus, and unorganized activities were the most frequent locations or activities; (2) *going to and from school*—accidents occurred most frequently in the form of falls on the street and the sidewalk; (3) *the home*—injuries resulted from falls, cuts, and scratches; (4) *miscellaneous category*—play activities, falls, and accidents involving bicycles and motor vehicles were the most common.

Many accidents occur on playgrounds, during recess periods, and at sports events and activities involving the physical education class. The unorganized games during recess and noon intermissions, according to the statistics gathered by the National Commission on Safety Education, are more likely to result in pupil injuries than the regularly scheduled activities which are a part of the physical education class.

Accidents that occur on playgrounds and in gymnasiums and other locations for children's play sometimes result in lawsuits.

Because accidents do occur in activities involved with the physical education program in the elementary schools, it is very important for the teacher to be informed and aware of her responsibility. The growth of these specialized programs in this country has brought the problem of legal liability to the forefront. There is always danger of accidents during various activities that comprise programs of physical education. The nature of this field of work involves such things as the use of special apparatus, excursions and trips, living in camps, utilizing first-aid practices, and a considerable number of other activities which have implications for liability.

The Teacher's Responsibility. Each classroom and physical education teacher has a moral and a legal responsibility to provide for the welfare of her pupils. Morally she is responsible for the child's safety and welfare while he is in her charge. The whole concept of education in this country revolves around the premise that education is designed to provide those experiences for children which will help them develop to their maximum capacities, further their pursuit of hap-

(Courtesy of Game Time Inc.)

piness, and guide them in such a way that will prepare them to be mature, healthy adults.

Legally, too, the teacher is responsible for the safety and well-being of her pupils. Each teacher is liable for her own negligence. If litigation occurs and negligence is established, the teacher can be forced to pay from her own funds the costs of such damages, except in a very few states where financial restitution can be made from school funds.

Even in states where "safe harmless" laws protect the teacher, the worry, nuisance, and loss of time, together with the possible reprisal in other ways by boards of education and parents, can cause hardship to a teacher involved in a legal dispute.

According to Bouvier's *Law Dictionary*, liability is "the responsibility, the state of one who is bound in law and justice to do something which may be enforced by action." Another definition by the National Commission on Safety Education is that "liability is the condition of affairs which gives rise to an obligation to do a particular thing to be enforced by court action." This authoritative source goes on to say, "All school employees run the risk of suit by injured pupils on the basis of alleged negligence which causes bodily injury to pupils. Such injuries occur on playgrounds, in athletics, in science laboratories, or in shop classes...."

The teacher is responsible for what he or she does. The Supreme Court of the United States has reaffirmed this principle and all should recognize the important implications it has. Immunity of the governmental agency such as a state, school district, or board does not relieve the teacher of liability for his or her own negligent acts.

Teachers are expected to conduct their various activities in a careful and prudent manner. If they do not do so, they are exposing themselves to lawsuits for their own negligence. Every teacher should know how far she can go with various aspects of her program and what precautions are necessary in order not to be held legally liable in the event of accident. The fact that approximately 50 per cent of the accidents involving school pupils occur in buildings, that more than 40 per cent occur on playgrounds, and 10 per cent occur in going to and from school has important implications for physical education and the teacher. The legal rights involved in such cases are worthy of study. Although the law varies from state to state, it is possible to discuss liability in a general way that has implications for all sections of the country.

Legal Aspects.[1] For many years the courts have recognized the hazards involved in the play activities that are a necessary part of the educational program. The courts have recognized the possibility and risk of some injury in physical education programs and generally have not awarded damages where negligence could not be proved. However, they have pointed out that care must be taken by both the participant and the authorities in charge. They have implied further that the benefits derived from participating in physical education activities offset the occasional injury that might occur.

Many of these decisions were handed down at a time when the attitude of the law was that a government agency, which categorically included the school, could not be held liable for the acts of its employees unless it so consented. Since that time the attitude of the courts has been gradually changing. As more accidents have occurred, the courts have frequently decided in favor of the injured party when negligence could be shown. The immunity derived from the old common law rule that a government agency cannot be sued without its consent is slowly changing in the eyes of the courts so that both the Federal Government and the state may be sued. The compulsory elements of a school curriculum, such as physical education, prompt judicial decisions on the basis of what is in the best interests of the public. Those who uphold the doctrine that a government agency should be immune from liability maintain that payments for injury to constituents is a misapplication of public funds. On the other hand, liberal thinkers feel that it is wrong for the cost of injuries to fall on one or a few persons; it should, instead, be shared by all. To further their case these liberals cite the constitutional provision that compensation must be given for the taking or damaging of private property. They argue that it is inconsistent that the government cannot take or damage private property without just compensation on the one hand, yet on the other can injure or destroy the life of a person without liability or compensation. The liberal view is being adopted more and more by the courts.

Tort. A *tort* is a legal wrong which results in direct or indirect injury to an individual or to property. A tortious act is a wrongful act and damages can be collected through court action. Tort can be committed through an act of omission or commission. An act of omission results when the accident occurs during failure to perform a legal duty, such as when a teacher fails to obey a fire alarm after she has been informed of the procedure to be followed. An act of commission results when the accident occurs while an unlawful act is being performed, such as assault on a student.

The teacher has not only a legal responsibility as described by law, but is also responsible for preventing injury. This means that in addition to complying with certain legal regulations such as providing proper facilities, she must comply with the principle that children should be taught without injury to them and that prudent care, such as that which a parent would give, must be exercised.

Negligence. The question of whether or not negligence is involved often arises in connection with the actions of teachers in physical education programs. Negligence implies that someone has not fulfilled his legal duty or has failed to do something which, according to common-sense reasoning, should have been done. Negligence can be avoided if there is common knowledge of basic legal principles and proper vigilance. One of the first things that must be determined in the event of an accident is whether there has been negligence.

Rosenfield in his book *Liability for School Accidents* defines negligence as follows: "Negligence consists in the failure to act as a reasonably prudent and careful person would under the circumstances involved."

Negligence may be claimed when the plaintiff has suffered injury either to himself or to his property, when the defendant has not performed his legal duty, and when the plaintiff has constitutional rights and is not guilty of contributory negligence. The teacher in such cases is regarded as *in loco parentis*, i.e., acting in the place of the parent in relation to the child.

Since negligence implies failure to act as a reasonably prudent and careful person, necessary precautions should be taken, danger should be

---

[1] Parts of this section on legal aspects are adapted from Charles A. Bucher, *Administration of School Health and Physical Education Programs*, St. Louis, The C. V. Mosby Co., 1963, Chapter 7.

anticipated, and common sense should be used. For example, if a teacher permits a group of very young children to go up a high slide alone and without supervision, that teacher is not acting as a prudent person.

In respect to negligence, considerable weight is given in the law to the *foreseeability* of danger. One authority points out that "if a danger is obvious and a reasonably prudent person could have foreseen it and could have avoided the resulting harm by care and caution, the person who did not foresee or failed to prevent a foreseeable injury is liable for a tort on account of negligence." If a teacher fails to take the needed precautions and care, he is negligent. Negligence, however, must be established upon the basis of facts in each case. It cannot be based upon mere conjecture.

Teachers must also realize that children will behave in certain ways, that certain juvenile acts will cause injuries unless properly supervised, that hazards must be anticipated, reported, and eliminated. The question that will be asked by most courts of law is "Should the teacher have had prudence enough to foresee the possible dangers or occurrence of an act?"

Although there are no absolute, factual standards for determining negligence, certain guides have been established which should be familiar to teachers. One attorney discussing negligence before a conference of physical education teachers suggested the following which have implications for teachers.

1. The teacher must be acting within the scope of his employment and in the discharge of his duties in order to obtain the benefits of the statute.

2. There must be a breach of a recognized duty owed to the child.

3. There must be a negligent breach of such duty.

4. The accident and resulting injuries must be the natural and foreseeable consequence of the teacher's negligence arising from a negligent breach of duty.

5. The child must be a participant in an activity under the control of the teacher, or put in another way, the accident must have occurred under circumstances where the teacher owes a duty of care to the pupil.

6. A child's contributory negligence, however modified, will bar his recovery for damages.

7. The plaintiff must establish the negligence of the teacher and his own freedom from contributory negligence by a fair preponderance of evidence. The burden of proof on both issues is on the plaintiff.

8. Generally speaking, the Board of Education alone is responsible for accidents caused by the faulty maintenance of plants (schools) and equipment.[2]

Defenses Against Negligence. Despite the fact that an individual was negligent, damages cannot be collected unless it can also be shown that the negligence resulted in or was closely connected with the injury. The legal term used in such a situation is whether or not the negligence was the "proximate cause" (legal cause) of the injury. Furthermore, even though it is determined that negligence is the proximate cause of the injury, there are still certain defenses the defendant may use. These are as follows:

ACT OF GOD. An act of God is a situation that exists because of certain conditions which are beyond the control of human beings. For example, a flash of lightning, a gust of wind, or a cloudburst may result in injury. However, prudent action must have been taken to establish a case on this premise.

ASSUMPTION OF RISK. Assumption of risk is a legal defense especially pertinent to games, sports, and other phases of the physical education program. It is assumed that a child takes a certain risk when engaging in various games and sports where bodies are coming in contact with each other and where balls and apparatus are used. Participants in such activity assume a normal risk.

CONTRIBUTORY NEGLIGENCE. Another legal defense is contributory negligence. A child who does not act like a normal individual of similar age and nature may thereby contribute to the injury. In such cases negligence on the part of the defendant might be dismissed. Individuals are subject to contributory negligence if they expose themselves unnecessarily to dangers. The main consideration in such cases is usually the age of the child and the nature of the activity in which he was engaged.

Contributory negligence has implications for differences in responsibility of elementary teachers

[2] City-Wide Conference with Principals' Representatives and Men and Women Chairmen of Health Education, *Proceedings*, New York, City of New York, Board of Education, Bureau of Health Education, 1953.

as contrasted, for example, with high school teachers. The elementary school teacher, because the children are immature, has to assume greater responsibility for their safety. In other words, accidents to elementary school children are not held in the same light from the standpoint of negligence as those to high school students who are more mature. The courts might decide that a high school student was mature enough to avoid doing the thing which caused him injury; whereas if the same thing occurred to an elementary school child, they would feel the child was too immature and the teacher should have prevented or protected the child from doing the act which caused injury.

Supervision. Children are entrusted by parents to physical education programs and it is expected that adequate supervision will be provided so as to reduce to a minimum the possibility of accidents.

Questions of liability in regard to supervision pertain to two points: (1) the extent of the supervision and (2) the quality of the supervision.

Regarding the first point, the question would be raised as to whether adequate supervision was provided. This is a difficult question to answer because it would vary from situation to situation. However, one would ask if additional supervision would have eliminated the accident and if it is reasonable to expect that additional supervision should have been provided?

Waivers and Consent Slips. Waivers and consent slips are not synonymous. A waiver is an agreement whereby one party waives a particular right. A consent slip is an authorization, usually signed by a parent, permitting a child to take part in some activity.

In respect to a waiver, a parent cannot waive the rights of a child who is under 21 years of age. When a parent signs such a slip, he is merely waiving his or her right to sue for damages. A parent can sue in two ways, from the standpoint of his rights as the parent and from the standpoint of the child's own rights which he has as an individual irrespective of the parent. A parent cannot waive the right of the child to sue as an individual.

Consent slips offer protection in that the child has the parent's permission to engage in an activity as specified by the consent slip.

What the Teacher Can Do to Provide a Safe Program. It is important to take every possible precaution to prevent accidents by providing for the safety of pupils who participate in programs of physical education. If such precautions are taken, the likelihood of a lawsuit will diminish and the question of negligence will be eliminated. Some precautions that the elementary school teacher should take follow.

The Place. Play should be fun, but it will not be fun if it isn't safe. The first consideration in avoiding accidents is to make sure that the field, swimming pool, sandlot, gymnasium, or playground is not a condemned area. A street is definitely off limits. The danger of automobiles, trucks, bicycles, and other vehicles, in addition to pedestrians, is too prevalent. Also, places where construction is going on and excavations are being made, the railroad tracks, bridges, and other nuisance spots should never be considered suitable play areas. The place that is chosen should allow ample room for movement and be free of any hazards which might involve injury.

Protective equipment such as mats should be utilized wherever possible. Any hazards such as projections or obstacles should be eliminated. Radiators should be properly screened and recessed into walls. Floors should not be slippery. Shower rooms should not have slippery surfaces.

The buildings and other facilities used should be inspected regularly for safety hazards such as loose tiles, broken fences, cracked glass, and uneven pavement. Defects should be reported immediately to the person responsible and necessary precautions taken.

In planning play and other instructional areas, the following precautions should be observed:

1. There should be sufficient space for all games.
2. Games which utilize balls and other equipment which can cause damage should be conducted in areas where there is minimum danger of injuring someone.
3. Quiet games and activities should be in places which are well protected.
4. Games where there is fast motion, such as basketball and soccer, should be played where they will not interfere with other activities and can be isolated from other play and games.
5. Boundary lines should be clearly marked.

The Equipment. The equipment is an important consideration in providing for a safe physical education program. Many accidents which occur

injury a child should be in good physical condition. A strong and healthy body which possesses the necessary stamina to engage in games and sports without becoming excessively fatigued and which has agility and flexibility to insure proper balance and mobility, together with other components of physical fitness, helps to lessen the possibility of injury. Many injuries occur when a boy or girl becomes tired and exhausted from his or her own physical inadequacies. There should be a periodic check-up by the family or school physician to make sure there is not a cardiac condition or other defect which could be aggravated through play.

It is always advisable for children to engage in competitive sports with other boys and girls of comparable size and ability. This not only results in a better but also a safer game.

The player will also find that he gains by mastering the basic fundamentals of play. Many injuries have occurred because participants did not know what to do. Regardless of the activity, a good knowledge of the fundamentals helps avoid or eliminate injuries.

Classes and Activities. Classes should be properly organized according to size, activity, physical condition, and other factors which have a bearing on the safety and health of the pupil.

Activities should be adapted to the age and maturity of the participants, proper and competent supervision should be provided, and spotters should be utilized in apparatus and other similar activities. The teacher should be familiar with the activities she conducts and supervises. She should be present at all organized activities in the program and should make sure that all the necessary precautions have been taken to provide for the child's welfare. Overcrowding should be avoided, building codes and fire regulations should be adhered to, and proper lighting should be provided. Children should not be requested to move heavy apparatus or otherwise engage in activities which may be detrimental to their health and safety.

A planned, written program for proper disposition of students who are injured or become sick should be followed. The teacher should understand the fundamentals of administering first aid.

The Rules. Game rules and regulations are made to protect the player and to insure a good contest. Therefore, they should be observed. A

in the school gymnasium and playground involve apparatus such as parallel bars, jungle gyms, slides, rings, and other equipment. All equipment should be in A-1 condition. A defective bar or a faulty rope can cause serious injury. When apparatus is being used, proper supervision should be present. In addition, spotters should be provided for equipment like the trampoline. Mats should be used whenever there is danger of a child's body striking the floor or wall hard enough to cause injury. Personal equipment should be such as to guarantee safety. Sneakers should be worn in the gymnasium. Eyeglasses should be taken off or protecting guards provided. Special equipment should be used in sports that involve blows to the head or other parts of the body. Safe, healthy, and proper methods of moving, storing, and cleaning equipment should be followed.

Regular inspections should be made of such items of equipment as apparatus, ropes, and chains by placing extra pressure upon them and taking other precautions to make sure they are safe. Equipment should also be checked for such things as deterioration, looseness, fraying, and splinters.

The Child. If he is to avoid accidents and

good sportsman, playing within the spirit as well as the letter of the rules, will not only receive greater respect from his opponents but will also help make the sport safer. It is the responsibility of the teacher to make the rules known to the players and to place good sportsmanship first during supervision of sports and play activities. Such actions as piling on, pushing, tripping, taking advantage of the small or weak players, cheating or using unethical tactics to win a game, not allowing certain unskilled or unpopular children to play, and other unsportsmanlike conduct should not be permitted.

Procedure in Case of Accident. In the event of accident the following or some similar procedure should be followed:

1. The teacher should go to the scene of the accident immediately, at the same time notifying the principal and nurse, if available, by messenger.

2. An immediate general examination of the injured child will give some idea as to the nature and extent of the injury and the emergency of the situation. If the injury is serious, the parents, a physician, and an ambulance should be called at once.

3. If the teacher is well versed in first aid, assistance should be given. Every teacher who supervises physical education is expected to know first-aid procedures. Everything should be done to make the injured person comfortable. He should be reassured until the services of a physician can be secured.

4. After the injured child has received all the necessary attention the teacher should fill out an accident form, take the statements of witnesses, and file this information for future reference. Reports of accidents should be prepared promptly and sent to proper persons. They should be accurate in detail and complete in information. Every accident report should contain at least the following essentials: (a) name and address of injured child; (b) activity engaged in; (c) date, hour, and place; (d) person in charge; (e) witnesses; (f) cause and extent of injury; (g) medical attention given; (h) circumstances surrounding incident. The National Safety Council publishes a standard student accident report form. This form is recommended for use in school systems.

5. There should be a complete follow-up of the accident with an analysis of the situation and eradication of any hazards that exist.

First Aid. First aid is the emergency care that is given to an injured or sick person until the services of a doctor can be procured. Each teacher should understand simple first-aid procedures. A teacher should avail himself of the opportunity to study first-aid procedures through the Red Cross training program or other authorized agency if he has not previously received this training or if a long period of time has elapsed since such training. Each teacher should own a first-aid manual or book for reference and study. Space permits a listing here of only a few general rules to follow in case of an emergency:

1. Have the victim remain in a lying position. Do not allow him to move around.

2. Examine patient for severe bleeding or asphyxia. Also be alert for injuries to various parts of the body. If multiple injuries exist, treat serious bleeding first. If patient is not breathing, start artificial respiration at once.

3. Make the patient as comfortable as possible and keep him warm. Do not allow bystanders to disturb by crowding or making unnecessary remarks. Do not let them attempt to give treatment.

4. Provide the person who is sent to call a doctor with general information as to nature of injury.

5. Do not give the patient anything to drink if he is unconscious. Do not move him unless it is safe and absolutely necessary.

6. Only a doctor can treat—the teacher administers first aid. This fact should always be kept in mind. The teacher should remain calm and do the preliminary job as well as possible.

Insurance. The teacher should be interested in at least two types of insurance. He should have a policy to protect himself against liability suits and should also be interested in seeing that the children and parents are adequately protected.

Until sane, harmless laws become a part of the legal structure of every state and thus make school districts financially responsible for all law suits, each teacher should be interested in having his or her own liability policy to protect against claims. Such insurance is available at a nominal fee. For $15 a year some policies give protection up to $25,000 against one's own negligence. This insurance is very important since damages awarded often run into thousands of dollars. In purchasing liability insurance, however, it is important to examine the various provisions very carefully. An attorney's advice would be helpful in obtaining the insurance that best protects the teacher.

The teacher should also be interested in seeing that the school has a written policy in regard to financial and other responsibilities associated with injuries. The administrator, parents, and students should be thoroughly familiar with the responsibilities of each in regard to injuries.

Every school should be adequately protected by insurance. In general there are five types of accident insurance in use. Two types are commercial insurance policies—those written on an individual basis and others written on a group basis in the form of student medical-benefit plans. The other three types are medical-benefit plans operated by specific school systems, high school athletic association plans, and self-insurance.

Before a school selects an insurance policy, a careful study should be made of the various types of policy available. After the type of policy which fits the needs of a particular school is selected, several insurance companies should be contacted to determine their coverage and costs. In light of this information, the one that best meets the needs of the school should be determined. After purchasing insurance there should be periodic re-evaluation of the protection that is being given. To help in this appraisal careful records should be kept in regard to all costs, claims, payments, and other pertinent data.

Teaching Health Education

Motivation, suggested methods, materials, challenge, and general hints for health and education are all most important in the successful teaching of health education. There are many suggestions for teaching health education, both directly stated and implied, in Chapter 15. Therefore, the reader should reread this material.

Motivation. Regardless of the excellence of planning, programs of health education will become meaningful to the child only when there is successful teaching. When learning or a mastery of facts can be taken out of context and become *his*, to accept and use, when he has developed desirable attitudes and demonstrates them by improved health practices, and when he is applying scientific knowledge that he has learned for the solution of his problems—only then may we feel we have succeeded.

Motivation, perhaps, is the key to successful teaching once well-planned units and lessons have been prepared. To motivate requires using incentives that are meaningful to the student—meaningful today and not concerned only with what he will need tomorrow. If we can show a direct relationship between the effect of desirable health habits and the ego needs and desires, we may be successful. When a child's immediate goal cannot be accomplished because of illness, lack of strength and vitality, or other health reasons, he will be more inclined to apply the knowledge he has learned to his behavior and use good health practices. For example, if a child is keenly interested in playing with the little league team and cannot do so because he missed too many practices and games because of bad colds or an upset stomach, he may well become interested in applying what he has learned to help prevent the disqualifying condition. But if he has no such intense interest in an activity or project, he may see no need to apply his knowledge of health.

If teachers can discover today's needs, interests, and hopes of children, these can be successfully exploited in teaching health education. Self-made goals are strong in motivation value. Tomorrow's goals and special desires are also very important. If a child wishes to become an athlete, to attend a military academy, to become a doctor or a nurse—these interests help as incentives. Teachers must remember that desires change with age, hence motivations and incentives must change also.

Health education deals with specific facts. These must always be carefully selected for the teacher's use. The results of years of research have given us these facts. A teacher must be able to interpret them and help students distinguish truth and fact from the untruths presented in print and in audio-visual media.

The approach in teaching health must be positive. If correct facts are taught, what effect will their application have on the child? How will they effect his life—directly and indirectly? What studies have been done to prove whether more cancer and heart disease occurs among heavy smokers? Answers to such questions are necessary in order to change the attitudes of students.

Effective health education is dependent to a large degree on the interest and enthusiasm of the teacher. A well-prepared and informed teacher enjoys teaching. Perhaps some teachers in elementary schools do not show interest and enthusiasm because they feel unprepared. These teachers need to seek help from the consultants in their school or district.

School administrators and teachers should work for a healthful school environment—safe buildings, equipment, and playgrounds; cleanliness within buildings, lavatories, and locker rooms; emergency services needed for illness and accidents; medical and dental examinations. In addition, the correct mental and emotional atmosphere and correct heating and lighting must be present in every classroom. These surely are minimal requirements to insure the possibility of practicing desirable health habits in correct environmental situations while children are attending school.

Methods of Teaching Health. Methods in health education will determine to a great degree the outcomes achieved. They should be adapted to the group being taught, be compatible with the objectives sought, stimulate interest among the pupils, be capable of being used by the teacher, be adaptable to available space, equipment, and time in the school program, and be capable of use with the health activities that comprise the educational offering. Children usually like variety, so several different methods should be used rather than just one. Some of the better-known methods for the elementary school health program are listed below.

Problem Solving. Problem solving is one of the most effective and best methods. It can be utilized with nearly all health topics. An example of a health problem is "What are the effects of smoking on health?" After stating the problem to the class a systematic approach is utilized by the pupils to obtain the answer. For example, a problem could be treated step by step in this manner:

1. Stating the nature and scope of the problem.
2. Defining the various possible solutions to the problem.
3. Collecting scientific information to support each of the various aspects of the problem.
4. Analyzing the information and data gathered as to their source, authoritativeness, date of origin, and other pertinent factors.
5. Drawing conclusions on the basis of the information gathered.
6. Applying conclusions to the solution of the problem.

Class Discussions. Probably the most common method used is class discussion and group interaction on a particular health topic.

Textbook. Assigned readings in a textbook with a discussion based on these readings is a common method.

Construction Activities. In construction activities, students build something which will help enlighten them on health problems. For example, they may build a model of an ideal kitchen showing provisions for proper cooking of food and food handling.

Field Trips. Trips to such places as a dairy, health clinic, hospital, police station, or some other place which has health implications are effective teaching methods.

Demonstrations. Demonstrations can provide a visual picture of certain health and safety concepts. For example, rules of the road could be demonstrated to a class of children who ride bicycles.

Experiments. An example of a common experiment is to see what happens to the growth of animals with different types of diets.

Panels and Forums. A panel of students or outside specialists presents reports or discusses some health topic during class.

Class Committees. The class is divided into

committees and topics are assigned for exploration.

Exhibits. An exhibit of various types of bandages that can be used in cases of first aid is an example of this method.

Dramatizations. A play can be put on by a class, for example, to bring to the pupils' attention the importance of safety on the playground.

Independent Study. Each student might go to the library after being assigned a particular health topic for which he or she is supposed to gather as much information as possible.

Resource People. A doctor, dentist, health commissioner, or some other specialist can be invited to speak to the class.

Audiovisual Aids. Films, tapes, recordings, movies, and other kinds of audiovisual aids can be used for class presentation.

The Joint Committee on Health Problems in Education of the National Education Association and the American Medical Association has listed some of the health instruction activities in which pupils in the intermediate grades can engage:

Conducting animal feeding experiments and experiments to test food nutrients.

Taking field trips to local dairies, markets, restaurants, bakeries, water supply and sewage treatment plants, and housing projects.

Visiting museums.

Preparing charts and graphs for visualizing class statistics, such as absences due to colds or school accidents.

Making pin maps of sources of mosquitoes, rubbish depositories, and slum areas.

Making health posters.

Setting up room and corridor health exhibits.

Preparing health bulletin boards and displays.

Making murals and dioramas.

Maintaining class temperature charts.

Arranging a library corner of health materials on the subject being studied.

Using sources of printed material—reference books, texts, bulletins, newspapers, and magazines—for the study of a particular topic.

Giving reports in various ways—chalkboard talks, dramatizations, role-playing, and panels.

Serving on the safety patrol.

Joining the bicycle safety club.

Participating in a home or school clean-up campaign.

Sharing health programs with primary grades.

Planning menus.

Preparing meals for class mothers or other guests.

Securing a health examination.

Having all dental corrections made.

Taking innoculations.

Keeping records of growth through charts or graphs.

Keeping diaries of health practices, studying texts or references to find answers to problems.

Thinking through solutions to problems. Applying health principles learned.[1]

Material Aids for Health Teaching. There are many material aids for health teaching. The elementary school teacher should be familiar with these various pictures, charts, films, and other materials that can be obtained from governmental sources, health agencies, professional societies, business groups, and other organizations. This section provides a brief discussion of the various aids that are available and where they can be obtained. The teacher should use material aids that are adapted to her students' interests, age, and experience and which help to clarify the health material covered.

Textbooks, Encyclopedias, Study Guides, Workbooks, and Printed Matter. Textbooks and other printed materials used in the elementary school must be selected with care if they are to be effective teaching aids. It would be wise for the elementary school teacher and the physical education specialist to review with the state education department the list of criteria they have developed for the adoption and use of textbooks. Also, some professional associations have prepared such criteria. The criteria commonly applied to the selection of printed materials include content which is scientifically accurate, good organization of material, material related to age group and needs of children, interest appeal, attractive presentation, and a layout that includes type which is easy to read with good paper stock and illustrations.

[1] Joint Committee on Health Problems in Education of The National Education Association and The American Medical Association, *Health Education*, Washington, D.C., 1961.

Posters, Flash Cards, and Flip Charts. There are many posters available for health teaching about various topics that are related to the elementary level. Such posters should be accurate in content, be simple, have appeal, possess balance, attract attention, and, of course, convey a message which is necessary for the child. Flash cards which can be used to flash certain information before the pupils and flip charts on nutrition and other such topics also have a place in the classroom.

Still Pictures. Still pictures include such illustrative material as filmstrips, lantern slides, charts, and prints. They are readily available from a number of sources for use in the schools. Filmstrips are increasingly being produced by professional health agencies as well as many commercial agencies. They are convenient, require little equipment, and usually carry 20 to 50 pictures on a strip, which makes it possible to cover considerable material. In connection with still pictures, the opaque projector has great value since charts, graphs, reports, and other materials can be projected on a screen in the classroom for all to see.

Motion Pictures. The motion picture attracts much interest among persons of all ages. The action that can be presented and the material covered has great value if proper pictures are selected. Films can motivate, inform, and educate youngsters in regard to health. They are available from state departments of health, university film libraries, commercial houses, and various health agencies. Furthermore, the *United States Office of Education Film Library Directory* lists a great many excellent films.

Flannelboards, Bulletin Boards, Chalkboards, and Magnetic Boards. A piece of velvet cloth stretched over a piece of wood or masonite provides an excellent place to attach pictures and other materials for use in the classroom. A bulletin board is also a suitable place to post materials that have been clipped from newspapers, magazines, and various periodicals. Furthermore, chalk-boards always provide an accessible spot in the typical classroom to record meaningful health material. Magnetic boards are also available to many teachers.

Radio and Television. Radio and television have many possibilities for the health education program. Radios in the classroom are inexpensive and there are many programs that feature health lectures and other programs worth listening to. Furthermore, there are many opportunities to broadcast school programs to the community at large. Television for health purposes has been enhanced by the great number of educational television channels that have been activated throughout the country. Furthermore, closed-circuit television has possibilities in many school systems that use it. Through such a medium, outstanding resource people and other programs can be utilized which otherwise might not be possible.

Recordings. Recordings on both phonograph records and tape have proved to be of value to health teachers. There are many fine records which are on the market and suitable for classroom work. Also, tape recordings can be made of speeches, radio programs, or special presentations and later played back to a class.

Collections. A health class can collect such things as insects, frogs, pictures, plants, teeth of animals, bones, and other items which have health implications. For children to see, at first hand, various animate or inanimate objects which have health implications makes it possible for them to identify much more readily with these objects.

Models. Models play a very important part in health instruction. To have a model of the human body that shows the various muscles and vital organs makes it much more interesting and understandable for children. There are other models which relate to health that can be made by the children themselves, such as houses, filtration plants, and traffic situations for safety purposes.

Stick Drawings, Cartoons, Sketches, and Related Materials. Many times, visual aids in the forms of cartoons, drawings, and sketches make it possible to present health material in a much more vivid form than would otherwise be possible. Such materials can be found in magazines, newspapers, and other periodicals or they can be made up by the school art department, teachers, or the pupils themselves.

Miscellaneous Materials. Some other materials which may be used in health education are scrapbooks, pamphlets, manikins, mobiles, question boxes, food samples, first-aid supplies, mirrors, microscopes, comics, puppets, health records, bicycles, museums, and writing pads.

Sources of Health Materials. There are many agencies, business concerns, health departments, and other organizations where free or inexpensive health materials may be procured by the teacher. It would take up much valuable space to list all these sources. Instead, a partial listing of where such materials are available is given. The teacher should investigate further if the list does not meet his or her needs.

Schools and Universities. The teacher should explore his or her own school library and public library. These often have needed materials or will order them upon request. In addition to books and other printed materials, many libraries stock such items as recordings and films. Any nearby university is an additional source of materials.

The elementary school teacher should be sure to determine the availability of materials from the health education specialist, the health coordinator, the physical education director, and the coordinator of audio-visual materials in the local school system.

Official Health and Educational Agencies. Official health agencies such as the local health department are excellent sources for help and materials. At the county, state, and national levels there are also many official agencies. State departments of education, state health departments, the United States Department of Health, Education, and Welfare, the Public Health Service, the Childrens Bureau, and the United States Office of Education are examples of source agencies that will be helpful in furnishing materials. On the international scene, such agencies as the World Health Organization will be of help.

Professional Societies and Voluntary Health Organizations. There are many professional societies and voluntary health organizations such as the American Dental Association, the American School Health Association, the American Association for Health, Physical Education, and Recreation, the American Academy of Pediatrics, the American Hearing Association, the American Public Health Association, the American Association for Mental Health, Inc., and the National Safety Council that will be happy to be of assistance.

Commercial Concerns. Several commercial concerns have made it a practice to publish health materials. This is especially true of insurance companies, cereal producers, toothpaste manufacturers, citrus growers, and athletic groups. Such material should be evaluated in light of the commercial and advertising purposes associated with it.

Some Sources of Free or Inexpensive Materials. Free or inexpensive materials are available from the following sources:

American Association for Health, Physical Education, and Recreation, 1201 16th Street, Washington, D.C. 20036.

American Automobile Association, Inc., 1712 G Street, N.W., Washington, D.C. 20036.

American Cancer Society, 219 East 42nd St., New York, N.Y. 10017.

American Dental Association, 211 East Chicago Ave., Chicago, Ill. 60011.

American Hearing Society, 919 18th Street, Washington, D.C. 20006.

American Heart Association, 44 East 23rd Street, New York, N.Y. 10010.

American Medical Association, 535 North Dearborn Street, Chicago, Ill. 60610.

American National Red Cross, Washington, D.C. 20036.

American Public Health Association, 1790 Broadway, New York, N.Y. 10019.

American School Health Association, 515 East Main Street, Kent, Ohio 44240.

Athletic Institute, 209 South State Street, Chicago, Ill. 60604.

Cereal Institute, Inc., 135 LaSalle Street, Chicago, Ill. 60602.

Child Welfare League of America, 44 East 23rd St., New York, N.Y. 10021.

Equitable Life Assurance Society of the United States, 1285 Avenue of Americas, New York, N.Y. 10019.

Joint Committee on Health Problems in Education of the National Education Association and the American Medical Association, 1201 16th Street, Washington, D.C. 20036.

Metropolitan Life Insurance Company, 1 Madison Avenue, New York, N.Y. 10010.

National Association for Mental Health, 10 Columbus Circle, New York, N.Y. 10011.

National Dairy Council, 111 North Canal Street, Chicago, Ill. 60606.

National Education Association, 1201 16th Street, Washington, D.C. 20036.

National Foundation, 800 Second Avenue, New York, N.Y. 10017.

National Safety Council, 425 North Michigan Avenue, Chicago, Ill. 60611.

National Society for the Prevention of Blindness, 1790 Broadway, New York, N.Y. 10023.

National Tuberculosis Association, 1790 Broadway, New York, N.Y. 10023.

Parke-Davis Company, Detroit, Mich.

Public Affairs Pamphlets, 381 Park Ave., South, New York, N.Y. 10021.

Science Research Associates, Inc., 57 West Grand Avenue, Chicago, Ill. 60610.

Some Publishers of Textbooks for Elementary School Health Education. The following publish textbooks for elementary school health education:

American Book Company, New York, N.Y.

The Bobbs-Merrill Company, Inc., Indianapolis, Ind.

Ginn and Company, Boston, Mass.

Laidlaw Brothers, River Forest, Ill.

Lyons and Carnahan, Chicago, Ill.

Scott, Foresman and Company, Chicago, Ill.

The L. S. Singer Company, Syracuse, N.Y.

The John C. Winston Company, Philadelphia, Pa.

The Teaching Challenge. A teacher should select various methods for health instruction and combine those she finds best applicable to her students with respect to their age, skills, and ability. The methods selected must reflect all that is known concerning the learning process and meet all educationally sound objectives and the objectives of her health unit. The teacher must take all individual differences into account and contribute the most possible to each child. Children must be wholly involved in problem solving and be given the opportunity to use the best available resource materials. The teacher must choose the methods which will be most adaptable to the time allotted for health teaching and to available facilities and teaching aids, and also those with which she feels most comfortable and which utilize her strengths. Her methods must be the best means for fulfilling the desired goals or objectives. Variety many times increases student interest.

The successful teacher, regardless of her methods and approach, not only contributes rewarding experiences to her children but creates happiness and enthusiasm and sees the application of their learning to everyday life.

The teacher may contribute to the educational experiences of children by having consultants visit the classroom. The teacher can be assisted by consultants in analyzing and interpreting data which she and her children have collected in their study and work. This becomes especially helpful in the problem-solving method. The use of consultants and field experiences are excellent links between the school and the community.

All teaching in health education must work toward operational and desirable health habits.

Some desirable basic health teaching guides are:

1. Emphasize the positive not the negative approach.
2. Endeavor to reach each individual in order to make him desire to use his findings for the improvement of his own health.
3. Use various teaching methods depending on age and ability of the children in your group and those with which you are most successful.
4. Teach that which is especially needed by your group and make it a meaningful reality, able to be applied after the learning period.
5. Correlate and integrate health education and experiences with other parts of the curriculum.
6. Avoid the measurement of knowledge per se.
7. Be certain all materials used and facts taught are correct.
8. Teach health education as a means of helping children live better today and tomorrow.
9. Teach health education so it is interesting and fun.
10. Help children to know the correct facts or where to find them in order that they may make meaningful decisions concerning their health today and continue the application to their family and community tomorrow.
11. Work closely with parents of children because children can effectually use only the knowledge and habits permitted by their parents. It is necessary for the parents to know each unit of work being presented in health in order for them to assist the child in the home.
12. Evaluate your teaching and change materials and methods according to your findings.
13. Make use of all audio-visual aids, consultants, field experiences, and meaning-

ful acceptable educational media to create interest.

These practices should be avoided:

1. Do not give awards of any kind or establish contests concerning health patterns and practices. Common among these are stars for clean teeth, charts indicating foods eaten each day, and recognition for good rest habits.
2. Do not try to shock children in the hope that they will become health conscious as a result.
3. Do not permit children to become overly critical of each other. This is particularly important when groups are from families in different areas and of different cultural and socioeconomic backgrounds.
4. Avoid overemphasis. Children tire of the same thing and constant drill. We know too much may be as ineffective as too little. If a teacher knows her group she can well realize how much emphasis will be accepted.
5. Do not teach one thing and do another, or fail to permit children to practice in school that which is taught. One example of this is found in schools where children are taught to wash their hands before eating, yet they are never afforded the opportunity before going to lunch. The lack of time cannot be accepted as a logical excuse. If it is important to teach and learn, it is important to use the learning in the school.
6. Never destroy children's natural desire to learn and their curiosity by making health education boring and dull. Today more than ever we have many opportunities to make health teaching interesting and meaningful. The care of an animal in the classroom, plots of land usable for gardens, visits by community doctors or dentists, field trips and audio-visual materials are but a few media which help create and maintain much interest.
7. Do not teach the same subject matter in all grade and age levels. Make the program progressive.
8. Do not present adages and superstitions as truths. If children question those learned elsewhere, use the opportunity as a means to teach.

Guides to Good Teaching. Good teaching does not just happen—it requires planning with meaningful concepts in mind.

Some general guides for successful teaching are:

1. Be mindful that teachers and students are striving for common goals—to find and identify problems and to learn through these experiences; to evaluate and put in use their findings.
2. Keep the individual differences and rates of learning of children in mind in all teaching.
3. Work toward accomplishments which will give challenge and bring satisfaction to each child.
4. Make all teaching purposeful by being reality-centered.
5. Use various means of motivation and inspiring interest in the problem at hand.
6. Try to keep the teaching environment pupil-centered, not teacher-dominated.

Questions and Practical Problems

1. Plan exactly how you would interest the children in your class so they would want to organize in squads.

2. How can squad organization be helpful in other parts of the curriculum?

3. Select three games from the primary, intermediate, and upper areas which are of the elimination type. Make necessary revisions in order that all children may participate throughout the playing of entire games.

4. "Joy and satisfaction accompany success and are desirous emotional responses" is an accepted educational belief. Relate this to physical education activities.

5. It has been believed that progress is apt to be more rapid and pleasurable when a child gains satisfaction and fun from his experiences. Can this be made possible in physical education? in health education? in safety education?

6. Investigate the laws of your state and

write a report on the legal responsibility of teachers to children.

7. List some instances under which a teacher would be negligent in his or her conduct of physical education classes. Show how the procedure could be corrected.

8. Make a list of safety procedures that should be followed by the teacher in the gymnasium, locker room, playground, swimming pool, halls, and classroom.

9. Prepare a health unit for the grade of your choice on a topic suitable for the age and grade level.

10. Select a health knowledge test and evaluate the health knowledge of a sixth grade.

Selected References

American Association of Health, Physical Education, and Recreation. *School Safety Policies: With Emphasis on Physical Education, Athletics and Recreation.* American Association of Health, Physical Education, and Recreation, Washington, D.C.: 1967.

BEYRER, M. K., A. E. NOLTE, and M. K. SOLLEDER, *A Directory of Selected References and Resources for Health Instruction.* Minneapolis, Minn.: Burgess Publishing Co., 1966.

BUCHER, CHARLES A. *Administration of the School Health and Physical Education Programs* (Fifth Edition). St. Louis: The C. V. Mosby Co., 1971.

GROUT, RUTH E. *Health Teaching in Schools for Teachers in Elementary and Secondary Schools* (Fifth Edition). Philadelphia: W. B. Saunders Company, 1968.

HAAG, JESSIE HELEN. *School Health Program* (Revised Edition). New York: Holt, Rinehart and Winston, Inc., 1965.

JENKINS, GLADYS G. "These are Your Children." *Journal of Health, Physical Education, and Recreation,* Vol. 37, No. 9, Nov–Dec. 1966, p. 34.

KURTZMAN, JOSEPH. "Legal Liability and Physical Education." *The Physical Educator,* Vol. 24, No. 1, March 1967, pp. 20–22.

LOCKHART, AILEENE. "Conditions of Effective Motor Learning." *Journal of Health, Physical Education, and Recreation,* Vol. 38, No. 2, Feb. 1967, pp. 36–39.

LONG, ALBERT C. "Integration of Safety in the Physical Education Curriculum." *The Physical Educator,* Vol. 25, No. 2, May 1968, pp. 82–84.

National Safety Council, School and College Conference, Elementary School Section, Lois Clark, editor. "The Distinctive Role of the Elementary School in Education for Safe Living, a Statement of Belief." *Journal of Health, Physical Education, and Recreation,* Vol. 37, No. 7, Sept. 1966, p. 32.

OLIVER, JAMES N. "Add Challenge with Variety in Activities." *Journal of Health, Physical Education, and Recreation,* Vol. 37, No. 4, April 1966, pp. 30–32.

PITCHFORD, K. "How You Can Become a Master Teacher." *Journal of Health, Physical Education, and Recreation,* Vol. 31, No. 2, Feb. 1960, pp. 30–31.

SALT, E. BENTON, et al. *Teaching Physical Education in the Elementary School* (Second Edition). New York: The Ronald Press Company, 1960.

SCHNEIDER, ROBERT E. *Methods and Materials of Health Education* (Second Edition). Philadelphia: W. B. Saunders Company, 1964.

STRASSER, MARLAND K., JAMES E. AARON, RALPH BOHN, and JOHN CALES. *Fundamentals of Safety Education.* New York: The Macmillan Company, 1964.

VANNIER, MARYHELEN, and MILDRED FOSTER. *Teaching Physical Education in Elementary Schools* (Third Edition). Philadelphia: W. B. Saunders Company, 1963.

WILLGOOSE, CARL E. "White House Conference on Health, November 3–4, 1965, Washington, D.C." *Journal of Health, Physical Education, and Recreation,* Vol. 37, No. 1, Jan. 1966, p. 14.

YOST, CHARLES PETER. "Total Fitness and Prevention of Accidents." *Journal of Health, Physical Education, and Recreation,* Vol. 38, No. 3, March 1967, pp. 32–37.

CHAPTER 18

Audio-Visual Materials and Other Special Aids

Auditory and visual materials are being utilized on an increasingly large scale in American schools and colleges. The current *Educational Media Index* lists over 60,000 entries of such nonbook instructional materials as flat pictures, graphs, maps, films, records, slides, video tapes, transparencies for the overhead projector, and charts. Each year finds more records, tapes, transcriptions, and other audio materials being used. The index of commercial enterprises that are involved in the manufacture and sale of such materials to schools and colleges is also growing rapidly with the increased demand for such materials.

The elementary schools utilize audio-visual materials and other special aids. Educators know that sensory experiences provided by such media make cognitive learning much more effective. Educators know that the teacher who merely gives reading assignments and talks in class will not provide the opportunity for learning that is necessary for the fullest development of the many concepts, skills, and attitudes that represent educational goals for children. Educators realize that children can profit greatly from listening and looking at selective audio-visual materials.

Teachers of physical education and health education, as is the case in other areas in the elementary school curriculum, also have found that they can profit from using the many materials and resources that are readily available. The teaching of skills, the development of concepts relating to good health habits, and a better understanding of the human organism can be brought about in a much more meaningful manner with the use of such materials. The health or physical education teacher who is familiar with and utilizes a variety of audio-visual materials is adding more interest and meaning to his or her teaching.

Purposes of Audio-Visual Aids

Some purposes for the use of audio-visual materials and other special aids include the following:

1. *They make possible a better understanding of concepts, events, and experiences that cannot be studied at first hand by the student.* The teacher may discuss how the human heart functions or how to play a new game, for example, but neither may be very clear in the pupil's mind because he cannot visualize what actually takes place. With

271

the use of a film, pictures, or other materials, however, a clearer understanding is developed in the mind of the student. He has actually seen or heard something take place. He now has a much better idea of what it is all about.

2. *They provide motivation for participation and further study.* As a result of getting a clearer picture of the topic under consideration together with information that affords personal identification with the subject, the student is more likely to be motivated to engage in a game or acquire a skill. His curiosity is aroused and he has a desire to learn more about the subject, whether it is developing skill in the broad jump or finding out what happens to an ice cream sundae after it enters his stomach.

3. *They help in the retention of material.* Presenting facts and information in different forms and settings enables the student to retain the material longer than when it is presented only in a classroom lesson. The utilization of various audio-visual techniques by the teacher along with other teaching methods assures more effective learning and greater retention of the material to which the student has been exposed.

4. *They help to provide a variety of teaching techniques.* The interest span of children can be extended and boredom more easily eliminated when a variety of techniques is used, including the use of audio-visual and other materials.

5. *They provide for economy of time on the part of both teacher and student.* Some materials will be learned more readily by using audio-visual aids with the result that both the teacher's and the student's time will be saved. The time consumed by the teacher in imparting information and the time consumed by the pupil in learning this information will therefore be reduced.

6. *They provide an extension of direct classroom experience.* The use of films and recordings, for example, enables the student to be taken to other lands, outside the world in which he lives from day to day, and other places where the scope of his experience can be broadened much more than through the traditional classroom approach.

7. *They can tell a story involving many experiences that have taken place over a period of time.* The impact of smoking on an individual over the course of several years, the results of effective training procedures on an athlete during a sports season, or other events that occur over a space of months and years can be condensed into a film that can be shown in one class period. A story can be told in a limited amount of time that carries a meaningful message for the student.

Classification of Audio-Visual Materials and Other Special Aids

The following represents a listing and classification of audio-visual materials and other special aids that the health or physical education teacher will find useful in his or her work.

Visual Aids

Reading Materials. Many reading materials can be utilized in both health and physical education—such as encyclopedias, almanacs, dictionaries, newspapers, magazines, and sport stories. This material will provide additional information on such health topics as dental caries or personal grooming or on such physical education activities as folk dancing in the Philippines or physical fitness in California. Of course, well-illustrated textbooks are also important teaching aids.

Chalkboards. Chalkboards are common equipment in the classroom and gymnasium. They have many uses such as presenting an outline that summarizes a class discussion, a quotation written by the teacher, a particular formation for a physical education activity, or the basic four groups of food in a study of nutrition.

Wall Charts. Wall charts are large displays that can be hung on a wall. They come in black and white and also in color. They can show, for example, several pictures, illustrating the sequence in performing a particular stunt such as a forward roll or the route of the blood through the heart.

Flat Pictures, Cartoons, Posters, Photographs. Black-and-white or colored pictures, photographs, cartoons, and posters secured from outside sources, when displayed in school, will add interest and color to the classroom on a variety of health and physical education topics from dancing to first aid.

Graphs. Graphs can be utilized to summarize a variety of health and physical education materials or to compare findings of research studies on various subjects. Bar, circle, and line graphs can be used effectively for showing, for example, death rates for those persons who smoke and do not smoke and for those who exercise regularly and those who do not.

Maps and Globes. Maps and globes can provide a better understanding of such things as where the Olympic Games are being held, where the best surfing waters are in the world, or where the world traffic in drugs and narcotics takes place.

Bulletin Boards. Bulletin boards provide a medium for notifying students of coming events, or posting schedules of activities, squad lists, club news, clippings of interesting events, achievement standards, health rules, safety mottoes, and other items that are important for any health and physical education program.

Magnetic and Flannel Boards. Magnetic and Flannel Boards are similar to bulletin boards but have additional qualities that make them functional in health and physical education programs. Magnetic boards are magnetized so that metal disks that represent players in a game or items of food, for example, may be organized so as to demonstrate a play or show what constitutes a well-balanced meal. Flannel boards are made of flannel, felt, velvet, or suede, permitting displays of cutouts backed with strips of sandpaper which will cling to the board.

Models and Specimens. Models, as of gymnasiums, playgrounds, or specialized facilities for various activities, can be used for planning a field day or special event. Model figures can be valuable as aids in the teaching of such things as body mechanics or movement principles. Specimens, as of baseball in various stages of manufacture (to show how it is made) or some kind of insect that transmits germs, may also be helpful.

Opaque Projector. The opaque projector is used to display on a screen an enlarged picture that is too small in the original for all students to readily see and understand its message. It can be used for flat pictures, cartoons, posters, etc. Also, handwritten material may be projected.

Overhead Projector. The overhead projector is a compact, lightweight machine that can be operated with ease. The material that is projected is in the form of a transparency, made of film that can either be purchased in prepared form or reproduced by a copying machine from the original document, such as a map, diagram, play, etc.

Stereoscopes. Stereoscopes are machines that project a picture in three dimensions and thus give a better understanding of the space relationships pertinent to some subjects that may be discussed in a health or physical education class.

Silent Films. Silent films are not as popular since the advent of sound but there may still be some use for them when students, for example, make their own films of subjects or activities that relate directly to what is being taught in the classroom or gymnasium. Such films may provide an excellent teaching device for the class.

Slides. Generally speaking, there are three types of slide. There is the regular 35 mm. individual slide encased in a cardboard holder; the lantern slide that is larger, usually $3\frac{1}{4}''$ by $4''$, and the lantern slide that may be prepared for immediate use by a Polaroid transparency film.

Filmstrips. Filmstrips provide a series of photographs that show a step-by-step process or procedure for illustrating such subjects, for example, as plant and animal life or how to float in the water.

Loop Films. Loop films are available in cartridges which can be inserted into a projector and shown with comparative ease, never requiring rewinding. Subjects are available pertaining to many activities in the physical education field. There are three types of loop films—a free 8 mm. loop film that can be shown in an 8 mm. projector, an 8 mm. cartridge film encased in a plastic cartridge that requires a special projector, and the super 8 mm. encased in a plastic cartridge that requires a still different type of projection. The cartridge type of loop film is gaining great popularity among physical education teachers in this country.

Motion Pictures. Many motion pictures in the fields of health and physical education are available for projection. Films may be obtained on a free or rental basis from voluntary agencies, industries, public or governmental agencies, and many other sources.

Television. Television offers many opportunities for more effective and dynamic teaching. Educational television stations, closed circuit television, and the use of the kinescope recorder have unlimited potential. Video-tape recording that enables a student to actually see how he performs a particular skill has proved effective in the teaching of motor skills.

Audio Aids

Radio. In addition to many interesting health, physical education, and sports programs that are regularly heard on the air, educational radio programs are scheduled periodically in many states. In some cases specialists in health or physical education do radio teaching and even supply teacher manuals to cover various topics like nutrition and rhythm and games.

Records and Transcriptions. Important events, speeches, musical productions, and the music for dances are recorded and made available at relatively low cost. Records and transcriptions may be stored easily and then used when needed.

Tape Recordings. Special events that are held in the school or community can be recorded and used to appraise student progress in conduct, skills, concepts, and appreciation and to cover current happenings pertinent to subjects under consideration in the classroom or gymnasium.

Other Resources. Other resources, in addition to the audio-visual aids that have been discussed, are usually readily available in the community where the school is located. The alert teacher will know how they can be most effectively used.

Human Resources. Most communities have residents who are specialists in various areas of health and physical education. These individuals may be persons who work in voluntary or official health agencies, in a dairy or manufacturing concern, or in some other specialty. In physical education it could be individuals like a professional dancer, a physical-fitness enthusiast, or a gymnast. To utilize such human resources most effectively, it is important to know how your visitor can best contribute, to explain to the grade level involved and the contribution he can make, to inform the children in your class about the visit, and to follow through after the visit to correct any misconceptions and to determine what has been accomplished.

Physical Resources. The field trip is a valuable teaching tool. A field trip to a police station, a doctor's office, or a dance studio can provide many new insights for the students. In planning a field trip the potential advantages should be considered, the purpose of the trip should be clear, and the concepts that will be reinforced by the trip should be understood by both teacher and students. Also, necessary arrangements with school authorities and representatives of places to be visited should be made in advance. There should also be an evaluation after the trip has been taken.

The Elementary School Library. Another resource that should not be overlooked is the school library. Books and other materials should be available in health and physical education that will meet the needs of all children—the culturally disadvantaged, the gifted, the average, the slow learner, etc. There should be a wide selection which offers opportunities for reference on class topics and also for the pleasure of reading. In addition to the necessary reading materials, there should be adequate guidance in how to use the library, proper leadership to supervise the library, and opportunities for teacher and librarians to discuss books with children.

Advantages and Disadvantages of Selected Visual Materials

Since there has been much interest in visual aids during recent years, many teachers of health and physical education are asking what visual aids they should use. In order to help the teacher to understand the various aids available and the advantages and disadvantages of each, this section is presented.

Chalkboards and Bulletin Boards
Advantages
1. To supplement instruction.
2. Will attract attention of students.
3. Inexpensive.
4. Easily transported from place to place.
5. Information and material on boards can easily be changed.

Disadvantages
1. Cannot be used to show movement realistically.
2. Use of color on a chalkboard is difficult even with colored chalk.
3. Individual teacher's skill and ingenuity is a limiting factor in some cases.

Wall Charts
Advantages
1. Will attract attention of students.
2. Inexpensive.

Audio-Visual Materials and Other Special Aids

3. Commercially available for many subjects and activities in health and physical education.
4. Provide for a sequence of pictures such as actions involved in the performance of a skill.
5. May be left on wall for as long a period of time as needed.
6. Artistically designed in many cases.

Disadvantages
1. Cannot simulate movement.
2. Usually made in black and white.
3. Student may have difficulty in identifying with activity illustrated and in a self-analysis of his difficulty.

The Opaque Projector

Advantages
1. Simple to operate.
2. Usually provides for a built-in pointer that can be used by instructor to identify points of interest.
3. Unlimited use in projecting anything from a page in a book to a picture that relates to the topic under discussion.
4. Provides a good picture for classroom use.
5. Newer models are convertible to lantern or 35 mm. projection.
6. Effective way of supplementing teacher's presentations.

Disadvantages
1. Cannot simulate motion.
2. More expensive than many still-action-projection media.

The Overhead Projector

Advantages
1. May be used without darkening setting.
2. May be projected on walls or screens from 30 to 40 feet away.
3. Permits projection of transparencies.
4. Transparencies may be superimposed for means of comparison.
5. Transparencies may be purchased commercially on a variety of subjects or can be made by the creative teacher.
6. Transparencies may be black and white or colored.
7. Transparencies are easily stored.
8. Equipment can be transported easily from setting to setting.
9. Equipment does not require a skilled operator.
10. Projector maintenance is minor.
11. Acetate rolls up to 30 feet permit the projection of a series of stunts or subjects.

Disadvantage
1. Transparencies do not permit the projection of movement.

Slides

Advantages
1. Pictures can be taken and made into slides by the average person.
2. May be projected on screens, walls of classrooms, and other places like gymnasium walls.
3. Equipment is easily transported from place to place.
4. May be ready for use shortly after pictures have been taken.
5. The order in which slides are shown may be changed at will.
6. Color adds to the attractiveness of the subjects being projected.
7. A single slide may be projected for as long as desired.

Disadvantages
1. Lack motion.
2. The performer can view only part of the performance—cannot see a sequence or pattern in performance of a skill.
3. The order of showing slides may be easily mixed up.
4. May be projected upside down thus causing lack of interest and delay in presentation.
5. Lantern slides require a special projector.

Filmstrips

Advantages
1. Have advantage over 35 mm. and lantern slides since they cannot be shown out of order.
2. Filmstrips on a variety of health and physical education subjects readily available.
3. Easy to store.
4. Provide a series of pictures that develop a single concept or idea.

Disadvantage
1. The order of the pictures cannot be changed.

Loop Films and Cartridge Films

Advantages
1. Readily procured commercially on a variety of subjects.

2. Subjects provide for excellent demonstrations of skills and other material.
3. Can provide for the continual repetition of a skill or activity, thus permitting a better understanding of the activity or skill.
4. Loop films may be produced by the average person.
5. Projectors are easy to operate.
6. Both black-and-white and color are available.
7. Equipment is easily transported from place to place.
8. Cartridge films are durable since they are very difficult to break by dropping, etc.
9. Projection may be on screens or walls.
10. Develop a concept very effectively.
11. Permit students to see entire skill or stunt.
12. Speed of projection may be altered—full speed, slow motion, or stop action.

Disadvantages
1. Cost more than many movement-projection media.
2. More than one stunt or skill may be on a film and thus cause loss of time in showing an activity not relevant to the lesson.

Motion Pictures
Advantages
1. Permit motion.
2. Motion pictures of student's performance permits comparison with that of model.
3. Provide demonstrations by experts.
4. Many health and physical education subjects available.
5. Sound and color add to the presentation.

Disadvantages
1. Films need rewinding after showing.
2. Experienced projectionist needed.
3. Expensive.
4. Require special projector.
5. Require a darkened room for best projection.

Television—Closed-Circuit
Advantages
1. Permits master teacher or performer to be seen and heard by many students located in many different classrooms or settings.
2. Closed-up shots permit a detailed and clear view of an experiment or skill, such as the ingestion of alcohol by mice or the position of hand or head in a wrestling hold.
3. Many different types of activities may be projected.

Disadvantages
1. Impersonal relationship of teacher or performer to students.
2. Does not permit interaction between students and teacher or performer.
3. Additional equipment needed in the form of TV monitors for each room or setting can prove costly.
4. Black-and-white is the usual form of projection because color is too costly.

Television—Video-Taping
Advantages
1. Permits instant replay so that performer is able to see his own performance immediately.
2. Permits slow-motion or stop-action playback so that points needing attention may be discussed by teacher.
3. Tape can be used repeatedly if desired.
4. Material can be taped previous to class for use in class presentation.

Disadvantages
1. Expensive.
2. Requires trained operators.
3. Equipment not as easily transported from place to place as some other media.

Guidelines for the Selection of Audio-Visual Materials and Other Special Aids

In health and physical education, as in any other area of the school curriculum, sound guidelines must be followed in the selection of a particular learning resource. Some that will help the health or physical educator are as follows:

1. The goals of learning should always be kept in the mind of the teacher when selecting an instructional resource. The particular material or aid should be designed to enable the children to achieve these goals more effectively. Audio-visual

materials and other special aids are educational tools and their selection should be guided by program objectives. They should also be free of objectionable commercial appeals.

2. The greater the number of sensory perceptions that are made possible through the use of a material, resource, or aid, the more effective the learning will be. Therefore, materials, resources, and aids should be selected that will add different types of sensory perception for the students' learning experiences.

3. The teacher must be involved in the use of the material, resource, or aid. No resource is automatically effective as a teaching device. In other words, materials cannot be any better than the teacher who uses them and therefore materials should be selected that enable the teacher to set the stage for effective learning.

4. The material, resource, or aid needs to be carefully evaluated before and after it is used. It should not be used just because it is available. Quality of the material should be a first consideration in its selection. Scientifically accurate content is a must.

5. The material, resource, or aid selected needs to be considered on the basis of the individual differences that exist within the class for which it is going to be used. The background experiences of each student, the skill level, the interests, and other factors are important considerations.

6. The material, resource, or aid selected must be suitable for the developmental level of the class for which it is going to be used. Young children, for example, need many concrete and firsthand experiences. The initial learning of concepts is best achieved by presenting to the learner the actual thing which the concept represents.

7. Most efficient learning takes place in motor skills when concepts are acquired prior to drill or practice on the skill. Therefore materials, resources, or aids should be selected that will help to develop underlying concepts.

8. Slow-motion and stop-action projection are best when a pattern of coordination of movements in a skill is to be taught.

9. The resource, material, or aid should appeal to the sensory capacities of the individual. Color, artistic design, and other qualities must be considered if students are to be sufficiently motivated through the use of these aids.

10. The resource, material, or aid should be timely and administratively feasible. Materials should relate to the lesson being taught or the concept being developed. They should not be injected without regard to the subject under discussion in the regular class period. Furthermore, they should be administratively feasible in light of such factors as the time it takes to utilize them effectively, the cost, and the personnel needed for their implementation.

Guidelines for Using Audio-Visual Materials and Other Special Aids

After selecting the appropriate aid or aids, it becomes imperative to use them intelligently. The following guidelines will help the teacher to obtain the greatest value from such aids:

1. Students should be prepared for the materials to be used by an adequate lead-up. The students should understand why they are being used, the concepts they are intended to develop, and what to look for in the material. As the materials are presented, points pertinent to the concept being developed should be especially mentioned. After the materials have been used an evaluation by the students should be made.

2. Teachers, other school personnel, or students who are to operate the equipment should be prepared to carry out this function efficiently and effectively. If a projector is to be used, for example, and the teacher is to operate it, the preparation for such a responsibility should take place prior to the time it is used. Furthermore, the room where the material, resource, or aid is to be used needs to be prepared.

3. Opportunities should be provided for the students to participate. When students participate during a film showing, for example, increased learning will result. Research has indicated that when questions are raised and answered while an aid is being used, when information regarding a skill is communicated to the student while the student is seeing that skill performed, and when mental practice is involved with physical practice, the learning that takes place is often increased.

4. The audio-visual materials and other special aids that are utilized should be carefully

evaluated. The materials are designed to achieve certain educational goals and therefore it should be determined whether or not these goals were accomplished. Has the utilization of this resource been worth the time and expense involved? Were the materials of a quality and accuracy that was desired? These and other questions should be asked in order to determine whether or not the material, resource, or aid should be used again.

5. Variety should be injected into the use of materials, resources, and aids. In addition to developing concepts and skills, aids can be used effectively as introductory and summary devices.

6. Materials, resources, and aids should be used to achieve educational outcomes rather than for their entertainment value.

7. Materials, resources, and aids will require different forms of presentation. The aid will need to be studied by the teacher to determine how it can be most effectively utilized in the learning situation for which it has been selected.

Evaluation Procedures

Although evaluation procedures were mentioned in the previous section, there is a need to cover them more thoroughly. An effective way for the teacher to evaluate materials, resources, and special aids is to ask a series of questions. Some of the questions that will help to determine the effectiveness of audio-visual materials and other special aids are:

1. Was the cost in terms of time and expense worthwhile?
2. Was the interest of students clearly in evidence? Was their attention held?
3. Did the students' reactions indicate they felt this was a worthwhile experience?
4. Was the material suitable to the achievement level of students?
5. Did the materials and resources present concepts in a concrete and tangible manner that was meaningful to the students?
6. Was the material or resource of high quality and accurate as to content?
7. Was the physical condition of the material satisfactory? If a film, for example, was it in good physical shape or were there constant interruptions because of physical deficiencies?
8. As a result of this experience, do the students understand better the concepts that you were trying to develop and reinforce?
9. Was the distribution of familiar material in the audio-visual aid properly allocated with respect to the new material so as to foster growth? In other words, did the student identify with the new material and associate it with past experiences?
10. Did the material or person communicate on the student's level or did the presentation "talk down" to the students?
11. Were such technical aspects as size of type, arrangement, format, color, and design of high quality?

Organizing Audio-Visual Programs

Each elementary school should have an audio-visual program, not only for the subjects of health and physical education, but also for all subject-matter areas in the curriculum. Some considerations in the establishment of such a program would include the appointment of an audio-visual committee and development of a plan of operation.

In order to get started in the right direction it is important to have several members of the faculty form themselves into an audio-visual committee. Members of the committee should include persons who are interested in and see the value of audio-visual aids, who are representative of different subject-matter areas and possibly of the school administration.

The work of the audio-visual committee would consist first of becoming well acquainted with the audio-visual field, finding out what other schools are doing and what professional associations recommend, and developing a library of excellent references on the subject of audio-visual education. Next might come a survey of what audio-visual education is currently offered in the school and the facilities, equipment, and supplies available. Selected materials might be brought in and a faculty meeting utilized to review them and their potential use in various subject-matter areas. After these preliminary steps have been taken a plan of operation should be developed.

To be workable, a plan of operation for an audio-visual program should be simple, practical, effective, meet local educational needs, be well defined, and have the support of a large segment of the school faculty and administration. Materials will be utilized slowly as their effectiveness is demonstrated for those members of the faculty who have followed a traditional approach for many years. However, through patience and understanding and making opportunities and materials readily available to the faculty, progress will be made. Any workable plan needs money so provision must be made in the school budget for the purchase of materials and for their effective use.

A workable plan of operation for an audio-visual program should also provide for the selection and purchase of audio-visual aids. The committee will therefore have to decide what materials and what pieces of equipment should be purchased: opaque projector, overhead projector, movie camera, slide and filmstrip projectors, etc. It will need to determine what items get priorities, what items can wait, what items will be used most extensively throughout the school curriculum, and what the teachers want. These are only a few questions that should be answered in deciding what materials and equipment should be purchased.

Other items that need attention in a workable plan of operation for an audio-visual program are implied in such questions as: Who will operate the equipment? What facilities will be needed? Who will form policies? How are teachers and/or students and/or staff to be trained for audio-visual work?

Health education and physical education can profit from a greater use of audio-visual materials. These aids will provide for more efficient use of instructional time, more meaningful and motivating demonstrations, fewer errors on the part of the students, and a significant increase in motor skill and health learning.

Questions and Practical Problems

1. Prepare a list of the advantages of utilizing audio-visual materials in teaching health and physical education as opposed to straight lecture and drill.
2. What are some of the purposes of utilizing audio-visual materials in the teaching of motor skills?
3. Discuss the advantages and disadvantages of each of the following media: opaque projector, overhead projector, magnetic boards, loop films, motion pictures, television, filmstrips, and slides.
4. What type of expert in the field of health and physical education might be brought to your classes to assist in developing concepts in your field of endeavor?
5. What concepts lend themselves to development particularly in the field of health and of physical education?
6. Prepare a list of reading materials that you would give to your school librarian for use by your students in health and physical education.
7. Develop a detailed plan for organizing an audio-visual program in your elementary school.
8. Develop a list of criteria for the selection of audio-visual materials for an elementary school.
9. Read one of the books listed in the Selected References at the close of this chapter and report to the class on its contents.

Selected References

BROWN, JAMES W., RICHARD B. LEWIS, and FRED F. HARCLEROAD. *A-V Instruction: Materials and Methods* (Second Edition). New York: McGraw-Hill, Inc., 1964.

COSTELLO, LAWRENCE F., and GEORGE N. GORDON. *Teach with Television* (Second Edition). New York: Hastings House Publishers, Inc., 1965.

DE KIEFFER, ROBERT E. *Audiovisual Instruction*. New York: Center for Applied Research in Education, 1965.

DIAMOND, ROBERT M., ed. *A Guide to Instructional Television*. New York: McGraw-Hill, Inc., 1964.

Educational Media Council. *Educational Media Index*. New York: McGraw-Hill, Inc., 1964.

ERICKSON, CARLTON W. *Fundamentals of Teaching with Audio-Visual Technology*. New York: The Macmillan Company, 1965.

HERMAN, LEWIS. *Educational Films*. New York: Crown Publishers, 1965.

KINDER, JAMES S. *Using Audio-Visual Materials in Education*. New York: American Book Company, 1965.

LUMSDAINE, A. A. "Instruments and Media of Instruction," in *Handbook of Research on Teaching*. Chicago: Rand McNally & Company, 1963, pp. 448–505.

SCHULTZ, MONTEN J. *The Teacher and Overhead Projection*. Englewood Cliffs, N.J.: Prentice-Hall, Inc., 1965.

Athletic Institute, The. *Sports Film Guide*. Chicago: The Athletic Institute, 1966.

TROW, WILLIAM CLARK. *Teacher and Technology: New Design for Learning*. New York: Appleton-Century-Crofts, 1963.

WILLIAMS, CATHARINE. *Learning from Pictures*. Washington, D.C.: Department of Audio-Visual Instruction, National Education Association, 1963.

WITTICH, WALTER A., and CHARLES F. SCHULLER. *Audiovisual Materials: Their Nature and Use* (Fourth Edition). New York: Harper & Row, Publishers, 1967.

CHAPTER **19**

Evaluation of Physical Education and Health Education Programs

Unless programs of health education and physical education are evaluated it is difficult to determine whether established goals are being accomplished. The staff and administration may feel that certain objectives, needs, desirable traits, habits, and attitudes are being achieved and developed, but to substantiate these claims objectively, valid techniques and procedures must be utilized.

Programs should be evaluated objectively to justify health education and physical education in the curriculum. Merely to plan a program of activities, make provision for time and facilities, and provide an opportunity for children to participate is not adequate. Beyond this it must be determined whether the activities, time, facilities, and participation on the part of children have accomplished educational goals. Health education and physical education are a part of the curriculum, usually established by law making it mandatory that they be provided in the school program. Therefore, evaluation is needed to ascertain if the mandate is meaningful and valuable to the students.

Evaluation, when conducted properly, may accomplish many desirable goals. It may have implications for the manner in which the program is organized and planned. It will help to determine if the program has been based on the needs, interests, and abilities of children. It will determine whether the objectives of organic power, neuromuscular development, good health habits, desirable social and personal adjustment, democratic attitudes, intellectual growth, and emotional maturity have been met. It will discover whether the program is meeting the needs of each child. It will find out whether the programs are an integral part of the educational process.

Evaluation should assist in showing the teacher where he is going, by what means he is going to reach established goals or objectives, how he is progressing, and what effects the program is having on each individual child. A sound evaluation program should assist the educational program to make a significant contribution to each child's growth and development.

Need for Evaluation

Special reasons for establishing a proper evaluation program include the following:
1. It gives evidence as to whether physical education objectives and health education objectives are being met.
2. It helps parents, teachers, and pupils to understand the worth of experiences provided in the physical education and the health education programs.
3. It provides a basis for modifying the

experiences provided in the programs in order to better meet the needs of the pupils.
4. It helps in the formulation of educational principles and policies for these programs.
5. It provides basic information for guidance purposes regarding individual pupils.
6. It acts as a means of motivation for students to reach desired goals. Each one should be encouraged to evaluate his individual progress rather than compare himself to others.
7. It acts as a means of motivation for teachers to find ways to assist children to meet desirable goals and needs.
8. It justifies needs for equipment, facilities, materials, and expenditure of money for personnel and other essentials in these programs.
9. It suggests preventive measures that should be taken in the interest of pupils.
10. It is a means of improving health education and physical education programs so that they contribute to greater child growth and development.
11. It is an aid in grouping pupils, predicting future performance, and determining where emphasis should be placed.

Evaluation will keep a teacher alert and it will help to make the teaching of health education and physical education valuable and meaningful. It is a means of making it possible for educators to understand their worth in the total educational offering. It will inform both the teacher and the pupil whether or not the objectives of the programs are being met.

Types of Information Desired

For a sound evaluation program for health education and for physical education, information is needed about the student, the program, and the teaching.

Information Needed About the Student. The type of information desired about the student centers on his health, skills, knowledge, and social status.

Health. Information regarding the organic development of the pupil is essential for planning and determining the effectiveness of health education and physical education programs. Needed information includes facts about his nutritional status, posture, feet, speech, behavior, attitudes, ears, nose, teeth and gums, lungs, scalp and skin, bones and joints, nervous system, throat and mouth, and eyes and lids. Furthermore, it is important to know how his various organic systems function in relation to exercise. This implies that facts about his muscular strength, vital capacity, cardiorespiratory endurance, and speed and power are also needed.

Skills. The development of physical skills represents a major goal of physical education programs and therefore the motor educability, physical capacity, and motor ability of the student should be known.

In the area of health and safety, information should be acquired on such skills as first aid, home nursing, and automobile driving.

Knowledge. There is much health content that needs to be acquired by elementary school students. A nationwide survey of grades Kindergarten through 8th grade conducted by the School Health Study Project (the most comprehensive study ever conducted on school health programs) indicated a great deficiency in such knowledge. Some of the health-content areas listed in this survey included accident prevention, alcohol, cleanliness and grooming, communicable diseases, dental health, exercise and relaxation, family life, food and nutrition, personality development, posture and body mechanics, rest and sleep, and vision and hearing.

Physical education knowledge that should be acquired by the student includes such topics as ingredients that make for physical fitness, personal regimen needed to develop physical fitness, place of physical education in our culture, rules and regulations concerning various games and activities, basic principles of movement, game strategies, principles of good body mechanics, and the place of dancing, games, and sports in the various cultures of the world.

Social Effectiveness. Social effectiveness implies an understanding and appreciation of such matters as good health habits and proper practices in regard to safety, rest, disease prevention, controlling one's emotions, respecting the rights of others, and good boy-girl relations.

Social effectiveness also includes such things as observing the rules of good sportsmanship, cooperating in the planning of group activities, assuming responsibility, playing within the framework of the rules, and taking an active part in games and other activities.

Information Needed About The Program. Information needed for an evaluation of a program includes objective answers to such questions as the following:

Administration. What kind of records are kept and are they accurate and up-to-date?

Have policies been developed and are they in writing and properly publicized?

Is the budget adequate?

What is the relationship of the program to the community at large and the various agencies and publics within the community?

Is the organizational structure of the program such that it permits the most effective accomplishment of educational goals?

Facilities. Are the facilities conducive to good health practices?

Is there a health suite?

Is the gymnasium and playground space adequate?

What about the lighting? Water? Heat? Ventilation?

Is there a library that has an ample supply of health and physical education books?

Leadership. What are the qualifications of the teachers in the program?

What about salaries—are they adequate?

Is the ratio of teachers to students appropriate?

Are the working conditions for teachers satisfactory?

Equipment and Supplies. What about indoor equipment and supplies? Outdoor equipment and supplies?

Are there a sufficient number of items for full class participation?

Have the equipment and supplies been selected with such qualities in mind as durability, safety, and adaptability to the needs of students?

Activities. Does the nature and scope of activities offered conform to standards set by the leading professional associations in health and in physical education?

Have the activities that are offered in the program been matched to the needs of students?

Are there a variety of activities?

Are the activities presented in a progressive sequential manner?

Is the methodology used in teaching activities appropriate?

Participation. Is the time allotted to the health education and to the physical education periods adequate?

Information Needed About the Teacher. The evaluation of the teacher in the health education and the physical education programs should be concerned with the teacher's effectiveness. Such questions as the following, when answered with objective facts, should provide this information.

What constitutes the teacher's performance? What the teacher does on the job should be the main point of reference in an evaluation program. Therefore, information pertaining to this question should be obtained.

What are the teacher's strengths and weaknesses? Evaluation is not designed to punish the teacher but instead to reveal his strengths and weaknesses and to help in eliminating his weaknesses and exploiting his strengths.

How will the evaluation of the teacher's effectiveness affect the program? The goal desired in evaluating the teacher's effectiveness should be development of a better health program and a better physical education program. Therefore, information should be obtained that will directly result in better programs such as more effective techniques and methods used by the teacher.

What role will the teacher play in the evaluation process? Evaluation is a cooperative process whereby the teacher and the administration develop cooperatively the criteria, the method, and use to be made of the findings.

Techniques Used in Evaluation

For sound evaluation programs for health and physical education it is important to use the right techniques to acquire the information that is needed.

Techniques for Gaining Information About Students

Health. Medical, psychological, dental, and physical fitness examinations are examples of effective techniques for gaining information about the health of the student.

MEDICAL EXAMINATIONS. Both periodic and referral examinations should be given to students. A periodic examination is one that is given at stated intervals and a referral examination is one that is given to a student who has a health problem needing special attention. It is recommended that the family physician, wherever possible, give the periodic medical examination. It is felt that through his more complete knowledge of the family history and closer personal relationship, a better job can be done by him. However, in those cases where families do not have a family physician, the school physician should conduct the examination.

WETZEL GRID. An example of an instrument that can be used by the teacher and can prove helpful is the *Wetzel Grid.* This is valuable in either school health education or physical education programs since it takes into consideration such elements as physique, developmental level, and nutritional progress with respect to weight, age, and height. These aspects of the student's health can be plotted on a graph by the teacher.

PSYCHOLOGICAL EXAMINATIONS. Psychological examinations are designed to help students to adjust satisfactorily to school, detect individual behavior problems, assist the teacher and parent to a better understanding of human behavior, and discover mental handicaps, emotional difficulties, and maladjustments.

DENTAL EXAMINATIONS. The dental examination in most schools is designed to bring to the attention of the child and the parent information concerning such conditions as decayed teeth, malocclusion, and periodontal diseases. A few schools also treat the childrens' dental problems but most schools feel that educational institutions should be concerned with educating the child, not treating him.

PHYSICAL FITNESS TESTS. Many tests have been developed to determine the physical fitness of elementary school children. Most of these tests attempt to measure certain components of physical fitness such as strength, endurance, agility, flexibility, power, speed, balance, and coordination. These tests use such measures as the following in determining how a student rates in regard to these components: *arm and shoulder strength,* by such tests as pull-ups and rope climb; *cardiorespiratory endurance,* by such tests as running and the step test; *agility,* by such tests as shuttle run and agility run; *flexibility,* by such tests as trunk flexion and trunk extension, *power,* by such tests as standing broad jump and vertical jump; and *speed,* by such tests as 50-yard dash and 100-yard dash.

The American Association for Health, Physical Education, and Recreation has developed a physical fitness test (with norms for elementary school children—see Teachers Manual for this test) consisting of pull-ups, sit-ups, shuttle run, standing broad jump, 50-yard dash, softball throw, and 600-yard run-walk.

Many states and cities have developed their own physical fitness tests including, New York, North Carolina, Oregon, Washington, and Tulsa, Oklahoma. The New York State Physical Fitness Test, for example, includes a posture test, target throw, modified push-up, side-step, 50-yard dash, squat stand, and treadmill.

Most of the state tests may be secured by writing directly to the State Department of education or of public instruction at the appropriate state capital.

Techniques for Gaining Information About Programs. Checklists and other techniques have been developed as a means of evaluating school health and physical education programs. Some references that contain techniques for evaluation are as follows:

American Association for Health, Physical Education, and Recreation. *Planning Areas and Facilities for Health, Physical Education and Recreation.* Washington, D.C.: American Association for Health, Physical Education, and Recreation, 1965.

BUCHER, CHARLES A. "Checklists for the Evaluation of School Health and Physical Education Programs," in *Administration of School Health and Physical Education Programs* (Fifth Edition). St. Louis: The C. V. Mosby Co., 1971.

Criteria for Evaluating the Elementary Health Program, Sacramento, Calif: California State Department of Education, 1962.

Evaluation Criteria, Health Education. Washington, D.C.: NSSD, American Council on Education.

LaPorte, William Ralph. *Health and Physical Education Scorecard No. 1 and No. 2.* College Book Store, 3413 S. Hoover Blvd., Los Angeles, California.

LaPorte, William Ralph, John M. Cooper, ed. *The Physical Education Program.* College Book Store, 3413 S. Hoover Blvd., Los Angeles, California.

Los Angeles City Schools. "Health Tests" (for various grade levels), *School Publication 673.* Los Angeles: *Division of Educational Services,* Los Angeles City Schools, 1962.

Michigan School Health Association. *Appraisal Form for Studying School Health Programs.* Michigan School Health Association, 1962.

Techniques for evaluating school health and physical education programs other than checklists and score cards include questionnaires to be sent to parents and students; rating scales; surveys of interested groups of people who know about the program; expert evaluations by authorities such as sanitarians, test experts, and curriculum specialists; analysis of health records; tests and inventories; and interviews and conferences.

Techniques for Gaining Information About Teachers. Some of the techniques that have been found to be valuable in evaluating teachers are the following:

Observation of Teacher's Performance. Observation is a commonly used method and obtains the best results when it is followed up by a conference of the teacher and supervisor or other person doing the evaluation. At this conference the teacher's performance is discussed. Most teachers indicate the observation, if conducted properly, can be a very helpful method.

Standardized Tests. Sometimes standardized tests to determine the progress the student has made in the class are assumed to constitute evaluation of the *teacher.* This technique may be somewhat misleading since there are other factors besides the teacher that affect the student's progress.

Ratings. The type of rating that is given varies with the school system that utilizes this particular technique. It may consist of an over-all estimate of a teacher's effectiveness or consist of separate evaluations of specific behaviors and traits. Self-ratings may also be used. Ratings may be conducted by administrative personnel, students, or the teacher's peers. Rating scales in order to be effective must possess such qualities as objectivity, reliability, sensitivity, validity, and utility.

Use of Evaluation Results to Aid Teachers and Students. Records of objective and subjective evaluation should be kept by the teacher and filed with the records of the individual children. They should accompany the child as he advances in school so he may see his growth and the teachers who receive him as a new student will know something of his ability and needs, how he has developed, and what he has accomplished.

Regardless of the type of evaluation, the child must know the result if he is to be able to help himself and adjust his work and endeavors in the correct direction. Self-appraisal is recommended which may be by means of a diary or appraisal forms. These are usually compiled by the teacher and the student together. The student must first be aided in establishing his goals or objectives so that he has an idea of what he wishes to accomplish. In this way, evaluation is possible. Self-evaluation and appraisal are excellent learning aids.

The carry-over of activities taught in the physical education program to the noon-hour, after-school, and leisure-time pursuits must not be overlooked in evaluation. If a child desires to participate in these programs, it shows they have made a favorable impression on him and have given him satisfying and pleasurable experiences.

Specific Points to Be Evaluated

Evaluation might start with the general objectives of the program and then extend to specific objectives. It should include the evaluation of the teacher, the facilities, the equipment and apparatus, the actual program—both the planning and administration—and last but not least, the effects the planned program has had on each individual and the group as a whole. Some specific questions relating to each phase are listed for the help of the teacher.

Evaluation of Program Planning. Regarding program planning, the teacher should answer such questions as the following:

1. Am I planning activities to meet the needs, interests, and abilities of my group as a whole?
2. Are the activities diversified sufficiently to meet the needs, abilities, and interest of each individual child?
3. Are the activities planned according to the available facilities, equipment, budget, personnel, apparatus, and space?
4. Do I have attainable objectives?
5. Are the objectives too general, or are they specific?
6. Is the program integrated with other parts of the school program?
7. Have I considered the indoor program of physical education for inclement weather?
8. Have I planned with the help of my students?
9. Does the program include all types of activities recommended for students comparable to my group?

Evaluation of Teaching. In respect to teaching, the teacher should answer such questions as the following:

1. Am I well prepared to present and teach this program?
2. Am I teaching and reaching each individual child? Do I recognize individual differences?
3. Is there a correct teacher-pupil relationship? Pupil-pupil relationship? Pupil-teacher relationship?
4. Are the children learning and having fun?
5. Are they interested?
6. Are they meeting the objectives?
7. Do I set a good example?
8. Am I efficient in my use of time, equipment, and facilities?
9. Am I aiding good group relationships?
10. Am I democratic enough in my teaching?
11. If the activity does not appear to be successful, do I blame the children or do I stop the activity and later make a self-analysis to find reasons?
12. Do I permit pupil choice?

Evaluation of Facilities and Equipment. In evaluating facilities, space, equipment, and apparatus, such questions as the following should be considered:

1. Am I using all of the play area to full advantage?
2. Is this area safe—free from debris? Are there well-established safety rules for the use of equipment, apparatus, and so on?
3. Am I getting the most from the available equipment?
4. Are children having opportunities to use all apparatus?
5. Are all pieces of equipment and apparatus inspected regularly and in safe condition?
6. Is the health suite adequate?
7. Do the facilities meet proper health and safety standards?
8. Are there provisions for audio-visual aids?

Evaluation of Program Results. In evaluating the effects of the program on the children, such questions as the following should be considered:

1. Is each child better in some way because he has participated in this program?
2. Is he in better physical condition?
3. Is he better in neuromuscular skills?
4. Is he better in his democratic attitude toward his fellow playmates?
5. Is he a better sport?
6. Does he use good judgment?
7. Is he a good leader?
8. Is he a good follower?
9. Is he happy and enjoying the activities?
10. Is he always finding excuses to stay away from the physical education program?
11. Does he use any of the activities in his leisure time? Does he assume self-direction?
12. Is he replacing an egotistical or "I" attitude with a cooperative or "we" one?
13. Does he have a sense of responsibility?
14. Has his over-all physical skill development improved?
15. Has his over-all social development improved?
16. Is he more stable emotionally?
17. Does he demonstrate good health practices?
18. Has he acquired sound health knowledge?

General Evaluation. At the close of each lesson, the teacher should discuss the activities with the class. What did they like best? Why? Would they like the activities again? If so, why? If not, why? The teacher will learn much from the students which will be of value to him or her and to them.

The teacher should evaluate each lesson. Why did it proceed exceptionally well, or why did it not? By so doing, he or she will not make the same error twice and will use good techniques again.

Above all the teacher should remember that health education and physical education are integral parts of education. They do not differ in their aims or objectives—merely in their means toward these ends. Unless they aid each individual and he is better for having participated, something is wrong. It is the teacher's challenge to ascertain this, and it may only be accomplished through honest, broad evaluation of the teacher and the program by the teacher and the group.

To summarize, evaluation will aid in keeping the programs of health education and physical education alive and challenging. This must be done if they are to meet the needs of children in a changing world and society.

Evaluation will tell whether the planned and established goals have been reached, whether the methods used to reach them were the most desirable, and whether the actual goals were the most valuable and practical for a given situation, program, or individual class.

Forms for Evaluating Physical Education Programs

Table 19–1. **Evaluation Chart for Story Plays, Kindergarten Through Grade Three**

Name_____
Grade_____
Year _____
Age _____
Teacher _____

Scoring key:
Satisfactory—S
Improved—I
Needs help—NH

Category	Scoring Period			
	Nov.	Feb.	April	June
Coordination of large muscles				
Throwing				
Bending				
Twisting				
Running				
Jumping				
Stretching				
Sportsmanship				
Friendliness				
Self-control				
Respect for others				
Enjoyment				
Imagination				
Participation				
Improvement				
Excellent				
Average				
Little				
None				
Average mark				
Special remarks				

Table 19–2. Evaluation Chart for Self-testing Activities and Stunts, Kindergarten Through Grade Three

Name _____
Grade _____
Year _____
Age _____
Teacher _____

Scoring key:
Satisfactory—S
Improved—I
Needs help—NH

Scoring Period

Category	Nov.	Feb.	May

Subjective evaluation
  Does he move quickly and safely?
  Does he have good balance?
  Is he getting strong?
  Is he having fun?
  Is he making friends?
  Does he like to try?

Objective evaluation
  Balancing: Walk across walking board, placing heel of one foot, at each step, against toes of other foot. Extend arms sideward, for balance. Look straight ahead. Turn around. Walk back. Walk backwards.
  Bouncing balls: Bounce and catch ball. Bounce to partner. Tap while standing. Tap while walking. Combine bouncing, catching, and tapping in a pattern.
  Catching: Catch, with two hands, a ball or bean bag thrown into the air. Catch ball after bounce. Catch ball or bean bag thrown by another child.
  Jumping: Jump in place, landing lightly on two feet. Jump to music. Jump individual rope 10–15 times. Jump rope in various ways— backward, legs crossed, or feet apart. Jump long rope to rhymes or verses. Jump long rope that is turning toward jumper or away from jumper. Jump long rope in various tempos. From standing position, jump over a rope placed at various heights. Take off from two feet and land lightly on two feet (this is a modified standing jump).
  Kicking: Manipulate ball with feet. Manipulate ball using either foot. Kick soccer ball, meeting ball with top of instep to direct ball along floor.
  Leaping: Leap over a 12-inch hurdle while running, taking off from one foot at a time and landing on one foot at a time. While running, leap over rope placed at various heights from floor. Take off from one foot and land lightly on one foot at a time (this is a modified running high jump).
  Throwing: Throw a bean bag into the air and catch it. Throw underhand to partner with vigorous arm swing. Increase distance. Place correct (opposite) foot forward when throwing. Throw bean bag through opening in easel target, using underhand throw. Throw bean bag over net using overhand. Throw volley ball, using shoulder throw. Throw ball at wall target.
  Balancing an object: Place block on the head. Walk while balancing it. The child should walk a distance sufficient to test his skill.
  Bouncing ball: Jump up and down lightly on toes, gradually lowering height until a stooping position is reached. Stunt may be performed to rhythmic accompaniment.
  Puppy run: Walk or run on all fours using short steps.

Evaluation of Physical Education and Health Education Programs 289

Table 19-3. Evaluation Chart for Games, Kindergarten Through Grade Three

Name _____	Scoring key:
Grade _____	Satisfactory—S
Year _____	Improved—I
Age _____	Needs help—NH
Teacher _____	

	Scoring Period			
Category	Sept.	Dec.	Feb.	May

Subjective evaluation
  Does he show good sportsmanship?
  Is he a cheerful loser?
  Does he control his temper?
  Does he accept decisions?
  Does he play fair?
  Does he follow directions?
  Does he participate actively?
  Is he a good leader?
  Is he a good follower?
  Can he skip?
  Does he tag properly?
  Can he dodge a thrown ball?
  Can he tiptoe?
  Can he dart?

Objective evaluation
  How many times can he catch a ball, out of 10 tries?
  How many times can he throw a ball to a partner in 10 tries? (Specific distances.)
  How many times can he jump a rope without missing?
  How long does it take him to run 60 feet without falling?

Table 19-4. Evaluation Chart for Individual-Dual Activities, Grades One Through Three

Name _____	Scoring key:
Grade _____	Excellent E
Year _____	Good—G
Age _____	Fair—F
Teacher _____	No improvement—NI

Category	E	G	F	NI

Activities, with skills involved
  Hopscotch: hopping, bending, keeping balance
  Marbles: shooting marbles
  Rope jumping: jumping on toes—using knees and ankles
  Ball: accurate underhand toss
  Rubber quoits: accurate toss

290 METHODOLOGY FOR PLANNING AND TEACHING

Table 19-4 (*continued*)

Subjective evaluation

He shows gradual development in skills.	_____
He uses games to gain relief from tension or physical fatigue.	_____
He participates daily in exercise which suits his personal needs.	_____
He enjoys performing a variety of activities he understands.	_____
He develops the power to adjust socially to the needs and wishes of his playmates.	_____
He finds satisfaction in a game well played whether he wins or loses.	_____
He has a sense of belonging to the group.	_____
He feels important to the group.	_____
He overcomes shyness or fear of being hurt.	_____
He gains security as skills increase.	_____
He develops a sense of coordination.	_____
His physical endurance can meet the daily demands put upon his body.	_____
He is willing to share equipment and take turns.	_____
He contributes his share as a group leader.	_____
He contributes his share as a group follower.	_____
He cheerfully participates in the activity selected.	_____
He plays fairly.	_____
He wins gracefully.	_____
He loses gracefully.	_____
He puts his whole effort into the activity.	_____
He appreciates the skill and sportsmanship of others.	_____

Table 19-5. **Evaluation Chart for Rhythms and Dances, Intermediate Grades**

Name _____   Scoring key:
Grade _____   Excellent—E
Year _____   Very good—VG
Age _____   Good—G
Teacher _____   Fair—F
                                   Poor—P

	Scoring Period		
Movements to Music	Sept.	Jan.	May
Walk			
Run			
Jump			
Hop			
Slide			
Gallop			
Slip			
Clap			
March			
Polka			
Waltz			
Two-step			

Evaluation of Physical Education and Health Education Programs 291

Table 19-6. Evaluation Chart for Objective Skills, Intermediate Grades

Name _____	Scoring key:
Grade _____	Excellent—E
Year _____	Improved—I
Age _____	Needs help—NH
Teacher _____	

	Scoring Period		
Category (Addition and substitution of other activities are encouraged.)	Sept.	Feb.	May
Dribbling—in each scoring period put in the time spent by each pupil dribbling by hand and/or foot a distance of 20 yards (by foot, not kicking forward more than 5 yards).			
Throwing—football, basketball, and softball, depending upon the season—how many times the student makes the target with each (football—a barrel from 60 feet) in 10 tries. Then try each for distance—longest in three tries.			
Batting—with a softball (in season); how many hits with 10 swings on pitches from a pitcher.			
Catching—with football, basketball, and softball, depending on season, how many times the student catches the object thrown in each (football—15 yards; basketball—width of basketball court; softball—60 feet) in 10 tries.			
Running—time taken to run the 30-, 40-, or 50-yard dash, full speed.			
Pushups—number of pushups possible.			
Jumping—(1) distance covered in broad jump (best of three attempts); (2) distance covered in hop, skip, and jump (best of three attempts).			

Table 19-7. Evaluation Chart for Team Sports, Intermediate Grades

Name _____	Scoring key:
Grade _____	Satisfactory—S
Year _____	Improved—I
Age _____	Needs help—NH
Teacher _____	

	Scoring Period				
Objectives	Sept.	Nov.	Jan.	Mar.	May
Sportsmanship Gets along well with others Plays fairly Accepts officials' decisions Uses good judgment					
Team play Plays for team, not self Good loser Understands rules Good winner					

Table 19–7 (*continued*)

Democratic attitude
  Helps others learn skills
  Encourages others
  Accepts own limitations
  Cooperates

Leadership
  Knows the job to do
  Does a good job
  Plans well

Followership
  Helps settle disputes
  Takes suggestions
  Takes proper turn

Participation
  Enjoys playing
  Uses time to good advantage
  Interested in learning new activities
  Interested in improving skills

Self-direction
  Uses activities in leisure time
  Applies learning in other situations

Responsibility
  Shares responsibility
  Plays to the end of a game no matter how it is going
  Shows respect for equipment

Emotional growth
  Accepts defeat
  Respects rights of others
  Feels he belongs
  Feeling of success
  Self-control

Table 19-8. Evaluation Chart for Individual and Dual Activities, Intermediate Grades

Name _____
Grade _____
Year _____
Age _____
Teacher _____

Scoring key:
Satisfactory—S
Improved—I
Needs help—NH

Category	Scoring Period			
	Nov.	Jan.	Mar.	June

Skills and fundamentals

Croquet
1. Hitting ball accurately
2. Knowledge of rules
3. Knowledge of terms

Deck tennis
1. Catching
2. Throwing
3. Movement on court
4. Rules of game

Horseshoe and Quoits
1. Pitching
2. Knowledge of rules
3. Knowledge of terms

Badminton
1. Volleying shuttlecock
2. Serving
3. Knowledge of rules

Tennis
1. Serving ball
2. Volleying ball
3. Knowledge of rules

Volley Tennis
1. Hitting
2. Knowledge of rules

Shuffleboard
1. Pushing disc
2. Knowledge of rules
3. Knowledge of terms

Sportsmanship
Fair play
Respect for others
Can play alone and as "we"
Enthusiasm
Uses equipment properly while playing
Assumes responsibility for returning equipment
Self-direction

Table 19-9. Self-evaluation Physical Education Chart for Students, Intermediate Grades

Name _____
Grade _____
Year _____
Age _____
Teacher _____

Scoring key:
Always—A
Usually—U
Sometimes—S
Never—N

Category	Report Card Periods				
	1	2	3	4	5

Desirable social learnings

Leadership
1. Am I interested in the welfare of others?
2. Do I encourage good practices of safety?
3. Am I just?
4. Am I fair?
5. Am I developing self-discipline?
6. Do I respect the rights of others?
7. Am I developing a sense of responsibility?

Followership
1. Am I loyal to my team?
2. Do I play for the good of all?
3. Do I accept and respect the judgment of others?

Sportsmanship
1. Do I avoid arguments over decisions?
2. Do I play for the good of all?
3. Do I put forth my best effort?
4. Do I play fairly and honestly?
5. Do I have a sense of responsibility?
6. Can I lose gracefully?
7. Can I win gracefully?

Organization
1. Am I prepared to play the game?
2. Do I foresee needed equipment?

Consideration
1. Do I win or lose with grace?
2. Am I fair to others?
3. Am I kind to others?
4. Do I know the rules which govern the game?
5. Do I remember to play quietly in the classroom?

Cooperation
1. Can I adjust to the interest of the group?
2. Am I willing to serve as an official instead of playing?
3. Do I play my best at all times?

Evaluation of Physical Education and Health Education Programs

| | Report Card Periods |||||
| Category | 1 | 2 | 3 | 4 | 5 |

Specific learnings (YES or NO)
1. Do I know the history of some of the games?
2. Do I know the rules of the games?
3. Can I score the games?
4. Have I improved in my accuracy in:
    a. Throwing balls?
    b. Batting?
    c. Catching?
    d. Running?
    e. Jumping?
5. Have I improved in my accuracy in pitching quoits?
6. Have I improved in my accuracy in throwing darts?
7. Do I play the games during my leisure?
8. Have I taught games to others?
9. Have I constructed games?
10. Do I have good rhythm in dances?

Games I have learned and can teach others:
1.
2.
3.
4.
5.

Checklist for Evaluating the Health Science Instruction Program[1]

General — Yes / No

1. The school has a clear statement of the philosophy and principles upon which an effective school health instruction program is based.
2. Teachers on the staff appreciate the importance of health instruction and understand the contribution it makes to the total education program.
3. The school administration has assigned a qualified person from the staff to coordinate the entire school health program and provides him time to carry out his duties and responsibilities.
4. The school has an active health committee that helps in planning and coordinating the school health program.
5. The school provides a physical environment and an emotional atmosphere that helps to make possible the achievement of the goals of the health instruction program.
6. Teachers and other school staff members set a good example, in terms of good physical and mental health habits and attitudes, as part of the health instruction program.
7. The health instruction program is based upon the health needs, problems, interests, and abilities of the pupils.
8. The school has developed a teaching guide outlining a progressive plan of health instruction from grades 1 through 12.
9. The school has established definite goals of achievement in relation to habits, understandings, attitudes, and skills for each.
10. The school administration promotes the integration of health and safety instruction with all curricular areas and extracurricular activities of the school.
11. The school includes in its in-service education program opportunities for its staff to become better qualified for conducting the health instruction program.
12. The school administration provides adequate materials, such as books, charts, filmstrips, and pamphlets needed for the program.
13. Textbooks used in health classes are authoritative, up-to-date, written in an interesting manner, and suitable for the grade level in which they are used.
14. The school evaluates its health instruction periodically to determine its effectiveness in achieving established goals.

Elementary program

15. In grades 1 to 3 sufficient time is provided during the school day for incidental and integrated teaching of health.
16. In grades 4 to 6 a minimum of three periods a week is allotted for direct health instruction.
17. The planned health instruction is supplemented in the upper grades by incidental teaching, correlation, and integration.
18. Classroom teachers meet the state's minimum standards relative to college preparation in health education.
19. The health instruction program centers around the daily living of the child instead of rote learning of health facts and rules.
20. The program provides many interesting and worthwhile activities that are helpful to the child in solving his health problems related to growth, development, and adjustment.
21. If the school attempts to integrate health instruction with large teaching units, the services of a health educator are utilized in planning those phases of unit dealing with health.
22. The health instruction program includes the major health areas and problems.

[1] From State of Ohio, Department of Education, *A Guide for Improving School Health Instruction Programs*, Columbus, Ohio, State of Ohio, Department of Education, Division of Elementary and Secondary Education, 1963.

Rating Scale to Evaluate Health Education Materials[2]

	Yes	No
Suitable material meets all of these criteria		
1. Is appropriate to the course of study.	___	___
2. Is a reinforcement of other materials.	___	___
3. Is significantly different.	___	___
4. Is impartial, factual, and accurate.	___	___
5. Is up-to-date.	___	___
6. Is nonsectarian, nonpartisan, and unbiased.	___	___
7. Is free from undesirable propaganda.	___	___
8. Is free from excessive or objectionable advertising.	___	___
9. Is free or inexpensive and readily available.	___	___

Pamphlets	Excellent	Good	Fair	Poor
1. Readability of type.	___	___	___	___
2. Appropriateness of illustrations.	___	___	___	___
3. Organization of content.	___	___	___	___
4. Logical sequence of concepts.	___	___	___	___
5. Important aspects of topic stand out.	___	___	___	___
6. Material directed to one specific group such as teachers, pupils, or parents.	___	___	___	___
7. Reading level appropriate for intended group.	___	___	___	___
8. Based on interests and needs of intended group.	___	___	___	___
9. Positively directed in words, descriptions, and actions.	___	___	___	___
10. Directed toward desirable health practices.	___	___	___	___
11. Minimal resort to fear techniques and morbid concepts.	___	___	___	___
12. In good taste; avoids vulgarity, stereotypes, and ridicule.	___	___	___	___
Total rating	___	___	___	___

Posters

	Excellent	Good	Fair	Poor
1. Realistic and within experience level.	___	___	___	___
2. Appeals to interest.	___	___	___	___
3. Emphasizes positive behavior and attitudes.	___	___	___	___
4. Message clear at a glance.	___	___	___	___
5. Little or no conflicting detail.	___	___	___	___
6. In good taste.	___	___	___	___
7. Attractive and in pleasing colors.	___	___	___	___
Total rating	___	___	___	___

Recommended for use

1. For use by:
   a. pupils ___ b. teachers ___ c. parents ___ d. adults ___
2. Appropriate grade level:
   a. primary ___ b. elementary ___ c. middle school ___

Not recommended for use and why

Date _____ Evaluated by _____

[2] From Barbara M. Osborn and Wilfred Sutton, "Evaluation of Health Education Materials," The Journal of School Health **34**: 72, Feb. 1964. (Rating scale prepared by members of the school activities committee.)

METHODOLOGY FOR PLANNING AND TEACHING

Checklist for Administrative Practices for a Healthful Environment[3]

Organization of the school day

LENGTH OF THE SCHOOL DAY   Yes No

1. The length of the school day should be adapted to the age of the child, starting with one-half day in kindergarten.
2. Play and rest periods are provided in accordance with pupil needs.

SCHEDULING

1. Subjects demanding diligent application are scheduled early in the day.
2. Subjects requiring more mental concentration and academic effort are interspersed with those requiring less mental effort.
3. The amount of time devoted to a specific task is assigned with regard to the age, readiness, and needs of the child.
4. There is ample time between classes to ensure student promptness without excess haste.
5. A leisurely lunch break is provided for each pupil.
6. The educational program is a flexible one, so that it is possible to schedule special programs or activities without hindering the regular program.

Student achievement

INDIVIDUAL DIFFERENCES

1. There is provision in the school program for individual differences among children in respect to physical handicaps, readiness to learn, academic ability, and environmental background.
2. Consideration is given to the physical and mental growth of each child.
3. The abilities of each child are recognized and instruction is adjusted to individual ability.

GRADES

1. Provision is made for clerical and special assistance in helping the teacher to spend more time with teaching responsibilities.
2. The program is planned so that each child experiences a series of educational successes.
3. Goals are adjusted to fit each pupil, and marks are used to indicate progress toward stated goals.
4. Provision is made for a descriptive evaluation along with the grade.

REPORTING PUPIL PROGRESS

1. The means used to report pupil progress include personal conferences, checklists, graphs, letters, progress reports, and report cards.
2. Problems, weaknesses, and potential of child are items for teacher-parent conferences.

TESTS AND EXAMINATIONS

1. Examinations are used as a means of helping pupil and teacher discover the progress that has been made in the acquisition of knowledge.
2. Tests help the learner attain satisfaction and a sense of achievement when he is doing as well as he should.
3. Tests help the teacher judge how effective his teaching methods are.
4. Tests assist in making administrative judgments in respect to grouping and other procedures.
5. Tests provide emphasis on diagnosis rather than on rating of over-all merit, upon individual improvement rather than comparison with others, and are used more as guides than as final measures.

INTELLIGENCE RATINGS

1. Intelligence tests are selected and administered by a trained person.
2. Tests are used with a view to how the children can profit with suitable instruction.

[3] From Charles A. Bucher *Administration of School and College Health and Physical Education Programs* (Fourth Edition), St. Louis: The C. V. Mosby Co., 1967.

Physical education and recreation

1. Physical education class size ranges from thirty to forty pupils.
2. Physical education is offered daily and stresses basic skills and movement experiences.
3. The physical education program is concerned with the social, mental, and emotional aspects of the child, as well as the physical.
4. Recreational activities are based on pupil interests.

Homework

1. Homework is assigned in accordance with the age, interest, ability, and needs of the child.

Pupil attendance

1. The school nurse determines whether the child should attend school and when he should be sent home.
2. The child does not return to school after sickness until he is able to attend all classes.
3. The nurse and attendance officer play a major role in communication with the parent regarding proper health practices.

Discipline

1. Behavior is evaluated with the knowledge that misconduct is a sign of maladjustment and an attempt is made to find the cause.
2. The staff upholds the same standards of behavior.
3. All pupil abilities are recognized and an effort is made to maintain the self-respect of the child through the use of praise.
4. Fear is not used as a technique of control.
5. Children are encouraged to assist in developing standards of behavior and to assist in their enforcement.

Student grouping

1. Grouping is flexible so that administration and organization exist only to expedite the process of learning.
2. Differences in learners and subject matter are considered in grouping.
3. Promotion practices are flexible.
4. Grouping is such that children do not bear labels, for example: "fast group" or "slow learner."

Teacher-pupil relationships

1. There is cooperative thinking and effort between teachers and pupils rather than emphasis upon the sole direction and authority of the teacher.
2. The teacher sets a good example for the pupil.
3. A primary teacher responsibility is that of pupil counseling.
4. The pupil is made to feel that he is part of the group and contributes to it.
5. The atmosphere of the classroom is relaxed and friendly.
6. The teacher shows interest in each pupil.
7. The teacher recognizes the various environmental factors that compose pupil personality and behavior.
8. The teacher has good relationships with his colleagues.
9. The teacher has an enthusiastic and confident attitude.
10. The teacher enjoys his work and takes pride in it.
11. The teacher is secure in his job.

Professional services

1. The administration provides for guidance, psychologist, psychiatrist, and social-worker services.
2. Specialists in "1" work closely with the home in providing necessary help for the child.

Checklist for Administrative Practices for a Healthful Environment (continued)

Personnel policies

1. Relationships between administrators and teachers are harmonious.
2. The administration promotes good social and professional relations among members of the staff.
3. Administrators help educate the public to its true responsibilities to the schools and seek the support of the public in the promotion of educational goals.

The teacher

1. The teacher likes children.
2. The teacher is well adjusted and mentally healthy.
3. The teacher understands the growth and development of children.
4. The teacher is able to identify children with serious problems and knows how and when to refer them for help.
5. The teacher helps pupils meet their basic emotional needs.
6. The teacher has a pleasing appearance and manner and is physically healthy, patient, and impartial.
7. The teacher respects the child's personality, understands his limitations, and creates an over-all atmosphere of security.

Working conditions

1. The physical conditions of the job are good (salary, sick leave, class load, etc.).
2. Administration is aware of factors that might affect the mental health of the teacher and helps to eliminate such problems.

Improving instruction

1. Administration utilizes opportunities to commend teacher achievement and effort.
2. The beginning teacher is helped over the rough spots and is also assisted in obtaining a broad professional orientation.

Yes   No

Questions and Practical Problems

1. Set up specific criteria for the evaluation of (a) the total programs of health education and physical education in elementary schools; (b) each specific part of the programs as recommended for early-childhood and middle-childhood grades.

2. Plan a lesson for one specific grade. Set up specific evaluation points for this lesson, using a chart.

3. Observe one or more classes in health education and physical education. Evaluate them on the basis of objectives, child-learning situation, child growth, and participation. Substantiate them as a valuable part of the total educational program.

4. Plan skill tests for each specific phase of the physical education program in the grade of your choice.

5. Outline a week's activities for the health education and physical education program for a particular grade including the time given to tests and evaluation, and on the basis of this schedule examine (a) the relevance of the program to the needs and special problems of various types of children; (b) whether the program offers a sufficient variety of activities to be interesting to all of the children; (c) if sufficient time is included in the week's program for tests and evaluation, and if the program could benefit from a greater amount of time given to planning and evaluation; (d) whether the program is sufficiently integrated with the other parts of the school's educational program.

6. What are some of the objectives in having the teacher and her class discuss their activities at the end of each lesson?

7. On the basis of an enlightened planning of the health education and the physical education program, what specific requirements would you ask for a child to meet before being promoted?

Selected References

American Association for Health, Physical Education, and Recreation. *Evaluation Standards and Guide in Health Education, Physical Education, Recreation Education*. Washington, D.C.: American Association for Health, Physical Education, and Recreation, 1959.

BACHMAN, H. M. "Let Your Students Set Their Own Goals," *Journal of Health, Physical Education, and Recreation*, Vol. 26, March 1955, pp. 19–20.

BROER, MARION R. "Evaluating Skill," *Journal of Health, Physical Education, and Recreation*, Vol. 33, Nov. 1962, p. 23.

California State Department of Education. *Criteria for Evaluating the Physical Education Program: Kindergarten, Grades One Through Six*. Sacramento, Calif.: State Department of Education, 1960.

CLARK, H. H. *Application of Measurement to Health and Physical Education*, 4th ed. Englewood Cliffs, N.J.: Prentice-Hall, Inc., 07632.

Criteria for Evaluating the Elementary Health Program. Sacramento, Calif. California State Department of Education, 1962.

JOHNS, EDWARD. "An Example of a Modern Evaluation Plan," *Journal of School Health*, Vol. 32, Jan. 1962, p. 5.

LASALLE, DOROTHY. "Evaluation," in *Children in Focus*, 1954 Year Book of the American Association for Health, Physical Education, and Recreation. Washington, D.C.: American Association for Health, Physical Education, and Recreation, 1955, p. 267.

LATCHAW, MARJORIE. "Measuring Selected Motor Skills in Fourth, Fifth, and Sixth Grades." *Research Quarterly*, Vol. 25, Dec. 1954, pp. 439–449.

LATCHAW, MARJORIE, and CAMILLE BROWN. *The Evaluation Process in Health Education, Physical Education, and Recreation*. Englewood Cliffs, N.J.: Prentice-Hall, Inc., 1962.

MATHEWS, DONALD K. *Measurement in Physical Education* (Second Edition). Philadelphia: W. B. Saunders Company, 1963.

MEANS, RICHARD K. "A Teacher Appraisal Scale," *Journal of Health, Physical Education, and Recreation*, Vol. 31, May-June 1960, pp. 36–37.

Michigan School Health Association. *Appraisal Form for Studying School Health Programs*. Michigan School Health Association, 1962.

SOLLEDER, MARIAN K. *Evaluation Instruments in Health Education*. Washington, D.C.: American Association for Health, Physical Education, and Recreation, 1965.

PART FIVE

Recommended Movement Experiences for Physical Education Programs

CHAPTER 20

Movement Experiences for Early Childhood (Ages Five and Six)

Dances and Rhythms

Children in early childhood should be able to execute the following movements in rhythmical patterns: the walk, run, hop, jump, leap, and combination movements of skipping, galloping, and sliding. These are locomotor movements. Comparable body movements are swinging, swaying, pushing, pulling, bending, and stretching. Records such as Bassett and Chestnut's "Rhythmic Activities" and Dietrich's "Rhythmic Play" are excellent to use when children perform these activities.[1]

MARJORIE DAW (BEND AND STRETCH)

Verse

See saw, Marjorie Daw,
Jack shall have a new master.
He shall make but a penny a day
Because he can't work any faster.

Directions

Two partners face each other and join both hands. The verse is chanted slowly and the partners mimic a seesaw. One child rises up on her toes while the other one does a deep knee bend. This action is then reversed and is continued throughout the chanting of the rhyme.

THE DUCKS (RUN AND WALK)

Verse

Some little ducks a walk did take
Out the yard, down toward the lake.
Under the fence they had to squeeze;
Then they waddled around two trees.
Finally they ran to the lake with vim.
They jumped right in for a good, long swim.

Directions

Children squat on their haunches and place their hands either on their hips or under their armpits, making their bent arms into wings. Children chant the verse and act it out while waddling like ducks. On line three they crouch as close to the ground as possible to make believe they are going under the fence. They then waddle around two trees, going by one side of one and the opposite side of the other, making a crooked path. On line five they waddle quickly to imitate a run. When they get to the lake they take one big jump and then pretend to swim.

[1] These records are available from Educational Records, 157 Chambers St., New York, N.Y. 10007.

THE SWINGS
(PUSH-BEND-STRETCH-RUN)

Verse

> Up, down, up in the swing,
> Up in the air so high.
> Isn't it a lot of fun
> To be so near the sky?
> Up, down, up, down,
> Watch us run under and turn ourselves round.

Directions

Groups of three children work together. Two face each other and join both hands, forming the seat of a swing. (Do not cross hands.) The third child stands behind the swing and acts as the person who pushes the swing to make it go higher. All swings stand in a double circle and all pushers face the same direction in the circle.

While chanting the verse, the pusher makes the swing go up and down in time with the chant. On "up" she pushes it away and lets go. On "down" the arms of the two players return to her, and so on. As she pushes she steps forward on one foot and as the swing returns to her she rocks back on the other foot. This makes her do a rocking motion. On the line, "watch us run under," the pusher runs under the swing. On "turn ourselves round" the partners wring the dish cloth by turning under each other's arms. Each pusher now has a new swing. Change swings and pushers so that all children will have a chance to act out both parts.

THE ELEPHANTS
(SWING AND SWAY)

Verses

> The elephant's walk is steady and slow.
> His trunk like a pendulum swings just so.
> But when there are children with peanuts around,
> He swings it up and he swings it down.

> This self-same elephant stands and sways
> His body back and forth this way.
> Sometimes he lifts his foot from the ground,
> But rarely, if ever, he makes a sound.

Directions

Children chant the verses, acting out the directions as follows:

First Verse: Both hands are clasped together in front of the child to represent the trunk of an elephant. He bends over at the waist. He walks slowly, swinging his trunk to the left and right in rhythm with his step and his chant. On line four, he stops walking and swings his trunk up as high as he can and then brings it down.

Second Verse: On lines one and two, children stand and sway in time to their chant. On line three they lift the left foot from the ground and replace it quietly. On line four they lift the right foot up and replace it quietly. Repeat as interest warrants.

HICKORY DICKORY DOCK
(RUN AND JUMP)

Verse

> Hickory Dickory Dock, tick tock,
> The mouse ran up the clock, tick tock.
> The clock struck one, the mouse ran down,
> Hickory Dickory Dock, tick tock.

Directions

One half of the children form a circle. The other half are arranged so that each child stands 4 to 6 feet in back of a child in the circle. The children in the circle represent the clocks. Those standing behind the clocks are mice.

The *clocks* clasp their two hands together in front of them and let them hang down to represent the pendulum of a clock. They bend slightly at the waist. As they chant the verse they swing their hands and arms back and forth. On the words "tick tock," they also stamp each foot. Clocks continue this motion throughout the verse. When the clock strikes one, children clap their hands once.

Mice stoop in a crouched position behind the clocks. On line two, mice run in front of the clocks and make believe they are climbing up by stretching up as high as they can reach. When the clock strikes one, the frightened mice run down the clock and scamper back to their original places. Clocks and mice then exchange positions and repeat the verse.

LITTLE MISS MUFFET
(STOOP AND JUMP)

Verse

> Little Miss Muffet sat on a tuffet
> Eating her curds and whey.
> Along came a spider and sat down beside her
> And frightened Miss Muffet away.

Directions

The verse is chanted and acted out. One half of the players form a circle, stoop in a squat position, and pretend to be eating. The other children are chosen to be spiders. They walk on all fours (hands and feet) and creep around the circle. On line three, "sat down beside her," the spiders each stop by someone in the circle. These children then jump up and run away. Repeat, changing spiders and Miss Muffets.

JACK BE NIMBLE
(SKIP AND JUMP)

Verse

Jack be nimble,
Jack be quick,
Jack jump over
A candlestick.

Directions

Children chant the verse. On lines one and two they skip around in a circle. On line three they jump as high and far as they can.

SALLY GO ROUND
(WALK—RUN—SLIDE)

Verse

Sally go round the sun.
Sally go round the moon.
Sally go round the chimney pots
Every afternoon—BOOM.

Directions

Children form a single circle and face so they move clockwise. As they chant the verse they may walk, run, or slide, moving around in a circle. On the word BOOM, they quickly squat, trying to keep their balance and not fall on the floor.

MOTION POEM
(BEND—STRETCH—SWING—SWAY)

Verses

Did you ever, ever see
Children stand as tall as we?
We can raise our hands up high,
And wave our fingers to the sky,
Quickly spread them open wide,
Then drop them down on either side.

We can raise our heels with ease,
Lower them and bend our knees,
Once again we stand upright,
Clap our hands with all our might.
Tap our feet upon the floor,
While we count 1 . . . 2 . . . 3 . . . 4.

Forward arms we can extend,
And our elbows stiffly bend,
Place our hands upon our hips,
Meet on heads our fingertips,
Spin around, just like a top,
Then sit down—it's time to stop.

Directions

The class stands and pantomimes the actions in the three verses. They learn the words as the teacher says them and, when they can, chant with her.

JACK AND JILL

Verses

Jack and Jill went up the hill
To get a pail of water.
Jack fell down and broke his crown
And Jill came tumbling after.

Up Jack got and said to Jill,
As soon as he was able,
"You're not hurt, brush off the dirt
And let's go get the water."

So up the hill went Jack and Jill
This time they got the water.
They took it home to mother dear
Who praised her son and daughter.

Directions

First Verse: The action is done with partners holding inside hands in a double circle. All face clockwise. One child represents Jack and one Jill. They move in the circle on the first two lines as they chant the words. On line three Jack falls down easily and then Jill follows him on line four.

Second Verse: Jack gets up and brushes himself off on lines one and two. On line three he turns to Jill and shakes his finger at her. Then he extends both hands and helps her up on line four.

Third Verse: Again they join inside hands and skip around the circle very happily.

TWO LITTLE BLACKBIRDS

Verse

> Two little blackbirds sitting on a hill.
> One named Jack, the other named Jill.
> Fly away Jack, fly away Jill.
> Come back Jack, come back Jill.

Formation

Single circle, partners facing each other. All Jacks face in the same direction and all Jills face in the opposite direction.

Directions

First Line: Both Jack and Jill kneel on both knees.

Second Line: Jack stands and claps his hands once. Jill stands and claps her hands once.

Third Line: Jack raises his arms and flies to his right. Jill raises her arms and flies to her right.

Fourth Line: Jack flies back to his original place. Jill flies back to her original place.

Singing Games and Folk Dances[2]

THE SNAIL SHELL

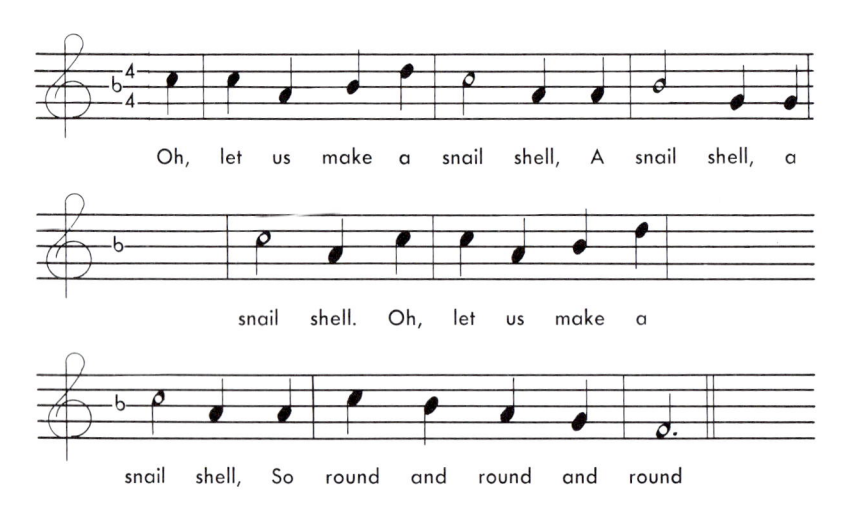

Figure 20-1. The Snail Shell.

Formation

Divide class into groups of ten children. Each group stands in a straight line and holds hands.

Verses

> Oh, let us make a snail shell,
> A snail shell, a snail shell.
> Oh, let us make a snail shell,
> So round and round and round.
>
> Oh, let's unwind the snail shell,
> The snail shell, the snail shell.
> Oh, let's unwind the snail shell,
> So round and round and round.

Directions

During the first verse, the first child in each line leads all children around in a large circle, which he gradually makes smaller.

During the second verse he leads them back again to a straight line. Start by walking, then change to skipping, and then to slide steps. Sing the first verse as many times as needed to make the shell and then repeat the second verse to unwind.

Variation

The entire class may play this together if desired.

[2] Diagrams of various dance formations may be found in Appendix C.

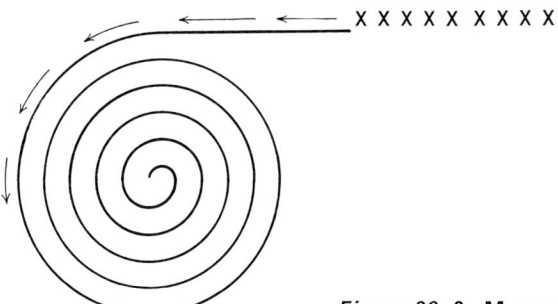

Figure 20–2. Movement during "The Snail Shell."

IMITATIONS

Figure 20–3. Imitations.

Formation
　　Single circle, holding hands.

Verses
Did you ever see a bunny, a bunny, a bunny;
Did you ever see a bunny,
Hop this way and that?

Hop this way and that way,
Hop this way and that way;
Did you ever see a bunny,
Hop this way and that?

Did you ever see a froggie, a froggie, a froggie,
(Repeat as above verse, substitute "jump" for "hop.")

Did you ever see a duck, a duck, a duck,
(Repeat as first verse, substitute "waddle.")

Did you ever see a car, a car, a car,
(Repeat as first verse, substitute "run.")

Did you ever see a jet, a jet, a jet,
(Repeat as first verse, substitute "fly.")

Directions

Children hold hands and skip around the circle on the first three lines of each verse. On lines four, five, and six they pantomime the action as the word suggests (i.e., bunny—hop), going around the circle the opposite way without holding hands.

MERRY-GO-ROUND

Figure 20–4. Merry-Go-Round.

Formation

Double circle. Partners holding inside hands.

Verse

The merry-go-round goes round and round,
One horse goes up and one goes down,
It's fun to reach as we go by,
To catch the brass ring, we will try,
We get a free ride if we do,
If not—one ride and then we're through,
The merry-go-round goes round and round,
One horse goes up and one goes down.

Directions

First Line: Eight skips clockwise around the circle. Stop; face partner and hold both hands.

Second Line: Inside partner goes way up on tiptoes as outside partner does a deep knee bend. Alternate four of each for each partner making a total of eight counts.

Third and Fourth Lines: Sixteen skips with partners behind each other in a single circle; each child pretends to grab the brass ring in rhythm to the skipping and the music. They stop, facing their partners, and hold hands.

Fifth and Sixth Lines: Repeat the up-and-down action of the merry-go-round horse as in line two for a total of sixteen counts.

Seventh and Eighth Lines: Drop one hand; sixteen skips with partner in double circle.

HEAD AND SHOULDERS

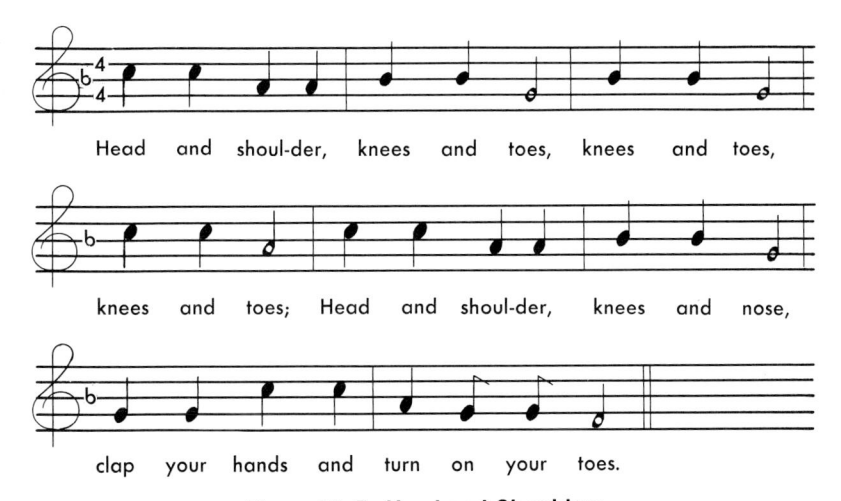

Figure 20-5. Head and Shoulders.

Formation
  Circle or line

Verse
  Head and shoulder, knees and toes,
  Knees and toes, knees and toes;
  Head and shoulder, knees and nose,
  Clap your hands and turn on your toes.

Directions
  Children touch the parts of their body as they name them.

Variations
  Change words using other parts of the body and different actions at the end. Changes in tempo may also be used.

OCTOBER'S LEAVES

(musical notation)

to-ber? Do you all love Oc-to-ber, With its bright co-lored leaves?

Figure 20–6. October's Leaves.

Formation
    Circle with children holding hands.

Verses

    Do you all love October,
    October, October?
    Do you all love October,
    With its bright colored leaves?

    First, will come the gold ones,
    The gold ones, the gold ones,
    First, will come the gold ones,
    Fluttering to the earth.

    Next, will come the red ones,
    The red ones, the red ones,
    Next, will come the red ones,
    Fluttering to the earth.

    Now, will come the brown ones,
    The brown ones, the brown ones,
    Now, will come the brown ones,
    Fluttering to the earth.

    All to earth have fallen,
    Have fallen, have fallen,
    All to earth have fallen,
    October's bright leaves.

    Now the wind comes blowing,
    Comes blowing, comes blowing,
    Now the wind comes blowing.
    And scatters the leaves away.

Directions
    All children choose the color leaf they wish to be. Children hold hands and skip around the circle on the first verse.
    Second Verse: All children who are gold leaves flutter down slowly with the music until they are as low as they can stoop.
    Third Verse: Red leaves fall.
    Fourth Verse: Brown leaves fall.
    Fifth Verse: Sung while children are still in the crouched position.
    Sixth Verse: As children sing they gradually rise moving their arms as the wind would blow them. On the last line, all the children scatter away from the circle as fast as they can.

Variation
    Change the name and use other words, such as the springtime with its bright colored birds.

THE BIRDS

(musical notation)

There stands a red bird, tra - la - la,

Figure 20-7. The Birds.

Formation

Single circle. One pupil is chosen to stand in the center as the "bird."

Verses

There stands a red bird, tra-la-la,
There stands a red bird, tra-la-la,
There stands a red bird, tra-la-lee,
Give me sugar, coffee, and tea.

(*Note:* Change the color of the bird depending on the color of clothing the "bird" is wearing.)

Let me see your motion, tra-la-la,
Let me see your motion, tra-la-la,
Let me see your motion, tra-la-lee,
Give me sugar, coffee, and tea.

A very good motion, tra-la-la.
A very good motion, tra-la-la.
A very good motion, tra-la-lee,
Give me sugar, coffee, and tea.

Now fly to your lover, tra-la-la,
Now fly to your lover, tra-la-la,
Now fly to your lover, tra-la-lee,
Give me sugar, coffee, and tea.

Directions

First Verse: Entire circle moves around clockwise, either with skip, walk, or slide step.

Second Verse: Child in the center pantomimes an activity in rhythm to the music. Players in the circle clap their hands in rhythm as they sing.

Third Verse: All children do the same motion the child in the center did in the second verse.

Fourth Verse: The child in the center flies to choose a new person. All children raise their arms and pretend to fly while singing.

TO THE CANDY SHOP

Hip-pit-y hop to the can-dy shop, To buy three bars of can-dy

314 RECOMMENDED MOVEMENT EXPERIENCES

One for you and one for me And one for sis-ter San-dy.

Figure 20–8. To the Candy Shop.

Formation

Double circle, facing clockwise. Boys and girls are partners, boys in outer circle.

Directions

Children hold hands and skip around the circle.
Second Line: Children may use free hand to hold up three fingers, to represent the "three bars of candy."

Third Line: Children stop and face each other and point their fingers as directed.

Fourth Line: "And one for sister Sandy," they turn and look all around for sister.

HOW DO YOU DO, MY PARTNER?

How do you do, my part-ner, How do you do to-day?
Will you dance in the cir-cle? I will show you the way.

Figure 20–9. How Do You Do, My Partner?

Records

Folkraft Record Co., #1190; Educational Record Sales, Record 10—"Folk Dances, Song Plays, Play Parties."

Formation

Double circle facing partners.

Directions

First Line: Boy bows to girl.
Second Line: Girl curtsies to boy.
Third and Fourth Lines: Partners join both hands and skip in a small circle taking 12 skips. Repeat tune singing "tra, la, la," and skip around the large circle clockwise.

RIDE A COCK-HORSE

Ride a cock-horse to Ban-bur-y Cross To

see a fine lady up-on a fine horse; Rings on her fingers and bells on her toes, She shall have music wherever she goes.

Figure 20-10. Ride a Cock-Horse.

Records
Educational Record Sales—"Nursery and Mother Goose Songs."

Formation
Double circle facing toward the center. Girls stand in the back with their hands on boys' shoulders.

Directions
First Line: Four quick glide steps toward the center of the circle.

Second Line: All face right, take partner's hand and skip four steps forward.

Third Line: "Rings on her fingers," partners face each other. Raise both arms high over head and return them in a fluttering movement. "Bells on her toes," partners hold hands and jump, each extending right foot forward and replacing it. Repeat.

Fourth Line: Partners face line of direction holding inside hands and skip. Repeat the entire dance.

THE MUFFIN MAN

Oh, have you seen the muf-fin man, the muf-fin man, the muf-fin man? Oh, have you seen the muf-fin man who lives in Dru-ry Lane, O!

Oh, yes I've seen the muf-fin man, the muf-fin man, the muf-fin man? Oh, yes, I've seen the muf-fin man who lives in Dru-ry Lane, O!

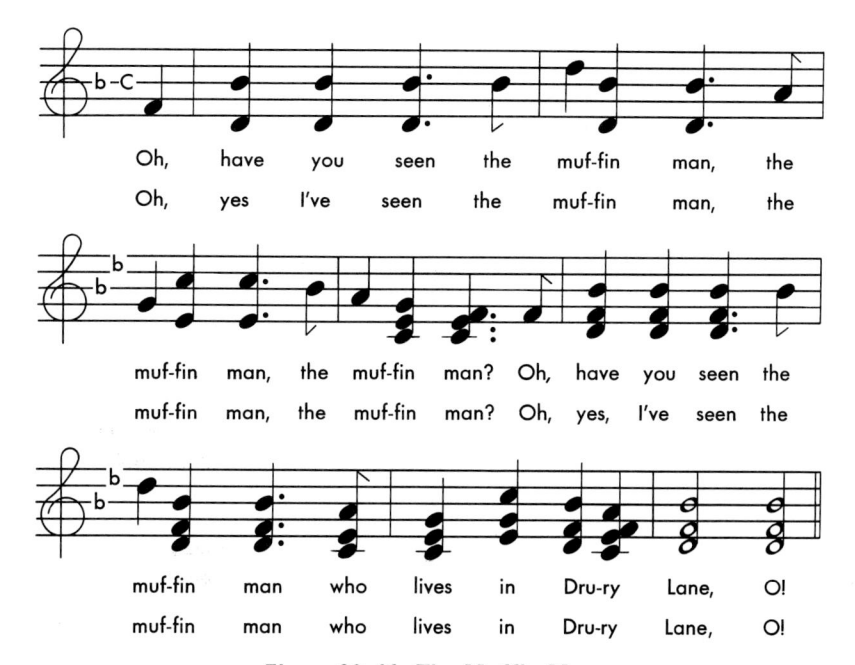

Figure 20-11. The Muffin Man.

316 RECOMMENDED MOVEMENT EXPERIENCES

Records

Folkraft Record Co., #1188; Educational Record Sales, "Kindergarten Album No. 1"; Educational Record Sales, Record 3—"Folk Dances, Song Plays, Play Parties."

Formation

Players hold hands in a single circle. One or more stand inside the circle.

Directions

First Verse: First and second lines: the circle skips in a counterclockwise direction while singing the first two lines; players inside the circle walk in the opposite direction. Third line: all stop and each child from inside the circle chooses a partner from the circle and takes him to the center. Circle children clap. Fourth line: the children in the center of the circle join both hands and skip around. Circle children clap.

Second Verse: Before starting the second verse, the players in the center choose partners from the outer circle to enter the circle with them; they clasp hands and dance around the circle singing the last two lines, while the outer circle does the same.

THE MULBERRY BUSH

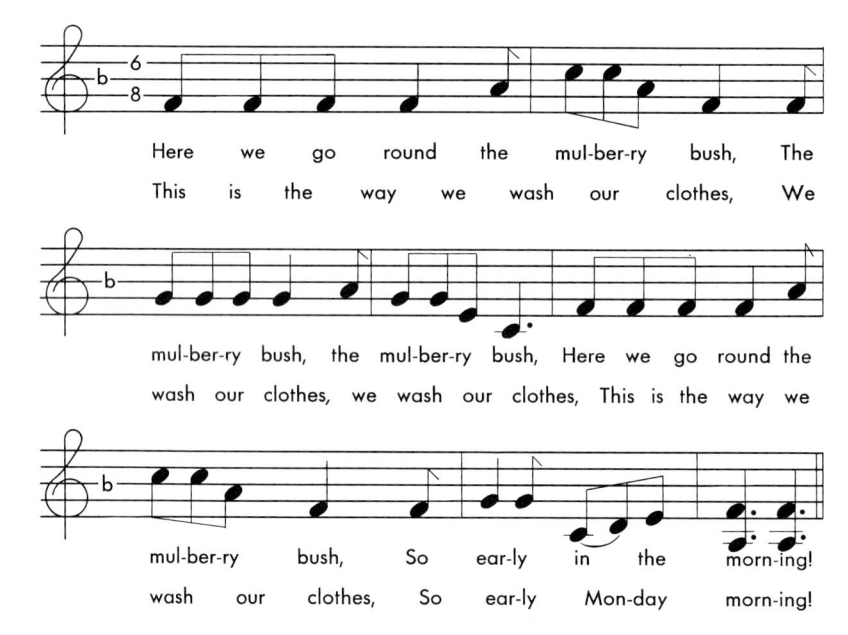

Figure 20–12. The Mulberry Bush.

Records

Folkraft Record Co., #1183; Educational Record Sales, Record 4—"Folk Dances, Song Plays, Play Parties"; Kismet Record Co., #111.

Formation

Single circle, holding hands.

Third Verse

This is the way we iron our clothes . . .
So early Tuesday morning.

Fourth Verse

This is the way we scrub the floor . . .
So early Wednesday morning.

Fifth Verse

This is the way we mend our clothes . . .
So early Thursday morning.

Sixth Verse

This is the way we sweep the house . . .
So early Friday morning.

Movement Experiences for Early Childhood

Seventh Verse
Thus we play when our work is done . . .
So early Saturday morning.

Eighth Verse
This is the way we go to church . . .
So early Sunday morning.

Directions
First Verse: Children sing first verse while skipping around circle in counterclockwise direction.

Other Verses: Children dramatize the action called for on each day, "ironing" on Tuesday, "scrubbing" on Wednesday, "mending" on Thursday, and so on.

DID YOU EVER SEE A LASSIE (LADDIE)?

Figure 20–13. Did You Ever See a Lassie?

Records
Folkraft Record Co., #1183; Educational Record Sales, Record 4—"Folk Dances, Song Plays, Play Parties."

Formation
Single circle, facing clockwise with hands joined. One child is in the center.

Directions
Dancers walk or skip to the left eight steps, then turn and walk eight steps to the right. As they sing line three, the child in the center does any action the children can imitate. On line four, they all imitate the action. Select a new child for the center and repeat.

LOOBY LOO

Figure 20-14. Looby Loo.

Records

Folkraft Record Co., #1102 and #1184; Educational Record Sales, Record 5—"Folk Dances, Song Plays, Play Parties"; Educational Record Sales, Record 10—"Honor Your Partner."

Formation

Single circle, all facing left with hands joined.

Chorus

Here we dance Looby Loo,
Here we dance Looby Light;
Here we dance Looby Loo,
All on a Saturday night.

First Verse

You put your right hand in,
You put your right hand out,
You give your hand a shake, shake, shake,
And turn yourself about.

Second Verse

You put your left hand in, etc.

Third Verse

You put your right foot in, etc.

Fourth Verse

You put your left foot in, etc.

Fifth Verse

You put your head way in, etc.

Sixth Verse

You put your whole self in, etc.

Directions

Start with the chorus. Children skip around the circle when chorus is sung. Pantomime the action as each verse is sung. Repeat the chorus after each verse, with children skipping around the circle.

HERE COMES A BLUEBIRD THROUGH MY WINDOW

Complete directions for "Here Comes a Bluebird Through My Window" are given in Chapter 9.

SHOEMAKER'S DANCE

Figure 20–15. Shoemaker's Dance.

Records

Folkraft Record Co., #1187; Kismet Record Co., VIC 45–6171.

Formation

Double circle, partners facing.

Verses

Wind, wind, wind the thread,
Wind, wind, wind the thread,
Pull, pull, and tap, tap, tap.

Wind, wind, wind the thread,
Wind, wind, wind the thread,
Pull, pull, and tap, tap, tap.

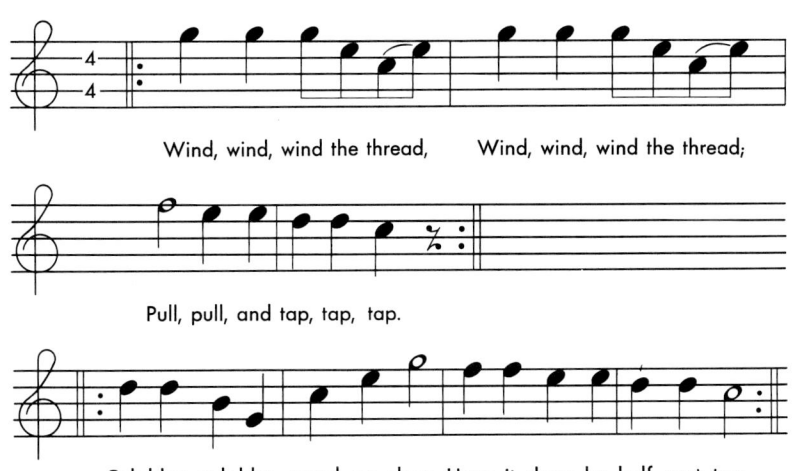

Cobbler, cobbler mend my shoe,
Have it done by half past two.
Stitch it up and stitch it down,
Make the finest shoe in town.

Directions

First Line: "Wind the thread" by raising arms to shoulder height in front of chest, clenching fists, and winding one arm over the other three times.

Second Line: Reverse wind by rolling fists in opposite direction.

Third Line: "Pull, pull" by pulling fists apart twice. "Tap, tap, tap" by clapping own hands three times.

Fourth, Fifth, and Sixth Lines: Repeat action.

Seventh and Eighth Lines: Double circle, facing counterclockwise, inside hands joined; all skip around circle, finishing with bow.

Creative and/or Interpretive Rhythms, Including Mimetics. After the child has learned the single fundamental movements and their combinations in a variety of specific rhythmical patterns, he can use them to create his own patterns or interpret the standard ones in order to convey an idea suggested to him by musical accompaniment.

Such interpretations may include fall winds blowing hard and scattering leaves; airplanes taking off, flying, and landing; a day at a circus; a parade; the toy shop; joyful fairies; sad elves; Santa's helpers in a gleeful mood; or snowflakes falling and being blown by the wind.

One excellent source of music for interpretation is the ever popular children's recording. Many records are available. Ruth Evans's "Childhood Rhythm Records," Series I, II, and IX, are excellent. Phoebe James's "Creative Rhythms," a 22-record series (AED1 through AED22), is also a rich source for creative dances. R.C.A. records offer many choices, too. Appendix A lists other sources and addresses.

The greater the rhythmical experiences of a child, the greater is his potential for self-expression. Also, activities which are specifically defined or identified by the teacher, another student, or the child himself can be imitated. The child borrows from actual observations and mimics those defined for him. Such imitations may be of tops, wooden soldiers, animals, birds, trains, prancing horses, or skating and swinging. Records for mimetics include "Animal Rhythms," the RR2 Educational Record Album; "The Merry Toy Shop," "I Am a Circus," "Let's Be Firemen," "Let's Play Zoo," Merry Toy Shop—Album 21, Modern Activities for Primary and Elementary Schools.[2]

Developmental Activities with Playground Equipment

Great fun and large-muscle activity may become an important part of the physical education program through the correct use of playground equipment. Children naturally love to climb. The jungle gym gives them the opportunity to do so. However, children must be taught correct and safe usage of equipment. Seesaws, swings, and slides give opportunities for the use and development of certain groups of muscles. Leg muscles are constantly used in climbing the ladder of the slides. The pulling movement of the arms on the swing and the use of leg muscles on seesaws are all recommended for the growth of children. Other desirable pieces of equipment include horizontal ladders, climbing bars of different heights, ropes for climbing, and large tiles or barrels for crawling through.

When children are taught the safe and correct way to use these pieces of equipment and to take turns in their use so they respect each other, they are learning important daily lessons in getting along together as well as gaining much fun and developing their large muscles.

Games of Low Organization

Games with Equipment

CALL BALL

Equipment
One ball.

Formation
Children form a single circle. One player is in the center with a ball.

Directions
The center player tosses the ball into the air and calls one of the children's names. The player called runs to catch the ball before it bounces more than once. If he catches the ball, he remains in the center and the one in the center takes his place in the circle. If he misses, he returns to his place in the circle and the center player calls someone else. Encourage children to toss the ball straight up and, also, as they improve, to catch it before it hits the floor.

TEACHER BALL

Equipment
One ball.

Formation
Several groups of eight or ten are formed. One

[2] Addresses of record companies are given in Appendix A.

player in each group is "teacher." The players line up facing the teacher.

Directions
The "teacher" tosses the ball to each of the players in turn and they return it to him. When the "teacher" has tossed it to and received it from each child he goes to the foot of the line and the child from the head of the line is the new "teacher." Continue as long as interest warrants. Distances may be made greater as children become better at tossing.

Variations
Bounce the ball to each other; catch a tossed ball and bounce it once to yourself before returning it.

DODGE BALL

Equipment
One ball (any size).

Formation
Circle.

Directions
Children form a single circle facing center. Place several players in the center of the circle. The players in the circle attempt to hit the players in the center below the waist by throwing the ball at them. The players in the center may run, jump, and dodge to keep out of the way of the ball. When a player in the center is hit, he exchanges places with the thrower who hit him.

HIT THE BOX

Equipment
One ball or bean bag and one cardboard box.

Formation
Circle.

Directions
Children stand in a circle facing the center where a box has been placed. They take turns trying to toss the ball or bean bag into the box. Each child runs in to retrieve his equipment and tosses it to the person who was on his right in the circle. One point is scored for each time the ball or bean bag stays in the box.

Distances may be increased as children become more skillful at hitting the box. If space is restricted, a smaller box may be substituted as the children improve.

CIRCLE STRIDE BALL

Equipment
One ball.

Formation
Circle.

Directions
The children stand in a single circle facing the center. The players stand in a stride position so that the outsides of their feet touch those of the player next to them. One player is "It" and stands in the middle of the circle with the ball.

"It" tries to throw or roll the ball between the legs of the players in the circle. The players must not move their feet, but they may use their hands to try to stop the ball. Knees must be kept straight. If "It" succeeds in getting the ball through a player's legs, he changes places with that player and the game continues.

Games Without Equipment

TABBY CAT

Formation
Circle.

Directions
One half of the class acts the part of tabby cats; the other half are hungry mice. Boys may represent one and girls the other, if desired. The tabby cats sit down in a circle, if the ground is dry. Otherwise, they may stoop. The mice make a circle around the tabby cats so each mouse is at least 10 feet from the cats. A safe home for the mice is marked on the ground away from the large circle. The tabby cats pretend to be asleep. The mice chant the following verse and do the following pantomime actions as they creep up behind the tabby cats:

Hungry mouse is creeping and walking all around.
He's wearing furry slippers and doesn't make a
  sound,
Tabby cat is sleeping and dozing in the sun,
Walk softly or you'll wake her and she will make
  you run.

On the last line—"And she will make you run"—the tabby cats jump up and chase the mice. All mice run for their home. The mice caught act as cats, and cats who caught a mouse act as mice for the next game. Every child should be given an opportunity to play each part.

BIRD CATCHER

Formation

Rectangular area with two goals marked at either end.

Directions

Two opposite goals are marked off at each end of the play area. One serves as a nest for the birds and the other as a cage. A mother bird is chosen and takes her place in the nest. Two other players take the part of bird catchers and stand midway between nest and cage. All other players stand in the cage. All of these players should be named for birds. Several players may take the name of the same bird. The naming of the players will be facilitated by doing it in groups.

The teacher calls the name of a bird, whereupon all of the players who bear that name run from the cage to the nest, but the bird catchers try to intercept them. Should a bird be caught it assists the bird catcher, but a bird is safe from the bird catchers if it reaches the nest and the mother bird. The players should be taught to make the chase interesting by dodging in various directions instead of running for the nest in a simple, straight line.

BEAR IN THE PIT

Formation

Circle.

Directions

Children are in a circle formation holding hands. Mark two goals 10, 20, or 30 yards from each side of the circle depending on the age of the children and the amount of playing space. One player stands in the center of the circle and is the bear. The bear tries to break through the ring by parting the hands of the players. When he breaks through, all players chase and try to tag him. If the bear is successful in reaching a goal before being tagged he may score a point and select the next bear. A player who tags the bear before he reaches the goal becomes the new bear.

CHARLEY OVER THE WATER

Formation

Circle.

Directions

One player is chosen to be Charley. If there are more than 20 players, there should be two or more Charleys to make the action more rapid. Charley stands in the center; the other players join hands in a circle around him and dance around, repeating the following rhyme:

> Charley over the water,
> Charley over the sea.
> Charley catch a blackbird,
> Can't catch me!

As the last word is said, the players stoop, and Charley tries to tag them before they can get into that position. Charley has three turns. His score is the number of children tagged before they stoop. After three turns a new Charley is chosen and the game continues. All children are challenged to see if they can be fast enough never to be tagged.

FLOWERS AND THE WIND

Formation

Rectangular area with a home line at each end.

Directions

The players are divided into two equal groups. Each group has a home marked off at opposite ends of the play area, with a long neutral space between. One group represents a flower. Children decide among themselves which flower they shall represent, such as daisies, lilies, lilacs, and so on. They then walk over near the home line of the opposite group. The opposite players represent the wind. They stand in a row on their line, ready to run as soon as they guess the name of the flower chosen by their opponents. As soon as the right flower is named, all flowers turn and run home. The winds chase them. Each player tagged by a wind before reaching his goal scores one point for the wind. The two groups then reverse and the wind group chooses the name of a flower. After an even number of times of being both wind and flowers the group with the higher score wins.

MERRY-GO-ROUND

Equipment
   None. (A record player may be used.)

Players
   10 to 30.

Directions
   Form a double circle, one inside the other. Choose from one to five children to go in the middle of the inner circle. These children are the ticket takers. At the signal "Go," the players in the outside circle walk around the inner circle. The inside circle stays in place but the children move up and down representing horses on the merry-go-round. At a given signal—a whistle, a clap, or stopping the music if a record is used—the children in the outer circle try to get a horse for a ride. They succeed by placing one hand on the head of a child in the inner circle. The ticket takers try to get a horse also. Those left with no horse become the new ticket takers.

THE GARDENER AND THE SCAMP

Formation
   Circle.

Directions
   All but two of the players form a circle and join hands. The circle is the garden. One of the odd players is assigned to be the scamp and stands in the circle. The other odd player, the gardener, moves around on the outside of the circle.
   The gardener calls to the scamp inside, "Who let you in my garden?" The scamp answers, "No one!" He then starts to run away and the gardener chases him. The gardener must follow the path of the scamp, in and out, under the arms of the players, who must lift their hands to let them pass. The gardener must also imitate every movement performed by the scamp, who may jump, skip, run, walk, hop, or do any other movement he wishes. When the scamp is caught, a new gardener and scamp are chosen.
   If the gardener fails to follow in the exact path of the scamp and/or to perform any of the feats or antics of the scamp, the gardener must at once join the ring. The scamp then has the privilege of choosing a new gardener. If the gardener has not tagged the scamp after a few minutes have passed, two others should be chosen.

GOOD MORNING

Formation
   Circle.

Directions
   Children form a circle holding hands. One child is "It" and stays outside the circle. He moves around the circle and separates the hands of two persons. "It" stays in the vacant place left by the two, standing with his back to the center of the circle and one arm extended full length. The two children run around the circle each in the opposite direction. When they meet they extend right hands, shake hands, and repeat aloud so that all may hear, "Good morning; good morning, good morning." They then continue around in the same direction to see who can tag the extended hand of "It" first. The winner becomes the new "It."
   Variations include different ways of moving, such as hopping, skipping, or galloping. Also, seasons of the year may change the greeting to "Merry Christmas," and the like.

SQUIRREL IN THE TREE

Formation
   Groups of three scattered over an area suitable for the number of players.

Directions
   Players stand in groups of two with hands clasped together, thus forming a tree. Trees are scattered in a large area. A squirrel is chosen to stand in each tree. One odd squirrel is without a tree. The leader of the game then claps his hands and the squirrels, including the odd player, run for a new tree. The squirrel left out becomes the odd squirrel for the next game. More than one odd squirrel may be used. Trees and squirrels change positions often.

OLD MOTHER WITCH

Formation
   Rectangular area with a goal line at one end of the rectangle.

Directions
   One child is chosen to be Old Mother Witch. The others stand within an area marked at one end of the play space. This is the children's home. Old

Mother Witch starts walking and the children follow her chanting:

> Old Mother Witch
> Fell in a ditch,
> Picked up a penny,
> And thought she was rich!

Each time the verse ends, Old Mother Witch turns and asks, "Whose children are you?" One child, who is the leader, answers anything he or she wishes, such as "The baker's," "The butcher's," and so on. After each answer, the witch continues and the children trail her again, chanting the rhyme. When the leader answers the witch's question with "Yours," the witch chases the children back to their goal. Her score is the number of children she tags. A new witch is then chosen and the game is repeated.

BROWNIES AND FAIRIES

Formation
Two goals are set 30 to 40 feet apart; the players are divided into two equal groups and stand in the goals. One group are the fairies and the other are the brownies.

Directions
One group (fairies) turn their backs, while the others (brownies) creep up as quietly as possible. One fairy is watching, and when the brownies are near calls, "Look out for the brownies." The fairies then chase the brownies to their goal and tag as many as they can. Each brownie caught scores one point for the fairies. Then the brownies turn their backs and the fairies come up quietly, and so on. The side having the greater number of points at the end of the playing time is the winner.

COME ALONG

Formation
The players join hands and form a single circle. One player who is "It" is on the outside.

Directions
"It" runs around the circle, taps one of the players on the shoulder, and says, "Come along." The one who is tapped starts in pursuit and tries to tag "It" before he gets into the place left vacant. If he succeeds he becomes "It" and challenges another player. If he does not tag him he takes his original place in the circle. The original "It" may have a second turn or may choose a new "It."

FOLLOW THE LEADER

Formation
Players form in single file behind a leader.

Directions
The players follow the leader and do whatever he does. When one player has been leader a reasonable length of time, the teacher indicates that he is to choose a new leader. Teachers may need to help in suggesting different activities for the leader.

HILL DILL

Formation
Two parallel boundary lines are drawn from 30 to 50 feet apart. One player is chosen to be "It" and stands in the center. The other players stand behind one boundary line.

Directions
The center player calls out "Hill, dill, come over the hill!" The players run to the new goal, and, as they run across the open space, "It" tags as many as he can. All who are tagged assist him thereafter in tagging the others. "It" then calls the players back to their original goal. The last player tagged becomes the new "It."

HUNTSMAN

Formation
Children stand in a group on a goal line. One player is chosen to be the huntsman.

Directions
The huntsman moves around in any way he chooses. All the players follow behind him and do the actions he does. When the huntsman sees that all are away from their goal he calls "Bang." This is the signal for all to return to their goal. The huntsman tags as many as he can. Each huntsman may have three turns. His score is the number he tagged during his three turns. All children continue to play. No one assists the huntsman. After three turns a new huntsman is chosen.

RINGMASTER

Formation

Players form in a circle around a player chosen to be the ringmaster.

Directions

The ringmaster makes believe he cracks a whip and calls out the name of some animal. All players in the circle mimic the actions of the animal—i.e., a tiger claws, stretches, snarls, walks rapidly back and forth. The one doing the best imitation is chosen to be the new ringmaster.

CAT AND RAT

Formation

Single circle facing inward. One player, the rat, inside the circle; another, the cat, is outside.

Directions

The cat tries to break through the circle and catch the rat. The circle does all it can to protect the rat. If the cat should break through, the circle must protect the rat by letting it out and keeping the cat in. When the rat is caught it returns to the circle. A new cat and rat are chosen. If the cat fails to catch the rat after a few minutes, reverse the names.

Individual and Dual Activities

Children should use different activities alone or with two or three friends to develop certain skills, to share with others, and to have fun while being active.

BALL BOUNCING

Use large balls. Children may bounce the ball and catch it or they may work with partners and bounce it to a partner who catches it and bounces it back. This may also be played with four players standing in a square.

BALL TOSSING

Follow the directions for ball bouncing, but toss the balls back and forth.

CONTINUED BALL BOUNCING

When children are able, they should be encouraged to bounce a ball more than once to themselves. This develops eye-and-hand coordination.

BEAN BAG TOSS

Mark a circle and have children toss bean bags from different distances, trying to make them land in the circle. Circles should be of various sizes. When the players become consistently able to hit a large circle, they should then be challenged to aim for a smaller one. Waste baskets and cardboard boxes are also challenging to hit.

ROPE JUMPING

Children of this age group start to learn rope jumping by having the rope turned by two persons. Some can gain the coordination necessary to turn their own rope and skip at that same time.

SIMPLE HOPSCOTCH

Very simple diagrams for hopscotch are usable with this age group. Diagrams and directions may be found in the activities for seven- and eight-year-olds.

Self-Testing Activities and Stunts

DOG WALK

Place hands on floor. Walk on hands and feet like a dog.

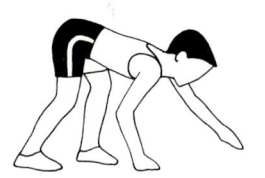

Figure 20–16. Dog Walk.

RECOMMENDED MOVEMENT EXPERIENCES

JUMPING JACK

Take squat position, touch hands on floor between knees, then suddenly jump up and at same time extend arms horizontally to sides.

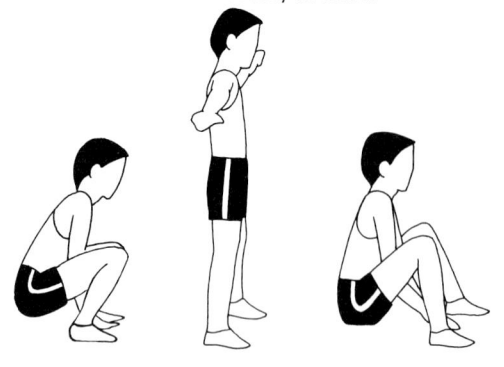

Figure 20-17. Jumping Jack.

DUCK WALK

Deep knee bend to squat position. Hands on hips or tucked under armpits. Walk without raising hips.

Figure 20-18. Duck Walk.

TIGHTROPE WALKING

Draw a 10-foot line on floor. Walk line using arms to balance.

Figure 20-19. Tightrope Walk.

MONKEY JUMP

On all fours, imitate a jumping monkey.

Figure 20-20. Monkey Jump.

ELEPHANT WALK

Bend forward keeping knees straight and place hands flat on the floor. Walk forward and backward keeping knees and elbows straight.

Figure 20-21. Elephant Walk.

RABBIT JUMP

Squat position. Place hands on floor in front of feet. Push off on the feet and lift hands from floor. Catch weight on hands and bring feet to hands to imitate a rabbit hop.

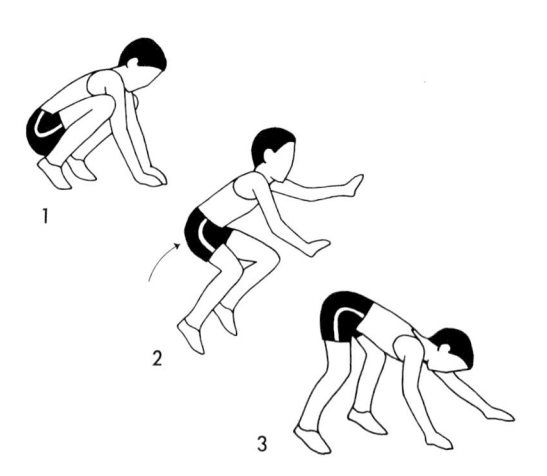

Figure 20-22. Rabbit Jump.

Story Plays

Titles for story plays may be planned on a monthly basis using seasons, holidays, and special occasions. The following are suggested by months. Teachers will readily find many more of interest to their children. Refer to Chapter 9 for a story play showing complete development, progression, and correlation.

Table 20–1. **Possible Themes for Story Plays**

September

Preparations for returning to school.
Taking a long hike through the woods.

October

Getting ready for Halloween.
Going to the country to get pumpkins.
Raking leaves and helping Mother and Dad.
Gathering autumn leaves.
Picking apples.

November

Thanksgiving—going to Grandma's house.
Going to a turkey farm to get a turkey.
Fixing and delivering baskets of food to ill and needy families.
Gathering nuts.
November winds.

December

Santa's helper.
Santa's reindeer.
Getting the Christmas tree from Farmer Brown's farm.
Christmas toys.
Trimming the Christmas tree.

January

Shoveling snow.
Making snowmen and knocking off their hats with snowballs.
Skating on a pond and up a creek.
Coasting.

February

Stories relating to Washington.
Stories relating to Lincoln.
Valentine's Day.
A snow storm.

March

The Easter Bunny's helpers.
March winds.

April

Raking and mowing lawns.
Planting a garden.
House cleaning.
Baby birds.

May

Going to the woods to pick flowers.
Preparing and delivering May baskets.
Trees in a storm.
Going swimming.

June

Getting ready and going on a picnic.
Getting ready and going to the lake or seashore for a swim.
Picking cherries.
Going fishing.

Classroom Games

SEVEN UP

Players
   Entire class.

Directions
   Pupils are all in their seats. A captain is in charge at the front of the room. The captain calls seven pupils to the front of the room and instructs all players in their seats to put their heads on their desks and close their eyes. The seven pupils at the front of the room then tiptoe around the room. Each one touches one person gently on the head. Then they return to the front of the room. The person touched raises his hand so that he will not be touched twice. All heads remain down until the captain tells them to raise them by saying "Seven up." The captain then asks each person with a raised hand to guess who touched him. If he guesses correctly, he exchanges places and goes to the front of the room. If he fails to guess who touched him, the toucher remains as one of the seven to play the next game.

TRAFFIC LIGHT

Equipment

   Three circles cut from 9-inch by 12-inch pieces of construction paper. One is red, one yellow, and one green. Music—any march.

Players
   Entire class.

Directions
   Choose one child to be a policeman and supply him with the red, yellow, and green circles. All children march around the room in time with the music. The policeman flashes first one color then another. Children must obey the traffic lights. Green light means "Go," and they march. Yellow light means "Caution," and they mark time in place. Red light means "Stop," and they move no part of their body. Various steps, such as skipping, tiptoes, giant strides, and so on, may be used. Change the direction and paths the children take.

THE LONE RANGER

Equipment
   A bandana to cover a child's eyes.

Players
   Entire class.

Directions
   The class chooses one child to be the Lone Ranger. He is blindfolded. The other children form a circle with the Lone Ranger in the middle. He whirls around three times, points to a person and calls "Hi ho Silver!" This person must answer, "Hi ho Silver." The Lone Ranger tries to identify the voice. He may have three tries. If he does not guess correctly, the player who fooled him is blindfolded and becomes the Lone Ranger.

YARN BALL DODGE BALL

Equipment
   One yarn ball.

Players
   Entire class.

Directions
   Divide the class into two groups. One group sits in its seats in the center of the classroom. The other group forms a square around them. The group which is standing up gets three minutes to hit as many sitters as it can with the yarn ball. Each hit is a point. The score is kept aloud by the leader of the throwing team. After three minutes the groups change. The higher score wins.

QUIET AS MICE

Equipment
   Five chairs; five blackboard erasers, bean bags, or objects of similar size.

Players
   Entire class.

Directions
   Five children are chosen to be big mice; each one sits on a chair in front of the room. One object representing a big cheese is placed under each chair.

All other children act as baby mice who try to steal the cheese from the big mice. The big mice close their eyes and five baby mice are selected to steal the cheese. They go up as *quietly as mice*. Even if the big mouse hears a baby mouse, he or she does nothing. When each baby mouse has a cheese, all children exchange seats very quietly so the big mouse cannot trace the sound and guess who stole his cheese. Each big mouse is given one guess to determine who stole his cheese. If he is successful, he remains a big mouse. If he fails, each successful baby mouse grows to a big mouse.

Selected References

See end of Chapter 24.

CHAPTER 21

Movement Experiences for Early Childhood (Ages Seven and Eight)

Dances and Rhythms

As children progress, their level of ability improves and the quality of skill movement should be much improved. For example, they can develop from a slow skip to a jig skip, to a fast skip. This progression enables them to cover a greater distance through space. The personal satisfaction is an individual reward because each one is moving as he feels and propels himself through space at his own level of ability. Their ability makes it possible for the children to combine various locomotor movements—such as slide, slide-hop; leap, run-run—and change direction on command during the performance of any movement without falling or colliding with another person.

The use of media such as lummi sticks, gretch drum, or tambourine is valuable in the development of the rhythmic pattern for each combined movement.

Dramatization and Creative Rhythms. Additional dramatizations and creative rhythms are an important phase of the rhythm program at this level. The child is encouraged to utilize the fundamental movements and combination movements to convey ideas suggested by the children's experiences, the teacher, or musical compositions. These age groups may be expected to develop movement compositions (floor patterns) by using combinations of the various fundamental movements to interpret ideas or suggestions conveyed by music.

New steps should include the basic schottische and modified polka, which are easily learned combinations of fundamental movements.

1. Schottische—4/4 time: step (L)–step (R)–step (L)–hop (L).

2. Modified polka—2/4 time: step (L)–together (R)–step (L). Counts: 1 and 2.

Other activities that may be included are rope jumping and ball bouncing to music. Suggested records for these rhythms are Evans, "Skip Rope Games," Series IV, Evans Childhood Records; and Durlacher, Album 12, "Rope Skipping."[1]

Singing Folk Dances

THE THREAD FOLLOWS THE NEEDLE
Records
Folkraft Record Co., V22760; Victor E–87–5064.

---

[1] The addresses of some record companies are given in Appendix A.

Movement Experiences for Early Childhood 331

The thread follows the needle, The thread follows the needle,

In and out the needle goes, As Mother mends the children's clothes.

Figure 21–1. The Thread Follows the Needle.

Formation
Children form a single line, all hands joined in a chain.

Directions
To sew the stitches, the leader guides the line under the raised arms of the last two children in line. When the complete line has passed under the last two children's arms, these two turn to face the opposite direction and cross their arms across their chests. The Leader continues guiding the children in and out, down the line. Each one passed turns about. This continues until all the children are facing in the opposite direction, with their hands crossed over their chests. To rip out the stitches, each child turns under his top arm and the line is straight again.

JUMP, JIM JOE

Jump, jump, oh jump, Jim Joe. Take a little whirl, and around you'll go.

Slide, slide, and stamp just so. Then take another partner and you jump, Jim Joe.

Figure 21–2. Jump, Jim Joe.

Records
Folkraft Record Co., #1180; Educational Record Sales, Record 1, "Folk Dances, Song Plays, Play Parties."

Formation
Dancers form a double circle with both hands joined. The girls are on the outside, boys on the inside.

Directions

First Line: Partners take five jumps in place.

Second Line: Hook right arms and turn in a small circle with partners with ten running steps.

Third Line: Face partners, both hands at sides. Each partner takes two slide steps to the right and three stamps in place on "stamp just so." They should then be facing new partners.

Fourth Line: Hook right arms with new partner and turn in a small circle with nine running steps. On "Jump, Jim Joe," partners jump three times in place. Repeat dance.

JOLLY IS THE MILLER

Jol-ly is the mil-ler who lives by the mill. The wheel goes 'round with a right good will; One hand in the hop-per and the oth-er in the sack, The right steps for-ward and the left steps back.

Figure 21–3. Jolly Is the Miller.

Records

Folkraft Record Co., #1192; Educational Record Sales, Album 10, "Honor Your Partner" Albums; Educational Record Sales, Record 12, "Folk Dances, Song Plays, Play Parties"; Decca, Set 283.

Formation

Double circle, with all of the children facing the line of direction. Partners join their inside hands.

Directions

First and Second Lines: Players march forward in time to music. On line two they also circle their free arm in a clockwise direction.

Third Line: Partners stop and pantomime action.

Fourth Line: Partner on the outside of the circle (R) steps forward and the partner on the inside circle (L) steps back. This should give them new partners. Repeat verse and action.

A-HUNTING WE WILL GO

Oh, a-hunt-ing we will go, A-hunt-ing we will go,

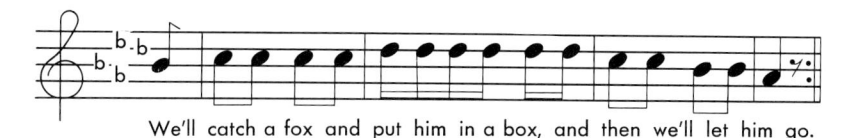

We'll catch a fox and put him in a box, and then we'll let him go.

Figure 21-4. **A-Hunting We Will Go.**

Records
Folkraft Record Co., #1191; Educational Record Sales, Record 11, "Folk Dances, Song Plays, Play Parties."

Formation
Two parallel lines, facing each other.

Chorus
Tra, la, la, la, la, la, etc.

Directions
First Line: Head couple joins both hands and slides to the foot of the line.
Second Line: Head couple slides back to the head of line.
Third Line: Repeat slide steps to foot of line.
Fourth Line: Repeat slide steps to head of line.
Chorus: Head couple drops hands and each marches around behind own line. Persons in each line follow their leaders. When leaders meet they form an arch and other couples pass through under the arch. A new head couple starts the dance again, repeating all the movements.

NUTS IN MAY

Tune
"Mulberry Bush"; see Figure 20-12, Chapter 20.

Records
Folkraft Record Co., #1183; Educational Record Sales, Record 41, "Folk Dances, Song Plays, Play Parties"; Kismet Record Co., #111.

Formation
Children form into two single lines facing each other about 10 feet apart.

Verses
Here we go gathering nuts in May,
Nuts in May, nuts in May.
Here we go gathering nuts in May,
So early in the morning.

Whom will you have for nuts in May,
Nuts in May, nuts in May?
Whom will you have for nuts in May,
So early in the morning?

We will have _____ for nuts in May,
Nuts in May, nuts in May.
We will have _____ for nuts in May,
So early in the morning.

Whom will you have to take (him or her) away,
Take _____ away, take _____ away?
Whom will you have to take _____ away,
So early in the morning?

We will have _____ to take (him or her) away,
Take _____ away, take _____ away.
We will have _____ to take _____ away,
So early in the morning.

Directions
Children in each line hold hands. One line is known as line one, the other as line two.
First Verse: Both lines skip toward each other and back in place two times in time with the music.
Second Verse: Line one repeats the action, singing the verse to line two.
Third Verse: Line two sings and repeats the action, naming the one child they wish from line one.
Fourth Verse: Line one sings and moves as before.
Fifth Verse: Line two sings and moves forward and backward and names the child in its line that will pull the other child away.

Then the children from lines one and two who were named drop hands and move to the center between the two lines. They join both hands and try to pull each other over a 1-foot line or mark placed on the ground or floor. The child pulled across the line joins the line of the puller and the rhythm is repeated from the beginning.

GO ROUND AND ROUND THE VILLAGE

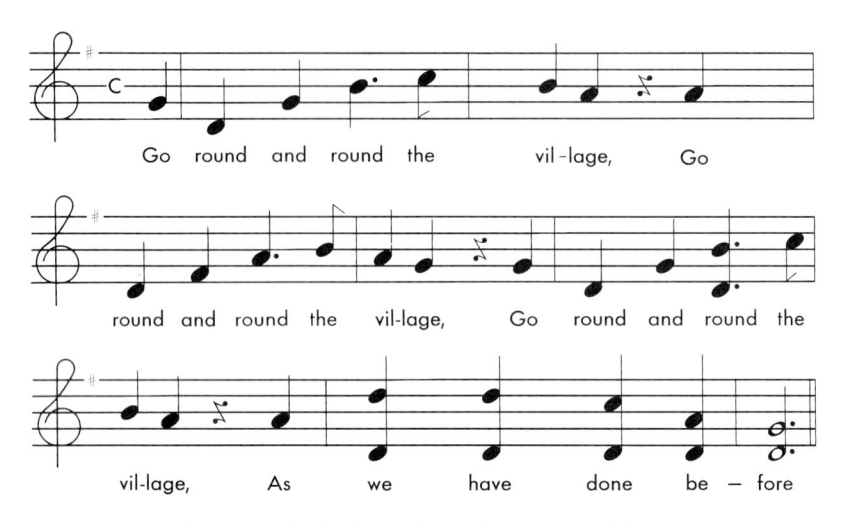

Figure 21–5. Go Round and Round the Village.

Records

Folkraft Record Co., #1191; Educational Record Sales, Album #1, "Singing Games and Folk Dances."

Second Verse

Go in and out the windows, etc.

Third Verse

Now stand and face your partners, etc.
And bow before you go.

Fourth Verse

Now go with me to London, etc.

Directions

First Verse: All players move around in a circle as they sing. Three children on the outside move the opposite way around the circle.

Second Verse: Circle stops and raises arms for windows. Players on outside go in and out the windows.

Third Verse: Each of the three players who went in and out the windows faces a partner. Children inside clap as they sing, and bow as they sing the last line.

Fourth Verse: Children and partners skip around the inside of the circle holding inside hands. Repeat all verses and actions.

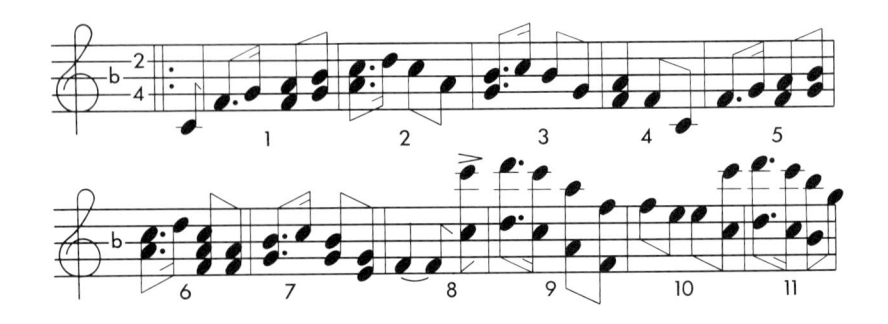

CHILDREN'S POLKA

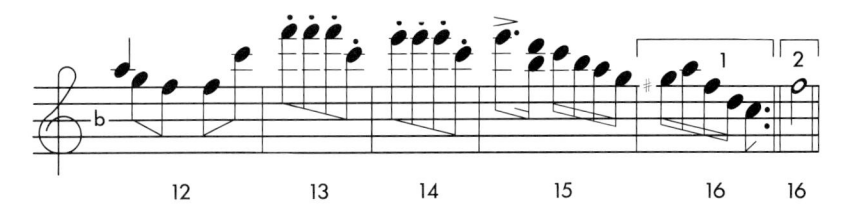

Figure 21-6. Children's Polka.

Records

Folkraft Record Co., #1187; Educational Record Sales, Album 3, "Folk Dances and Singing Games."

Formation

Single circle, partners facing each other, hands joined and arms extended shoulder high.

Directions

a. *Measures 1–2*: Partners take four slides to center of circle.
b. *Measures 3–4*: Four slides back to places.
c. *Measures 5–8*: Repeat a and b.
d. *Measure 9*: Clap own thighs, then clap hands in front of chest.
e. *Measure 10*: Clap partner's hand three times.
f. *Measures 11–12*: Repeat d and e.
g. *Measure 13*: Point right toe forward and resting right elbow in left hand, shake forefinger of right hand at partner three times.
h. *Measure 14*: Repeat g with left foot and hand.
i. *Measure 15*: Jump four times in place, making a quarter turn each time and turning away from partner.
j. *Measure 16*: Stamp three times, beginning with right foot.

Measures 1–16: Repeat all.

DANCE OF GREETING

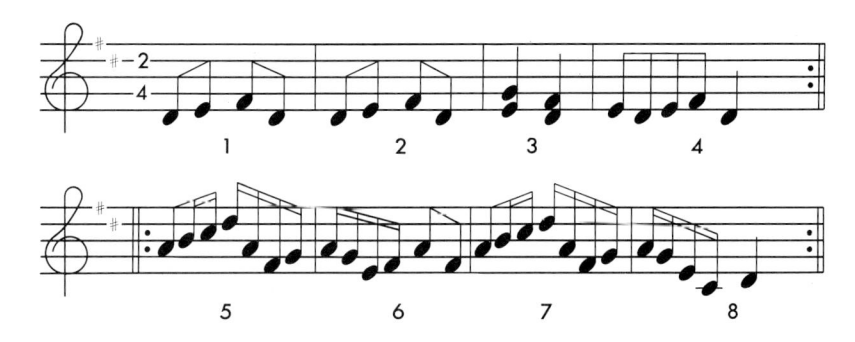

Figure 21-7. Dance of Greeting.

Records

Folkraft Record Co., #1187; Kismet Record Co., VIC 45–6173; Educational Record Sales, Album 2, "Singing Games and Folk Dances."

Formation

Single circle. Partners facing center, hands on hips. Boy on left of each couple.

Directions

Measure 1: Clap hands twice, turn to partner and bow.
Measure 2: Clap hands twice, turn to neighbor and bow.
Measure 3: Stamp twice (right, left).
Measure 4: Turn around in place to left, with four quick running steps.

Measures 1–4: Repeat.

Measures 5–8: Join hands in circle, and, starting with the left foot, run 16 steps clockwise.

Measures 5–8: Turn and run 16 steps counterclockwise.

Repeat all actions.

CHIMES OF DUNKIRK

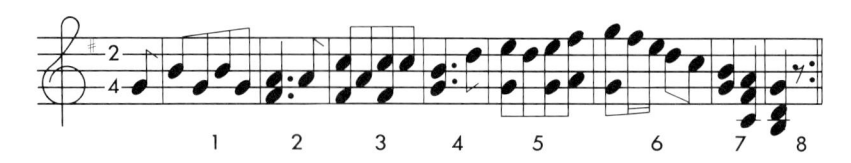

Figure 21–8. Chimes of Dunkirk.

Records

Folkraft Record Co., #1188; Kismet Record Co., VIC 6176.

Formation

Double circle, partners facing each other, hands on hips.

Directions

Measures 1–2: Stamp right, left, right, hold.

Measures 3–4: Clap one, two, three, hold.

Measures 5–8: Partners take hands and turn each other around once with running steps in place.

Measures 1–8: Repeat all. If desired, at end of turn, partners may change, going forward one place.

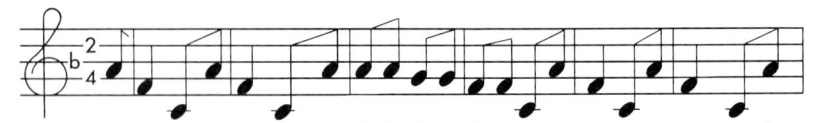

I SEE YOU

I see you, I see you, Tra,-la,-la,-la,-la,-la,-la. I see you, I see you, Tra, la, la, la, la, la, la. You see me and I see you, Then you take me and I'll take you. You see me and I see you, Then you take me and I'll take you.

Figure 21–9. I See You.

Records

Folkraft Record Co., #1197; Educational Record Sales, Record 17, "Folk Dances, Song Plays, Party Plays."

Formation

Two double rows facing each other and about 6 feet apart. In each of the double rows, those in front are No. 1 and those in back are No. 2. Each No. 1 places hands on hips; each No. 2 places hands on the shoulders of his partner, No. 1.

Verses

I see you, I see you,
Tra, la, la, la, la, la, la.
I see you, I see you,
Tra, la, la, la, la, la, la.

You see me and I see you,
Then you take me and I'll take you.
You see me and I see you,
Then you take me and I'll take you.

Directions

First Part:

1. No. 2 bends first to the left and then to the right, looking over No. 1's shoulder at No. 2 in the opposite line. Sing "I see you, I see you," measures 1–2.

2. No. 2 makes three quick movements of the head, leaning left, right, left, looking at No. 2 opposite. Sing "Tra, la, la, la, la, la, la," measures 3–4.

3. Repeat the directions accompanying measures 1–2 and 3–4, above, while singing measures 5–8.

Second Part:

1. All clap hands on the first beat of the measure, and No. 2 skips forward, meets No. 2 from the opposite line. Joining hands, both swing around once to the left. Sing "You see me and I see you, Then you take me and I'll take you," measures 5–8.

2. All clap hands on the first beat of the measure and join hands with partner and swing around to the left, finishing with No. 1 in the rear of No. 2. Sing "You see me and I see you, Then you take me and I'll take you," measures 1–4.

Repeat all, with No. 1 in rear.

PAW PAW PATCH

Figure 21–10. Paw Paw Patch.

Records

Folkraft Record Co., #1181.

Formation

File formation, set of six to eight couples.

Second Verse

Come on boys, let's go find her . . .
Way down yonder in the paw paw patch.

Third Verse

Pickin' up paw paws, put 'em in her pocket . . .
Way down yonder in the paw paw patch.

Directions

First Verse: The first girl in the line skips clockwise in a circle around the set. (*Note:* Use the name of the girl involved.)

338 RECOMMENDED MOVEMENT EXPERIENCES

Second Verse: The same girl skips around the set again, and is now followed by the entire line of boys until they all return to their places.

Third Verse: Head boy and head girl again lead their lines in a circle clockwise around the original set. When the head couple meet they form an arch and, as each couple meet, they go through the arch. A new lead couple comes through and restarts the dance.

Variation

First sing girl's name. Next time sing boy's name and change words and actions accordingly.

Developmental Activities

Activities with Equipment. Continued use of playground equipment and indoor equipment, such as ropes, horizontal ladders, and horizontal bars, is important to the further development of children at this age level. Time should be allotted in the program for this with instruction and encouragement. Some children are not as agile or as strong as others and special body types should be considered in terms of achievement.

Activities Without Equipment

RUNNING IN PLACE

Start slowly and increase speed. Increase time as children become conditioned.

JUMPING IN PLACE

Do for one minute. As children get conditioned, increase time.

HOPPING IN PLACE

Hop on alternate feet. Stress lightness in landing.

BICYCLE

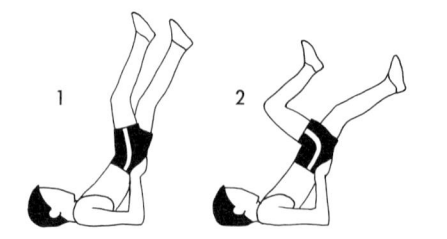

Figure 21–11. Bicycle.

Lie on floor with feet high in the air. Back is supported by hands, with weight of body placed on shoulders. With legs and feet, imitate the motions of pedaling a bicycle.

JUMPING JACK

Child jumps with feet apart to a stride position and claps hands over his head by moving arms sideward. He then returns to an erect standing position. Repeat and gradually increase number of times as children become conditioned.

SIT-UP

Figure 21–12. Sit-Up.

Lie flat on back, legs straight out, and feet together. Clasp hands over head or behind neck. Come to a sitting position by keeping feet on floor and legs straight. Slowly lie down again.

ABDOMINAL CURL

Child lies on floor on back, arms at side of body or extended sideward at shoulder level. Lift both legs from the floor and attempt to touch the floor above the head with the toes.

BOUNCING BALL

Figure 21–13. Bouncing Ball.

Assume pushup position by bending forward, extending the arms, and placing the hands on the floor, shoulder width apart, fingers pointing forward, and extending trunk and legs backward in a straight line. The body is supported on the hands and toes.

Bounce up and down by a series of short, upward springs. (Try clapping hands together while body is in the air.)

FROG STAND

Figure 21–14. Frog Stand.

Assume squat position, hands on floor, fingers pointing forward. The elbows are inside of, and pressed against, the knees.

Lean forward slowly, transferring body weight to hands, raising feet clear of the floor. Maintain balance, keeping head up. Hold for several seconds, then return to starting position. Repeat, maintaining balance for increasingly longer periods.

WHEELBARROW

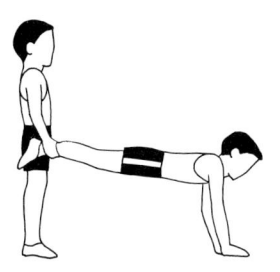

Figure 21–15. Wheelbarrow.

Children pair off. One takes "hands and knees" position. The hands are directly under the shoulders, fingers pointing forward. His partner grasps the kneeling pupil's ankles, raising his legs.

The first pupil walks forward on his hands. His feet and legs are supported by partner walking between the outstretched legs.

PROPELLER

Child stands erect, arms extended sideward at shoulder height, palms down. Maintaining this position, he inscribes small circles with the hands. Circles can be inscribed forward and backward.

Games of Low Organization

Games with Equipment

FOX AND RABBIT

Equipment
Two balls or bean bags.

Formation
Circle.

Directions
Two bean bags or two balls should be used. One should be white; the other, a different color. The white one represents the rabbit; the other represents the fox. One child in the circle is given the rabbit, which he sends around the circle by passing it quickly to the child next to him, and so on. A moment later the fox is started, giving chase to the

rabbit. The rabbit must reach the starting point before the fox overtakes it.

RUN AND HIT

Equipment
One rubber ball for each group.

Players
Five to ten in a group; two groups.

Directions
Groups line up horizontally on a square or rectangular playing area. Half of each group is on each side of the area. A goal is marked across the two ends of the play area. The running group occupies its place behind these goal lines—half on each side. The other group is given a ball. At the signal "Go," the running group endeavors to exchange goals. The throwing group endeavors to hit as many players as possible before they cross the goal lines. Each one hit before he crosses the line safely counts as one out. Throwers retrieve the ball and make as many throws as possible while other team is running. If all cross the lines and no one is hit, the team scores a run. Each hit constitutes an out. Three outs constitute one half an inning and the groups exchange places. The highest score of the last complete innings declares a winning group.

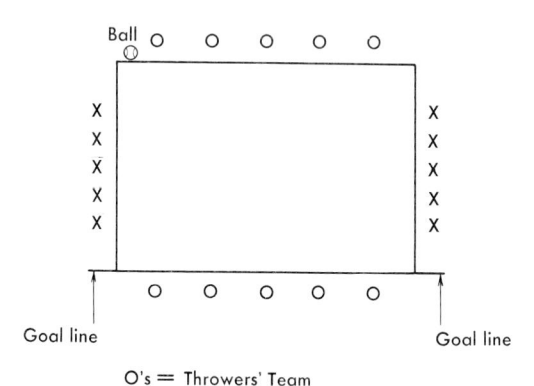

```
Ball O   O   O   O   O
  X                     X
  X                     X
  X                     X
  X                     X
  X                     X
      O   O   O   O   O
Goal line            Goal line

    O's = Throwers' Team
    X's = Runners' Team
```

Figure 21-16. **Run and Hit.**

WESTERN ROUNDUP

Equipment
A piece of rope 4 to 5 feet long and a bean bag for every five children.

Players
Fifteen to twenty-five.

Directions
Five children are chosen to be steers. Each steer is given one piece of rope and a bean bag. He ties the bean bag to the end of the rope. This represents the tail of the steer, and each steer drags it. The other children are either horses or cowboys and are paired off. Each couple makes a horse and a cowboy or cowgirl. Couples hold hands. The game begins by permitting the steers to wander off. Cowboys and horses must wait behind a line until the steers call "Ready." Then the cowboys and horses gallop off and try to catch a steer by catching its tail. Only the cowboy—*not the horse*—may attempt to catch the steer. When one steer is caught, all players return to the original starting position. Children then choose a new role and start the game again.

JOHN BROWN

Equipment
One Indian club, empty salt box, or milk carton for each group.

Players
Divide all players into groups of 10 each.

Directions
Place a club, milk carton, or salt box in a square about 30 feet from the starting line. Draw another square 5 to 10 feet away from it. Leave it empty. The ten children on each team or squad stand in a straight line facing the objects and the squares. They number themselves from one to ten. Each child must remember his number. At the signal "Go" number one on each team runs forward, picks up the object, and puts it in the other square. He then runs back to the line and calls out "One." This is the clue for number *two* to run. He puts the object back in its original square. When he returns to his starting position he calls out "Two," the signal for number *three* to run. The game continues in this manner until all ten children have had one turn. After number *ten* returns to the line and calls out "Ten," the game is only half completed. His call of "Ten" is the signal for number *nine* to run again, his call of "Nine" is the signal for number *eight*, and so on

Group I 1 2 3 4 5 6 7 8 9 10

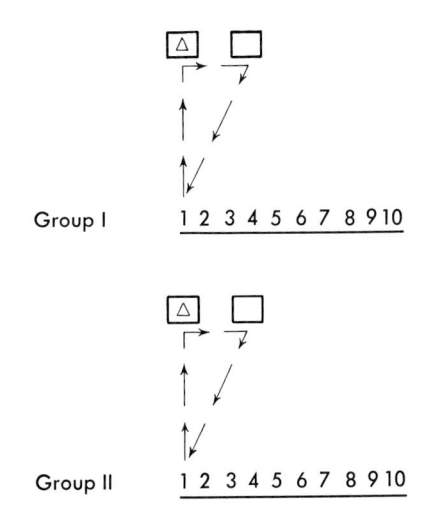

Group II 1 2 3 4 5 6 7 8 9 10

Figure 21-17. John Brown.

back to number *one*. When number one returns to the starting line he raises his hand and calls out "John Brown." The first group to finish is the winner.

CHASE THE BONE

Equipment
One rubber dog bone for each group.

Players
Eight to ten in a group.

Directions
Each group forms a circle. In the center of each circle, a 3-foot circle is drawn on the ground. One child is chosen for the thrower and one for "It." The thrower takes the dog bone, stands in the 3-foot circle, and throws it as far as he can. All players, except "It," then run and hide. "It" chases the bone, retrieves it, and runs back with it to the 3-foot circle, where he drops it. He may then start calling the names of all people he can see. They are caught and return to the area. He must search for the others. As he finds them, he calls them out by touching his foot on the bone in the circle. While he is away from the bone, a player whom he has not found may sneak in, get the bone, and throw it out of the circle again. If this happens, all persons who were caught are again free to run and hide. "It" must then secure the bone, place it back in the circle, and start the hunt all over. "It" may call all players in at any time by calling "chase the bone." To do this he throws the bone from the circle and those who are still hiding may come in and are all free. A new thrower and "It" are chosen and the game begins again.

CIRCLE RUN

Equipment
Two rubber balls and four colored flags.

Players
Four squads, four to eight players each.

Directions
Squads one and two are arranged on opposite sides of the circle. They play together. Squads three and four are on opposite sides and they play together. The flags are placed in the center of the circle. All players face left, the direction in which they will run. The first players on squads one and three are given balls. At the signal "Go," they pass the balls back over their heads until they reach the last child. When he receives it, he runs around to the opposite squad, stands in front of it, and passes the ball over his head back again to the last person (i.e., number *one* runs to squad two; number *three* to squad four). The game continues until squads one and two have changed places and squads three and four have done the same. When all players of a squad arrive at their new home, number *one* of that squad goes to the center of the circle, picks up the flag, and raises it in the air. The two squads that raise flags first are the winners.

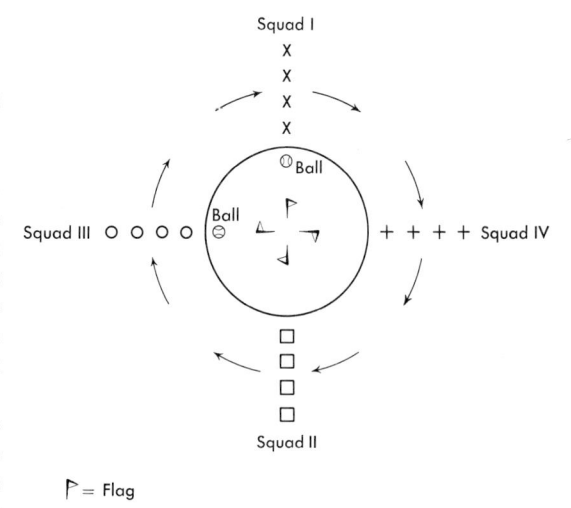

⌐ = Flag

Figure 21-18. Circle Run.

BOUNCE BALL

Equipment
One 8- or 10-inch rubber ball for each group.

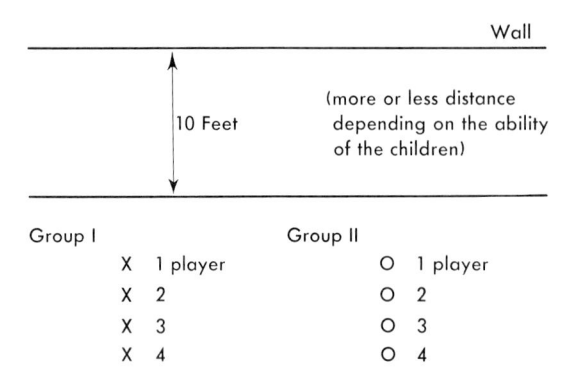

```
                                                    Wall
_____
           ↑
           |         (more or less distance
  10 Feet  |         depending on the ability
           |         of the children)
           ↓
_____

Group I               Group II
   X   1 player          O   1 player
   X   2                 O   2
   X   3                 O   3
   X   4                 O   4
```

Figure 21–19. Bounce Ball.

Players
Four to six players in each group.

Directions
The first child, from behind the 10-ft. line, bounces a ball against the wall. Number *two* runs forward and tries to catch it on the first bounce. If he catches it, he scores a point. Number *two* throws the ball and number *three* runs to catch it. As each child throws it, the next one tries to catch it. The team that has the most successful catches at the end of a given amount of play time wins.

CENTER BASE

Equipment
One ball.

Directions
The players stand in a circle formation. One player is "It" and stands in the center of the circle. He tosses a ball to a player in the circle who catches it, brings it to the center, and places it in the base. The base is a small circle marked in the center of the circle of players. After he has placed the ball in the base, he chases the player who threw the ball to him. Both the runner and the chaser must leave the circle through the space left in the circle by the player catching the ball.

The runner is safe by coming back into the circle through this same space and touching the ball. If the chaser tags the runner, he becomes "It." If not, a new "It" is chosen.

CENTER CIRCLE PASS BALL

Equipment
Bean bag or ball.

Formation
Single circle facing the center. One person stands in the circle and has the equipment.

Directions
The center player throws ball or bean bag to a player in the circle, who immediately returns it. He then tosses it to another player and this continues until all players in the circle have had a turn. Another player is then chosen to be center player.

As soon as the game is learned, three or four circles should be playing to give more activity. Variations of passing a ball may include underhand, overhand, and bounce pass.

OVERHEAD TOSS

Equipment
Volley or other inflated ball.

Formation
Groups of not more than eight children. One player with a ball stands on a throwing line. He stands with his back to the group. The other players stand around in the playing space. They may be at different distances from "It."

Directions
The player with the ball tosses it with both hands, backward, over his head. The other players attempt to catch it before it hits the ground. When a player is successful in catching the ball he changes places with the thrower and the game continues.

If the class has difficulty catching the fly ball, it may be caught on one bounce for a change of leaders.

CIRCLE TOSS

Equipment
A ball or bean bag for each of the players except one.

Formation
All the players form a circle facing center. They are separated from one another by a space of 3 or 4 feet.

Directions

At a signal from a leader, each player turns toward his right-hand neighbor and tosses his ball or bean bag to him. He then turns at once to receive the bag or ball which is coming to him from the left. The game should move rapidly. If children are not quick enough, it may be advisable at first to play the game with a smaller number of balls or bean bags. Do this until the children grow accustomed to tossing and turning quickly to catch. Change directions of the tossing when you wish—and when the children least expect it—to add interest once the basic movements are learned.

DAYS OF THE WEEK

Equipment
A ball.

Formation
The class stands side by side in seven groups. Each group is named for a day of the week. A child stands in front of the group and is the leader.

Directions
The leader throws the ball in the air and calls out one of the days of the week. The players from this group run forward. Each one attempts to catch the ball in the air or on the first bounce. The one who catches it becomes the new leader. The others return to their places.

Games Without Equipment

COWBOY AND INDIAN

Formation
Double circle facing center.

Directions
The class forms a double circle facing the center. The children in the circle represent trees. Two players are selected from the group and take their places outside the circles. One is named the Indian and the other is the cowboy. At the signal "Go," the cowboy chases the Indian around the circle and attempts to tag him. The Indian may avoid being tagged by stopping *in front* of a group of two. This makes three in the group, and the third one (the one on the outside) becomes the new Indian. The chase continues. If, at any time, the cowboy catches the Indian, the chase is reversed and the Indian attempts to catch the cowboy. Change cowboys and Indians often. Some may never be tagged.

MIDNIGHT

Formation
Rectangular area.

Directions
One player is the fox and the others are sheep. The fox may catch the sheep only at midnight. The game starts with the fox standing in a den marked in one corner of the playground, and the sheep in the sheepfold marked in the diagonally opposite corner. The fox leaves his den and wanders about the playground, whereupon the sheep also come forth and scatter around approaching as close to the fox as they dare. One player is designated as the leader of the sheep and asks, "What time is it?" The fox answers any hour he chooses. Should he say "Three o'clock" or "Eleven o'clock," the leader asks again; but when the fox says "Midnight!" all sheep run for the sheepfold as fast as possible. The fox chases them. Any sheep caught changes places with the fox, and the game is repeated.

LAME FOX AND CHICKENS

Formation
Rectangular area with two goals.

Directions
One player is chosen for the fox and stands in a den marked off at one end of the playground. The rest are chickens and have a chicken yard at the opposite end of the ground. The chickens advance as near as they dare to the den of the fox and tease him by calling out, "Lame fox! Lame fox! Can't catch anybody!" The lame fox may take only three steps beyond his den, after which he must hop on one foot, trying to tag the chickens while hopping. All tagged chickens become foxes and go home with him, thereafter sallying forth with him to catch the chickens. They must all then observe the same rule of taking but three steps beyond the den, after which they must hop. Should any fox put both feet down at once after his three steps while outside the den, the chickens may drive him back. Care should be taken that the hopping be always done on one foot, though a fox may change his hopping from one foot to the other. The last chicken caught wins the game and becomes the first lame fox in the new game.

CHINESE WALL

Formation
Rectangular area with a middle area marked for a "wall" and a goal at each end of the area.

Directions
The Chinese wall is marked off by two parallel lines straight across the center of the playground, leaving a space between them about ten feet in width. This space represents the wall. On each side of the wall, at a distance of from 15 to 30 feet, a parallel line is drawn across the ground. This marks the safety point or home goal for the besiegers.

One player is chosen to defend the wall and takes his place in the area. All of the other players stand in one of the home goals. The defender calls "Start!" All of the players must cross the wall and go to the opposite goal. The defender tries to tag as many as he can as they cross, but he may not overstep the boundaries of the wall himself. All players tagged join the defender in trying to tag future players exchanging goals. The game ends when all have been caught. The last player tagged becomes defender for the next game.

FROG IN THE MIDDLE

Formation
Circle.

Directions
One player is chosen to be the frog and sits in the center of the circle with his feet crossed in tailor fashion. If there are more than 20 players, it is well to choose at least two frogs. Other players stand in a circle around the frog, repeating "Frog in the sea, can't catch me!" They dance forward toward the frog and back, tantalizing him, and taking risks in going near him. The object of the game is for the frog to tag someone. When he does he changes places with the tagged player. The frog may not at any time leave his sitting position until he has tagged another player. If the frog or frogs are unsuccessful after a few minutes, more frogs should be chosen or new ones should replace the first ones.

BLACK AND WHITE

Formation
Small area.

Directions
One player is chosen as leader. The remainder of the players are divided into two equal groups. Each player in one group should tie a handkerchief on his left arm to indicate that he belongs to the Whites; those in the other division are called the Blacks. The players stand around the playing ground at random, the Whites and Blacks being mingled indiscriminately.

The leader is provided with a flat disk which is white on one side and black on the other, and hung on a short string to facilitate twirling the disk. He stands at one side of the playing area and twirls this disk, stopping it with one side only visible to the players. If the white side should be visible, the party known as the Whites may tag any of their opponents who are standing upright. The Blacks should drop instantly to the floor, as in Stoop Tag. Should the black side of the disk be shown, the party of Blacks may tag the Whites. Any player tagged scores one point for the tagger's side. The side wins which has the most points. The leaders should keep the action of the game rapid by twirling the disk frequently.

HOUND THE RABBIT

Formation
Couples holding hands.

Directions
A considerable number of the players stand in couples, holding hands. Each couple makes a small circle which represents a hollow tree. In each tree is stationed a player who takes the part of a rabbit. There should be one more rabbit than the number of trees. One other player is chosen to be the hound.

The hound chases the odd rabbit who may take refuge in any tree. But no two rabbits may lodge in the same tree. As soon as the hunted rabbit enters a tree the rabbit already there must run for another shelter. Whenever the hound catches a rabbit, new players are chosen for the hound and rabbit. Trees change places with rabbits so each child has a chance to be both a rabbit and a tree.

BLACK TOM

Formation
Rectangular area.

Directions
Two parallel lines are drawn on the ground with a space of from 30 to 50 feet between them. All of the players except one stand beyond one of these lines. In the middle territory between the lines the

one player who is chosen to be "It" takes his place. He calls, "Black Tom! Black Tom! Black Tom!" (repeating the words three times), whereupon the other players must all run across to the opposite line. "It" chases them and tags all that he can. Anyone so caught joins him in chasing the others.

The particular characteristic of this game lies in the fact that the center player, instead of saying, "Black Tom!" may trick or tantalize the runners by crying out, "Yellow Tom," or "Blue Tom," or "Red Tom," or anything else that he may choose. Any player who starts to run upon a false alarm is considered captive and must join "It" in the center. This is also true for any player who starts before the third repetition of "Black Tom." The last one to be caught is "It" for the next game.

BLIND MAN'S BUFF (WARM WEATHER GAME)

Formation
Circle.

Directions
One player is chosen to be blindfolded and stands in the center. The other players join hands and circle around him until the blind man claps his hands three times. The circle stops moving and the blind man points toward the circle. The player at whom he points must at once step into the circle. This player will naturally try, by noiseless stepping, dodging, and so on, to give the blind man some difficulty in catching him, but when once caught he must stand without struggle for identification. The blind man must then guess who the other player is. If the guess is correct, they change places. If not correct, or if the blind man has pointed at an empty space instead of at a player, the circle continues and the game is repeated.

RED LIGHT

Formation
Two parallel lines, 50 feet apart. One is the starting and one the finishing line. One player, the policeman, stands behind the finish line. He has his back to the group. The other players stand on the starting line.

Directions
The policeman calls out, "Green light, one, two, three, four, five, red light." When he says "Green light," the players may start to advance toward the finish line. When he says "Red light," all must stop and stand still. The policeman turns around quickly. All players he sees moving their feet must return to the starting line and begin again. The policeman turns again and counts. The players move. The object is to move to the line the policeman is on and return to the starting line. The first one back to the original goal is the new policeman.

RUN FOR YOUR SUPPER

Formation
Players hold hands in a single circle. One player is inside and is "It."

Directions
"It" breaks the hands of two players in the circle and says, "Run for your supper." The two run around outside the circle in opposite directions. The one who first returns to his original place wins. He is "It" for the next game.

MOVING DAY

Formation
In a relatively large area, circles are drawn on the ground to represent houses.

Directions
Each player except "It" must have a house and stand in it to start the game. One player is chosen to be "It." He walks up and down the streets between the circles. At intervals the teacher calls "Moving day." The residents along the street change houses and "It" tries to get a house while it is vacant.

After any one player has been "It" for a reasonable length of time and has been unable to secure a house, a new "It" should be chosen. Winners are those who were never caught without a house. More than one "It" may be used if desired.

SCAT

Formation
Players form a circle. One child is chosen to be "It" and stoops in the middle of the circle. Several bases are marked away from the circle.

Directions
All players move around in the line of direction in the circle. When "It" calls out "Scat!" players drop hands and run to the bases. If "It" catches any of the players they become his aids and help him. The last one caught is the winner.

TOUCH

Formation
Form two parallel lines with an equal number of players in each. All face the same direction.

Directions
The leader or teacher gives a direction such as "Touch wood," "Get a stone," or "Touch the fence." All players obey the command and return to their places quickly. The line in position first, providing all carried out directions, wins. Repeat as long as interest warrants.

TRADES

Formation
The players are divided into two groups. Lines are drawn about 40 feet apart. Teams stand on the two lines facing each other.

Directions
One group decides upon a certain trade. They advance to within several feet of the other group and announce, "Here we are from New York." The group staying at home says, "Have you a trade?" The first group replies, "Yes." The second group then orders, "Get to work." The first group imitates the trade to which they belong. The second group tries to guess it. When the correct trade is guessed the players representing the trade run for their home line and the guessers chase them. Each player tagged before reaching his home line gives one point to the tagging team.

The other side now has a chance to represent a trade. At the end of the game, the side with the greater number of points wins.

COOKIES IN THE JAR

Formation
The baker marks out several 2-foot circles in a clearly defined territory. These are his cookie jars. One parallel line is marked "Home," from which the children leave and return.

Directions
The children leave their home as the baker moves around the area. The baker chants:

> Dear children, dear children,
> You dare not go far,
> For if I catch you,
> You'll land in my jar.

When the baker catches a child, he places him in the cookie jar. Any child may be freed if tagged by another player, if he is the only one in the jar. When the baker gets two cookies in each jar, the game is over and may be restarted.

Individual and Dual Activities

HOPSCOTCH

Equipment
A stone or a button.

Formation
Various diagrams may be used—see Figure 21–20.

Directions
A player tosses a stone or button into the spaces in numbered order. After each toss, he hops into the space, picks up the stone, and then hops out. The stone or the foot must not touch the line. He repeats, going from number one to as high a number as possible until he misses by tossing the stone in the wrong area, losing his balance and touching both feet to the ground, or stepping on a line. When one is through, the next player starts. Only three or four children should use one hopscotch area at one time. In areas two-three and five-six, one foot may be placed in each.

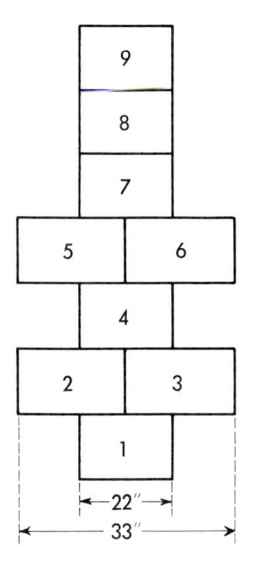

Figure 21–20. Hopscotch

LADDER HOPSCOTCH

1. In one version, the player tosses the stone into space one and hops over space one into space two. He picks up the stone and hops out, touching

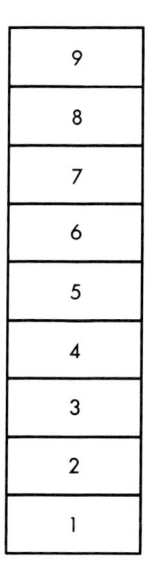

Figure 21–21. Ladder Hopscotch.

space one. Next, he tosses the stone into space two, hops into space one, over space two, and into space three. Picking up the stone, he hops into space two, space one, and out. He continues up the ladder, then down the ladder.

2. In another version, the procedure is the same except the player kicks the stone into the next space instead of picking it up. He hops into the area with the stone and kicks it up the ladder and back.

FINLAND HOPSCOTCH

Toss the stone or button into space one. Then hop into space one, pick up the stone, and hop out. Toss the stone into space two and hop into space one, then into space two, pick up the stone, and hop out. Continue up and back. In spaces four-five and seven-eight, both feet may touch, one in each square. A player misses by touching lines, using two feet in other than allowed squares, changing feet, or tossing the stone into the wrong section.

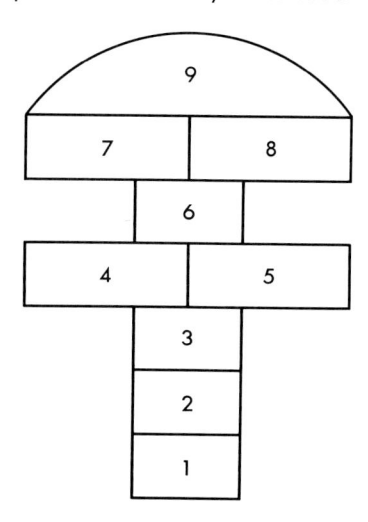

Figure 21–22. Finland Hopscotch.

ITALIAN HOPSCOTCH

Toss the stone into space one and hop into space one. Then kick the stone into space two and hop into space two. Continue with space three, and so on, up to space eight. In space eight, both feet may be put down. The player picks up the stone and hops out a winner. Start again in the opposite direction, from space eight to space one in the same manner, if desired.

Figure 21–23. Italian Hopscotch.

PICK-UP HOPSCOTCH

The stone is always tossed into the center block. The player tosses the stone into the center and hops into block one. He picks up the stone and hops out. He again tosses the stone into the center block, hops into block one, then into block two, picks up the stone and hops out, touching block one. He continues advancing from block to block and picks

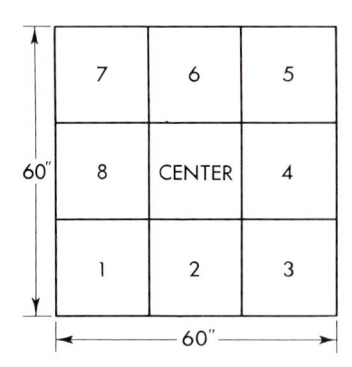

Figure 21-24. Pick-Up Hopscotch.

up his stone each time from the correct block. The winner is the one who is able to go from block one to block eight without missing the center square with his stone, or losing his balance when picking up the stone, or hopping on any lines. A miss permits the next player to start.

TOURNAMENT HOPSCOTCH

The stone is kicked as many times as necessary to move it from number one to number ten. It is a miss if it lands on a line. A double-foot landing may be used in areas one-two and four-five, and both feet may land in area seven. The stone is kicked at first with the free foot. After children become good at this, encourage them to kick it with the foot on which they hop.

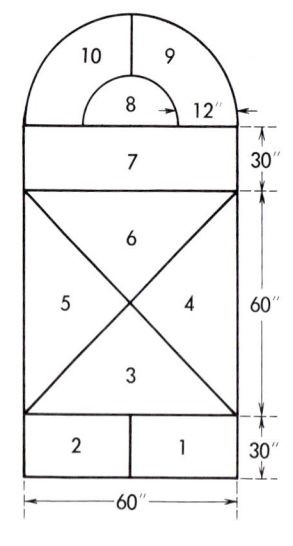

Figure 21-25. Tournament Hopscotch.

SNAIL HOPSCOTCH

Snail Hopscotch is played the same way as regular Hopscotch. Endeavor to move from number one to ten without tossing the stone in wrong area, touching both feet to the ground, or stepping on a line.

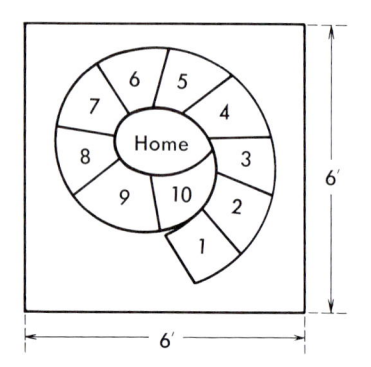

Figure 21-26. Snail Hopscotch.

JUMP ROPE GAMES

Jump Rope is a very fine activity for children of all ages and is especially enjoyed by the seven- and eight-year-olds. Many jump ropes may be had at a minimum cost by buying a hundred feet of clothesline and cutting it into various lengths—for two to turn and for individuals to use alone. Tie knots at the ends of each length to keep the rope from raveling.

Records for Jump Rope are available.

Rhymes that children may chant are plentiful. Children should also be encouraged to make up rhymes and actions to combine with jumping.

TEDDY BEAR JUMP ROPE

Verse

> Teddy bear, teddy bear, turn around;
> Teddy bear, teddy bear, touch the ground;
> Teddy bear, teddy bear, show your shoe;
> Teddy bear, teddy bear, please skidoo!

Directions

Two players turn the rope and one child jumps at a time. Others await their turn and one moves in on the word "skidoo." The child jumping acts out the words in the verse.

STRAWBERRY SHORTCAKE JUMP ROPE

Verse

Strawberry shortcake, huckleberry pie,
V-I-C-T-O-R-Y,
Can you jump it?
I'll say, "Yes."
Salt and pepper, and now take a rest!

Directions

Two players turn the rope. One jumps as the verse is chanted. On the last line, "salt and pepper . . .," the rope is turned rapidly. On the word "rest," the player jumps out and a new one starts at the beginning of the verse.

DUAL ROPE TURNING

When two people turn the rope, jumping variations are plentiful.

1. Jumper starts by standing in the middle.
2. Jumper runs in while rope is turning, jumps a designated number of times, and runs out.
3. Jumper runs in, drops a stone or a button, and picks it up on the jump number designated by the group.
4. Jumper runs in and bounces a ball while jumping. Number of times should be designated by the group. Start with two and work upward.

INDIVIDUAL ROPE TURNING

Variations for individuals who are capable of turning their own rope are challenging.

1. Turn the rope forward and jump.
2. Turn the rope backward and jump when it is in back of the feet.
3. Jump on one foot.
4. Jump on two feet.
5. Jump first with one foot and then with the other in a stepping fashion.
6. Hold hands with a partner. Each holds one end of the rope with the free hand and turns. Then they jump together.
7. Face your partner and jump together.
8. Jump covering the ground in various formations—squares, lines, and so on.

MARBLES

Area

A circle 10 feet in diameter.

Equipment

Thirteen marbles arranged in a cross in the center of the circle. One shooter for each player, not less than one half of an inch or more than three quarters of an inch in diameter.

Players

No less than two, no more than six.

Directions

Players stand on a line approximately 6 to 8 feet from the circle and toss their shooters, one at a time. A line extended beyond the circle is called the lag line, this is where the players try to land their marbles. The one whose marble is nearest to the lag line is the first shooter. The first player knuckles down at any place outside the circle line he chooses and shoots at the marbles. He continues to shoot as long as he knocks a marble from the ring and his shooter remains in the ring. Each marble knocked from the ring is his for a score of one. He takes his next shot from where his shooter stayed in the circle. When he is unsuccessful in knocking a marble from the ring or when his shooter leaves the ring, he is through and picks up his shooter. The next player starts from whatever place he wishes around the ring. The player with the most points when all 13 marbles have been shot out of the circle is the winner. Players do not keep the 13 marbles.

Tournaments are very popular in this sport in the spring and summer.

BOWLING

Area

Smooth surface.

Equipment

Six or 10 Indian clubs, plastic pins, or milk cartons, and one 6- or 8-inch ball.

Directions

Set pins up in a triangular formation (see Figure 21–27). Mark a starting line 20 to 30 feet from the pins. Each person bowls the ball in turn at the pins. The score is the number of pins that are knocked down. One child starts as the pinsetter. After the first bowler rolls, he becomes pinsetter. Two to four players may play on one court. The score may be determined by number of pins hit in 10 tries (the number of tries may be lessened or increased, depending on the interest of the players and the time available).

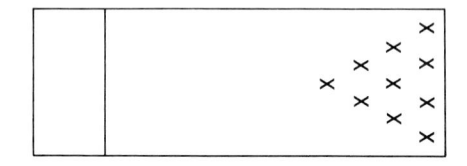

Figure 21-27. Bowling Games.

Self-Testing Activities and Stunts

ROCKING CHAIR

Two children of near equal size and weight sit on the floor facing each other. They extend their legs and each then sits on the feet of his partner. They clasp their hands on the upper arms of their partners. One pulls back and lifts his partner a little distance from the floor. This is then reversed in a rocking fashion.

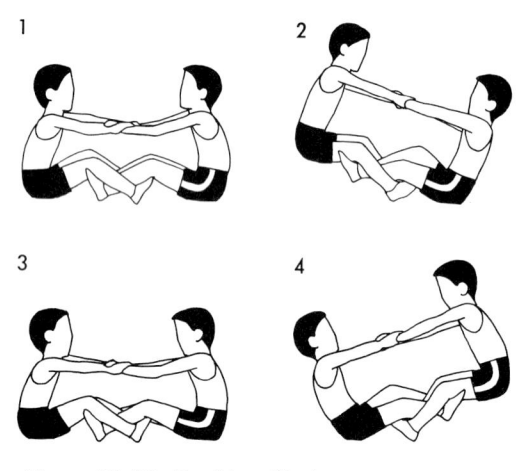

Figure 21-28. Rocking Chair.

SEAL CRAWL

Prone position, hands on floor, legs together, weight on toes and hands. Walk on hands, drag feet.

Figure 21-29. Seal Crawl.

SIAMESE TWIN WALK

Stand back to back with partner. Lock arms together. Walk together with partner. Permit each one to walk forward and backward.

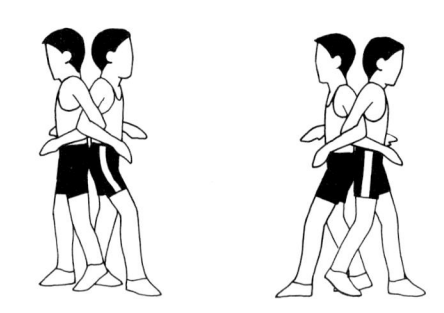

Figure 21-30. Siamese Twin Walk.

COCKFIGHT

Each child has a partner. Partners face each other and fold their arms across their chests. They practice hopping on one foot. When they are ready they bump each other, endeavoring to make one lose his balance and place both feet on the ground or floor.

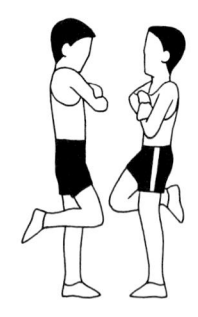

Figure 21-31. Cockfight.

CHURN THE BUTTER

Children stand back to back with partner of near size and hook arms. One leans over and takes weight of partner on his back, lifting partner's feet off the ground. He places him back on his feet and the "partner" will then raise the first child the same way. They work together in slow rhythm.

Figure 21–32. Churn the Butter.

HAND WRESTLE

Two children face each other and grasp right hands. Each raises his right foot balancing himself on the left. At a signal, each endeavors to make the other child place his right foot on the ground.

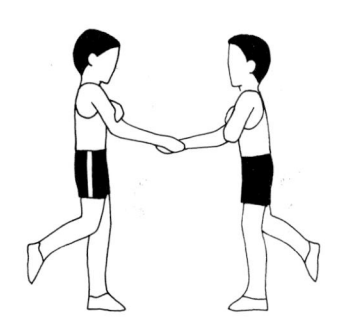

Figure 21–33. Hand Wrestle.

CRAB WALK

Sit on floor, face up. Raise body and support its weight by keeping hands and feet on floor; keep back straight. Walk backward, forward, and sideward using hands and feet.

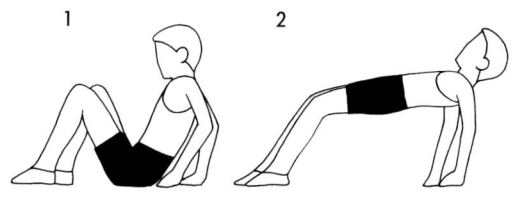

Figure 21–34. Crab Walk.

FROG HOP

Take squat position. Place arms between legs and hands on the floor. Take short hops by placing hands on floor ahead of feet and bringing feet up to hands.

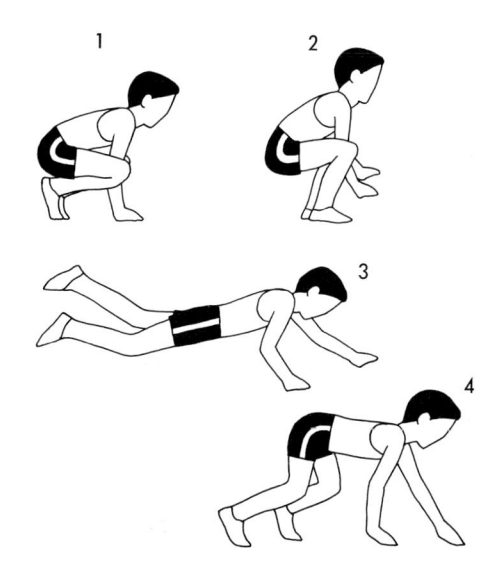

Figure 21–35. Frog Hop.

INCH WORM

Hands on floor, shoulder-width apart, extend legs to rear, feet together, supporting body on hands and toes. Arms are straight and body straight from head to heels. Keep hands stationary. Using little steps, move feet to hands keeping knees straight. When they are as close to hands as possible, walk with hands as far as possible. Repeat bringing feet to hands, and so on.

Note: Hands and feet move alternately not at same time. Body must not sag. Progress forward by repeating activity.

Figure 21-36. Inch Worm.

INDIAN GET-UP

Sit on floor with feet crossed and arms folded shoulder high. Rise to an upright position without losing balance or unfolding arms. Return to sitting position.

Figure 21-37. Indian Get-Up.

JUMP AND SLAP HEELS

From standing position, jump up, extending heels backward and to the side, and reach backward to slap heels.

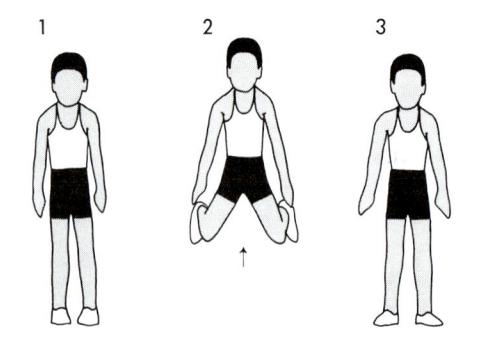

Figure 21-38. Jump and Slap Heels.

KANGAROO HOP

Fold arms over chest, squat; jump up keeping knees flexed, then go back to squat position.

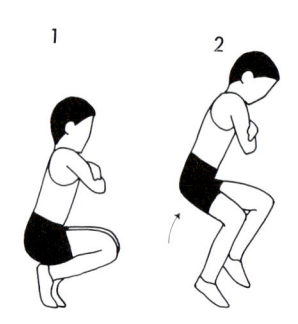

Figure 21-39. Kangaroo Hop.

KNEE LIFT

Stand with feet apart, hands forward at hip level; jump up making knees touch hands.

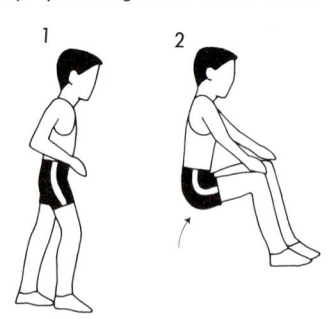

Figure 21-40. Knee Lift.

LAME DOG WALK

Same as Dog Walk only hold up one foot, first right and then left.

Figure 21–41. Lame Dog Walk.

Story Plays

Story plays may be enjoyed by seven-year-olds. However, teachers must use their judgment with respect to story plays for the eight-year-old since children mature at different ages. The use of this part of the program must be determined by each individual teacher. Selection of topics and materials for story plays will also depend upon the background, experience, and maturity of the children.

Classroom Games

DRAWING OBJECT RACE

Equipment

One piece of drawing paper fastened on the wall or bulletin board for each group. One colored crayon for each group.

Players

Entire class divided in groups of six to eight players each.

Directions

Choose an object to be drawn. It may be a school, barn, farmyard, and the like. Decide the number of lines each artist may draw, depending on the subject. For example, he may be given a chance to make two lines or four. Each group stands the same distance from its paper which is on the wall. The game starts with the first person going to the paper and drawing the given number of strokes or lines. He returns and gives the crayon to the second player, who does likewise. The winning group is the one with the best recognizable drawing, not the one finished first.

LEAF HUNT

Equipment

Many autumn leaves should be hidden in the room. They may be either real leaves or made from colored paper. Separate bare trees are drawn on the blackboards. Each tree is named—for example, Oak, Maple, or Ash.

Players

Entire class.

Directions

The types of trees and leaves are those the children have studied and know. The object is for each child to find as many leaves as possible in an allotted time. When the time is up, all players sit down. Then each child has a chance to place his leaves in the chalk tray under the correct tree. The child who has the most leaves will *not* win if he places them on the wrong tree. If this game is to be played a second time, the children may close their eyes with heads on the desk while the leaves are again hidden.

THE LOST CHILD

Formation

All children are seated.

Directions

This is a quiet game designed to test the memory. The players are all seated, with the exception of one who is sent from the room. When this player is well out of sight and hearing, the leader or teacher beckons one of the players, who leaves the group and hides. In the schoolroom, this may be done under the teacher's desk or in a wardrobe. The rest of the players then change their seats and the one who is out is called back. He tries to tell which player is hidden. He may have one, two, or three guesses depending on grade level. If he guesses correctly he scores a point and may choose another player to be the guesser. If he fails to identify the hidden child, the hidden child becomes "It" and is allowed to leave the room for the new game while the teacher chooses another hider.

NUMBER TOSS

Equipment
Ten pieces of oaktag or construction paper, approximately 4 inches by 6 inches, for each group. Number each piece from one to ten, or use higher numbers depending on the mathematical ability of the group. Three rolled socks for each group.

Players
The entire class is divided into groups of four, five, or six each.

Directions
Each group lays its ten papers on the floor so the edges touch each other. They make no specific pattern regarding number placement. Mark a line 10 feet away. The distance may be lengthened or shortened depending on the ability of the group. Each group of children lines up behind a leader. The first child has the three rolled socks and tosses them on the paper. His score is taken from wherever the socks land. He writes his score on the board and tosses the socks to the second child. Each child recovers the socks he tossed and writes his own score on the board. The last person totals the scores. One round is played and the winner is the group with the highest score. The game may be played as many times as the group wishes to play it.

CLOTHESPIN RACE

Equipment
Two clothespins for each group and a length of clothesrope which will reach the width of a classroom.

Players
Any number.

Directions
The children are divided into groups of from four to eight each. The first child on each squad holds two clothespins. Any distance away, and facing the squads, are two children holding the rope taut between them. At the signal "Go," the first child in each group starts the race by running up to the rope and putting the clothespins on it. He runs back and tags the next person in line who runs up and carries the pins back and hands them to the third child. Each child has a turn either to pin them on the line or take them off. The squad finished first wins. All clothespins must stay on the line. If one falls off, the child must return and pin it up again.

Variations
Give something for them to hang up such as socks or hankies (Kleenex).

ROLL BALL

Equipment
A golf ball or ping-pong ball for each squad or group. Three blackboard erasers for each squad or a cereal box cut to form an arch.

Players
Five to six in each group.

Directions
Set up an arch about 10 feet in front of each group. Mark a line for contestants to stand behind. The first one in each group has a ball. He endeavors to roll the ball through the arch. He recovers it and tosses it back to the second person and then takes his place behind the last player in his line. Each player rolls the ball in turn and recovers it as the first player did. One point is scored each time the ball passes through the arch. Play for five minutes. The group with highest score is the winner. The game may be repeated.

I AM TIRED OF STIRRING THE MUSH

Formation
Children in seats.

Directions
Player who is "It" stands in front of the room pretending to stir a pot of mush. "It" says, "I am tired of stirring this mush." The class asks: "Why?" "It" says, "Because (name of a child) won't walk around the room like a dog and bark like a dog." "It" may suggest anything he wants the child to do such as sing, dance, skip, hop, jump, recite, or run. The child called upon does the action and then becomes "It."

Variation

"It" may call upon an entire row to perform. The more varied the acts are, the more enjoyable the game becomes. The new "It" would be the person from the row who did the best imitation.

HAT IN THE RING

Equipment

Record player; record—a march; an old straw hat or other type of hat.

Directions

Divide the class into two groups. The two groups line up facing each other. Each group counts off consecutively from number one on. Group members must remember their numbers. Each group makes a circle or, if space will not permit, two circles. The groups may follow their leaders around the room or up and down aisles. The old hat is placed in the middle of the room. When the music starts, the players march around either in their circle or up and down the aisles. Suddenly the music stops. Number *one* from each group runs to try and get the hat and take it back to the place where he was when the music stopped. The one who succeeds scores a point for his group. At the next music break, number *twos* race for the hat and so on. The group first totaling ten points wins.

CAT AND MICE

Formation

Children seated.

Directions

One player is chosen to be cat and hides behind or under the teacher's desk. After the cat is hidden, the teacher beckons to five or six other players to be mice. They creep softly up to the desk, and when all are assembled, scratch on it with their fingers to represent the nibbling of mice. As soon as the cat hears this, he or she scrambles out from under the desk and gives chase to the mice, who may save themselves only by getting back to their holes (seats). If a mouse is caught, the cat changes places with him for the next round of the game. If no mouse is caught, a new cat is chosen.

A different set of mice should be chosen each time in order to give all of the players an opportunity to join the game.

Selected References

See end of Chapter 24.

CHAPTER 22

Movement Experiences for Middle Childhood (Ages Nine and Ten)

Dances and Rhythms

Dances and rhythms for the nine- and ten-year-old child include folk dances, square dances, interpretive and creative dances, and mixers.

Today, many companies have records available with accompanying directions. Square dance records are available with specific directions and calls on one side for teaching. The actual dance music and calls are on the reverse side of the record. Names and addresses of some record companies are listed in Appendix A.

Dances listed in Table 22-1 are recommended for this specific age group. Sources for procuring the records and the country from which the dance originates are given to assist the teacher with correlation to other parts of the curriculum.

Basic Steps. Steps for this group include the bleking, buzz step, draw step, grapevine, mazurka, pas-de-basque, polka, promenade, step-hop, shuffle, two-step, touch step, and waltz. These steps are executed as follows:

BLEKING (2/4 TIME, EVEN RHYTHM)

Bleking is a hop step in which the free foot is extended forward with the heel touching the floor. A quick change brings the forward foot back for the hop and extends the opposite foot forward.

```
    1       and     2
  Hop step   —    Hop step
```

BUZZ STEP (2/4 OR 4/4 TIME, UNEVEN RHYTHM)

A pivot step is used that is much the same as though a person is riding a scooter. The weight is on one foot and the free foot pushes the person around. The foot with the weight is lifted slightly on each push.

DRAW STEP (EVEN RHYTHM)

The draw step is a sideward step with one foot followed by a "draw" which brings the other foot over to the one used for the sideward step.

```
  1     and    2     and
 step  draw  step  draw
```

GRAPEVINE STEP (2/4 TIME, EVEN RHYTHM)

Count 1: Step left to side.
Count 2: Cross right behind left.
Count 3: Step left to side.

MAZURKA (3/4 TIME, EVEN RHYTHM)

Step left (slight stamp), bring right foot up to left with a cut step displacing left, hop right while bending knee so that left foot approaches right ankle. Repeat on same side.

```
  1    2    3
 step cut  hop
```

356

PAS-DE-BASQUE (3/4 TIME, EVEN RHYTHM)

Count 1: Leap to side on left foot.
Count 2: Slide right foot across in front of left foot, weight held on right foot.
Count 3: Step left in place.
Count: 1   2   3
Sequence: Leap slide step

POLKA STEP (2/4 TIME, UNEVEN RHYTHM)

Count And: Hop on right foot.
Count 1: Step forward on left foot.
Count And: Bring right foot up to left foot.
Count 2: Step forward on right foot.
Count: And 1 And 2
Sequence: Hop step together step

PROMENADE (4/4 TIME, EVEN RHYTHM)

The promenade step is used by couples in American square dances to move around their set. It is a shuffle step smoothly performed as a step-together-step.

STEP HOP (2/4 OR 4/4 TIME, EVEN RHYTHM)

Count 1: Step on left foot.
Count 2: Hop on same foot raising right knee forward.

SHUFFLE (2/4 OR 4/4 TIME; EVEN RHYTHM)

Shuffle is the basic step for all square dance. It is a smooth walking step forward, the feet not leaving the floor. Avoid skips, bounces, and runs. This leads to rowdyism as well as fatigue for dancers and is not in keeping with the spirit of this type of dancing.

TOUCH STEP (2/4 TIME)

Count 1: Raise left forward and touch the floor with the toes.
Count 2: Raise left foot and step forward on it. Repeat counts 1 and 2 with the right foot.

TWO-STEP (2/4 TIME; EVEN RHYTHM)

Count 1: Step forward with right foot.
Count 2: Bring left foot to right foot, transfer weight onto left foot.
Count 3: Step forward with right foot and hold position. Repeat with left foot starting on count 1.
Count: 1 and 2 and
Sequence: Step together step hold

WALTZ STEP (3/4 TIME; EVEN RHYTHM)

Count 1: Step forward on left foot.
Count 2: Step right foot forward to the right side.
Count 3: Bring left foot to the right and take weight on left foot. Repeat three counts starting with right foot.

   1   2   3
Step step together

Basic Formations. Basic forms for the American folk dance include circle, progressive circle, quadrille, and line or contra sets.

Circle sets call for partners to form a double circle with the lady on the gentleman's right. All couples face in the same line of direction. An example of this type is the favorite "Here We Go Round the Mountain."

The *progressive circle* formation places two couples facing each other. They dance specific calls together and then on command each couple moves in the opposite direction to meet a new couple.

The *quadrille* formation is a hollow square made by four couples facing each other. The couple with their backs to the music are always known as the head couple. If "head couples" are called for, the couple facing the head is the additional one. Side couples are the partners on the other side of the square. If a quadrille calls for couple number one, this means the head couple. In sequence, couple number two is to the right of couple one, number three is to the right of two, and number four is to the right of number three.

Line or contra sets are formations that usually call for from four to eight couples facing each other in two straight lines. The couple nearest the music is the head couple and those at the opposite end are the foot couple.

Table 22-1. Folk Dances

Dance	Nation	Formation	Step Used	Record No.
Ace of Diamonds	Denmark	Double circle Partners facing	Polka step-hop	Folkraft 1176
Bleking	Sweden	Single Circle Partners facing	Bleking step	Folkraft 118
Captain Jinks	U.S.	Double circle Girls outside	Walk-skip slide	Victor 45:6169 Folkraft 1240
Children's Polka	Sweden	Single circle Partners facing	Run-side step	Folkraft 1187
Csebogar	Hungary	Single circle Couples	Slide, skip, step, draw	Victor 45:6182 Folkraft 1196
Donkey Dance	Mexico	Contra Couples	Grapevine	Burns and Evans Album 123
Dutch Couples	Holland	Double circle Partners facing	Step, swing, hop	Burns and Evans Album 333
Gustaf's Skol	Sweden	Quadrille (square)	Walk, skip	Victor LPM-1622 Folkraft 1175
Heel and Toe Polka	U.S.	Double circle Girls outside	Hop-step Two-step (polka)	MacGregor 400 Old Timer 8005
Horse and Buggy Schottische	U.S.	Double circle 2 couples to a set	Step-hop (schottische)	MacGregor 400 Imperial 1046
Klappdans	Germany	Double circle Girls outside	Polka step	Victor 45:6171 Folkraft 1175
Mexican Hat Dance	Mexico	Couples file formation	Leap-buzz step	Folkraft 1038
Norwegian Mountain March	Norway	Threes	Waltz step-hop	RCA Folk Dance Educational Record Sets #5
Sellengers Round	England	Single circle	Walk-slide, step-balance	Folkraft 1124
Seven Jumps	Denmark	Circle, no partners	Step-hop, skip	Methodist 108 Victor 45:6172
Sicilian Circle	U.S.	Sets—2 couples Facing (circle)	Shuffle walk	Folkraft 1115 Folkraft 1242 (calls)
Tinikling	Phillipine Islands	Sets of 4 contra	Leap, hop	RCA Victor LPM 1619
Virginia Reel	U.S.	Long set (contra)	Walk-slide, skip	Folkraft 1141 Victor LPA 4138
Yankee Doodle	U.S.	Contra—6 couples	Walk-slide	Windsor A-751

Developmental Activities

Developmental activities started in previous grades should be continued. As children grow older and stronger they are capable of and interested in doing more difficult types. The following are recommended.

PULLUPS—(BOYS)

Equipment

A bar, of sufficient height, comfortable to grip.

Starting Position

Grasp the bar with palms facing forward; hang with arms and legs fully extended. Feet must be free of floor. The partner stands slightly to one side of the pupil being tested and counts each successful pullup.

Figure 22–1. Pullups for Boys.

Action

1. Pull body up with the arms until the chin is placed over the bar.
2. Lower body until the elbows are fully extended.
3. Repeat the exercise the required number of times.

Rules

1. The pull must not be a snap movement.
2. Knees must not be raised.
3. Kicking the legs is not permitted.
4. The body must not swing. If pupil starts to swing, his partner stops the motion by holding an extended arm across the front of the pupil's thighs.
5. One complete pullup is counted each time the pupil places his chin over the bar.

MODIFIED PULLUPS—(GIRLS)

Equipment

Any bar adjustable in height and comfortable to grip. A piece of pipe, placed between two stepladders and held securely, may be used.

Starting Position

Adjust height of bar to chest level. Grasp bar with palms facing out. Extend the legs under the bar, keeping the body and knees straight. The heels are on the floor. Fully extend the arms so they form an angle of 90 degrees with the body line. The partner braces the pupil's heels to prevent slipping.

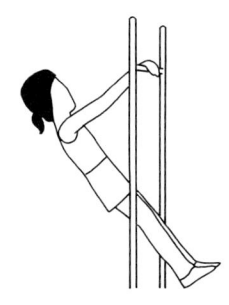

Figure 22–2. Modified Pullups for Girls.

Action

1. Pull body up with the arms until the *chest* touches the bar.
2. Lower body until elbows are fully extended.
3. Repeat the exercise the required number of times.

Rules

1. The body must be kept straight.
2. The chest *must* touch the bar and the arms must then be *fully extended*.
3. No resting is permitted.
4. One pullup is counted each time the chest touches the bar.

PUSHUPS

Starting Position

Boys: Extend arms and place hands on the floor, just under and slightly to the outside of the shoulders. Fingers should be pointing forward. Extend body so that it is perfectly straight. The weight is supported on the hands and toes. See Figure 22–3.

Girls: Extend arms and place hands, fingers pointing forward, on ground just under and slightly outside of the shoulders. Place knees on floor and extend body until it is straight from the head to the knees. Bend knees and raise the feet off the floor. The weight is supported by the hands and knees. (Also for boys who cannot do regular pushups.) See Figure 22–4.

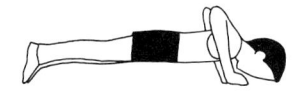

Figure 22–3. Pushups for Boys.

Action

Count 1: Keeping body tense and straight, bend elbows and touch chest to the floor.

Count 2: Return to original position. (The body must be kept perfectly straight. The buttocks must not be raised. The abdomen must not sag.)

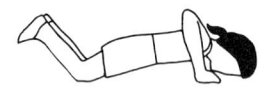

Figure 22–4. Modified Pushups for Girls.

SAWING WOOD

Starting Position

Pupils pair off, face each other, and grasp hands with fingers interlaced.

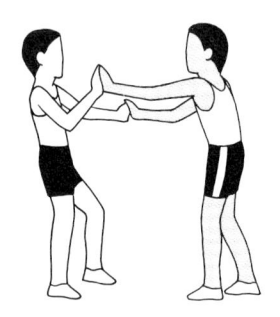

Figure 22–5. Sawing Wood.

Action

With a vigorous action, pupils pump the arms alternately as if they were sawing wood. (See diagram.)

WING STRETCHER

Starting Position

Pupil stands erect. Raise elbows to shoulder height, fists clenched, palms down, in front of chest.

Figure 22–6. Wing Stretcher.

Action

Thrust elbows backward vigorously and return. Be sure head and neck remain erect.

HEAD UP

Starting Position

Pupil lies on back, knees bent, feet flat on floor close to buttocks, hands clasped behind neck, elbows on floor.

Movement Experiences for Middle Childhood

Figure 22–7. **Head Up.**

Action
Tighten abdominal muscles. Raise head and press chin to chest. Keep the lower back flat and arms on floor.

SIDE FLEX
Starting Position
Pupil lies on side, arms extended over head. The head rests on the lower arm. Legs are extended fully, one on top of the other.

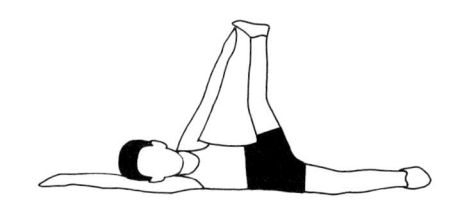

Figure 22–8. **Side Flex.**

Action
Count 1: With a brisk action, raise the topmost arm and leg vertically. Attempt to make contact with hand and foot, without bending elbow or knee.
Count 2: Return to starting position.
Repeat for several counts, then change to other side.

Note: Continued use of rope jumping and the start of circuit training should be used with this age group for additional development activities.

THE SCISSORS
Starting Position
Pupil sits against wall, legs extended with knees straight. Hips, back, shoulders, and head touching wall.

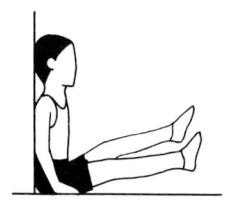

Figure 22–9. **The Scissors.**

Action
Raise and lower legs alternately in a scissors fashion. Gradually increase the tempo of the movement.

BEAR HUG
Starting Position
Pupils stands, feet comfortably spread, with hands on hips.

Figure 22–10. **Bear Hug.**

Action
Count 1: Take a long step diagonally right, keeping left foot anchored in place; tackle the right leg around the thigh by encircling the thigh with both arms.
Count 2: Return to the starting position.
Counts 3 and 4: Repeat to the opposite side.

Games of Low Organization, Including Relays and Lead-Up Activities

PASS AND SHOOT
Equipment
Two basketballs and two basketball goals.

Players
Two teams.

RECOMMENDED MOVEMENT EXPERIENCES

Directions

Divide the class into two teams. Each team has a ball and lines up in front of the baskets. The ball is passed back through the legs of the team members. When the last person in line receives it he dribbles the ball to the front and shoots at the basket. After each person receives his shot he runs to the front of his line and passes the ball back through his legs. This continues until the leader of each team returns to his original position. Each basket made scores two points. The team with the most points at the end of a set time is the winner.

RACE THE BALL

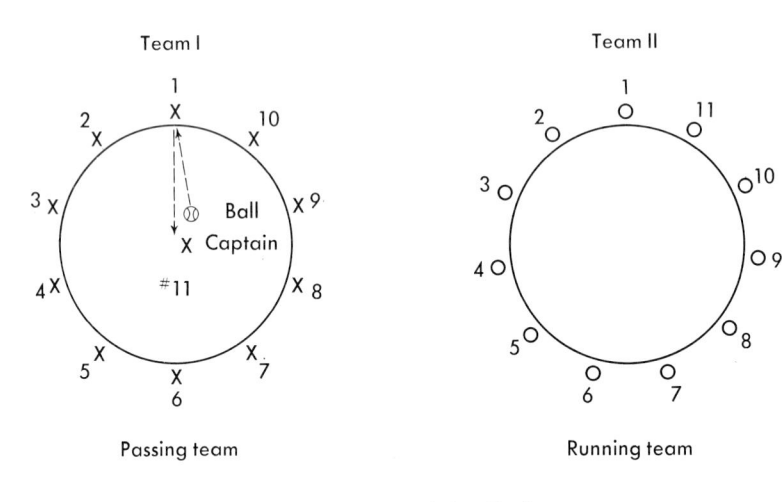

Figure 22–11. Race the Ball.

Equipment

One volleyball or inflated ball of that size.

Players

Two teams, an equal number on each.

Directions

Children are arranged in two circles of equal size. The game is started by the captain of the passing team. He throws the ball to number *one* in his circle. Number *one* catches it and returns it to the captain who passes it to number *two*, receives it from him, and so on, until the captain has passed the ball to each of his players. As soon as the passing team throws the ball, number *one* of team two starts running around his circle. When he returns to his place, he tags number *two* who runs around. On his return he tags number *three*. Team two keeps running until the captain of team one has passed the ball to each member of his team. The captain then calls "Stop!" Team two counts its score. Every runner who made a complete trip around his circle scores one point for his team. Team two now receives the ball and team one becomes the scoring team. When the ball changes teams, the next runner to start is the one next to the last runner. For example, if number *four* was running when "Stop" was called, number *five* would be the first runner in the next inning.

JUMP THE SHOT

Equipment

A rope about 12 feet long to which a bean bag or an old sneaker has been attached at one end.

Formation

Single circle facing inward, one player within the circle.

Directions

The odd player swings the object around the circle and the players jump over the rope. The rope should not be more than one foot above the ground. Whoever misses his jump and stops the rope changes places with the center player.

Variations

1. Use a long pole instead of rope.
2. Players walk or run about the circle, either in the same direction or the opposite direction to that in which the rope is moving.

RAPID TRANSIT

Equipment

Two objects for throwing—balls, bean bags, or erasers.

Players

Two teams of six to twelve each.

Directions

Each team forms a column in back of the team line. Opposite the first player for each team is the catcher facing his team at a distance of 10 feet or more from the team line. The first player holds the ball. At the signal "Go" the first player throws the ball to his catcher, who throws it back to him. When he receives it, he runs to the back of his team and passes the ball, with both hands overhead, from the rear to the front of the line. When the ball reaches the front, the second player throws it to the catcher who returns it to him and he repeats the action. The game continues in relay form, until the catcher has received the ball ten times. The first catcher who calls out "Ten" is the winning team.

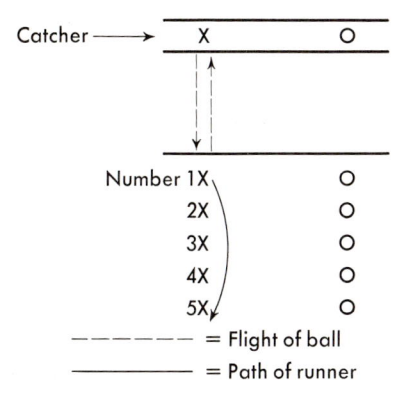

```
Catcher ────►   X               O
                ▲
                │
                │
                ▼
     Number 1X                   O
            2X                   O
            3X                   O
            4X                   O
            5X                   O
       ─ ─ ─ ─ ─ = Flight of ball
       ─────────  = Path of runner
```

Figure 22–12. Rapid Transit.

CLOTHESPINS AWAY

Equipment

Three boxes for each squad; three clothespins for each child.

Players

Two squads or more.

Directions

Players are arranged in squads behind a starting line. Each player is given three clothespins. At the command "Go," the first player in each squad runs to a given point, trying to drop a clothespin in each of the three boxes which are distributed along the running path. He returns to the starting line, tags the next person, and goes to the end of his line. The next player does the same, and so on, until all have had a chance to run. Five points are given to the squad finishing first and one point for each clothespin in the boxes.

CIRCLE RELAY

Equipment

Two large rubber balls.

Players

Twenty children or more; two teams.

Directions

The group counts off so each person has a number. Those persons having odd numbers make up team A and those with even numbers constitute team B. They form a circle and face the center. Two players, one from each team, stand in the circle, each holding a large rubber ball. They may be children who are not able to participate in strenuous physical activity, or any two team members. The A team member calls odd numbers, and B calls even numbers. A may call "Three," and B will quickly call "Six." As they call the numbers they throw the balls in the air. The students whose numbers are called run to catch the balls. Each one then returns to his place in the circle, lays the ball down, and runs around the circle. The first player back to his place scores a point for his team. These two players are the next to toss the balls and call the numbers. The team that scores ten points first wins the game.

BALL ROLL

Equipment
Two soccer balls, volleyballs, or basketballs.

Players
Two teams.

Directions
Each team has a ball. Team players line up behind each other. Team one rolls first. As the first player of team one rolls the ball, the first player of team two rolls his and endeavors to hit team one's ball. If the ball is hit, there is no score. If number one's ball crosses the goal line without being hit, his team scores a point. Each person in team one rolls for a goal, while each in team two endeavors to hit their ball. Then the play is reversed.

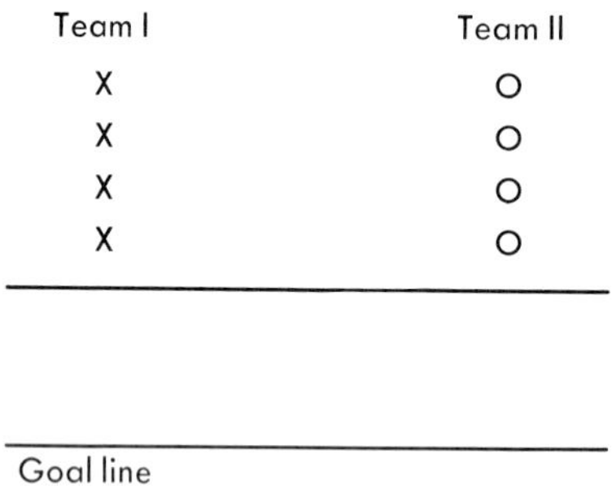

```
     Team I           Team II
       X                O
       X                O
       X                O
       X                O
    _____
           Goal line
```

Figure 22–13. Ball Roll.

MEDLEY RELAY RACE

Equipment
The amount of equipment depends on the number of teams. Each team needs a tenpin, a block of wood, a ball, and a stick.

Players
Unlimited number of teams. Four or eight players on a team.

Directions
Players line up in straight lines with a tenpin placed 20 to 30 feet in front of each. The leader of each team puts a block of wood on his head and runs around the tenpin, returns, and gives it to the next player in line. If he drops it, he must stop, replace it and continue. Each player has a turn. When the leader is again at the front of his line, he dribbles the ball around the tenpin and back. Each player does the same. The third time the leader is in front, he hops on one foot up to the club and back. All players have their turn. The fourth time the leader uses the stick and ball. He hits the ball with the stick up around the tenpin and back. Each player follows suit. The first team to finish the entire activity wins.

WICKET BALL

Equipment
A croquet ball for each team. One mallet for each team. Five wickets for each team. Old hockey balls or softballs may be used, and hockey sticks may be used in place of mallets.

Players
Four to eight on a team.

Directions
Set up the wickets in straight rows about 3 feet apart. Each player hits the ball through *each* wicket on the way down to the goal line and back to his team. The ball must go through each wicket. Each player in line takes his turn and the team through first wins.

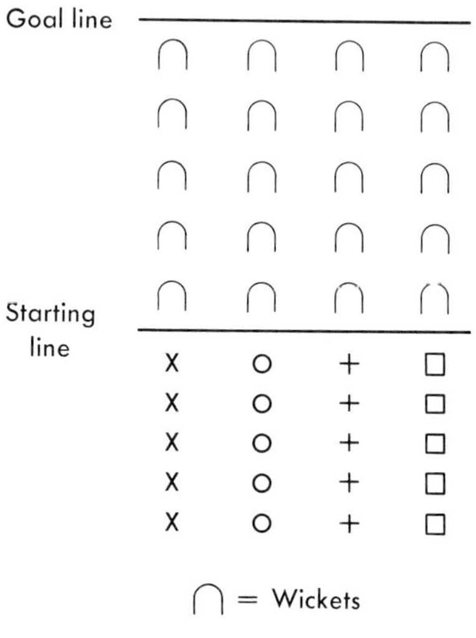

```
Goal line _____
              ∩   ∩   ∩   ∩
              ∩   ∩   ∩   ∩
              ∩   ∩   ∩   ∩
              ∩   ∩   ∩   ∩
Starting      ∩   ∩   ∩   ∩
  line    _____
              X   O   +   □
              X   O   +   □
              X   O   +   □
              X   O   +   □
              X   O   +   □

              ∩ = Wickets
```

Figure 22–14. Wicket Ball.

CROWS AND CRANES

Formation
Large rectangular area with a goal line at each end.

Directions

The players are divided into two teams. One team is the Crows and the other is the Cranes. The players of each team are lined up on their own goal line. They move toward each other walking, running, jumping, or skipping, as directed by the leader. The teacher stands at the center of the area and calls either "Crows!" or "Cranes!" if the teacher calls "Crows!" the Crows run home chased by the Cranes. A Crow tagged by a Crane before he reaches safety behind his own goal line scores a point for the Cranes. The Cranes are chased by the Crows when the teacher calls "Cranes!" The team which has the highest score at the end of the playing period is the winner.

Variations

1. Permit children to cross into each other's half of the playing area.
2. Change movement to hopping, walking, skipping.
3. Do not call each name in sequence. Call Crows several times before Cranes. However, give each team an equal number of times to tag.
4. Try to trick children by calling Crabs or other names beginning with Cr. Those who run score points for opponents.

DARE BASE

Formation
Rectangular area.

Directions

A rectangular playing space with a goal marked off across each end is used. The class is divided into two equal teams, A and B, and each team takes its place on its own goal. Each group selects a name for identification.

Three players from team A step forward and dare three specific players from team B to tag them. Approximately one minute is allowed for the chase and each player caught scores a point for team B. If a player has not been tagged when time is called, he returns to his own team. Tagged players also return to their original goal. The game continues with team B daring three other members of team A. This alternates back and forth until the end of the playing time. The team having the greater number of points at that time wins the game.

CIRCLE TOUCH BALL

Equipment
One ball.

Formation
Circle.

Directions

Players stand in a circle, several feet apart, with an odd player in the center. He tries to touch the ball, which is tossed rapidly from one circle player to another across the circle in any direction. Should he be successful, the one who last touched the ball changes places with him.

CATCHING AND THROWING RELAY

Refer to Chapter 11.

HOT POTATO

Refer to Chapter 11.

DOG CATCHER

Refer to Chapter 17.

Individual and Dual Activities

Children of this age group continue an interest in hopscotch, jump-rope games, marbles, and throwing-and-catching games involving specific skills. They gain great enjoyment in challenging themselves to improve.

Additional games of this type follow.

TETHER BALL

Equipment

In a circle 3 feet in radius, mount a pole 10 feet high with a 7.5-foot card or rope attached to the top of the pole. Paint a 1-inch line 4 feet from the top of the pole. This pole may be attached to a broad base so that it will stand safely, or it may be anchored in the ground. A ball is attached to the rope. This may be a volleyball or a tennis ball in a sack or net. Two paddles are needed if a tennis ball is used. A court diagram is included in Appendix C, Figure C–8.

Directions

Players stand on a line which bisects the circle and extends beyond it. One player stands on the line outside the circle and hits the ball, endeavoring to wind it around the pole above the painted line. If a volleyball is used, it is served with the hand; if a tennis ball is used, each player uses a paddle and serves the ball by hitting it with the paddle. As soon as the ball is hit (served), the opponent tries to hit it and send it back so it will not wind around the pole. Neither player may step into the circle. A game is won when one player is successful in winding the rope completely around the pole above the painted line. The loser serves first in the second game. The greatest number of games won out of three, five, or seven games, as agreed on before play, wins.

BALL PITCHING

Equipment

One old tire, a rope, and a ball. Attach the tire to the rope and hang it from a horizontal bar or tree limb. The height of the tire may differ depending on age and size of participants.

Directions

Mark distances of 10, 15, and 20 feet on the ground on each side of the tire. A football, volleyball, softball, or basketball may be used. One child stands on a line with the ball and attempts to throw it through the tire. Throws may start either underhand or overhand. The second player stands on the opposite side of the tire to catch the ball. A point is scored for each successful throw through the tire. The highest number of points wins.

JACKS

Equipment

Six to twelve jacks and a small semihard rubber ball the size of a golf ball. Children use six jacks to start. As they develop and grow older, as many as twelve jacks may be used.

Directions

A smooth surface is needed to play on. There are many different ways to play Jacks. Each is discussed under its name.

Rules

Fouls are the same for each type and are as follows:
1. Switching hands to catch the ball.
2. Failure to pick up number of jacks required in the game.
3. Catching ball with two hands.
4. Dropping either the jack, or jacks, or ball.
5. Hitting a jack other than the ones supposed to be picked up.
6. Double bounce of ball before catching.

Baby Game—Ones

Scatter all jacks upon the playing surface with a single movement of the right hand. Toss the ball, pick up one jack, and, after the ball has bounced once, catch the ball in the same (right) hand. Transfer the jack to the left hand and proceed as before until all six jacks are in the left hand.

Twos

Jacks are picked up by twos; otherwise, proceed as in Ones.

Threes

Jacks are picked up by threes; otherwise, proceed as in Ones.

Fours

Jacks are picked up four and then two, or two then four; otherwise, proceed as in Ones.

Fives

Jacks are picked up one and then five, or five then one; otherwise, proceed as in Ones.

Sixes

Jacks are picked up all at once; otherwise, proceed as in Ones.

Downs and Ups

All jacks and ball in one hand. Toss ball upward, lay down all jacks, and catch ball in right hand. Throw ball up again, pick up all jacks, and catch ball in same hand.

Eggs in the Basket

Scatter jacks, toss ball, pick up one jack, using only the right hand, and while the ball bounces once, transfer jack to the left hand, then catch ball with the right hand. When all jacks have been picked up and transferred to the left hand, the jacks are all put in the right hand and scattered again. Proceed through twos, threes, fours, fives, and sixes.

Crack the Eggs

Scatter jacks with right hand. Toss ball with right hand and while ball bounces once, pick up one jack with right hand, "crack" (tap) it on the playing surface, and catch ball in right hand, which is still holding the jack. Transfer the jack to the left hand and proceed as before until all jacks are picked up. Scatter again and proceed by twos, threes, and so on, through sixes.

Downcast

Scatter jacks with right hand. Toss ball with right hand, pick up one jack with right hand, and catch the ball in the right hand after it has bounced once, as was done in the Baby Game. Bounce the ball downward and transfer the jack to the left hand, then catch the ball with the right hand. Proceed through sixes.

Double Bounce

This is played the same as the Baby Game, but ball must bounce twice before it is caught. Play through sixes.

Bounce, No Bounce

Scatter jacks with right hand. Toss ball upward, pick up one jack while ball bounces once, and catch the ball in the right hand. With jack still in right hand, toss the ball upward with the right hand, transfer the jack to the left hand, and catch the ball in the right hand without allowing it to bounce. Continue until all jacks have been transferred to the left hand, then scatter them again and proceed by twos, threes, and so on, through sixes.

CROQUET

Equipment

Croquet set, grass plot.

Players

Two or four.

Directions

Each player drives his own ball with his mallet through the arches in the prescribed manner (see Figure 22-15) and reverses it to come home. The first player to reach home and hit the goal with his ball is the winner.

Each player has one shot to start and gains an immediate additional shot each time he makes a successful shot through a wicket. He also gains two additional shots if he is able to hit an opponent's ball. If a player wishes, he may use one of his strokes gained by hitting an opponent's ball with his to knock the opponent's ball further away from the playing area. This is accomplished by placing his ball so it touches his opponent's, holding his ball with his foot, and hitting the ball with the mallet. This causes an indirect hit to his opponent's ball and sends it away. One must be certain that his foot holds his own ball securely or else it, too, will roll far away from the playing area.

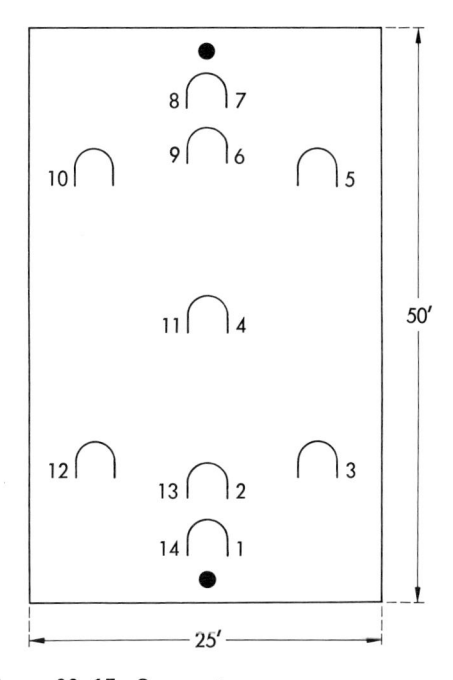

Figure 22-15. Croquet.

Self-Testing Activities

HEEL JUMP

Assume a squat position. Fold arms across chest. Spring quickly, placing weight on heels in a stride position. Return to squat. Repeat rapidly.

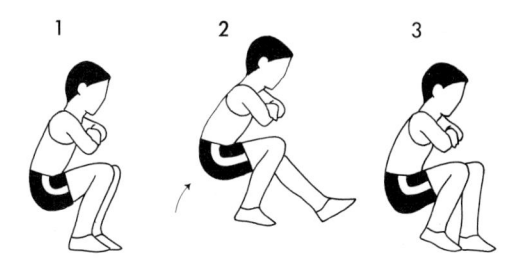

Figure 22-16. Heel Jump.

368 RECOMMENDED MOVEMENT EXPERIENCES

BEAR DANCE

Squat position with arms folded across chest. Jump and extend the right foot forward, quickly bring it back, and extend the left foot forward at the same time.

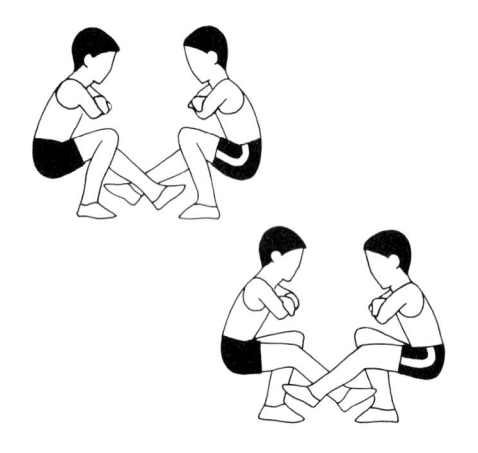

Figure 22–17. Bear Dance.

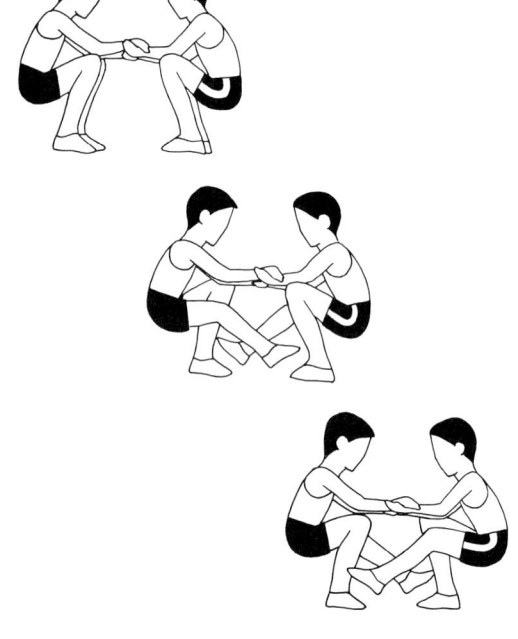

Figure 22–19. Couple Bear Dance.

HEAD PUSH

Stand about 2 feet from a wall, place hands and head against the wall. Remove hands and come to erect position without using them.

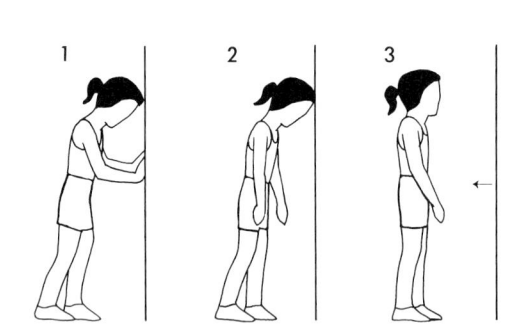

Figure 22–18. Head Push.

TOE KICK

Stand in a straight position, feet together. Jump and raise feet forward touching toes with hands.

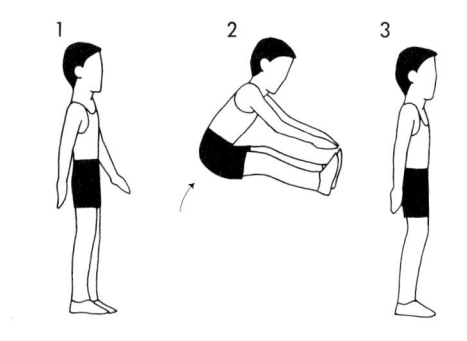

Figure 22–20. Toe Kick.

COUPLE BEAR DANCE

Partners assume squat position facing each other and grasp hands. Each extends his right leg forward, then quickly exchanges his right leg with the left. Do in rapid rhythm.

TWISTER

Partners face each other and join right and left hands respectively. One steps over the joined hands with left foot and the other does the same with his right. This brings them back to back, straddling their joined hands and arms. The first puts his right foot

Movement Experiences for Middle Childhood

over the joined arms, the other one his left foot. They should now be facing each other as when they started.

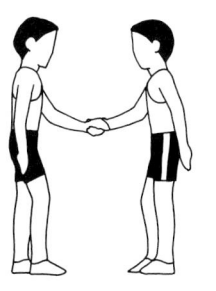

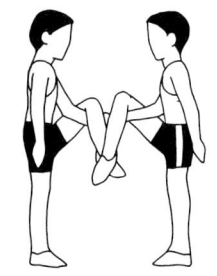

Figure 22-21. Twister.

RING CHAMPION

Players stand on one leg in 5- or 6-foot circles with arms folded across chest. They challenge another player and endeavor to make him lose his balance or leave the circle.

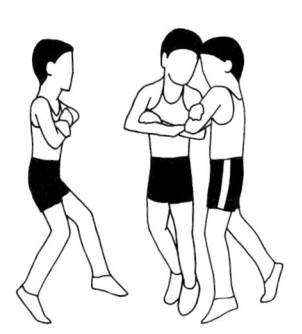

Figure 22-22. Ring Champion.

ROOSTER FIGHT

Partners assume a squat position in a circle about 5 or 6 feet in diameter. Arms are folded across their chests. They move in this position endeavoring to force one off balance or push him out of the circle.

Figure 22-23. Rooster Fight.

SIAMESE HOP

Partners stand with backs together. Each grasps the ankle of his partner's left foot. Couples hop on right foot to a given distance. Each should have a chance to move both forward and backward. Sideways is fun also.

Figure 22-24. Siamese Hop.

Team Games

CENTER CATCH BALL

Equipment
Two balls.

Directions
Divide the group into two teams. Each team stands in a circle. One player from each is chosen to stand in the center of the other circle. Each ball is passed back and forth across each circle. The center player tries to intercept. When he succeeds, he runs back to his team and the next player takes his place in the other circle. Winner is the first team to "play around."

CORNER SPRY

Equipment
Four balls.

Directions
Mark a circle about 10 feet in diameter in the center of a rectangular playing area. Four teams of

370 RECOMMENDED MOVEMENT EXPERIENCES

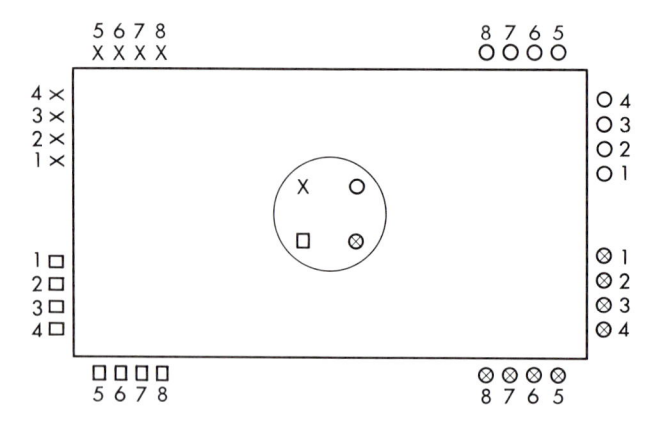

Figure 22–25. Corner Spry.

equal number play. A captain is chosen for each team. One team is in each corner of the playing area and the captains take their places in the circle. Each captain has a ball (see Figure 22–25).

At a signal, the captain of each team starts passing the ball to each member of his team in succession from one to the last number. As each player receives the ball, he tosses it back and squats. When the captain tosses the ball to the last player in the group he calls, "Corner spry," and runs to the head of the team as all members stand up. The last player runs to the circle and becomes captain and repeats the performance. This is done until all members of the team have been captain. The team whose original captain first returns to the center wins.

BEAT THE BALL

Equipment
One volleyball.

Players
Ten to thirty children.

Directions
Two teams of equal number line up facing each other about 30 to 60 feet apart. This distance varies depending on the abilities of the children. Draw a circle in the middle of the area about 3 feet in diameter. Team one has the ball. Number *one* rolls the ball forward. It must roll through the circle. If it does not, he is out. If successful in his roll, he runs and touches the circle with one or both feet and returns to his starting position. Number *one* of the receiving team recovers the ball *after* it has rolled through the circle. He may not leave his starting position until the ball has gone *through* the circle. He attempts to hit the running player before he returns to his position. Each player of the rolling team who crosses the safety line without being hit scores a point. Each hit

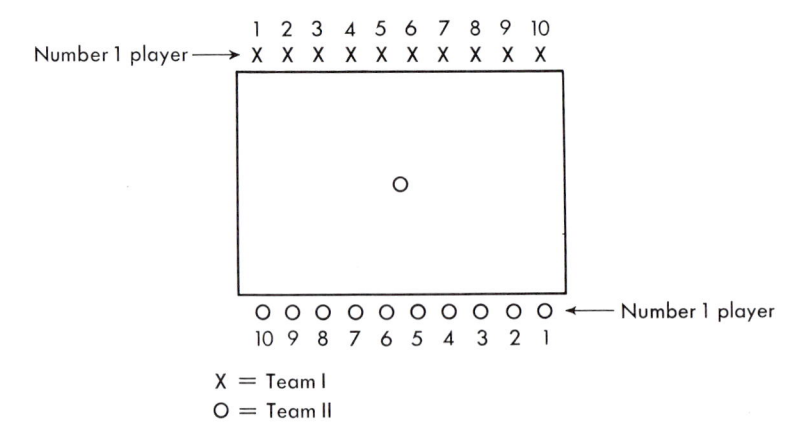

X = Team I
O = Team II

Figure 22–26. Beat the Ball.

HIT THE MALLET OR BAT

Equipment
One softball and one mallet or one softball and bat.

Directions
Fielders from team A scatter in the playing area and one child from team B is up at home base. The ball lies on the home base. The playing area is the size suited to the class. One home base and one first base are all the markings needed. The first player of the batting team hits the ball out in the field, lays the mallet down on the home base, and attempts to run to first base and return home before a fielder can recover the ball and roll it *from where it was fielded* to home base and hit the mallet. If the fielder succeeds in hitting the mallet before the runner gets home, the runner is out. If the runner beats the ball, he scores a run. The game is played by innings. If the ball misses, another player may run and get the ball and attempt another roll at the mallet or bat. The game may be played for five, seven, or nine innings. High score at the end of the last complete inning is the winner

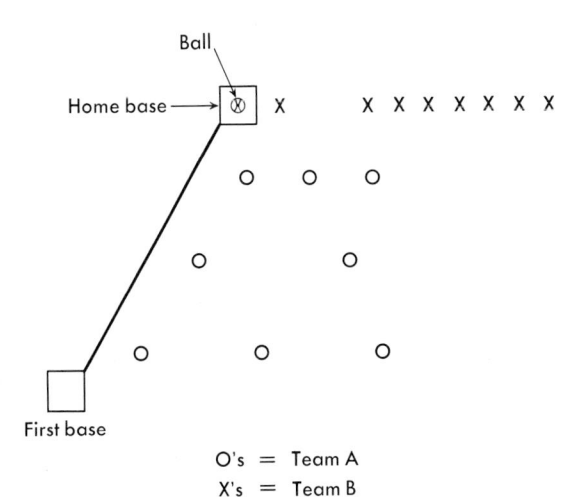

Figure 22-27. Hit the Mallet.

WARM-UP

Equipment
One basketball, volleyball, soccer ball, or large rubber ball.

Directions
Two teams consisting of an even number of players. Playing area is diagrammed in Figure 22–28. Distance of goal line from team A may vary depending on children's ability. Team A has the ball. Number *one* throws it out in the field toward the team B players. He immediately runs to the goal line and returns to his original place, tags number *two*, and so on. The object is for as many members as possible of team A to run across the goal line, one at a time, before team B calls "Stop." Each one who succeeds scores a point for team A. Any member of team B recovers the ball as soon as possible and stands still. All of his teammates run and line up behind him. The ball is then passed back to each person in line. When the last player receives it, he runs to the front of his line and calls "Stop." The team A player who is running stops where he is. A's score is counted. Each person who ran to the goal line and back scores a run. Team B scatters and number *two* of team A throws the ball. The runner is the next one in line after the one running when B called "Stop." If number *three* was running when team B called "Stop," number *four* would be the first runner after number *two* throws the ball. The game continues until three team A players have had a chance to throw the ball. This is one half an inning. It is then team B's turn to throw and team A is in the field. The highest score of the last complete inning wins.

Variations
Variations may be made in the way the fielding teams move the ball back to the last player. A caught fly may be considered an out or not, depending on the class.

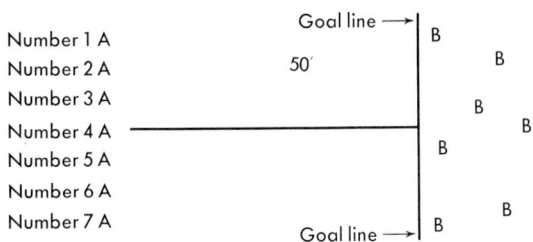

Figure 22-28. Warm-Up.

372 RECOMMENDED MOVEMENT EXPERIENCES

```
Number 1 — X  — — — — — — — — — — — — — — — — — — =  → O — 1 Number
Number 2 — X  = = = = = — — — — — — — — — — — — = =  → O — 2 Number
Number 3 — X  = = = = — — — — — — — — — — — — — = =  → O — 3 Number
Number 4 — X  = = = = — — — — — — — — — — — — = = =  → O — 4 Number
Number 5 — X  = = = = — — — — — — — — — — — — — — —  O — 5 Number
```

Figure 22–29. **Stop Ball.**

STOP BALL

Equipment

One volleyball, or a rubber ball of about that size.

Directions

Two teams or squads line up facing each other. The distance between the two depends on the ability of the children. Number *one* of team X is given the ball. At the signal "Go" he passes it to number *one* of team O. This number *one* passes it across to number *two* of team X, and so the ball continues. (Dotted line shows the direction of the ball.) The teacher or leader, with her back to the group so she does not know who has the ball, suddenly calls out "Stop!" The ball must be held by the person until the signal "Go" is given again. If an X player has the ball the O team scores one point, and if the O team holds the ball the X team scores. The class and teacher may decide before starting how many points will win a game.

Variations

Various methods of passing may be used, such as the two-hand chest pass, one hand throw, and the bounce pass.

BAT BALL

Refer to Chapter 11 for complete directions.

DODGE BALL

Refer to Chapter 17 for complete directions.

KICKBALL

Refer to Chapter 11 for complete directions.

UNDER LEG BALL

Equipment

Softball and four bases.

Formation

Two teams with positions as in softball. Teams may vary in number from eight up. If space is limited, base lines may be as short as 20 to 25 feet.

Directions

The pitcher pitches the ball underhand. The batter catches the ball. If he misses, it is counted as one strike. If the batter fails three times to catch the ball, he is out. When the batter catches the ball he throws it under his leg and runs the bases as in regular baseball. Fouls and outs are the same as in regular baseball.

PIN SOCCER

Equipment

Two or four Indian clubs and one soccer ball.

Formation

A court 20 feet by 30 feet with one or two Indian clubs standing in a 3-foot circle drawn at each end of the court. Two teams of five to eight players are scattered in their halves of the court.

Directions

One player of each team stands at the center with his foot on the ball. At the signal, the two center players suit the action to the words, "Ground, ball; ground, ball; ground, ball; kick," whereupon play begins.

Each team attempts to knock over the pin in their opponent's court by kicking the ball. They may not go over the center line. The ball may not be caught. When a ball goes out of bounds, the opposite team throws it in to start play. One point is scored each time a pin is knocked over by a legal kick.

Track and Field Events

In working with track and field events, children need to be taught the correct form for each event and then should be permitted to practice in small groups of from four to eight children. No competition should be planned until enough time has been spent in practice to assure one that each child is in condition for it.

Each event gives a child opportunities to improve if he or she keeps a record at the beginning of participation and again at the end. A dash need not be run in competition. A stop watch used by a classmate or a teacher will check the time for the dash. This may be recorded by the child. Six weeks later, after much participation, a second check can be made on speed. Such individual improvement checks may be used for all track and field events with great enjoyment and much physical growth.

STANDING BROAD JUMP

Equipment

A line can be marked on the ground, or a take-off board 6 or 8 inches wide and at least 2 inches deep may be sunk firmly in the ground. Either the line or board serves as a scratch line. A jumping pit from 5 to 6 feet wide and 25 to 30 feet long is dug in front of the scratch line and filled with sand or sawdust.

Direction

The contestant stands on the take-off board or line, bends his knees, and sways his body and arms backward and forward to get impetus. He may not lift his feet until he takes off. He should land on both feet.

The measure of the jump is taken from the front edge of the take-off board or line to the first break the child has made in the sawdust or sand with his feet or any other part of his body.

THREE STANDING BROAD JUMPS

This event is exactly like the Standing Broad Jump, except that instead of stopping when he lands, the contestant jumps again immediately, making a second and then a third jump. He may not stop between jumps even for any of the preparatory movements made before a first jump. Each jump is made with both feet and the measurement is made from the outer edge of the take-off board or scratch line to the heel mark made on the last jump, unless some other part of the body has touched the ground nearer to the take-off. All rules and fouls are the same as for Standing Broad Jump.

RUNNING BROAD JUMP

The Running Broad Jump requires a long runway, a take-off board, and a jumping pit. There is no rule limiting the distance of the preliminary run. The jump is made at the finish of the run and is a spring on one foot from the forward edge of the take-off. For the foot to touch the ground in front of the take-off as the jump is made counts as a foul. The jump is measured to the first mark the jumper makes in the pit. The jumper should have good balance in landing and fall forward to avoid lessening the measurement of his jump. Each contestant is given three or four trial jumps.

RUNNING HOP, STEP, AND JUMP

The Running Hop, Step, and Jump is exactly like the Running Broad Jump except that the first movement is a hop, followed without stopping by a step, and then by a jump. All rules, fouls, and procedure are the same as for the Running Broad Jump.

The landing from the first spring is made on the foot that made the take-off—the hop. The second landing is made with the opposite foot—the step. This step should be as long as possible, propelled by the foot that remains on the ground. The spring to the third and final effort (the jump) is made from the one foot then on the ground, but the landing is on both feet. There must be no stop between any of the three efforts.

The measurement is made from the scratch line or forward edge of the take-off board to the final mark of the heels, unless the body has fallen backwards and made other marks closer to the scratch line.

HIGH JUMP

Equipment

Jump standards and a line or light stick for a bar, and a pit filled with sand or sawdust.

Directions

Distance is needed for the contestant to run at least 20 feet. The bar is raised after each successful jump in competition. However, as a child practices, he may wish to keep it at the same level for several tries.

JUMP AND REACH

Equipment
A wall and piece of chalk.

Directions
The child holds a piece of chalk and, jumping as high as possible, either from a crouch or a standing position, marks the wall.

STEP JUMP

From a standing position the child steps with one foot as far as possible and then jumps from both feet.

SOCCER KICK FOR DISTANCE

The ball is placed on a baseline and the player may make a standing or running kick. The distance is marked from the baseline to the point where the ball first touches the ground.

In competition, the play may be between individuals or teams.

BASKETBALL THROW FOR DISTANCE

Equipment
A basketball.

Directions
Mark a starting line. Players may stand at or start back and move up to the line. The ball is held between the hand and arm. Measure the distance from the starting line to where ball first hits the ground.

SOFTBALL THROW FOR DISTANCE

Equipment
A softball.

Directions
Both underhand and overhand throws may be used and recorded in the same fashion as the basketball throw.

DASHES

Equipment
A flat, stoneless area is needed. A string is held by two people at the end of the measured distance.

Directions
Distances recommended: (1) grade four—boys, 30 yards; girls, 30 yards; (2) grade five—boys, 45 yards; girls, 40 yards.

WALKING RACES

Arrangements for Walking Races are the same as those for Dashes, except, of course, that students walk the distance. Start with short distances and gradually increase.

Classroom Activities

SITTING BALL GAME

Equipment
A softball or ball of similar size for each squad, a chair for each person.

Players
Two or four squads of equal number.

Directions
Divide the group into two or four squads and place the rows of chairs so that contestants will be facing each other. Contestants fold their arms and extend their legs out straight in front of them feet off the floor. The ball is placed on the legs of the first person in each row, close to the ankles. Without the use of his hands or having any help whatsoever, each player tries to place the ball on the next contestant's legs, and so on down the row. If the ball falls off it must be picked up and started where it fell. All teams play at the same time. The first team to pass the ball to its last player is the winner.

This and the other games described in this section may of course be repeated as often as time and interest permit.

RUBBER HEELS

Equipment
Three rubber heels for each group.

Players
Groups of four or five each.

Directions
If tiled floor is available use six blocks for each group; if not, the target may be drawn with chalk on the regular floor. Number the blocks from one to six. Players stand on a line 6 to 10 feet from the target area and toss the rubber heels one at a time. Their score is determined by where the heels fall. A plywood or wallboard target may be used with numbers painted in the squares. If enough targets are available, the game may be played outside. Chalk-marked targets may also be made outside on concrete or asphalt pavement. Bean bags may be substituted for the heels if necessary.

Variations
Toss clothespins into numbered boxes. Toss spools into old shoes which are numbered.

NUMBERS ARE FUN

Equipment
None.

Players
Two teams. One team is designated *number one* and one *number two*.

Directions
Two teams are formed and stand back to back. One person in team one calls out a number in a false voice. Then he changes his place in line and in a different voice calls out his number again. The first person on team two tries to guess who called the number. If he succeeds, his team scores a point and may guess again. If he fails, the play is reversed. The team with highest score wins.

FINDING URANIUM (ADAPTATION OF HUCKLE BUCKLE BEANSTALK)

Equipment
Small pebble or stone.

Players
Entire class.

Directions
One child is chosen to be "It" and leaves the room. The class agrees on a hiding place for a small pebble which represents the uranium ore. When "It" comes into the room, the class makes a slow clicking noise with their tongues. They increase the speed of the "Geiger counter" as "It" gets closer to the uranium. When he is far away it becomes a very slow click, barely audible. The point of the game is to develop the hearing sense of "It," so that he can find the uranium when the "Geiger counter" reaches its highest speed. When "It" finds the uranium, he may choose the next "It."

TRAVELING

Equipment
Chalk and blackboard.

Directions
Teams work according to the rows in which they are seated in the classroom. Each must have an equal number. Each team chooses the name of a car. The names of these cars are written on the board in front of each row. The children in each row join hands. All children except the leader in each row put their heads down on the desk so they may not see the blackboard. The teacher or leader writes a number on the blackboard which represents the miles the cars are to travel, and erases it again. The leader passes this number to the one holding his hand by squeezing his hand the number of times that corresponds to the number on the board. If they are to travel six miles he squeezes his hand six times. The second child squeezes the hand of the third and so on down to the last person in the row. As soon as the last person receives the number, he goes to the blackboard and under his team's car writes the number of miles. The first row finished with the correct number of miles wins the race. The teacher needs to stress quietness in this game. Naturally, if a child tells the number of miles to anyone, there is no game. There must be absolutely no talking until all cars have registered mileage. If the row finished first has the incorrect mileage, the winner will be the next with the correct mileage. Change leaders for each successive game. For mileage of double numbers, i.e., 62, the number 6 would be passed

then there would be a pause—then 2. Thus the last one would read the mileage 62, not 6 plus 2, or 8.

COFFEE, TEA, AND MILK

Equipment
None.

Directions
On the floor mark three or more spaces, each about 3 square feet. Mark one with a "T" for tea, one "C" for coffee, and the third "M" for milk. All children start moving around the room in a line, varying their steps as the teacher or a leader directs. They may walk in giant strides, tiptoe, hop on both feet, hop on one foot, skip, and so on. The direction around the room is changed frequently. All aisles or parts of the room should be used. The teacher or leader does not watch the children. At various times he or she claps. This is the signal for the children to stop. Children standing in the area marked "M" for milk get one point; children standing in coffee or tea areas have a minus one. All children remain in the game until it is over. The child with the highest score wins. Children must be sure to stop as soon as the clap is heard. As soon as the teacher claps, he or she turns around. Children caught moving may also have a minus one score. The reason the teacher has his or her back to the class when he or she claps is so that he or she will not know where any child is and thus no one will feel that the teacher has been unfair. More areas may make the game more fun.

FOX AND RABBIT

Equipment
Clean blackboard erasers or similar objects. If there are six teams or rows of children, three erasers would be left as is and three would have some identifying mark.

Directions
The leader of row one is given a plain unmarked eraser. This is the rabbit. The leader of row two receives a marked eraser which is the fox. Each two rows are competitors. The object is for the rabbit to catch the fox or vice versa. The eraser is passed back over the head of each child to the last one in the row, who places it on the desk of the row with which he is competing. If the fox is placed on the last desk in the rabbit row before the rabbit is on the last desk of the fox row, the fox wins. If six rows are competing there would be three winners. Teams or rows may wish to change from fox to rabbit. At the end one can determine if the foxes or rabbits (all totaled scores) won.

Variations
Require the fox and rabbit to travel up and down a designated number of times.

HANDWRITING IDENTIFICATION

Equipment
Chalk and blackboard.

Directions
One child is chosen "It" and is seated in the back of the room with his eyes closed. A leader points to a child who goes to the blackboard and writes a word. All children then exchange seats so "It" may not be able to tell who wrote the word from the mere direction of sound. "It" is then asked to turn, look at the word, and identify the writer. He has three guesses. If he guesses correctly, he is "It" again. If he does not, the writer is the new "It."

Selected References

See the end of Chapter 24.

CHAPTER 23

Movement Experiences for Middle Childhood (Ages Eleven and Twelve)

Dances and Rhythms

It is necessary to introduce dances more complex in pattern and vigorous in movement at this age level in order to maintain the interest of the boys in particular.

A mixture of contra dances, rounds, and couple dances which will prepare this age level for social dance steps on a simplified scale is included in this chapter, giving formation and type.

Steps for this group include allemande left and allemande right; balance step; do-si-do; grand right and left; ladies' chain; Texas star; and the three-step turn. Some of the steps described in Chapter 22 are used in the dances listed below.

The addresses of the record companies are given in Appendix A.

The meter for American square dancing is generally either 2/4 or 4/4 time.

ALLEMANDE LEFT

Boy joins left hand with the girl on his left. They walk completely around each other and back to their original positions.

ALLEMANDE RIGHT

Boy joins right hand with the girl on his right. They walk completely around each other and back to their original positions.

BALANCE STEP

Step right forward, close left foot to right and rise on toes. Keep weight on right in place. Step left backward, close right foot to left and rise on toes. Weight on left in place.

DO-SI-DO

Partners walk toward each other, pass right shoulders, continuing around each other back to back and return backward to original position.

GRAND RIGHT AND LEFT

Facing partners, extend right hand to partner. Walk toward each other passing right shoulders. Extend left hand to next person and pass left shoulders. Continue around the circle weaving in and out until you meet your original partner. Boys always walk counter-clockwise and girls clockwise in circle.

LADIES' CHAIN (SQUARE SET)

Head couples face (couples 1 and 3). Ladies walk toward each other, clasp right hands, pass

378 RECOMMENDED MOVEMENT EXPERIENCES

Table 23–1. International Folk Dances

Dance	Nation	Formation	Steps Used	Record No.
Boston Two-Step	England	Double circle	Pas-de-basque two-step, step, draw	Folk Dance MH 3001
Black Nag	England	Contra	Walk-slide, skip	Folkraft 1174
Gay Gordons	Scotland	Circle, couples	Two-step, walk	Folkraft 1162
Hora	Israel	Single circle	Grapevine step	Folkraft 1110B
Spinning Waltz	Finland	Double circle, couples	Waltz step, 3-step turn	Imperial 1036
Minuet	France	Contra, or double circle	Walk, Step-balance	RCA-LPM 1621
Miserlou	Greece	Single circle (broken)	Grapevine, two-step	Folkraft 1060
Norwegian Polka	Norway	Double circle	Walk, pivot, turn	Folkraft 1411
Sicilian Tarantella	Italy	Two couple sets	Step-swing-hop	RCA LPM 1621
Troika	Russia	Circle sets of 3	Running	Folkraft 1170
Varsouvienne	Sweden	Double circle, girls outside	Mazurka step, waltz step	Folkraft 1130

right shoulders and exchange partners who turn them clockwise. Ladies repeat the chain returning to original partner. Partners again turn in clockwise direction. Side couples (2 and 4) repeat same figure.

TEXAS STAR (Right and Left Hand)

Two or more couples join right hands in center of set and walk clockwise. Two or more couples join left hands in center of set and walk counterclockwise.

THREE STEP TURN

Step forward on left foot, pivot on left foot turning the body counterclockwise and step back on right foot; pivot on right foot, turning the body clockwise and step forward on left foot.

Table 23–2. Dances for Special Events

Dance	Formation	Steps Used	Record No.
Festival (processional)	Single or couple formation	Walk	Folkraft 1179
Maypole Dance	Single circle	Walk-skip	Folkraft 1178
Minuet	Double circle	Walk-balance	RCA Victor 20440
Swedish Weaving Dance	Progressive circle	Grapevine step	Folkraft 1172
Grand March	Twos, fours, and eights	Walk	Any march Record

Table 23–3. Square, Contra and Round Dances

Dance	Nation	Formation	Steps Used	Record No.
Black Hawk Waltz	U.S.	Progressive circle	Waltz-balance	Folkraft 45:1046
Circle Waltz (Mixer)	U.S.	Double circle	Waltz-turn	Folkraft 1046
Cotton-Eyed Joe	U.S.	Double circle (round)	Polka—Two-step	Folkraft 1035-1124
Dud's Reel	U.S.	Longways (contra)	Balance, buzz, walk, step-swing	Folk Dance M.H. 508
Glow Worm (Gavotte)	U.S.	Double circle, girls outside	Walk-turn	Folkraft 1158
Haymaker's Jig	U.S.	Longways (contra)	Step-swing, walk, balance, pivot	Folk Dance M.H. 1071
Josephine	U.S.	Double circle (round)	3-step turn, two-step	Windsor 4502
Laces and Graces	U.S.	Double circle (round)	Slide-pivot, 2-step turn	Folkraft 1047
Oh, Johnny	U.S.	Single circle	Shuffle step, buzz step	Folkraft 1037
Progressive Two-step	England	Double circle, girls outside	Two-step	Folkraft 1161
Put Your Little Foot	U.S.	Double circle, girls outside	Mazurka	Folkraft 1165
Spanish Circle (Waltz)	U.S.	Progressive circle	Waltz-balance	RCA LPM 1620
Teton Mountain Stomp	U.S.	Double circle	Step, draw, swing	Windsor 7615
Texas Schottische	U.S.	Circle, couples	Grapevine, schottische step, two-step	RCA LPA 4235
Varsouvienne	U.S.	Progressive circle	Mazurka	Folk Dance 3012

Developmental Activities

Continue circuit training and rope jumping planned and selected to meet the needs of children.

SQUAT THRUST

Starting Position

Pupil stands at attention.

Action

Count 1: Bend knees and place hands on the floor in front of the feet. Arms may be between, outside, or in front of the bent knees.

Count 2: Thrust the legs back far enough so that the body is perfectly straight from shoulders to feet (the pushup position).

Count 3: Return to squat position.

Count 4: Return to erect position.

Figure 23–1. Squat Thrust.

380 RECOMMENDED MOVEMENT EXPERIENCES

KNEE RAISE (SINGLE AND DOUBLE)

Starting Position
Pupil lies on back with knees slightly flexed, feet on floor, arms at sides.

Action
Count 1: Raise one knee up as close as possible to chest.
Count 2: Fully extend the knee so the leg is perpendicular to the floor.
Count 3: Bend knee and return to chest.
Count 4: Straighten leg and return to starting position.

Alternate the legs during the exercise. The double knee raise is done in the same manner by moving both legs simultaneously.

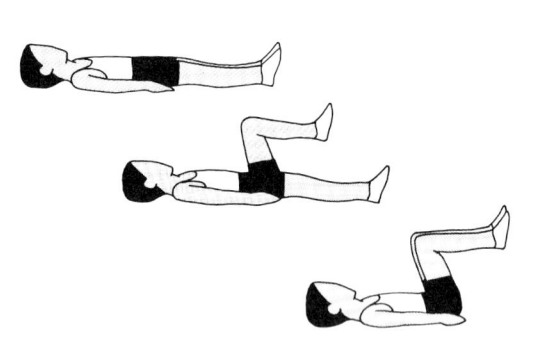

Figure 23-2. Knee Raise (single, center left; double, below right).

PULL STRETCHER

Starting Position
Two pupils sit facing each other, legs apart and extended, so that the soles of their feet are in contact. Pupils grasp hands with fingers interlocked and take alternate turns pulling each other to a bending and an erect position.

Figure 23-3. Pull Stretcher.

LEG EXTENSION

Starting Position
Pupil sits, legs extended, body erect and hands on hips.

Action
Count 1: With a quick, vigorous action, raise and flex the knees by dragging feet backward toward the buttocks with the toes lightly touching the ground.
Count 2: Extend the legs back to the starting position.

The head and shoulders should be held high throughout the exercise.

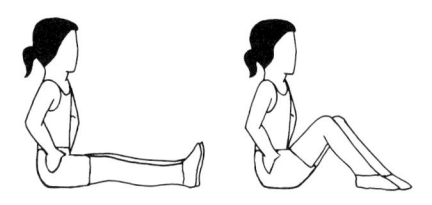

Figure 23-4. Leg Extension.

UP OARS

Starting Position
Pupil lies on back with arms extended behind head.

Action
Count 1: Sit up, reach forward with the extended arms, meanwhile pulling the knees tightly against the chest. Arms are outside the knees.
Count 2: Return to starting position.

The exercise is done rhythmically and without breaks in the movement.

Figure 23-5. Up Oars.

HEAD AND SHOULDER CURL

Starting Position
Pupil lies on the back with hands clasped, palms down, behind the small of the back.

Action
Count 1: Lift the head and pull the shoulders and elbows up off the floor. Hold the tense position for four counts.
Count 2: Return to starting position.
Repeat the exercise.

Figure 23-6. Head and Shoulder Curl.

RECLINING PULLUPS

Starting Position
One pupil lies on back. His partner stands astride of him, face to face, feet beside reclining pupil's chest. Partners grasp hands, with fingers interlocked. Reclining pupil's arms are fully extended.

Action
Count 1: Pupil on floor pulls up with arms until chest touches partner's thighs. His body remains straight, with weight resting on heels. The standing partner supports but does not aid action.
Count 2: Return to starting position.

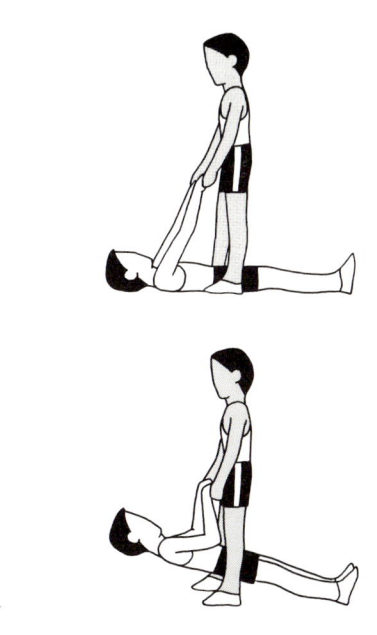

Figure 23-7. Reclining Pullups.

Games of Low Organization, Including Relays and Lead-Up Activities

Teachers should analyze each team game to determine what specific skills are needed for its enjoyment and success. These skills may be practiced many times in game formations known as relays or lead-up activities. For example, in analyzing Kickball, one finds that the skills needed are catching, throwing fast and accurately, running fast, and kicking a stationary ball. In Volleyball the skills needed are serving and volleying. Practice situations may well be planned by teachers and children. Many games formulated by combined thinking serve practice needs well and develop the skills desired.

SQUEEZE OUT

Formation
A double circle is formed, with partners facing each other. There are two extra players, the chaser and the runner.

Directions
The chaser and runner run around or through the circle. The runner is safe if he stops between the members of a couple. When the runner stops, he stands with his back to one of the players. This player is "squeezed out," and he becomes the

chaser, while the former chaser becomes the runner. If the runner is caught, the chaser becomes the runner and the runner the chaser. Encourage the players to keep the game moving by not running too long, and to make surprise stops between the couples.

BROAD JUMP RELAY

Formation
Several teams with equal numbers of players.

Directions
Teams are in single lines behind a starting line. Mark off a space 1 yard wide a good running distance away from the starting line. About 20 feet beyond this, mark off an end line. The first player in each line runs forward, jumps over the area marked off, runs to the end line, and returns to his starting place repeating the actions. He tags the second player and so on. The first team finished wins. Should a player fail to jump the marked area he must repeat his run.

KEEP IT UP

Equipment
One volleyball for each team.

Directions
Teams of eight to ten players. Each team forms a single circle facing inward. One player in each team starts the play. The ball is volleyed from player to player, the object being to keep it in play. One point is counted for each successful volley and one point deducted for each miss. The team having the highest score in a given time wins. Score is kept aloud.

THREE DEEP

Formation
Double circle facing inward, one player standing directly behind the other. One player is chosen to be "It" and another to be the runner.

Directions
The runner may save himself by stepping in front of any two players; the rear player of the three then becomes runner. The runner should not run for a long period before stepping in front of a player. If there are many players, several runners and "Its"

may be chosen. Runners may run in any direction and through the circle.

CIRCLE PURSUIT TAG

Formation
Players form a single circle facing counterclockwise. Players should not be closer to each other than 8 feet.

Directions
At a signal, all start to run following the general outline of the circle. Each tries to tag the runner directly in front of him. Each player tagged drops out of the game and starts a new circle and another game as soon as there are three or four tagged. The last player tagged in the first circle wins. At a signal from a leader or teacher, the circle faces about and runs in the opposite direction. As this reverses the relative position of runners who are gaining or losing ground, it is a feature that may be used by a judicious leader to add much merriment and zest to the game.

Variation
Form the players in a large circle facing toward the center and count off by fours. The number ones then take two steps backward and face to the right. Upon command these pupils (the ones) run forward, each one trying to tag the one in front of him. As soon as one is tagged he must step into the circle. Continue until only one is left. Repeat with "twos," "threes," and "fours," and finally with the four winners.

ARCH GOAL BALL

Equipment
A ball or bean bag and a basket or box for each team.

Formation
Two or more teams of equal number, in columns, with a basket or box placed 15 feet in front of the first pupil of each team.

Directions
The first player in each team has a ball or bean bag. At the signal "Go," he throws for the basket or box. Regardless of whether his throw is successful he retrieves the ball, runs to the rear of his team and passes the ball overhead to the player in front of him.

The ball is passed on to the front pupil who repeats the action. The race is finished when all have had a turn and the ball has been returned to the first player in line. The team making the greatest number of successful pitches at the basket or box wins. Each successful toss counts one point.

SQUARE RELAY

Equipment

Four Indian clubs or milk cartons for each team.

Formation

Four Indian clubs are placed in position to form a square. The players are divided into two teams. The teams are in single file each facing a square. The distance the teams are from the clubs differs according to the space available.

Directions

At the signal "Go," the first runner of each team starts and runs around the clubs. He must circle each club. Each runner upon completing his run touches off the next runner. The first team to finish wins.

KANGAROO RELAY

Equipment

An eraser, bean bag, volleyball, or basketball for each team.

Formation

Divide players into two or more equal teams. These teams line up in columns behind a starting line drawn on the ground. On the playing space draw another line parallel to the starting line 10 to 20 feet from it.

Directions

The first player of each team places a volleyball (or whatever is used) between his knees and at the starting signal jumps to the line on the other side of the playing space, keeping the ball between his knees without touching it with his hands. If the ball falls out he must pick it up and replace it at the point in his running space where he dropped it. Upon reaching the line he takes the ball in his hands and runs back to the starting line, where he gives it to the next player on his team who should be toeing the starting line. He then takes his place at the rear of his team. This mode of playing continues until all players have run. The winning team shall be the one that has each one of its members complete the run and is standing at attention first.

BASKETBALL RELAY

Equipment

One basketball for each team. Basketball goal for each two teams.

Formation

Teams of equal numbers lined in single file, 20 feet from the goal.

Directions

Teams are in basic relay formation facing a basketball goal. On the signal "Go," the first player dribbles up to his basket and attempts a shot. He recovers the ball and throws it back to the next player in his line. He then runs to the end of his starting line. Each basket made counts a point for the team.

SOCCER-DRIBBLE RELAY

Equipment

One soccer ball for each team.

Formation

Teams of equal numbers in file formation. One line 20 feet from starting line.

Directions

Players stand in a basic running-relay formation. The first player in each team has a soccer ball in front of him. At the "Go" signal, the first player dribbles the ball with either foot to the turning point and back. The second player in line may not start until both ball and player have crossed the finish line. The use of hands is prohibited.

FIVE TRIPS

Equipment

Two balls, any size desired by class or teacher. If more than two groups are used, more balls will be needed as each group needs two. Balls should be approximately the same size but should be easily distinguishable. One white volleyball and one red rubber ball would be an example of this.

Directions

Groups line up as shown in Figure 23–8. Number *one* of each team has a ball. At the signal

```
Start Number 1 X          O Number 1
              O           X
              X           O
              O           X
              X           O
              O           X
```

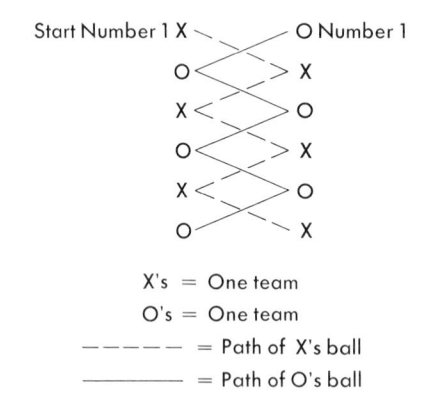

X's = One team
O's = One team
— — — — = Path of X's ball
────── = Path of O's ball

Figure 23–8. Five Trips.

"Go," he passes the ball to the opposite person on his team. Dotted line shows the path of the ball for team X. The ball travels down the entire line in zigzag formation and comes back to the starter. This makes one trip. The leader calls "One" out loud so all may hear. He immediately starts the ball on its second trip and so it continues until the ball has made five trips and is back in the leader's hands. Both teams pass their balls at the same time. This will work well if one leader is designated to make the first pass low while the other is asked to pass it high. From then on no one need worry about the passes. Distances between lines depend on the ability of the children and the type of pass used. Various types may be used. If a ball is lost the person who missed it recovers it and starts it again from his place in line. The number of trips may be varied by the teacher and pupils.

CLUB SNATCH

Equipment
One Indian club.

Directions
A goal is marked off across each end of the playing area, 50 to 100 feet apart. An Indian club is placed midway between the goals. (A stone or dumbbell laid on the ground may be substituted.)

The players are divided into two equal teams and are distributed, one half standing on one goal line and the other half on the other. Each member has a number, from one up. Each must remember his number. The object of the game is for the runners whose numbers are called to snatch the club and return to the goal before they are tagged by a runner from the opposite goal. Both runners leave their starting bases as the same time when their number is called. Should one succeed in reaching the goal with the club before the other player can tag him, his team scores one point. Should he be tagged before he can return with the club, there is no point. The club is replaced after each run. Both players return to their original teams.

The team wins which has the highest score at the end of the playing time. It adds fun to the game to call out two numbers at one time.

Individual and Dual Activities

DECK TENNIS

Players
The game may be played as either singles (two players) or doubles (four players).

Equipment
The doubles court is 40 feet long and 20 feet wide. It is divided across the middle by a net, the ends of which are attached to posts standing one foot outside of the court on either side. The width of the court is divided in half by a line drawn the full length of the court, thus forming the half courts. A neutral ground is marked off by lines drawn parallel to, and two feet from, the net.

The singles court is 40 feet long and 15 feet wide. It is divided the same as the doubles court. The court may be marked out with tennis marker or tapes cut to the proper lengths.

The net is 22 feet long and 36 inches wide with a 2-inch top binding of white canvas. The height of the net is 6 feet at the posts. A rope may be substituted for the net.

The ring shall have a 4.5-inch inside diameter and 7-inch outside diameter. It is made of soft molded rubber. A rope ring may be substituted.

Object
The game is similar to tennis except that a ring is tossed, instead of a ball being batted back and forth.

Rules

1. Choice of sides and the right to serve in the first game shall be decided by toss.
2. The players shall stand on opposite sides of the net; the player who first delivers the ring shall be called the server and the other the receiver.
3. When serving, the server shall stand behind the base line and within the limits of the half court. The server's partner and the receiver's partner may take any position in their own court.
4. The service shall be delivered from the right and left courts alternately, beginning from the right in every game. The ring served shall drop within the half court line and the side line of the court which is diagonally opposite to that from which it was served, or upon any such line. Each player serves a game.
5. The ring must always be played or served with an upward tendency no matter whether the ring be taken high or low. No balking or hesitating is allowed.
6. Either forehand or backhand play is allowed, except for the serve, which must be forehand.
7. A ring touching the net in going over during the service is a "let" and the service is taken over.
8. The ring must be caught with only one hand and delivered with the same hand immediately.
9. Scoring is like tennis.

QUOITS (OUTDOOR)

Equipment

One set (four) of quoits or horseshoes and two metal pegs. Level area 50 feet by 10 feet.

Players

The game may be played singles (two players) or doubles (four players). In doubles one player of each team pitches from each peg.

Rules

1. The standard distance apart for pegs is forty feet. For younger players the distance may be shortened. Pegs shall extend 6 inches above the ground.
2. When pitching, contestant's forward foot shall be in the rear of the peg and within 3 feet of either side.
3. At the beginning of a game the contestants shall toss a coin for first pitch, the winner having his choice of first or follow pitch.
4. At the beginning of any game other than the first, the loser of the preceding game shall have first pitch.
5. Except at the beginning of a game, the winner of the preceding pitch shall have first pitch.

Scoring

1. A regulation game shall consist of twenty-one points and the contestant first scoring this number shall be declared the winner.
2. The most points a contestant can score in a single game are 21. Therefore, if a contestant has 19 points, he cannot get full credit for a ringer, but only the necessary points required to bring his total up to 21. Should he make a ringer, in that case it would count only two points.
3. The closest shoe to the peg shall score one

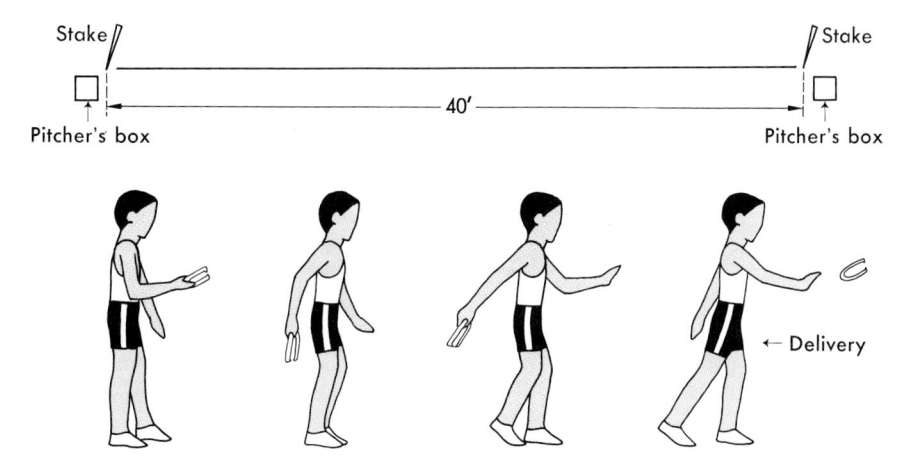

Figure 23–9. Quoits.

point. If both shoes are closer than either of an opponent's they shall score two points.

4. A ringer shall score three points. To be a ringer, a shoe must encircle the peg for enough to permit a straight edge to touch both calks and clear the peg.

5. A leaner shall score two points. To be a leaner, a shoe must be supported by the peg, and more than one-half of it should be clear of the ground.

6. Two ringers is the highest score a pitcher can make with two shoes and shall count six points.

7. All equals shall be counted as ties. That is, if both contestants have one shoe each equal distance from the peg or against it, they are tied, and the one having the next closest shoe shall score one point.

FLOOR OR BEACH TENNIS

Equipment
A tennis ball or sponge rubber ball.

Formation
Mark on the floor or ground a rectangle 6 feet by 12 feet. No net is needed. Draw a line across the court dividing it into two equal parts.

Directions
The game is usually played by two players (singles). It may be played by four (doubles). The player starts the game by batting the ball with his hand to his opponent. It is played with the open hand. Players must remain outside of the marked area and make each play by reaching in. Winning score may be set at 13, 15, or 21 points.

HANDBALL

Equipment
One small rubber ball.

Players
Two to four players constitute a team.

Field
Flat piece of ground 20 feet deep in front of a wall 10 feet wide and 10 to 15 feet high. (Mark off with line on brick wall of a building or wall of gymnasium.) Line drawn on the ground parallel to the wall and 8 feet from it called the *short line*.

Directions
To start the game, a player from team A steps up to the short line, bounces the ball on the ground, and bats (serves) it with his hand against the wall so that the ball rebounds beyond the short line, and within the playing area. He has two chances to do this. If on the second trial the ball falls short of the short line, hits the player, or goes outside the playing area, he is out and another member of team A serves.

As soon as a member of team A succeeds in batting the ball so that it rebounds beyond the 8-foot line, the ball is considered in play and a member of team B must return it before it has bounced twice.

Rules
1. The ball must be batted first by a member of one team and then by a member of the opposing team.
2. Failure to return the ball scores one point for the serving team.
3. If the serving team fails to return the ball, it makes an out.
4. Two outs put the side out.
5. Twenty-one points constitute a game.

PADDLE BADMINTON

Equipment
One paddle for each player, one shuttlecock, one net. Area 25 feet by 50 feet with a net 4 or 5 feet in height attached to poles outside the court.

Players
Two or four.

Directions
A player from one side serves the shuttlecock from behind the end line into the court across the net. Play is then started and the object is to hit the shuttlecock back and forth from one side to the other, keeping it within the bounds of the court. If doubles are being played, the partners must hit alternately.

One point is scored for the opponents when a player:
1. Hits the shuttlecock out of the court.
2. Fails to return it to his opponent.
3. Hits the net with his paddle or his body.

The same player serves as long as his side or he, as an individual, scores. If he or his partner fail to score or to return the shuttlecock, hit the net, or hit the shuttlecock out of bounds, his serve ends and the opponent becomes the server. The serving side is the only side which can score a point. Partners alternate services. Points may vary for winning a game. They may be 13, 15, or 21, as set before play.

TABLE TENNIS

Equipment

One table-tennis table, one paddle for each player, three balls, and one net.

Players

Two or four.

Directions

One player serves the ball across the net to his opponent. The ball is served as in tennis except that it must bounce on the server's side of the net before crossing onto the opponent's half of the table. The object is to hit the ball back and forth across the net keeping it on the table. The same player serves until five points have been scored. Service then changes sides. Points are made when a player:

1. Hits the ball off the table.
2. Fails to serve the ball correctly in two turns.
3. Hits the table with his body.
4. Fails to return the ball to his opponent.

The winning score of a game is 21 points.

Self-Testing Activities

COFFEE GRINDER

Assume a deep knee bend position and place the left or right hand on the floor by the side of the body. Keep the elbow stiff and place weight on the arm. Extend both legs either to the right or left depending on which arm is used. Use the arm as a pivot and walk in a circle.

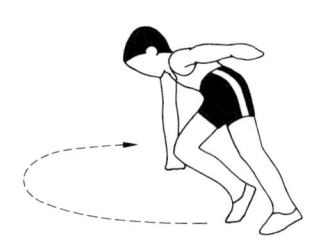

Figure 23–10. Coffee Grinder.

ANKLE TOSS

Hold a tennis ball or bean bag between ankles. Jump and toss it so you may catch it.

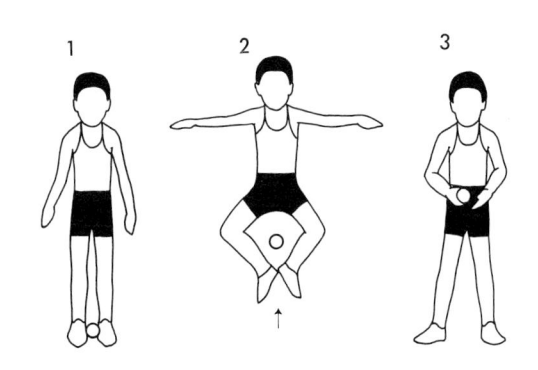

Figure 23–12. Ankle Toss.

ANKLE JUMP

Feet together. Grasp ankles with hands. Jump as far as possible. May be done from a squat or standing position.

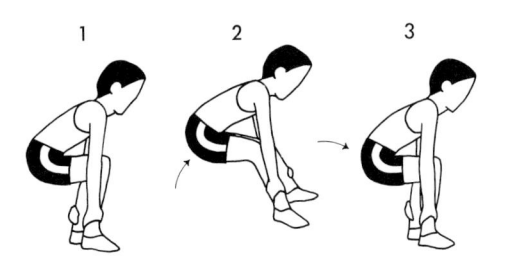

Figure 23–11. Ankle Jump.

KNEE WRESTLE (MATS NEEDED)

Partners assume a kneeling position on the mat and face each other. They hold right hands and endeavor to push or pull each other off balance.

Figure 23–13. Knee Wrestle.

CRANE DIVE

Stand a piece of paper on the floor about 4 inches to 6 inches in height. Stand in front of it. Balance on one foot, raise the other to the back. Place arms sideward for balance. Bend forward and pick up paper with teeth. Come to standing position without losing balance.

Figure 23-14. Crane Dive.

FISH HAWK DIVE

Kneel on one knee. Stand a folded paper about the size of an envelope on the floor. Raise one leg backward, balance on the knee, bend forward, and pick up the paper. Come back to kneeling position without loss of balance.

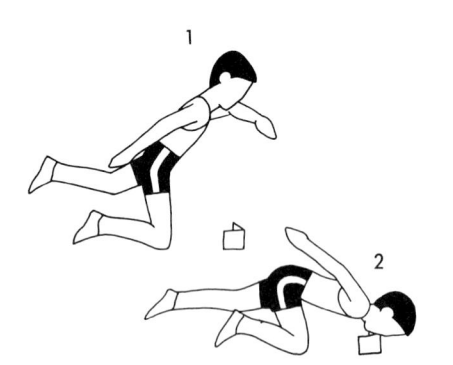

Figure 23-15. Fish Hawk Dive.

HAND WRESTLE

Partners stand facing each other with right hands joined and right feet placed against each other. Each endeavors to make the other lose his balance by moving one or both feet from the floor.

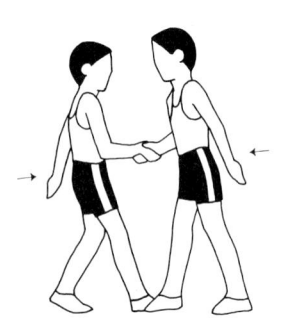

Figure 23-16. Hand Wrestle.

HEEL CLICK

Stand erect, both feet together. Jump in the air and endeavor to click heels together two or three times before landing back on the floor.

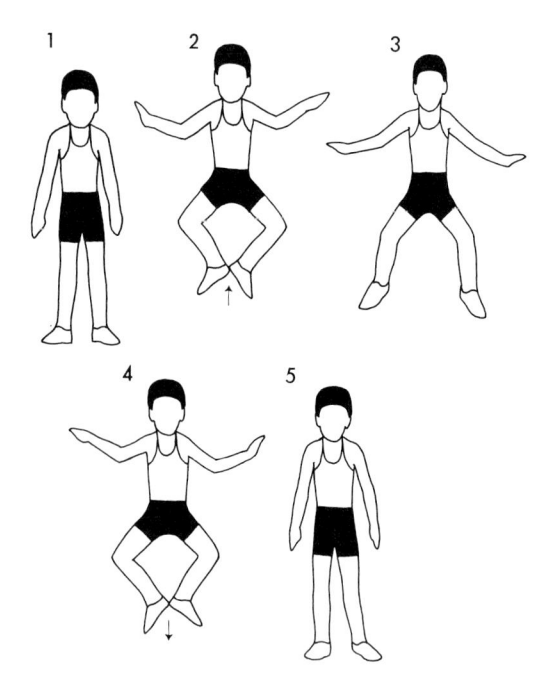

Figure 23-17. Heel Click.

JUMP THE STICK

Hold a broomstick or wand in both hands and jump over it without releasing either hand. Try this forward and backward.

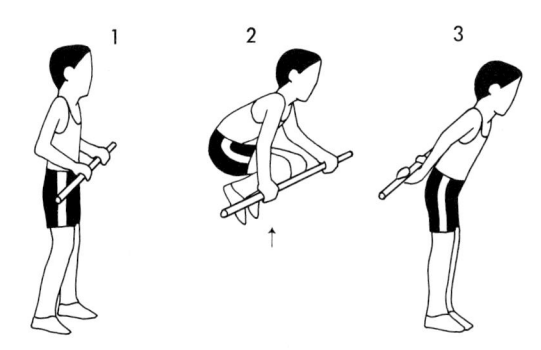

Figure 23–18. Jump the Stick.

SITTING BALANCE (MATS NEEDED)

One player lies on his back, bends his knees to his chest, and extends his feet. The second child stands with his back to him and sits on the soles of his feet. The first lifts him by straightening his knees upward.

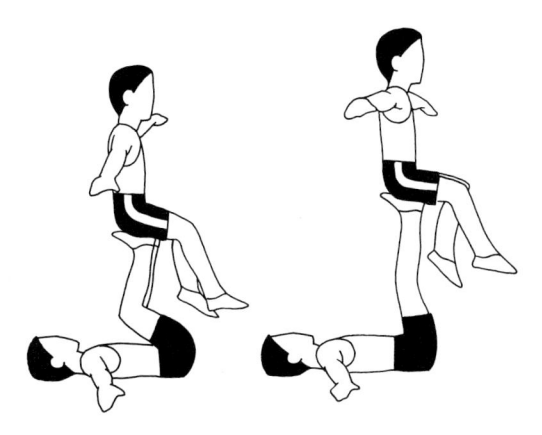

Figure 23–19. Sitting Balance.

TANDEM

Three players stand one behind the other. The last one assumes a semisquat position. The one in front sits on his knees. They walk forward using left and right feet together.

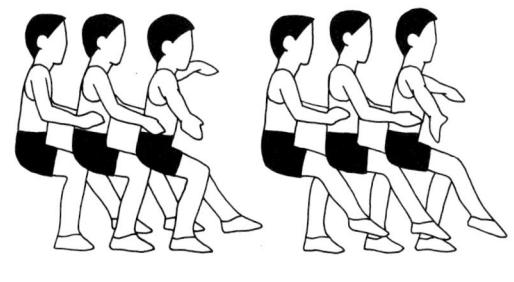

Figure 23–20. Tandem.

KANGAROO FIGHT

Each partner stands with a tennis ball or folded newspaper between his knees. Arms are folded across chests. Each endeavors to make the other drop the object by bumping shoulders.

Figure 23–21. Kangaroo Fight.

TEAM FORWARD ROLLS (MATS NEEDED)

Three or more people stand at the edge of mats and do forward rolls at the same time, endeavoring to keep in rhythm.

Team Games

Achievement Skills and Tests for Various Team Games. The following will suggest a number of tests to use in determining individual skills:

1. Baseball activities: (a) baseball throw for accuracy, (b) baseball throw for distance, (c) baseball batting for accuracy, (d) fielding grounders and fly balls.

2. Basketball activities: (a) basketball throw for distance; (b) basketball goal throwing—free throw, goal in one minute, goal throw for accuracy; (c) relays to help develop skills—shuttle, dribble and shoot, dribble.

3. Soccer activities: (a) soccer kick for goal, (b) soccer kick for distance, (c) soccer kick for accuracy, (d) dribbling.

4. Touch football activities: (a) drop kick for goal, (b) punting for distance, (c) forward pass for distance and accuracy.

5. Volleyball activities: (a) serving for accuracy, (b) return for accuracy, (c) volleying with a partner across a net, (d) volleying against a wall to oneself.

BUNT SOFTBALL (OUTDOOR)

Bunt softball is played exactly the same as baseball except for two rules: (1) six men on a side, eliminating the outfield; (2) the batter may do nothing more than bunt; if he swings at a ball, he is out whether he hits it or not.

This game will develop real bunters.

PADDLE BASEBALL

Equipment
A wooden paddle, similar to a ping-pong paddle, a tennis ball or rubber ball, a diamond marked like a baseball diamond only smaller, depending on the children.

Directions
This game is played like softball and may be played in a smaller area and in areas where rules do not permit baseballs or softballs to be used. If boys hit too hard they may be required to bat the opposite way from their regular way of batting. (A left-handed batter would bat right-handed and vice versa.)

PUNCH BASEBALL

Equipment
One volleyball or a rubber ball of approximately the same size and a baseball diamond of a size to meet the children's ability.

Directions
The directions are the same as for softball. The pitcher pitches the ball and the batter *punches* it. This is a *must* so the child does not hurt his arm or hand. Children may play this game in a smaller area than softball, get much enjoyment, and satisfy the desire for a team game in the spring when area and regulations will not permit softballs to be used.

BASEBALL NEWCOMB

Equipment
Softball and volleyball net, the top 10 feet from the ground.

Formation
An area 30 feet by 60 feet divided into two courts by the net. One team on each side of the net spaced as in volleyball.

Directions
A server pitches the ball underhand, over the net. The ball is caught and returned by the receiving side and the play continues until a miss occurs. Players may not run with the ball. Each player should keep his own position on the court. The ball must always be pitched underhand.

Scoring
One point for the opposite side when (1) the ball is improperly thrown; (2) the ball is missed; or (3) the ball is thrown into the net or out of bounds.

BAND BOX BALL

Equipment
One volleyball and four Indian clubs.

Directions
Two teams of five each, divided into three forwards and two guards. More players may be used by enlarging the playing area and using more than one goal. The game is played on a rectangle. The size will depend on the ability of the children. The ball is put in play by jumping it at center between an A and B player. Forwards try to score a point by knocking down their opponents' pins. Guards attempt to intercept and pass the ball to their forwards. If the ball rolls over the band area, the team responsible for it must give its opponents a point. Two points are scored when a forward succeeds in knocking over the Indian club in the goal. They may either throw or roll the ball. Balls which go out of bounds are thrown in by the team not responsible for causing it to go out of the playing area. Balls may not be knocked from an opponent's hand. If this occurs, a

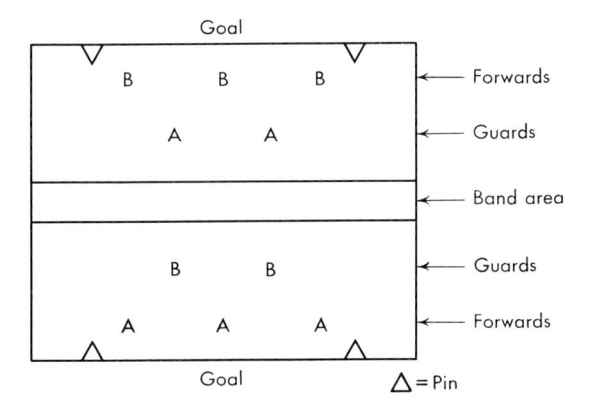

Movement Experiences for Middle Childhood   391

```
         Goal
  ▽       ▽
┌────────────────────┐
│  B    B    B       │ ←── Forwards
│                    │
│    A     A         │ ←── Guards
├────────────────────┤
│                    │ ←── Band area
├────────────────────┤
│    B    B          │ ←── Guards
│                    │
│  A    A    A       │ ←── Forwards
└─△──────△────△──────┘
         Goal           △ = Pin
```

Figure 23-22. **Band Box Ball.**

forward may have a free shot at his opponent's goal. Teachers and pupils may set the number of points for a game, or it may be played by a time limit in quarters or halves.

LONG BASE

Equipment
Softball bat and a softball.

Formation
The softball area may be used for the area of this game. To the right of the pitcher's box and 65 feet away from home plate is marked a square; this is the long base. The pitcher's box is marked 30 feet away from home plate. The players, preferably from eight to twelve, are divided into two equal groups. The players on each of the teams are numbered in consecutive order. Each of the teams chooses a pitcher, a catcher, and a long-baseman. The remainder of the players are the fielders or the batters, depending upon the playing position of the team. The teams alternate their positions when three outs are declared.

Directions
The first batter of the batting team stands at home base and attempts to hit the ball thrown underhanded to him by the pitcher. If the batter hits the ball, it is fair no matter where it goes. The batter runs to the long base and may return to home base. If the batter does this successfully without being tagged by one of the fielders, he scores one run. If a batter reaches the long base safely, he may remain there until another batter of his team hits a ball. During the process of the game, several batters may stand on

the long base at once. Once the ball is hit by the batter, the fielders try to tag the batter before he reaches long base or to throw the ball to long base before the runner reaches it. All of the fielders, including the pitcher and the catcher, may move anywhere on the field. When the batted ball is retrieved by one of the fielders, he may throw the ball to any fielder who is closer to home base or long base. The team at bat remains at bat until three outs are declared. An out occurs when the fielders catch a fly ball, when the ball beats the runners to long base or a runner is tagged with the ball, when the batter is not within the area of long base and is tagged with the ball, and when the batter throws his bat instead of dropping it as he runs to long base. The game consists of seven innings. The team having scored the largest number of runs wins the game.

KICK BASEBALL
Refer to Chapter 11 for complete directions.

KICK PIN BASEBALL
Refer to Chapter 11 for complete directions.

SCRAM

Equipment
One volleyball and individual markers for one team.

Players
From ten to thirty children.

Directions
Players take their places in a rectangular playing area of suitable size for age level. A suggested size is 50 by 40 feet. One player from each team comes to the center of the area, faces his teammates, and attempts to tap a ball which is tossed straight up in the air by the leader. When the ball is tapped, anyone may catch it and players are then free to move in

```
┌─────────────┬─────────────┐
│  X  X  X    │   O  O  O   │
│    X  X     │    O  O  O  │
│           O │ X           │
│  X  X  X    │    O  O     │
│  X  X  X    │   O  O  O   │
└─────────────┴─────────────┘
```

Figure 23-23. **Scram.**

both courts. The object is to hit players on the opposite team below the waist with the ball. Each hit scores a point for the throwing team. *However, if the opponent can catch the thrown ball, there is no score and he in turn throws it back at his opponents.* Rebounds do not count as hits. Anyone may pick a ball up off the floor and throw it. No one may run or step with the ball. To aid players in knowing teammates, one team should wear markers of some kind. When a player is hit he goes to the side of the court and rests until another of his teammates is hit and comes out; then he returns. This helps to make scoring easy and also enables a child to rest for a few seconds which is often necessary during this game. When a class plays this well, two balls may be used. The game is played in quarters of three, five, or six minutes each, depending on the children.

NEWCOMB

Equipment
Volleyball, junior-sized basketball, or an 8-inch or 10-inch playground ball.

Formation
A court 25 feet by 50 feet in size is marked on the playing area. A net or rope 7 feet from the floor is stretched across the center of the playing area, dividing the court into two equal parts. The players are divided into two equal teams. Eight to twelve players are recommended for each team although the game may be played with smaller or larger numbers.

Directions
One player is designated to throw the ball across the net. The game continues with the object being to throw the ball over the net, to catch the ball, and to continue throwing and catching the ball back and forth across the net. Any player may catch the ball. The ball may be relayed among team members. The play continues until one point is scored. Points are scored when the following occurs: the ball drops to the ground on the opponent's side; the ball hits the net, rope, or standards holding the net; the ball is thrown under the net by a player; the ball is thrown outside the playing area; the ball is held for more than ten seconds. After a point has been scored, the ball is immediately thrown by the side in possession and the game continues as before. The game is played in two 10-minute periods or may be played for points.

SIMPLIFIED VOLLEYBALL

Equipment
Volleyball and net.

Formation
Teams of six to ten players on either side of the net as in volleyball. Each player should be assigned a position.

Directions
Regular volleyball rules should be followed with the following exceptions:
1. Two serves are allowed.
2. An assist on a serve is allowed.
3. Any number of players may play the ball before it goes over the net.
4. A player may hit the ball twice in succession but may not hold it.
5. For very small players the ball may be allowed to bounce once after passing over the net.
6. Any one or all of these exceptions may be allowed.

MASS VOLLEYBALL

Equipment
Volleyball, giant volleyball or cage ball, and net.

Formation
As many players as can be accommodated on the court, one team on either side of the net as in volleyball.

Directions
The ball is thrown or batted over the net. As many as can are allowed to play on the ball in succession or at the same time. The objective is to keep the ball in play and to get it back over the net. Players are not allowed to hold the ball. When the ball hits the ground or is knocked out of bounds a point is scored.

SQUARE SOCCER

Equipment
Soccer ball.

Formation
The players are divided into two teams, each team occupying the two adjacent sides of a large square, with clearly marked boundary lines. A soccer ball is placed in the center of the square.

Directions

At the leader's command the player at the right end of each team runs to the center and endeavors to kick the ball through the opposing side. The players on the lines stop the ball with hands or body, throwing or kicking it back to the center, or, if possible, through the other team, the two center players assisting. If the ball is kicked over the heads of the players on the line, the opposing center player is given a free kick from the center of the square, the other center standing in back of him. After a team scores a point, the center players take their place at the foot of their teams, and two new players enter the square. One point is scored each time the ball is kicked through the opposing team; the team wins that first scores 21 points.

SOCCER KEEP-AWAY

Equipment
One soccer ball.

Formation
A playing area 25 feet by 50 feet is marked on the playground or gymnasium floor. Across this area are marked parallel lines at 10-foot intervals; five zones are thus formed. The zones at each end are called *end zones*. The middle zone is named the *center zone* and the other two zones of each court are the *neutral zones*. Players are divided into three teams: A, B, and C. One team, B, occupies the center zone, the second and third teams, A and C, occupy the end zones. The neutral zones are unoccupied. One of the team A players in the end zone has possession of the ball at the beginning of the game.

Directions
The end zone team A players, with the ball, attempt to kick the ball through the neutral zones and the center zone to team C stationed in the end zone at the opposite end of the playing area. If successful, the kicking team scores one point, and the game is started by team C. After each point has been scored, sides and players on the team alternate in kicking the ball through the center zone. If team B players, stationed in the center zone, stop the ball, the team B player closest to the ball gives it to the end zone team that did not kick the last ball. Each time the center players intercept the ball, one point is scored for their team. If a team player kicks the ball over the heads of both the center zone and the opposite end zone players, both of the latter teams score one point. The end zone teams may score one point each if the center players step into the neutral territory. If the players in any of the zones touch the ball with their hands, the other two teams each score one point. The team having scored the greatest number of points within a designated playing time is declared to be the winner of the game.

CAPTAIN BALL

Equipment
Basketball, volleyball, or soccerball.

Formation
A playing area is marked as diagramed in Figure 23–24. Each of the circles is approximately 2.5 feet in diameter. Fourteen players are divided into two teams. Each team is made up of three circle players, or forwards, who stand within the three circles of their side of the playing area, three guards who stand outside the opponents' circles, and one player who is designated as the center and who stands behind the center line within the center circle facing his forwards. The captain of each team is the forward player who is stationed in the circle that is farthest away from the center line. The players who serve as jumping centers face each other as the teacher holds the ball between them.

Directions
The referee tosses the ball into the air between the two jumping centers. They attempt to bat the ball to one of their own guards, who in turn attempts to throw the ball across the center line to one of his team forwards. If a forward player secures the ball, he attempts to throw it to his forward captain. All of the circle forwards are guarded by the opponents'

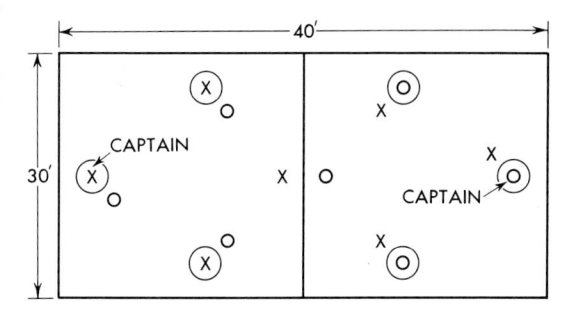

Figure 23–24. Captain Ball. O = Team I
X = Team II

guards. The guards may intercept the ball at any time and then throw it to one of their forward players. A point is scored each time the captain receives a throw from one of the forward players. No points are scored if the guards or the jumping center throw the ball directly to the captain. The game is played in two halves of 10 minutes each. At the beginning of the second half the guards and forwards exchange positions so that all players have an opportunity to receive experience in playing the various positions. After the toss up, the running centers cross the line and assist the guards of their own teams. The guards may not step on or inside the circle lines, and the forwards may not step on or outside the circle lines; if this foul is committed, the ball is given to the opposite jumping center who takes it to the center line and resumes play by throwing the ball to a guard on his own team. The team with the highest number of points at the end of the playing time is declared to be the winner of the game.

TALLY BASKETBALL

Equipment
Basketball goal, basketball, or volleyball.

Formation
If the game is played out of doors, a playing area about the size of a standard basketball court is marked on the play field. If the gymnasium is used, the basketball court lines serve as boundary lines. A center circle is marked in the center of the play area. The game is played by two teams composed of six to ten players per team. One half of the team are forwards and the other half are guards. The players are arranged in couples on the court. The forwards of one team remain in one court, and the guards of the same team are stationed in the opposite court; each of the guards has one forward to guard. The same procedure applies to the opposite team.

Directions
The referee awards the ball to a forward who stands in the center circle of the playing area. This forward passes the ball to a teammate. This pass may not be intercepted. After the first pass from the center, the forwards, as they receive each pass, call out "One," "Two," and so on, for each completed pass until five consecutive passes are made. The guards may intercept the ball at any time during these passes and pass it to their own team forwards, the guards' passes are not counted. When a forward receives the first pass from another forward, he starts counting in a manner similar to that of the opposing team. When a team has made five consecutive passes, one point is scored. The player who is credited with the fifth consecutive pass walks to the basket and attempts to make a basket. The player may select his own place on the floor from which to shoot. If he scores, one additional point is given. Whether he makes the basket or not, the ball is dead, and the referee gives the ball to the center forward of the team which did not score. The game is played in four quarters of five minutes each. Teams receive the ball alternately from the referee for a center throw each quarter. The team that has gained the greatest number of points at the end of the playing time is the winner. A rest period of two minutes is given between each of the quarters. Fouls occur if the players walk or run with the ball, push or hold a player, or hand the ball to a teammate. A free shot at the basket is granted for a foul which involves personal contact; other fouls are penalized by not counting the passes made. If two opposing players are holding the ball simultaneously, the referee calls a "tie ball," and the ball is thrown up between the two players for a jump ball.

Variations
Change number of passes to 10 before scoring.

RECEIVE AND RUN

Equipment
A junior football or substitute.

Formation
Two teams of six to twenty, each on each half of the rectangular playing field. Goal lines marked at the ends of field. Suggested size of field is 40 feet by 70 feet.

Directions
One team throws a forward pass from the middle of the field. If playing on a small field it may be thrown from the end instead of the middle.

The opposing team receives the ball and attempts to run forward. They may pass the ball in any direction at any time. No tackling or blocking is allowed. The ball is dead when the player carrying the ball is tagged by a member of the opposing team.

The ball is returned to the facing team and passed again from the point at which it was declared dead. After a second pass, the ball goes to the other team.

A point is scored if the ball is carried over the goal line.

FORWARD PASS BASEBALL

Equipment
Junior football.

Formation
Baseball diamond with baselines of approximately 50 feet. There are two teams of eight to twelve players each. One team is "up," the other in the field. The team in the field consists of a catcher and fielders. There are no basemen or pitcher.

Directions
The player who is up throws a forward pass, then runs the bases. The fielders retrieve the ball and pass it to the catcher. When the catcher has the ball and has his foot on home plate, any runner off a base is out. The runner may not take a lead off bases. His foot must be in contact with the base until the next ball is thrown. Note that on all plays the ball is thrown to the catcher.

A thrower is out on a caught fly and all runners must return to their bases.

A ball thrown outside the base lines is a foul. Two fouls constitute an out.

FLAG FOOTBALL

Flag football is a variation of varsity or touch football. Rules should be adapted to suit the needs and safety of the participants (number of players, size of field, length of game, and so on).

Kickoff
The kickoff should be made from the kicking team's equivalent of the 20-yard line of a regulation field. (*Examples:* 75-yard field, kickoff from 30-yard line; 50-yard field, kickoff from the goal line.)

Scoring
Six points for a touchdown.

Scrimmage
There shall be no tackling of ball carrier, passer, or kicker. (Penalty, 15 yards enforced from spot of foul.) The man carrying or in possession of the ball is considered down when the flag has been removed from his back belt area. There shall be no strenuous or violent blocking, such as leaving the feet. (Penalty, 15 yards enforced from spot of foul.) Blocking in line play is permissible.

Downs
There shall be four downs required in a series of downs. Option 1: If a team fails to score after a series of downs the ball shall be turned over to the defensive team. Option 2: If a team completes three out of four passes it may be awarded another series of downs. Option 3: A predetermined distance of ball advancement may be considered necessary before a new series of downs is awarded.

Forward and Lateral Passes
Forward and lateral passes are permissible exactly as in regular football. Forward passes behind the line anywhere are permissible, but only one to a play. A forward pass thrown beyond the line of scrimmage is illegal. (Penalty, loss of 5 yards from spot of foul.) All men on playing field, both offensive and defensive, are eligible to receive passes at all times. Lateral passes recovered by the defense may be advanced farther than point of recovery only when the ball has not touched ground. Offensive players may advance their own fumbled lateral at any time.

Dead Ball
When a player in possession of the ball steps out of bounds the ball is dead. The ball is declared dead when a defensive player succeeds in obtaining the flag from the back belt area of the offensive player carrying the ball. Whenever the whistle blows, the ball is dead.

Flags
Flags can be easily made of heavy cloth and should be worn so all players have the same amount of cloth exposed.

Advantages of Flag Football
Flag football eliminates much of the roughness which often takes place with either one- or two-handed tagging in touch football. It eliminates any indecision as to whether the offensive player was actually tagged, since the defense must actually have the evidence in his hand—the opponent's flag.

Track and Field Events

Events worked on in the previous age group continue to be challenging with the eleven- and twelve-year-old child; see Chapter 22.

Different distances are recommended for dashes: (1) grade six—boys, 60 yards; girls, 50 yards; (2) grades seven and eight—boys, 75 yards; girls, 60 yards.

Classroom Games

CIRCLE PUSH

Equipment

Yardsticks, broomsticks, wands or similar sticks, and blackboard erasers. One stick and one eraser for each team or squad.

Directions

A circle is drawn on the floor in front of each team or squad. Each is the same size. Inside each circle two smaller circles are drawn. Each circle is numbered. A straight line is drawn in front of each team. The eraser is placed on this line. The leader of each team is given a stick which he uses as a pusher. His object is to push the eraser with his stick (while remaining behind the line himself) so it goes to and remains in the circle. He scores according to which circle it remains in. He gives his stick to the next person in line, recovers the eraser, and tosses it back to the starting line. He then takes his place at the blackboard and records his points and the points of each succeeding player of his team. Each succeeding player, as he has his turn, recovers the eraser, tosses it to the next player, and then goes to the rear of the line. The line or team scoring the most points wins the round. As many rounds may be played as time and interest permit. The team which has the highest score at the end of the playing time is the winner.

Variations

Many variations exist using this idea. Bean bags may be used for tossing into these circles without the use of sticks for pushers.

IN THE BOX

Equipment

Three or four rolled-up socks for each group.

Players

Three or four squads.

Directions

A box is placed 6 to 10 feet in front of each squad. Members line up behind a leader. Each person takes a turn and endeavors to toss the socks into the boxes. Every time a player succeeds he scores one point for his squad. After each person tosses his three socks, he retrieves them and throws them to the next player in his line. Number *one* is score keeper. At the end of a specified time the team with the highest score wins.

CLASSROOM GOLF

Equipment

Indoor golf ball. Yardstick, broomstick, wand, or golf club cut out of plywood. Objects to be used as obstacles on the course may be blackboard erasers, pencils, a pencil box with the two ends cut out for a tunnel, pieces of colored paper, lines drawn on the floor, or any available object that would be appropriate and not take up too much room. Set up the course in the back of the classroom or in the recreation room.

Players

Two or more depending on the space available and ability of children to control their own activity.

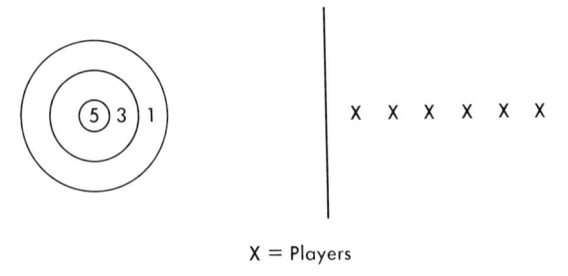

X = Players

Figure 23–25. Circle Push.

Directions

Play as miniature golf.

CROSSING THE BROOK

Equipment

Four or six paper plates for each team.

Players

Four teams. Seven or eight players in a team.

Directions

Lay the brook out as in Figure 23-26. Use paper plates for stones. At the word "Go," the first person on each team steps from rock to rock crossing the stream to the far goal line and returns the same way. This is played as a relay, each person having a turn. The winning team scores 10 points; second team, 7 points; third team, 5 points; last team, 3 points.

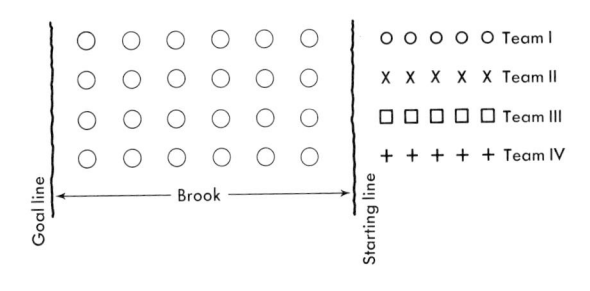

```
             |  O O O O O Team I
O O O O O O  |
             |  X X X X X Team II
O O O O O O  |
             |  □ □ □ □ □ Team III
O O O O O O  |
             |  + + + + + Team IV
O O O O O O  |
Goal line
   ← Brook →   Starting line
```

○ = Paper plates

Figure 23-26. **Crossing the Brook.**

WORD GAME

Equipment

Pencil for the leader of each squad, team, or unit. Piece of paper on the first desk in each row or on a table or desk placed in front of each row of children.

Directions

The group is divided into as many equal squads as the teacher wishes. Each squad lines up behind its leader. Each leader is given a pencil. A piece of paper is placed on the desk in front of him. At the signal "Go," the leader in each group writes a word on the paper. He takes the pencil and runs to the back of his line and passes the pencil down the line to the first person. When the latter receives the pencil he writes another word on the paper, goes to the rear of the line, passes the pencil forward, and so

the game continues until the captain is again in front of the line. The team finishing first with no misspelled words is the winner. No word may be repeated. All must be legible.

Variations

This game may be varied many ways. A specific number of letters may be required for each word; numbers may be used; initials of children; states; rivers; proper names; countries; and the like. Children may walk, hop on one foot, skip, or vary the method of reaching the end of the line.

UPSET THE UNION

Equipment

None.

Directions

Each child selects the name of a state. One child is "It." The only seats used in the game are the ones occupied by the children at the beginning of the game. Extra seats must be marked in some way so they are not used. "It" calls the names of two states. These two must change seats while "It" tries to get one of the seats. If "It" succeeds, the player with no seat becomes "It." More than two states may be called. This is up to the leader or to "It." If "It" wishes all children to move, he calls "Upset the Union." Winners of this game will be those who were never "It." This challenge makes "It" always trying for a seat and thus keeps the game very active.

Variations

Many variations are possible for this game. For example, names of cars, flowers, birds, rivers, and cities may be used.

OVER AND UNDER RELAY

Equipment

One ball or bean bag for each team.

Formation

Even number of children standing in relay formation.

Directions

Teams stand in lines of equal numbers. The first player in each line holds a ball or bean bag. At the signal "Go," he passes it over his head to the second player. The second player passes it between his legs to the third player. The object continues to be passed alternately over and under until it is received by the last player in line. When he has the object he runs to the front of the line and restarts it always *over the head*. When each person has had a turn to be the leader and the original starter is at the head of the line the game is over. The first team to complete this is the winner.

TELEGRAMS

Formation
Even number of children in each row. They may be sitting or standing. Each holds the hand of the person in front and back of him.

Directions
All students must close their eyes except the first one in each line. The teacher writes numbers on the board corresponding to his or her wishes, e.g., 4–7–6. As soon as all *number one* players see it, the teacher erases it. Each number *one* passes the telegram to the corresponding number *two* by squeezing his hand as follows: four squeezes, then a pause, seven squeezes, a pause, and six squeezes; then each number *one* unclasps his hand from number *two*. Thus the telegram is passed from one to the other in this manner. When the last person receives the telegram he runs to the blackboard and writes it on the board. Then he must decipher it. Each number means the letter of the alphabet, i.e., 4 = D, 7 = G, 6 = F. From the coded letters he must write a message, e.g., *Don't go fast*. The first to finish with the correct answer wins the game.

Variations
All variations must be written on the board by the leader.

1. *Long and short codes*, e.g., 6–7. Six is a long, even squeeze. Pause. Seven is a rapid, light squeeze. Answer is read "six long and seven short."
2. *Addition:* Two or more numbers sent as directed. Last person adds them and gives the sum.
3. *Multiplication:* Two numbers sent. Last person multiplies them and gives the product.
4. *Fractions:* Addition or subtraction, whichever is directed.
5. *Division:* Two numbers sent. Last person divides and gives the quotient.

Note
After each game, the last child should move to the front of the line and be the new starter.

BIRD, BEAST, AND FISH

Formation
The entire class is divided into two equal sections.

Directions
One person on each team is selected to be the score keeper. The teacher may be "It" until the class learns the game. "It" points to a student and calls either "Bird," "Beast," or "Fish." "It" immediately starts to count aloud, 1–2–3–4–5–6–7–8–9–10, as rapidly as possible. The student whom "It" selected must give the name of whichever group "It" called for. For "Bird" the response may be "robin." For "Fish" the response may be "bass." For "Beast" the response may be "horse." If the selected player cannot say a name before "It" reaches 10, a point is scored for the opposite side. The game may be set for five points or more depending on interest. No duplication may be used.

Variations
As the class becomes accustomed to the game it may be made more challenging by adding various categories. For social studies ask for rivers, mountains, states, capitals, and so on. For nature ask for trees, flowers, stones, and so on. In a general category often called "the sky is the limit," the leader, or "It," is privileged to call for anything. Examples are makes of cars, modes of travel, holidays, and Presidents' names.

Selected References

See end of Chapter 24.

CHAPTER 24

Movement Experiences for Upper Grades (Ages Thirteen and Fourteen)

Many of the activities used in the earlier years will be continued in these grade levels. The skills learned, and the strength, agility, balance, rhythm, grace, and poise developed all add to the potential of more highly organized activities requiring specific patterns of combined skills.

Dances and Rhythms

Folk and Square Dances. Boys and girls in this age group are mature enough to be able to grasp such intricate dance patterns as The Highland Fling, The Sailor's Hornpipe, and Kreuz-Konig. Many times the teacher is called upon to have students perform for a particular school function. Most of the dances listed in Table 21–1 can be used for exhibition purposes.

Social Dance. It is important to establish the correct attitude toward this type of dancing. Style and performance will vary because of the age group, the current music, and the interest and popularity of the dances. Therefore, it would be best to introduce those basic forms of dance which will appeal to this age group such as the Lindy, slow fox trot, and the "fad dances," as they appear on the scene.

Latin American dances such as the Cha Cha Cha, Samba, and the Merengue appeal to this age level because they afford opportunities for individual creativity.

Before steps in the social dance can be learned it is important for students to understand dance positions, footwork, leading and following.

Closed Position

1. Partners stand facing each other (good body alignment).
2. Feet together, weight over ball of foot.
3. Boy's right hand placed off the center of girl's back slightly toward her left side.
4. Girl's left hand rests lightly on boy's upper arm.
5. The free hand (both boy's and girl's) is halfway between them at girl's shoulder level. The boy's arm should be bent at the elbow.

Open Position. Partners stand side by side. The girl is on the boy's right. Both face in the same direction, that is counterclockwise. The boy's right arm is around the girl's waist. The girl's left hand rests on the boy's upper arm. Boy's left hand and girl's right hand are hanging free.

Leading. When boy wishes to lead a girl in a step towards him, gentle pressure with fingertips of right hand are used; away from him the heel of the right hand is used. If a turn or a side step is planned the shoulders initiate the lead along with the heel of the right hand.

Following. The girl's response to a lead is often determined by her ability to follow the actions of the man's shoulder and hand. The importance of maintaining the right amount of resistance without becoming rigid should be emphasized. In many instances the girl should be able to anticipate each step before the lead.

Footwork

1. Boys feet should be pointing either straight ahead or straight back depending on direction of movement. The girl should be slightly to boy's left.
2. When moving the feet, pass them as close together as possible, maintaining stable balance, especially when changing direction. Emphasize to boys that the steps should not be long strides.
3. Steps should be shortened when a fast number (fox trot) is being danced.

Introductory Steps. The following are introductory steps for this age group. They are the cha cha cha, foxtrot, Lindy (swing), and merengue.

CHA CHA CHA (4/4 TIME)

Closed position: Partners are standing facing each other with boy's right hand on girl's waist, girl's left hand on boy's right shoulder—the free hands are clasped.

Open position: Partners facing, hands dropped, no contact.

Forward Basic (*Use open position*)

		Rhythm	Count
Step L forward— Weight forward	Rocking Motion	Slow	1
Step R backward in place, weight backward		Slow	2
Step L backward	3 short	Quick (cha)	3
Step R backward	running	Quick (cha)	and
Step L backward	steps	Slow (cha)	4

Back Basic (*Same as forward basic*)

		Rhythm	Count
Step R backward		Slow	1
Step L forward in place		Slow	2
Step R forward	3 short	Quick (cha)	3
Step L forward	running	Quick (cha)	and
Step R forward	steps	Slow (cha)	4

Note: Make sure that feet keep in contact with the floor at all times.

Cue: Forward, back and cha cha cha or (run–run–run).

Butterfly

Holding inside hand only, start with boy's left foot (girl's right). Step left foot over right foot in crossover position (weight forward). Step back right in place, weight on right foot while turning to face partner. Step L, R, L in place facing each other. Drop hands and clasp other hand while leading right foot to cross over boy's left foot (weight forward). Step back on left foot (weight backward). Step R, L, R—facing each other and in place.

Repeat butterfly step as many times as boy wishes.

Cue: crossover, back, and cha cha cha.

How to return to basic cha cha cha pattern from butterfly step: After L crossover step and 3 cha cha cha steps in place, boy's R foot is free. Gently draw girl toward him while stepping back on his R foot. Complete the basic step pattern.

Creative Steps (*Use open position*)

The boy may lead with basic forward and back steps into a fancy variation by changing direction, turning, etc. The girl may either follow his pattern or create her own. Encourage both to create their own variations.

FOX TROT (4/4 TIME)

Conversation Step (*Open dance position*)

	Rhythm	Count
Step L forward	Slow	1
Step R forward	Slow	2
Step L forward	Slow	3
Step R forward	Slow	4
(Continue any length of time)		

Westchester Step

	Rhythm	Count
Step L forward	Slow	1–2
Step R past left	Quick	3
Step L to R	Quick	4

Quarter Turns

	Rhythm	Count
Turn one quarter with L foot	Slow	1–2
Step R sideward	Quick	3
Close L to R, take weight on L	Quick	4
Step back R (in place)	Slow	1–2
Step L sideward	Quick	3
Close R to L., take weight on R	Quick	4
(Repeat 3 more times turning L on counts 1)		

Table 24–1. International Dances

Dance	Nation	Formation	Steps Used	Record
Black Nag	England	Longways	Walk-slide-skip	Folkraft 1174
Call to the Piper	Scotland	Double circle	Walk, pas-de-basque	Folkraft 45:1065
Circle from Sarid	Israel	Single circle	Jump	Folk Dancer MH 1053
Galopede	England	Contra	Walk-polka	Folkraft 1331
Gerakina	Greece	Single circle	Walk, step-hop	Folkraft 1060
Gypsy Wine (Pustza)	U.S.	Double circle	Two-step and waltz	RCA 25.0038
Hambo	Sweden	Double circle	Hambo polska	Folk Dancer MH 2002
Highland Fling	Scotland	Individual dance, single line	Leaps, hops, and kicks	Folkraft 45:1036, RCA LPM 1621
Il Codiglion	Italy	Couple, double circle	Walk and pas-de-basque	Folkraft 1172
Italian Quadrille	France	Square	Walk	Harmonia H-2051B
Jefferson's Reel	U.S.	Contra	Walk	Folk Dancer MH 10073B
Kreuz Konig	Germany	Two file sets	Leap, draw, mazurka	Folk Dancer MH 1022
Lady of the Lake	U.S.	Quadrille	Balance, swing, ladies' chain	Folk Dancer MH 1028B
Milanova Kolo	Yugoslavia	Single circle	Kolo step (a hop step), walk	RCA LPM 1620
Oxdans	Sweden	Contra (men)	Step, draw, stomp	Folk Dancer MH 1055B
Rye Waltz	U.S.	Couples in ballroom position	Hopping, touching heel and toe, and waltz	Folkraft 1044
Ten Pretty Girls	U.S.	Couple mixer	Walk, grapevine	MacGregor 605
Virginia Reel	U.S.	Contra	Walk, slide	RCA 45-6180
Tschukessia	Israel	Single circle	Grapevine	RCA EPA 4140
Sailor's Hornpipe	England	Single line (recommended for boys only)	Hop-leap	RCA LPM 1621

402 RECOMMENDED MOVEMENT EXPERIENCES

Twinkle Steps (quick side steps)

| Step L sideward | Quick | 1 |
| Close R to L | Quick | 2 |

(Repeat 3 more times)
Note: The quick steps are very small.

MERENGUE (4/4 TIME)

Basic Side Step (closed position)

	Rhythm	Count
Step L sideward (small step)	Slow	1
Close R to L, take weight on R	Slow	2

Cue: Side, close

Box Step (closed position)

Step L forward	Slow	1
Close R to L, take weight on R	Slow	2
Step L backward	Slow	1
Close R to L, take weight on R	Slow	2

Cue: Forward together, back together

Box Turn (closed position)

Step L, toeing out to L a quarter turn counterclockwise	Slow	1
Close R to L, take weight on R	Slow	2
Step L backward	Slow	1
Close R to L, take weight on R	Slow	2

Cue: Turn, close, back, close
Repeat 3 times to make one full turn counterclockwise.

Merengue Variations

Teachers are encouraged to permit students to use their creative efforts to work out variations as done in cha cha cha.

SINGLE LINDY (4/4 TIME)

Step L sideward	Slow	1–2
Step R sideward	Slow	3–4
Rock Step:		
Step L backward, a little behind R heel	Quick	1
Step R in place	Quick	2

Cue: Side Side Rock Rock

The boy relaxes his right arm to a position at the girl's waist. He uses both right hand and left hand to guide the girl out to open position. Semi-open position for all steps. When stepping back on the rock, roll outward quickly to position side by side, then return to original position. The knees should bend easily on each step.

Single Underarm Break

Boy leads girl under L arm, turning her clockwise into an open position. The turn is started on counts 1 and 2. The rock step (quick-quick) is done at the end of the turn.

Recommended Dances. The list on page 401 includes international dances which have been chosen for their vigorous and challenging step patterns. Dances from many countries have been listed and could be used for folk festivals and/or correlation with other areas of the curriculum.

Developmental Activities

In addition to the developmental activities listed in this chapter, the continuation of rope skipping, in more difficult sequential patterns and for longer periods of time to develop endurance, should be a part of the program. Circuit training should also be used and should be planned to meet the specific objectives of individuals.

Track and field events are also excellent for development and are popular. Those activities suitable for track and field meets are also listed in this chapter.

If apparatus and competent teachers are available, gymnastics are thoroughly enjoyed and add much strength, agility, balance, and fun. Chapter 26 discusses gymnastics.

RUN AND STRIDE JUMP

Stand erect with the feet together and the arms at sides. Run in place, raising knees high so that feet are four inches or higher from the floor. Count one each time the starting foot touches the floor. After fifty runs, do ten stride jumps. Repeat each series two times.

Begin the stride jump with feet together and arms at side. Jump so feet are about eighteen inches apart and the arms are raised sideward to shoulder height. Jump again returning to starting position—feet together and arms at sides. This constitutes one stride jump.

Variation: Continue the activity for two minutes.

Movement Experiences for Upper Grades   403

Figure 24-1. Run and Stride Jump.

Attempt to increase the number of repetitions possible in the two-minute period.

THROUGH THE STICK

Stand erect, holding a light, round stick about three feet long (broom handle is good) parallel to the chest, palms facing body. Squat and place the right foot over the stick and between the hands and the stick. Raise the stick over the head with the left hand, and then down behind you. Return to the upright position by stepping backward over the stick with the left leg.

Note: It may be necessary to roll on the ground to complete the stunt.

CHAIR VAULT

Stand facing the side of a sturdy straight chair. Place one hand on the seat and the other on the back of the chair. Jump through the space between the arms without touching the chair with the feet. Hands may leave the chair when feet are beyond the seat of the chair.

This may be reversed by placing hands on chair behind you and jumping backward.

SEAL SNAP AND CLAP

Starting position: Lie face down on mat with toes curled and touching the mat and hands directly under shoulders on mat, palms down.

Push off from mat with hands and toes and snap yourself up as high off the mat as possible. Clap the hands while body is in the air. Return to starting position breaking fall with hands and curled toes. Strive for more than one clap while in air.

Figure 24-2. Seal Snap and Clap.

V-SIT

Starting position: Lie on back with arms at sides, palms facing mat.

Simultaneously raise trunk and legs (straight) forward and upward. Grasp lower legs and hold position for five seconds. (Note: Legs remain in extended position with knees not flexed.) Return to starting position slowly, taking five or more counts.

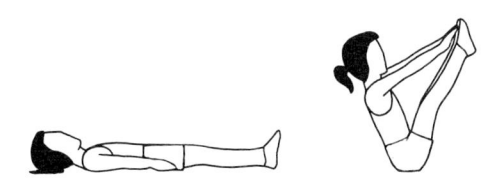

Figure 24-3. V-Sit.

KIP

Starting position: Lie on back with arms at side and legs extended.

From this position raise the legs, bend knees, and rock back until knees are above the head. Hands should now be at side of head, palms down, thumbs close to ears, fingers pointing toward body. Vigorously thrust legs forward and upward and push off with both hands ending in a partially crouched position. Strive for maintenance of balance.

Figure 24-4. Kip.

HUMAN ROCKER

Lie on stomach. Bend the knees and reach back with both hands and grasp the ankles. Raise the head high, arch the back, and rock forward to chest, then backward toward thighs.

Figure 24–5. Human Rocker.

FOREARM BALANCE

Kneel on the mat. Place the hands and forearms parallel and flat on the mat, shoulder width apart. Lean body forward and bring legs up by an overhead kick. Stiffen legs, arch back, point toes and hold the balance. Come out by lowering feet to floor or pushing harder with arms, duck head under and roll over.

HITCH KICK

Stand erect, arms forward. Kick the left leg forward and upward with straight knee, as high as possible. Before left foot touches the floor, kick right leg forward and upward. This makes a scissors kick with both feet in the air at once. The left foot will hit the mat first, then the right.

Track and Field Events

Table 24–2. Recommendations for a Track and Field Meet for Upper Elementary School Boys and Girls.[a]

Boys' Events	Girls' Events
50-yd. dash	50-yd. dash
75- or 100-yd. dash	75- or 100-yd. dash
standing broad jump[b]	standing broad jump
running broad jump[b]	running broad jump
running hop, step, and jump[b]	running hop, step, and jump
240-yd. relay	240-yd. relay
high jump[b]	high jump
220-yd. run	150-yd. run
softball throw for distance[b]	softball throw for distance
basketball throw for distance[b]	basketball throw for distance
sling ball throw	sling ball throw
low hurdles (50 yds.)	low hurdles (50 yds.)
tug-o-war	tug-o-war

[a] The order of the events is suggested as a format for scheduling.
[b] Descriptions in Chapter 23.

WALK, JOG, RUN

Mark off a small track using chairs, rubber markers, etc. In response to a verbal signal to start, class begins to walk around the track. On a sequence of whistle signals the class responds as follows: 1st signal—jog; 2nd signal—run at top speed; 3rd signal—jog; 4th signal—walk. Continue this sequence. During first performance allow a longer time between the walk and jog phases. After class has been practicing the activity for a number of periods, increase the time at full speed. The object is to reduce the time necessary to make one or more complete circuits of the track.

OVERTAKE

Object: To develop a fast start. Arrange the class into line formations of 4 runners each, 6 feet apart. Each runner in a line is a member of a different

MULTIPLE JUMPS

Arrange the class along starting line(s) from 10 to 20 feet long. Participants' toes should touch the line. Draw a finish line 30 feet in front of the starting line. On a starting signal, each attempts to cover the distance between start and finish line with as few broad jumps as possible. The object is to reduce the number of jumps necessary to cover the distance in repeated trials. The second and each additional jump starts from where heels touched. Use partners to mark landing positions.

BATON RACE

Mark three 10-yard zones an equal distance apart on a 240-yard segment of a track or improvised track. Place one member from each team in each 10-yard zone. Each must stand in the same area of the zone. On signal, the first runner from each team, with baton, runs to the next position and passes baton to his teammate within the 10-yard zone. The teammate in turn runs to the next position and repeats the action until the baton is in the possession of the fourth member of the team, who carries it across the finish line.

Note: Baton is a 12 inch by 1 inch dowel made from broom handle. It is passed with the left hand and received with the right hand.

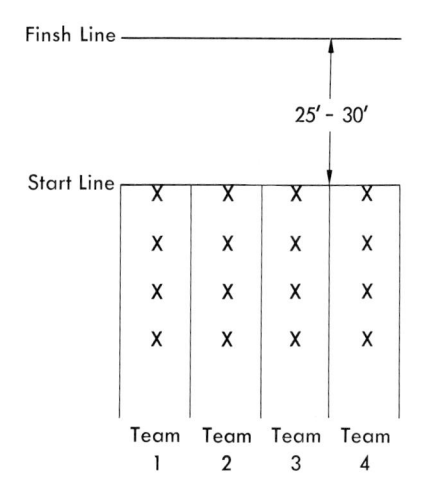

Figure 24–6. Overtake.

team. On the signal, each runner makes a fast start and attempts to overtake the runner in front of him before he reaches the finish line which is 25 to 30 feet in front of the starting line. If he can do this a point is scored for his team. Repeat, rotating the order of starting positions until each player has started in each position.

Note: The starting signal should be "Take your marks; get set; go." Practice both standing and kneeling starts.

Lead-Up Activities

Team games and individual and dual activities require specific skills. These can be taught and offer much fun and challenge by the use of lead-up activities.

Teachers can plan many more of these by analyzing the skills needed for the sports that are to be taught in the program. Students, if challenged, create many excellent activities.

Since the team sports suggested for use in this age group include basketball, volleyball, soccer, touch football, softball, and fieldball, lead-up activities which include the skills needed in these sports are presented in this chapter.

TWENTY PLUS ONE

Equipment
Basketball and goals.

Players
Six to eight on a team. Teams unlimited—each must have one basketball and one basket.

Directions
Each player takes a long shot and a follow-up shot. A long shot scores 2 points; the follow-up scores 1 point. The long shot is taken from a line 15 feet from the basket and the follow-up from the spot where the ball is recovered following the long shot. If this is too close to the basket, one dribble may be taken for better shooting position. In order to be eligible for the short shot the ball must be recovered on the first bounce. More than one bounce forfeits the second shot. Each team participates at its own basket. Individual scores are totaled toward a team score and the first team to reach 21 points wins the game.

In repeating the game, specify various shots to be used.

NINE COURT BASKETBALL

Equipment
Basketball and goals.

Area
Gymnasium or playground 40 feet by 60 feet.

Directions
Each team has a player in each division of the court. One goal is designated for each team. Players in the three divisions closest to their goal are forwards. Players in the three divisions farthest from their goal are guards. Players in the remaining divisions are centers. The game starts with a jump ball between opponents in division 9 (see Figure 24–7). The ball is put in play in the same manner following each goal. All players attempt to pass the ball among their teammates, thus advancing it to their forwards who attempt to score a basket. Opponents attempt to intercept and guard the ball in an effort to keep the other team from scoring. Only forwards are permitted to shoot. After each goal, players rotate to the next higher numbered court. A goal scores 2 points for a team. Basketball rules apply except that dribbling is not permitted.

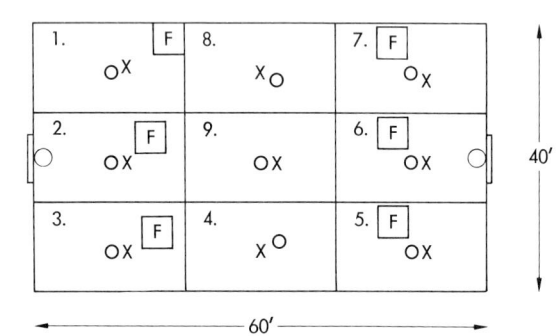

```
1.    F    8.         7.  F
   OX        XO          OX
2.    F    9.         6.  F
 OX        OX            OX      40'
3.    F    4.         5.  F
   OX         XO         OX
         ────── 60' ──────
```

O—Designates one team
X—Designates other team
F—Designates Forwards

Figure 24–7. Nine Court Basketball.

TRIANGLES

Equipment
Hockey sticks and balls, soccer balls, volleyballs.

Area
Playing field.

Players
Unlimited. Three in each group.

Directions
Groups of three players each are positioned 15' to 20' apart to form a triangle. On a starting signal each group will attempt to hit the ball in a clockwise direction as often as possible. At the end of a given period of play (e.g., one minute) the groups are awarded points as follows: 5 for the greatest number of hits; 3—second high; 3—third high. The group with the highest score at the end of a given number of rounds is the winner.

In successive periods, hits should be made alternately clockwise and counterclockwise.

Variation
One of the three in each group becomes a defense player in each triangle and attempts to intercept the ball. He scores a point for his team for each interception.

This may also be used to practice kicking and stopping a soccer ball and both serving and volleying a volleyball, i.e., serve to partner who catches and serves to next, or volley to partner who volleys to next partner without stopping the ball. Use badminton racket and shuttlecock in the same way to develop skills in serving and hitting.

COURSE WORK

Equipment
Hockey sticks and balls, soccer balls, or basketballs; 3, 5, or 7 obstacles (which may be cone markers, boxes, pinnies, etc.).

Area
Playing field or gymnasium.

Players
Eight to ten on team. Teams unlimited.

Directions
Teams assemble in squad formation behind the starting line. The obstacles are placed in line with each team, 5 yards apart beginning 20 feet from the starting line. On the signal "Go," the first player from each team dribbles toward the obstacles. He goes to the left of the first, to the right of the next, etc.—weaving through to the last, dribbles around it and

weaves his way back to the starting line. The next player then does the same thing. The first team to return to its original position is the winner.

Play several games allowing 5 points for first place, 4 for second, 3 for third, etc. The team with the greatest number of points is the winner.

This may be used with a soccer ball or basketball to develop dribbling and control of the ball.

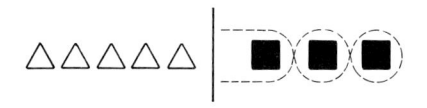

Figure 24–8. Course Work.

DIAMOND SOCCER

Equipment
Soccer ball(s).

Area
Playground or gymnasium.

Players
Unlimited; ten on a team.

Directions
All but two players defend two sides of diamond as diagramed in Figure 24–9. The two active players attempt to kick the ball below shoulder level through the other team line. Each plays in his half of the diamond. The line players serve as guards. They may block, trap, and kick the ball but may not use their hands. The team scored against puts the ball in play. After each score, players are rotated and two new players become "active." A point is scored each time the ball goes through opponents' team line below shoulder level.

Note: Keep kick below waist level for girls. Use more than two active players for faster game.

CRAB SOCCER

Equipment
Soccer or cage ball.

Area
Gymnasium or playground; rectangular—approximately 40 feet by 60 feet.

Players
Fifteen on a team; two teams. Reduce playing field for lesser number on team.

Directions
The object of the game is to move the ball over the opponent's end line by kicking it. Players must maintain the crab-walk position. Each team is lined up on its own end line and the ball is in the middle of the playing area. On the starting signal both teams move toward the ball and attempt to kick it over the opponent's end line. Balls which go out-of-bounds over the sidelines are tossed back in from that spot by the official. One point is scored each time the ball crosses the opponent's end line. The game is more exciting if a cage ball is used.

Variations
Use soccer goals, scoring 5 points for a goal and 1 point for ball over the end line.

Divide team into forwards and guards. The forwards roam the field while the guards protect the line. Rotate positions after a score.

PEPPER CIRCLE

Equipment
Softballs and bats.

Area
Playground or gymnasium, large enough for one or more circles of 30′ radius.

Players
Unlimited.

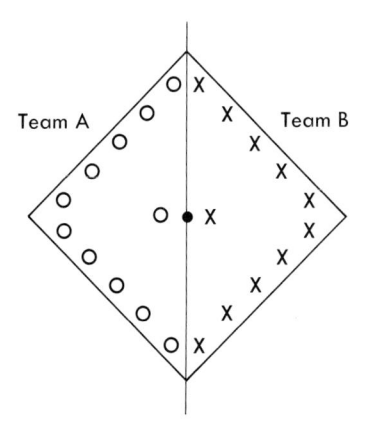

Figure 24–9. Diamond Soccer.

Directions

Organize class into teams of 8 to 10 players each assembled in a circle of 30-foot radius. One member of the team, the batter, is in the center of the circle. Each player in turn pitches the ball to the batter who hits it to the person on the thrower's left. If the ball is missed, it must be replayed. A game is completed when everyone has had a turn at bat. If there are two or more circles, and the children have had ample opportunity for practice, the first team to finish may be declared the winner.

Variations

Use batting and fielding of ground balls, flyballs, and bunts. Change size of circles. Change formation to a straight line.

Note: Plastic equipment may be used. This game may also be played with volleyballs. The player serves the ball to the center player who in turn volleys it back to the next one in the circle.

PACE-A-BALL

Equipment
Softball(s) and bat(s).

Area
Playground, gymnasium.

Players
Unlimited, 6 to 8 on team.

Directions

The object of the game is for the batter to run as many bases as possible after hitting the ball into fair territory. This must be done before the catcher gains possession of the ball and calls "Stop." The batter hits his own toss. The fielders throw the ball to the catcher. There are no outs. An inning consists of a turn at bat for each member of the team at bat. A fly ball caught is played as any ball fielded and a foul ball counts as a turn at bat. One point is scored for each base touched before the catcher receives the ball. Four points are scored when a batter touches all four bases before the catcher stops him.

Variations

Bat the ball from a tee; throw the ball instead of batting it; use a pitcher and bat the ball when pitched.

KEEP IT UP

Equipment
Volleyball(s).

Area
Playground or gymnasium, to accommodate marked circles of 10-foot to 15-foot radius.

Players
Unlimited.

Directions

Divide class into groups of 7 to 9 players per circle. Players should be approximately 3 or 4 feet apart. On a starting signal, a player tosses the ball into the air. Players attempt to keep the ball in the air by striking it with both hands. The ball may not be hit twice in succession by the same player. Each hit scores one point. The team with the highest number of points at the end of a playing period is the winner. The ball is dead when it touches the floor and the count begins again with the number one in any given playing period.

Note: Encourage players to follow ball with eyes and body; to move out of position to play ball and return immediately.

Variations

Circles may compete with themselves to score higher than in a previous game; the team keeping the ball up for the longest period of time is the winner; striking the ball with one or both hands may be permitted.

V-BALL

Equipment
Volleyball; net and standards.

Area
Playground or gymnasium, rectangular court 30 feet by 60 feet with net across center of court, top 6'8" from floor. (Size may be reduced for less skilled players.)

Players
Two, three, or four on a team.

Directions

V-Ball is played like its parent game, volleyball. A team may consist of 2, 3, or 4 players. This encourages more active play and develops skills faster. Game, point, or time can be adjusted if advisable.

Movement Experiences for Upper Grades 409

PUSH AWAY

Equipment
Rolled mats (tied), cage ball, or other large bulky object.

Area
Playground or gymnasium, playing surface 40 feet by 60 feet, marked with side and end lines.

Players
Eight to ten on team.

Directions
Players attempt to advance the mat or cage ball or other object from the center of the playing area over the opponent's goal line in a specified length of time. Both teams are on their respective goal lines at the start of the game. On signal each team rushes to the mat and attempts to advance it to the opposite goal. There are no rules other than prohibition of unnecessary roughness. For this players are disqualified for one minute and team plays short. The team succeeding in getting the mat over the goal line is the winner.

N-ZONE

Equipment
Footballs.

Area
Gymnasium or playground; playing area 40 feet by 60 feet.

Players
Six to eight on a team.

Directions
The object of the game is to pass the ball into the opponents' end zone. Players are permitted in the zone only to retrieve dead balls. A ball is dead when it touched the ground in the end zone or outside the playing field. Players are restricted to their half of the field. The game is played with two footballs. One point is scored for each ball passed into the end zone.

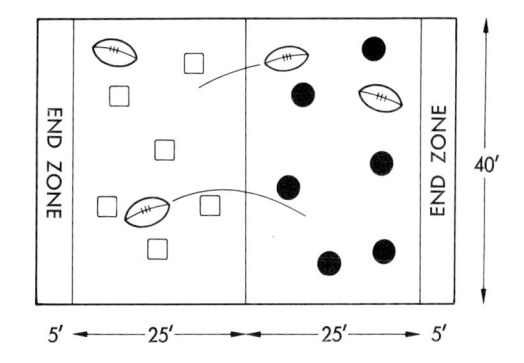

Figure 24-10. N-Zone.

Individual and Dual Sports

Interest in individual and dual sports increases as children grow older. In fact most leisure activities of youth and adults are those of an individual and dual nature. Most of these sports can be learned progressively through participation in lead-up or modified activities designed to develop the skills and understanding necessary to engage in the parent sport. These activities are sometimes referred to as recreational games and are excellent in providing for social experiences and relationships.

As in team sports, the skills and modified activities should be taught in the physical education class and extra time for the activity or sport should be provided in the extracurricular program. Archery, bowling, paddle tennis, and tennis are examples.

Though the activities listed below are introduced at an earlier level, they continue to be of interest to 13- and 14-year-olds. In fact they carry over into later life. The rules and description of these activities can be found in Chapter 23.

Deck Tennis
Quoits and/or Horseshoe Pitching
Floor or Beach Tennis
Handball
Paddle Badminton
Table Tennis

Additional activities which interest this age group follow.

BOUNCE BALL

Equipment
Regulation volleyball or 6-, 8-, or 10-inch playground ball.

Area

Turf, wood, cement, tile, or blacktop with a regular deck tennis court of 40 feet by 18 feet and a 3-foot net dividing court into two equal parts.

Players

Game may be played with 1 or 2 players on a side.

Rules

1. The ball is put into play by the server who stands anywhere behind the rear line and bounces the ball with one or both hands so that it rebounds from the playing court on his side across the net into the opponent's court. Two attempts at service are permitted.
2. Feinting is not permitted.
3. The server continues to serve until five points are scored as in table tennis (i.e., First serve would change when the total of his and his opponents' score ends in 5 or 0). Term of service alternates between teams and individuals.
4. The ball can be played only once by one player while on his side.
5. The ball shall be returned by batting it with either one or both hands against the playing surface on the player's side of the net so that it bounces over the net into the opponent's court.
6. Balls which touch the net are in play except on service. Should the ball touch the net and go into opponent's court on service, it is served again.
7. Balls which touch boundary lines are in play.
8. The ball may be contacted for return after or before the first bounce. It must be contacted before the second bounce.
9. The ball may not be caught or held.
10. A player may not touch the net with any part of his body.

Scoring

A point is scored by the opponent each time the receiving team fails to return the ball properly in bounds. Game consists of 21 points.

Note: Players can agree to play for a lesser number of points.

FLOOR PADDLE TENNIS

Equipment

One table-tennis ball and one table-tennis paddle for each player.

Area

Wood, cement, tile, or blacktop surface with a court 10 feet by 5 feet divided into two equal parts of 5 feet by 5 feet by a 2-inch line.

Players

Two or four.

Rules

Rules are the same as for Bounce Ball with the following exceptions: (1) Ball is put into play from behind end line by server who strikes it with paddle so that it hits in his half of court and rebounds into opponent's half. (2) Returns must be played after the first bounce directly to opponent's side of net.

Scoring

Same as Bounce Ball.

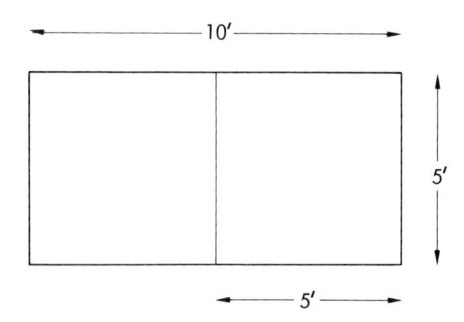

Figure 24-12. Floor Paddle Tennis Court.

DUEL RINGS

Equipment

Four deck-tennis rings or rubber or soft plastic rings 6" in diameter.

Area

Two circles 5 feet to 6 feet in diameter, 15 to 20 feet apart.

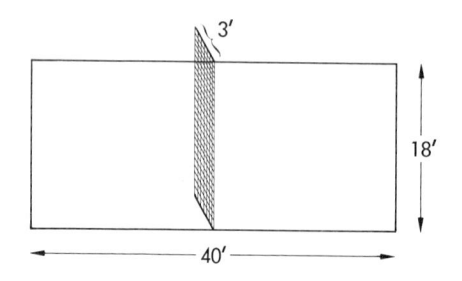

Figure 24-11. Bounce Ball Court.

Movement Experiences for Upper Grades

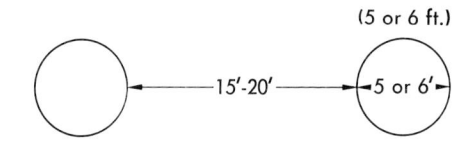

Figure 24-13. Duel Rings.

Players
Two.

Directions
Each player stands in one of the circles. One player holds all four rings and attempts to throw them, one at a time, hoping they will land in the opponent's circle. The opponent attempts to "hook" the rings with his hand or foot. The game consists of an equal number of innings (turns to throw) for each player. The winner is the player with the highest number of points.

Scoring
One point for each ring "hooked" with hand; two points for each ring caught with foot; one point for receiver if ring lands outside of circle providing the receiver did not touch it; one point for tosser for each ring landing in circle. Lines are considered part of the circle.

Variation
Play for total of 11, 15 or 21 points.

SHUFFLE BOARD

Equipment
Eight discs and four cues per set. Four discs are painted one color and four another (usually red and black). The discs are 6 inches in diameter and 1 inch thick. Cue handles are 5' to 6'3" long with a 3" broadened blade curved to fit the disc. Official sets may be purchased at sporting goods stores or sets can be made.

Players
Two or four.

Directions
If two play, they stand at the same end of the court and take turns propelling their discs to the opposite court, endeavoring to dislodge opponent's disc and to keep own in scoring area. If four play, partners are at opposite ends of the courts. Discs are propelled with the cues from within the "10 off" area. Disc which remains entirely within a marked area, not touching a line, scores the points marked in that area. If a disc rests within the "10 off" area, 10 points must be subtracted from the score. The game score may be set at 50, 75, or 100 points. This should be decided before play begins.

Note: Official rules may be obtained from National Shuffleboard Association, Kissinee, Florida.

SIMPLIFIED BADMINTON

Equipment
Net is 5'1" at posts and 5' at center.

Court
20 feet by 44 feet (see Figure 24-15).

Directions
The winner of the toss before the game has a choice of serving first or choosing ends. The server drops the shuttlecock held in nonracket hand so he may hit it with racket in an underhand stroke to start the game and for each serve thereafter. The object is for the players to return the shuttlecock

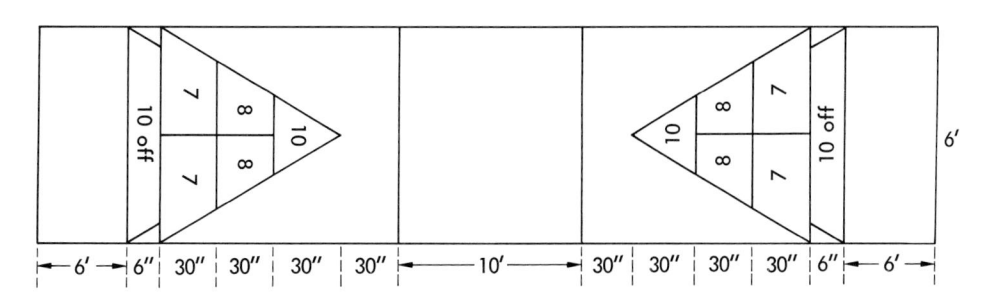

Figure 24-14. Shuffle Board Court.

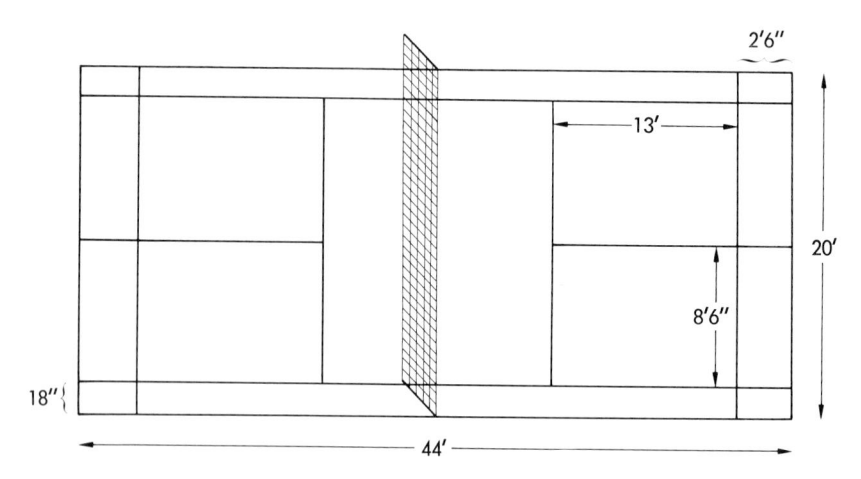

Figure 24-15. Simplified Badminton Court.

back and forth across the net by hitting it with their rackets. It may be hit once only by one player on each side of the net.

Games and Match

Ladies singles—11 points; all doubles and men's singles—15 or 21 points as arranged; match —2 out of 3 games.

Scoring

1. Points may be scored only by the player or the side which is serving.

2. Each player continues to serve, alternating courts, until an error is committed.

3. Singles. On an error by the server, "service over" is called, no points are scored, and the receiver becomes the server.

4. Doubles. When an error is committed by the serving side when the first server is serving, "second service" is called, no point is scored, and the partner of the first server becomes the server. When an error is committed by the serving side when the second server is serving, "service over" is called, no point is scored, and the opposing side becomes the serving side.

5. Setting. If the score is tied, the game may be extended by the player or side first reaching the tied score. In a 15-point game, when the game is tied at 13, it may be set 5 points; when tied at 14, it may be set 3 points. In a 21-point game, substitute 19 and 20 for 13 and 14. In an 11-point game, when the game is tied at 9, it may be set 3 points; when tied at 10, it may be set 2 points.

6. A set game continues as previously, but the score is now called "love-all." The first side or player to reach the set score wins the game.

Doubles Play

1. The side serving first in the game has only one term of service in the first inning. If the serving team commits a fault in the first inning, "service over" is called.

2. Throughout the following innings, each partner on each side has a turn at service.

3. Whenever a side becomes the serving side, the partner in the right service court serves first. The partners rotate courts only after winning a point. A partner who in the first innings served from the right service court, should be in this court when his side is serving whenever the score for his side is zero or even.

Singles Play

1. The first serve of the game is made from the right service court and received in the diagonal right service court, as are all serves when the server's score for his side is zero or an even number.

2. When the server's score is odd, the serve is made from the left service court and received in the diagonal left service court.

Faults

A fault committed by the player or side serving in singles results in "service over," and in doubles results in either "second service" or "service over" depending upon whether one or both partners have served and what the inning of play is. A fault committed by the player or side receiving results in a point for the serving player(s). It is a fault if:

1. During the instant the shuttle is contacted on the serve if the shuttle be above the server's waist or the racket face be above the racket hand.

2. During the serve the shuttle does not fall within the boundaries of the diagonal service court.

3. During the serve the feet of the server and the receiver are not within the boundaries of their respective service courts. Feet on the boundary lines are considered out of bounds.

4. Before or during the serve any player feints or balks his opponent(s).

5. During the serve or rally the shuttle contacts the wall, the ceiling, the player, or his clothing; passes through or under the net; fails to pass the net; or does not fall within the court boundaries.

6. Any player reaches across the net to contact the shuttle, other than on the follow-through.

7. During play any player's person, clothing, or racket touches the net or supports.

8. The shuttle is hit more than once in succession by a player or is hit in succession by partners or caught or slung when struck. Wood shots and simultaneous striking of the base and feathers of the shuttle are legal if no slinging or catching occur.

9. A player obstructs an opponent or invades an opponent's court.

10. In play, a player standing in bounds or out of bounds contacts the shuttle with any part of his person or is struck on any part of his person by the shuttle.

General

1. A serve may not be delivered until the receiver is ready.

2. Some part of both feet of the server and the receiver must remain in contact with the court inside the boundary lines until the shuttle leaves the racket of the server.

3. A serve which touches and passes over the net and falls within the diagonal service court and a shot during a rally which touches and passes over the net and falls within the legal boundary lines are both good.

4. Shuttles falling on the line are in bounds.

5. It is not a fault if server completely misses the shuttle on the serve.

6. "Let" is called when the receiver is not ready for the serve and when, after passing over the net on a serve or a rally, the shuttle is caught in or on the net.

Team Games (Sports)

The description of the games given here is basic and concerned only with the elements necessary for play. Since official rules may change frequently, the reader is referred to the current official Rules Guides for these activities. Those governing girls' play may be obtained from the American Association of Health, Physical Education, and Recreation, 1201 Sixteenth St., N.W. Washington, D.C. The National Federation of State High School Athletic Associations, 7 S. Dearborn St., Chicago, Ill., is responsible for publication of the official rules for boys.

Team Games found in Chapter 23 continue to be interesting to this age group also and should be used in addition to those discussed in this chapter.

BASKETBALL

Equipment

Basketball, 2 blackboards, 2 goals.

Area

Playing court 42 feet by 74 feet (minimum) to 94 feet by 50 feet (maximum).

Players

Boys, 5 on a team; girls, 6 on a team.

Game

Each team attempts to outscore the opponent by throwing the ball into a basket guarded by the opponents. Players move the ball by passing, batting, rolling, or dribbling it in any direction according to certain regulations. Two points are awarded for each field goal scored. One point is awarded for each free throw. The game is divided into four equal parts of 6 minutes each. Rest between quarters is 2 minutes and between halves 10 minutes. Boys play the whole court. However, in the girls' game at least two players from a team must be in each half of the court at all times.

414 RECOMMENDED MOVEMENT EXPERIENCES

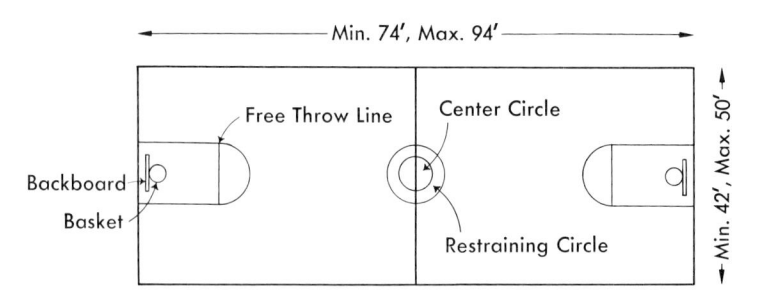

Figure 24–16. Basketball Court.

Basic Rules

Play begins with a tossup between two opposing players in the center restraining circle:

1. At the start of each period of play.
2. After the second of two free throws following a double foul.

Play begins with a toss between two opposing players in the nearest restraining circle:

1. When the ball lodges in basket supports.
2. When the ball goes out of bounds after being touched simultaneously by opponents.
3. When a tie ball occurs.
4. When officials are in doubt as to who last touched ball.
5. When officials disagree as to who last touched the ball.

The ball is put in play by a throw in from out of bounds by a player when an opponent:

1. Commits a violation of the rules.
2. Scores a field goal or free throw.

The ball is dead:

1. After a violation occurs.
2. When there is basket interference.
3. When a basket is made.
4. When a foul is called.
5. When a tie ball occurs.
6. At expiration of playing time.

Violations are minor infractions of the rules for which the opposing team is awarded the ball out of bounds. Some common violations are causing the ball to go out of bounds, traveling (walking or running) with the ball, kicking the ball, stepping over free-throw line or lane line; jump ball infractions, using more than ten seconds for a free throw, stepping into lane on a free throw.

Fouls are serious infringements of the rules, the penalty for which is one or more free throws awarded opponents. These include delaying the game; leaving court without permission; unsportsmanlike conduct; illegal substitution; spectators or coach entering team without permission; pushing, tripping, or blocking progress of opponent with any part of the body; obstructing; charging.

A player is disqualified after five fouls. A single disqualifying foul is one which in the judgment of the officials is a willful foul.

A free throw is an unguarded shot for basket from the free-throw line. Other players line up alternately behind the lane lines when a free throw is taken. If the foul is committed by the opposing team while a player is in the act of shooting and the goal is made, it shall count and one free throw is awarded. Two free throws are awarded if the goal is missed.

In the girls' game, all individual fouls during the last two minutes of play and in overtime periods carry a penalty of two free throws.

In the boys' game, following commitment of the fourth foul by a team during either half of the game the opposing team is awarded a second free throw each time a foul is committed against them provided the player makes the first free throw attempted.

SOFTBALL

Equipment

Bats, ball (12-inch circumference), homeplate, 3 bases.

Area

Radius from home plate: 135 feet. Diamond: homeplate, first, second, and third bases 60 feet apart. Pitcher's rubber 35 feet from homeplate for girls; 46 feet for boys.

Players

Nine on a team.

Game

The object of the game is to score more runs than the opposing team. The game is divided into portions called innings during which each team has a turn at bat and a turn in the field. The game consists of seven innings unless the team second at bat has more runs in six innings than its opponent has in seven innings. A team at bat is retired after three outs. The team at bat attempts to score runs while the team in the field tries to prevent runs being scored. Team members are responsible for playing certain positions. These positions are catcher; pitcher; first, second, and third basemen; shortstop; left, center, and right fielders.

"Playball" is the official signal for play to begin at the start of a game and after a team has been retired. A batter of the one team, standing within the batter's box, attempts to hit an underhand throw (pitch) from the opposing pitcher. The batter immediately becomes a base runner following a fair hit.

A batting order (the sequence in which players will bat) is established before the game begins and must be followed throughout the game. For example, should the team be "retired" after the fifth batter in the first inning, the sixth player in the batting order would "lead off" (be the first batter) in the next inning.

Upon becoming a base runner the player attempts to run around as many bases as possible on the hit. The runner may stop on any base and run on the next fair hit. When he reaches homeplate, a run is scored.

A batter is out:

1. After three strikes if the catcher catches the third strike.
2. On a foul tip legally caught on the third strike.
3. On a fair or foul ball legally caught. A foul fly is a ball rising higher than the batter's head.
4. If he interferes with the catcher intentionally.
5. If he is hit by a legally batted ball while out of the batter's box.
6. If he hits the ball while out of the batter's box.
7. If he bats out of turn (the error must be discovered before the ball has been pitched to the next batter).
8. If he attempts to bunt on the third strike or he bunts foul.

A batter becomes a base runner:

1. When he hits a ball into fair territory and reaches first base safely.
2. When he is hit with a ball by the pitcher. He is then permitted to take first base.
3. If the catcher does not catch the third strike, and he reaches first base which is vacant, before being tagged or thrown out. Note: This rule should be used only when there is a backstop behind home plate.
4. If the catcher interferes with his batting (he is given first base).
5. When the umpire calls four balls against the pitcher.

A base runner is out:

1. If he fails to tag the bases when running.
2. If he attempts to avoid being tagged by running three feet out of the base line.
3. If he leaves the base before the ball leaves the pitcher's hand.
4. If he is tagged by an opponent with the ball while off base.
5. If he fails to remain or return to the base occupied when a fly ball is hit. *Note:* The baseman must tag the runner when he is off base or tag the base occupied by the runner before he returns to it.
6. If he fails to reach first base after a fair hit before an opponent can touch the base with the ball in his possession.
7. If he does not touch the base on a forced run before an opponent touches the runner or the base with the ball in his possession.
8. If he is struck by a fair-hit ball not touched by a fielder.

The ball is dead and determined a foul ball when a pitched ball hits the batter's bat providing he makes no attempt to strike at the ball. All base runners must return to the bases previously occupied if they have advanced on a foul ball. The runner may advance one base on an overthrow or a wild pitch. He may not "lead off" the base but must remain in contact with it until the ball leaves the pitcher's hand.

Definitions

Strike—A pitched ball that goes over home plate between the batter's knee and armpits.

Ball—A pitched ball which does not travel over home plate between the batter's knees and armpits.

Fair ball—A legally batted ball that travels through or within the area between home plate and first base and home plate and third base.

Foul ball—A ball outside of fair territory.

Foul tip—A foul that goes off the batter's bat directly to the catcher's hand and which is not higher than the batter's head. It is called a strike when held by the catcher.

Fly ball—A ball batted into the air higher than batter's head. If caught the batter is out.

Bunt—A legally batted ball not swung at. Instead of swinging the batter shortens his grip on the bat as he meets the ball with a pushing motion, tapping it slowly within the infield.

SPEEDBALL

Equipment

Soccer ball; goal posts 18 feet apart with crossbar 8 feet from ground.

Area

Forty yards by eighty yards.

Players

Eleven players on a team.

Game

Speedball is a combination of basketball and soccer. The object is to kick or pass the ball over the opponent's goal line.

Players are as follows: forward—left and right wing, left and right inner and center forward; backs—left, center, and righ halfback, left and right fullback, and goalkeeper. At kickoff the players are positioned as indicated in Figure 24–17. The goalkeeper has no special privileges as in soccer.

The game consists of four 6- to 8-minute quarters with 2 minutes' rest between quarters and 10 minutes between halves.

A kickoff (place kick) in the direction of opponent's goal by the center forward at the center of the field puts the ball in play at the beginning of each half and after each score. The team scored against kicks following a goal.

A ground ball may be advanced by heading, kicking, or bouncing the ball off the body. It may not be played with the hands. A ground ball must be kicked by the foot to make it an aerial ball. A bouncing ball must be headed or volleyed with the hip or shoulder. An aerial ball may be blocked with the body, caught and passed with the hands, or knocked down to become a ground ball. It may also be kicked or kneed.

An out-of-bounds ball which passes over the side line is put into play by an opponent with a throw-in from the point at which the ball went out of bounds. A one-hand or two-hand pass may be used and the ball is played as an aerial or ground ball. All players must be six yards away. A score cannot be made with a throw-in. A ball going out of bounds over the end line is returned to play by an opponent, from the outside of the field, using a punt, drop kick, place kick or pass. Usually attackers pass and defenders punt. A ball kicked out of bounds by opposing players is put in play by a tossup taken one yard in from the spot at which the ball crossed the line.

A ball held simultaneously by two opponents results in a tossup between them as in basket ball. Opponents must be six yards away on a tossup, free kick, or out-of-bounds play.

To convert a ground ball into an aerial ball:

1. Place the instep of the foot under the ball and lift it into the air to be directed to another player.

2. Kick the ball "up" to one's self. This is done by placing the sole of the foot on the top of the ball and rolling it rapidly toward one's self until it rolls to the top of the instep. It can then be lifted higher by knee action.

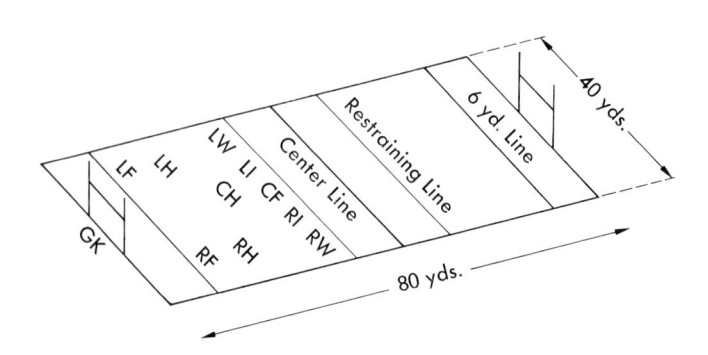

Figure 24–17. Speedball Field.

3. Hold the ball between both ankles, take a quick jump from both feet and release the ball with an upward twist so that it can be caught with the kicker's hands.

4. Permit an approaching ball to roll onto the instep of the foot and with upward action of the knee elevate the ball into the air so that it can be caught with both hands.

All rules infractions are called fouls. They are classified as team, individual, and disqualifying fouls. Individual fouls are kicking, tripping, charging, pushing, blocking an opponent without the ball, holding; unnecessary roughness which includes knocking the ball out of a player's hand, touching a ground ball with the hands, running with the ball, holding the ball more than three seconds on the field, juggling the ball more than once, drop kick within penalty area, boxing up players. Team fouls are illegal substitution, more than 11 players on field, taking more than 3 time-outs in a game. Disqualifying fouls are unsportsmanlike conduct, rough and dangerous play.

Penalties:

1. For foul by an individual outside of his own penalty area: free kick (place kick) awarded to opponent at the point where the foul occurred.

2. For foul by an individual within his own penalty area: a penalty kick is awarded to opponents.

3. For team foul: penalty kick awarded to opponents.

4. For disqualifying foul: player removed from game and a free kick or penalty kick awarded opponents.

The penalty kick is a drop kick taken at the penalty mark (12 yards from the goal line). Only the goal keeper is allowed to guard the goal. All other players must be 6 yards from the kicker and out of the penalty area until the kick is taken. For a penalty kick to score it must pass over the crossbar between the goal posts.

Scoring

1. A drop kick: 3 points. Kick must be made from outside the penalty area and ball must travel between the goal posts above the crossbar.

2. A field goal: 2 points.

3. A touchdown: 2 points.

4. A penalty kick: 1 point. The ball must pass between the goal posts and over the crossbar.

Definitions

Aerial (fly) ball—One that has been raised into the air by a kick.

Dribble—Control and direction of the ball by use of the inside and outside of the foot and instep.

Drop kick—A kick made when a player, with or without preliminary steps, drops the ball and kicks it just as it rebounds from the ground.

Ground ball—One in contact with the ground.

Kick-up—Converting a ground ball into a fly ball.

Juggle—A throw to one's self. The ball is thrown and caught by the same player to gain a better playing position.

Place kick—A kick of a stationary ground ball, with or without preliminary action.

Punt—Player drops the ball to instep and kicks it before it strikes the ground.

Field goal—A ground ball kicked or legally pushed with the body between the goal posts under the crossbar.

Touchdown—A completed forward pass across the opponent's penalty area by a player outside the penalty area to a player of his own team behind the goal line.

SOCCER

Equipment

Soccer ball, two sets of goal posts with crossbars, whistle, four corner flags.

Area

Maximum 80 yards by 60 yards; see Figure 24–18 for details.

Players

Eleven on a team: five forwards, three halfbacks, two fullbacks, one goalkeeper. Teams should consist of boys or girls, not mixed groups.

Game

The game consists of four quarters of 6 to 8 minutes each with 2 minutes' rest between quarters and 10 minutes' rest between halves. Teams are assembled on the playing field as follows. The forwards take position along their side of the center line; the halfbacks stand a short distance behind the forwards; the fullbacks are near to the goal, and the goalkeeper is within the goal area.

The ball is put into play with a place kick from the center of the field by the center forward. The kick is directed toward the opponent's goal. Opponents must be 10 yards away when this kick is made and players from either side may not cross the

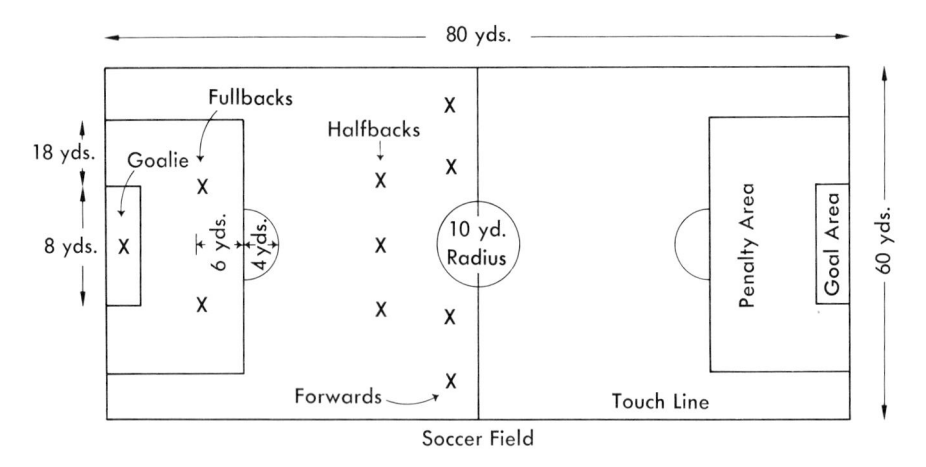

Figure 24–18. Soccer Field.

center line until the kick is made. On the kickoff, the ball must travel forward more than its own circumference. It cannot be played by the kicker again until touched or played by another player.

The object of the game is to make goals by dribbling, heading, or volleying the ball over the opponent's goal line between the goalposts and beneath the crossbar. Opponents attempt to defend their goal. Players, except for the goalkeeper, may not use arms or hands to advance the ball. After a goal is scored the team scored against puts the ball in play with a kickoff. A point is scored for each legal goal.

Definitions

The following definitions will assist in interpreting the rules.

Place kick—A kick of the ball while it is on the ground in the center of the field. This kick is made in the direction of the opponent's goal and is used to "kickoff" or put the ball in play at the beginning of a game and following a goal.

Free kick—A kick awarded for an infraction of a rule. It can be made in any direction and ball is resting on the ground when kick is taken. It is kicked from the spot at which the infraction occurred. A direct free kick is one from which a goal can be scored while an indirect free kick is one which must be played by another player before a goal can be scored.

Hand—Advance or strike the ball with hands or arms.

Holding—Using the hands, arms, or knees in any way against an opponent.

Tackling—Use of legs or feet in attempting to get the ball away from an opponent.

Dribbling—Advancing the ball up or down the field by using the feet.

Heading—Use of the head to propel a ball above shoulder level.

Passing—Kicking the ball to a teammate.

Charging—Use of the body weight in personal contact against an opponent to prevent him from dribbling, passing, or receiving a ball.

Touch—Touch the ground outside the playing field.

Rules

A ball played over the end lines, other than between the goal posts, by the attacking team is awarded to the defending team. A player of that team then kicks the ball into the field from within the half of the goal area nearest the point at which the ball left the field. Players on the attack may not be closer than 30 feet until the ball is kicked. The ball must be kicked forward beyond the penalty area and cannot be played again by the kicker until touched by another player.

If the ball is played over the goal line, not between goals, by the defending team, a corner kick is awarded the attacking team. That is, one member of the attacking team kicks the ball into the field from the corner nearest the point at which the ball went out. A goal may be scored direct from a corner kick and the defending team is not allowed nearer than 10 yards until after the ball is kicked.

A free kick is awarded the opponents when a player is offside. A player is offside if he is ahead of the ball and there are fewer than two opponents between him and the opponents' goal.

When playing a ball from out of bounds, the player must have both feet behind the touch line and must face the playing field. He may kick in any direction. The ball must be touched by another player before a goal can be scored from this kick-in.

A goalkeeper:

1. May, within his own penalty area, handle the ball; carry the ball for two steps in playing it; catch and throw the ball with his hands or arms. Becomes a regular player when outside his area.

2. Becomes a regular player when outside his area.

3. May be changed if notice is given the referee.

4. May not be charged except for holding the ball, obstructing an opponent, or an infraction when out of his goal area.

A free kick is awarded when the following fouls take place outside the defending player's penalty area: striking, tripping, jumping on, kicking, pushing, or holding an opponent who is handling the ball. A goal may be scored from this kick.

A free kick is also awarded the opposing team for being offside, failure to kick the ball forward from a penalty kick, charging the goalkeeper, carrying the ball by the goalkeeper, an improper kick-in from the touch line, and playing the ball before it touches the ground after a kick-in. A goal cannot be scored on a free kick awarded for these fouls.

A penalty kick is awarded the opposing team when a defending team member trips, kicks, pushes, strikes, holds an opponent, or handles the ball in his penalty area.

A penalty kick is taken from a mark 12 yards in front of the goal line, midway between the goal posts. Except for the goalkeeper, players remain outside the penalty area until the ball has been kicked. Goal if made scores a point, otherwise the ball remains in play.

VOLLEYBALL

Equipment
Volleyball; net and net posts.

Area
Court 30 feet by 60 feet with net across center. Net should be from 6 feet to 8 feet high at center, depending on experience and height of players. See Figure 24–19 for details.

Players
Six on a team.

Game
The object of the game is for each team, playing in their respective half of the court, to play the ball legally over the net by volleying it with their hands so that it cannot be returned.

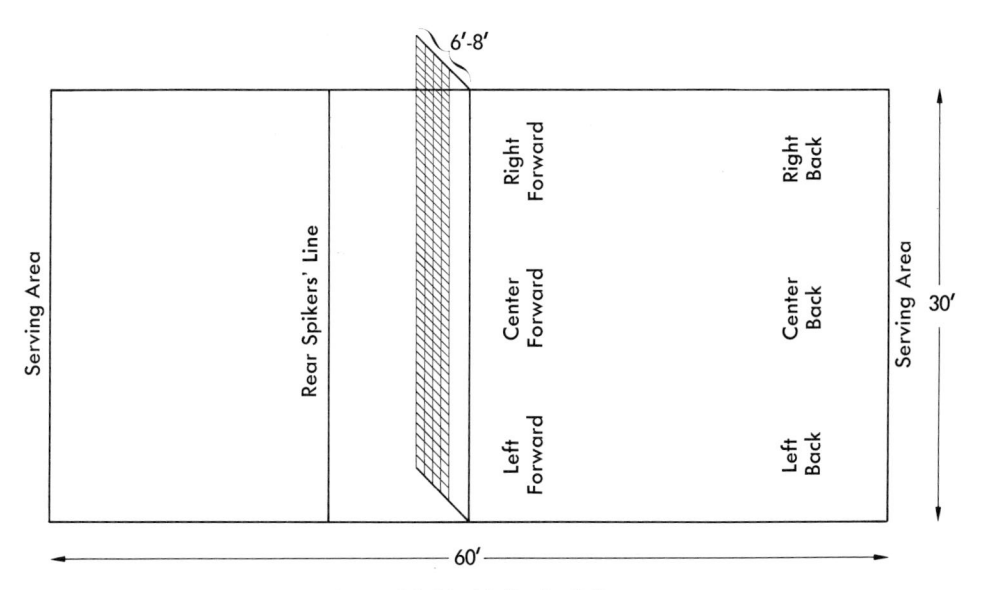

Figure 24–19. Volleyball Court.

The game is started with a service by the player in the right back position, standing behind the end line. He attempts to hit the ball over the net with the hand or forearm and has only one attempt to achieve this. The ball is then played back and forth across the net in a series of volleys, attempting to hit the ball over the net so that it cannot be returned. Points are scored by the serving team only. Team members serve in succession. The server continues to serve until his team loses the ball to the other team. Rotation of players for a turn at service occurs when a team wins the service following a side-out. Rotation is clockwise.

"Side out" is called when the serving team fails to win its point. This automatically gives the ball to the other team which becomes the server. The ball is dead after a point is made and when "side out" is called. "Double hit" (illegal play) is called when a player hits the ball two or more times in succession. "Holding" (illegal play) refers to a scoop, lift, or shove. The ball must be batted and cannot be held or caught.

A regulation game consists of 15 points, or if desired the highest score in 8 minutes of play (whichever occurs first). However the game must be won by a margin of two points over the opponent.

The ball may be volleyed in any direction. A volley consists of one hit of the ball by a player. The ball may be volleyed only three times by a team before it is returned over the net. Though a player may not touch the ball twice in succession, he may be the first and third player to hit the ball.

Should any of the following acts be committed by the serving team, "side out" is called; one point is awarded to the serving team by the receiving team.

1. Serving illegally.
2. Failure to return serve.
3. Holding (catching, holding, scooping, lifting, or shoving ball).
4. Double hit.
5. Ball touching person or clothing other than hands and forearms.
6. Player touching net.
7. Player stepping over center line.
8. Ball being hit by more than three players on the same team.
9. Ball being hit more than once in succession by same player.
10. Player reaching over the net.
11. Player reaching under the net and touching ball or player of opposing team.
12. Hitting the ball out of bounds.
13. Illegal substitution—substitution can be made by serving team only.

Classroom Games

Rope jumping, self-testing activities which require no mats, dancing, and quiet games are all good for use in the classroom when the weather does not permit outdoor activity and the "all-purpose" room or other indoor area is not available.

BALLOON BALL

Equipment

Several inflated balloons (use two at a time).

Directions

Divide the class into four groups. Groups 1 and 2 stand on one side of the room and 3 and 4 on the opposite side. Group 3 faces 1 and is part of their team. Group 4 faces 2 and is part of their team. The end person of groups 1 and 2 each receive a balloon. At the signal "Go," they each toss it in the air and tap it to the line facing them. The object is to keep the balloon in the air by hitting it back and forth from line to line and not permit it to leave the designated playing area or hit the floor. Each time it goes into the wrong area or hits the floor, one point is scored. When this occurs the balloon is restarted at once by the person nearest it. The team with the *lowest* score after a 5-minute period is the winner.

Variations

1. Permit only left or right hand to be used, not both.
2. Play sitting in seats.
3. Play over a rope which acts as a net.

BEAN BAG OVERTAKE

Equipment

Two or four bean bags.

Directions

Players are divided into either two or four even

groups, depending on number of students and size of room. One or two circles are made as large as the room will permit. One circle will consist of all number 1 and number 2 players standing alternately around the circle (i.e., 1–2–1–2–1–2–etc.). If two circles are used, arrange numbers 3 and 4 in another circle the same way. Captains should face each other on the opposite sides of the circles. Each captain receives one bean bag. Players must know their teammates *well*. At a "Go" signal, the captains begin the game by passing the bean bags to their right to their next teammates. They are caught and passed around the circle in the same manner. The object is for a team to overtake and pass the bean bag of the other team. Each time this is successfully completed, the overtaking team scores one point.

ADAGES

Equipment

One pencil and one sheet of paper for each player.

Directions

Old adages are used and only a part is read to the players. Players number each adage and complete it on their paper. For example, the leader reads, "A stitch in time," and stops. The players should write on their paper, "saves nine." The one with the largest number correctly completed wins. Or players may be formed into teams, 1 point being given each team for each correct completion by each player. Of six players, four complete one adage correctly; the score is 4. In preparation for this game, students may be given an assignment to bring in as many adages as possible.

Variations

1. Foods (eggs and bacon; hotcakes and syrup).
2. States and capitals (New Jersey—Trenton; New York—Albany).
3. States and rivers (Pennsylvania—Delaware).
4. Countries and capitals.

BOX TOSS

Equipment

An empty carton or wastebasket for each group; a bean bag, whiffle ball, or yarn ball for each group.

Directions

Players are divided into 4 or 6 equal groups, depending on area. A box or basket is set 10 feet in front of a line marked for each No. 1 player to stand on. A whiffle ball, bean bag, or yarn ball is given to No. 1 player in each line. At the signal each No. 1 tosses his ball or bean bag into the box or basket. If it goes in, it scores 1 point. Whether it goes in or not the thrower retrieves it, tosses it to No. 2, and returns to the end of his line. Five minutes is the time allotted. The team with the highest score wins. A captain must be designated for each team and he or she must keep score.

VARIETY TRAVEL

Equipment

None.

Directions

Each player is seated alone. One player is chosen to be "It" and one to be the "Traveler." At the signal "Go," the Traveler starts to move around the room in any manner he desires. "It" must follow in same manner. "It" endeavors to catch up and pass the Traveler, following the same route, before the Traveler sits down in a seat beside another person. If "It" passes the Traveler, "It" wins. If the Traveler sits with another person without being tagged, he wins. Either way a new "It" is chosen. The new Traveler is the one by whom the original Traveler sat. Each new Traveler must originate a different method of moving around the room and "It" must use the same method. If any Traveler repeats a mode of movement, he must immediately give his place to a new Traveler.

Variations

1. If space permits, two Travelers and "Its" should be on the floor at the same time.
2. Rules such as crossing between seats, or the time permitted for each Traveler and "It" to participate before a new couple are selected may vary according to the age and interest of the group.

PING-PONG RELAY

Equipment

One Ping-pong ball and one paddle for each group.

Directions

Divide players into four or more groups of equal number. Arrange them in relay formation. The first person in each row is given a paddle and ball and stands on the starting line. Ten feet (more or less) may be used according to the space available. In front of the starting line, draw a line or place a chair, box, or wastebasket at an equal distance from each team. At the signal "Go," the first player places the ball on the paddle and "juggles" it with the paddle up to the line or around the marker and back to the second person. Each in line has a turn. The first group back wins. If the ball is lost on the floor, the juggler must recover it and start at the place where it dropped.

QUOIT RELAY

Equipment

Three quoits or rings for each group. Deck-tennis rings or 6-inch to 8-inch rope quoits may be used or rings can be made from a coat hanger and small garden hose.

Directions

Groups are lined up in relay formation. One from each group moves to the front about 10 feet and faces his team. He is known as the "peg." Lines or marks must be visible for the starting group and for the ones who must work 10 feet from their groups. The first person in each group is given three quoits. At the "Go" signal, he pitches them one at a time to the player facing him in such a manner that his "peg" may catch them on his arm—over his open hand, fingers closed together pointing upward. In other words, the pitcher endeavors to ring his teammate's hand. Each rings scores one point. Rings on the floor are recovered and the "peg" may move his hand and body to endeavor to help the thrower make a point. However, he may not move his feet. After the first player has pitched his quoits he runs up to be the "peg," the old "peg" runs to the line, gives the quoits to the player on the line, and places himself at the end of the line. Each one has a turn pitching and being the "peg." The game is played for five minutes (longer if desired). Winning team is the one with the highest number of points.

Variation

Use straight chair turned over so legs face players. Ring leg of chair.

SKIP ROPE RELAY

Equipment

One 8-foot jump rope for each group.

Directions

Divide class into equal teams of 6 to 8. Place them in relay formation. The first person on each team is given a rope which he must use to skip forward to a marked line and back. The second person repeats and so on until each has had a turn.

Variation

Designate type of skip to be used (i.e., skip while traveling; two feet, both close together; legs crossed; jump on both feet with one foot crossed over ankle of other).

Selected References

American Association for Health, Physical Education, and Recreation. *Skills Test Manual*. Washington, D.C.: American Association for Health, Physical Education and Recreation, Manual available for each sport, current year.

American Association for Health, Physical Education, and Recreation, Division for Girls' and Women's Sports. *Basketball Guide*. Washington, D.C.: American Association for Health, Physical Education, and Recreation, current year.

———. *Soccer-Speedball Guide*. Washington, D.C.: American Association for Health, Physical Education, and Recreation, current year.

———. *Softball Guide*. Washington, D.C.: American Association for Health, Physical Education, and Recreation, current year.

———. *Volleyball Guide*. Washington, D.C.: American Association for Health, Physical Education, and Recreation, current year.

AMES, JOSELYN. *City Street Games*. New York: Holt, Rinehart and Winston, Inc., 1963.

Athletic Institute. *Track and Field for Elementary School Children and Junior High Girls*. Chicago: Athletic Institute.

BANCROFT, JESSIE. *Games* (Revised Edition). New York: The Macmillan Company, 1952.

BLAKE, O. WILLIAM, and ANNE VOLP. *Lead-Up*

Games to Team Sports. Englewood Cliffs, N.J.: Prentice-Hall, Inc., 1964.

Division for Girls' and Women's Sports. *Track and Field Guide.* Washington, D.C.: American Association for Health, Physical Education, and Recreation, current year.

———. *Tennis and Badminton Guide.* Washington, D.C.: American Association for Health, Physical Education, and Recreation, current year.

EDGREN, HARRY D., and JOSEPH J. GRUBER. *Teacher's Handbook of Indoor and Outdoor Games.* Englewood Cliffs, N.J.: Prentice-Hall, Inc., 1963.

FISHER, HUGO, and D. SHAWBOLD. *Individual and Dual Stunts.* Minneapolis, Minn.: Burgess Publishing Co., 1955.

GILB, STELLA. *Games for the Gymnasium, Playground and Classroom* (Revised Edition). Lexington, Ky.: Hurst Printing Co., 1962.

HARRIS-PITTMAN-WALLER. *Dance A While.* Minneapolis, Minn.: Burgess Publishing Co., 1968.

JACKSON, NELL. *Teaching Track and Field for Girls and Women.* Minneapolis, Minn.: Burgess Publishing Co., 1968.

JAEGER, ELOISE and HARRY LEIGHTON. *Teaching of Tennis for School and Recreational Programs.* Minneapolis, Minn.: Burgess Publishing Co., 1963.

KRAUS, RICHARD. *A Pocket Guide of Folk and Square Dances and Singing Games for the Elementary School.* Englewood Cliffs, N.J.: Prentice-Hall, Inc., 1966.

LATCHAW, MARJORIE, and JEAN PYATT. *A Pocket Guide of Dance Activities.* Englewood Cliffs, N.J.: Prentice-Hall, Inc., 1958.

McCUE, BETTY F. *Physical Education Activities for Women.* New York: The Macmillan Company, 1969.

MILLER, KENNETH, Ed. *Physical Education Activities.* Dubuque, Iowa: Wm. C. Brown, 1966.

MURRAY, RUTH L. *Dance in Elementary Education.* New York: Harper & Row, Publishers, 1963.

NAGEL, CHARLES. *Play Activities for Elementary Grades.* St. Louis: The C. V. Mosby Co., 1964.

ORLICK, EMANUEL, and JEAN MOSLEY. *Teacher's Illustrated Handbook of Stunts.* Englewood Cliffs, N.J.: Prentice-Hall, Inc., 1963.

PORTER, LORENA. "Volleyball for Classroom Teachers." In *Volleyball Guide 1965–1967.* Washington, D.C.: American Association for Health, Physical Education, and Recreation, Division for Girls' and Women's Sports, p. 36.

PRENTUP, FRANK B. *Skipping Rope.* Boulder, Colo.: Pruett Press, Inc., 1963.

SAFFRAN, ROSANNA. *First Book of Creative Rhythms.* New York: Holt, Rinehart and Winston, Inc., 1963.

SCHURR, EVELYN L. "Developing Basketball Skills in Elementary Grades." In *Basketball Guide 1964–65.* Washington, D.C.: American Association for Health, Physical Education, and Recreation, Division for Girls' and Women's Sports, p. 19.

STUART, FRANCES R, and JOHN S. LUDLAM. *Rhythmic Activities, Series I (Gr. K–3).* Minneapolis, Minn.: Burgess Publishing Co., 1963.

———. *Rhythmic Activities, Series II (Gr. 4–6).* Minneapolis, Minn.: Burgess Publishing Co., 1963.

———. *Rhythmic Activities, Series III (Gr. 5–8).* Minneapolis, Minn.: Burgess Publishing Co., 1963.

STUART, FRANCES R., VIRGINIA L. GIBSON, and ARDEN JERVEY. *Rhythmic Activities, Series IV (Grades 1–9).* Minneapolis, Minn.: Burgess Publishing Co., 1963.

VERMES, HAL G. *The Boy's Book of Physical Fitness.* New York: Association Press, 1961.

VERMES, JEAN. *The Girl's Book of Physical Fitness.* New York: Association Press, 1961.

CHAPTER 25

Activities for Special Occasions and Holiday Fun

Programs for assemblies, demonstrations, play days, sports days, dance festivals, field days, and May Day are special occasions which offer excellent opportunities for teachers and students to plan and present interesting educational events. They give parents and the community opportunities to see some of the learning that takes place in the program of physical education. These programs must be well understood by the children. They are educationally sound when children are given a part in planning and administering them.

All programs are more colorful if costumes are worn. These can be made by children as part of their learning experience. One must be mindful that certain activities may be dangerous when children wear special costumes. When such activities are presented children should wear the correct safe apparel. For example, some frilly costumes could be dangerous in stunts, self-testing activities, and gymnastics.

Assembly Programs

Activities taught in the regular physical education class can well be organized into interesting programs for assemblies. Assembly programs may be presented for the school children themselves, for parent-teacher groups, for a special "educational week" when parents attend school, or for a specific parents' day or night.

Children must be included in all planning and a genuine understanding of the objectives must be theirs if programs are to be successful. Special attention must be given to choice of suitable activities based on children's interest, to the space available, to the number of children who may participate on stage at one time, and to planning something for each child's participation. The time element is important. The program should be neither too long nor too short.

Dances and rhythmic activities are always fun for children and well received by audiences. Singing games and folk dances, creative and interpretive rhythms, rhythmic work with ropes, wands, and hoops, square dancing, and the social dances may be presented.

Self-testing activities, stunts and tumbling done by individuals or couples, gymnastics, free exercise, and pyramid building are interesting to spectators. Story plays and dramatics may be part of a program for the kindergarten, and first- or second-grade children.

Space does not usually permit games to be played in assembly programs. If they are desired, teachers and children must choose them with great care for safety. Novelty games and relays without running are usually safe.

Demonstrations

Demonstrations usually include different parts of the physical education program such as dance, gymnastics, games, track and field events, and individual and dual activities. They are prepared and presented to audiences to show the experience children acquire and what they achieve in the physical education program. They show parents and interested community leaders the nature and content of the programs, this in turn should give them a better understanding of values and objectives.

A typical demonstration for a school of eight grades might include:

Rhythms	Grade 1
Games of different types—circle, running and tagging, employing equipment	Grade 2
Self-testing activities and stunts	Grade 3
Developmental activities	Grade 4
Creative movement and dance	Grades 5 & 6, Girls
Team games	Grades 5 & 6, Boys
Individual and dual activities	Grades 7 & 8, Girls
Gymnastics	Grades 7 & 8, Boys

Programs are at their best when they are truly an outgrowth of the program and not planned especially for show. However, children are very eager to practice and they gain valuable skill from it when they have as an incentive the knowledge that their parents and friends are coming to see their program.

Playdays

Playdays make it possible for a number of students from one or more schools to meet and participate in one or more common activities. They may be planned for specific age groupings on different days or combine fifth, sixth, seventh, and eighth grades with separately planned activities for boys and girls on the same day. The availability of space, equipment, and facilities will be the determining factor in the number of children to be invited at one time.

Some playdays are planned for two hours in the afternoon when school has been dismissed, some for a half day, and some for an entire day on a Saturday or a holiday when schools are not in session. Playdays give large numbers of children the social experience of meeting and participating with students from other schools within a given city, a district, or from completely separate districts and towns. School rivalry is not present because children are mixed with others from different schools and do not participate with their own group against another grade or school.

The program for a playday may include only one activity or several, such as swimming, bowling, archery, volleyball, and kickball.

Planning. The hostess school acts as chairman. It is advisable to have a representative from each participating school on the committee to plan for the playday. This committee should include children from the grades or age groups which will participate in the program. After deciding to have a playday and agreeing on the program, much work remains to be completed.

The hostess school needs committees to prepare facilities and mark them well, to plan for equipment (deciding whether each school must bring some), to organize registration, and to prepare for supervisors or officials for each activity. Decisions must be made concerning lunches (whether each child shall bring his own), with soup and milk provided by the hostess school, or luncheon be prepared for all at the hostess school, whether it shall be free or paid for by each school or each child.

Invitations must be issued three or four weeks in advance, accompanied by appropriate entry

Table 25-1. **Example of a Playday Program**

9:00–9:30	Registration and assignment to groups.
9:30–10:00	Welcome, announcements and questions, assignments of groups to areas.
10:00–10:30	Icebreakers (singing, fun relays, mixers, etc.)
10:30–12:30	Activities—may be worked on a rotation basis in time blocks of 30 minutes. Hence, each group would change three times. Permit 8 to 10 minutes for rotation and rest so all may start together and have equal time for participation. (Each group may play 3 different groups in the same game if the playday calls for one activity only. Each may play three different games with three different groups if the playday includes three activities such as kickball, newcomb, and bombardment.)
12:30–1:00	Preparation for lunch.
1:00–1:45	Lunch.
2:00–3:00	Activities chosen by participants based on master planning and facilities (i.e., dancing—gym; sports film—auditorium; individual and dual activities: tetherball, archery, quoits—play field; quiet games: checkers, canasta, Chinese checkers—classroom.)

forms, in order for each school to send back the names of students attending and indicate who will be participating in each activity of the daily program. A date must be set for the return of entry blanks for participants in order for the hostess school to have sufficient time to make name tags, arrange groupings, and assign each participant to a specific group.

At registration each child will receive a sturdy tag to wear for the day, showing his name and his team or group's name and number (Frank Smith—Blue #1. Marjorie Stubbs—Gold #4).

During the group meeting, after registration, each participant must be informed of the location of playing areas. A large diagram is helpful; also each group captain or leader may be given a small copy.

The rotation plan must be understood. Again each captain may be given a copy. Groups may be rotated in many ways. One example for a playday with one activity or sport and with two color groups working together for the day would be to start Red group #1 playing with Blue #1 on area #1. Red #2 playing with Blue #2 on area #2 and match numbers until all are assigned. The first change for the second round could move all odd group numbers to the next consecutive numbered play area (one to two, three to four, etc.). The third round would move all even-numbered groups to prevent a group from playing in the same area more than twice. Note that #1 Red on first move would play #3 if there were only three groups of reds and three of blues. There are many ways to rotate groups participating in a playday, whether one activity or three or four activities are programed for the day.

Mixing players from all schools by placing one or more children from each in a group enhances the social experience. A special theme for the day may be selected and groups named accordingly. For example, for a circus theme groups could be tigers, lions, elephants, etc. For fall playday, groups could be named for leaves such as oak, maple, chestnut, etc. A spring theme suggests using the names of flowers for groups—tulips, daisies, roses, etc. In this plan if ten schools participated and ten groups were desired, one child from each school could be in each group.

The above mixing is often the basis for color groups when only two colors are designated for the day and composite scores for various activities are recorded for each color group. At the end of the activity period, a color winner is announced. However, note that the winners would represent every school present. Ten groups would permit five red and five blue groups of teams. At the end of the activities the total scores for each color are announced. This plan leads to much fun and activity. New friends are made and there is no competitive stress on one school against another.

Sports Days

Sports days differ from playdays in that each team consists of players from one school. Thus the competition is between teams representing different schools (two or more). There may be many teams from the same school, divided according to age and grade levels. These teams may also be grouped according to skill level. This provides competition for many children from each school with those from other schools with whom they are fairly evenly matched.

Sports days are usually limited to sixth-, seventh-, and eighth-grade students. Occasionally fifth grades are included. Team schedules are organized so sixth grades play against each other, seventh with seventh, and eighth with eighth. Boys and girls are on separate teams and activities may be different for each sex. Some individual activities such as badminton, archery, tennis, table tennis, and so on may be coeducational.

Dance Festivals

Dance is always a very interesting part of the physical education program and tends to make a fine public event.

Festivals may be international in nature. Such programs might offer dances from Denmark, Switzerland, Poland, Sweden, England, Norway, and Germany and be planned and produced in correlation with the social studies the various age groups are engaged in. All folk-dance records and materials note the place of origin of the dance. A learning process takes place for children in researching the types of dress used, making costumes, and making programs.

American dance festivals could be planned and presented to show dances popular in various periods of our country. These could include dances from colonial days, post-Civil War days, and the gay nineties as well as modern country dances and new dances of the 1960's and 1970's.

Field Days

Field days permit children to run, play, and compete within a planned program. They offer a chance for some competition which must be well planned and organized according to age and ability grouping.

Younger children, from kindergarten through third or fourth grades, usually participate in the program by demonstrating some of the activities they have learned in the physical education program. These could include special dances, rhythms, games of low organization, and hopscotch and rope jumping.

Grades four through eight might also devote some of the day to demonstration and the balance to competition in whatever events they wish to take part in. Participation in competitive events *must be voluntary.* Competitive events might include:

Dashes:	20-yard, 30-yard, 40-yard, 50-yard, 60-yard—according to age groupings (separate heats for girls and boys in grades four through eight).
Throws:	Softball throw for distance. Basketball throw for distance. Football throw for distance.
Kicks:	Placement kick for distance. Football punt for distance (boys).
Archery:	Shooting from 20 yards or 30 yards.
Jumps:	Standing broad jump (girls). Hop, step and jump (boys and girls). Running broad jump (boys and girls). High jump (boys and girls).

Team events: Relays (various kinds).
Games such as kickball, volleyball, newcomb, punchball, and softball.

Entrance in events must be well understood by children and a limit as to the number of events and activities each one may enter must be established in order for the child not to be overburdened.

Refreshments (free) make a nice ending for this day.

May Day Programs

May Day programs are fun and can be a meaningful climax to the year's program. Usually a theme is selected for a May Day and a king and queen are elected to reign. Costumes applicable to the theme are used, especially in the processional which is lead by the king and queen.

It is traditional to have one or several Maypoles with dancers participating at one time. This dance makes a nice climax, regardless of the theme used.

A program may consist of:
Processional—King and queen with attendants, followed by all the children
Dances portraying theme of the day
Games portraying theme of the day
Contests portraying theme of the day
Maypole Dances
Recessional

The following suggestions are but a few of the many possible themes which may be used for May Days.

1. The circus.
2. Various countries. Dances, games, and activities appropriate to these countries, plus costumes and programs with their colors or flags on them, make this a very interesting and educational experience.
3. Historical event or period. Carry it through with activities suitable for the period and occasion.
4. A favorite story.
5. Changes in our country. Portray through activities popular in and appropriate for different eras.
6. The months of the year. Have each class depict an activity appropriate for the month.

These are only a few ideas. Teachers will think of many more. May Day may be used to interest parents in the various types of activities their children are taught during the physical education program.

Children should help with all of the plans, costumes, invitations, and everything that is to take place during the program. *Every child* should be given a chance to participate in the day's activities.

May Days may be climaxed with various sports and games. Refreshments planned to fit the theme tend to add interest.

Activities for Holiday Fun[1]

Parties and special occasions are often headaches for teachers. Yet, they are a valuable part of the social life of each child and provide valuable learning experiences.

If parties involve refreshments, the preparation and planning of them may have an interesting and valuable correlation with health. Committee work brings in our democratic idea of working together. Finances may be approached as part of the math work. If the party involves invitations, programs, and the like, the language arts are involved.

Teachers should remember that the names of games and activities may be changed to suit special holidays and occasions. As their programs progress, they will think of many games to use. Children are eager to accept the challenge of making up new games, individually or in groups. One idea may often result in several different activities.

---

[1] *Rhythmic Activities* (Series IV), listed under selected references, contains dances especially planned for holidays. *Holiday Funfest* (listed under selected references) contains activities and games especially planned for holidays and special occasions.

Do not be afraid to use ingenuity. Norman G. Shidle has this to say about ideas:

> Ideas have much in common with rubber balls. The way they bounce depends on where they start from; the force with which they are thrown, dropped, tossed or pushed; the character of the surface on which they hit; the "texture" of the ball or idea itself; the ambient temperature in which the bounce takes place. All of these influence the bounce of a ball—and the rebound of an idea.

Halloween Activities

The names of games and characters can be changed to suit the occasion. For example, brownies and fairies can be called witches and goblins.

CAT TAIL

Draw a large cat without a tail. Have each child make a tail. They may be long, short, fluffy, etc. Post the cat on a bulletin board. Blindfold children one at a time and permit them to tack their tails on the cat. Nearest one wins.

WITCH HAT

Draw a picture of a witch, omitting her hat. In art class have the children make hats. Fasten the witch on a bulletin board. Blindfold children one at a time and permit them to thumbtack their hats on the witch. The one nearest her head wins.

PUMPKIN STEM

Draw a pumpkin minus the stem and fasten it on the bulletin board. Blindfold children one at a time and permit them to fasten their pumpkin stems on the pumpkin. The one nearest the correct place wins. Each child may make his own stem in art class.

DRAWING CONTEST

Each child is given paper and a crayon. Within a specified time, they must draw a witch or a goblin. The winners may be those who draw the ugliest or prettiest witch or goblin, whichever has been decided before the start of the game.

FINDING PARTNERS

To group couples, print a familiar saying such as, "A stitch in time saves nine," on a paper witch. Cut the witch into two pieces so that part of the saying appears on each half of the witch. Place each piece in a separate box. The number of pieces must correspond with the number of persons present. Each person draws a piece from a box and then endeavors to locate his partner. This method may be used to pair children for refreshments or games. Use one box for boys and one for girls.

Foods may also be used for pairing groups. Type names of foods that go together on a piece of paper. Cut each one in two pieces and permit children to draw for partner. Bread and butter, hot cakes and syrup, pork and beans, bacon and eggs, soup and crackers are but a few possibilities.

SEED GUESSING

Place pumpkin seeds in a jar. Have the children guess the number in the jar and write it on a piece of paper on which they have also written their names. Prizes may be given to the person who guesses the nearest correct number and a booby prize to the one who was farthest off.

BLINDFOLDED ARTIST

Blindfold certain children. Give them paper and a crayon. Instruct them to draw pictures of ghosts, goblins, black cats, corn shocks, or anything appropriate for Halloween. Much fun will result when the art is exhibited.

OLD MOTHER WITCH

This is a group game with a verse to chant. See Chapter 20.

CAT ON THE FENCE

Organize the children in squads or groups. Draw a line on the floor the length of the room in front of each squad. Each child who can walk the line by measuring his feet (place heel of advancing foot against the toe of the other foot) scores a point for his group.

WITCH RELAY

Ride a broom to a given goal and return. Give the broom to the next person. The group which completes the ride first is the winner.

Thanksgiving Activities

CORN GAME

Give ears of corn to certain children or to each child. In a given time limit, see who can shell off the most kernels. They must count their kernels. The winner is the one with the highest number of kernels. Use the kernels for Bingo-type games. They may also be used for a kernel hunt.

TURKEY

Play this the same as Bingo, except the winner must have six numbers or names in a row, not *five*, and must call "Turkey," not "Bingo." Kernels left from the corn game may be used for this game. Cards may easily be prepared by folding sheets of paper to make the squares. Each person may write his own numbers in each square, or cards may be prepared in advance.

TURKEY PASS

Cut small turkeys out of paper. Divide the group into squads. Give each person a straw. Give the leader of each squad a paper turkey. With the straw in his mouth, he must hold the turkey on the end of his straw by sucking in. At the signal "Go," he transfers it to the next person's straw and so on until the last person in line has the turkey. No one may use his hands in this game. The winning group is the one which succeeds in passing the turkey to each child.

TURKEY GUESS

This game is played like blindman's buff, except "It" asks, "Where is a turkey?" and the person must gobble like a turkey in reply.

STUFF THE TURKEY

Use a box to represent the turkey. This may be done by pasting a large picture of a turkey on the side next to the group. Organize the children into groups. Give each person one ingredient which is used to stuff a turkey. Ingredients may be drawn in the art class or may be cut out of magazines—for example, pictures of bread, salt, pepper, celery, oysters, etc. The children line up an equal distance from the turkey. At a signal, each one runs up and drops his paper in the box to stuff the turkey. Play this in relay formation.

PUMPKIN TOSS

Cut a large hole in the top of a pumpkin and remove the cut section. Clean out center so the pumpkin is hollow. Set it on a desk or table or on the floor. Arm each child with six bottle caps or other small objects. Permit children to stand on a line or around a marked circle and toss their caps into the pumpkin. Highest number in wins.

THANKSGIVING WORDS

Twelve children are placed on each team. Give the first person on each team a piece of paper and a pencil. At the signal "Go," he must write a word starting with the letter *T*. He then passes the paper to the next person who writes a word starting with the letter *H*. This continues down the row until all the letters in "Thanksgiving" have been used. The first line finished with all words correctly spelled wins. The length of words may be specified if desired. For example, they may be only five-letter words. The number of letters for each word would depend on the grade level and the ability of the group.

This same idea may be used for Christmas, Valentine's Day, Easter, and all holidays.

Christmas Activities

HERE WE GO ROUND THE CHRISTMAS TREE

Tune: "Here We Go Round the Mulberry Bush." Use toys and pantomime the appropriate actions, following the same directions as for "Here We Go Round the Mulberry Bush." See Chapter 20.

SANTA'S TOYS

Pantomime the actions of dolls, soldiers, tops, and all toys. These may be presented as mimetics, story plays, or self-testing activities, depending on the age of the children.

SANTA'S PACK

Give each child the name of a toy. One acts as Santa. He calls the names of two or more toys. The people representing the toys called must exchange seats. Santa tries to claim a seat. If he does, the child without a seat is the new Santa. If Santa wishes all children to exchange places, he calls, "Upset Santa's Pack."

REINDEER

One child is Santa. He goes to the front of the room and calls the names of his reindeer. As he calls each name, he beckons a child to come up. When he has called all of his reindeer, each child reindeer places his hands on the shoulders of the one ahead. Santa is in the back. He gives the signal for them to walk by saying "Get Up!" They move around the room. When Santa calls "Merry Christmas" they must run to their seats. The first one to sit down is the new Santa.

CHRISTMAS ORNAMENTS

Make different ornaments out of paper, in art class. On the back of each one place a number. Fasten these ornaments on the wall, on a string, or place all of them in a box. Organize the children in several groups. Each child may choose one ornament at a time. The group adds up the numbers on the back of the ornaments and the group with the highest score wins. A variation of this game may be played by blindfolding different children and letting them try to find ornaments which have been placed around the room. They add their scores when time is called. The highest score determines the winner.

PIN THE WHISKERS ON SANTA

A large picture of Santa is on the wall. Children are blindfolded, one at a time, and given whiskers which they pin on Santa. The person whose whiskers are nearest the correct place on Santa's face wins the game. Transparent tape may be substituted for pins.

PIN THE HORNS ON REINDEER

Directions same as above except use reindeer without horns. Have children pin or tack horns on while blindfolded.

SANTA CLAUS GUESSES

Same as blindman's buff. Santa is "It" and asks, "What do you want for Christmas?" The person answers a present of his choice and Santa tries to guess who is speaking.

INTERPRETIVE DANCES

1. All toys in Santa's pack.
2. Santa's reindeer.
3. Skater's waltz.

Valentine's Day Activities

WALKING ON HEARTS

Divide the group into equal teams. Two hearts drawn on 9-inch by 12-inch construction paper are needed for each group. At the signal "Go," the first person in each group lays one heart on the floor and steps on it, then he lays the next heart down and steps on it. He picks up and lays down the hearts until he reaches a goal. He may not walk on any part of the floor except the hearts. When he reaches the goal, he picks up both hearts, runs back, and gives them to the next player in his group who repeats the action. The first group finished wins all the hearts.

AUTOGRAPH ARTIST

Permit children to make hearts (6 inches by 9 inches with one side uncolored. Give each child a pencil. At the signal, "Go," they begin collecting autographs. At a given signal the one with the most legible signatures wins.

THE MISSING HEART

Fasten fewer hearts upon the walls of the room than there are children participating. Play the game like Going to Jerusalem, except when the music stops, children must put one hand on a heart to be safe. The winner is the one never left without a heart during the playing time. No one is eliminated.

VALENTINE HUNT

Send the group to another place in the building. Hide small hearts all over the room. These may be the small commercial paper hearts which are purchased to stick on envelopes or used in making valentines; they may be tiny hearts cut out of red construction paper; or they may be candy hearts. When the group returns the game is played like Peanut Hunt. The one who finds the most hearts in a specified time wins the game.

If moderately-sized paper hearts are used, this game may be varied by putting a number on the back of each heart and determining the winner by adding. This game aids children with number concepts.

FILL THE CUP

Each child has a little paper cup, a straw, and 25 or 30 little red candy hearts. The hearts are placed on a napkin beside the paper cup. Each person endeavors to fill his cup with the candy hearts, picking them up on the end of his straw by drawing in on the straw which is in his mouth. They may not use their hands. The first one to succeed stands up and is the winner.

Easter Activities

PIN THE TAIL ON THE RABBIT

A large picture of a rabbit is fastened on the wall. Children are blindfolded and given a bunny's tail, which they endeavor to pin on the rabbit. The one who pins it nearest the proper place for the tail is the winner. Transparent tape may be substituted for pins.

EASTER RABBIT

All children form a circle. One child is the Easter rabbit and has a plastic Easter egg. He runs around the outside of the circle and drops the egg in back of a child. He then weaves in and out among the children hopping like a rabbit. The player who picked up the egg follows in the same manner and tries to tag the Easter rabbit before he returns to the runner's place. If successful, he is the new Easter rabbit; if not, the original "It" chooses a new rabbit.

EGGS IN THE BASKET

Use an empty Easter basket or box covered with Easter paper. Three paper eggs are needed for each player. Golf balls or Ping-pong balls may be used. Place the box in the center of the floor and line the children up around it in a circle. They must all be an equal distance from the box. Each one attempts to toss his three eggs into the basket, one at a time. The winner is the first person to do so. Children may recover eggs which missed the basket and throw again after they have returned to their starting place.

EGG WORDS

Each player must give three words, each starting with the letters in *egg*. For example: *Everyone goes gunning*. At the beginning of the game, players need not be required to form a sentence. As the game progresses, especially for more mature groups, there is more fun and challenge if players are required to make a complete sentence. This game may be played orally to see who can make the funniest sentence, or it may be used in a relay with each player required to write a sentence and pass the paper to the next one, and so on, until each person has written a sentence. A variation could be based on the letters in the word *Easter*. Each person may be asked to give only one word. The first a word which starts with *E*, the second a word beginning with *A*, and so on.

A DOZEN EGGS

Divide the players in groups of twelve. Give the first person in each group a large piece of paper and a crayon. The game is started with this rhyme:

> Draw an egg,
> Draw it fast,
> So your team,
> Won't finish last.

The first player of each group draws an egg, colors it, and passes the crayon to the next. Each person must repeat this. The team who completes the dozen eggs first is the winner.

BASKET TOSS

Place an empty Easter basket in a marked circle several feet in diameter. The size will depend on the age of the children. Supply each child with 6 to 10 jelly beans. Standing with toes on the edge of the circle, each one has a turn to toss his jelly beans into the basket. Winner is the one who succeeds in having the most beans stay in the basket.

EGGS IN THE BASKET

Two large Easter baskets are drawn on oaktag or wrapping paper and fastened to the wall. The children line up in two even groups the same distance away from the baskets. The first person in each group has a crayon. At the signal "Go," he runs to his basket, draws an egg, returns, and gives the crayon to the second player, and so on. The team which has the best looking basket of eggs wins.

DUCKS AND CHICKS

This game is played like Crows and Cranes, or Brownies and Fairies. Players are either ducks or chicks. See Chapter 20–21.

BARNYARD SQUABBLE

Hide candy Easter eggs (jelly beans) all over the room. Divide the class into four groups. One group is chickens, one group ducks, one group geese, and one pigeons. All children join the hunt for the eggs, but only the leader of each group may pick them up. When the chicks find an egg, they peep until the leader comes and picks it up. The ducks quack, the geese honk, and the pigeons coo. A time limit is set and the team with most eggs wins.

Birthday Party Games

CUT THE BIRTHDAY CAKE

Arrange the children in a circle with hands joined. The honored guest is "It" and stands in the center. He walks around and cuts the hands of two children. As he does so, he says, "I cut the birthday cake." These two children walk with giant steps, each in the opposite direction, around the circle. The first one back wins and may cut the next piece of cake.

FIND THE CANDLES

Hide small cake candles around the room. Designate one specific colored one as the prize candle. For example, all may be blue except one which is yellow. The yellow one would be the prize candle. Each candle found scores one point for the finder. The prize candle scores ten points. The person with the highest score wins.

NUMBER GUESSING

Divide the class into four groups. Permit each group to select one number. Each group is then given one guess to try for the lucky number. The correct number is the age of the honored guest. If no group guesses it the first time they may have a second try or as many tries as are necessary.

CANDLE PIN

Draw a picture of a large birthday cake on paper and hang it on the wall. Blindfold children and give each a paper candle to try and put on the cake. The one coming nearest to the center of the cake wins.

GIFT GIVERS

Divide the class into four groups. Show them a fancy wrapped package. The object is for a group to guess its contents. Each group agrees on one object. Each group is given a turn to guess in rotation. Select a funny article such as a dill pickle, pretzel, or the like, for the package. If the guessing is far from the object, hints may be given, such as the first letter of the article, or the number of letters in the word.

UNWRAP THE PRESENT

The class stands in a circle. Music is played either on a record or piano. A very securely wrapped package tied with several layers of wrappings and string is passed around the circle from one child to the next. Each time the music stops, the child who has the package may unwrap a bit of it. When the music starts again, it must be passed on. Each time the music stops, it is unwrapped a little bit more. Make the stops very short. The player who completely unwraps the present is permitted to keep it.

Questions and Practical Problems

1. Plan a thirty-minute assembly program for grades one, two, and three from a hypothetical physical education program.

2. Your school is host to five schools in a playday. Plan for this completely, assuming twenty-five children from each school, grades seven and eight, either boys or girls.

3. Select a theme and organize a May Day program for two classes in each grade, one through eight. What benefits would we gain if two were planned, one for kindergarten through third grade and one for fourth grade through eighth? Plan for this type also.

4. Discuss educationally sound philosophy and principles concerning the organization and practice of special programs. Are there valid reasons for having no special programs for parents?

Selected References

Allen, Catherine L. *Fun for Parties and Programs.* Englewood Cliffs, N.J.: Prentice-Hall, Inc., 1957.

Bancroft, Jessie. *Games* (Revised Edition). New York: The Macmillan Company, 1952.

Eisenberg, Helen, and Larry Eisenberg. *The Handbook of Skits and Stunts.* New York: Association Press, 1953.

Gibson, Virginia L., and Arden A. Jervey. *Holiday Funfest.* Minneapolis, Minn.: Burgess Publishing Co., 1964.

Harris, Jane A. *File of Fun.* Minneapolis, Minn.: Burgess Publishing Company, 1962.

Hunt, Sarah, and Ethel Cain. *Games the World Around.* New York: A. S. Barnes and Company, 1950.

Latchaw, Marjorie. *A Pocket Guide of Games and Rhythms.* Englewood Cliffs, N.J.: Prentice-Hall, Inc., 1956.

Mason, Bernard S., and Elmer D. Mitchell. *Social Games for Recreation.* New York: A. S. Barnes and Company, 1937.

Stuart, Frances R., Virginia L. Gibson, and Arden Jervey. *Rhythmic Activities, Series IV.* Minneapolis, Minn.: Burgess Publishing Co., 1963.

Stuart, Frances R., and John S. Ludlam. *Rhythmic Activities* (*Series I and II*). Minneapolis, Minn.: Burgess Publishing Company, 1963.

CHAPTER **26**

Movement Experiences in Stunts, Tumbling, and Gymnastics

This chapter is dedicated to bridging the gap from basic movement experiences to problem-solving approaches and to definite structured movements necessary to accomplish specific outcomes in tumbling and gymnastics.

In describing sequentially organized experiences that elementary children should be taught, it is obvious that movement education is an approach to teaching stunts, tumbling, and gymnastics and not a replacement. Movement education should be the catalytic effector that guides our programs progressively through series of lessons from unit to unit, in an effort to achieve individual success. It explores simple patterns that eventually evolve to complex patterns requiring greater skill.

It seems apparent that a child learns in many ways about himself and the world about him. He learns by seeing, hearing, smelling, feeling, tasting, jumping, stretching, and turning. Also accepted today is the fact that kinesthetic "feedback" produced by body movement plays an important part in the learning process. The capacity an individual has to move his body effectively and efficiently through space is closely related to the more finely developed neurological phenomena associated with memory, perception, and problem solving. The more senses involved in the learning process, the better the understanding and retention appear to be.

Stunts, tumbling, and gymnastics can be an avenue for learning because they provide (1) enjoyment and challenge, (2) excellent means of developing agility, balance, elasticity, flexibility, and strength, (3) opportunities for each individual to achieve relative degrees of success in new skills, (4) opportunities for the development of mental traits such as self-confidence, courage, determination, decisiveness, initiative, and perseverance, (5) learning experiences involving safety factors such as how to fall and land without injury.

Basic principles of physics must be kept in mind when teaching these activities. They are (1) Bodies rotate around three axes which intersect at the center of gravity of the body. (2) The horizontal axis passes through the hips from side to side. (3) The vertical axis passes down the center of the body from head to feet. (4) The sagittal axis passes through the midsection from front to rear. (5) For every action there is an equal and opposite reaction. (6) The longer the lever the greater the angular momentum and the greater will be the force needed to initiate the movement. (7) The point of support should be under the center of gravity. (8) The trajectory of an object in flight cannot be changed.

Movement exploration as an approach to teaching stunts and tumbling requires detailed preparation in order to afford meaningful experiences. Movement in stunts, tumbling, and gymnastics will aid the child in (1) learning about himself, (2) learning about space, (3) learning about his body in space.

Outcomes Desired

Stunts, tumbling, and gymnastics should develop strength, flexibility, self confidence, and courage, and provide safe enjoyment.

Some experiences to develop balance and to help develop strength and good movement may come from the following problems.

1. Can you walk on a line?
2. Can you hop on a line on only one foot?
3. Can you balance yourself on one foot for ten seconds?
4. Can you squat, jump, and land softly?
5. Can you bounce and land with a half turn?
6. Can you jump and land facing the opposite direction from which you started?
7. Can you jump and make a three-quarter to full turn in the air?
8. Can you jump and touch your heels?
9. Can you jump and touch your toes?
10. Can you jump and click your heels? How many times?

More difficult experiences which develop strength, flexibility, coordination, challenge, and fun include the following:

1. Walk through hands.
2. Knee dip.
3. Turk seat.
4. Single leg balance.
5. Fish hawk dive.
6. Snap up to stand from knees.
7. Human ball.
8. V-seat.
9. Jump through from front lean.
10. Body bridge.

Individual and partner stunts and activities help children to develop concepts by:

1. Learning about animals and how they move.
2. Learning about relationships with themselves and others.
3. Learning about people.

Having children move by imitating animals is a very effective technique for helping them to understand body structure and different forms of movement. The following imitations are suggested:

1. Rabbit hop.
2. Duck walk.
3. Dog run.
4. Frog hop.
5. Elephant walk.
6. Measuring worm.
7. Crab walk.
8. Mule kick.
9. Kangaroo walk.
10. Guess what kind of animal.

Partner stunts involve social experiences as well as awareness of how an individual relates spatially with someone else. Activities which help children to develop this awareness include the following:

1. Chinese get-up.
2. Wring the dishrag.
3. Rocking chair.
4. Wheelbarrow.
5. Bear dance.
6. Leap frog.
7. Tandem walk.
8. Seesaw.
9. Partner balances bike ride.
10. Partner balances angel.

Learning about people and developing strength and balance, are both possible through combative activities such as the following:

1. Indian arm wrestle.
2. Rooster fight.
3. Tug-of-war.
4. Leg wrestle.
5. Hand push.
6. Chinese pull.
7. Indian leg wrestle.
8. Back-to-back push.
9. Duck fight.
10. Hand wrestle.

Music interpretations can be used to combine stunts into organized movement patterns utilizing learned skills. A creative atmosphere will come from a properly set stage when the teacher:

1. Is receptive to questions and unusual ideas.
2. Recognizes original and creative behavior patterns.
3. Asks questions that require thought.
4. Builds onto the learned skills.
5. Uses movement to develop ideas and concepts from the child's experiences in the classroom and playground and at home.

Movement Experiences in Stunts, Tumbling, and Gymnastics

Basic Tumbling

Tumbling, including the "basic ten," is the next part of the gymnastics program to follow problem-solving movement, individual and couple stunts, and self-testing activities.

In addition to tumbling, children should be able to use various pieces of apparatus—some of which may be found outside and some inside the building. Balance beams, mini-tramp, horizontal ladders, rings, ropes, parallel bars, and vaulting equipment are those most often available. The presentation of the basic ten in tumbling and the safe and correct use of each piece of apparatus are broken down for ease of teaching. Each breakdown includes the skills, teaching hints, and the safety factors necessary for successful experiences. Teachers will start children where they presently are in terms of ability, and will work with them as individuals in each area. As is true in all movement experiences, children will develop at varying rates because of many factors. The fact that these experiences make possible individual development and progression makes them most acceptable and challenging to children of various age levels.

The Basic Ten in Tumbling, Including Directions, Safety Factors, and Common Errors

FORWARD ROLL

Directions

1. Assume a squat position with the hands placed on the mat just outside of the legs and in front of the body. The knees should be pressed tightly together and touching the chest. The chin is tightly tucked.
2. Lift the hips backward and upward over the head.
3. Stay in a tight tuck during roll and return to a squat position.

Safety Factors

1. The spotter assumes kneeling position beside the student and assures safety by placing one hand on the back of the student's neck and head, thus forcing him to remain in tuck position.
2. The other hand is placed on the back at the thigh and lifts the student's hips.

Common Errors

1. Student not remaining in tight tuck position.
2. Not jumping hips over the head.
3. Attempting roll with legs in straddle position.
4. Not returning to squat after execution of forward roll.

BACKWARD ROLL

Directions

1. Assume squat position with back to mat.
2. Place back of hands on the shoulders with fingers pointing to the rear, thus the palms are facing upward.
3. Remain in tight tuck position throughout backward roll.
4. Fall off balance backward keeping knees in contact with chest.
5. Once on upper portion of back, place the palms on the mat. Keep the elbows pressing inward and the knees against the chest. Chin continues in tuck position.
6. As the palms contact the mat, the student must push against the mat, rotating the hips over the head, and continue into a tight tuck squat position on the feet.

Safety Factors

1. Spotter must lift student's hips upward as student rolls onto hands and upper back so that the pressure is removed from the neck.

Common Errors

1. Incorrect hand placement on mat.
2. Pupil not remaining in tight tuck throughout roll.
3. Student completing roll on knees instead of feet.
4. Spotter not lifting student's hips properly.
5. Elbows allowed to flop outward, thus causing student to roll sideward.

FROG STAND

Directions

1. Assume a squat position with knees straddled and hands placed on mat in front of and between knees. Fingers are spread and pointing forward.
2. Place forehead on mat in front of and between the hands, thus forming a tripod with the hands and forehead.
3. Place the inside of the left knee on the left elbow and the inside of the right knee on the right elbow.
4. Find balance position, point the toes sharply and hold.

Safety Factors

1. Spotter must support student's hips by lifting gently upward.

Common Errors

1. Forearms not perpendicular to floor and student not on forehead.

HEAD STAND

Directions

1. Assume frog-stand position.
2. Stretch legs upward through a tuck position to a full extension.
3. Tighten stomach muscles, hips, and thighs and point toes sharply.

Safety Factors

1. Spotter places one hand on back of student's ankles and the other hand on front of ankles and pulls upward, thus assisting student in gaining full extension and balance.

Common Errors

1. Student balancing on top of head rather than forehead.
2. Hands and head not forming tripod.
3. Arching too hard and remaining tight.

MOMENTARY HANDSTAND

Directions

1. From a standing position, bend at the hips and place the hands on the mat, shoulder width apart with the fingers spread and the second knuckle of each finger slightly raised as though attempting to play a piano.
2. The eye level should fall between the hands and just in front of the fingers.
3. Arms straight, elbows locked, and the shoulders squeezed into the neck. This arm position and shoulder squeeze must continue throughout the skill.
4. Kick one leg up and over the head, jump off the opposite leg and bring legs together in an upward extension of the body.
5. Continue squeezing shoulders into neck, tighten abdominal muscles, hips, and thighs and point the toes sharply.
6. Return to standing position by piking hips.

Safety Factors

1. Spotter should stand to side of performer and grasp ankles as in headstand.

Common Errors

1. Allowing arms to bend and shoulders to sag.
2. Fingers and palms not placed in proper position.
3. Head not slightly in front of hands.
4. Muscles loose.
5. Body arched or piked.

DIVING FORWARD ROLL

Directions

1. Assume a standing position with the arms and hands held at the sides.
2. Bend slightly forward at the hips and knees and reach upward and outward with the hands.
3. As performer loses balance forward he must push off with the feet, reaching a point of momentary midair suspension.
4. As the hands contact the mat, the performer must assume a very tight tuck position with the chin on the chest.
5. The arms flex and allow the rounded back to contact the mat first.

Safety Factors

1. The spotter rests on one knee and extends the opposite leg toward the approaching direction of the performer.
2. As the performer's hands touch the mat the spotter places his far hand on the back of the performer's head and his near hand on the back of the performer's thigh.

Common Errors

1. Not pushing off with feet.
2. Starting with hands extended upward over the head and not at the sides.
3. Tucking the chin into the chest before the hands touch the mat.
4. Grabbing shins after completion of roll.

BACKWARD EXTENSION SNAPDOWN

Directions

1. The first steps are the same as the progression for the backward roll.
2. With the performer on his upper back and the hands placed properly on the mat, the legs should be pulled into a tightly compressed pike position. Legs are fairly straight and the knees are pressed into the nose.
3. From this compressed position the legs and feet should be punched directly upward as the arms are fully extended and the head is driven out of its tucked position and pressed backward very quickly.
4. Upon attaining the handstand position, the performer should pike at the hips to drive the feet down toward the hands as he pushes off the mat. The performer is now in a standing position with the arms stretched upward over the head.
5. Keep the feet and legs together at all times.

Safety Factors

1. Spotter should stand to the side of the performer's path with legs straddled.
2. As the performer rolls to his upper back, the spotter should place the inside of his far forearm on the performer's shins just above the ankles and the near hand should grasp the back of both ankles.
3. As the performer begins to extend upward, the spotter should allow his far hand to grasp the front of the ankles and the spotter assists the performer by lifting upward on the ankles.
4. After the performer has arrived at the handstand position, the spotter should move his far hand to the front portion of the hips, causing the performer to flex. The near hand should push on the backs of the ankles so that the snapdown is initiated.

Common Errors

1. Not enough initial force in the backward roll.
2. Improper hand placement.
3. Poor compression in pike position.
4. Not extending arms at proper time.
5. Failure to drive head backward.
6. Leg thrust not vertical.
7. Bending knees on snapdown.
8. Failure to push off mat with hands during snapdown.

HANDSTAND ROLLOUT

Directions

1. Assume handstand position.
2. Lean forward, keeping eyes on mat in front of hands.
3. As balance is lost, bend arms and pull into tight tuck position, landing on upper back.
4. Continue as in forward roll.

Safety Factors

1. Spotter must assume spotting position as in momentary handstand.
2. As performer loses balance forward, the spotter should lift upward gently on the ankles to remove pressure from back of performer.

Common Errors

1. Performer not off balance forward.
2. Tucking chin too early.
3. Back not rounded.

CARTWHEEL

Directions for the Left Hand

1. Face in the direction of the path that you wish to take. *Do not turn either side in direction of path at this time.* Extend the arms straight upward by the ears. Raise the straight left leg forward and upward to the horizontal or above and push forward with the right foot causing a step outward to be taken onto the left foot. The left leg should be bent at the knee at this point.
2. Place the left hand on the mat well in front of and in line with the left foot. The fingers should be pointing outward so that they are perpendicular to the projected path of the cartwheel. As the left hand is placed on the mat, the straight right leg should be driven directly back and upward over the head. The bent left leg is forcefully extended.
3. The body is now in an upward motion and the right hand is placed on the mat in line with the left hand. The hands are shoulder width apart and the fingers are pointing in the same direction. The head is forced back and the legs are in a hyper-straddle position.

4. As the body starts downward, the performer should come off the left hand and the left hip should be rotated outward.

5. As the right hand leaves the mat, the right foot should make contact with the mat and remain in line with the left and right hand placement.

6. The performer steps onto the left foot with a continued outward rotation of the left hip.

7. The performer should end with his left side to the direction of his path, standing in a straddle position, the arms stretching upward by the ears.

Points to Remember
1. Step onto a bent left leg.
2. Keep the elbows locked and the shoulders squeezed into the neck.
3. Maintain a hard straddle of the legs.
4. Maintain rhythmical patter of hands and feet.
5. Keep feet and hands in line down the center of the mat.

Safety Factors
1. The spotter should take up a position facing the left side of the performer.
2. As the performer begins the hand placement, the spotter should place his near hand on the left hip at the top of the student's pelvic girdle and exert an upward lifting pressure.
3. As the performer comes into a handstand position, the spotter must place his far hand on the right hip of the performer and exert the same upward pressure.

Common Errors
1. Hands and feet not traveling down a center line.
2. Performer not stepping onto a bent left leg and then extending forcefully.

3. Hands too close together or too wide apart and arms bent while passing through handstand.
4. Legs not maintained in a straddle position.
5. Outward rotation of the left hip not employed.
6. Nonrhythmical patter of the hand and foot placement.

ROUNDOFF

Directions
1. The beginning of this skill is the same as the cartwheel up to the placement of the left hand.
2. The left hand should be placed on the mat in front of the right foot with the fingers pointing perpendicular to the path taken by the performer.
3. In placing the right hand on the mat, the performer must reach across the left hand and place it in front of the left foot. The fingers of the right hand should be pointing back in the direction that the performer has come from. This placement of the hands on the mat causes the body automatically to twist into the handstand position in preparation for the snapdown of the feet to the mats.
4. The snapdown is the same as that which was explained in the backward roll extension snapdown.

Safety Factors
1. The spotter must follow the same procedure that was explained for the cartwheel.

Common Errors
1. Placing left hand in front of the left foot instead of the right foot.
2. Performer not reaching across the left hand with the right hand.
3. Not pushing off the mat with the hands while initiating the snapdown.

Apparatus Activities, Including Directions, Safety Factors, and Common Errors

The use of apparatus is very fascinating to children. They must be taught the safe and proper use in order to enjoy it and to develop ability to use it. The following pieces of apparatus are especially interesting to elementary children.

Horizontal Bar

HANDGRIP

Regular
The thumb and fingers should grip the bar so that they are working in opposition to one another with the fingers toward the performer. Fingers are over the bar.

Reverse
Grip the bar with the thumb and fingers in opposition and the fingers turned away from the body. Fingers are under the bar.

Mixed
One hand is in regular grip and the other hand is in reverse grip.

"L" HANG

Directions
1. The child assumes a regular grip with the hands and pulls straight up toward his chest. Hold this suspended position for approximately three seconds. Repeat aim three times.

Safety Factors
1. Spotter can assist child by raising his legs and taking some of the weight thus affording some measure of success.

Common Errors
1. Child swings legs into position. They must be lifted.

CHIN-UPS

Directions
1. Employing a regular grip, the performer flexes the arms and pulls downward on the bar until the chin has arrived above the bar. Repeat this at least three times.

Safety Factors
1. Spotter can assist child by gently lifting him and taking some of the weight.

KICKOVER

Directions
1. Grasp the bar with a regular grip.
2. Stand away from the bar so that the arms are fully extended.
3. Take one step onto your pushing foot. This foot must be placed directly under the bar.
4. Kick the opposite leg under, up, and over the bar at the same time as the arms flex and pull downward.
5. Pull the bar into the hips and bring the legs together above the bar.

Safety Factors
1. The spotter must take up a position that is perpendicular to the bar, facing the path that the performer will take and on the opposite side of the bar from the performer.
2. As the student steps under the bar the spotter places his near hand on the performer's back just above the pelvic girdle and his far hand on the back of the performer's near thigh.
3. Spotter lifts upward with both hands.

Common Errors
1. Attempting aim with arms straight throughout.
2. Not allowing the legs to come together as they reach over the top of the bar.

FRONT SUPPORT

Directions
1. Hands are in a regular grip.
2. The arms are straight and extended downward to the sides of the performer on the bar holding the body in a front resting position.
3. The shoulders should be extended downward and the elbows locked. The chest is pressed outward and the hips are squeezed together tightly.

Safety Factors
1. Spotter stands in front of performer, places his hands on performer's rib cage and lifts upward.

Common Errors
1. Allowing arms to bend, shoulders to sag, and hips to be loose.

BACK HIP CIRCLE

Directions
1. *Beat*—From the front support position, the performer must sag the shoulders by squeezing them into the neck while reaching under and forward of the bar with the legs. This is the power stroke that must precede the next phase of the back hip circle which is known as the *cast*.
2. *Cast*—Force the legs backward and upward until the entire body reaches a horizontally suspended position on the hands with the arms straight.
3. As the body moves back into the bar, the stomach will be leading and will reach the bar first. The legs should be straight.
4. As the stomach touches the bar the performer must flex hard at the waist, driving the legs under, upward, and over the bar until he has returned to a front support position.
5. Squeeze the hips, extend the shoulders downward, push the chest out, and lift the head.

Safety Factors
1. Spotter assumes the same position as for the kickover.
2. As the performer's body starts back into the bar, the spotter places his near hand on the small of

the back and his far hand on the back of the near thigh.

3. Spotter holds performer's hips into the bar and forces legs under and over the bar.

Common Errors

1. Bending arms during the beat or cast.
2. Piking before the stomach touches the bar.

FRONT HIP CIRCLE TUCK

Directions

1. Front support position, upper thighs resting on bar.
2. Arms extended sideward and upward.
3. Eyes focused on an object that is level with them.
4. Arms are fully extended and generate circular motion around bar.
5. Body falls off balance forward with eyes remaining focused on spot.
6. Legs begin to drive up behind performer.
7. As the upper body reaches a vertical position under the bar, the performer must tightly tuck with the hands grasping the shins.
8. Performer will continue up and over the bar, arriving in a resting position on the forearms.
9. Change to a regular hand grip and extend the body to a front support.

Safety Factors

1. Spotter stands behind performer, facing the side of his hip.
2. Reach under bar with near hand and place it on the small of the performer's back.
3. As performer loses balance forward, the spotter holds the hips into the bar.
4. As the student arrives under the bar, the spotter places his far hand on student's upper back for added support.

Common Errors

1. Resting on bar at waist.
2. Arms not extended side-upward.
3. Eyes not remaining focused on spot of same height.
4. Tucking too soon.

SINGLE KNEE SWING UP

Directions

1. From an under hang position, hands in regular grip, place one leg through arms and under bar.

2. Hook knee over bar.
3. Use free leg as lever and kick it back and forth from the hip.
4. Keep arms straight.
5. Continue kicking leg until you arrive in a stride support position on the top of the bar.

Safety Factors

1. From side-stand position to rear of performer, place far hand in small of back and near hand on near wrist.
2. Assist performer in arriving at stride-support position.
3. Near hand may also be placed on front of performer's thigh to assist in kicking motion.

Common Errors

1. Swinging free leg from knee rather than from hip.
2. Bending arms severely.

SINGLE KNEE CIRCLE FORWARD

Directions for Right Knee Forward

1. Change hands to a reverse undergrip.
2. Lift body until hips are well above bar.
3. Extend chest forward.
4. Focus eyesight on spot that is level with eyes throughout first part of aim.
5. Lose balance forward and attempt to build a full circle around bar.
6. Reverse side of knee circle is the same as a single knee swing up.

Safety Factors

1. Spotter assumes a position to the rear of the bar and facing the side of the performer.
2. With near hand, reach under, up, and over bar, grasp wrist of performer, being sure that spotter's thumb is downward.
3. As performer arrives under bar, place your far hand in small of back and exert effort upward.

Common Errors

1. Not maintaining high support position at beginning of aim.
2. Tucking chin into chest too early.

Rings

BALANCE HANG

Directions

1. Grasp the rings with the fingers and thumbs in opposition.

2. Pull to a semi-chin.
3. Pull the legs straight, forward and upward over the head until the body is in a tight pike position.
4. Extend the arms and keep the chin tightly tucked into the chest.
5. Hips are carried just above the horizontal.

Safety Factors
1. Provide double to triple thickness of mats directly under the rings.
2. Spotter faces side of performer.
3. Grasp wrist with near hand and place far hand on back of performer's near thigh.
4. Pull upward on thigh.

Common Errors
1. Hips not gaining above horizontal position.
2. Chin not tucked into chest.
3. Not arriving in a tight pike position.

"L" HANG CONDITIONING EXERCISE
Directions
1. Arms fully extended, body in underhang position.
2. Pull straight legs forward to a horizontally extended position.
3. Hold this position for three seconds.

CHIN-ONE ARM PUSH
Directions
1. From underhang position, pull downward until arriving at a full chin-up position.
2. Keep one arm fully flexed and extend the opposite arm directly sideward.
3. Hold this position for three seconds.
4. Pull both arms to full flex and repeat extension to opposite side.

INVERTED HANG
Directions
1. From underhang position, pull the hips and legs forward and upward to an inverted vertical position.
2. Eyes peer down at mat as in the handstand position.

Safety Factors
1. Spotter stands to front side of the performer.
2. Grasp wrist with near hand.

3. Support rear of hips with far hand and lift upward.

Common Errors
1. Too much arch when in inverted position.
2. Chin tucked.

NEST HANG
Directions
1. From vertical underhang, pull hips and legs forward and upward to a balance hang position.
2. Place right foot through right ring to the instep and left foot through left ring.
3. Force head backward and arch the back.
4. Hold position for three seconds.

Safety Factors
1. Stand to front side of performer.
2. Grasp wrist with near hand and support back with far hand.

Common Errors
1. Not arriving at a fully arched position.

SKIN THE CAT
Directions
1. From balance hang position, press feet and legs downward and backward over the head.
2. Continue downward until body is fully extended.
3. Finish in an arched position.

Safety Factors
1. Near hand on wrist.
2. Far hand on front of hips.

Common Errors
1. Lack of a full extension in arch position.

Ropes

ONE ROPE
Directions
1. Ascend the rope using a hand-over-hand method. Descend employing a hand-under-hand method.
2. Rope should be carried between the thighs from the front of the body, wrapped around the back of the calf of the lower leg, around the outside of the ankle and over the instep of the foot.

3. Step onto the rope with the arch of the opposite foot, thus pinching the rope between the feet.

Progression

1. From reclining position, pull body to standing position.
2. Climb one half of the way to the top and return, employing previously discussed methods for ascending and descending the rope.
3. Climb to top using legs and hands.
4. Climb to top using just hands.
5. Climb to top of rope in sitting position.

Safety Factors

1. Mats placed under ropes.
2. Spotter holding rope taut.

Common Errors

1. Not using suggested hand-under-hand descent.

Minitramp

REBOUNDING

Directions

1. Child must maintain full extension of legs while rebounding.
2. As performer leaves the bed of the tramp, he must point the toes sharply downward.
3. Hands and arms reach forward and upward as feet leave trampoline bed.
4. Hands and arms circle backward and downward as child returns to trampoline.
5. Children must learn to hurdle from one foot to two feet.
6. After rebounding from the mini-tramp, the performer must learn to absorb the shock by bending the knees and executing a forward roll.

Progression

1. *Rebounding* on mini-tramp several times in succession while grasping a spotter's hands.
2. *Hollow-back*—Hurdle onto and rebound from mini-tramp, maintaining upright, slightly arched body position throughout. Extend arms forward and upward.
   Spotter—Stand to front side of trampoline. Place far hand on performer's abdomen and near hand on back.
3. *Squat touch*—Same as hollow-back except when highest point of rebound is reached the performer must pull to momentary tuck. Return to hollow-back position prior to landing.
   Spotter—Same as for hollow-back.
4. *Straddle touch*—Hollow-back. At peak of rebound extend straight legs sideward and forward to touch feet with hands. Return to hollow-back position prior to landing.
   Spotter—Same as for #2 progression.
5. Perform progressions 2, 3, and 4 and initiate a half turn prior to landing.

Safety Factors

1. Provide a double thickness of mats in landing areas.
2. Have children initiate a roll upon landing.
3. Close spotting.

Common Errors

1. Hurdle step improperly initiated.
2. Improper use of hands and arms.
3. Flexing knees greatly while on mini-tramp.
4. Not pointing toes and extending ankles for greater rebound height.
5. Looking down or tucking chin to chest while in rebound descent.
6. Not flexing knees and absorbing shock upon landing.
7. Not rolling after landing.

Balance Beam

Progression

1. Walk forward.
2. Walk backward.
3. Run forward.
4. Walk forward raising rear leg to forward extended horizontal position, clap hands together under extended thigh. Repeat to opposite side and continue.
5. *Step on forward foot and hop* on same foot, repeat to opposite side. Hopping action should be vertical rather than forward.
6. *Sashay*—Leap forward from both feet. Keep one foot in front of the other foot at all times. Land on trailing foot and step to forward foot.
7. *Forward Roll*—Bend at waist, keeping legs straight. Reach forward and place hands so that the thumbs are on the top of the beam and the fingers are on opposite sides of the beam. Place chin on chest, bend arms and place the back of the head on the beam. Roll forward to the back, changing the hands to an undergrip position on the beam. Keep the legs over the head and squeeze the elbows

inward. Continue rolling forward and arrive on the feet in a squat position.

8. Use combinations of the above for simple routine composition.

Teaching Hints

1. Place feet on beam with toes pointed out to the side while walking.
2. Press the shoulders downward.
3. Squeeze hips together.
4. Hold chin flat.
5. Arms to sideward extended position at shoulder height.
6. Hands—Palms down, thumb carried opposite middle finger as if squeezing small ball.
7. Stretch through the waist.

Safety Factors

1. Use a low beam for beginners.
2. Hold performer's hand for balance.
3. Support hips while performer is initiating forward roll.

Common Errors

1. Not landing on the balls of the feet while walking, running, jumping, and leaping.
2. Not pointing toes downward while walking.
3. Not stretching while performing.
4. Performer watches feet rather than the end of the beam.

Parallel Bars

Progression

1. *Hand support*—With bars set at low level, from a cross stand at one end, jump to a support position between the bars and resting on the hands. Arms extended downward and the body held in a vertical support position.

Spotter—Stand outside of parallel bars, facing the performer. Grasp front of forearm with far hand and triceps of upper arm with near hand.

2. *Hand support walk*—From hand support position, walk on the bars from one end to the other.

Spotter—Same as for the hand support.

3. *Dismounting from hand support*—Initiate a quarter turn of the body to either the right or left and change both hands to the same bar as you are facing. Drop between bars to landing on the feet.

4. *Hand support swing*—From hand-support position, swing legs forward and upward toward the head. Keep the arms straight and the shoulders in line with the hands. Swing legs downward, backward, and upward until body arrives at a position that is at the horizontal or above. Continue swinging.

Spotter—Same as in the hand support.

5. *Straddle travel*—From hand-support position, swing legs forward and upward. As legs arrive at a position above the bars, separate them to the sides and allow back of thighs to rest on the bars. From this straddle-seat position, reach forward with the hands and place them on the bars in front of the hips and between the thighs. Swing the legs backward and upward while leaning forward on extended arms and force the legs together and down between the bars. Repeat procedure until you arrive at the end of the bars.

6. *Forward roll*—From the straddle-seat position with hands grasping bars in front of hips and inside of the thighs, lean forward, raise hips backward and upward over the head which is tucked tightly into the chest. Press the legs outward in a hard straddle position throughout execution of the routine. As performer arrives at a back resting position, the hands must be transferred from behind the shoulders to the starting position, grasping bars in front of hips and between thighs. Return to a straddle-seat position.

Spotter—stand outside of bars and facing the side of the performer. As performer arrives on back, place your far hand in the small of his back and your near hand on his upper back. Remember to spot by reaching under the bars and never over the bars.

Vaulting Apparatus (Horse, Buck, Swedish Box)

REUTHER BOARD TAKE-OFF

Directions

1. Performer must approach the board at a sprinting pace, running on the balls of the feet, arms working vigorously forward and backward by the sides.
2. Hurdle onto the board should be at a low angle and initiated off one foot and approximately 36" to 54" away from the near end of the board.
3. Performer lands on the board with both feet together, on the balls of the feet, knees slightly flexed, back vertical, hands pressing downward at the sides, and toes about 12" from the far edge of the board.
4. At this point the arms drive forward and upward until they are touching the ears. The performer should come off the board vertically.

5. Press the heels together, upward, and backward, attempting to drive the body into a horizontal position.

Common Errors
1. Approaching take-off board too slowly.
2. Running on the flats of the feet.
3. Hurdle step too short, too long, or too high.
4. Back not vertical while on the board.
5. Hands and arms not pressing downward as feet land on the board out of the hurdle step.
6. Not lifting arms upward as take-off is initiated.

SQUAT ON—JUMP OFF

Directions
1. From take-off the reach is upward; as the body rotates to the horizontal, the reach of the hands is downward and onto the horse.
2. At this point the hips must be pulled forward and downward and the knees tucked into the chest as the hands rest on the horse.
3. Performer should then stand and spring from the horse to the floor. An attempt at straightening the body prior to landing is important.
4. Performer should land on the balls of the feet and flex the knees to absorb shock and maintain balance. Sink back to the heels.

Safety Factors
1. Proper matting on far side of horse only.
2. Spotting—Assume a standing position on the far side of the horse facing the performer's approach. As the performer places his hands onto horse, grasp the biceps of his near arm with your far hand and his forearm with your near hand. Assist the performer until he is securely standing on the mat.

Common Errors
1. Dropping head and eyesight level while in the squat position.
2. Not fully extending prior to landing.
3. Improperly initiated landing.

SQUAT VAULT

Directions
1. This vault is the same as the "squat on" except that the performer does not rest on or touch the horse with the feet at any time.

2. As the performer's hands touch the horse, he must immediately push backward with the hands and arms and extend the chest.
3. The arms should not bend throughout this entire action.

Safety Factors
1. Same *spot* as in the squat on, jump off.

Common Errors
1. Allowing hands to remain on horse too long.
2. Landing in a forward pike position.

STOOP VAULT

Directions
1. Same as for the squat vault except the knees should not bend at all throughout completion of vault.
2. Raise hips backward and upward as the feet are drawn between the arms.

Safety Factors
1. Same as for previous vaults.

Common Errors
1. Bending legs at any time during vault.
2. Other points are the same as in the squat.

STRADDLE VAULT

Directions
1. After upward lift of the body from the take-off board, the hips and legs are pressed tightly together and upward to the rear. Once the horizontal position is attained the legs are forced to separate very quickly to the sides as the hands push vigorously from the horse.
2. The legs will pass to the outsides of the arms as the body passes over the horse.
3. Legs are brought together once again prior to landing.

Safety Factors
1. Spotter—Stand directly in front of the performer's path but on the far side of the horse.
2. As performer places his hands on the horse the spotter must grasp both of performer's biceps with both of his hands and lift vigorously upward.
3. Remain in contact with performer until proper landing is assured.

Common Errors
1. Lifting hips too high while straddling.
2. Straddling legs to the sides too early.

QUARTER TURNS AND HALF TURNS

All of the previous vaults should be learned with quarter and half turns prior to landing.

Horizontal Ladder

LONG HANG

Progression
1. Hands in regular grip on same bar. Thumbs in opposition to fingers, hands shoulder width apart, and body extended downward with feet suspended. Body facing length of ladder.

REVERSE LONG HANG

1. Hands in reverse grip on same bar.
2. Same as long hang.
3. Back toward direction of length of ladder.

SIDEWARD HANG

1. Regular grip on one bar and a reverse grip on next bar.
2. Body facing side outward.

LONG HANG ON TWO BARS

1. Body facing length of ladder and in long hang position.
2. Both hands are in regular grip but on opposite bars.

LONG HANG TRAVEL

1. Assume long-hang-on-two-bar position.
2. Reach forward with rear hand to next empty bar and grasp with regular grip.
3. Continue with rear hand until end of ladder is reached.

REVERSE LONG HANG TRAVEL

1. Same as in long hang travel except a reverse grip is employed.

SKIN THE CAT

1. Regular grip on same bar.
2. Same procedure as for rings.

INVERTED HANG

1. Regular grip on same bar.
2. Same procedure as for rings.

NEST HANG

1. Regular grip on same bar.
2. Same procedure as for rings except that the instep of each foot is hooked on bar.

MIXED GRIP TRAVEL

1. Assume sideward-hang position.
2. Reach toward length of ladder to next rung with rear hand and grasp rung with reverse grip. Allow body to rotate half turn as new rear hand reaches to next rung with regular grip, allowing body to rotate half turn. Continue to end of ladder.

Selected References

BALEY, JAMES. *Gymnastics in the Schools*. Boston: Allyn and Bacon, Inc., 1965.

JOHNSON, BARRY L. *A Beginner's Book of Gymnastics*. New York: Appleton-Century-Crofts, 1966.

KEENEY, CHARLES J. *Fundamental Tumbling Skills Illustrated*. New York: The Ronald Press Company, 1966.

MOSSCROP, ALFREDA, et al. *Apparatus Activities for Girls*. Minneapolis, Minn.: Burgess Publishing Co., 1961.

MOSSTON, MUSKA. *Developmental Movement*. Columbus, Ohio: Charles E. Merrill Books Inc., 1965.

MUSKER, FRANK F., DONALD R. CASADY, and LESLIE R. IRWIN. *A Guide to Gymnastics*. New York: The Macmillan Company, 1968.

ORLICK, EMANUEL, and JEAN MOSLEY. *Teachers' Illustrated Handbook of Stunts*. Englewood Cliffs, N.J.: Prentice-Hall, Inc., 1963.

O'QUINN, GARLAND, JR. *Gymnastics for Elementary School Children*. Dubuque, Iowa: William C. Brown, 1967.

PROVAZNIK, MARIE, and NORMA B. ZABKA. *Gymnastic Activities with Hand Apparatus for Boys and Girls*. Minneapolis, Minn.: Burgess Publishing Co., 1965.

CHAPTER 27

Movement Experiences in Swimming and Water Safety

Needs

It is essential for children to be taught water safety and swimming. Each year well over 100 million persons engage actively in some kind of aquatic recreation. Opportunities and needs for water sports are greater today than ever. State and national governments are developing park areas near rivers, lakes, and seacoasts. Local communities are building more pools than ever before. More YMCA's, YWCA's and YMHA's are being built and are including swimming pools in their facilities. Public schools are adding permanent pools as a teaching facility at both the secondary and the elementary levels. Portable pools are being used on elementary school playgrounds in many parts of the country. Some of them may be taken down and set up on another playground in four hours, making it possible for one facility to serve children in many areas. Home owners are annually buying more pools than had ever been predicted. These include both the permanent and the temporary seasonal type.

Recreational activities requiring water-safety programs are increasing. Boating, skin diving, water skiing, surfing, and the winter sports of skating, ice boating, kite skating, and cross-country skiing are becoming more popular annually. Camping is also increasing as a family recreation and, since many camps are by water, children and adults have opportunities to swim and engage in water sports.

Deaths from drowning total 7,000 annually, according to the American Red Cross. Over 60 per cent of these drownings are of persons who are in the water because of accident. Most of these deaths could be prevented if people were taught to swim and to practice water-safety techniques.

Hence, since today's recreational trend places many persons in areas where water and water sports are available, swimming and water safety should be a vital part of educational programs.

Values

While 7,000 lives may be saved annually through the ability to swim and knowledge of water safety, this is not the only value that justifies including such instruction as an important part of the elementary school program. If one is catapulted from a speedboat in the middle of a lake or river, regardless of excellence in swimming ability, one could probably not make the shore simply because of distance. Hence, survival techniques are equally as important as being able to swim.

Swimming has been recognized as an activity which is one of the best in inducing all-round physical development. It uses most of the muscles in the body and also aids in the development of an efficient cardiovascular system. It contributes to general physical fitness. It also leads to controlled relaxation better than most forms of activity.

As one of the few activities which can be coeducational for all age levels, if proper dressing facilities are available, this sport has natural social advantages. Studies conducted in schools where swimming is a part of the program, find it is rated by the children as one of the most popular activities. Interest and desire surely act as incentives for learning and perhaps account for the prevalence of success in this activity at early age levels.

Swimming and water sports have great carry-over value. They are enjoyed by millions as recreational activities. They are sports which can be included for the entire family at home, during weekends, and on vacations.

Handicapped persons, including the amputee, the spastic, the blind, and the paralytic, are able to gain much enjoyment and physical exercise in the water. Because the buoyancy of the water makes it possible for them to move in the water in ways impossible on land, they are especially benefited. This participation also makes them feel a part of either a family or a peer group.

Qualifications of Instructors

As should be the case in all teaching, but which is mandatory in swimming, only well-qualified persons should attempt to teach swimming and water safety. While swimming can be a relatively dangerous activity, statistics indicate it has been a very safe part of the programs in which it is included. This is undoubtedly because of well-qualified teachers.

The generally acceptable qualification is an instructor's rating or its equivalent as prescribed by the American Red Cross. This title not only gives the assurance of capability in swimming, but also in survival and teaching techniques.

If facilities are available in the school or community and qualified instructors are not available within the school faculty, assistance may readily be gained from qualified persons in the community. The American Red Cross will gladly assist schools in locating qualified teachers.

The successful teacher must have a thorough knowledge of swimming, and be able to demonstrate swimming skills and techniques. She must teach about water conditions and safety as well as swimming skills.

In addition, according to the American Red Cross, a teacher must (1) Be familiar with the logical progressions to fit any level of students and teach from the known to the unknown; (2) Possess confidence, enthusiasm, and patience; (3) Be able to see what is being done and analyze it immediately in order to assist the student; (4) Be able to demonstrate.

The teacher must build positive attitudes in students in order for them to enjoy and be successful in this sport.

Recommended Starting Age Level

The swimming program in the primary grades consists of teaching the bare fundamentals. Results of experiments at all age levels tend to support the fact that the teaching of swimming is most efficient when it is a part of the six-year-old child's program. Fear is less prevalent in this age group and its absence helps the learning process. While studies prove that this age is most receptive to teaching, starting at an earlier age is not ruled out. Here again, individual differences of children must be considered.

The six-year-old child does not have sufficient

motor coordination for us to expect highly skilled results, but he can learn the fundamentals and at least one stroke. Children eight and nine years old show much improvement in skill and motor coordination. The ten- and eleven-year-old group usually has developed sufficiently to acquire good coordination, poise, and timing. This advanced motor coordination development makes it possible for them to become quite proficient in various strokes.

Class Organization

The organization of students for swimming classes is most important. Good organization makes it possible to accomplish more successful work. It saves valuable time and it will help maintain attention because all students are placed in positions where each can *see*, *hear*, and *move*. This is important always but even more so when working with younger children in the elementary school who have a short interest span.

Minimum principles to be observed in class organization are:
1. Organize for the safety of students.
2. Organize to save time.
3. Organize so all can *see* and *hear* the instruction.
4. Organize so all can see the demonstrations.
5. Organize so each child will have the opportunity for maximum movement, practice, and fun without interfering with another.
6. Organize so you, the teacher, can check readily for skill assistance needed.
7. Organize so students will not be facing the sun.

Patterns. Specific organizational patterns need to be planned for land discussion and practice, static formation in the water when students are practicing nonlocomotor movements, such as bobbing and breathing, and fluid formation for the actual movement in the water of techniques and strokes.

Patterns must be selected to make the best use of the space available, both in and out of the water. Selection will depend on such factors as a large or small group, plenty of deck space or a little area, long narrow area or a short wide area, large pool, small pool, same water depth or shallow and deep areas. The semicircle, V formation, L formation, parallel lines, circle, circle within a circle, and multiple lines where the first line sits, the second kneels, and the third stands are all beneficial patterns for good teaching results. Some are applicable for both land and water instruction and some for land only, such as the multiple lines.

Recommended Skills, Teaching Techniques, and Hints

Classification of Students. The following skills are suggested for an elementary school program. The letter to the right of the skill (second column, "Class Level") suggests the stage of advancement at which the skill should be taught, the students being classified as follows.
A. *Nonswimmer*—Lacks basic skills, may or may not be afraid of water.
B. *Beginner*—Has conquered fear of water and has acquired basic water-safety skill. Able to swim a few feet.
C. *Intermediate swimmer*—Possesses a variety of safety skills and can swim on both front and back.

Teaching Aids. Teaching aids which will assist students include the hand support by the teacher or "buddy," kickboards, water wings, cannister-type floats, and life preservers.

Artificial supports can be used effectively in teaching beginners. They help the body to maintain proper position in the water and aid in the development of the skill. They also aid in giving the student a kinesthetic feel for the movement he is striving for.

Flotation devices such as water wings and cannisters should not be used by those who *fear the water*. Should anything happen such as losing them or their becoming useless due to loss of air, the child would panic because he is completely dependent on them.

Table 27–1. Aquatic Skills

Skill	Class Level	Teaching Techniques	Common Errors and/or Teaching Hints
Wading and submerging	A	1. Walk in water waist deep, bob to chest level. 2. Walk in water chest level, bob submerging head.	Join hands with students to give them confidence.
Breath holding	A	1. Inhale, place face in water or submerge, hold breath. 2. Increase time for holding breath. Have students count. Try to count to 10 while holding breath. 3. Add exhaling through mouth, blowing bubbles.	Tendency to jump up as soon as water touches face. Concentrating on counting will help overcome this. Blowing bubbles will aid exhaling through mouth.
Opening eyes	A	1. Hold breath, submerge and open eyes under water. Count partner's fingers. Pick up objects from bottom.	Tendency for nonswimmers to keep eyes tightly closed.
Bobbing and rhythmic breathing	A B C	1. Inhale above water, submerge and exhale. Keep repeating—aim to get a rhythmic cycle of inhaling and exhaling. 2. Do same but place face in water to exhale—roll to side to inhale. 3. Progress to deep water.	Tendency to hold breath while submerged or while face is in water. This prevents a rhythmic cycle.
Prone float	A B C	1. In knee-deep water, start prone float with hands on bottom. Inhale, place face in water—extend legs—take hands from bottom. 2. Hold on to gutter, take breath—place face in water—let feet float to surface—release hold on gutter. 3. Same can be done by holding on to buddy's hand. 4. Stand in chest-deep water, gently push into prone float. Regain standing position by bringing head up and tucking knees under body.	Throwing body forcefully into water causes body to sink and detracts from feeling of buoyancy that accompanies easy, gentle movement. Pushing with too great a force.
Jelly fish float	A B	1. From standing position in chest-deep water, place hands on thighs—bend over, place face in water and slide hands down to ankles. 2. Hang suspended in water: feet should leave bottom and body bob in water with back showing above surface. 3. Regain footing by raising head.	Assuming position too fast, without relaxation.

(continued)

Table 27-1. (contd.)

Skill	Class Level	Teaching Techniques	Common Errors and/or Teaching Hints
Back float	A B C	(Student should be assisted by partner or instructor placing hands under learner's shoulder blades.) 1. In chest-deep water, submerge until shoulders are under water, then lean back placing head on water with arms extended and legs extended. 2. To regain footing bring chin forward, drop hips, and draw knees back with arms reaching forward.	Throwing head back forcefully in water causes body to sink.
Kicking on front and back	A B	1. Hanging on to gutter or partner's hands, alternate up and down movement of legs.	Overkicking—too great a bend in knees.
Prone glide and recovery	A B	1. Go into prone-float position with more of a push from the bottom. 2. Hold breath and keep face in water. 3. Recovery same as from front float.	Jumping rather than pushing gently from bottom.
Back glide and recovery	A B	1. Go into back float with more of a push from the bottom, relax and glide. 2. Recovery same as from back float.	Throwing body back into water rather than pushing gently from bottom.
Prone glide with kick	A B	1. Push into a prone glide and add kick. May be done with aid of kickboard or with arms extended. Rhythmic breathing can be added.	Heavy, jerky movements and overkicking.
Back glide and kick	A B	1. Push into back glide and add kick.	Heavy, jerky movements and overkicking.
Sculling	A B	(Usually done on back in direction of the head. Hands and arms are used to propel swimmer. 1. From back-glide position with arms at sides, extend hands and arms sideward and bring them back to body. 2. Continue movement rhythmically, keeping arms fairly close to body with hands performing the movement.	Arms becoming too involved in movement. Arm movement too far from body.
Arm stroke on front	A	1. This is the crawl stroke with the hand entering the water in front of the shoulder and pressing backward to the thigh. 2. The arm is then lifted from water by the shoulder and extended forward for next cycle of movement.	Pulling beyond thighs makes it difficult to recover arms and is negative action.

(continued)

Table 27-1 (contd.)

Skill	Class Level	Teaching Techniques	Common Errors and/or Teaching Hints
Combined stroke on front	A	1. Push off into prone-glide position, begin kicking and then add arm stroke. 2. Start with the number of strokes that can be done with one breath. Then add breathing to cycle.	Rhythmic breathing must be practiced as part of all lessons or poor performance of this element presents a definite hindrance to progress at this point.
Arm stroke on back or finning	A B	1. Beginning movement on back is called finning. Starting with arms extended along sides, draw hands up to about hip level with fingers extended and then press hands backward toward feet to original position.	Hands and arms too far from body.
Combined stroke on back	A B	1. Push off into a back glide. 2. Begin alternating movement of legs and then add finning movement of arms.	Movements are apt to be jerky and rigid. Aim for smooth relaxed movements.
Elementary backstroke	A B	1. Done on back with body submerged except for head. 2. Arm movement: From glide position with arms at side, draw hands up sides with elbows flexed. At a point just below shoulder level, extend arms and press downward toward feet to original position. 3. Leg movement: In glide position legs are together and extended fully. Flex knees and drop heels down back toward hips. Turn feet out and position outside knees and then thrust to original position. 4. In coordinating the arms and legs, the legs will begin the movement when arms reach the waist. Both arms and legs will exert thrust at same time.	All movements should be slow and kept below surface. Position of feet prior to thrust is important Glide at end of stroke is important. Glide position—legs extended, arms at side close to body.
Sidestroke	C	1. Start in glide position: Body comfortably on side with back flat and legs extended; under arm extended beyond head and upper arm extended along body and thigh. 2. Arm movement: Press bottom arm down toward feet and when it passes point in line with shoulder recover close to body and return to extended position. Draw upper arm hard up close to body to a position in front of shoulder and then press it back to original position. 3. Leg movement: Legs move in a scissors kick with top leg moving forward and bottom leg backward. Legs separated, knees are flexed and both legs pressed back to original extended position.	It is important to stress that the movement of the top arm and the legs coincide. Exhale as top arm and legs are exerting their thrust. Legs should end action together. Avoid passing each other in thrust. Keep under arm close to body Glide at end of stroke is important.

(continued)

Table 27–1. *(contd.)*

Skill	Class Level	Teaching Techniques	Common Errors and/or Teaching Hints
Breast stroke	C	1. Start with body in prone position with back flat; arms and legs extended. 2. Arm movement: Palms are pressed diagonally downward to a position just outside the shoulder line. Keep the hands inside the elbows and reach under the body fairly close together and return to extended position. 3. Leg movement: From freely extended position draw heels up over knees, point toes to side with feet rotated to a position outside the knees. Extend hips, knees, and ankles into original position. 4. Breathing is coordinated with the stroke by inhaling during the pressing movement of the arms. Raise the head just high enough to clear the surface of the water. Stroke is started by arms with the legs starting as arms are finishing their pressing movement.	Arms pulling in too wide an arc. Body not kept in streamlined prone position. Hips coming out of water. Glide at end of stroke with arms and legs extended.
Methods of entering water	A	1. Jump into shallow water	1. Use low elevation; make slight spring from bottom and go into swimming position.
	B	2. Jump into deep water	2. In beginning, make certain that after leveling off a few strokes will bring swimmer to edge of pool or dock.

	B
	C
		3. Diving
		Suggested progression:
		  a. From sitting position
		  b. From one knee
		  c. From one leg
		  d. From two feet (without spring)
		  e. From two feet (with spring)
			3. Keep eyes open and focused on entry spot.
			Keep arms in line with head.
			Contract abdominal and leg muscles.
			When entirely in water, raise head and arms to surface.

Personal safety skills	A	1. Changing direction: While swimming, reach with forward arm in new direction and then turn head in that direction.	1. Maintain kicking action.
	B	2. Turning over: To turn from front to back, roll on arm extended in front, drop shoulder and turn head away from shoulder. Other arm is drawn across body to opposite side.	2. Continue stroking as soon as turn is finished to prevent body from sinking in water.

(continued)

Table 27–1. (contd.)

Skill	Class Level	Teaching Techniques	Common Errors and/or Teaching Hints
	B C	3. Treading water: Arms just below shoulder level, hands move easily in wide circles. legs do an exaggerated Flutter kick.	3. Keep kick slow and wide.
	A B C	4. Release of cramp: Stretching muscle, rubbing, and kneading will help to relieve cramp.	4. Cramps are of little danger if swimmer does not panic.
	A B C	5. Use of life jacket and preserver: (*a*) Swim and float wearing life jacket. (*b*) Jump in wearing life jacket. (*c*) Use seat cushion preservers.	5. Stress the use of Coast Guard-approved equipment.
Rescue skills	A	1. Assisting nonswimmer to feet: Have nonswimmers work with a buddy and learn to help each other regain footing in skill practice.	1. Working alone, many nonswimmers become unnecessarily frightened and progress is halted.
	A A, B C	2. Nonswimming rescues: (*a*) Reach with arm. (*b*) If victim is beyond arm's reach use towel, shirt, or pole. (*c*) Throw a line or ring buoy if victim is far from shore.	2. Reaching and extension assists can be made by untrained swimmers or nonswimmers.
	A B C	3. Artificial respiration: Procedure for mouth-to-mouth resuscitation. a. Clear mouth of any foreign matter. b. Tilt head back, chin pointing upward. c. Open your mouth wide and place it over mouth of victim. Pinch victim's nostrils shut and blow into his mouth. d. Remove your mouth and let air escape. e. Rate: About 12 breaths a minute for an adult and 20 for a child.	3. Many good films are available that demonstrate this technique, also dolls on which technique can be practiced.
	B C	4. Wading Rescues Singly In pairs With extensions In chain formation With free floating support	4. Rescuer stays between victim and shore. Take firm grip on victim. Use interlocking grip on chain rescue. Push support to victim and then pull to safety.

Water Games

Recreational aquatic activities have a very important place in any swimming program. They may be used to alleviate fear, which is often a problem of a nonswimmer, and thereby hasten the learning process. Through games children gain confidence in their aquatic ability and skill in the techniques involved. Long periods of concentrated practice are effectively spared by the use of games and novelty events.

The following games are recommended for the various classes of swimmer.

Nonswimmer (A) Simon Says, Number Retrieve, Number Change, Black and White.

Beginner (B) Touch, Cork Game, Neptune's Call, Poison, Ball Tag.
Intermediate (C) Tag, Follow the Leader, Touch, Balloon Battle, Treasure Hunt, Water Push Ball, Retrieving, Water Basketball.

Relay races are fun and must be chosen to suit the ability of the swimmers. They include novelty events such as disrobing, candle relay, egg and spoon, reading newspaper, flag relay, swim the duck relay.

These games and relays may be found in *Swimming and Water Safety* by the American National Red Cross, Washington, D.C., and *Aquatics Handbook* by Gabrielsen and others, published by Prentice-Hall, Inc.

Water-Safety Hints

1. Respect the water.
2. Learn to swim.
3. Never swim alone.
4. Swim at a safe place—preferably where lifeguards are present.
5. Do not swim when overtired.
6. Do not swim when overheated.
7. Do not swim immediately after eating.
8. Know your ability and do not try for too great a distance in open water.
9. Have a boat accompany you if you are trying for distances.
10. Be considerate of the safety of others. Many persons have been so frightened by "horseplay" they have been forced to give up the sport.
11. Be careful of overexposure to the sun. Also remember you can sunburn and windburn even on a cloudy day.
12. Do not dive into unknown water. Make certain it is deep enough and has no dangerous hidden objects.
13. Learn to handle boats and canoes before going out in them.
14. Insist that companions abide by safety rules.
15. Carry life preservers in all small craft.
16. Remember most small craft will float when upset. Hence, stay with your boat or canoe.
17. In case of drowning, start artificial respiration at once.

Selected References

American National Red Cross. *Swimming and Diving* (Revised Edition). Washington, D.C.: 1962.

———. *Teaching Johnny to Swim* (Revised Edition). Washington, D.C.: 1963.

———. *Water Safety Instructor's Manual.* Washington, D.C.: 1962.

ARMBRUSTER, D. A., R. H. ALLEN, and H. S. BILLINGSLEY. *Swimming and Diving* (Fourth Edition). St. Louis: The C. V. Mosby Co., 1963.

BARR, ALFRED S., BEN F. GRADY, and JOHN HIGGENS. *Swimming and Diving*. New York: A. S. Barnes and Company, 1950.

BROWN, RICHARD L. "Finding and Using the Aquatics Resources in Your Own Community." *Journal of Health, Physical Education, and Recreation*, Vol. 134, No. 5, May 1963.

CURRETON, T. K. *Fun in the Water*. New York: Association Press, 1957.

EMPLETON, BERNARD. "Water Games Add to Control, Confidence and Competence." *Journal of Health, Physical Education, and Recreation*, Vol. 134, No. 5, May 1963.

GABRIELSEN, M. A., BETTY SPEARS, and B. W. GABRIELSEN. *Aquatics Handbook*. New York: Prentice-Hall, Inc., 1960.

KAUFFMAN, CAROLYN. *How to Teach Children to Swim*. New York: G. P. Putnam's Sons, 1960.

LUKENS, PAUL W. *Teaching Swimming*. Minneapolis, Minn.: Burgess Publishing Co., 1952.

MACKENZIE, M. M., and BETTY SPEARS. *Beginning Swimming*. Belmont, Calif.: Wadsworth Publishing Co., 1963.

MANN, CHANNING. "Swimming Classes in Elementary Schools on a City Wide Basis." *Journal of Health, Physical Education, and Recreation*, Vol. 134, No. 5, May 1963.

Official Aquatic Guide (Latest Edition). National Section for Girls' and Women's Athletics, American Association for Health, Physical Education, and Recreation, Washington, D.C.

ORPHAN, MILTON, JR. "Motivating Beginners to Increase Learnings in the Basic Skills." *Journal of Health, Physical Education, and Recreation*, Vol. 134, No. 5, May 1963.

SMITH, HOPE. *Water Games*. New York: The Ronald Press Company, 1962.

VANNIER, MARYHELEN, and HALLY BETH POINDEXTER. *Individual and Team Sports for Girls and Women* (Second Edition). Philadelphia: W. B. Saunders Company, 1968.

Appendixes

APPENDIX A

Audio Visual Aids and Records

Visual Aids

Teachers may wish to know sources of various visual aids useful in physical education programs. Film catalogues are available from some of the following companies. This list is not exhaustive.

Coronet Instructional Films, Coronet Building, Chicago, Ill. 60600

Encyclopaedia Britannica Films, 20 N. Wacker Drive, Chicago, Ill. 60600

International Film Bureau, Inc., 332 S. Michigan Ave., Chicago, Ill. 60604

H. W. Wilson Company, 950 University Ave., New York, N.Y. 10452

National Section on Women's Athletics, 1201 Sixteenth Street, N. W., Washington, D.C. 20036

Popular Science, Audio-Visual Division, 355 Lexington Ave., New York, N.Y. 10017

The Athletic Institute, Merchandise Mart, Room 805, Chicago, Ill. 60600

United States Government Printing Office, Washington, D.C.

Magnetic boards are of great help as teaching aids for team games. They may be obtained from:

The Program Aids Company, Inc., No. 1 Physical Fitness Drive, Garden City, N.Y. 11530

Records

Records for dances may be secured from the following companies. This is not an exhaustive list.

Bownar Records, Dept. J169, 622 Rodier Drive, Glendale, Calif. 91201

Chevoit Corporation, Dept. F. A. Whitney Bldg., Box 34485, Los Angeles, Calif. 90034

Childrens Music Center, Inc., 5373 West Pico Blvd., Los Angeles, Calif. 90034

Educational Activities, Inc., Box 362, Freeport, N.Y. 11520

Educational Recordings of America, Inc., P.O. Box 6062, Bridgeport, Conn. 06606

Freda Miller Records for Dance, 131 Bayview Ave., Northport, N.Y. 11768

Kimbo Records, Dept. J., Box 55, Deal, N.J. 07723

Leo's Theatrical Co., 125 N. Wabash Ave., Chicago, Ill. 60602

Stanley Bowmar Co., Inc., 4 Broadway, Valhalla, N.Y. 10595

Stepping Tones Records, Dept. J-6, P.O. Box 64334, Los Angeles, Calif. 90064

The Dancer's Shop, Children's Music Center, 5373 W. Pico Blvd., Los Angeles, Calif. 90019

APPENDIX B

Sources of Equipment and Supplies

Various equipment and supplies may be secured from the following sources. This is not an exhaustive list. Catalogues are available and are great aids for teachers and administrators.

American Athletic Equipment, Box 111, Jefferson, Iowa 50129

Creative Playthings, Inc., Princeton, N.J. 08540, and Los Angeles, Calif. 90034

Game-Time, Inc., 900 Anderson Rd., Litchfield, Mich. 49252

Lind Climber Co., 807 Reba Place, Evanston, Ill. 060202

MacGregor Co., Interstate 75 at Jimson Rd., Cincinnati, Ohio 45215

Miracle Equipment Co., Box 275, Grinnell, Iowa 50112

Nissen Corp., 930 Twenty-seventh Ave., S. W., Cedar Rapids, Iowa 52406

Premier Athletic Corp., Rivervale, N.J. 07675

Rawlings Company, 2300 Delmar Boulevard, St. Louis, Mo. 63166

Spalding Sales Corp., Div. of A. G. Spalding & Bros., Inc., 360 Sylvan Ave., Englewood Cliffs, N.J. 07632

The Delmer F. Harris Co., P.O. Box 288, Dept. J, Concordia, Kansas 66901

Universal Bleacher Co., P.O. Box 638, Champaign, Ill. 61820 (Maker of Port-A-Pools)

W. J. Voit Rubber Corp., 29 Essex St., Maywood, N.J. 07607

APPENDIX **C**

Formations for Games, Dances, and Individual and Dual Activities

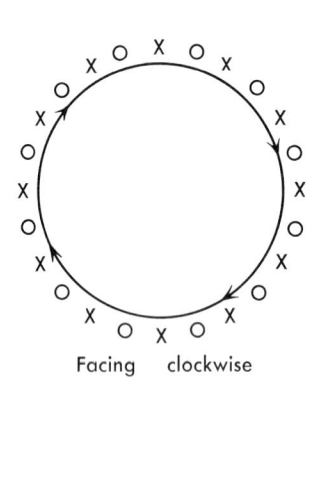

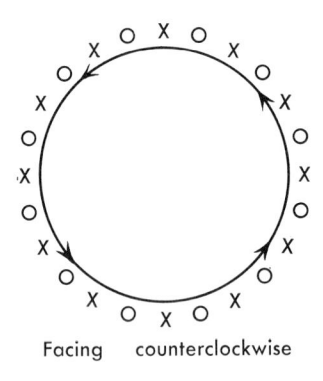

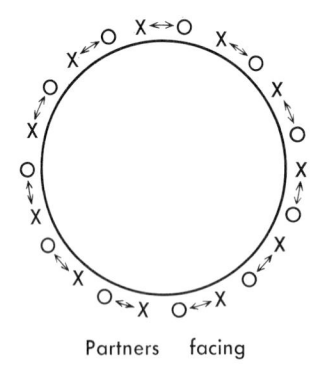

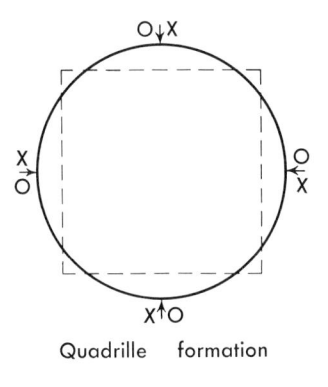

Facing clockwise

Facing counterclockwise

Partners facing

Quadrille formation

X = Boy
O = Girl

Figure C–1. Single circle dance formations commonly used for folk dances, singing games, and rhythms.

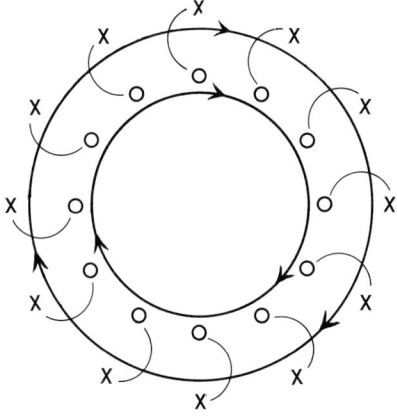

Partners facing clockwise

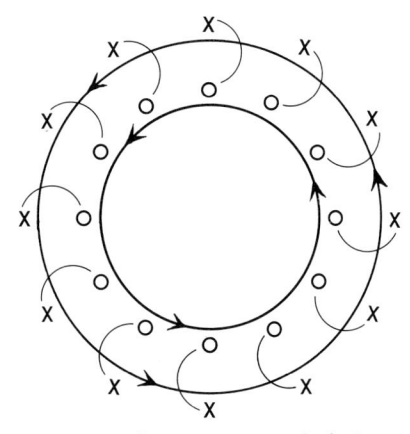

Partners facing counterclockwise

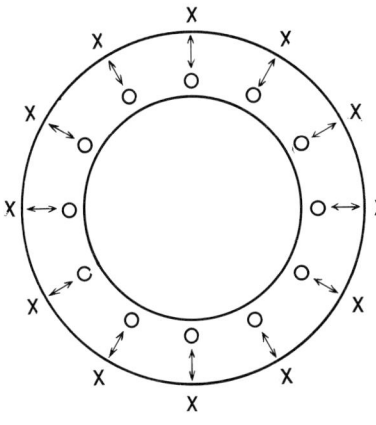

Partners facing each other

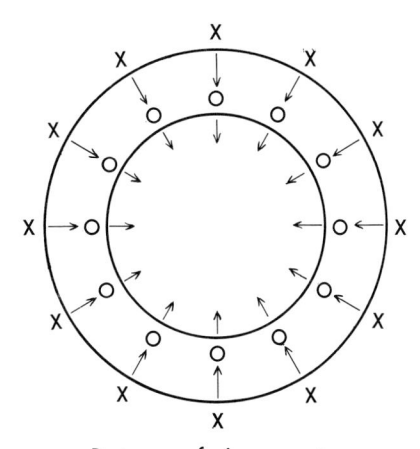

Partners facing center

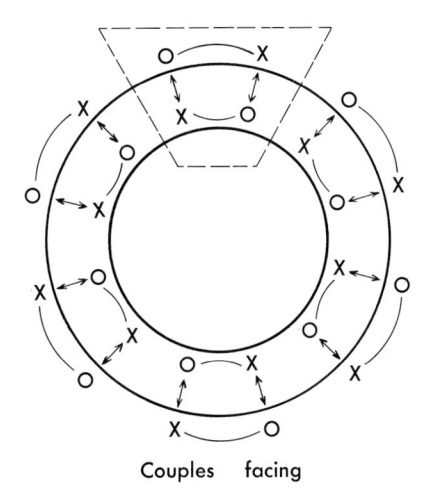

Couples facing

Figure C–2. Double circle formations used for folk dances, singing games, and rhythms.

X = Boys
O = Girls

466 APPENDIXES

```
X    X    X    X    X    X    X    X
─────────────────────────────────────
O    O    O    O    O    O    O    O
─────────────────────────────────────
            Double  line  formation


X ─ O         X ─ O         X ─ O         X ─ O
  ↕             ↕             ↕             ↕
O ─ X         O ─ X         O ─ X         O ─ X
        Partners  side  by  side  facing  center


X    X    X    X    X    X    X    X
↕    ↕    ↕    ↕    ↕    ↕    ↕    ↕
O    O    O    O    O    O    O    O
            Partners  facing  center


X ←→ O       X ←→ O       X ←→ O       X ←→ O

X ←→ O       X ←→ O       X ←→ O       X ←→ O
        Couples  facing  each  other


               X = Boys
               O = Girls
```

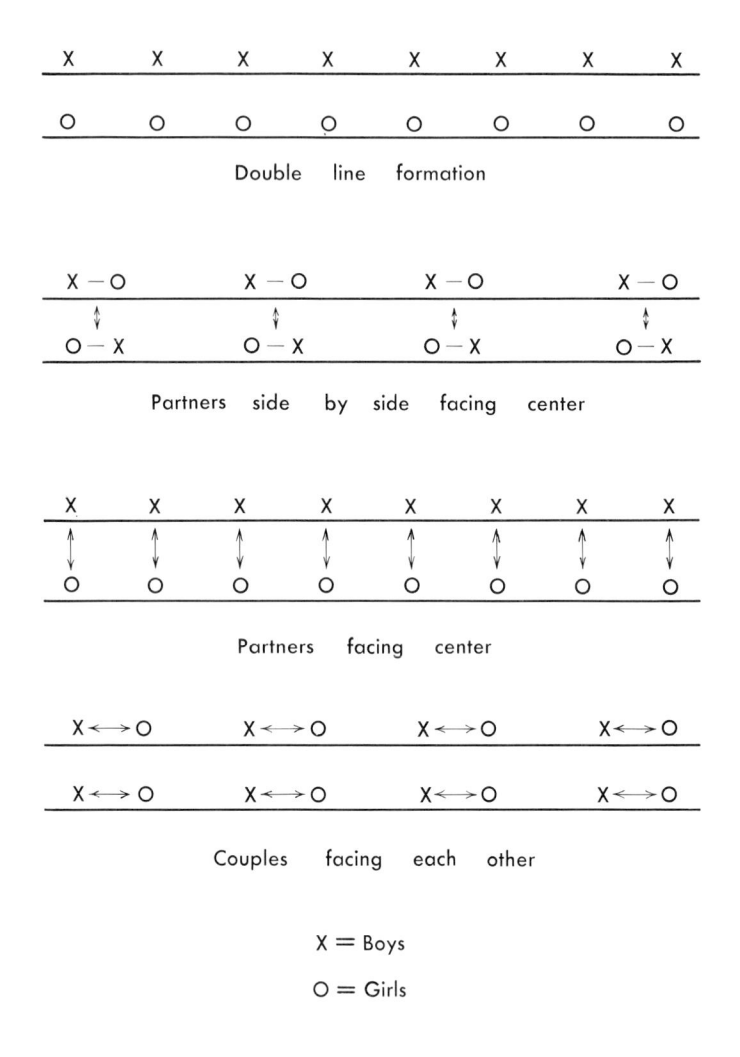

Figure C–3. Double line dance formations.

Formations for Games, Dances, Activities   **467**

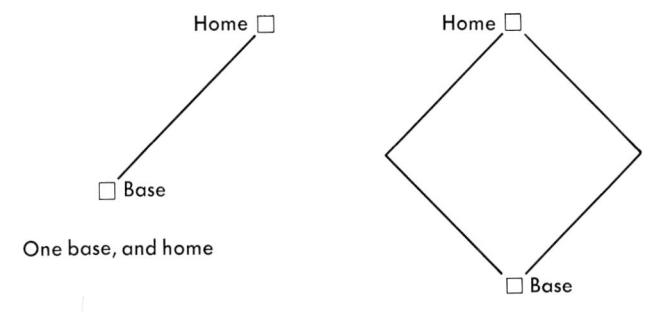

Home ☐
☐ Base

One base, and home

Home ☐
☐ Base

One base opposite home

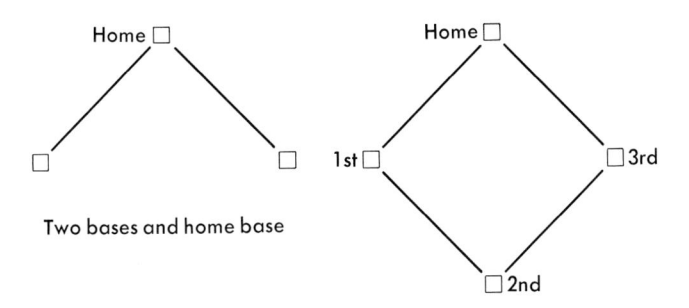

Home ☐
☐   ☐

Two bases and home base

Home ☐
1st ☐   ☐ 3rd
☐ 2nd

Diamond formation, four bases

Figure C–4. **Base diagrams for games.**

468 APPENDIXES

Goal   Goal

Two goals at opposite sides

Goal line   Goal line

Section I   Section II

Two goals at opposite sides, area split in two sections

Goal line

Home

Home base and goal line

Home

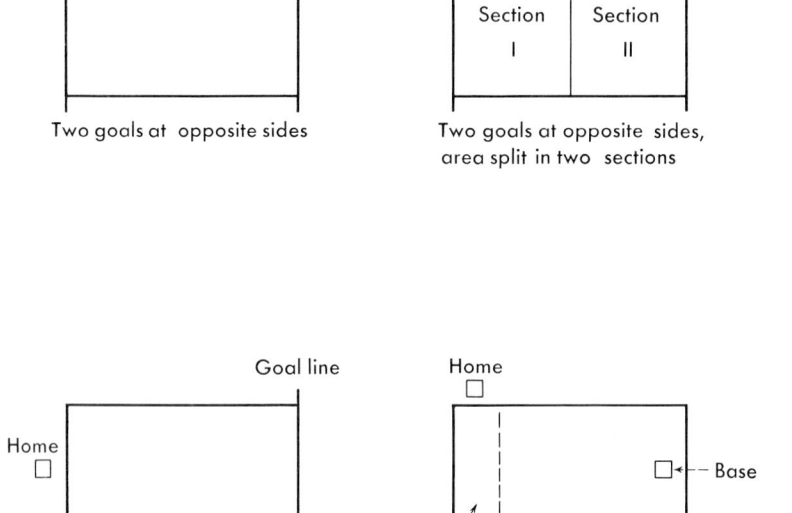

Base

Safety area

Home safety area and one base

Figure C–5. Diagrams of general playing areas.

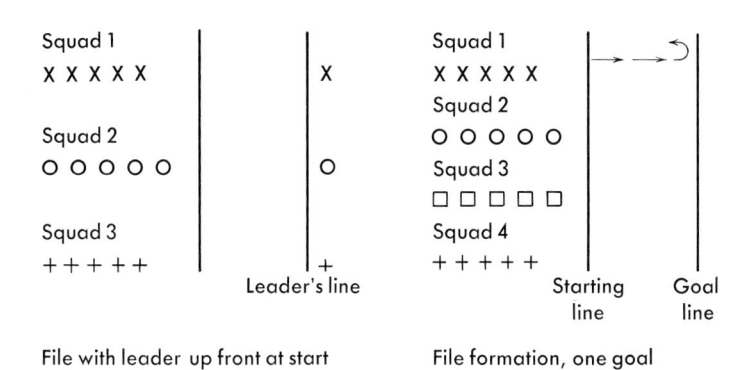

Formations for Games, Dances, Activities **469**

```
Squad 1                               Squad 1
X X X X X          X                  X X X X X      → →  ↩
                                      Squad 2
Squad 2                               O O O O O
O O O O O          O                  Squad 3
                                      ▢ ▢ ▢ ▢ ▢
Squad 3                               Squad 4
+ + + + +          +                  + + + + +
             Leader's line                      Starting  Goal
                                                line      line

File with leader up front at start    File formation, one goal


Squad 1                               Squad 1
X X X X X    ← ←                      4 3 2 1               5 6 7 8
| | | | |                             X X X X      ←        X X X X
X X X X X      →

Squad 2                               Squad 2
O O O O O      →                      4 3 2 1               5 6 7 8
| | | | |                             O O O O               O O O O
O O O O O    ← ←
            Starting  Goal
            line      line

Double file, used                     Shuttle relay formation
for partner participation
```

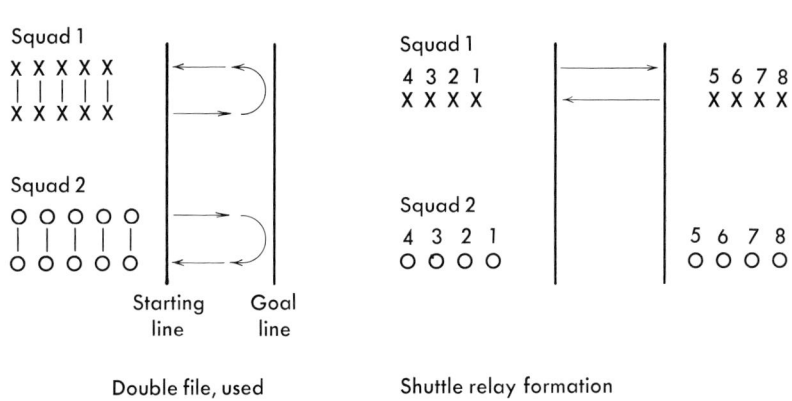

Figure C–6. **Relay formations.**

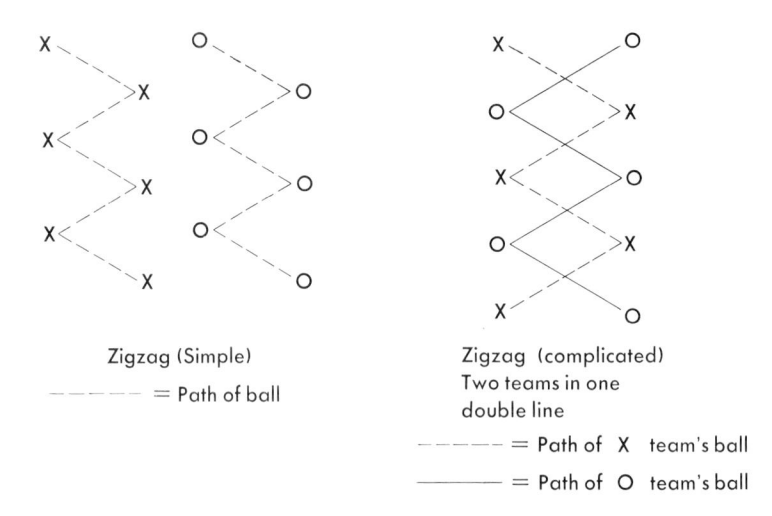

470 APPENDIXES

Zigzag (Simple)

------ = Path of ball

Zigzag (complicated)
Two teams in one
double line

------ = Path of X team's ball

⎯⎯⎯ = Path of O team's ball

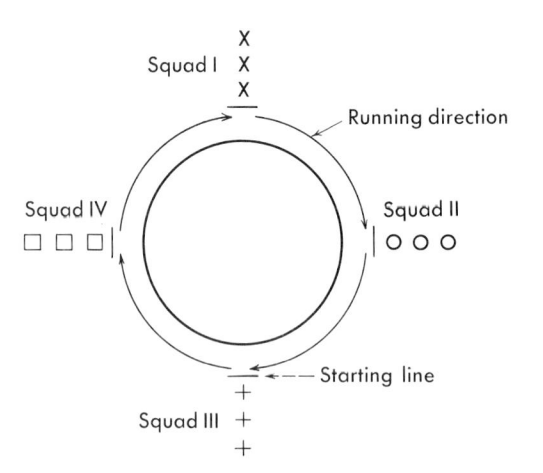

Circle relay with four teams

Figure C–7. Relay formations (cont.).

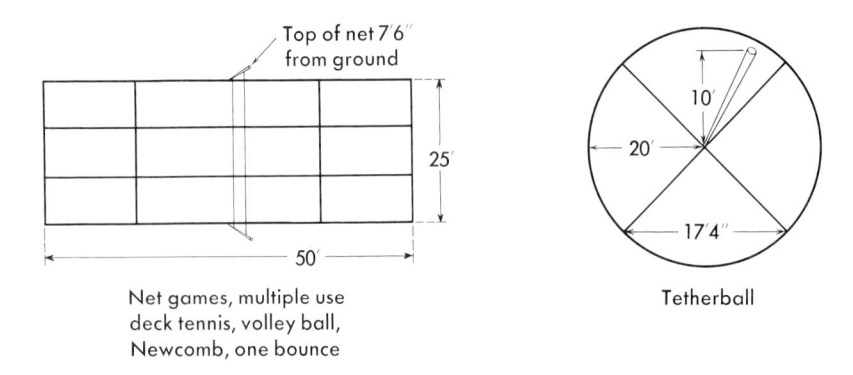

Net games, multiple use
deck tennis, volley ball,
Newcomb, one bounce

Tetherball

Figure C–8. Individual and dual game diagrams.

APPENDIX D

Suggestions for Making Equipment

1. Bowling pins may be secured free from your local alley. Contact the local manager and ask him to save those which are not good enough to be refinished. These may be used for many games, for marking playing areas, and so on.

2. If the school is in an area where there are sewing mills or hosiery mills, ask them to save for you the spindles or cones which the thread comes on. They may be used in place of Indian clubs, for bases, for bowling games, and so on.

3. Ask your children to bring in large tin cans. Be sure that they have smooth edges. They may be used for target tossing games in the classroom and on the playground in warm weather.

4. Your school cafeteria or your favorite sweet shop will save for you the ice cream cartons bulk ice cream is packed in. Wash, dry, and have your class paint them. They may be used for games, to store small balls, bean bags, and the like, and to carry outside for marking play areas.

5. Children may bring in dried ears of corn and heavy cloth material to make bean-bags under your guidance. They are much better than those which can be purchased and naturally are cheaper.

6. Ask your children, local farmers, and poultrymen for empty feed bags. Put clean hay, straw, or dry lawn clippings in them. Tie them with binder twine and use them for bases in softball, to mark play areas, and for bases in all other games. Carry them out and in each time so they do not get wet and muddy. They are light, clean, and require little storage space.

7. Use plain paper plates to mark your playing area for running and tagging games. A little sand or dirt placed on the center of each will prevent them from blowing away. These may also be used for indoor tossing games.

8. Ask your children to bring in bottle caps. Use them for target tossing games. Toss them into the tin cans, onto marked floor targets, or into the ice cream cartons already mentioned.

9. Make quoits out of rope. The rope must be heavy enough to hold its shape and may be taped with tire tape. These quoits may be thrown over homemade pegs made by crossing two sticks of wood with an upright piece in the center or over an old bowling pin. They may also ring a person's arm. The human target bends his arm at the elbow, makes a fist, and endeavors to catch the ring on his arm.

10. Volleyball nets are costly. If you have none, use a piece of rope—clothesline will do very nicely. Attach it to two posts or trees. Tie strips of white cloth every few inches on the rope and permit them to hang down 3 or 4 feet. This makes it very easy to ascertain whether the ball goes over or under the rope.

11. Ask your children to bring in smooth pieces of board or ask for them from your manual arts room. They may vary in size from 12 by 12

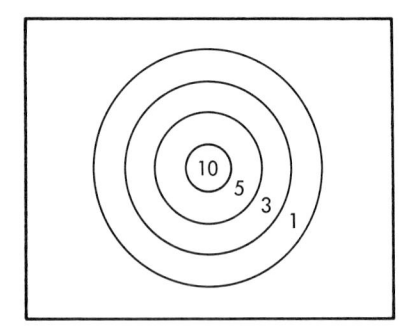

Figure D–1. Dart Board.

inches to 24 by 24 inches. Have your children paint circles on them for dart games. Use suction or regular darts.

12. Mark pieces of board of any appropriate size in squares. Paint numbers in each square. Next, drive a nail in each square at an angle. Use mason-jar rubber rings for tossing at the board. Rings must hook over nails and remain on. Each person has five turns. His score is then recorded. Make the game any score you desire. See Figure D–2.

Figure D–2. Ring Toss Board.

13. To mark players for two teams in games where they intermingle, use any colored cloth or red or blue bandanas. Tie on the arm of the players of one team. These may also be used to mark boys or girls in dances where your group is uneven.

14. Cut rings from round cereal boxes. Use them to toss short distances for ring games. They may also be used on the floor or ground to toss bottle caps or pebbles into for target games.

15. Use rolled socks for classroom games so no damage will be done if they are missed. These socks may be sewn so they do not come unrolled. Mothers or children may knit or crochet a cover and stuff it with socks.

16. Pieces of red material may be fastened on heavy wire or pieces of wood. One end may be pushed into the ground to mark playing areas. See Figure D–3.

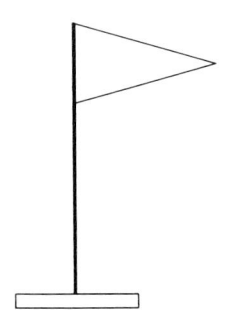

Figure D–3. Playground Marker.

17. Use pieces of wall board to make target games of various kinds.

18. Fill an old dishpan or round basin with wet cement and stand a piece of 2-inch pipe about 12 inches long in the center of it so it will dry there. When it dries you have a standard to hold up nets for Paddle Tennis, Deck Tennis, Badminton, and the like. Insert a 1-inch pipe in this 2-inch pipe and tie the net to it. The cement is a heavy enough base to hold the nets satisfactorily.

19. Collect quart milk cartons. Wash them thoroughly and use them in place of Indian clubs for games. They make fine quiet pins for indoor bowling games. They may be used to mark play areas. If they are partially filled with sand, the wind will not blow them away when used out of doors.

20. Collect cloth salt or sugar sacks and fill them with shredded newspapers. Sew them securely to use for indoor games and activities.

Index

A Dozen Eggs, 432
Abdominal Curl, 338
Active play, 104
Activities
 classroom, 374–76
 developmental, 338–39, 359–61
 movement, 131–62
 selection of, 247–51
 self-testing, 136–37, 154–55, 325–36, 350–53, 367–69, 387–89
 special and holiday, 424–34
 stunts, tumbling, and gymnastic, 435–47
 water, 448–57
Adages, 421
Adapted program, 18
Adler, Alfred, 13
Administration, health programs and, 29–30
After-school programs, 180–81
Age, physiological, 93
A-Hunting We Will Go, 332–33
Alcohol, health education curriculum and, 210–12
Allemande Left, 377
Allemande Right, 377
American Association for Health, Physical Education, and Recreation, 53, 55
American Association of School Administrators, 5n, 66
American Council on Education, 24
American Medical Association, 53
Anderson, C. L., 33

Ankle Jump, 387
Ankle Toss, 387
Aquatics
 childhood, 139, 159
 games and, 455–56
 skills and (*tables*), 451–55
Arch Goal Ball, 382–83
Assembly program, 424–25
Atypical children, *see* Children, atypical
Audio-visual aids, 86, 271–80
Autograph Artist, 431

Baby Game, 366
Back Hip Circle, 441–42
Backward gymnastics, 437, 439
Badminton, 411–13
Balance gymnastics, 442–45
Balance Step, 377
Ball Bouncing, 325
Ball games, 370
 Arch Goal, 382–83
 Bat, 153–54, 372
 Catch, 369–70
 Circle, 153
 Dodge, 153, 250, 321
 Kick, 156–59, 372
 Relay, 152–53
 Stop, 372
 Under Leg, 372
Ball Pitching, 366

473

Ball Roll, 364
Ball Stand, 142
Ball Tossing, 325
Balloon Ball, 420
Band Box Ball, 390–91
Barnyard Squabble, 433
Baseball, types of, 156–59, 390–91, 395
Basket Toss, 432
Basketball, 374, 406, 413–14
Basketville Relay, 382
Bat Ball, 153–54, 372
Beach Tennis, 386
Bean bag games, 325, 420–21
Bear Dance, 368
Bear games, 322, 361
Beat the Ball, 370–71
Bicycle, 338
Bird games, 312–13, 322, 398
Birthday party games, 433
Black Tom, 344–45
Black and White, 344
Bleking, 356
Blind Man's Buff, 345
Blindfolded Artist, 429
Block plans, physical education (*table*), 220–21
Blue Book, 54
Body movement, 12, 13
Bouncing ball games, 339, 342, 409–10
Box Toss, 421
Bowling, 349–50
Broad Jump Relay, 382
Brouha, L., 53
Brownies and Fairies, 324
Bucher, Charles A., 9*n*
Bunt Softball, 390
Buzz Step, 356

Call Ball, 140, 142, 320–21
Camping, 189–97
Candle Pin, 433
Candy Shop, 313–14
Captain Ball, 393–94
Cartwheel, 439–40
Cat games, 325, 355, 429
Catching and Throwing Relay, 152–53
Center ball games, 342, 369–70
Circle Toss, 342–43
Cha Cha Cha, 400
Chair Vault, 403
Chamberlain, Wilt, 15

Chapman, J. Crosby, 5*n*
Charley over the Water, 322
Chase the Bone, 341
Children
 atypical, 116–27
  physical education program for, 163–74
 body knowledge and, 13
 exceptional, 36
 growth and development of, 9–10, 91–107
 health of, 25
 judgment of, 12–13
 school objectives and, 4
Children's Polka, 334–35
Chimes of Dunkirk, 336
Chin-One Arm Push, 443
Chin-ups, 441
Chinese Wall, 344
Christmas, 430–431
Chronological age, 93
Churn the Butter, 351
Circle games, 153, 321, 341, 363, 382, 396
Civic responsibility, 6–7, 17
Class organization, 243–51
Classroom games
 childhood
  early, 138–39, 250, 328–29, 353–55
  middle, 374–76, 396–98
 upper grade, 420–23
Classroom Golf, 396–97
Clothespin games, 354, 363
Club Snatch, 384
Cockfight, 350
Coffee Grinder, 387
Coffee and Tea, 250
Coffee, Tea, and Milk, 376
Come Along, 324
Contra Dances (*table*), 379
Cookies in the Jar, 346
Corn Game, 430
Corner Spry, 369–70
Counseling, health, 35–36
Counts, George, 5
Couple Bear Dance, 368
Course Work, 406
Cowboy and Indian, 343
Crab Soccer, 407
Crab Walk, 351
Crack the Eggs, 366
Crane Dive, 388
Creative children, 122
 physical education program for, 170–72
Croquet, 367

Index

Crossing the Brook, 397
Crows and Cranes, 364–65
Cuturally disadvantaged children, 117–18, 172
  physical education program for, 163–65
Curriculum
  health education, 198–213
  physical education, 227–32
  See also Programs
Cut the Birthday Cake, 433

Dance of Greeting, 335–36
Dances and rhythms
  early childhood, 305–19, 330–38
  middle childhood, 356–59, 377–79
  upper grades, 399–402
Dances, special event (*table*), 378
Dashes, 374
Days of the Week, 343
Deck Tennis, 384–85
Democracy
  physical education and, 18, 69
  play and, 14
Demonstration, 425
Development
  child, 91–107
  physical, 11–12
Developmental activities
  childhood
    early, 338–39
    middle, 359–61, 379–81
  upper grade, 402–4
Dewey, John, 5, 6, 11, 102
Diamond Soccer, 407
Did You Ever See a Lassie?, 317
Directed play, 102–4
Disadvantaged children, 117–18, 172
  physical education and, 163–65
Disease, 15, 37
Disruptive children, 120–21
  physical education and, 168–69
Diving Forward Roll, 438–39
Dodge Ball, 153, 250, 321
Dog games, 249, 325
Do-Si-Do, 377
Double Bounce, 367
Double elimination tournaments, 185
Downcast, 367
Downs and Ups, 366
Drawing games, 353, 356, 429
Drugs and health education (*table*), 209–10, 239–40
Dual activities, childhood
  early, 136, 325, 346
  middle and upper, 151–52, 365–67, 384–87
Dual Rings, 410–11
Dual Rope Turning, 349
Duck games, 305, 326, 432

Early morning program, 176
Easter activities, 432
Economic efficiency, 6, 16–17
Educational Policies Commission, 5–6, 24
Egg Words, 432
Eggs in the Basket, 366, 432
Elementary and Secondary Education Act, 74
Elephant games, 306, 326
Elimination factor, 249–51
Elimination tournament, 184–85
Émile (Rousseau), 11
Environment, health and, 25, 33–35
Evaluation, programs and, 281–301
Exceptional children, 36
Exercise, 11–12
Equipment
  playground, 320
  program, 20

Facilities, 20
Family life, 3, 16
Field days, 427–28
Field events, *see* Track and field events
Fill the Cup, 432
Films, 275
Find the Candles, 433
Finding Partners, 429
Finding Uranium, 375
Finland Hopscotch, 347
Fish Hawk Dive, 388
Five Trips, 383–84
Flag Football, 395
Floor Tennis, 386
Flowers and the Wind, 322
Folk dances, 358, (*table*) 379, 399
  International (*tables*), 378, 401
Follow the Leader, 324
Football, Flag, 395
Forearm balance, 404
Forward Pass Baseball, 395
Forward Roll, 437
  Diving, 438–39

Fox and Rabbit, 376
Fox Trot, 400
Froebel, Friedrich, 11
Frog games, 339, 344, 351, 438
Front Hip Circle Tuck, 442
Front Support, 441

Gallagher, J. R., 53
Games
　baby, 366
　birthday, 433
　circle, 153
　classroom, 138–39, 159, 250, 328–29, 353–55, 420–23
　creative, 226–28
　jump rope, 348–49
　lead-up, 152
　low organization, 135–36, 150, 249, 361–65
　out-of-doors, 151
　relay, 152–53, 363–65
　team, 153–59, 250, 369–72, 389–96, 411–23
　water, 455–56
Gardener and the Scamp, 323
Giesell, Arnold, 13, 101
Gift Givers, 433
Gifted children, 122
　physical education and, 170–72
Givens, Willard, 6
Go Round and Round the Village, 334
Golf, 396–97
Good Morning, 323
Government, federal, health education and, 73–74
Grand Right and Left, 377
Grants, government, health education and, 74
Grapevine Step, 356
Growth, children and, 9–10, 91–107
Gymnastics, 155, 436–47

Halloween activities, 429
Hand Wrestle, 351, 388
Handball, 386
Handgrip, 440
Handicapped children, 118–19, 172
　physical education and, 165–67
Handstand rollout, 439
Handwriting Identification, 376
Hangs, gymnastic, 441–43, 447
Happiness, play and, 14
Hat in the Ring, 355
Head and Shoulder Curl, 381

Head Up, 360–61
Head gymnastics, 311, 361, 438
Health
　education and, 15
　factors of, 25
　importance of, 24–25
　objectives of, 25–26
Health coordinator, program and, 31–32
Health counseling, 35–36
Health council, school, 27
Health education
　approach to, 26–27
　curriculum for, 198–213
　drugs and (*table*), 209–10, 239–40
　federal government and, 73–74
　guides for, 32–35
　physical education and, 37–38
　preventive medicine and, 71–72
　principles of, 84–87
　teaching of, 27–29, 74, 263–70
　trends in, 61–68, 72–74
Health practices, 26
Health programs, 29–30
Health services, 35–37
Health teams, 28–32
Heating, 34
Heel Click, 388
Heel Jump, 367
Here Comes a Bluebird Through My Window, 133–34, 319
Here We Go Round the Christmas Tree, 430
Heredity, 25
Hickory Dickory Dock, 306
High Jump, 373–74
Hill Dill, 324
Hit the Bat, 371
Hit the Box, 321
Hit the Mallet, 371
Hitch Kick, 404
Hoffmaster, P. J., 191
Holiday activities, 428–34
Hopping in Place, 338
Hopscotch, 346–47
Hot Potato, 153
Hound the Rabbit, 344
How Do You Do, My Partner?, 314
Human relationships, 6, 16
Human Rocker, 404
Huntsman, 324

I Am Tired of Stirring the Mush, 354–55

I See You, 336–37
Imitations, 309–10
In the Box, 396
Inch Worm, 351–52
Indian Get-Up, 352
Individual activities
  childhood
    early, 136, 325, 346
    middle and upper, 151–52, 365–67, 384–87
  upper grade, 409–13
Individual Rope Turning, 349
In-service classes, health education and, 74
Instructors, water, 449
International Folk Dances (*tables*), 378, 401
Intramural programs, 18
Inverted Hang, 443
Italian Hopscotch, 347

Jack and Jill, 307
Jack Be Nimble, 307
Jacks, 366
John Brown, 340–41
Jolly Is the Miller, 332
Joseph P. Kennedy, Jr. Foundation, 190
Jump games, 326, 331, 338, 348–49, 352, 362–63, 374, 389
Jumps, 373–74

Kangaroo games, 352, 382, 389
Keep It Up, 382, 408
Kennedy, John F., 59
Kick games, 157–59, 371, 391, 441
Kip, 403
Knee Lift, 352
Knee Raise, 380
Knee Wrestle, 387

"L" Hang, 441, 443
Laban, Rudolf, 40
Ladder Hopscotch, 347
Ladder tournament, 183–84
Ladies' Chain, 377–78
Lamb Dog Walk, 553
Lame Fox and Chickens, 343
Lead-up games (*table*), 152
Leaf Hunt, 353
Learning, 8, 108–12
Lee, Joseph, 102, 105

Leg Extension, 380
Leisure, 15
  children and, 4
  health and, 62–64
Lesson plans, physical education, 224–25
Lighting, 34
Little Miss Muffet, 306–7
Locke, John, 11
Locomotor skills (*table*), 49–50
Long Base, 391
Long Hangs, 447
Looby Loo, 318
Lost Child, 353–54
Low organization games, 249
  childhood
    early, 135–36, 320–25, 339–41
    middle and upper, 150, 361–65, 381–84
Lucas, Jerry, 59

Marbles, 349
Marjorie Daw, 305
May Day programs, 428
Mazurka, 356
Medicine, preventive, 71–72
Medley Relay Race, 364
Melby, Ernest O., 191
Menninger, Dr. William, 104
Mental development, 15
  play and, 12–13
Mentally retarded children, 119–20, 172
  physical education and, 167–68
Merengue, 402
Merry-Go-Round, 310–11, 323
Middle school program, 22
Midnight, 343
Missing Heart, 431
Mixed Grip Travel, 447
Modified Pullups, 359
Momentary Handstand, 438
Monkey Jump, 326
Motion Poem, 307
Motor learning, 108–12
Motor skill development, 96–98
Movement activities, childhood
  early, 131–45
  middle and upper, 146–62
Movement education, 40–51, 70
Movement experiences
  childhood
    early, 305–55
    middle, 356–98

Movement experiences (*cont.*)
  gymnastic, 436–47
  special and holiday, 424–34
  upper grade, 399–423
  water, 448–57
Moving Day, 345
Muffin Man, 315–16
Mulberry Bush, 316–17

Namath, Joe, 59
National Education Association, 5n, 6, 24
Nest Hang, 443, 447
Neuromuscular skill, 12
Newcomb, 392
Nine Court Basketball, 406
Noon-hour program, 176–80
Number Guessing, 433
Number Toss, 354
Nonlocomotor skills (*table*), 49–50
Numbers Are Fun, 375
Nuts in May, 333

Obedience to law, physical education and, 18
October's Leaves, 311–12
Old Mother Witch, 323–24, 429
Olympics, 3
One Rope, 443–44
Organization, class, 243–51
Outdoor education, 67, 189–97
Out-of-doors games (*table*), 151
Over and Under Relay, 397–98
Overhead Toss, 342

Pace-a-Ball, 408
Paddle games, 386
Palmer, Arnold, 15
Parallel bars, 445
Parents, physical fitness and, 58–59
Pas-de-Basque, 357
Pass and Shoot, 361–62
Passive play, 104
Paw Paw Patch, 337–38
Pepper Circle, 407–8
Pestalozzi, Johann Heinrich, 11
Physical development, 11–12
Physical education
  basic principles of, 76–84
  curriculum, 227–32
  definition of, 7–9

education and
  general, 15–18
  health, 37–38
family, 3
need for, 3
objectives of, 9
philosophy of, 3–87
sports and, 3
teaching of, 3, 13, 243–63
  game skills, 251–56
  legality, 256–63
  organization, 243
  safety, 256–63
trends in, 61–72
Physical education programs, *see* Programs, physical education
Physical fitness, 52–60
  definition of, 53–54
Physically handicapped children, 118–19, 172
  physical education and, 165–67
Physiological age, 93
Physiological principles, education and, 76
Pick-Up Hopscotch, 347–48
Pin games, 431–32
Ping-Pong Relay, 421–22
Play
  active, 104
  democracy and, 14
  development and, 10–15
  directed, 102–4
  happiness and, 14
  motivation of, 232–33
  success and, 14
  trial and error, 13
Playdays, 425–26
Polka Step, 357
Poorly coordinated children, 121–22
  physical education and, 169–70
President's Council on Physical Fitness and Sports, 52
Preventive medicine, health education and, 71–72
Programs, 64–68
  adapted, 18
  assembly, 424–25
  camping, 192–95
  children's, 163–74
  evaluation of, 187
  health education, 27–37, 218, 234–42
    whole curriculum (*tables*), 236–39
  involvement, 45–50
  physical education, 18–23, 77–84, 218

Index 479

creativity, 223–27
evaluation, 281–301
supplies (*table*), 78–80
types, 218–34
whole curriculum, 227–32
school day, 175–81
special and holiday, 424–34
supplies, 20, 78–80
tournaments and, 181–87
Projectors, 275
Promenade, 357
Propeller, 339–40
Pull Stretcher, 380
Pullups, 359
Pumpkin games, 429–30
Punch Baseball, 390
Puritanism, play and, 10–11
Push Away, 409
Pushups, 359–60
Pyramid tournament, 184

Quiet as Mice, 328–29
Quoits, 385–86
  Relay, 422

Rabbit Jump, 326
Race the Ball, 362
Races, 362
  Clothespin, 354
  Drawing Object, 353
  Walking, 374
Rapid Transit, 363
Reading, physical education and, 15–16
Rebounding, 444
Receive and Run, 394–95
Reclining Pullups, 381
Recreation, 19
Red Light, 345
Reindeer, 431
Relationships, human, 6, 16
Relays, 152–53
  middle childhood, 363–65, 381–84, 397–98
  upper grade, 421–22
Required class program, 18
Retarded children, 119–20, 172–73
  physical education and, 167–68
Reuther Board Take-Off, 445–46
Rhythms, dances and, *see* Dances and rhythms
Ride a Cock-Horse, 314–15
Ring Champion, 369

Ringmaster, 325
Rocking Chair, 350
Rooster Fight, 369
Rope jumping, 325
Round Dance (*table*), 379
Round-robin tournaments, 181–83
Roundoff, 440
Rousseau, Jean Jacques, 11
Rubber Heels, 375
Running games, 338, 340, 345, 373, 402–3

Safety, 65, 85, 440
Sally Go Round, 307
Sanitation, school, 34
Santa games, 430–31
Sawing Wood, 360
Scat, 345
School
  environment of, 33–35
  function of, 4–7
  physical education and, 3
  programs in, 175–87
  site of, 34
School districts, consolidation of, 66–67
Scissors, 361
Scram, 391–92
Scrambled Words, 227–28
Seal games, 350, 403
Seed Guessing, 429
Self-realization, 6, 15–16
Self-testing activities
  childhood
    early, 136–37, 325–36, 350–53
    middle, 367–69
    upper grade, 154–55, 387–89
Services, health, 35–37
Seven Up, 328
Sex education, 73
Shoemaker's Dance, 319
Shuffle, 357
Shuffleboard, 411
Siamese Hop, 369
Siamese Twin Walk, 350
Side Flex, 361
Simple Hopscotch, 325
Single Lindy, 402
Single knee gymnastics, 442
Sitting Balance, 389
Sitting Ball Game, 374
Sit-Ups, 338

Skill development
    motor, 96–98
    play and, 12
Skills
    aquatic (*tables*), 451–55
    health, 26
    locomotor (*table*), 49–50
    neuromuscular, 12
Skin the Cat, 443, 447
Skip Rope Relay, 422
Sliepcevich, Dr. Eleana M., 73
Smith, W. R., 102
Snail Hopscotch, 348
Snail Shell, 308–9
Soccer, 48, 49, 372, 374, 383, 392–93, 407, 417–19
Social Dances, 399–402
Softball, 374, 414–16
Special activities, 424–34
Specialists, program, 20–22
Speedball, 416–17
Squad class organization, 243–47
Square dances (*table*), 379
Square Relay, 383
Square Soccer, 392–93
Squat On—Jump Off, 446
Squat Thrust, 379
Squat Vault, 446
Squeeze Out, 381–82
Squirrel in the Tree, 323
Standing Broad Jump, 373
Step Hop, 357
Step Jump, 373
Stoop Vault, 446
Stop Ball, 372
Story Plays, 137–38, 327, 253
Straddle Vault, 446–47
Strawberry Shortcake Jump Rope, 349
Stunts, 436–47
Supplies
    physical education (*tables*), 78–80
    program and, 20
Swimming, 448–57
Swings, 306

Tabby Cat, 321–22
Table Tennis, 387
Tag, 382
Tally Basketball, 394
Tandem, 389
Teacher Ball, 140

Teachers
    health education and, 27–29, 73
    physical education, 3, 68
        influence, 13
        program, 20–22
Team Forward Rolls, 389–90
Team games
    childhood
        early, 153–59, 250
        middle, 369–72
        upper grade, 413–23
Teddy Bear Jump Rope, 348
Telegrams, 398
Tennis
    Beach, 386
    Deck, 384–85
    Table, 387
Tether Ball, 365–66
Texas Star, 378
Thanksgiving activities, 430
Thread Follows the Needle, 330–31
Three Standing Board Jumps, 373
Three Step Turn, 378
Through the Stick, 403
Thurston, Lee M., 191
Tightrope Walking, 326
Time, programs and, 19–20
Tobacco smoking, health education and, 207–9
Toe Kick, 368
Toss Ball, 226–27
Total-child development concept, 66
Touch, 346
Touch Step, 357
Tournaments
    evaluation of, 186–87
    Hopscotch, 348
    school and, 181–87
Track and field events
    middle childhood, 159, 396, 373–74
    upper grade, 404–5
Trades, 346
Traffic Light, 328
Traveling, 375–76
Trial and error play, 13
Triangle, 406
Tumbling, 436–47
Turkey games, 430
Turns, gymnastic, 447
Twenty Plus One, 405
Twister, 368–69
Two Little Blackbirds, 308
Two Step, 357

Under Leg Ball, 372
Unit plans, physical education, 222–23
Unwrap the Present, 433
Up Oars, 380
Upset the Union, 397

V-Ball, 408
V-Sit, 403
Valentine's Day activities, 431–32
Variety Travel, 421
Vaults, 446
Visual aids, 272–73
Volleyball, 392, 419–20

Wall charts, 272–75
Walking games, 47–49, 374, 431

Waltz Step, 357
Warm-Up, 371
Water activities, 448–57
Western Roundup, 340
Wheel and Spoke, 232
Wheelbarrow, 339
White House Conference on Education, 7, 24
WHO (World Health Organization), 24
Wicket Ball, 364
Wing Stretcher, 360
Witch Hat, 429
Witch Relay, 429
Word Game, 397
World Health Organization (WHO), 24
Wrestling, 387–88

Yarn Ball Dodge Ball, 328
Yastrzemski, Carl, 15